Poetry and Culture in Middle Kingdom Egypt

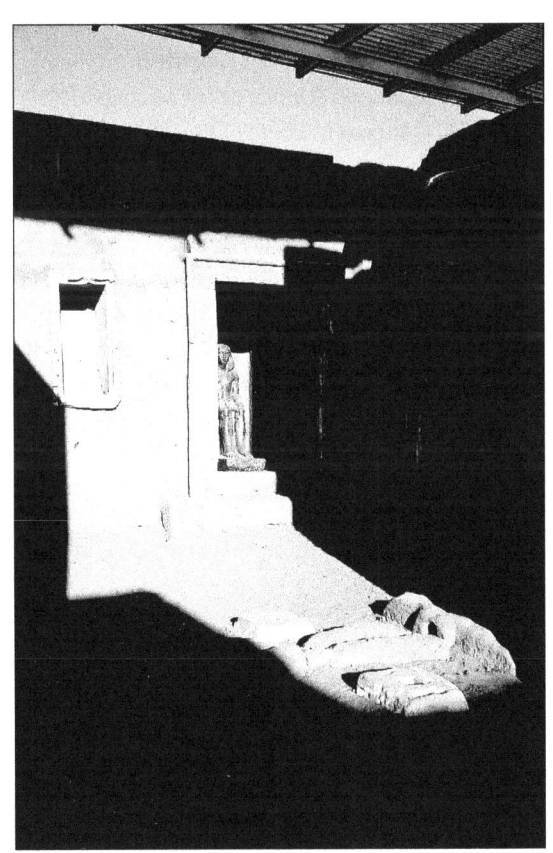

Studies in Egyptology and the Ancient Near East
Edited by Professor John Baines,
The Oriental Institute, University of Oxford

This interdisciplinary series publishes works on the ancient Near East in antiquity, including the Graeco-Roman period and is open to specialized studies as well as to works of synthesis or comparison.

Editorial Board:
Alan Bowman (University of Oxford)
Erik Hornung (University of Basel)
Anthony Leahy (University of Birmingham)
Peter Machinist (Harvard University)
Piotr Michalowski (University of Michigan)
David O'Connor (Institute of Fine Arts, New York University)
D.T. Potts (University of Sydney)
Stephan Seidlmayer (Aegyptologisches Seminar, Berlin)
Dorothy Thompson (University of Cambridge)
Pascal Vernus (Ecole Pratique des Hautes Etudes, Paris)
Norman Yoffee (University of Michigan)

Also published in the series:
Myth and Politics in Ancient Near Eastern Historiography
Mario Liverani
Edited by Zainab Bahrani and Marc Van De Mieroop

Local Power in Old Babylonian Mesopotamia
Andrea Seri

Poetry and Culture in Middle Kingdom Egypt

A Dark Side to Perfection

R.B. Parkinson

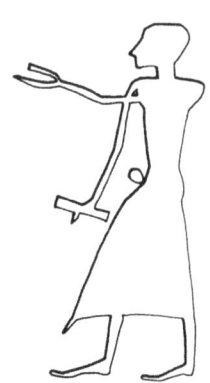

LONDON   OAKVILLE

Published by Equinox Publishing Ltd.

UK: Office 415, The Workstation, 15 Paternoster Row, Sheffield, S1 2BX
USA: ISD, 70 Enterprise Drive, Bristol, CT 06010

www.equinoxpub.com

First published in hardback by Continuum International Publishing Group Ltd. in 2002.
This paperback edition published in 2010.

© R.B. Parkinson 2002

All rights reserved. No part of this publication may be reproduced or transmitted in any form or by any means, electronic or mechanical, including photocopying, recording or any information storage or retrieval system, without prior permission in writing from the publishers.

British Library Cataloguing-in-Publication Data
A catalogue record for this book is available from the British Library.

Library of Congress Cataloging-in-Publication Data
Parkinson, R. B.
  Poetry and culture in Middle Kingdom Egypt : a dark side to perfection / R.B. Parkinson.
      p. cm. -- (Studies in Egyptology and the Ancient Near East)
  Originally published: New York : Continuum, 2002.
  Includes bibliographical references and index.
  ISBN 978-1-84553-770-8 (pb)
  1. Egyptian poetry--History and criticism. 2. Egypt--Civilization--To 332 B.C.
  PJ1487.P37 2010
  893'.1109--dc22
                              2010001500

ISBN 978 1 84553 770 8 (paperback)
ISBN 978 1 78179 192 9 (eBook)

Typeset by Centraserve Ltd, Saffron Walden, Essex
Printed and bound in Great Britain and the USA

Page i: The chapel of Heqaib at Elephantine in 2001, showing the shrine and statue of Sarenput II (1841 BCE). Photo: R. B. Parkinson.

Page iii. The draftsman and lector priest Sasobek holding a papyrus roll and reciting, from from the mid-13th Dynasty stela of the official Senebsuma, from Abydos (British Museum EA 215 = ANOC 25.1). Drawing by R. B. Parkinson.

Contents

Preface ix

Acknowledgements xiii

Chronology xv

Abbreviations xvii

PART ONE: APPROACHES

1 The study of Middle Kingdom 'literature'	3
1.1 Introduction	3
1.2 The literary tradition in Egyptology	10
1.3 The propaganda model	13
1.4 Models and approaches	17
2 General considerations: Definitions, genre, interpretation	22
2.1 Introduction	22
2.2 Defining 'literature'	22
2.2.1 General	23
2.2.2 Egyptian literature	29
2.3 Genre	32
2.4 Interpretation	36

PART TWO: CONTEXT AND INTERTEXT

3 Texts and intertext	45
3.1 The date of the compositions	45
3.1.1 History and texts	45
3.1.2 Possible strategies	46
3.2 Textual transmission	50
3.2.1 Attitudes to text	50
3.2.2 New Kingdom manuscripts	53

	3.3 The oral and textual context of literature	55
	3.3.1 Oral and written prototypes	55
	3.3.2 Intertext	60
4	The social context	64
	4.1 Middle Kingdom society	64
	4.2 Literary manuscripts in society	66
	4.3 Authors and authorship	75
	4.4 Audience and performance	78
	4.5 The literary response	81
5	Literature in culture	86
	5.1 Literature and ideology	86
	5.1.1 Texts and ideology	86
	5.1.2 Literature as imaginary	87
	5.2 The differentiated nature of literary decorum	91
	5.3 Programmatic and other models for contextualization	98
	5.4 Complex models: Play and mediation	101
6	Literary form	108
	6.1 Formal aspects of social practice	108
	6.2 Literary genres	108
	6.3 Metrics	112
	6.4 Style	118
7	The cultural themes of literature	129
	7.1 The thematic range	129
	7.2 Theodicy: The great argument	130
	7.3 The low tradition	138

PART THREE: READINGS

8	Tales	149
	8.1 High and low narratives	149
	8.2 *The Tale of Sinuhe*: The search for a voice	149
	8.3 *The Eloquent Peasant*: Eloquence's answer	168
	8.4 The range of responses: From *Cheops' Court* to	
	The Shipwrecked Sailor's island	182
9	Discourses and dialogues	193
	9.1 Discourses: The world's recreation	193
	9.2 *The Words of Khakheperreseneb*: Struggling with silence	200

9.3	*The Dialogue of Ipuur and the Lord to the Limit*: The architecture of the great argument	204
9.4	*The Dialogue of a Man and His Ba*: Representing death	216
9.5	*The Sporting King* and *Fishing and Fowling*: Recreational discourses	226
	9.5.1 Compound genres	226
	9.5.2 The end of discourse	232

10 Teachings   235
  10.1 Learning nothing: The problem of context   235
  10.2 *The Teaching of Amenemhat*: Rewriting history   241
  10.3 *The Teaching for Merikare*: Shepherding rebellion   248
  10.4 *The Teaching of Ptahhotep*: Fragmenting the ideal life   257
  10.5 *The Loyalist Teaching(s)*: Imagining social solidarity   266
  10.6 *The Teaching of Khety*: Learning laughter?   273

11 Reading the poems   278
  11.1 Introduction   278
  11.2 Images for reading   278
  11.3 The modern reader: Responses and evaluation   283
  11.4 Answering voices   288

Appendix 1: Survey of the Middle Kingdom literary corpus   293
  A.1 The extant corpus   293
    A.1.1 Tales   294
    A.1.2 Discourses and dialogues   303
    A.1.3 Other wisdom texts   310
    A.1.4 Compound genres   311
    A.1.5 Teachings   313
  A.2 Lost works and attributions   320

Appendix 2: *Kemit*   322

References   326
  Egyptian compositions   326
  Bibliography   328

Index   385

Addenda

The literary fragments from el-Lahun are now published in M. Collier and S. Quirke, *The UCL Lahun Papyri* [2]: *Religious, Literary, Legal, Mathematical and Medical* (BAR International Series 1209; Oxford: Archaeopress 2004), 34–5. These include a new fragment of a manuscript of *Sinuhe* from el-Lahun (P. UCL 32106C), to be added to the listing on p. 297 (see R. Parkinson, *Reading Ancient Egyptian Poetry: Among Other Histories* (Chichester: Wiley-Blackwell 2009), 122.

Preface

> Please do not fear vibrato, liveliness, subjectivity . . . but please be very afraid of coldness, purism, objectivity and empty historicism.
> Nikolaus Harnoncourt, *The Musical Dialogue* (1989),
> 'Monteverdi Today'

As ever, my thanks are due to John Baines, a superlative High Steward, for almost everything; he has inspired and sustained, as well as edited, this study. I have also benefited greatly from the encouragement of many others, including Jim Allen, Elke Blumenthal, Alec Dakin, W. V. Davies, Philippe Derchain, Biri Fay, Hans-Werner Fischer-Elfert, Detlef Franke, Erhart Graefe, Tom Hare, Erik Hornung, Friedrich Junge, Christian Klotz, Lisa Leahy, Antonio Loprieno, Andrea McDowell, Lynn Meskell, Piotr Michalowski, Gerald Moers, Janet Richards, William Kelly Simpson, Claire Thorne and Ursula Verhoeven. The idea of this book was first developed in the Griffith Institute, now demolished, which was a home for so long. Writing was begun during a Junior Research Fellowship at University College, Oxford (1990–91), and since then has continued in leisure-time and often in isolation from an academic institutional environment. I am therefore most grateful to those friends and colleagues who have engaged in dialogue with me and kept the project alive: in particular, those who have allowed me to consult their work before publication. Without their kindness and interest, the book would have been abandoned in despair at my inability to complete it.

The study is necessarily shaped by meditation as well as philological research, and various non-institutional locations have left their imprint, including several favourite Italian cities, the Yourcenarian sites of Tivoli and Bruges, and (thanks to Bales Worldwide and Dietrich Raue) the White Chapel at Karnak, Qubbet el-Hawa at Aswan, and above all the chapel of Heqaib at Elephantine. Most influential perhaps have been the landscapes of the dale where I was born and brought up. A surprisingly large amount of this book has been written on public transport in various countries, and much of the final stage of writing was done in the earthly paradise of the British Library at St Pancras, and in the Department of Egyptian Antiquities, British Museum, thanks to Vivian Davies' support for the project. It goes without saying that I am also immensely grateful for the publisher's patience over the long years.

My thanks are, as ever, due to my late parents – on a minor level the entire book has been written on a pc that was a gift from my father. They did not live to see the project finished, but their influence permeates it, and loss of them has intensified my concern for reading as a dialogue with the dead. Gratitude is also owed to Gwen, a better typist than myself, for her persistent help in word-processing the manuscript.

Many of the arguments outlined here have been indicated in previous articles; this book aims to provide an overview, intended for a more general academic audience than specialists in Middle Kingdom texts, since I believe that (to paraphrase T. Ziolkowski on Vergil) the poems are too important to be left to the Egyptologists. Since this book is intended for a mixed audience, different audiences will find some passages redundant. It complements recent collections of studies (Loprieno 1996a; Assmann and Blumenthal 1999), and provides an integrated discussion from a single western viewpoint. It remains an overview, sketching arguments rather than expounding them in detail, and references to other scholars' discussions are selective and have been cut to the minimum; my disagreements with many other studies are left implicit and are not analysed, except for particular points of philology that are crucial for my readings. Details of the poems and discussions are included in Appendix 1 (**A.1**). I am painfully aware that these treatments are far from comprehensive. I have concentrated on reconstructing some of the original experience of reading; this necessitates a certain amount of paraphrase, while readers are referred to the Oxford World's Classics anthology (Parkinson 1999f) for passages and aspects not mentioned here. The need for reliable text editions, newly collated with all extant original manuscripts, and for fully referenced interpretive commentaries cannot be overstressed.

I have drawn on a few schools of literary theory which seem to be relevant to the present priorities of Egyptological research, within a general framework of theoretical concerns. The work of Stephen Greenblatt has been particularly inspirational. The book is a response to old historicist approaches to Middle Kingdom texts, in order to argue for the aesthetic aspects of these poems, and to foreground the original Egyptian actors' perspectives. It is, like all academic study, a subjective and personal work, shaped by personality, family, institutions, and my sympathies with 'les hommes obscures' of literature who must find a voice and a personal equilibrium as parts of a hierarchy of power over which they have no control; nevertheless, I hope that it represents a fuller western engagement with these Egyptian poems than has sometimes been the case.

The deepest debts are to my parents in the land of the dead, and above all to my partner Tim Reid in the land of the living. As well as being the centre and support of my life, his labour has saved the text from many inconsistencies. This book is thus both 'un verre aux morts' (in Pascal Quignard's phrase), and, since it was begun around the time we met, an anniversary present for Tim.

R. B. P.
Milton Park
May 2000

Note to the paperback

This paperback is an unrevised reprint and, in particular, does not address a hypothesis of recent years: a few scholars have proposed that several compositions included here are to be re-dated to the early New Kingdom; I remain unconvinced by this. However, ongoing research by Andreas Stauder argues convincingly that *Amenemhat* and *Neferti* are likely to date later, rather than earlier, in the Middle Kingdom.

The literary fragments from el-Lahun that were listed as unpublished in Appendix 1 (p. 294, 300–3, 311) are now published in M. Collier and S. Quirke, *The UCL Lahun Papyri [2]: Religious, Literary, Legal, Mathematical and Medical* (BAR International Series 1209; Oxford: Archaeopress 2004). This includes a new fragment of a manuscript of *Sinuhe* from el-Lahun (P. UCL 32106C), to be added to the listing on p. 297: see R. B. Parkinson, *Reading Ancient Egyptian Poetry: Among Other Histories* (Chichester and Malden, MA: Wiley-Blackwell 2009), 122. Also to be added to Appendix 1 are small fragments of a papyrus, apparently containing a narrative, from a late 12th Dynasty tomb in the Asasif (see *idem*, 91 n. 19).

Acknowledgements

I am grateful to the following copyright holders for their kind permission to reproduce lines of modern poetry:

W. H. Auden: 'A Walk after Dark' © W. H. Auden 1966; 'The Truest Poetry Is the Most Feigning' © 1954 by W. H. Auden; 'Letter to Lord Byron' © 1937 by W. H. Auden; 'Secondary Epic' © 1960 by W. H. Auden. All from *W. H. Auden: Collected Poems*. Used by permission of Random House, Inc., and Faber and Faber, London.

T. S. Eliot, *Four Quartets* (Faber and Faber, 1959). Used by permission of Faber and Faber, London, and Harcourt Inc. (HBT), Orlando, Florida.

Louis MacNeice, *Collected Poems* (Faber and Faber, 1979). Used by permission of David Higham Associates, London.

Myfanwy Piper, Libretto for *Death in Venice* (Benjamin Britten, 1973). Used by permission of Faber Music Limited, London.

W. B. Yeats: The Poems (Everyman's Library, 1992). Used by permission of Michael B. Yeats, Co. Dublin.

Waldo Williams, *Cofio*. Used by permission of Gwasg Gomer, Llandysul.

Chronology

All dates are approximate.

EARLY DYNASTIC PERIOD	
3rd Dynasty	2650–2575
OLD KINGDOM	
4th Dynasty	2575–2450
5th Dynasty	2450–2325
6th Dynasty	2325–2175
7th/8th Dynasty	2175–2125
FIRST INTERMEDIATE PERIOD	
9th Dynasty	2150–2080
10th Dynasty, ruling in the north	2080–1975

    Includes various kings called Khety, among them:
    Nebkaure Khety
    Merikare Khety

MIDDLE KINGDOM	
11th Dynasty, initially ruling in the south	2080–1975
Intef I	
Intef II	
Intef III	
Rulers of all Egypt	
Nebhepetre Montuhotep (II)	2010–1960
Sankhkare Montuhotep (III)	1960–1948
Nebtawire Montuhotep (IV)	1948–1939
12th Dynasty	
(Overlapping dates indicate co-regencies.)	
Sehotepibre Amenemhat I	1938–1908
Kheperkare Senwosret I	1918–1875
Nubkaure Amenemhat II	1876–1842
Khakheperre Senwosret II	1844–1837
Khakaure Senwosret III	1836–1818

Nimaatre Amenemhat III		1818–1770
Maakherure Amenemhat IV		1770–1760
Sobekkare Nefrusobek		1760–1756

13th Dynasty 1756–1640

A series of ephemeral kings; only the most important are listed, with their approximate position in the Dynasty, according to the Turin Royal Canon

4	Sekhemkare Amenemhat (V)	
12	Khaankhre Sobekhotep (I)	1725
16	Amenemhat-Sobekhotep (II)	
17	Khendjer	
21	Sekhemreswadjtawi Sobekhotep (III)	
22	Khasekhemre Neferhotep (I)	1710–1700
24	Khaneferre Sobekhotep (IV)	1700–1690
25	Khahotepre Sobekhotep (V)	1690–1685
27	Merneferre Iy	1685–1670

Abbreviations

Abbreviations for frequently cited periodicals, series and volumes:

ÄA	Ägyptologische Abhandlungen (Wiesbaden: Harrassowitz)
ÄAT	Ägypten und Altes Testament (Wiesbaden: Harrassowitz)
AcOr	Acta Orientalia
ADAIK	Abhandlungen des Deutschen Archäologischen Instituts Kairo (Glückstadt, Hamburg, New York: J. J. Augustin)
AHAW	Abhandlungen der Heidelberger Akademie der Wissenschaften zu Berlin, Philosophisch-historische Klasse (Heidelberg: Carl Winter)
AL	D. Meeks, *Année lexicographique: Égypte ancienne* 1-. Paris: published by author, 1980-
APAW	Abhandlungen der Preussischen Akademie der Wissenschaften (Berlin: Akademie Verlag)
ASAW	Abhandlungen der Sächsischen Akademie der Wissenschaften zu Leipzig, Philosophisch-historische (Berlin: Akademie Verlag)
ASE	Archaeological Survey of Egypt (London: Egypt Exploration Fund)
AV	Archäologische Veröffentlichungen, Deutsches Archäologisches Institut, Abt. Kairo (Mainz am Rhein: Philipp von Zabern)
BAe	Bibliotheca Aegyptiaca (Brussels: Fondation égyptologique Reine Élisabeth)
BdE	Bibliothèque d'étude, L'Institut français d'archéologie orientale (Cairo: Institut français d'archéologie orientale)
BEHE	Bibliothèque de l'École pratique des hautes études (Paris: Honoré Champion)
BES	*Bulletin of the Egyptological Seminar*
BIFAO	*Bulletin de l'Institut français d'archéologie orientale*
BiOr	*Bibliotheca Orientalis*
BSEG	*Bulletin de la Société d'égyptologie de Genève*
BSFE	*Bulletin de la Société française d'égyptologie*
CdE	*Chronique d'Égypte*
CRIPEL	*Cahier de recherches de l'Institut de papyrologie et égyptologie de Lille*

CT	A. de Buck, *The Egyptian Coffin Texts* (7 vols). Chicago: University of Chicago Press, 1935–61
DFIFAO	Documents de fouilles de l'Institut français d'archéologie orientale (Cairo: Institut français d'archéologie orientale)
GM	*Göttinger Miszellen*
GOF	Göttingener Orientforschungen (Wiesbaden: Harrassowitz)
HÄB	Hildesheimer ägyptologische Beiträge (Hildesheim: Gerstenberg)
HÄS	Hamburger ägyptologische Studien (Hamburg: Borg)
JAOS	*Journal of American Oriental Society*
JARCE	*Journal of the American Research Center in Egypt*
JEA	*Journal of Egyptian Archaeology*
JEOL	*Jaabericht van het Voorasiatisch-Egyptisch Genootschap (Gezelschap) "Ex Oriente Lux"*
JNES	*Journal of Near Eastern Studies*
JSSEA	*Journal of the Society for the Study of Egyptian Antiquities*
KRI	K. A. Kitchen, *Ramesside Inscriptions* (8 vols). Oxford: B. H. Blackwell, 1968–1990
KÄT	Kleine Ägyptische Texte (Wiesbaden: Harrassowitz)
LÄ	W. Helck *et al.* (eds), *Lexikon der Ägyptologie* (7 vols). Wiesbaden: Harrasowitz, 1975–92
LÄS	Leipziger ägyptologischen Studien (Glückstadt, Hamburg, New York: J. J. Augustin)
LingAeg	*Lingua Aegyptiaca*
MÄS	Münchner ägyptologische Studien (Munich and Berlin: Deutscher Kunstverlag)
MÄU	Münchner ägyptologische Untersuchungen (Munich: Peter Lang)
MBP	Münchner Beiträge zur Papyrusforschung (Munich: C. H. Beck)
MDAIK	*Mitteilungen des Deutschen Archäologischen Instituts, Abteilung Kairo*
MDOG	*Mitteilungen der Deutschen Orientgesellschaft*
MIFAO	Mémoires publiés par les membres de l'Institut français d'archéologie orientale (Cairo: Institut français d'archéologie orientale)
MIO	*Mitteilungen des Instituts für Orientforschung*
OBO	Orbis Biblicus et Orientalis (Fribourg: Editions Universitaires, Göttingen: Vandenhoeck und Ruprecht)
OLA	Orientalia Lovaniensia Analecta (Leuven: Peeters)
OLZ	*Orientalische Literaturzeitung*
Or	*Orientalia*
OrSu	*Orientalia Suecana*

PÄ	Probleme der Ägyptologie (Leiden: E. J. Brill)
PM	B. Porter, R. L. Moss et al., *Topographical Bibliography of Ancient Egyptian Hieroglyphic Texts, Reliefs, and Paintings* (1st ed. 7 vols, 2nd ed. ongoing). Oxford, 1927–
PSBA	*Proceedings of the Society of Biblical Archaeology*
PT	K. Sethe, *Die altägyptischen Pyramidentexte* (4 vols). Leipzig: J. C. Hinrichs, 1908–22
Ranke, *PN*	H. Ranke, *Die altägyptischen Personennamen* (2 vols). Glückstadt: J. J. Augustin, 1935–52
RdE	*Revue d'égyptologie*
RIDA	*Revue internationale des droits de l'antiquité*
SAGA	Studien zur Archäologie und Geschichte Altägyptens (Cairo, Heidelberg: Heidelberger Orientverlag)
SAK	*Studien zur altägyptischen Kultur*
SAOC	Studies in Ancient Oriental Civilization (Chicago: University of Chicago Press)
SSEA	Society for the Studies of Egyptian Antiquities
StudAeg	*Studia Aegyptiaca*
TAVO	Tübinger Atlas des Vorderen Orients, Reihe B (Geisteswissenschaften), Nr. 1, Beihefte (Wiesbaden: Ludwig Reichert)
TT	Theban Tomb
TTS	The Theban Tomb Series (London: Egypt Exploration Society)
TUAT	Texte aus der Umwelt des Alten Testament (Gütersloh: Gütersloher Verlagshaus)
UGAÄ	Untersuchungen zur Geschichte und Altertumskunde Ägyptens (Leipzig: J. C. Hinrichs)
Urk.	K. Sethe *et al.*, *Urkunden des aegyptischen Altertums* (8 vols). Leipzig and Berlin: J. C. Hinrichs and Akademie-Verlag, 1904–61
VA	*Varia Aegyptiaca*
VIO	Deutsche Akademie der Wissenschaften zu Berlin, Institut für Orientforschung, Veröffentlichungen (Berlin: Akademie Verlag)
Wb.	A. Erman and H. Grapow (eds), *Wörterbuch der ägyptischen Sprache* (12 vols). Berlin: Akademie Verlag; Leipzig: J. C. Hinrichs, 1925–1963
WdO	*Die Welt des Orients*
WZKM	*Wiener Zeitschrift für die Kunde des Morgenlandes*
ZÄS	*Zeitschrift für ägyptische Sprache und Altertumskunde*
ZAW	*Zeitschrift für die Alttestamentliche Wissenschaft* (Berlin: Walter de Gruyter)
ZDMG	*Zeitschrift der Deutschen Morgenlandischen Gesellschaft*

O genedlaethau dirifedi daear,
    A'u breuddwyd dwyfol a'u dwyfoldeb brau,
A erys ond tawelwch i'r calonnau
    Fu gynt yn llawenychu a thristau?

(O countless generations of the land,
    With their divine dream and fragile divinity,
Does anything remain but silence for the hearts
    That once rejoiced and lamented?)
Waldo Williams (1904–71), *Cofio*

For Tim, l'homme qu'il me faut
Once in a while the odd thing happens

PART ONE
Approaches

1
The study of Middle Kingdom 'literature'

1.1 INTRODUCTION

un vrai trésor historique
J.-F. Champollion, *Lettres écrites d'Egypte
et de Nubie en 1828 et 1829* (1868: 19)

In the late afternoon, with the birds singing, it is still possible to walk through the remains of the Middle Kingdom town on the island of Elephantine, go down an alley, turn across the broad street, and enter the small enclosed chapel dedicated to the local saint Heqaib, which was once filled with statues of worshippers and donors. This chapel was rebuilt in the reign of Senwosret I around 1880 BCE and was continually developed until it was abandoned some three centuries later during the 17th Dynasty. It thus embodies the material culture of most of the Middle Kingdom, a period which is often regarded as the Renaissance of Ancient Egypt and an era characterized by literary masterpieces (Franke 1994, 1995). Both the literary works and the architecture are artefacts of their culture, and both belong to the same context, but the poetry that was once read in these buildings is now in many ways less tangible and accessible. Modern study has often resulted in an archaeology of texts for these 12th and 13th Dynasty poems, rather than of the original impulses that determined their composition or the responses that they aroused in their audiences: intellectual and emotional responses are more fugitive and fragile than any manuscript, but attempts to reconstruct such aspects from the original actors' perspectives remain integral to any understanding of the compositions and the culture they represent. Direct evidence for their precise social context is lacking, and their role in their culture is uncertain.

In this respect, these ancient works pose interpretive problems relevant to contemporary critical debates concerning the status and role of such discourse in many cultures. They also raise general questions about modern responses to, and interpretations of, the words of the past in an extreme form since the time of their composition is so distant. Unsurprisingly, these works have produced radically varied reactions among modern readers, including incomprehension and functionalist analyses in terms of political propaganda. Analyses have rarely considered the act of reading and experiencing the poems, which is an activity that is common to both ancient and modern audiences, albeit very differently constructed. Discussion of such material is necessarily embedded in the specifics of Egyptology, but it can address the poems from a broad perspective to assess the role of 'literary' discourse in a society. This book complements an anthology of translations (Parkinson 1997a, 1999f), and explores the richness of the corpus for interpretation. It proposes strategies for reading that are derived from a consideration of these particular texts, but it also forms a meditation on our possible relationship with the ancient dead. It suggests ways in which we can attempt to read in the dark of history.

As with the English Elizabethan age, 'literature' is one of the characterizing features in historians' views of the Middle Kingdom, and the compositions have shaped modern conceptions of it. The literary corpus is a significant portion of the texts known from that period, and they are among the most widely read and cited Egyptian texts. In specific terms, their study is hindered by manuscript lacunae, philological difficulties and incomplete publication of the corpus: new discoveries are probably to be made in most major museum collections of papyri and ostraca (cf. Fischer-Elfert 1997). Reading the texts has often been a matter of slowly battling against these difficulties rather than reading as the word is normally understood (see, e.g., Erman 1927: xliv n.2); aesthetic pleasure is not commonly recorded as a reader's reaction. The fragmentary nature of the corpus is compounded by the lack of ancient inherited paradigms for reading and defining literature, since Egyptian criticism and meta-commentaries are almost non-existent. In comparison with the literature of classical antiquity, this break in interpretation is a major obstacle in the production of modern readings.

I discuss the literary texts as components of a coherent corpus that can be defined in terms of fictionality, genre, and social and discursive context, and which occupied a distinctive place in the mainstream tradition of Egyptian written high culture. Much discussion has attended the problem of defining 'literature' in any context or cultural tradition, while critical discussion on this topic has also increased within Egyptology.[1] 'Literature' itself is a comparatively recent term (e.g., R. Williams 1977: 45–54), but in assessing the ancient world we cannot reject our own language and culture as anachronistic, and I retain the term as an approximation, in notional quotation marks, recognizing that 'literary studies have been based ... on a highly specific concept of literature, a concept which is unlikely to have more than rough parallels within Ancient Egyptian culture' (Gumbrecht 1996: 9). While still recognizing the differences between the Egyptian cultural constructs and our own, I have tried to

[1] E.g., J. Assmann 1974; Loprieno 1988; Parkinson 1991b; Gumbrecht 1996; Loprieno 1996b.

acknowledge the modern and subjective aspects of interpretation; the epigraphs are intended to encourage readers to 'only connect' between this most dead of literatures and their experience of their own (modern and usually western) culture's literature.

Modern knowledge of the period remains fragmentary in many respects, although the general historical outline is comparatively clear. The Middle Kingdom was a period of cultural renewal, especially after the succession of a new dynasty, the 12th. This was a generation after the country's unity was restored following a period without central rulership, the First Intermediate Period, which was characterized by local patron governors in semi-independent provinces. The 11th Dynasty Theban king Nebhepetre Montuhotep II had reunified Egypt around 1975 BCE, ousting the Heracleopolitan rulers who had dominated the north of the country in continuation of Old Kingdom rule. Montuhotep II's second successor, Montuhotep IV, was followed by Sehotepibre Amenemhat I (*c.* 1938 BCE), who had probably been his vizier; the circumstances of the transition of power – usurpation or succession – are unclear. He actively consolidated the country's borders and, perhaps in his twentieth year of reign, moved the court to a new site near el-Lisht, a little south of the Old Kingdom capital of Memphis (D. Arnold 1991: 15–16). The 12th Dynasty was known in later periods as 'the kings of the Residence of Itj-tawi'. His descendants ruled for two centuries, occasionally adopting a practice of co-regencies between father and designated successor.

After a probably turbulent reign of 30 years Amenemhat I was assassinated, and his son and co-regent Kheperkare Senwosret I succeeded (*c.* 1918 BCE), continuing the process of renaissance proclaimed in the choice of his father's royal titulary. Senwosret intensified the cultural and political renewal with an assertion of the king's divine creative powers (e.g., Franke 1996), perhaps in order to enhance the dynasty's legitimacy. He also reorganized the provinces and created new administrative titles (in general: Gestermann 1987). The reign was marked by internal strife and military campaigns to the east; to the south Senwosret completed the conquest of Lower Nubia. His 34 years of sole rule formed the climax of the early phase of the Middle Kingdom with the establishment of a unified material culture (e.g., Franke 1994: 8–29; Obsomer 1995). There was an extensive building programme, and a conscious re-creation of elite culture, drawing on Old Kingdom models and centred around the royal Residence; this official art provided models for following periods. The 35-year reign of Senwosret I's son, Nubkaure Amenemhat II, seems to have been less spectacularly productive and may have been a period of consolidation. His son, Khakheperre Senwosret II, died after probably only eight years on the throne.

The succession of Senwosret II's son Khakaure Senwosret III

(c. 1836 BCE) marks the start of the high Middle Kingdom (e.g., Gestermann 1995, 1997). This period is often seen as one of tension between central authority and local rulers. Senwosret III's 19-year sole reign (Wegner 1996) saw the gradual dying out of the powerful provincial governors (Franke 1991), as wealth and power increasingly centred around the court, in a process that had begun in earlier reigns and that was finally completed in later ones. Senwosret pursued an extremely active foreign policy, notably in Nubia. The reign was also marked by distinctive trends in architecture and funerary practices, and in particular in sculpture, including visual expression of the king's role (Tefnin 1992; Polz 1995; J. Assmann 1996e: 71–9). Major social and political changes seem to have occurred at this period. The lower officials of the central bureaucracy gained greater wealth and were able to dedicate monuments; social levels may have become more varied and mixed, although society remained highly unequal, and the elite was still a very small group of the population. The 46-year reign of Senwosret III's son, Nimaatre Amenemhat III, has left no record of military campaigns abroad and is noted for the magnificence of its works of art, as well as the king's land reclamation works within Egypt, both suggestive of great prosperity. Intense bureaucratic activity monitored equilibrium between the Residence and the provinces, and the Eastern Delta witnessed immigration and integration of peoples from Palestine.

The late Middle Kingdom began with the accession of Amenemhat III's successor Maakherure Amenemhat IV (c. 1770 BCE), who may or may not have been his son. After a 9-year reign he appears to have died, and a daughter of Amenemhat III, Sobekkare Nefrusobek, succeeded him. Her accession is probably an indication of a dynastic crisis, and her 4-year rule apparently marked the sudden end of the family's dominance. The 13th Dynasty (c. 1755–1630 BCE) is essentially a continuation of the 12th in administrative and cultural terms. It was known in later Egyptian historiography as 'the kings [who followed?] after the [house? of Sehot]epibre (Amenemhat I)' (Ryholt 1997: 69), and comprised a sequence of some 50 kings in a period of 150 years (e.g., Quirke 1991b; Ryholt 1997). For part of this period, kings did not succeed one another on the basis of kinship. The rapid succession of rulers and the prominence of high officials in the dynasty suggest that the bureaucracy was more influential in maintaining the stability of the country than were the kings.

A sequence of longer reigns of members of a single family around the middle of the dynasty witnessed attempts to maintain 12th Dynasty traditions (c. 1710–1685 BCE, Neferhotep I and Sobekhotep IV) and marks the high point of the dynasty in terms of royal monuments. Although the monuments of minor officials show their increasing access to high material culture, there was also a general decrease in the country's wealth, and the central traditions of the high court culture eventually declined both in influence on private monuments and in the quality of royal monuments. Some elite families of provincial Upper Egypt gained in importance in relation to the ruling elite, while the Eastern Delta became increasingly separate, with continuing immigration from the east. The dynasty ended with a succession of 24 kings, with individual reigns averaging just over one year each.

Local rulers in the Delta had formed the contemporaneous 14th Dynasty, possibly from early in the 13th Dynasty. A separate and distinct state was established by the Canaanite rulers, known as the 'Hyksos', and their vassals (the 15/16th Dynasties, *c.* 1640–1532 BCE), centred at Avaris (Tell el-Dab'a). The 13th Dynasty rulers lost control over a unified country, and may have withdrawn to Thebes in the south; from there independent kings opposed the Hyksos and ruled as the 17th Dynasty (*c.* 1630–1540 BCE). The material and written remains from the Theban area suggest a provincial polity cut off from the traditional cultural resources of the 12th Dynasty Residence in the north (Quirke 1991b: 127–8). Campaigns of the 17th Dynasty rulers from the mid-sixteenth century onward brought their control of the north, driving the Hyksos rulers out of Egypt into Palestine. The continuing 17th Dynasty royal house established the New Kingdom (18th Dynasty, *c.* 1550–1307 BCE).

At least since the time of scholars such as François Chabas (1858), Middle Kingdom literature has attracted attention as including some of 'the oldest books in the world' (e.g., Gunn 1906), although approaches to literary studies tend to take the genres of the classical world as their point of departure. It is, however, difficult to site Egyptian literature more broadly, when little enough is known of its chronological and cultural position within Egypt. The texts have provided a rich source for lexicography and linguistic analysis, and are a testimony to the events and beliefs of the culture; as with all ideologically patterned texts, any assessment of the reality behind them needs to be correlated with other evidence ranging from archaeological data to anthropological models (cf. Kemp 1989: 130; see further Kemp 1984). Such circumspection is applied to ancient historiography, but is less fully absorbed by those analysing literary texts, with notable exceptions (e.g., Björkman 1964 on *The Teaching for Merikare*). Individual texts are frequently analysed as sources for various topics on the basis of unstated modern expectations of history and literature that distort the assessment. Only rarely have they been subjected to detailed literary criticism. Marxist criticism has recognized that if a text is a mirror of historical reality, it is inevitably (albeit perhaps consciously) partial and selective, and that the text reveals as much about its own nature as about the socio-economic and political forces 'reflected' in it (Newton 1990: 102–29). The work of writers such as Louis Althusser has suggested that such compositions are rather 'overdetermined' and 'the product of a complex network of factors that cannot be interpreted in simple terms' (Newton 1990: 103). Without resorting to an essentialist or substantialist definition of literature or to extreme anachronism, it is possible to propose agreement with general literary scholarship that the text had no simple or direct mimetic relationship with history; the acknowledgement that 'the truest poetry is the most feigning' (*As You Like It*, 3.3) is not exclusively modern.

As Piotr Michalowski has commented of Sumerian writings, 'faced with bare texts with no metadiscourse about them, we simply read them, as if they were strictly referential, or more precisely, as if strictly referential texts were possible' (1989: 4). The need to consider the referential nature of the texts can be exemplified with one much-discussed instance where historical data and a literary text apparently contradict each other: *The Teaching of Amenemhat*. There was probably a co-regency between Amenemhat I, the king to whom this poem is ascribed, and Senwosret I, although scholars such as Claude Obsomer argue that the old king was killed before any co-regency was instituted.[2] In the teaching the old king claims from the grave that he was fatally attacked in his son's absence:

> when the entourage had not yet heard that I would hand over to you,
> when I had not yet sat (i.e., been enthroned) with you, that I might make
>   plans for you.
>
> (8b–c)[3]

For scholars who support the existence of a co-regency, this dichotomy between literature and the historical event has sometimes been difficult to elucidate. William J. Murnane maintained the absolute historicity of the text by proposing two separate attacks, of which the first would be recorded in the teaching, only the hypothetical second one ten years later being fatal (1977: 246–9). Karl Jansen-Winkeln (1991) concludes that the teaching is propaganda for the co-regency and describes a failed assassination attempt that was not repeated.[4] Such a reading requires the deceased

---

[2] For the early stages of the controversy see: Murnane 1977: 2–5, 245–50; 1981; Delia 1979, 1980, 1982; Eaton-Krauss 1980. Obsomer (1993; 1995: 45–145) has argued against a co-regency, with the agreement of Franke (1994: xi–xii; cf. Franke 1988: 115–6), Vandersleyen (1995: 50–2), and Grimal (1995b); overview with references: Jansen-Winkeln 1997: 116–7. Dieter, Dorothea and Felix Arnold assert that the balance of evidence supports the co-regency, citing evidence such as the building history of the pyramid of Senwosret I (e.g., F. Arnold 1990: 30–1). Dorothea Arnold (1991) suggests that the start of the co-regency coincided with the move of the court to Itj-tawi.

[3] See Grimal 1995b: 275–6; Burkard 1999: 161.

[4] Jansen-Winkeln's philological readings are rather strained (Burkard 1999). The attack happens 'without' Senwosret, which tallies with the description in *Sinuhe* that Amenemhat I died in sudden circumstances while the prince was on an expedition: Jansen-Winkeln's argument that

king to announce a decade-old event both as a warning to his son – the fictional audience – and in order to bring the event into the sphere of public discourse – the actual audience of the text. Carolyn Thériault (1993) reaches a similar conclusion about the assassination, but argues for an extreme historicist reading in which Amenemhat I was the actual author of the work, despite later Egyptian claims that the teaching was written by a scribe Khety. Nicholas Grimal also gives a historicist reading, but dates the composition of the text to the New Kingdom, reading it as a commentary on a troubled mid-18th Dynasty co-regency (1995b).

If one relates the discussion to the specific nature of the text, it is possible to resolve these dilemmas without redating, denying the existence of the co-regency, or ignoring the teaching's explicit statement that the king died before the co-regency was instituted. The teaching has a clear historical dimension, but we cannot make assumptions about the manner in which it is related to history, or to what extent it is historiographic. There is always incongruency between social and political developments on the one hand and symbolic and textual systems on the other. Dorothea Arnold (1991) has argued that Amenemhat I's reign was marked by more continued changes than the textual and iconographic evidence might at first suggest. Confusion may arise because we do not know the historical details of co-regency,[5] but it is also possible that rules of decorum dictated the presentation of the two anomic events referred to in the teaching: an assassination, and the earlier establishment of the first co-regency.[6] As *The Tale of Sinuhe* shows, the killing of a king was a deeply problematic matter to express, and the language of the teaching seems to presuppose the existence of the institution of co-regency in denying that this first example had taken place. The teaching is marked as 'fictional', since the author could not have been the dead king. Fictional texts do not necessarily present historical information as literally accurate, as, say, commemorative annals purport to do, although standards of historical accuracy are notoriously changeable. Rather, the presentation will be shaped by the aims of the literary text, as in Dante's *Divina Commedia* or Shakespeare's history plays (Olsen 1987: 170–4). The historicist critic Jeremy Hawthorn (1996: 87–157) discusses the various ways in which literary works have appropriated and written the history of another unexpected and shocking disaster whose circumstances were not reliably known: the sinking of the *Titanic*

---

the two texts describe two similar but unrelated happenings posits an unlikely coincidence (as noted by, e.g., Obsomer 1993: 139; 1999: 234–6).

[5] Eaton-Krauss (1980: 45–6) tries to resolve the dilemma by suggesting that the verses quoted above describe how Senwosret was a junior, rather than a full, co-regent until the end of his father's reign.

[6] On the ideological difficulties of articulating the pragmatically desirable co-regency in official discourse see Murnane 1977: 239–65. See also Schaefer 1986.

in 1912. The emplotments of the event in literary works embody the diverse cultural concerns of different authors and occasions, changing with time. In the case of *The Teaching of Amenemhat*, the exact date and context of composition can only be guessed, preventing any certain analysis, but like the modern text, it may have emplotted the events it describes in a sophisticated and indirect manner, within the constraints of decorum as well as political expediency, and of both general cultural and particular class concerns (see **10.2**).

As with texts from classical antiquity, methodological awareness is needed to assess different interpretations, to test their validity, and to minimize distortion (e.g., Sourvinou-Inwood 1991: 3–23). The scarcity of the Egyptian evidence, and its possibly unrepresentative character, increases the need for careful modelling of contexts (Baines 1996b: 339–45). The problems of historical interpretation are essentially the same as those of reading texts (cf. Newton 1990: 10–11); western literary studies have developed partly in response to practical problems such as those that face the Egyptologist in an extreme form. In literary theory, however, there is no consensus about the status or practice of interpretation that could be adopted wholesale by Egyptology – as is also the case in Assyriology (Michalowski 1996). This pluralism brings with it, in David Robey's words, an awareness

> that it may be a mistake to try to define the essential features of literature in absolute and objective terms; that such definitions as one may devise are likely to be relevant only to certain kinds or features of literature, or merely constitute one among a number of possible ways of approaching the subject. (1986b: 90)

Despite such difficulties, these texts cannot be dismissed simply as curiosities, as evidence of merely historical value, or as evidence for theoretical models: they are enduring poetic works in themselves. The expectations and preoccupations which can produce a 'deafness' to the literary nature of these texts can be traced back to the time of their discovery, and can be related to the assumptions of literary and Egyptological scholarship in that period.

1.2 THE LITERARY TRADITION IN EGYPTOLOGY

> I. A Professed Critic has a right to declare that his Author *wrote* whatever he thinks he *ought* to have written, with as much positiveness as if He had been at his elbow.
> II. He has a right to alter any passage which He does not understand.
>
> Thomas Edwards, *The Canons of Criticism* (1748)

On 22–23 July 1828 Jean-François Champollion saw the collection of François Sallier and realized that it contained non-funerary manuscripts, including 'deux rouleaux contenant des espèces d'odes ou litanies à la louage d'un Pharaon' (1868: 18; see also Sallier 1828; Lepsius 1849: 49).[7] The text was *The Teaching of King Amenemhat*. The classical tradition of Egyptian writings as either historical or hermetic 'sacred writings' constrained the expectations of first 'hierologists': they were not expecting to find anything resembling 'literature'. Emmanuel de Rougé first realized the possibility of literature in 1852, describing the Late Egyptian *Tale of the Two Brothers* as 'la premier échantillon du génie égyptien dans un genre purement littéraire', and 'un ouvrage de pure imagination' (1852: 306, 319). Although the texts had begun to escape from the inherited preconceptions, other comparisons and expectations were influential: François Chabas was struck by the tale's similarity with the Biblical story of Potiphar ([1859]: 317), and Gaston Maspero by its similarity to the Arabic *Thousand and One Nights* (1911: vi). A concise current summary of attitudes is provided by Samuel Birch's *Introduction to the Study of the Egyptian Hieroglyphs* for the Great Exhibition in London, in which he referred to Egyptian writings as 'peculiarly monumental' (1857: 211), but admitted that 'even works of imagination were extant in Pharaonic time' (1857: 279).

A central group of the Middle Kingdom literary corpus, including *The Tale of Sinuhe* and *The Tale of the Eloquent Peasant* (see **4.2**), had already been known for some years, and was published in facsimile by Richard Lepsius in 1859 without commentary (1859: pl. 104–14). A few years later Chabas identified some of these compositions as 'récits d'il y a quatre mille ans' (1865). He gave partial translations and recognized that the papyri were 'de nature anecdotique'. In the same year Charles Goodwin produced an article on *Sinuhe* in *Fraser's Magazine*, later reprinted as a pamphlet entitled *The Story of Saneha, an Egyptian Tale of Four Thousand Years Ago*, including a translation. He suggested that these 'Berlin' papyri had been placed in the tomb of their owner who had 'delighted to peruse (them) when alive' (1866: 11). He considered the tale to be 'short and simple' with 'little claim upon the attention of the modern reader, plied with sensation novels' (1866: 44). The discoverers of the texts saw them as almost 'pre-historic', comparable to primitive folktales and to the more inspired biblical compositions. These predominantly classicist approaches (Loprieno 1996b: 39–40) betray a lack of comprehension of the implications of the loss of the language for interpretation, and a lack of engagement with the cultural otherness of the texts. This was evident in critics' evaluation of many non-western texts: in 1835 Thomas Macaulay could

---

[7] Schenkel (1996) provides a general discussion of the study of literature in Egyptology in a broader framework: here I concentrate on the interpretive and evaluative background.

write that 'I have never found one (orientalist) who could deny that a single shelf of a good European library was worth the whole native literature of India and Arabia'.[8]

At the beginning of the twentieth century literary studies in general were dominated by the positivist school of criticism, in which literature was considered in relation to factual causes, such as the historical context, the cultural environment, and its sources – and thus itself required little explicit definition. The school acknowledged that literary texts were distinctive, but 'in practice it treated them as if they were indistinguishable from other sorts of historical document' (Jefferson and Robey 1986: 9). Its approaches were euhemeristic, making direct connections between literature and history, and adductive, making assumptions about individual texts without any consideration of typology (Loprieno 1996b: 40; see also Mitchell 1985b: 6). Philological knowledge of a text was often taken as providing 'an unmediated access to the consciousness that produced a text' (Dellamora 1995: 145). In this general context Adolf Erman produced in 1923 a comprehensive anthology of Egyptian literature, including lyrics and commemorative and religious texts (see Blumenthal 1996b), for which he claimed a threefold significance, given in a revealing order: first, their age; second, their 'insight into an active intellectual life'; and third, an insight into ancient Egyptian 'poetry' (1927: xliii). A sense of texts as historic curiosities is embodied in T. Eric Peet's comparative study (1931), where he states that Egyptian texts could have no value as literature (131–2), because they lacked the power of 'conjuring with words', and commented that 'there is more poetry in each line of Keats' *Ode to a Nightingale* than in the whole of the Egyptian lyric' of *The Dialogue of a Man and His Ba* (130–42, especially 135). Romantic assumptions about what constitute literary qualities also have proved influential elsewhere (Kermode 1971). These positivist attitudes found expression in the more enduringly influential work of Alan H. Gardiner, whose *Notes on the Story of Sinuhe* devoted scarcely two pages to the tale's 'literary aspect' (1916: 164–5). Despite this, it was *Sinuhe* that he singled out for praise, and recommended to Rudyard Kipling as a world classic (Gardiner 1942: 74 n.1). Gardiner's choice of Kipling as a judge reveals more about his attitude towards literature than about the tale: Kipling (who concurred) was eminently suitable as a writer of stories about civilized men amid foreigners, but he is not a representative of the whole of English literature, still less of its high tradition.[9]

---

[8] Minute of 1835 on Indian Education (quoted in Said 1984: 12). For the phenomenon of 'orientalism' and the pervasiveness of eurocentrism in older studies of eastern cultures, see Said 1978.

[9] The influence of this evaluative tradition should not be underestimated. E.g., the *editio princeps* of *The Sporting King* describes it as 'a clumsy, dull and poor parody of literature' (Caminos

The work of the great Georges Posener published from 1950 onwards remains a landmark of studies of Egyptian literature, establishing the literary corpus, especially in a series of articles entitled 'Recherches littéraires' (1950a, 1951a, 1951d, 1952a–b, 1955, 1960). He did not use an explicit definition of literature, despite being familiar with Russian Formalist critics (J. Assmann 1999a: 2), but he regarded the texts as part of world literature (1971: 220).

1.3 THE PROPAGANDA MODEL

> Notre arrogance, qui sans cesse refuse aux hommes du passé des perceptions pareilles aux nôtres . . .
> Marguerite Yourcenar, *Archives du Nord* (1977), 'La nuit des temps'

The lack of a group of identified authors for Middle Kingdom poems has had a marked effect on Egyptological approaches. Egyptology has tended to adopt a traditional and positivist line, seeing the text as a direct result of an author's personal and historical experience. The matter is compounded by the fact that the protagonist of a text often takes on the role of the implied author (as in teachings, discourses, and the first person tales; see **4.3**), and there has been a continuing readiness to accept the protagonists of discursive texts as the individuals who actually composed the texts (the actor as author). This is perhaps a result of the critics' aversion to dealing with an authorless literary tradition (cf. Forster 1965: 85–96), and also a desire to enliven a blank historical record with touches of human interest (as acknowledged by de Buck 1938a). Scholars such as Hans Goedicke have attempted unsuccessfully to attribute many of the poems to a historical individual author (cf. Parkinson 1991e: 175; a similar fate has befallen Shakespeare: e.g., Wells and Taylor 1987: 134–41). There are convincing reasons for thinking that almost all of the supposedly 'authored' wisdom texts are pseudonymous and that the author-protagonists or actors are not the actual authors.

The emphasis on literature as a reflection of political history is in part a response to this specifically modern problem in reading the texts. Their anonymity makes them difficult to date, but if they can be attributed to a defined function and be regarded as a reflection of a specific historical event, they can be situated in a context. The aims of Posener's influential study of Middle Kingdom literature were summarized as follows (1956: ix):

1956: 25; compare Posener's description of these compositions as 'full of inane talk': 1971: 234). Resistance to theoretically informed analyses endures: e.g., Kitchen 1988: 280; 1996.

pour la littérature, la recherche cessait de se cantonner dans l'esthétique et la morale: elle pouvait aborder les questions de critique interne, l'étude des intentions et des tendences de l'écrivain, des motifs qui ont suscité la création de l'œuvre. Considérés comme documents historiques et replacés dans le cadre de leurs temps, les textes recevaient un sens concret et acquéraient une vie qu'ils n'avaient pas auparavant.

He identified the phenomenon of 'l'utilisation de la parole écrite à des fins politiques' (1956: 14) as having arisen in a time of political and intellectual confusion in the First Intermediate Period, when 'l'actualité a fait son intrusion dans la littérature, et on a appris à se servir des écrits pour influer sur l'opinion' (1956: 15). Subsequently the Middle Kingdom availed itself of literature to reaffirm its challenged values (1956: 17).

His placing of literature within a cultural context was thus primarily in political terms. The reading as propaganda has been subsequently adopted as a comprehensive framework to discuss the totality of literature, although Posener himself had reservations (Schenkel 1999).[10] This has proved a limiting strategy, favouring an interpretation of *The Shipwrecked Sailor* as 'ein Text der Opposition' because anything written in the Middle Kingdom must be political propaganda (Helck 1992, esp. 73–4). The unspoken motive of reading literature to recover otherwise sparse evidence for political reality compromises the methodology of such an approach; William Kerrigan has scornfully dismissed attempts to 'reconstruct political situations from the scattered topical details of an age that had not yet found the good sense to invent the daily newspaper or, better yet, the weekly news magazine' (1992: 73). Critics such as A. P. Foulkes (1983) have argued that propaganda is a complex phenomenon, while Jaques Ellul's influential study (1973) argues that it is ubiquitous, distinguishing four pairs of types: political (a government aiming at precise aims) and social (from within); agitation (subversive) and integration (affirming the social setting); vertical (from a leader to the masses) and horizontal (inside the group); rational and irrational. Complexities of this broad model have often not been fully integrated into discussions of the Ancient Near East.

Literature's responses to and interaction with state ideology range from the apparent social conformity expounded in the teachings to the apparently non-conformist laments in reflective wisdom literature. Some scholars have analysed this variety in historicist terms as reflecting differing political periods, the teachings the settled Kingdoms, and the laments the Intermediate Periods. This approach underestimates the complexity of art's relationship to ideology, and tacitly assimilates the Egyptian model of

---

[10] E.g., R. J. Williams 1964: 14–30; Spycher 1982: 1120–2; contrasting overviews: Eyre 1996a; Simpson 1996.

events, with its binary opposition of order and chaos. Posener's dating of *The Teaching for Merikare* and other texts to the First Intermediate Period, and his schematic view of that period as one of intellectual freedom, are now widely challenged,[11] as is the dating of many other texts to the periods of their settings. The make-up of the audience and levels of literacy are problematic, and largely unaddressed by the propaganda model (cf. Baines 1996c: 353–60). If literacy rates were as low as has been suggested, the audience will have been limited to the elite, who are not the audience he envisaged, although the elite were perhaps the source of opposition that the king and ruling group most needed to neutralize or persuade (cf. Liverani 1990: 28–9). The possible audience for such horizontal 'persuasion' is also problematic for specific texts, as in Goedicke's readings of *Amenemhat* and *Neferti* (1988b: 5; cf. 1977a: 8–14) as propaganda *to*, and not from, the king – the reverse of Posener's understanding of their purpose. Such specifically political readings also leave the later dissemination of these works largely unexplained. 'Propaganda' as a framework for interpreting Middle Kingdom literature thus remains problematic, not only because of the social restrictions to literary communication but also because it ignores distinctive features of the poems, which are diverse, ambiguous and ironic, involving a dialogue between reader and text. They are thus the opposite of the intentional and unqualified advocacy of state values that is often implicit in 'propaganda', a term that implies a one-way message.

The propaganda model is a reductive view of the texts, their audience and their artistry. Even unequivocal statements of cultural and ideological values are different from 'propaganda' in a narrow sense. In this latter, broader sense one might affirm that 'all artists are propagandists' as did René Wellek and Austin Warren (1962: 35–6). The relevance of such a broad undifferentiated concept of cultural propaganda is undeniable, but its analytical usefulness is questionable, since it means little more than that the texts are 'part of the system of signs that constitutes a given culture' (Greenblatt 1980: 4–5). The same interpretive dilemma is posed by more familiar works of western representational art: although Michelangelo's *David* has strong, specifically political aspects in iconography, subject matter, commission, and positioning in the Piazza Signoria in Florence (e.g., de Tolnay 1975: 13–15), the statue has not usually been seen as primarily 'propaganda'. A strategy of differentiating literary texts rather than of assimilating them to a single model fosters awareness of their complexity, allowing one to explore the interaction of different types of

---

[11] E.g., Schenkel 1975a; Junge 1977; J. Assmann 1983a, 1991: 259–87; overview: Willems 1988: 244–9 on Coffin Text evidence; general overview of period: Blumenthal 1996a: 130–2.

discourse, to site the interpretation of literary – and other – texts in a specific cultural system, and to 'reconstruct the nodes of perception which a given text can be observed to have affirmed or challenged' (Foulkes 1983: 106–7). The experience of Classical scholars exploring the multivalency of works such as Vergil's *Aeneid* suggests that such approaches are rewarding for the modern reader of ancient texts (Alpers 1979: 246–7).

The concern with propaganda among Egyptologists is determined partly by the political circumstances of twentieth century scholars and the application of the term is potentially anachronistic. The use of such a negatively value-laden term places the reader outside the ancient cultural system: 'propaganda' is the expression of cultural views one does not approve of. Without underrating the texts' public purposes for their contemporary audiences, one can usefully refine and qualify the term 'propaganda' (with Ellul), or use other terminology, such as royalist advocacy (Simpson), legitimation (Baines), loyalism, or prestige and interest (Liverani). One influential adaptation of this model has been to recast it in more general terms of culture rather than politics (see below).

Two related tendencies of old historicist treatments of literary texts can also be noted. One is with the phenomenon which the New Critics termed the 'heresy of paraphrase' (Brooks 1949: 176–96). In this, literary texts are not read as artefacts, but 'paraphrased' for their content, as cultural as well as political history. This tendency is particularly evident in the critical history of *The Dialogue of a Man and His Ba*, whose dialogue form evoked the classical Platonic dialogues and gave rise to expectations of a 'philosophic' content that could be decoded from a poetic form. This approach has persisted (e.g., Barta 1969), and only in the late twentieth century were anti-paraphrastic interpretations advanced. A second tendency is to adopt formal textual criticism, according to which any inconsistencies in the text are seen as pointers to a textual evolution (e.g., Herrmann 1957; Seibert 1967; Fecht 1972). Redactional activity is well attested in the transmission of texts, but redactional criticism in an extreme form relies on a severe and anachronistic view of the exclusive unity of genres (see **2.3**). Such textual analysis is very often a substitute for engaged interpretation of elements in a composition that do not match the modern reader's expectations. Almost all the texts of the Middle Kingdom literary corpus were presented as unified wholes, including those which display a diverse variety of genres and modes, which suggests that a redactional approach is not generally appropriate (Parkinson 1992: 164–6).

1.4 MODELS AND APPROACHES

> The essential vocation of interpretive anthropology is not to answer our deepest questions but to make available to us answers that others ... have given, and thus to include them in the consultable trend of what man has said.
>
> Clifford Geertz, 'Thick Description' (1973: 30)

In the 1970s, there was a movement towards a more detailed study of the literary qualities in individual texts (e.g., Purdy 1977) developing gradually into a general acceptance of a hermeneutic approach (Loprieno 1996b: 41). Much literary work was accomplished in anthologies of translations, although these rarely address theoretical or typological issues. Miriam Lichtheim's influential anthology resists western expectations of 'literature' with a selection of wider types of text than Posener's canon (1973: vi), while the fluency of her translations foregrounds their aesthetic aspects. I here select and review three broadly complementary trends in late-twentieth-century analyses featured in *Ancient Egyptian Literature: History and Forms*, edited by Antonio Loprieno (1996a), which has provided a diverse new paradigm.

1. One approach is that of scholars who use formalist and structuralist theories of text and language. Jan Assmann's review (1974) of *Das Handbuch der Orientalistik* was a turning point in published Egyptological treatments of genre. Although his approach was schematic and limited in its equation of genre with *Sitz im Leben*, the review was influential in raising theoretical awareness (cf. Loprieno 1996a: ix). One suggested criterion for literariness was the relationship of the text to function: genres are determined by function, but in a narrow definition those of literature are functionally non-specific (J. Assmann 1992a), which suggested that literary texts are written forms that have been transposed into a more autonomous state of existence (for Andre Jolles, *Einfache Formen* [1930] see, e.g., A. Fowler 1982: 151–2). This basically formalist and structuralist idea of the differentiation of literature as a transposition of non-literary texts (*Ausgangtyp*) also occurs in a study by Wolfgang Helck (1972; see also Fecht 1991). J. Assmann has emphasized the importance of literature's role of expressing cultural norms – rather than, for example, expressing or evoking spontaneous feeling – and the influence of the tomb on written literature (1983c), together with the 'great tradition' of intellectual discourse (1984a, 1990). Assmann's studies show a growing dissatisfaction with the concept of 'literariness'. His subsequent work shows a renewed emphasis on literature as primarily 'cultural texts' with an 'identity function' of expressing a culture's self-understanding, rather than as functionally

or contextually unbounded writings (1996b, 1999a, 1999b; cf. A. Assmann 1999: 89). Thus, Middle Kingdom compositions acted as 'a kind of normative and formative cultural program which conveys and reproduces cultural identity from one generation to the other' (1999a: 7). He assigns literature to the institutional frame of the school, with the court as the generator of such texts, arguing that literature represents the programmatic codification of social norms, to be 'learnt and not read' (1999a: 7). He views literature's 'entertainment' aspect as a development only of the later New Kingdom, when it became separate from official discourse and 'countercultural' (1993). This recantation is part of a schematic and evolutionary view of Egyptian civilization (1996a).[12]

Loprieno's *Topos und Mimesis* (1988) expounds the thesis that literature is essentially mimetic, that is, concerned with the individual rather than with social norms or nomos. This schema draws on the characterization of literature as 'transposition' (1988: 97). His treatments of literature are highly developed theoretically, but his model of topos and mimesis encounters problems in the treatment of wisdom literature, since the siting of texts along this continuum of social and personal concerns does not match the pattern of formal genres: non-royal and royal teachings are purely topical; discourses, dialogues and loyalistic teachings are intermediary to varying degrees; exclusively narrative tales occupy the mimetic pole (1996f: 538–9; cf. A. Assmann 1999: 85–7). I therefore prefer to discuss the texts intertextually, in terms of looser areas of official and literary discourse, rather than to adopt his terminology. Loprieno has argued that multilevel ambiguity is a sign of literature, defining its characteristics as fictionality, intertextuality and reception (1996b: 43–58), while placing this schema within J. Assmann's evolutionary framework (1996e: 517–8). Gerald Moers (1999b, 1999c, 2001) has developed Loprieno's characterizations of literariness in a study of tales of travel that has implications for Egyptian literature as a whole, proposing that the motifs of travel and boundary crossing can be taken as paradigms of literary fictionality.[13]

2. Another approach continues and modernizes the philological tradition of editing and commentary exemplified by Posener. The importance of traditional philology in shaping readings of a text is evident in studies such as Robert Parant's valuable examination of the juridical aspects and terminology of *The Tale of Sinuhe* (1982). Notable in this respect are the literary studies of Elke Blumenthal, which are concerned with literature in a historical and ideological context, analysing genre and structure (e.g., 1980a, 1982a, 1984b, 1985, 1998a), and of Hans-Werner Fischer-Elfert

---

[12] On such tendencies in Near Eastern studies in general see Baines 1996c: 383. J. Assmann's use of 'cultural texts' originates in Geertz (1973: 412–53), but differs significantly from Geertz's.
[13] Comparable theoretical studies include, e.g., Junge 1994.

(e.g., 1996a, 1999). While emphasizing that literature is not abstract (e.g., Blumenthal 1996a: 133), such approaches admit a relative abstraction from situations (e.g., L. Morenz 1996: 111).

3. Another line of approach includes the 'new British school', as it is termed by William Kelly Simpson (1996: 438), which shares aspects of both the approaches already outlined. Less explicit in terms of theory than the work of Loprieno, its presentation of readings of individual works is more explicitly grounded in philology. These readings emphasize the relative autonomy and complexity of literary texts as works of art. The articles of John Baines (e.g., 1982, 1990a) can be considered turning points in the analysis of the texts as aesthetic artefacts. This approach emphasizes literary criticism more than literary theory. It employs anthropological models and strategies of contextualization, and remains based on methodologically informed assessments of textual form, context and aesthetic aspects, rather than on the application of theoretical models. In this respect, it has close affinities with Philippe Derchain's brilliantly personal and perceptive analyses of cultural artefacts (e.g., 1969, 1987, 1996a). It shares with Gerald Moers' work an emphasis on fictionality and aesthetic qualities, as opposed to socio-functionally determined analyses.

I summarize here a few aspects that I address in this study, which are developed in subsequent chapters.

Although 'not many scholars spend time defending the literariness of literary works' (Lipking 1995: 2), this remains a priority in Egyptology. Many scholars have acknowledged a degree of autonomy in the Egyptian literary corpus, which tends towards the self-referential and self-contained, while scholars such as J. Assmann and Blumenthal argue rightly against anachronistically 'aesthetic' approaches. Critical works have emphasized the danger of overestimating the autonomy of art, an idea that derives from nineteenth century aesthetics. 'Notions of literature transcending society, history, and politics then (are) in themselves ... ideological manoeuvres' (Sinfield 1994: 29). Terry Eagleton argues that this elevation of literary studies is itself (in part) a response to the social context of criticism in the nineteenth century (1984: 39–40), when the romantic image of the poet as unacknowledged visionary sage was formulated, and some critics have claimed that capitalism is the perpetrator of separate discursive domains (cf. Greenblatt 1990: 146–59). This has a material parallel in the enormous growth of museum collections, uprooting works of art from their context (Iser 1989: 204–5); the Bloomsbury image of all writers writing while seated together 'in a sort of British Museum reading-room' (Forster 1927: 18) is now problematic. Much recent work in literary theory has been marked by a turn towards history (e.g., Cox and Reynolds 1993: 3–38; Newton 1990: 102–29; Hamilton 1996; Hawthorn

1996) without, however, going as far as some Egyptologists' return to the view that literary texts were both bound to socio-functional contextually-defined roles in culture and were undifferentiated parts of a monologistic tradition. Historical and contextual evidence suggests that literature was a differentiated form of discourse within Middle Kingdom culture. As Stephen Greenblatt remarks 'differentiation is not the same as autonomy' (1990: 112).

While literature creates its own world, it embodies and is an active part of the cultural values of its period; it is 'part of the system of signs that constitutes a given culture' (Greenblatt 1980: 4). Comparison with other contemporaneous fields of discourse allows one to model the distinctive social and cultural ('functional') context of literary discourse, aiming for a balance between isolation and homogeneity (Gumbrecht 1996: 15). I assume that the texts aroused in the original audience distinctive and culturally circumscribed interpretive responses. I seek to demonstrate possible approaches that can be induced from the texts and suggest possible relationships between the putative original responses and modern ones. One aim is to reconstruct the texts – to recontextualize them – in a system of cultural values, rather than to provide a narrowly historical analysis. In keeping with the limited evidence, I aim at a broadly synchronic study within the Middle Kingdom, drawing on theoretical frameworks to identify gaps in the evidence.

Loprieno warns against a 'prehistoricism' in interpretation (1996b: 42) that is common to early literary analysis (see above) and modern deconstructionism: 'the illusion that there can be an unfiltered hermeneutic continuity between Egyptian literary text and Egyptological interpretation'.[14] All approaches are influenced by their modern context, and a degree of hermeneutic continuity has to be assumed if interpretation is to take place at all. I thus focus on literature as in part a personal discourse. I emphasize the intertextual and cultural context of the texts and the textuality of culture in order to foreground specifically 'literary' features that can only be explained by aesthetic considerations. One aim is to reclaim the concept of accessible 'literary' meaning. While I do not deny the importance of cultural difference or underestimate criticism's role of seeking, in Greenblatt's phrase, a 'poetics of culture' (see **2.4**), I adopt a strategy of dwelling on similarities as well as differences. In attempting to assess the compositions' impact on their audiences it is a productive heuristic strategy to draw self-consciously on modern parallels: our experience of reading the writings of our own culture can inform our attempts to reconstruct and to imagine the original, at first unimaginably different,

---

[14] For example, B. Lesko's characterizing Egyptian lyric art as the 'romantic outpourings of the human soul' (1986: 97).

reception of an ancient culture in their fullness, and can help by reminding us of the life that the texts once had but have now lost. Such an approach is inevitably anachronistic, but all historical scholarship involves anachronism.

In this book, I consider the distinctive strategies of literary discourse primarily within the interpretive framework provided by studies of early modern literature as cultural artefacts, attempting to approach the texts in a personal dialogue, governed and inspired by empathy, to explore their role within the intertext (**3**) as a form of discourse that diverges from the norms of ideology, and to demonstrate that this differentiation was integral to expectations of literary practice in the Middle Kingdom (**4–5**). This social practice is formalized in literary style and presentation (**6**) and in literature's manners of presenting its subject matter (**7**). I then present readings of texts from different genres (**8–10**). Any overview must be inductive, and the outline of literature proposed here must remain hypothetical. I adopt a pragmatic rather than a theorizing interpretive strategy and do not intend to exemplify any particular critical school; 'the aggressive use of theory tends to introduce historical distortions' (Lipking 1995: 10). My study may thus be termed 'post-paradigm thinking'. An open, multidimensional approach[15] can attempt to encompass the complexity of the phenomenon under discussion without fragmenting closely integrated aspects of study. I use hermeneutic approaches since it concerns relevant problems (drawing on the work of critics such as E. D. Hirsch and A. Fowler); reader-response criticism as a guide to readers' expectations, particularly in matters of fictionality and the possible purposes of fictional literature (Wolfgang Iser); and the New Historicists, who address the question of literature's role within the early modern state (Stephen Greenblatt), addressing issues similar to those envisaged by Posener (1956: ix). Theory is much needed (e.g., Trigger 1998; Baines 1996c: 344; Lustig 1997), but is a means to the end of comprehending the ancient material and cultural artefacts themselves,[16] which can claim a certain primacy especially since they have, as Battiscombe Gunn (1906: 12–13) remarked at the start of the twentieth century, 'for the most part, . . . cried in the wilderness of neglect hitherto, or fallen on ears filled with the clamour of more instant things'.

---

[15] Cf. the remarks of R. Bagnall on writing history from Greek papyrological sources: 1995, esp. 6–8; on literary history: Nemoianu 1995.
[16] See Fischer-Elfert 1996a on the priority of source-publication. One can suggest another more cynical consideration: in the end, theoreticians and theories come and go – in the late twentieth century with great rapidity (e.g., Perkins 1995).

2
General considerations: Definitions, genre, interpretation

Les théories passent; la grenouille reste.

Anon.

2.1 INTRODUCTION

Modern literary theory is plural and diverse.[1] For Egyptian texts the primary problem is that their historical and cultural context is alien and inaccessible: this is less true for many of the texts around which literary theory clusters. Parallel concerns are however voiced by critics dealing with early modern works, such as the New Historicists.[2] Many of their studies analyse the relationship between power and literature in Elizabethan culture, addressing concerns similar to those that have been prominent in treatments of Middle Kingdom texts since the work of Georges Posener. In this chapter I review three aspects of reading Middle Kingdom literature with respect to general issues: the nature of what is 'literary'; the role of genre; and the nature of interpretation.

2.2 DEFINING 'LITERATURE'

Je veux ici entasser aucunes façons anciennes que j'ai en mémoire, les unes de même les nôtres, les autres différentes, a fin qu'ayant en l'imagination cette continuelle variation des choses humaines, nous en ayons le jugement plus écairci et plus ferme.

Montaigne, *Essais* I (1580), xlix

---

[1] Convenient surveys include: Jefferson and Robey 1986; D. Birch 1989; Newton 1990; Greenblatt and Gunn 1992.
[2] See, e.g., Montrose 1986, 1988, 1989, 1992; Lützeller 1990; Felperin 1992: 142–69; Hamilton 1996; Hawthorn 1996; Brannigan 1998.

2.2.1 GENERAL

Definitions of Egyptian 'literature' have varied from narrow to broad (Baines, in press). Georges Posener's enumeration of the Middle and New Kingdom corpus (1951a, 1952a) implied a narrow definition. A broader definition includes the totality of Egyptian transmitted written elite culture, which has been termed 'the stream of tradition', adopting a phrase of the Assyriologist A. Leo Oppenheim (1977: 13). This can be described as a recorded body of statements of cultural value, beyond the immediate and practical conveying of information, as it has been for eighteenth century England (e.g., Eagleton 1983: 17). The literary texts I discuss here correspond to Posener's grouping (listed in **A.1–2**) and were an integral part of the wider body of written culture. Nevertheless they appear to have been differentiated, since they display a coherence on various intrinsic and extrinsic levels, distinguishing them as a group within that culture (Parkinson 1991b).

Concepts of 'literature' are mutable, whether formed by contemporaneous authors and readers or by later critics. For example, in the mid-twentieth century the Anglo-American New Critics (Robey 1986b) contracted literature to a few major genres (A. Fowler 1982: 11–14), whereas many subsequent critics have expanded it to the point of declaring the end of literature as a restricted corpus. As the Marxist critic Raymond Williams stated, 'the crucial theoretical break is the recognition of "literature" as a specialising social and historical category' (1977: 53; see also Arac 1995). The often intuitive assumption of a narrow definition of literature is largely a product of nineteenth century aesthetic, cultural and social attitudes and is thus potentially inappropriate to early civilizations such as that of ancient Egypt (see, e.g., J. Assmann 1999a). Yet while pre-nineteenth century characterizations of literature relate to a broader body of writings, they make internal distinctions. For example, among the wide body of Renaissance literature there is a narrower class of 'poesy', a term that is not limited to verse compositions (Fowler 1982: 9). The written stream of tradition in any culture is varied and differentiated. Thus, although 'literature' is a potentially anachronistic term, it is worth retaining to distinguish a narrow range of Egyptian discourse. As Walter Benn Michaels remarks (1995: 189–90):

> Since the distinctive literariness of literary texts must itself be understood as a historical fact, any attempt to characterize it will inevitably take the form of historical explanation. Poems, in other words, may be different from statutes, but they are not less historical than statutes, so questions about the distinctive nature of literature, like questions about the distinctive nature of statutes, will be historical questions producing historical answers.

Many theories have aimed at universal definitions of literature, often operating exclusively with a western, modern or early modern corpus. This tendency is extreme in autotelic definitions, in which literary texts were regarded as autorcferential in terms of their language and their relationship to reality (Robey 1986a; D. Birch 1989: 110–15). These limit the involvement of literature with the social and political world, and often ignore the political implications of their assumptions, separating the concerns of literary criticism from those of politics (e.g., Said 1984: 2–5, 31–53). The twentieth century saw a movement towards autotelic definitions, in which the determining features of literariness were sought within the text as aspects of language, style and structure, rather than in social or personal aspects. The literary text was often regarded as a thing in itself, an autonomous 'verbal icon' (Wimsatt 1964) or a 'well wrought urn' (Brooks 1949) unbound by its culture. This approach tended to treat all texts as if they were lyric poems (especially metaphysical ones), and thus made no great distinction between different types of text. As Charles Martindale notes, 'a stress on aesthetic autonomy always tends to narrow the range of what poetry can treat' (1997c: 117).

In the more recent 'turn to history' from formalism, several schools have built on formalist and structuralist criticism to argue that art is not autonomous but 'differentiated' from the surrounding world, and that authorial 'intention and genre are as social, contingent, and ideological as the historical situation' (Greenblatt 1990: 112). This movement is towards a more anthropological approach, in which literature is 'functional rather than ontological, as designating a kind of writing whose difference from other kinds is a matter not of its essential being but of its cultural function' (L. Patterson 1990: 256).

In their *Modern Literary Theory: A Comparative Introduction*, Ann Jefferson and David Robey suggest a broad definition of literature which can be paraphrased as involving a literary communication about reality from an (implied) author to an audience in language (1986: 13). I consider here the relevance of these factors to Egyptian compositions.

The concept of authorial identity has played a prominent role in some definitions of 'literature', but this is a legacy of the romantic period, and modern theory has often downplayed the role of the author. The New Critics in particular argued against the 'intentionalist fallacy', by which a text would be interpreted in terms of the author's (avowed) intentions (Wimsatt and Beardsley 1964), which attached the supposedly autonomous text to a particular moment in history. Any approach centred around the historical identity of the author (the 'biographical fallacy') is problematic for Egyptian texts, since the identity of the author is inaccessible and not central to the literary tradition (see **1.3**, **4.3**). However, one can posit an 'implied author' who is involved in creating the unitary meaning of a text: although a surviving Egyptian text may have been written by various individuals, it has a single implied author (see Derchain 1996a). The return to history in some sense marks a reinstatement of the role of the author, in opposition to the structuralist schools who proclaimed the 'death of the (historical) author' (see Jefferson 1986b: 111–12). It also includes consideration of broader questions, as Michel Foucault (1977: 138) evoked:

> We can easily imagine a culture where discourse would circulate without any need for an author. Discourses, whatever their status, form, or value, and regardless of our manner of handling them, would unfold in a pervasive anonymity. No longer the tiresome repetitions:
> 'Who is the real author?' . . .
> New questions will be heard:
> 'What are the modes of existence of this discourse?'
> 'Where does it come from; how is it circulated; who controls it?'
> 'What placements are determined for possible subjects?'
> 'Who can fulfil these diverse functions of the subject?'

Similar questions attend the role of the 'reader'. There has been controversy about the nature of the audience for ancient literary texts, how wide access was to them, and whether they were privately read or performed. In the context of the Middle Kingdom, a neutral term such as 'audience' is more appropriate than 'reader'. One can posit an 'implied audience', whose nature can be induced from the ancient text. Past audiences formed different interpretive communities with different conventions from those of modern readership. Reader-response and reception theory stress the importance of the cultural context of the audience, which shapes the meaning of the text (e.g., Newton 1990: 141–53). Work of that style has explored the interactive role of the audience in the creation of meaning, which is variously created by different audiences: 'interpretation is not the art of construing but the art of constructing. Interpreters do not decode poems; they make them' (Fish 1980: 327). Critics such as Wolfgang Iser argue that the reader responds to a specifically literary text in a distinctive manner, notably in the interpretation of gaps (Iser 1989, 1993; Newton 1990: 138–41).

What 'reality' does the communication concern? This reality can be ideological as well as belonging to the material world. The psychoanalytic school of critics is concerned with psychological reality (e.g., Wright 1986), while Marxist schools concentrate on the political reality (e.g., Forgacs 1986). The experienced 'reality' of ancient Egyptian life is largely inaccessible except in its self-conscious cultural formulation in surviving artefacts; in many areas of Egyptian and other civilizations only a 'history of discourses' can be attempted (Foucault 1981: 69). No imitation or representation of reality (mimesis) is unmediated by cultural discourse, just as all representations of something as apparently 'objective' as landscape are 'the product of a country's craving and culture's framing' (Schama 1995: 7). Louis Montrose writes of the 'textuality of history' (1989: 20):

> We can have no access to a full and authentic past, a lived and material existence, unmediated by the surviving textual traces of the society in question – traces whose survival we cannot assume to be contingent but must rather presume to be at least partially consequent upon complex and subtle social processes of preservation and effacement; ... those textual traces are themselves subject to subsequent textual mediations when they are construed as 'documents' upon which historians ground their own text, called 'histories'.

The relationship of a text to reality is complex, something Egyptologists have tended to underestimate (**1**). Egyptologists such as Georges Posener also tended to express awareness of the relationship between literature and ideology in exclusively sociopolitical terms, yet a more intertextual approach in terms of discourses is practicable.

The communication of an ancient text can appear to be inaccessible due to philological problems, but the issues are really at another level. Many theoretical schools have suggested that literature is an inherently more highly patterned, or more highly expressive, form of communication; such an approach makes lyric verse the quintessential form of literature. The patterning can be in either form or content, both of which are intrinsic to the text. Semantically oriented theories have identified certain linguistic features of a text as the distinguishing marks of literary composition. 'Semantic density' is one such proposed feature, and yet this can be lacking in a supposedly literary text and present in a supposedly non-literary one (e.g., Eagleton 1983: 1–14). Similarly, some literary narratives are simple, while others are semantically complex. The Russian Formalists analysed literature in terms of its linguistic deviation from normal language (e.g., Jefferson 1986a). Roman Jakobson asserted the prime importance of 'literariness', that which makes a text a literary work, and argued 'the set toward the *message* as such, focus on the message for its own sake, is the *poetic* function of language' (1960: 356). Literature was characterized by its 'defamiliarization', that is, 'how works of art create devices which undermine habitual modes of perception and allow the reader to see the world from a fresh perspective' (Newton 1990: 15). Such a general focus on literature as a form of discourse, rather than the analysis of individual works, also characterizes structuralist criticism, for example of Tzvetan Todorov (Newton 1990: 64–73). In Egypt, the style of literary language and diction is shared by other types of text and must be analysed through comparison with other grapholects of varying formality and artificiality. The difficulties attending such issues for dead languages can be exemplified by the comparatively simple question of whether the letters of the early 12th Dynasty funerary priest Heqanakht were colloquial or not (J. P. Allen 1994).

In much Formalist and structuralist criticism literary language is seen as inherently non-referential and aesthetically over-determined (e.g., D. Birch 1989: 110–16). Literary language is also often characterized as non-predicative and truth neutral (e.g., Fry 1995), so that literary texts pretend to assertions rather than making them, and this definition has been influential in Egyptology (e.g., Loprieno 1996f: 539). However, this approach often makes literature synonymous with poetic language and ignores the literary character of many types of writing, such as much expository prose in modern Europe. Even Todorov (1973: 7–8) considered fictionality to be 'one of the consequences of literature', rather than its definition. Wolfgang Iser (1993) moves from a dichotomy between the real and the fictional to a more complex range of real, fictive and imaginary, regarding fictionality as a means to fulfil literature's basic human and cultural role as providing a space for 'play'. Fictionalization is the product of a suspension agreed between author and audience, in which the represented world is 'separated from the reality in which it is normally embedded' (Iser 1989: 238–9).

Later twentieth century critical theory saw a movement away from semantic and structural definitions of what is literary to more historically circumscribed definitions. Structuralist theory 'recognized that the literary work, like any other product of language, is a *construct*' of its culture (Eagleton 1983: 106), that it is not an essentially unique form of discourse but part of a system (e.g., Olsen 1987: 73–87; Eagleton 1983: 1–16). The epistemological principle that meaning is created through context and relationships is relevant to the study of all phenomena, including ancient cultures (e.g., Sourvinou-Inwood 1991). Such approaches downplay the distinctiveness of literature from other texts, in favour of a concern with what Raymond Williams termed 'cultural materialism': the analysis of 'all forms of signification, including quite centrally writing, within the actual means and conditions of their production' (1981: 64–5). More generally, scholars such as Jack Goody (1987) and Walter J. Ong (1982) have also argued that writing itself is not monolithic, and that its potential varies from culture to culture. Literature must thus be considered not as the essentialist category of all literary works but as an aggregate, 'the cultural object of which they are part' (A. Fowler 1982: 3), and as a social practice. The analysis of literature as a cultural institution has particular relevance for ancient texts:

the specifically artistic features of a literary work are defined by the institutional conventions and have no existence independently of the institution; ... therefore the literary work has no objectively given distinguishing features, but ... these features are a product of a set of descriptive and classificatory possibilities created by the institution. (Olsen 1987: 22)

This culturally specific criticism is compatible with more general approaches such as Iser's analysis of the phenomenology of reading which addresses both the general issue of why any culture has literature at all and the manner in which literary discourse can operate as an intersection of texts, discourses and values (Iser 1989: 237–8; cf. Greenblatt 1990: 158–9).

The New Historicist critic Stephen Greenblatt too has argued for a more anthropological criticism, in contrast to 'a conception of art as addressed to a timeless, cultureless, universal human essence, or, alternatively, as a self-regarding, autonomous, closed system – in either case, art as opposed to social life' (1980: 4). Such criticism denies literature's supposed ability to transcend politics and situates it within social acts (e.g., Brannigan 1998: 153). For Greenblatt (1980: 4), literature functions in interlocking ways within the cultural system of codes of behaviour, both expressing these codes and consciously reflecting upon them. Texts are cultural artefacts that have acquired aesthetic power through encoding rhetorical 'social energy' by negotiation between various aspects of their culture (Greenblatt 1988: 1–20).

New Historicism is poststructuralist and anti-essentialist. Intertextuality is central to its style of interpretation: a common strategy is to compare literary and non-literary treatments of a theme (e.g., Greenblatt 1988; review Nuttall 1990). As well as drawing on anthropology, the movement is influenced by Marxist theory, including Williams, and by Foucault (Brannigan 1998: 19–54). Such criticism rehistoricizes and repoliticizes to varying degrees, as is exemplified in different readings of a Keats' sonnet (see Hawthorn 1996: 170–9; radically different perspective: Fry 1995: 122–32). The political aspects of this style of analysis are more central to the related but distinct approach of Cultural Materialist criticism. Central to this is the assertion that the 'texts we call "literary" characteristically address contested aspects of our ideological formation ... Through diverse literary genres and institutions, people write about faultlines, in order to address aspects of their life that they find hard to handle' (Sinfield 1994: 3). Literature is only one site of such discursive struggle, although it is a 'relatively authoritative one' (1994: 4).

The extent to which literature is a distinct form of discourse is a central question for such approaches. Both the Russian Formalists and the Marxist philosopher Louis Althusser saw literary art as something distanced from ideology, revealing the 'gaps' in ideology (Hawthorn 1996: 67–70), and

Althusser claimed that literature possessed 'relative autonomy' (Newton 1990: 103). New Historicism has also tended to view early modern literature as a differentiated form of discourse, characterized in part by its aesthetic playfulness. Critics such as the Cultural Materialist Alan Sinfield have noted that these analyses can take the concept of literature and ideology to be givens and monolithic entities (1994: 27–30). In contrast, Raymond Williams argued that 'we cannot separate literature and art from other kinds of social practice, in such a way as to make them subject to quite special and distinct laws. They may have quite specific features as practices, but they cannot be separated from the general social process' (1980: 44). As such, they cannot be entirely distanced from ideology. Similarly, Sinfield argues that the modern idea of literature 'is not an objective category of value, but a discourse we have been constructing – in order to assert, and contest, certain ranges of values in our cultures' (1994: 29).

In historicist terms, the definition of literature becomes less of an ontological problem and more a question of the historical reconstruction of a social institution. As Piotr Michalowski argues for ancient Near Eastern literature, the aims of New Historicists are compatible with aims of structuralism and formalism, both attempting 'to situate expressive acts within historical frameworks and to distinguish varieties of discourse' (1996: 181).

2.2.2 EGYPTIAN LITERATURE

Egyptian writing can be analysed as a mode of cultural self-definition and presentation and can be discussed in terms of 'decorum' (Baines 1985: 277–305; 1994a), which patterned written discourse as firmly as it did the decoration of tombs and temples, determining the position and manner of representation and of the recording of topics. Such rules were 'probably based ultimately on rules and practices of conduct and etiquette, of spatial separation and religious avoidance' (Baines 1990b: 17–21, quote p. 20; 1996c). The definition and reconstruction of the ancient institution and social practices of literature remain problematic, not least because no distinct descriptive terminology – such as 'literature' – metadiscourse, or even listing of categories is extant from the Middle Kingdom. Most Middle Egyptian terminology, such as $sšw$ 'writings', relates to the materiality of the texts. The same is true of abstract or generalizing categories like 'religion'. Cultural practices can, however, be analysed in the absence of an explicit analysis from within the culture (e.g., Baines 1985).

Evidence for the institution of Egyptian literature is implicit in the archaeological context of manuscripts and provenances, in the cultural context, and in the poems themselves and their intertext. Much of the surviving contextual evidence, however, derives from the use of the texts in the Ramessid Period and may not apply well to the original Middle Kingdom setting. The provenances and groupings of literary documents in archives associate them with other writings in an undifferentiated manner, but since in other cultures distinctively literary and non-literary texts generally circulate inseparably, this is no indication that differentiation did not exist. These literary texts can be examined for implicit attitudes, and are in many cases self-reflexive, describing their own fictional staging and commenting on their own production and qualities.

Egyptian writings also contain several direct and indirect commentaries on literary texts and figures. All are from the Ramessid Period and thus embody the later reception of the Middle Kingdom texts rather than the original context.

1. Two passages from a composition in praise of scribedom are preserved on the verso of P. Chester Beatty IV (= P. BM EA 10684; Gardiner 1935a: 38–44, pl. 18–19; the recto contains hymns). Scholars have suggested that it may be part of a work composed by the Scribe of the Necropolis Amennakht of Deir el-Medina (see Bickel and Mathieu 1993: 37–8), but this is uncertain. The composition as extant is an ostensibly didactic Miscellany text (see Caminos 1954), teaching apprentice scribes the value of writing and wisdom; such Miscellanies are not just school-texts, but also literary anthologies (see Quirke 1996b: 382–3). This one offers reflections on wisdom and particularly on the advantages of being a scribe. One passage can be termed a 'Eulogy of Dead Writers' (vso 2.5–3.11; translations: Parkinson 1991a: 148–50; McDowell 1999: 137–8; see also Brunner 1966a; Wildung 1977: 25–7). It shows the period's attitudes to some protagonists of Middle Kingdom wisdom texts, since it acclaims them as 'sages' (*rḫ-ḫwt*, see, e.g., L. Morenz 1996: 142–3) and as examples of how writing ensures success and cultural continuity. The eulogy extols the past scribes as exceptional, and different from contemporaneous writers:

> Is there any here like Hordedef?
> Is there another like Imhotep?
> There is none among our people like Nefer⟨t⟩i,
> or Khety their chief.
> I shall make you know the names of Ptahemdjehuty and Khakheperreseneb.
> Is there another like Ptahhotep,
> or likewise Kaires? (vso 3.5–7)

Among extant works, these figures relate to the teachings of *Hordedef*, *Khety*, and *Ptahhotep*, and *The Words of Neferti* (see **A.2** for other figures). They are acclaimed for their wisdom, which is evident in that 'they foretold what comes' which then 'happened' (vso 2.6, 3.7–8), and which they concealed in 'teachings' (vso 3.9–10).³ The categorization of the discourse *Neferti* as a teaching probably reflects its usage in Ramessid scribal training rather than its genre. The figures are presented as authors (see **3.1.1**, **4.3**), but not explicitly in literary terms, although a later passage in the text urges the scribal audience to make offerings to the scribe Khety, 'their chief', who is here acclaimed both as someone 'whose verses are choice' – a phrase used of literary language (see **6.4**) – and as the author of *The Teaching of Amenemhat* (vso 6.11–7.2; trans: Parkinson 1991a: 150).

2. 'The Harpist's Song from the Chapel of Intef' is known from a full copy in the Ramessid literary manuscript of P. Harris 500 (= P. BM EA 10600 rto 6.2–7.3; M. V. Fox 1985: 378–80; Wildung 1977: 21–5; trans: Parkinson 1991a: 145–6), from the west bank at Thebes (Mathieu 1996a: 22). An earlier fragmentary monumental copy is known from a late 18th Dynasty tomb chapel at Saqqara (PM III.2², 709–11). The text belongs to a genre well-attested in the New Kingdom,⁴ other examples of which include closely related songs in the early 20th Dynasty tomb of Inherkhau in Deir el-Medina (PM I.1², 423; e.g., McDowell 1999: 123–6), and the 20th Dynasty tomb of Amenpahapy (PM I.1², 419; Wildung 1977: 22). It claims to be copied from a scene in a funerary monument of King Intef, who could belong to either the 11th (2080–1975 BCE) or 17th Dynasty (1640–1635 BCE). It is uncertain whether this attribution is fictional or real,⁵ and, if the latter, which Intef is meant. The date remains controversial, but it is likely to be a composition of the New Kingdom (e.g., J. Assmann 1977b: 975–6). While lamenting the impermanence of human achievement the harpist mentions:

> the speech (*mdwt*) of Imhotep and Hordedef,
> whose sayings (*sḏdwt*) are so told.   (P. Harris 6.6–7)

These two protagonists are thus presented as renowned but ancient figures.

3. Two blocks from a wall of a 19th Dynasty tomb-chapel at Saqqara, known as the 'Daressy Fragment', contain a scene listing kings and illustrious ancestors.⁶ The surviving fragment of historical – possibly

---

³ This tradition of the figures as foretellers of the future apparently derives from the manner in which *Neferti* foretells the way in which his speech about the future will be received (15g; see **9.1**).
⁴ E.g., Brunner 1966b; J. Assmann 1977b, 1977d; M. V. Fox 1982; Osing 1992c; Fitzenreiter 1995: 122–4; Kákosy and Fábián 1995.
⁵ The king's name may have been chosen because it could be reinterpreted as 'he is taken away, i.e. departed' (cf. Goedicke 1977b: 192–3).
⁶ PM III.2², 571–2; Yoyotte 1952: 67–72; Wildung 1977: 28–9; 1984: 14, fig. 4; Redford 1986: 26. See also J. Assmann 1985: 39 n.13, 42–3; L. Morenz 1996: 87–8 n.387.

Memphite – personages, who include the viziers Imhotep and Kaires (see **A.2**), are not all arranged in chronological sequence (Fischer 1976: 64 n.26). The scene also includes a 'lector priest Khakheperreseneb', and an 'Overseer of Singers (*jmj-r₃ ḥsw*) Ipuur', that is, the protagonists of *The Words of Khakheperreseneb* and *The Dialogue of Ipuur and the Lord to the Limit*. One figure may represent the scribe Khety, but this is uncertain.[7] They are presented as eminent men from the past, despite being arguably fictional, and their pseudo-historical status is presumably due to their literary fame.

4. A magical spell on the Ramessid P. Athens 1825 (Fischer-Elfert and Hoffmann, in preparation) includes a vignette showing ten standing figures and twelve seated figures (rto col. X+10), who are described in the spell as 'these excellent spirits, and great officials' (X+10.3). Some of the figures, whose names are cursively written, can be identified as known literary protagonists. The standing figures include: Imhotep (1), Hordedef (2), Ipy (perhaps Ipu⟨ur⟩, 6), Djadjaemankh, a character in *The Tale of Cheops' Court* (7), Nefer (perhaps Nefer⟨ti⟩, 9). The seated ones include two figures named Ptah (2, 8) and one named Hotepu (3, perhaps deriving from Ptahhotep?), Khery (perhaps Khety, 6) and Uba (perhaps Uba⟨iner⟩, another character from *Cheops' Court*, 7). This group seems to mingle the protagonists of literary teachings and discourses together with wonder-working protagonists of tales. All are presumably invoked for their authoritative status as wonder-workers, developing the tradition of the protagonists of wisdom texts as wise men and possessors of 'magic' attested in the 'Eulogy of Dead Writers' to include magicians from tales.

5. The Ramessid *Satiric Letter* of P. Anastasi I (Fischer-Elfert 1986a, 1992a) is a literary letter, known from five papyri and numerous ostraca from Memphis and Thebes, which was copied by apprentice scribes. In it a scribe named Hori humorously berates his correspondent Amenemope for his ignorance and incompetence. In the course of this, the letter makes more or less explicit references to such issues as style and textual unity, also mentioning *The Teaching of Hordedef* as a text that the addressee should know (10.9–11.2; quoted on pp. 51–2).

2.3 GENRE

> Men's words have an age like themselves; and though they outlive their authors, yet have they a stint and period to their duration.
>
> Thomas Browne, *Religio Medici* (1643), sect. 23

---

[7] 'The Master of Largesse (*ḥrj-wḏb*) *s₃-ḫtj*'; the name must be an unattested Sakhety, an error for 'Khety' or '⟨X's⟩ son Khety', or the patronym 'Khety's son'.

The idea of literature as an institution is closely allied to genre theory (e.g., A. Fowler 1982: 18). The difficulties of assessing ancient genres are a specific example of the general difficulties of approaching texts. The apparent and often surprising immediacy of literary texts of times and cultures alien to the reader can blind one to their alterity (Parkinson 1999f: 7). Features of *The Tale of Sinuhe* that are vaguely similar to modern narratives have tempted readers into assuming that 'it deserves to be called a novel' (Posener 1971: 232), when it is something very different (**8.2**). Similarly, a reading of *The Eloquent Peasant* in terms of modern genres, with which it is not comparable, does not produce a satisfactory identification as a novel, lyric or satire, so that Alan H. Gardiner considered that its author was 'anything but a literary artist' (1923: 6–7). More generally, critics describing works from earlier periods often see faults of composition when what is present is a genre which is no longer current (A. Fowler 1982: 259). The attested Egyptian genres have no equivalents for the familiar western ones of epic, tragedy, comedy or pastoral.

A general definition of genre is problematic (e.g., Dubrow 1982), but not irrelevant to Egyptian culture, although caution is necessary as Piotr Michalowski warns in relation to Mesopotamian literature (1989: 4):

> Generic categorizations, however, are closely linked with reception, and the reading of ancient texts, when no continuous tradition of reading has survived, presents particular problems that are different from those encountered in old texts belonging to a living stream of interpretation. . . . By placing together certain texts we create a close and closed intertextuality, which, in turn, provides us with a false sense of security in reading.

Middle Kingdom compositions – like all domains of Egyptian written high culture – share a strong commonality of form and content (e.g., Eyre 1990: 162–3), and suggest that there was a strong adherence to a tradition of decorum, with a consistent use of formulae and established motifs. They are particularly susceptible to generic analysis. Although the number of literary texts originally belonging to the corpus is unknown, the typological nature of the surviving material is remarkably consistent. Recent literary theory acknowledges that types of literary text are historical and institutionalized forms, in contrast to the system of prescriptive genres of neoclassical theory, which regarded the genres of the corpus of classical texts as universals: 'each era has its own system of genres' (Todorov 1976: 161). Raymond Williams (1977: 185) has argued that genre is

> neither an ideal type nor a traditional order nor a set of technical rules. It is in the practical and variable combination and even fusion of what are, in

abstraction, different levels of the social material process that what we have known as genre becomes a new kind of constitutive evidence.

I use 'genre' as a convenient term to categorize the 'multiplicity of notations and conventions, evident in actual writing' (R. Williams 1977: 180). A broad period-based approach has to be taken for the Middle Kingdom, because it is difficult to date the literary texts; inevitably the constant variation and the diachronic development of the genres will be underestimated.[8]

A genre is not a mutually exclusive class, not 'all (of whose) characteristic traits need be shared by every other embodiment of the type' (Fowler 1982: 38). The variety displayed by even a well-recognized form such as 'tragedy' has led to a theory of genres as showing family resemblances produced by literary tradition. Since genres are mutable and frequently overlap, a rather imprecise terminology has advantages over a highly precise one. For example, the 1609 quarto text of Shakespeare's *Troilus and Cressida* terms it a comedy, whereas the 1623 Folio intended to group it among the tragedies (Orgel 1987: 4). One can propose a system of genres and subgenres, as well as modes, which refer to emotional and tonal features that cross various genres, such as comic or tragic (A. Fowler 1982: 106–29).

Thus, the system of genre is not an aggregate of fixed categories. Genre can be understood through relations between types. The term need not refer to a particular level of abstraction, but rather is best viewed as part of a scale ranging from a narrow definition, in which a single unique text is its own genre, to an extremely broad genre in which the whole institution of literature is a genre of writing. Different breadths of definition are determined by the requirements of the groups of texts being studied; there is no sharp or fixed division between genre and subgenre. Genre is a dynamic phenomenon (cf. Mathieu 1996a: 131), and genres are fluid and flexible; although they are ratified by tradition, each new work alters and adapts the system. The genres of a single culture are mutable, as is exemplified by the changing histories of the novel and the tragedy (A. Fowler 1971; Fowler 1982: 45–8, 134–6): genres are established, accepted, and often abandoned.

In assigning texts to genres, the Egyptologist should adopt a historical approach that uses ancient sources such as titles and context, together with an inductive approach in which the genres are elucidated from the works themselves. Not all of these sources are available for the Middle Kingdom. As Fowler notes (1982: 52), the last method of 'indirect constructive

---

[8] In my discussion I draw extensively on A. Fowler 1982; Parkinson 1996b gives more detailed references.

inference' is often the most informative. Some critics have defined genre in terms of an established pattern of inner and outer form (e.g., Wellek and Warren 1962), while others have attempted to be more exact. A. Fowler (1982: 54–74) provides a fuller list of types of features that may be shared by a particular genre; these are not necessarily relevant to all individual genres, nor to a particular generic system. His list includes: representational mode (narrative or discourse); external structure; metrical structure; size; scale; subject; values expounded; mood; occasion; attitude adopted toward the audience; setting; characters; unity or otherwise of the action; style (including diction); the task of the audience. These features are of course generic signals by which the text communicates, as well as formulates, its identity. Some may not apply to Egyptian literature, while Egyptologists are not yet in a position, for example, to distinguish types of text by metrical patterns (cf. Fecht 1982: 1139–40).

Those studying ancient literatures have often concentrated on 'occasion' (*Sitz im Leben*), despite the fact that the social occasion and setting are often inaccessible (cf. Longman 1991: 17–18, drawing on A. Jolles). This approach is not restricted to a crudely historical view of the text's origin – the specific event, such as a coronation, which inspired a composition – but draws on broader social and cultural considerations. It does not, however, acknowledge fully that literary genres can occupy many settings and that a single setting can produce many genres. The original perlocutionary setting or function does not determine the nature of literary genre, and many important kinds of literature have 'no discernible occasion' (A. Fowler 1982: 152). The subject matter of Egyptian literary texts is often at the juncture between the different spheres of sacred and profane, royal and private (e.g., Franke 1993: 351–2). Jan Assmann argues that Egyptian literary compositions were functionally specific to education (**1.4**). Against this style of analysis, discussions of other types of discourse suggest that they were less contextually determined than has often been assumed: for example, letters did more than communicate information, had performative and celebratory aspects and could be monumentalized (Baines 1999a: 24–5 on Old Kingdom examples). Literature itself can be interpreted not as a lack of function but as a cultural function and context in itself, which need not be identified with other institutions that are better attested in socio-functional terms. The literary context that I propose in Chapter 4 is a poorly documented social practice, even as the process of reading leaves no traces (Derchain 1987: 1). Many similarly inaccessible social practices existed.

Related to this widespread tendency to assimilate literature to specific occasions or functional contexts is an assumption that genres were 'pure', discrete, and determined by distinct contexts; but that neoclassical ideal is irrelevant to much literature. A literary work often includes another genre within itself, sometimes forming a hybrid; genres can be aggregated, in which one text is added to another. Genres can also be subverted by parody, or the tone or mode of one genre can be mixed with another. The intense fusion of genres is part of the highly intertextual nature of literary discourse.

Genre 'constitutes a field of reference within which ... the author can direct the specificity of his texts and the addressee can recognize it' (Conte 1994: 4). The act of reading is an institutionalized response that can be compared to genre, and the recognition of genre is imperative, because 'the [often unconscious] processes of generic recognition are ... fundamental to the reading process' (A. Fowler 1982: 259). Failure to recognize genre produces misunderstanding: '"Oh! you've been talking about a book all the time. I thought it was about a restaurant..."' (Hirsch 1967: 71). This relationship which is so vital to the reading process has been variously described as a sort of contract, a game or an institution.

2.4 INTERPRETATION

> Both read the Bible day and night,
> But thou read'st black where I read white.
> William Blake, *The Everlasting Gospel* (c. 1818), iv

Interpretation is fundamental to reading and understanding literary discourse, including editorial practice, to the extent that Marguerite Yourcenar's claim that 'nos fantaisies d'interprétation laissent intacts les textes eux-mêmes, qui survivent à nos commentaires' (1982: 540) is valid only in respect of the original material manuscripts. The establishing of a text from a manuscript is itself interpretation (e.g., Wells and Taylor 1987: 7; Newton 1990: 7–9). Interpretation has been a central concern especially in the English-speaking world, in the work of the New Critics and the hermeneutic school, despite tendencies to meta-historical definitions of literature and anti-interpretive movements that have arisen in opposition to the dominance of these schools.

The interpretation of a literary text has often been opposed to simple reading and experiencing of the text as an object in itself. The New Critics considered that form is meaning and both are beyond rational paraphrase (e.g., Wellek and Warren 1962: 110–24; Robey 1986b; Newton 1990: 10–39). They regarded the work of art as an individual object having 'an achieved harmony' between opposing connotations, attitudes and interpretations (Brooks 1949: 178–9). The aim of interpretation was to convey awareness of the harmony of an individual work. Later New Criticism aimed to accommodate as many features as possible of a text into a single coherent meaning, and to demonstrate the thematic unity of a work of art. This assumption of unity is problematic: unity and comprehensiveness are not universally integral to literary institutions and practices. Moreover, the New Critics had few rigid criteria for assessing the validity of an interpretation beyond its comprehensiveness.

Although in the late twentieth century New Criticism shaped many readers' supposedly intuitive ideas of what literature is, it has been attacked for being anti-historical, asserting the semantic autonomy of literary texts, producing too many possible interpretations, and being too essentialist (e.g., from the perspective of oral cultures: Ong 1982: 160–4). In contrast, the hermeneutic school of criticism was concerned with the determinacy of meaning, drawing on the tradition of biblical interpretation (e.g., Hamilton 1996: 51–98). E. D. Hirsch considered the question of authorial intention, and defined the aim of interpretation as to discover 'that aspect of a speaker's "intention" which, under linguistic conventions, may be shared by others' (1967: 163, 218). 'Authorial intention' is a problematic formulation for anonymous Egyptian works, although it can be redefined as 'realized intention' or 'the verbal meaning as it was available to the audience' (A. Fowler 1982: 256–83; Olsen 1987: 27–8). Much of the information required for assessing realized intention is inaccessible for Egyptian texts, but the Egyptian tradition of interpretation seems to have given much weight to authorial intention (P. Anastasi I 1.7, cited on p. 83).

The goal of interpretation is the historical understanding of the text's original intended meaning, as opposed to its 'significance' for the modern reader.[9] Hirsch's evaluation of interpretive strategy remains in part cogent (e.g., Maclean 1986: 136). His criteria are legitimacy – the reading is permissible in terms of language and grammar; correspondence – it accounts for each linguistic component; generic appropriateness; and coherence within context (1967: 236–7). In a similar manner Adele Berlin (1996) formulates six pieces of advice for the literary historian: respect the integrity of the text; assume that the text makes sense in its present form; take the wording of the text seriously; take the literary context seriously; take the historical and social context seriously; ask whether the text is to be read literally or metaphorically; decide which features of the text are hermeneutically significant and how they are to be used in the interpretive process.

Such an approach presupposes that interpretation can be objective and neutral. The idea of interpretation as 'reconstruction' is appropriate for

---

[9] Hirsch 1967: 211; compare Fowler 1982: 261; Fokkema and Ibsch 1986: 7; Newton 1990: 46–7.

readers of ancient texts, but history's status as an objective discipline is deeply problematic (e.g., Fay *et al.* 1998), and there are inevitable divergences between the original meaning and the meaning as a modern critic reconstructs it. Such divergences are well documented in better understood traditions: later Classical critics allegorized the Homeric poems in order to accommodate what they perceived as absurdities, and to provide evidence for their own cosmological truths (Hardie 1986: 26–8). This allegorization of epic was drawn on by Vergil, elements of whose own works were subsequently allegorized in the Middle Ages, but in ways he certainly did not intend that accommodated him into Christianity (Burrow 1997: 79–82). He has been continually reinterpreted by modern readers (e.g., Kennedy 1997). Such (re)interpretations belonged in a comparatively unbroken tradition, whereas modern readers of Egyptian literature have no inherited paradigms to guide the reader's response, apart from those of previous Egyptologists.

Hirsch's distinction between meaning and significance is problematic since it implicitly denies that interpretation is trapped in the hermeneutic circle.[10] The past cannot be interpreted except through its modern significance, and postmodern theory has in general asserted that the circle is inescapable and that modern readers cannot escape their own historical situation. In contrast, the philosopher Hans-Georg Gadamer's hermeneutics involves a 'fusion of horizons' (1979) 'in which the language and perspective of the interpreter is extended in order to understand the text that is being interpreted' (Newton 1990: 57; cf. Maclean 1986; Hamilton 1996: 81–98). For readers of ancient texts, the original meaning, so far as it was ever stable, almost certainly contrasts with the appropriation of the text by the modern interpreter; yet the two cannot be separated (Kennedy 1997: 53–5).

Is the original meaning of a work — regardless of whether it can be reconstructed — its total meaning? Can any reading be judged valid or invalid? Many critics have viewed the literary text as characterized by 'intrinsic plurality' (Kermode 1975: 129), and advocated a New Critical 'principle of plenitude' in which the most valid interpretation is the one that 'account(s) for the greatest quantity of data in the words of the poem' (Beardsley 1958: 144–5). A multiplicity of meanings is often seen as a characteristic or indeed defining feature of literature, with, for example, Charles Altieri viewing it as 'a function of the depth with which (the work) renders actions and their possible significance' (1978: 90). Poststructuralist criticism has tended to go further, opening up the text to multiple

---

[10] 'A concept based on the contradiction that in order to understand a part of a text one needs to have knowledge of the whole, while understanding the whole text depends on understanding every part' (Newton 1990: 45).

interpretations, embracing indeterminacy, arguing that a text is a 'play of undecidable meaning' (Newton 1990: 78), and making interpretation 'free play'. Roland Barthes argues that 'to interpret a text is not to give it a (more or less justified, more or less free) meaning, but on the contrary to appreciate what *plural* constitutes it' (1975: 5).

> The plurality of the text is also emphasized in reader-response and reception theory. Reception-theory highlights the ways in which textual meaning changes through time. It lets us see more sharply the indeterminacy of the text, the potential for different appropriations by different interests, and the competing canons which result.... And if (Mikhail) Bakhtin's ideas are employed, even individual interpretations become fissured when they are perceived to respond to the contrary and disunified voices already implying different audiences from within a single text. (Hamilton 1996: 206)

Readers of ancient Egyptian texts have tended to avoid 'free play', although a plurality of meaning is appropriate. For example, the reader's finding many local ambiguities in a text can be accidental, which can be resolved by knowledge of factors such as the generic context, but such ambiguities are sometimes deliberate: Antonio Loprieno (1991a) convincingly interprets several modern interpretive cruces in *The Shipwrecked Sailor* as intentional ambiguities. Similar dilemmas attend the interpretation of humour and irony in general (see, e.g., Booth 1974).

New Historicism advocates a return to interpretation in terms of historical and political content, although it retains a modern perspective fusing 'a Gadamerian form of hermeneutics with a political and cultural critique' (Newton 1990: 128–9). In a study of drawings by Albrecht Dürer of proposed monuments for a victory over the peasants, which may be serious, ironic or subversive, Greenblatt (1990: 99–130) considers how the meaning of the original may have been complex and potentially ambiguous, and attempts to reconstruct and assess the various possibilities for representing rebellion within the cultural context. Like poststructuralism, New Historicism explores gaps and tensions, just as deconstructive criticism involved 'the careful teasing out of warring forces of signification within the text itself' (Johnson 1980: 5). For Greenblatt, the aim of criticism is a 'poetics of culture', which he defines as the 'study of the collective making of distinct cultural practices and inquiring into the relations among these practices' (1988: 5; an example of this is B. Smith 1991). This can appear as a 'practice which hermeticizes culture as a self-contained sign system and which considers any notion of reality and history as an effect of this sign system and determined entirely by representations' (Brannigan 1998: 93). Such an approach is conscious of its own status as interpretation, and admits no escape from the hermeneutic circle.

New Historicism originated in work on the early modern period, when current political practices were starting to evolve, and its interpretations politicize these texts for the modern audience whose perspective it privileges:

> The production and consumption of such works (of art) are not unitary ... they always involve a multiplicity of interests, however well organized, for the crucial reason that art is social and hence presumes more than one consciousness. And in response to the art of the past, we inevitably register ... the shifts in value and interest that are produced in the struggles of social and political life. (Greenblatt 1990: 112)

The movement has been criticized for asserting that subversion is co-opted by power (Brannigan 1998: 76–7), and for avoiding historical and cultural specificity, and producing a totalized view of history (Porter 1988) instead of engaging with the specific issues of an individual text.

Cultural Materialist interpretations, by contrast, are more committed to overt and contemporary political ends, and can be deeply engaged, as in the 'queer reading' of canonical texts (e.g., Sinfield 1994). They are interested in how past works become legitimizing agents for present ideology. As poststructuralist theory has emphasized, 'no text ... can contain within its project all the potential significance that it must release in pursuance of that project. Closure is always inadequate' (Sinfield 1994: 37). Since all texts are to some extent indeterminable, 'faultlines' – conflicts and contradictions within ideology – may be present in them that can inspire counter-cultural readings:

> If new historicists believe that every culture or discourse finds the means of making safe the subversive voices which emerge from textual representations, cultural materialists work from the more positive belief that even where subversion is contained, traces of it remain which enable the dissident (i.e., cultural materialist) critic to raise the spectre of this subversion again, and thereby context the location and interpretation of that text in current discourses. (Brannigan 1998: 166)

This critical debate has implications for assessing the role of discourse in any culture. Middle Kingdom texts can, for example, be interpreted as directly unquestioning, but inevitably fissured, expressions of their ideology, that is propaganda. Alternatively, they can be interpreted as exploiting faultlines, integrally within their discourse, differentiating themselves from other forms of ideological utterance, either to voice subversion or to co-opt and entrap it. The oscillation of possible meaning(s) within literary texts suggests a more complex phenomenon than

General considerations: Definitions, genre, interpretation 41

the struggle between a dominant culture and a dissident reader that is often envisaged in recent historicist readings. Analysis of the distinctive qualities of literary reading by critics such as Iser, which seems appropriate for many Middle Kingdom compositions, suggests a possible tension and differentiation between literary texts and ideology. Such a relationship is a complex interplay of changing social forces that are difficult to analyse for ancient works, for which we largely lack the evidence that might indicate contemporaneous awareness or unawareness of complicity between the text and the dominant culture/hegemony. Close intertextual reading of a text in relation to other social practices becomes essential. As Kiernan Ryan (1996: xvii) notes:

> in the end only a precise local knowledge of a literary work, acquired through a 'thick description' of decisive verbal effects, will allow the critic to determine how far the work's complicity with power truly extends.

The interpretation of another culture is inevitably made through the values of the interpreter's own culture (see, e.g., Said 1978), even when those values are committed to respect the (possibly rebarbative) alien culture, as in the postmodern world where 'the acknowledgement of alterity, the acceptance of differences, has become the foremost ethical claim' (A. Assmann 1996: 98). Criticism must contextualize and historicize itself as well as the texts it analyses, since 'there is no disinterested reading' (Sinfield 1994: 4). Responses to Middle Kingdom literature have been largely determined by the traditional Egyptological preoccupations with social and political history rather than addressing broader issues of interpretation.

A fundamental question is whether the modern interpreter can escape from his/her historical situation at all (Hirsch) or cannot (Barthes). Readers of ancient literature are perhaps inclined to assert neither, assuming that some fusion inevitably takes place, as Charles Martindale comments on reading Vergil (1997b: 8):

> Antiquity cannot be studied merely *in itself*, because there is always a 'fusion of horizons' . . . between text and interpreter. It is not merely that in practice we cannot read Vergil like a Roman (which Roman?); it would not be desirable if we could, since it would no longer be 'we' who were doing the reading. Interpretation is situated, contingent upon time and place and ideological preoccupation, is always made from within history.

Although it is not appropriate to reconstruct a text's original meaning as if this were ever an objective and stable entity, the historicist reader must retain an awareness of the original actor's possible perspectives

(Geertz 1973: 3–30). Interpretation always involves translation and negotiation between cultures. The interpretive question is not 'what did the text say?' but rather 'what did the text say to me and what do I say to it?' (Jauss 1982: 146).

PART TWO
Context and Intertext

3
Texts and intertext

3.1 THE DATE OF THE COMPOSITIONS

> Their morals were not ours; not their poets; nor their climate; nor their vegetables even. Everything was different.
>
> Virginia Woolf, *Orlando* (1928), chap. 1

The passage of time has produced many problems for the reader who seeks to interpret an ancient text, compounding those of cultural alterity. These include the pervasive difficulties of dating a poem, of assessing the state of the text, and of assessing the oral and written contexts of the poem. These factors are integral for any engagement by the reader.

3.1.1 HISTORY AND TEXTS

There is little unequivocal evidence that the Egyptians were concerned with the accurate siting of their texts in past periods, beyond the attitude that what was old was good (Baines 1989; Aufrère 1998; for examples, see L. Morenz 1996: 16, 190–3). However, behind many texts' assertions of the antiquity of their original, unknown realities of editing, dating and creation are concealed, and complex pragmatic considerations surrounded the institution of literature. In the Ramessid 'Eulogy of Dead Writers' (**2.2.2**), the grouping of the wisdom authors into pairs suggests some historical awareness (for general awareness see McDowell 1992). While Hordedef and Imhotep, and Ptahhotep and Kaires are grouped together, presumably by their Old Kingdom settings, the fictional, supposedly 4th Dynasty Neferti is paired with the 12th Dynasty Khety, suggesting that both were regarded as Middle Kingdom figures. The Ramessid scribes may, however, have paired the two figures by their associations with Amenemhat I, and not by the poems' dates of composition.[1]

The relative and absolute dating of the Middle Kingdom corpus has aroused controversy – for which one can compare the chronology of the Shakespearean canon (Wells and Taylor 1987: 89–109). Literary works

---

[1] In P. Athens (**2.2.2**) no distinction is made between fictional characters in narratives and supposedly 'historical' protagonists of wisdom texts.

employ 'historical' settings, but few texts can be reliably dated by their ostensible setting or content; exactly or specifically 'contemporary' settings are a relatively recent phenomenon in fiction. Low dates are increasingly preferred.[2] Discussion has been hampered by problems of circular arguments, historical subjectivity, and a hyper-literal approach (see 1). No literary texts from the Old Kingdom are known as yet, but fewer papyri survive from the period than from the Middle (see lists of Posener-Kriéger 1972, Simpson 1972), and a single new find could necessitate reappraisal. Copies of literary works begin to appear in the surviving record during the 12th Dynasty. The political aspects of *Neferti* and *Amenemhat* are so marked that they probably belong to the early part of the 12th Dynasty. The earliest manuscripts are perhaps *The Shipwrecked Sailor* and P. Prisse (*Ptahhotep* and *Kagemni*), which can be dated to the mid- to late 12th Dynasty, and the manuscript of the *Herdsman*, all from non-royal tombs at Thebes. At the settlement of el-Lahun (see Quirke 1990b: 155–9), administrative documents are attested from the mid-12th Dynasty, yet no literary manuscripts are found before the later 12th Dynasty (Quirke, pers. comm.). The late appearance of literary manuscripts at el-Lahun and Thebes may show that literature was disseminated slowly from the highest court circles into the lower social levels attested at those sites, as well as illustrating the chances of preservation.

3.1.2 POSSIBLE STRATEGIES

The lack of securely dated literary texts makes the identification of style for particular periods (*Zeitstil*) hazardous. Attempts to correlate textual styles and 'mood' with specific periods is over-schematic (Parkinson 1991e: 174–5, with references). One example is *The Tale of the Eloquent Peasant* which was previously assigned to the First Intermediate Period by its setting and by plausible thematic grounds (such as its attitude to 'greatness'); the text has now been assigned to the later 12th Dynasty (Berlev 1987; Vernus 1990a; Parkinson 1991e; Roccati 1993). The positive or pessimistic aspects of a text are not due to its being composed in a certain period, as has often been argued, but spring from considerations of genre and authorial choice. A stable regime is arguably more likely to propagate fictional 'laments' than one only clinging onto order, for which pessimistic compositions might be too close to the bone.

A review of attested historical settings suggests that various options were available to Middle Kingdom authors, who made a choice among them for a variety of aesthetic reasons (cf. L. Morenz 1996: 41–2):

---

[2] E.g., on *Merikare* see Quack 1992: 116–8, review of opinions; Bickel 1994: 219.

1. For idealistic accounts of wisdom, there was the golden age of the far past, as in *Kagemni*, *Ptahhotep*, and the prologue of *Neferti* (cf. Blumenthal 1996a: 127). Related to this is the exotic and fantastic past of 'once, long ago', which was suitable for tales of wonder (*Cheops' Court*).

2. The more recent troubled age of the First Intermediate Period occurs in accounts of more problematic life, as in *Merikare* and *The Eloquent Peasant* (cf. Parkinson 1991e: 173). The reign of Neferkare, probably Pepy II of the late Old Kingdom, which is the setting for the scandalous events of *Neferkare and Sasenet*, may belong here.

3. The very recent past is appropriate to an equivocal view of the world, as in *Sinuhe* and *Amenemhat*.

4. The timeless setting of some compositions either embodies an anonymous fabulous world, as in *The Shipwrecked Sailor*, or the loyalistic world of *The Teaching of a Man*, which is both contemporaneous and timeless and conforms quite closely to the decorum of official texts of the period.

It is desirable to develop specific dating criteria (Björkman 1964; van der Plas 1984) that will allow comparison with more securely dated non-literary and literary materials within the framework of the individual composition. Linguistic features are providing vital criteria as they are studied in more detail. I summarize possible evidence here.

1. Manuscripts. The date of manuscripts can provide a relatively secure indication of the period by which a text must have been composed, although it can be taken to implausible extremes with the earliest manuscript being equated with the date of composition (e.g., van der Plas 1986; Grimal 1995b; cf. Burkard 1999: 164). Few papyri can be dated absolutely, however, so that palaeography is an uncertain criterion; the recent tendency has been to favour later absolute datings.[3] The existence of different styles of hieratic script both in different types of documents and in vertical and horizontal lines within a single manuscript, as well as possible geographic variations in writing styles, renders dating by palaeography uncertain (e.g., P. Westcar containing *Cheops' Court*). Orthography has hardly been studied since Dévaud (1924). Here even the published conclusions may be compromised by the fact that a manuscript's palaeography or orthography may have copied its older archetype; in the case of P. Prisse, for example, a later date by over a century is suggested by the orthography than by the ostensible style of the palaeography. The level of variants between contemporaneous copies and a text's redactional history

---

[3] E.g., the redating of the Heqanakht papers to the early 12th Dynasty (e.g., Do. Arnold 1991: 35–8).

may also provide rather approximate evidence for the length of previous transmission (e.g., Burkard 1977: 115, 316–17; Parkinson 1991e; Kahl 1998).

2. Allusions. Extrinsic features such as the names and titles of non-royal protagonists can offer specific evidence, as can incidental background information in a text. Our ignorance of the details of history renders topical references to dated events of little use. An example is a suggested – but very uncertain – allusion to the assassination of Amenemhat I in *The Teaching of a Man* (3.7; Brunner 1978); this compares unfavourably with the better documented allusions in Vergil, for example (e.g., Farrell 1997). Datings have often relied on identifying hypothetical political or historical allusions in the texts (e.g., Goedicke on *Cheops' Court*: 1992b: 32–6; Jenni 1998), but these presuppose the 'propaganda' model for literature. More reliable specific correlations are the administrative structure incidentally alluded to in the poems, such as the 12th Dynasty title 'High Steward', which features anachronistically in the Heracleopolitan setting of *The Eloquent Peasant* (Parkinson 1991c: 178; F. Arnold 1991).

3. Intertextuality and Quotations. While assessments of a text's general tone and thematic content, such as its treatment of loyalism or of predestination, are often hazardous, comparison of thematic treatments remains valuable, provided that the distinctiveness of literary discourse is accommodated. Correlations between the formulae of wisdom literature and datable texts such as biographies have not yet been fully exploited (exceptions are Blumenthal 1987, Vernus 1995b on *Ptahhotep*).

Quotations of one text in another have attracted discussion, but explicitly marked examples, such as the quotation of *Kemit* in *The Teaching of Khety* (2d–e), are very rare. It is difficult to tell which text is the quoter and which the quoted. Since the total corpus of literature was comparatively small, it is plausible that one text could have alluded specifically to the words of another, even without marking the allusion. However, similarities between different compositions could be reflections of a common source, or a common literary phraseology, in which formulae were standardized in relation to motifs.[4] The intertextual nature of literature, discussed below, is a complicating factor (on the comparable use of quotations to establish the chronology of the Shakespearean canon see Wells and Taylor 1987: 93).

In many cases the supposed quotations presuppose high dates for literary texts, but almost all of the examples proposed can be explained in other ways. Thus, the suggested quotations of *Merikare* on the 11th Dynasty

---

[4] See, e.g., Brunner 1979; Guglielmi 1984b; Eyre 1990: 153–60; Derchain 1994, 1996a: 93; Jasnow 1999: 194, 196–200; on formulae in literature see, e.g., Ong 1982: 23–7, 34–6, 60–70.

'Hound stela' of Intef II and in the inscription of Montuwoser dated to Year 17 of Senwosret I (Quack 1992: 135) are examples of the common formulaic phrases 'to drive a man from the goods of his father' and 'be partial toward a lord of payments'. Similar arguments affect the alleged quotations from *Hordedef* in a Coptos Decree of Pepy II and a First Intermediate Period stela (Brunner 1979: 117–19).

4. Linguistic. An example of grammatical evidence is Pascal Vernus' analysis of a progressive verbal construction (1990a, b). He proposes three stages in its development during the Middle Kingdom, with the absolute dating of the second stage being supported by examples in administrative documents of the reign of Amenemhat III. It is often difficult to convert the relative chronology into an absolute one, and there are few fixed points for comparison. Moreover, it is always possible that grammatical constructions were used archaistically, while literary language can be distinct from other registers (as Silverman 1980: 96–7).

5. Literary form. The evolution of literary form cannot yet be charted in detail. The contrasting features of Middle Kingdom and Ramessid literature provide a broad impressionistic framework for dating (J. Assmann 1985: 48–9), if one assumes that those Middle Kingdom compositions which show 'Ramessid features' are later than those which do not. As with the linguistic features mentioned above, one must allow for the existence of different contemporaneous stylistic registers.

Gerhard Fecht has proposed a clear distinction between the metrical rules of the Old and Middle Kingdoms, and has used this distinction to posit that an Old Kingdom archetype for *The Teaching of Ptahhotep*, composed in Old Egyptian, was later translated into Middle Egyptian and, in all but one manuscript, into Middle Kingdom metre (not fully published; see Fecht 1965: 125 n.109, 1986: 246–7). However the use of Old Kingdom metre could be an archaizing device comparable to such a phenomenon of representational art. The script of the 12th Dynasty P. Prisse, which contains the only copy of the teaching composed in Old Kingdom metre, may itself be archaistic (**A.1.5**, under *Kagemni*). Any aspect of a composition can be archaistic, but the effect can be more fully attained in metre than in the linguistic idiom of a whole text. The linguistic evidence is therefore likely to be more reliable, and I prefer to regard *The Teaching of Ptahhotep* as a Middle Kingdom composition written in an archaizing style, rather than a partially modernized Old Kingdom text.

I tentatively suggest a chronology based on the possible datings reviewed and summarized in Appendix 1. None of the poems predate the 12th Dynasty. The educational text *Kemit* (Appendix 2) is from very early in the dynasty. *Neferti* is from the final decade of the first reign, that of Amenemhat I. From the sole reign of Senwosret I comes *The Teaching of Amenemhat*, and perhaps *Khety*. From the following reign of 34 years

(Amenemhat II) comes *The Tale of Sinuhe*. A similarly early date can be suggested for *The Tales of the Shipwrecked Sailor* and *The Herdsman*. *The Teachings of Ptahhotep* and of *Hordedef* may come from the early 12th Dynasty. By the reign of Amenemhat II, *The Loyalist Teaching*, *The Teaching of a Man* and *The Teaching of Kagemni* had been composed, with *Kagemni* perhaps late in the group. The poems enumerated above were all composed in a period of about a century. *The Eloquent Peasant* was perhaps composed in the seven-year reign of Senwosret II, and a broadly similar date can be proposed for *Sasobek* and the *Fowler*. *The Dialogue of a Man and His Ba* comes from late in this phase.

The high Middle Kingdom perhaps saw the composition of *The Teaching for Merikare*, and *The Tale of Hay* and *The Tale of Horus and Seth*. All the canonical genres were established by this phase of the 12th Dynasty. From the final reigns of the 12th Dynasty and the 13th Dynasty (a period of 130 years) come *Khakheperreseneb*, *Ipuur* and the *Accounts*. The 13th Dynasty also saw *The Tale of the Court of Cheops* and *The Tale of Neferkare and Sasenet*.

3.2 TEXTUAL TRANSMISSION

> la beltà che prim'era si rimembra . . .
> Michelangelo, fragment of a Sonnet (*c.* 1545; *Rime*
> ed. Girardi, no. 237)

3.2.1 ATTITUDES TO TEXT

For the Egyptians the transmission of a text was an exemplar of cultural permanence, and was privileged over oral transmission (L. Morenz 1996: 21–32; Baines 1983, 1984): *The Teaching of Khety* presents society as divided into a scribal class and lowly illiterate workers, and the Elephantine inscription of Senwosret I dismissively refers to the oral transmission of ritual skills (Schenkel 1975b: 117 [SoNr 2, l. x+4]; Redford 1987: 53 n. 110). Written literature partakes of writing's role of 'proclaiming all that is forgotten',[5] and as cultural memory (J. Assmann and A. Assmann 1983; J. Assmann 1992b). The teachings assert that they teach according to the enduring words of the past (*Ptahhotep* 37), a theme that is developed in the later 'Eulogy of Dead Writers' which assimilates literary texts with 'heirs' and memorial monuments (P. Chester Beatty IV vso 3.3–4).

Nevertheless, in teachings the sage speaks to his children, and the subsequent transmission is often envisaged as passing orally from children

---

[5] 18th Dynasty hymn to Thoth: Winlock 1924: pl. 4; J. Assmann 1999c: no. 222.

to children (e.g., *Ptahhotep* 588–95). The end of *Kagemni* makes clear the equivalence for the literary context of performance/speaking and writing: the maxims are presumably spoken, and are then presented to the children as an already existing papyrus roll. The original pronouncement and the recited text are assimilated, as the Vizier summons his children:

> And at last he said to them:
> 'As for all that is in writing on this roll,
> hear it even as I said it'. (2.4–5)

In *Ptahhotep*:

> Memory of (the teaching's maxims) will ⟨not⟩ depart from the mouths of mankind,
> because of the perfection of their verses.[6] (510–11)

The words are transmitted by written means; repute comes through recital and word of mouth, as also in the biography of the Steward Montuwoser (Sethe 1928a: 80, ll.1–3; quoted on p. 87).

In practice, textual transmission was fragile, both during and after the dynastic period, as is also true of literature from classical antiquity (e.g., Reynolds and Wilson 1991: 101–2). Awareness of the means of transmission is important for general interpretation; the dangers of reading a text away from the original copies can be seen, for example, in editors' combinations of two distinct performing versions of Shakespeare's *Lear* and *Hamlet* into single plays (Wells and Taylor 1987: 1–68; Hibbard 1987).

The modern reader is accustomed to reproductive transmission, as against a productive transmission by which texts are copied and recast in terms of their type and function (e.g., Schenkel 1986; J. Assmann 1995: 4–9). The diachronic and synchronic variety in the Middle Kingdom Coffin Texts (overview in Willems 1996a) exemplify 'productive' transmission. The predominance of model phraseology and use of formulae in many types of Egyptian texts reflects this productive possibility (Eyre 1990: 157–60). Nevertheless, the copies claim to transmit a specific form 'found in writing' (see **4.2**), implying a relatively fixed ordered text that could rely on processes of collating and textual emendation (as are attested for some later funerary texts: e.g., L. Morenz 1996: 54; see also Nordh 1996: 132–44). An example of textual attitudes to Middle Kingdom poems is in the Ramessid *Satiric Letter*.

---

[6] I differ from L. Morenz (1996: 37), who interprets this passage as referring to the earlier oral transmission of the teaching.

You have come, provided with great secrets,
and have quoted to me a verse of Hordedef.
You do not know whether it is good or bad,
which stanza is before it, which after it.

(P. Anastasi I 10.9–11.2; Fischer-Elfert 1986a: 95–7)

Theory and practice may have diverged: colophons such as that to *The Shipwrecked Sailor* claim proficiency in copying that is not total in the actual manuscript. Günter Burkard's analysis of variants and/or errors in mostly New Kingdom manuscripts (1977: 320–2) indicates that most non-redactional variants were due to copying from an original manuscript or copying from memory, not dictation. The transmission of the corpus is predominantly written, and is thus predominantly reproductive – although reproductive and productive are not mutually exclusive. The performative setting of literary texts would allow easy redactional activity, to adapt the text to a new audience; such adaptations could have been subsequently discarded or preserved and transmitted. This was true of classical plays, which may be a relevant parallel for the performative examples of Egyptian works (e.g., Reynolds and Wilson 1991: 14–15, 19–20): authorial revisions can be detected in the works of dramatists 'from Euripides to Stoppard' (Wells and Taylor 1987: 16–17). The textual history of *The Loyalist Teaching* shows the potential extent of redaction, when a literary text was adapted for a monumental context in the Middle Kingdom (**A.1.5**). In a manuscript culture, the concept of an absolutely 'correct' ideal *Urtext* is often inappropriate, and authorization is irrelevant, especially where, as in Egypt, relatively little value was attached to the notion of named authorship (cf. O'Keeffe 1993 on editorial strategies for Old English texts). For the modern reader, however, their often fragmentary state requires a use of conflated texts, as opposed to a return to the study of individual manuscripts (cf. Middleton 1992).

Redactional activity is attested: the variant Middle Kingdom manuscripts of *Ptahhotep* constitute the most extreme example,[7] displaying two significantly different texts. There is a lesser extent of textual variation in the 13th Dynasty R(amesseum) manuscripts (*c.* 1600 BCE) of *The Eloquent Peasant* and of *Sinuhe* from around two and a half centuries after the original composition, compared with the earlier B(erlin) manuscripts (*c.* 1790 BCE; **4.2**). The R manuscripts contain additions in comparison with earlier manuscripts, but there is no thoroughgoing revision. The

---

[7] Various explanations have been adopted, such as assuming an Old Kingdom composition with loss of manuscripts in the First Intermediate Period, or oral transmission before the Middle Kingdom; Cannuyer 1986: 44–5 (a survey of explanations); Quack 1994: 20; see L. Morenz 1996: 38 n.158; Fischer-Elfert 1997: 22–3. Burkard (1977) underestimates the number of variants which are coherent redactional alternate readings.

mid- to late 12th Dynasty 'Berlin Library' contained two partial manuscripts of *The Eloquent Peasant* which form a semi-conflated but complete unity, in which minor variant texts existed side by side a century or so after the composition. Thus, there was some variation in the Middle Kingdom when living works were adapted slightly for different contexts of performance; in contrast, the transmission in the New Kingdom of the then 'canonical' texts was more rigidly reproductive. While some genres may have been more open to variation in the Middle Kingdom, such as the monostichic maxims of *P. Ramesseum II* (**6.2**), the extent of the variations is not enough to justify a general analysis as 'open transmission', whether written or oral (see Quack 1994: 18–23). In the Classical world, corruption and variants entered traditions within a century or so of composition (Reynolds and Wilson 1991: 26–7). In Egypt geographical factors may also be present: the presence of two redactions may reflect not only the period between the single archetype and the copies, but also differing transmissions in different regions, as is known for the Coffin Texts (e.g., Hoffmeier 1996). The survival of any manuscript suggests a degree of prestige, so that one cannot draw conclusions about the unpopular (or subversive) character of an individual poem from the paucity of copies (pace, e.g., Renaud 1991: 14).

3.2.2 NEW KINGDOM MANUSCRIPTS

The preserved textual record is more extensive from the Ramessid Period, when some texts from the corpus were much copied on papyri and ostraca, including tales, teachings and discourses. Non-literary texts were also copied together with the literary corpus, such as the Kamose inscriptions, or the Building Inscription of Senwosret I. Ostraca and writing boards provide the most numerous copies of much of the corpus, but they also include non-literary texts and genres. Ostraca are attested from the New Kingdom at various sites in Egypt and Nubia, but the large majority are from the Ramessid settlement of Deir el-Medina, although the exact original context is usually unknown (overview: Quirke 1996b: 392–4; see also McDowell 1999: 25–7). In the Institut Français d'Archéologie Orientale collection of these ostraca in Cairo, the most frequently occurring texts are, in descending order: *Khety*, *Amenemhat*, *Kemit*, *The Satiric Letter*, *The Nileflood Hymn*, *The Loyalist Teaching* (Gasse 1992: 52–3). Less frequent are hymns and prayers, and still less *Sinuhe* (seven examples).

The selection of literary texts for copying was probably determined by the context in which the copies were made, relating to teaching practices that drew on a codified group of 'set texts' in Middle Egyptian. Although the hands of the copies are generally too skilled for schoolboys learning to write (van der Plas 1986: I, 11–14; J. J. Janssen 1992: 86), the copies may be made at an advanced stage of training in literary Middle Egyptian, and dates mark many ostraca excerpts as training exercises (McDowell 1996). These copies are unlikely to have been intended primarily for reading. They are always excerpts of a greater or lesser extent. There are, however, some numbered ostraca, where the numbers do not correspond with the stanzas of the text (Posener 1975), that could mark 'the "pages" of "paperbacks" – the papyri being the "hardback" editions' (J. J. Janssen 1992: 86), but such examples are rare (e.g., the Late Egyptian *Tale of the Ghost*: von Beckerath 1992; McDowell 1999: 149–52). Moreover, the texts of many ostraca are corrupt enough to be only partially intelligible, due to the corruption of the available textual tradition and not the personal ignorance of the apprentice scribes, and must have been rote exercises (Burkard 1977: 318–21). The scribe's personal copies on papyrus and apprentice work on ostraca and papyri both drew on the same, often corrupt, textual traditions. A correlation between a corrupt tradition and the teaching context is possible, as texts used in school would be copied and recopied more frequently. Some degree of corruption in a manuscript, however, need not indicate that the text was copied exclusively by rote in training: scribes might keep bad copies beyond their teaching purpose out of respect for their literary value even if they were largely incomprehensible; the Elizabethans published and presumably read what we would consider 'bad' quartos of Shakespeare (e.g., *Hamlet* Q1, Hibbard 1987: 67–89), and plenty of contemporary middle-class British households have a copy of the *Works of Shakespeare*, often a relic of schooldays, which is infrequently read or fully understood. Scholastic or cultural use of a literary text can give it an 'encyclopaedic' function regardless of its legibility.

Wisdom texts, especially teachings, were the literary texts most copied on ostraca, while Middle Kingdom tales are rare, except for ones with some historical content such as *Neferkare* or *Sinuhe* (the best attested: Baines 1982: 31–2; Koch 1990: vi). This selection was presumably determined by educational concerns, although the nature of such concerns is inaccessible. The educational corpus seems to have often excluded earlier lighter and entertaining works, such as *Cheops' Court*, and concentrated on edifying texts in the classical language, although love-songs are occasionally included on educational ostraca (see **10.1**). The known literary corpus was broader than the educational corpus of set texts. Thus, *The Tale of the Eloquent Peasant*, which was apparently not in this corpus, was quoted in a Ramessid literary letter by the Deir el-Medina littérateur Menna (Simpson 1958a; Parkinson 1991c: xxix–xxx; McDowell 1999: 144–7; L. Morenz 1998). The Ramessid tradition as a whole reflects a general codification of earlier poems into a corpus of 'classical' compositions (J. Assmann 1985; Loprieno 1996b: 55–8) that were hallowed by their age and distinguished from contemporaneous literary activity. Their transmission continued into the Late Period and probably beyond (e.g., Jasnow 1999).

3.3 THE ORAL AND TEXTUAL CONTEXT OF LITERATURE

> On ne se livrera jamais assez au travail passionnant qui consiste à rapprocher les textes.
> Marguerite Yourcenar, *Carnets de notes de 'Mémoires d'Hadrien'*
> (1982: 530)

3.3.1 ORAL AND WRITTEN PROTOTYPES

A history of written discourses is the principal possible approach to the orality of a dead culture. As Jack Goody remarks, no study of oral literature was possible before the tape-recorder, since transcription distorts (1987: 80–1). By the end of the Old Kingdom a limited variety of types of text are attested in various media (e.g., Baines 1983: 577–8). There are copies of religious and ritual texts, preserved in the funerary Pyramid Texts. Private tomb-inscriptions exist, and commemorative inscriptions recording, e.g., mining expeditions. Fragments of administrative texts, letters, accounts and orders survive to show the extensive use of papyrus, presumably also used for the originals of many inscribed texts (L. Morenz 1996: 12 n.51, 199). Kinglists and annals (e.g., Baud and Dobrev 1995, 1997) bear witness to the existence of technical texts, and claims from later periods for the antiquity of technical treatises such as magical and medical papyri may well be in part valid: the biography of the 5th Dynasty vizier Ptahwash mentions a 'box of writings', apparently to do with healing (*Urk.* I, 42, l.8; Roccati 1982a: 108–11).

The balance of current evidence suggests that no literary works were written down in the Old Kingdom (see above), a lack which John Baines (1999a) addresses. In contrast to the slow and visible development of the funerary biographies (Lichtheim 1988; Gnirs 1996; Doxey 1998), the rapid emergence of the system of written literary genres in the Middle Kingdom in a full and stable form suggests considerable oral prehistory. As Tzvetan Todorov remarked, 'a new genre is always a transformation of one or several old genres' (1976: 161; cf. A. Fowler 1982: 149–69; Mathieu 1996a: 217). Since written literature was almost certainly performed at least in part, a transition between oral and written poetry might not have seemed as drastic as it does to us. Whether oral poetry before the Middle Kingdom comprised prototypes of later composition, or the actual texts which were later written down, has been debated (see L. Morenz 1996:

38). It is possible that the texts existed in an oral form before being committed to writing, but although genres present themselves as 'transcriptions' from oral compositions, the relationship between oral and written forms is very complex.[8] The exact oral transmission of oral compositions is unlikely (contrary to many studies; see Goody 1987: 110–22 on the ancient Indian Vedas).

Middle Kingdom Egypt was a predominantly oral 'face to face' culture in many respects, and the dynamics of oral performance are visible in many of its genres. The patterning of expression is often additive rather than subordinative and the use of formulae is prominent and aggregative rather than analytic, as when epithets appear in long sequences. Since an oral composition cannot be reread (with turning back pages) to remind the reader, the style may be repetitive or copious. An oral work conceptualizes knowledge with close reference to the specific life-world, and consideration of opposed ideas is formulated in agonistic fashion. The relationship of performer and audience with the literature is empathetic and participatory. This brings a tendency toward narratives that are objectivizing in style: because the reaction is communal and given, it need not be spelled out.

A parallel and older culture of songs, folktales and folk wisdom certainly existed in the Middle Kingdom, but evidence for the oral arena is sparse. Scenes on tomb walls provide a few harpist's songs, and workmen's songs (e.g., Parkinson 1991a: 27), but these are unlikely to be a direct transcription. There is sparse evidence for oral performers in written sources: the late Middle Kingdom *Ipuur* (4.11–13) and *Cheops' Court* (L. Morenz 1996: 42–3) mention singers and musicians. Oral story-telling is implied by a reference in a funerary inscription to travellers returning home 'to tell your campaigns to your wives' (Sethe 1928a: 88, ll.22–3). The influence of oral literature is perhaps detectable in the literary travesty of lowly (and thus illiterate) wise men (see **4.3**), although within high culture there was also oral performative literature, such as the song of the princesses in *Sinuhe*. In wisdom texts and compositions such as *The Eloquent Peasant*, the role of proverbial maxims and formulae suggests the influence of oral poetry, as do folkloric elements of *The Shipwrecked Sailor* (Baines 1990a: 57–61). In *A Man and His Ba* the atmosphere of the third lyric is suggestive of later love-songs,[9] perhaps pointing to an otherwise unrecorded type of lyric in the Middle Kingdom.

---

[8] Recent account: L. Morenz 1996: 20–57. In general see Goody 1987; on the impact of writing on the ancient Near East see Vanstiphout 1995.

[9] See Kaplony 1970 for a possible example of such a lyric in Coffin Text spell 671 (*CT* VI, 299); his reading, however, relies on a very uncertain rendering of VI, 299d. The earliest manuscript for the Late Egyptian love-songs is from the early 19th Dynasty (Mathieu 1996a: 22–3; for the date of P. Harris see Gardiner 1932: ix).

While the style of much Middle Kingdom writing reflects an oral/performative setting (Eyre and Baines 1989; Eyre 1990), the poems display signs of textuality, as against a status as transcriptions, although they consistently present themselves as copies of what was 'found in writing' and often integrate their own writing down into their self-description (e.g., the prologue of *Neferti*). This prominence of the idea of transcription can be interpreted as a self-textualization. Walter J. Ong (1982: 103) characterizes early writing as explicitly providing roles for the audience – roles which need no definition in an oral context. The texts thus provide fictional 'audiences' with whose responses the actual audience – whether an individual reading or a group at a performance – can identify. The same framing-device of an audience is found as late as Chaucer and Boccaccio, whose compositions were certainly textual but in a semi-oral context. A further indication of textuality is that the supposed authors of wisdom texts were certainly dead, since 'spoken utterance comes only from the living' (Ong 1982: 102). Moreover, some specific details suggest textual composition. In the first lyric of *A Man and His Ba*, the prevailing imagery of crocodiles at one point continues on a purely graphic level with the word 'sovereign' (*jtj*: Tobin 1991: 350 n.50; Parkinson 1999f: 163 n.27), while in *Ptahhotep*, the verse 'it is the spirit which extends his hands' (139) alludes to the graphic form of the sign writing 'spirit' (*k3*: Fischer-Elfert, pers. comm.). Thus, literature is created as a written phenomenon with an oral ancestry, out of oral poetic forms that were more extensive than written ones, but influenced by already existing written types. It was written to be heard, but was not composed aloud: it was aural, not oral, literature.

Literature is not simply a 'transposition' of workaday or religious discourse into an aesthetic realm (pace Helck 1972: 14). For example, the teaching genre presents itself as a transcribed, fictionalized version of actual advice, but the contents of the texts in the genre cannot be considered direct transcriptions of the sort of advice that would have been given from a paternal death-bed or when a son reached the age of discretion. Monumental prototypes for literature have also been proposed. Jan Assmann has argued that literature was a form of institutionalized discourse expounding cultural values that resulted from the social collapse of the Old Kingdom (1990: 54–7; compare the approaches of Herrmann 1957, 1977). The dominance of 'interregnum' motifs in many of the earliest compositions from a period of political troubles (cf. Quack 1992: 120–34) suggests a high degree of engagement with socio-political concerns, but does not necessarily provide a determining factor for the creation of literature. J. Assmann has also argued for the 'tomb as the school of Egyptian literature' (1983c; 1996c), seeing literature as resulting from the same 'dur désir de durer' as motivated monumental texts (Paul

Eluard, quoted by J. Assmann). This analysis derives literature primarily from the tomb biography. Literature appears at first in a period when there were substantial developments in the biographical genre (Gnirs 1996: 223–8; Coulon 1997), and literary and funerary texts show common themes and language, including such features as role-playing. Common to both is the concern for the transmission of elite culture, and literature in general has been characterized as the 'necropolis of stories' (Conrad 1985: 5). In Egypt, however, literature is differentiated from monumental, official discourse in terms of reception and decorum. J. Assmann's model probably underestimates the influence of areas of Egyptian cultural life and related social institutions that have not survived, such as oral poetry or even administrative documents. All of these may well have provided space for roles that written literature subsequently filled (Baines 1999a).

Literature is a complex phenomenon and its forms are unlikely to relate to a single prototype (cf. Goody 1987: 60). One example will suffice:[10] several scholars have suggested that the origin of the antithetical 'then-now' formulations common in pessimistic poems lies in funerary laments and orations;[11] most of these do not appear in the written record until later, but are likely to have existed earlier. A relatively early recorded example is in the late 18th Dynasty tomb of Neferhotep (Theban Tomb 49), in a caption above a scene of mourning women:

> Woe, woe!
> Safe, safe, safe, safe!
> . . .
> the multitude of mankind is taken from you (the deceased),
> and you are in the land which loves solitude!
> He who loved to stretch his legs to move
> is enclosed, bound, walled in.
> One rich in fine linen, who loved clothes,
> sleeps in the cast-offs of yesterday.
> (N. Davies 1933: pl. 24; Lüddeckens 1943: no. 49)

Such statements are strikingly similar to those of poems such as *Ipuur*:

> Look, the lords of robes are in rags;
> he who could not weave for himself is a lord of fine linen.   (7.11–12)

---

[10] Compare the analysis of Mathieu on the origin of the Ramessid love-song genre in 1996a: 217–41.
[11] Seibert 1967: 20–3; Schenkel 1984; J. Assmann 1990: 217 (quoting *Neferti* 12d: 'one lives in the necropolis'). See also Luria 1929.

However, sources for the so-called lament motif other than the observation of death are also possible. There are strong similarities between the descriptions of the land in laments and a New Kingdom hymn to the Nileflood (ODeM 1675; Fischer-Elfert 1986b: 45 n.1, 57), in which the prosperity brought by the flood is the exact opposite of their vision. The verse 'When (the Nileflood) delays, noses are blocked' in *The Nileflood Hymn* (2.5) parallels verses in teachings where the king is compared to the Nileflood (*The Loyalist Teaching* 3.5), and also a verse in a lament of *The Eloquent Peasant* on the consequence of social injustice (B1 264).[12] A core social context is perhaps the transition from king to king – the interregnum which threatens individual death, social disruption and cosmic chaos, as in Amennakht's hymn on the coronation of Ramses IV from Deir el-Medina:

> They who were naked, they are clad in fine linen.
> (O Turin 57001 rto l. 2–3; KRI VI, 68–9; Bickel and Mathieu 1993: 41–3; McDowell 1999: 158–9)

The association between the cycle of the year and political events is explicit in this eulogy:

> The troublemakers in this land, they have become peaceful;
> great Nilefloods have come forth from their caverns to refresh the people's hearts. (l.4)

And in another Ramessid hymn acclaiming King Merenptah's appearance as a 'happy time (*h3w-nfr*)', when

> Truth has driven off Falsehood;
> evildoers have fallen ⟨on⟩ their faces and all the greedy are forsaken.
> The water keeps up and does not subside,
> the Nileflood lifts high. (Gardiner 1937: 86.11–87.1; Caminos 1954: 323–5)

The same imagery occurs in the Ramessid *Satiric Letter*, where a littérateur says

> I will pour out for you choice things (*stpw*) like the flowing of the Nileflood,
> the shining waters in the Inundation-season, when it has seized the mounds;
> all my words are sweet,
> and pleasant in speech. (P. Anastasi I 7.8–8.2)

---

[12] The next stanza acclaims the Nileflood as 'one who makes greed until the whole land suffers (*mn*)' (3.1), which parallels the description in *Neferti*: 'the land in a state of suffering (*sn-mnt*)' (8e). In 3.7 'every tooth begins to laugh' parallels the grim state in *Neferti* where 'one laughs outright at suffering' (9b), and in *Ipuur* where 'laughter has perished' (3.13).

This image of plenitude embodies not only expansiveness, but also exuberance and pleasure, presenting this season as a metaphor for successful literary activity. Ramessid 'satiric' pictorial papyri and ostraca, with their travesties of the normal representation of men and women and the portrayal of animals in inverted contexts (e.g., Omlin 1971), have been connected with the period of merrymaking and chaos at the New Year (Kessler 1988; J. Assmann 1993). Mentions of such times of rejoicing at the New Year are attested from the Old Kingdom (L. Morenz 1999a: 132). Perhaps significantly, the literary descriptions of social upheavals in *Ipuur* include a contrasting reference to the idyllic conditions of New Year's Day (14.3–4). The entertainment of such festivals can serve as a broad, non-specific model for literary activity.

Thus, the 'then-now' motif can be related neither to specific historical events nor exclusively to a single functional textual prototype such as funerary laments or Nileflood hymns. Rather it is comparable with various textual expressions of life-situations, including the death of the individuals and the threatening phase of the yearly cycle in a constellation of imagery centred around these events, not around a single oral form. Literature's usage of forms derived from elsewhere is best assessed as one of intertextuality, not simply of transposition and transcription.

3.3.2 INTERTEXT

Intertextuality, an important component of poststructuralist literary theory, implies that 'a text is never a truly original creation of its author, but is inevitably part of a dynamic "universe of texts" with which it dialectically interrelates' (Loprieno 1996b: 51; Moers 2001: 106–54). It is not, however, a modern phenomenon; as Ong notes, 'manuscript culture had taken intertextuality for granted' (1982: 133). The literary canon apparently displays more pervasive intertextuality than other, more functional, types of discourse, an aspect of its contextual role in culture. The integration of other texts is often wholesale and explicit, as well as consisting of allusion and fusion of types. A composition's intertext depends on authorial choice and is vital for shaping any reading. Work here on Egyptian texts is in its infancy: one can contrast the exceptionally well-documented intertext of Vergil, which is pervasive, analytical, thematically motivated and wide-ranging (Farrell 1997).

The range of the Middle Kingdom intertext can be assessed from a brief review of types (general selection of translations: Parkinson 1991a) from the contexts of the royal court, the administrative elite and the temple (cf. J. Assmann 1999a). Utilitarian material in hieratic – the same script as literary manuscripts – included administrative documents, such as accounts, daybooks and reports (e.g., Quirke 1990b; Redford 1986:

97–126). The influence of these can be detected in *The Shipwrecked Sailor* (Blumenthal 1977a, b). Legal records may have influenced the dialogue genre, which can present itself as recording a sort of court case being enacted before an audience. Letters (Wente 1990: 24–5, 43–4, 68–88) can display a non-utilitarian level of rhetoric; model letters (Wente 1990: 69–70) were used in scribal training. Royal letters ('decrees'), which were disseminated on papyrus and often transferred into monumental memorials (Vernus 1991), also have a rhetorical aspect.

Texts of cult and courtly ritual were also prominent in the literary intertext; eulogies such as are included in literary and other texts (e.g., J. Assmann 1977a) probably derive from semi-cultic contexts. Mythical discourse occurs in hymns and in some specialized iconography (Baines 1996b), and is also utilized in literary tales about the gods. Divine hymns and eulogies for liturgical use, such as the Hymns to Sobek in P. Ramesseum VI (Gardiner 1957), are stylistically poetic, and are almost non-utilitarian despite their ostensible liturgical function, as are more recent examples of 'devotional verse'. Liturgical and religious texts are thus often the most difficult to distinguish from fictional literature although copies of some ritual utterances (such as the Ritual of P. Ramesseum B: Sethe 1928b: pl. 1–22) are more clearly contextually determined. Praise songs and ritual utterances to the king in court or temple are attested in papyrus copies, such as the Hymns to Senwosret III on P. Lahun LV.1 (= P. UCL 32157; e.g., Osing 1992a: 101–9), which is an apparently liturgical manuscript (Parkinson 1999d: 187–8). A context for lyrical songs in courtly ritual as well as in temples is suggested by the princesses' song in *Sinuhe*, which is also known in part from funerary monumental copies (B 269–79; L. Morenz 1997b). Other performative lyrics, such as harpist's songs (e.g., L. Morenz 1996: 58–77), were transcribed in tombs, and may have existed in archival copies, although the songs of workmen that are inscribed in tombs as illustrations of their activities were probably not archived as poetic compositions. A praise song of a Theban ruler carved as a formal graffito by a desert road may indicate how an occasional composition could move from improvised performance on a particular occasion to a commemorative monument (Darnell 1997b).

Written versions of performative ceremonies and 'spells' are also attested in the Coffin Texts, which include ritual texts and texts about rituals.[13] Manuscripts of liturgical funerary rites also existed (e.g., P. Ramesseum E). The performative aspects of such ritual texts, which include such situations as monologue, description and dialogue, would have made them

---

[13] See Wente 1982; Willems 1996a; Hornung 1999: 7–12. Hieratic manuscripts of Coffin Texts are apparently copies of master copies (e.g., P. Gardiner I–II from the early Middle Kingdom: Goedicke 1988c: xxi–xxii; Bourriau 1988: no. 64; see also Lapp 1988). The only instance of a direct relationship between such texts and literature is that of *The Herdsman*: see **A.1.1**.

suitable models for literary genres, while religious texts served as one model for literary manuscript presentation (**4.2**, **6.3**). Magical texts, such as Execration Texts, are included in literary works (e.g., Fischer-Elfert 1996b on *Sinuhe*).

Technical texts included calendars of lucky and unlucky days (unpublished: P. UCL 32192 from el-Lahun), as well as handbooks of healing (magical-medical) for treating men, women and animals (e.g., P. Ramesseum III–V), and mathematical books (e.g., P. Lahun IV.2–3, XLV.1, LV.3–4 = P. UCL 321659–62, 32134A). Such texts are alluded to in the teachings; their evocation in literature reaches prominence in the Ramessid *Satiric Letter* (Fischer-Elfert 1986a, 1992a). While technical texts ostensibly have a practical utilitarian purpose, they acquire encyclopaedic tendencies.[14] Lists, tables and 'onomastica' – thematically organized lists of words – are an integral part of the textual stream of tradition (Gardiner 1947; Kemp 1989: 29; Baines 1988; Hare 1999: 155–9). *The Eloquent Peasant* incorporates a list of goods (B1 1–14) and a sequence of fish-names (B1 257–62), both similar in type to the onomasticon of P. Ramesseum D. Particularly in monumental contexts, the stream of tradition also existed in captions to representational scenes, although visual material seems to have had little influence on literary texts. Esoteric treatises such as 'The King as Sunpriest' (J. Assmann 1970, 1995: 16–37), and the royal Underworld Books (e.g., Hornung 1967), which may derive in part from Middle Kingdom models,[15] were later inscribed in temples and royal tombs, integrated with visual forms of presentation.

Commemorative and funerary inscriptions on stelae, architecture and natural rock surfaces comprise a form of 'monumental discourse' (a phrase of J. Assmann's: e.g., 1996c), addressed to posterity as well as an audience of viewers and listeners, formulating central cultural values most explicitly, often with an ostensibly didactic aspect similar to literary teachings (e.g., Fischer 1982). Temple inscription and decoration was royal, while non-royal commemorative inscriptions included both funerary biographies (Gnirs 1996) and non-funerary inscriptions recording expeditions (e.g., Eichler 1994).

Royal texts also included the 'annals' which enumerated events by years (*gnwt*; Schott 1990: 379–81 [1655]; Redford 1986: 65–96). A section of the Annals of Amenemhat II is preserved in an inscription from a temple at Memphis (Altenmüller and Moussa 1991; Malek and Quirke 1992; Obsomer 1995: 595–607; Dautong 1999; Baines in preparation). Royal

---

[14] Thus a New Kingdom Onomasticon is entitled a 'teaching' (Schott 1990: 301–2 [1392]), but perhaps because it was attributed to an individual authority.
[15] A Middle Kingdom dating is considered unlikely by Hornung (e.g., 1999: 27–8; cf. J. Assmann 1995: 7 n.32). See also Borghouts 1989 for a possibly royal underworld guide from the Middle Kingdom.

commemorative inscriptions with a narrative aspect (*Königsnovellen* or Royal Tales: Loprieno 1996c, in preparation) are first attested in the 11th Dynasty (such as those of Nebhetepre Montuhotep II: Clère and Vandier 1948: 37–8; Schenkel 1965: 213–6). Building inscriptions of Senwosret I survive at Thebes (Gabolde 1998: 40–3, pl. 5), Elephantine (Schenkel 1975b, 1999) and Tod (Barbotin and Clère 1991); the latter follows the Royal Tale scenario. The most complete example, however, is that preserved on an 18th Dynasty leather roll.[16] Non-royal examples of such texts are attested in the stelae of Sarenput I (temp. Senwosret I) in the chapel of the local saint Heqaib on Elephantine (Franke 1994). Commemorative inscriptions from temple and tomb are tied to their monumental presentation, as is explicitly acknowledged in the standard 'address to tomb visitors' and the relation of the Semna and Uronarti stelae of Senwosret III to their emplacement in border fortress chapels with an image of the king (Seidlmayer 2000). However, both these and royal inscriptions probably had a potentially more mobile context of performance as well (Eyre and Baines 1989: 109–10; Eyre 1990; Derchain 1996a: 88).

Much of the material listed above is highly aesthetic in style and non-utilitarian, and identical with 'literature' in many respects, especially commemorative and religious texts, eulogies and narratives. Many are susceptible to a common 'literary' analysis. Nevertheless, they can be differentiated from works of literature in the narrow sense by their contextually determined manner of reception, by their decorum, and by not being fully fictionalized. The seventeenth century in England shows a similar fluidity: Andrew Marvell's 'occasional poems', such as *An Horatian Ode upon Cromwell's Return from Ireland* (1650), are historical, but are not historical reports. The boundary between literary and non-fictional exposition in texts is fluid, both over time and within a given period.[17] In the early 12th Dynasty *Sinuhe*, a royal eulogy is included within a clearly marked frame, whereas texts in similar genres, including royal eulogies and prayers to gods, seem to be more integral parts of the Ramessid literary corpus of the Late Egyptian Miscellanies. Like other forms of discourse, literature is a complex phenomenon and not the result of a single textual impetus, nor can it be circumscribed with a single pan-historical explanation.

---

[16] See Parkinson 1991a: 40–3; Osing 1992a: 109–19; Shirun-Grumach 1993: 147–73; Franke 1994: 180 n.487. Derchain (1992) suggests that the composition dates to the New Kingdom, but his arguments are controversial (see Obsomer 1995: 133–5; Piccato 1997: 137–42). For the probable existence of royal inscriptions commemorating expeditions, see Baines 1987.

[17] Some modern gardening and cookery books reveal high levels of artifice and fictionality, in contrast to books expounding more narrowly utilitarian information.

4
The social context

4.1 MIDDLE KINGDOM SOCIETY

> War das Antike doch neu . . .
>
> Goethe, *Römische Elegien* (1789), xiii

As well as being part of a wider intertext, 'the written word is self-consciously embedded in specific communities, life situations, structures of power' (Greenblatt 1980: 7), and cannot be understood 'without understanding the orientation of its evaluations in the ideological environment' (Bakhtin and Medvedev 1978: 121). The social context of Egyptian literature is difficult to determine, but its written nature places it in the centre of Egyptian culture. Alan Sinfield notes (1994: 29):

> When we ask: What are the truly literary qualities? we should also ask: Who says these are literary qualities, and why? Not just: What is it about this text that makes it literary? but: What is it in the social organisation that makes some people regard this text as literary? Literature becomes one set of practices within the range of cultural production.

I review here social features that are relevant, and in part distinctive, to the practice of literature, without assigning a primary significance to any one as a determining factor.

1. Social differentiation. Views of Middle Kingdom society have varied between seeing some of its texts as evidence of a democratic age (Wilson 1951: 123–4) and conceiving it as a highly prescriptive society driven by royalty (Helck 1963: 67–9; Kemp 1989: 149–80). The social structure of the period is still poorly understood. The First Intermediate Period shows increasing evidence for social networks probably between local patrons and their followers (Seidlmayer 1990; Franke 1990), but such networks existed in all periods, appearing in the record then due to increasing access in the provinces to literacy and to the means of cultural production. The 12th Dynasty experienced a complex set of tensions rather than a simple or conscious struggle between central and local control or individual and state tendencies (summary: Franke 1991: 51–2); the early and late Middle Kingdom are sharply differentiated from each other. Texts present a

schematic vision of a differentiated society in terms of 'patricians' and 'folk', 'great' and 'small', with limited indications of a subelite. It is unlikely that society was as uniform as it is often presented as being (Baines 1996c: 362–3), and moreover classes are never monolithic (e.g., Sinfield 1994: 31). Various texts refer to parvenus and admit social change (Vernus 1970, esp. 33–41). Some textual evidence records people who bear no official title except the descriptive 'townsmen' (Quirke 1991c; Andrassy 1998). From a survey of cemetery evidence Janet Richards (1992, 1997) argues that by the start of the Middle Kingdom there was a considerable degree of social differentiation, and that a 'middle class' existed in a more flexible and differentiated society than is usually deduced from society's self-presentation (see also O'Connor 1985: 175–7; on the high officials: Grajetzki 2001).

The creation and flourishing of literature has been linked to the rise of an intellectual, liberated 'middle class' at this period (Loprieno 1988; 1991a: 212–13). The extent to which this hypothetical group can be identified with the 'officials' (*srw*) mentioned in texts is uncertain (Quirke 1990a: 92; Doxey 1998: 157–9). Detlef Franke (1998a) has also argued that this hypothetical group cannot be identified in the 'little men' (*nḏsw*: cf. Doxey 1998: 196) of Middle Kingdom texts, and he reaffirms the economic and cultural dependence of the elite and subelite on the king. The Middle Kingdom was arguably a patronage society (Gnirs 2000b; Junge 2000). While the existence of literature is probably related to social changes, this group is problematic as an explanation of literature.

2. A culture of individuality. The 'theme of loneliness and isolation' (J. Assmann 1982b: 965) gains prominence in texts of the 10th–12th Dynasties. The concern with individual experience in the texts is a concern similar to what Stephen Greenblatt (1980) has termed 'self-fashioning' in the English Renaissance. One aspect is an emphasis on ethical behaviour as expressing the consciousness of individuality, which is embodied in the motif of 'following the heart' (Loprieno 1988: 86–91). A second aspect is religious, partly embodied in the concepts of the heart and the *ba* ('soul'; Loprieno 1988: 91–7; see also J. Assmann 1982b, 1984a: 215–20), and partly in the relationship between human individuals and the divine and royal spheres. In literature, the divine is presented in terms of its relationship to the human world, both in wisdom texts which express 'the way of god' (*Khety* 30a), and in narratives that tell of the divine's impact on individual lives, including 'personal piety' (Blumenthal 1998b). A third aspect is the 'culture of celebration' attested in First Intermediate Period later biographies (L. Morenz 1996: 110–11). For example, the late 13th Dynasty statue of the brewer Renefseneb-Dagi, probably from the Heqaib chapel at Elephantine, describes him as

a man of festival,[1]
beloved of myrrh,
who associates with holiday.

          (Berlin ÄMP 10115; Wildung *et al.* 2000: no. 75; Franke 1994: 103)

These phenomena are not necessarily signs of the evolution of individuality, but evidence of the history of discourses.

3. Expanding literacy and access to written culture. The early Middle Kingdom saw a 'media revolution', and the increased use of writing was an enabling factor for literature (L. Morenz 1996: 3, 201). Access to funerary texts offers a means of charting this: Middle Kingdom memorials at Abydos and non-royal tombs show an increasing use of funerary texts, but this was not a single or simple progression. In the late 12th Dynasty expansion and diversification in burial practices (Bourriau 1991), the memorials at Abydos come from rather lower levels of society than hitherto, but although a few inscriptions belong to individuals who had no titles (Quirke 1991c) such memorials do not include the Coffin Texts themselves, suggesting that some categories of texts were no less restricted than earlier. These changes in mortuary practice suggest that throughout the Middle Kingdom full literacy continued to be restricted principally to the male titled and official classes. The impact of increasing literacy on cultural artefacts was probably considerable: writing allows a dialogue which 'may relativize significant tenets of ideology, so that discordant conceptions come to be present in one and the same context ... Pluralization of this sort is characteristic of cultures with [writing], but not necessarily unique to them' (Baines 1984: 697). It is likely that the textualization of a new form of discourse in terms of looser decorum was formulated in the ambient of the royal court, rather than being a subversive movement due to an increased spread of literacy.

4.2 LITERARY MANUSCRIPTS IN SOCIETY

L'une des meilleures manières de recréer la pensée d'un homme: reconstituer sa bibliothèque.

          Marguerite Yourcenar, *Carnets de notes de 'Mémoires d'Hadrien'*
          (1982: 524)

Literary texts are composed in a grapholect – a means of essentially written communication (**3.3.1**). Thus a prime concern for siting them is the level of full literacy in society, assessed by Baines and Eyre (1983) at approxi-

---

[1] See Doxey 1998: 361.

mately under 1 per cent.² Literacy is never a monolithic phenomenon and such estimates can only model an order of magnitude for a complex and varied range of usage (compare Thomas 1986 on early modern England). The appearance of literature seems to coincide with the 'fixation of a particular register of written language', a formal, socially marked, official language (Loprieno 1996e: 518–20; Moers 2000: 59–80). Literary texts are thus in part a phenomenon of the male central elite and royal court, and a unitary part of the 'restricted' elite cultural apparatus (Eyre 1990: 162–4). Written literature is a medium created near the core of the literate state, and excludes the lower, non-literate levels of society; as such it is concerned in part with prestige and ostentation (L. Morenz 1996: 52). The attitudes towards the lower non-literate classes in *The Teaching of Khety*, for example, recall the effects of expanding literacy in Elizabethan England, which 'reinforced the existing social hierarchy by enabling the upper classes to despise their inferiors' (Thomas 1986: 117). Within the limits set by literacy, it is unknowable how restricted access to literature was, but the ability to become literate seems not to have been available to many levels of society, despite a presentation of the social order as meritocratic (Baines 1983: 585–6). The extent of upward social mobility is uncertain, and such mobility seems to have been conformist, with self-made men adapting to elite standards.

Indirect evidence for the social nature of literature is supplied by the groupings of texts in archives, where literary texts are not obviously distinguished or classified as separate entities. Literature shows affinities with various institutional spheres – temple, tomb, palace, administration. The principal means of circulating literature was by manuscript: many texts are described as being 'found' as a result of archival investigations (L. Morenz 1996: 52–5), and the content of colophons suggests the same for literary texts (see below). One can only speculate by what means, and how extensively, copies of literary texts were circulated: in the Roman Republic publication was 'casual and fluid' while 'most readers depended on borrowing books from friends and having their own copies made from them' (Reynolds and Wilson 1991: 23–4). Some poems are attested in manuscripts from throughout the country, such as *Sinuhe*, with Middle Kingdom manuscripts from Haraga in Middle Egypt and Thebes in the south, but it is possible that some may have been circulated only locally: examples of such may include some of the tales from el-Lahun, which are

---

² Their estimate has been much disputed (e.g., L. H. Lesko 1990). J. J. Janssen (1992: 84–6) has estimated that perhaps no more than 10 per cent of ostraca from Deir el-Medina are preserved, implying that Eyre's estimate of literacy there is too low (Baines and Eyre 1983: 86–91). Quirke (pers. comm.) estimates that 10 per cent of Lahun's population of about 3000 was literate, but like Deir el-Medina, this is an exceptional and specialized settlement.

known only from that site.³ The Ramessid community of Deir el-Medina provides a later example of local literary production (Bickel and Mathieu 1993). This pattern may well reflect a distinction between works commissioned and/or approved by the royal court and regarded as canonical, and local, lesser-known works. The texts of commemorative inscriptions are likely to have been circulated officially through the country (L. Morenz 1996: 139), and the same may have applied to canonical literary texts. In this context, institutional libraries may have been focal points for circulating copies and for individuals who obtained manuscripts for themselves (see Nordh 1996: 155–6).

Little is known about the nature and scope of institutional libraries (Burkard 1980; Quirke 1996b: 394–9); the principal sources derive from and relate to much later temple libraries (e.g., Tait 1977). How comprehensive such archives could be is suggested by Roman Period archival copies of Middle Kingdom commemorative inscriptions from Asyut (Osing and Rosati 1998: 55–100; Kahl 1999), and a 26th Dynasty copy of *The Teaching of Amenemhat* possibly from a temple context in Elephantine (P. Berlin 23045: Burkard 1977: 7–8; Verhoeven 1999: 259). This papyrus indicates that literature may have been stored in temple libraries, at least in the Late Period.⁴ Temple libraries are attested from the Middle Kingdom and Second Intermediate Period (e.g., L. Morenz 1996: 13, 84–6, 170–8). In the mid-13th Dynasty Abydos stela of King Neferhotep I, the king declares his desire to see the religious 'writings of Primeval times of Atum: Open (them) for me, for a great inventory (*sjpt-wr*)' (Helck 1983: 21, ll.6–7); he is answered:

'May your person proceed to the Houses of Writings and see the Divine
    Words!'
His Person proceeded to the House of the Book.
And then his Person opened the writings with these Friends.
Then his Person found the writings of the House of Osiris Foremost of
    Westerners.   (22, ll.12–16)

This is probably a temple library, although there is some New Kingdom evidence for palace libraries (Parkinson 1999e: 51–3). Such palace libraries could have included literary texts; quotations from, and allusions to,

---

³ Cf. L. Morenz 1996: 13–14. The attestation of literary texts from the Ramessid Period in the papyri from Memphis and from Deir el-Medina gives the impression of a fairly uniform availability of the canonical texts through the country (Quirke 1996b: 382–3).
⁴ In addition, an unpublished late Ramessid papyrus listing religious compositions includes a 'Teaching of Amen(em)o[pet(?)]', perhaps the well-attested *Teaching of Amenemopet*. This may derive from a temple (P. Berlin P. 15779; Burkard and Fischer-Elfert 1994: no. 180).

literary texts occur in royal inscriptions. For example, *Loyalist* 1.5–7 may be quoted in the inscription of King Neferhotep I (Helck 1983: 23, l.10).

Another important institution was the House of Life, which was both a scriptorium and an institution for advanced learning (Nordh 1996: 106–84, 193–215) that was attached to temples, but also closely associated with palaces and courts. Ritual and official texts are attested in connection with it and it very probably also contained literary texts, but it was not necessarily their primary place of composition or circulation.[5] Jan Assmann (1996b: 71–2) assigns literature to the institutional frame of the school, but there are few references to the 'school' in literature, even in the teachings (although Djedi in *Cheops' Court* has pupils: L. Morenz 1996: 117). The use of literary texts in scribal training is arguably at least partly secondary (see **3.2.2**, **10.1**).

Thus literature appears not to be tied to any particular institution (*Institutionsabstrakte*: L. Morenz 1996: 201). It is uncertain how far compositions would have been programmatically circulated under the instructions of the ruling group and royal court, or independently through members of the elite interested in belles lettres. Since the literate elite was small and had strong institutional ties, these two alternatives are not exclusive; the dichotomy between institutional and individual spheres may be inappropriate. A late New Kingdom example of a composition occurring in more than one context is the 'Qadesh poem' of Ramses II, which was 'published' on temple walls and was also apparently disseminated in manuscript form soon after the event it commemorated (1285 BCE), being attested in non-royal archives (von der Way 1984: 34–43; see below).

There is firm evidence for individual as well as institutional 'libraries' in the Middle Kingdom (L. Morenz 1996: 142–58); a fictional example is Djedi, who brings his 'writings' with him when summoned by Cheops (8.3–4). The Ramessid settlement of Deir el-Medina remains the only site from which non-royal archives have been recovered with any detailed archaeological or social context: the library of P. Chester Beatty begun in the late 19th Dynasty by the Scribe of the Tomb Qenherkhepshef (Pestman 1982; Nordh 1996: 165–8; McDowell 1999: 134–5) is the most extensive. It contained a wide range of material including: an archive of letters, memoranda and inheritance-documents of its various owners' families; various papyri with the following genres, often on the same roll: hymns, including *The Nileflood Hymn*; magical and medical texts; a manual on the interpretation of dreams; Miscellany-texts (including the *Satiric Letter* and the Miscellany containing the 'Eulogy of Dead Writers'); teachings (including *The Teaching of Ani* and *The Teaching of Khety*); Late

---

[5] Nordh (1996) assigns the transmission of literary texts to the world of the career scribe and non-royal initiative rather than to the House of Life.

Egyptian tales; love-songs; the Qadesh poem; and a ritual text. The lack of any Middle Kingdom compositions apart from *Khety* might suggest that 'the owners did not read the classics for pleasure' (McDowell 1999: 134). This collection was built up over more than a century by successive owners, and was eventually deposited in or beside a tomb-chapel in the necropolis of the village, presumably for safe-keeping (Posener 1978: vii; see also Parkinson and Quirke 1995: 64; Bickel and Mathieu 1993: 48–9 n.103). The textual sources drawn on by the collectors remains unknown (in general see Aufrère 1998: 49–53), but some love-songs are described as having been 'found in a book-container' (P. Chester Beatty I 16.9; Iversen 1979: 78); this particular manuscript seems to have been a personal gift from one scribe to another.[6]

Extant Middle Kingdom archives come from comparable non-royal and not very elevated spheres, suggesting that Middle Kingdom literature was not exclusively courtly. The lack of archaeological provenances for many manuscripts, however, is a severe problem. The presence of copies of some literary texts in non-royal tombs – from which come most substantially intact manuscripts – has suggested early on that they were intended to give pleasure in the afterlife as in this life (Goodwin 1866: 11). P. Prisse (*Kagemni* and *Ptahhotep*) was said to be from the necropolis of Dra Abu el-Naga, Thebes; a manuscript of *The Tale of Sinuhe* has a similar provenance from the necropolis of Haraga, near el-Lahun, and *P. Lythgoe* came from the Residence cemetery at el-Lisht. The placing of manuscripts in tombs was clearly secondary, but it is uncertain how far it gives evidence for their primary usage: they can hardly have been intended only for otherworldly pleasure, since administrative texts have also been found in tombs (the very early 12th Dynasty P. Reisner I–IV, placed on a coffin in tomb N 408 at Naga el-Deir: Simpson 1963a: 17, frontispiece). The meaning of this practice is unknown; perhaps the papyri formed part of the deceased's professional equipment – as has been suggested for the Ramesseum papyri – or were status symbols of literacy. It is hard to imagine that the specific contents of these administrative texts were any longer meaningful. The placing of non-funerary papyri in tombs continued occasionally after the Middle Kingdom (Quirke 1996b: 391; his R23 is an intrusive deposit). Four examples provide evidence of private archives.

1. Private individual ownership is exemplified by the colophon to *The Shipwrecked Sailor*, which describes it as 'the writing' of a named 'scribe, Ameny son of Amenyaa' (P. Leningrad 1115, 186–9), as became standard practice in the New Kingdom. The same scribe may have written

---

[6] McDowell 1999: 152. Another manuscript claims that 'this book was found in the old House of Books of the temple' (P. Chester Beatty VIII rto 4.3), but this may be an authentication of the spell rather than a reference to the source of the copy.

P. Prisse, and the two may thus have been found together in their owner's tomb at Dra Abu el-Naga, Thebes. The name in the colophon may be that of a copyist rather than of an owner, but later colophons show that the copyist and owner could be the same individual.[7]

2. Papyri excavated in the settlement site of el-Lahun include late 12th Dynasty literary manuscripts, now in the Petrie Museum, University College London (Griffith 1898, and unpublished). *The Tale of Hay* and *The Tale of Horus and Seth* were parts of archives of official and priestly documents; these papyri were excavated not in the great mansions, but in middle-ranking houses in Rank N (Gallorini 1998; on the types of housing in el-Lahun see Kemp 1989: 149–57; F. Arnold 1989: 75–93). It remains uncertain, however, whether the finds of papyri were primary or secondary archive deposits. The contents of one lot from a middle-ranking house is suggestive of the owner's being a lector priest (Quirke, pers. comm.).

3. The Ramesseum papyri are an archive, ranging over about a century (Gardiner 1947: 6), from a plundered 13th Dynasty burial in the late Middle Kingdom cemetery now beneath the later funerary temple complex of Ramses II at Thebes (Loyrette *et al.* 1994; Kalos *et al.* 1996: 75). They form a more subject-specific archive than any of the el-Lahun excavation lots, and include literary compositions together with an onomasticon, hymns, rituals, and medical and magical texts (Parkinson 1991c: xi–xii; L. Morenz 1996: 144–7). The administrative texts among the papyri are incidentally present, as texts that were reused or as personal records of their owner (Quirke 1990b: 187–95). The papyri were found in a chest (now lost) with a jackal drawn on the lid, and some items of magical equipment were scattered around the chest together with funerary artefacts (Parkinson 1991c: xi–xiii; Bourriau 1991: 20; Ritner 1993: 222–32; L. Morenz 1996: 144–7). Such a chest was probably the normal means of storing private collections of manuscripts (e.g., L. Morenz 1996: 144 n.622; Parkinson 1999e: 52). The jackal was perhaps a funerary symbol, or it may have been connected with the title 'Master of Secrets', which can be written with the hieroglyph of a jackal.[8] Several of the papyri may ultimately derive from a temple library.[9] The owner was probably of priestly rank, either a lector priest (and 'Master of Secrets') or

---

[7] P. D'Orbiney (*The Tale of the Two Brothers*) is dedicated to the apprentice scribe's master Qageb, but was 'made by the scribe Inena, the owner of this manuscript' (19.7–10; Gardiner 1932: 29).

[8] Ritner 1992: 194 n.42 and 1993: 231–2; L. Morenz (1996: 145–6) interprets differently, as indicating a temple provenance.

[9] Ritner suggests that the papyri were temple property and were buried with a man because they had been rendered unfit for temple usage by damage (1993: 232 n.1077). Modern damage, however, is so extensive as to suggest that ancient damage may have been very limited. L. Morenz's (1996: 147–54) attempt to identify a specific temple source for some of the papyri is very speculative.

embalmer, perhaps wealthy enough to have a household that used accounts (Quirke 1990b: 187–9). He was a provincial, not a member of the royal court at Itj-tawi. It is unclear to what extent the literary papyri belong to a professional assemblage of texts, or represent a more personal choice.

4. Another archive can be posited from the late 12th Dynasty Theban papyri, possibly the reign of Amenemhat III, now in the Berlin Museum (the 'Berlin library'; Parkinson 1991c: x–xi, xxv–xxvi). Four manuscripts comprise copies of *Sinuhe*, *A Man and His Ba* (including a reused copy of *The Herdsman*), and *The Eloquent Peasant* (two partial manuscripts), written by three different scribes. If these represent the full extent of the archive, then this is a library of three purely literary works. Given the state of preservation, the papyri must have been found in a burial, but nothing is known of the owner, except that he was wealthy enough to have had a tomb, and that he was not a member of the royal court (like 3 above). Ludwig Morenz's proposed identification of the owner (1996: 135–41) – the Steward Buau, the owner of coffin T9C discovered in a tomb beside the 11th Dynasty temple of Montuhotep at Deir el-Bahri (CGC 28027; PM I², 656) – is implausible for several reasons.[10]

The papyri were apparently first listed in the d'Athanasi sale catalogue of 1837 among 'rolls of papyrus found in tombs at Thebes' (d'Athanasi 1837: 23, nos 268–71) which Giovanni d'Athanasi is known to have acquired from the Dra Abu el-Naga area, where similar finds were apparently made (see 1 above). If the papyri were discovered in a reasonably well-preserved burial – as their state of preservation suggests – it is possible that the coffin might also have survived and have been collected. Very few late Middle Kingdom coffins were known at this date (John Taylor, pers. comm.). The same d'Athanasi sale included a coffin of one Sobekaa, discovered in an intact burial of the late 12th Dynasty beside the much later temple at Deir el-Medina (coffin T3Be; PM I², 821; Willems 1988: 114–15); the brief contemporaneous description of this find, however, makes no mention of any rolls of papyri (d'Athanasi 1837: 75–7).[11]

---

[10] The identification is based on the links between Coffin Text spell 836 (*CT* VII, 36i–s), which is known only from this coffin and *The Tale of the Herdsman*, but it requires the implausible assumption that the *Herdsman* manuscript is a thematically integral part of the 'library' (1996: 124–5), rather than being a discarded papyrus, written anterior to the main library, which was reused to strengthen the roll of *A Man and His Ba*. The identification is also problematic due to dating considerations: J. P. Allen dates Buau to the reigns of Montuhotep III, IV and Amenemhat I (forthcoming; cf. Willems 1988: 114), well before the date of the papyri; the papyri also appeared in London in 1843 (Parkinson 1991c: x), half a century before the first reported discovery of the find-spot of the coffin in 1896 (L. Morenz 1996: 136 n.588).

[11] Other possible candidates include: the coffin of the Montuhotep from Thebes, datable to the early/mid(?) 12th Dynasty (coffin T2L [BM EA 6655]; PM I², 827; Willems 1988: 115) which was in the collection of Joseph Sams of Darlington in 1834, but probably came ultimately from d'Athanasi's work (Taylor, pers. comm.); the coffin of the priest Amenhotep,

Two further cases suggest personal familiarity with literary works:

5. A graffito apparently from late in the reign of Amenemhat III, in the Wadi el-Hol by the desert road from modern Luxor to Farshut, appears to contain a quotation from *Sinuhe* (Darnell and Darnell 1996: 63–4). It names a priest (*hm-ntr*) Dedusebek travelling to participate in a festival at Deir el-Bahri. This provides a named and titled individual who was familiar with *Sinuhe*. Several other graffiti have literary characteristics, and some refer to 'spending a holiday' (*jr-hrw-nfr*) at the spot.

6. The high-ranking official Sehotepibre, an intimate member of the royal court under Amenemhat III, included a version of one literary text, *The Loyalist Teaching,* on his Abydos memorial stela (see A. 1.5). Supposed allusions to literary texts in many commemorative inscriptions can also be taken as evidence of the owner's familiarity with literature (e.g., L. Morenz 1996: 178–9), but most of these are very uncertain and the composer of an inscription may have been a different person from the owner.

Literary manuscripts are almost invariably written in the everyday cursive hieratic script used for documents such as letters and administrative documents. The compositions were thus not part of monumental discourse. The use of hieratic further distinguishes literary texts from those written in the linear hieroglyphic script, which was usually reserved for religious, liturgical and funerary texts connected with the temple sphere, although technical texts were written in either script form (e.g., L. Morenz 1996: 62, 70–1). There are only a few examples of Middle Kingdom literary works copied in linear script; most are later copies of *The Teaching of Amenemhat* on ostraca, written in linear hieroglyphs between ruled lines.[12] The choice of script probably derives from the ostracon being an apprentice exercise, written in the same script as the educational text *Kemit* (Appendix 2), and not from its being copied from an otherwise unattested type of literary papyrus, a copy in linear hieroglyphs from a temple library.

In the 12th Dynasty there were two styles of hieratic, one used for administrative and practical texts, and a less cursive one used for broadly literary texts, including technical treatises such as Onomastica. The el-Lahun papyri also show that different types of documents were formatted differently in terms of hand and layout. It is, however, unlikely that an exclusively literary format can be identified, except that literary texts,

---

datable to the late 12th Dynasty (coffin T18 [BM EA 12270]), which was acquired in 1839 from Giovanni Anastasi.

[12] ODeM 1175 vso (Posener 1951c: pl. 26a); O. Michaelides 50 (Goedicke and Wente 1962: pl. 1-2), ROM Toronto Ostracon 907.18.14 (B.3635), from Deir el-Bahari (unpublished). ODeM 1175 has *Khety* on the recto.

unlike many other types, are always unillustrated.[13] The literary manuscripts are not isolated from other domains of written culture. Literary manuscripts are not presented as esoteric, unlike texts that were inscribed in places of limited access and unlike sacred texts (cf. L. Morenz 1996: 78–87; in general Baines 1990b), nor does anything suggest that they were ever transmitted orally in restricted circles, as suggested by the courtly epithet: 'one who hears what only one person hears' (J. M. A. Janssen 1946: 110 [Fo.19]). As Jack Goody (1987: 118) remarks, written texts can be circulated with less authorial control than orally transmitted ones.

The transmission of a text in multiple manuscripts in itself is not a distinguishing feature of the literary corpus: there are numerous examples of funerary, magical and technical texts, and commemorative inscriptions, such as that of the Semna and Uronarti stelae, which were contextually bound to display in a royal chapel at a border (Eyre 1990: 138), are known to have existed in more than one copy. The physical means of copying literature does not correspond to an absolute distinction between it and other texts preserved on other media. *The Loyalist Teaching* was transferred from literary manuscripts to a stela, and performative ritual texts were transferred onto tomb walls (e.g., L. Morenz 1996: 58–70).[14] Conversely, texts could be transferred from a monumental context to a manuscript, such as the Building inscription of Senwosret I preserved on the 18th Dynasty Berlin leather roll;[15] such monumental texts were also drafted and stored in manuscript form. The usage of hieratic manuscripts is nonetheless relevant in placing the literary canon in an intertextual context, and is indicative of literature's situational mobility. The distinctiveness of literary transmission is explicitly acknowledged in the Ramessid 'Eulogy of Dead Writers' :

> The roll is more excellent than the carved stela.
>
> (P. Chester Beatty IV vso 3.1)

The devices used to label manuscripts also provide evidence for attitudes towards literary texts. Titles introduced by 'Beginning of' (*ḥȝt-ʿ*) occur in

---

[13] H. Altenmüller 1980: 39. Various scenes on Ramessid ostraca have been taken as illustrations to love-songs (see Fischer-Elfert 1997: 161–3, 161 n.85), but none is convincing; the only exception known to me is an apprentice scribe's informal doodle of a lion in the desert illustrating *The Teaching of Khety* 16b on the verso of P. Anastasi VII (P. BM EA 10222).

[14] Later examples of a Teaching on a funerary monument are 'The Teaching of Aamethu' on the walls of his son Useramen's tomb (Theban Tomb 131) together with an inscription describing his son's appointment and the 'Installation of the Vizier' text (Dziobek 1998; teaching: 23–54, pl. 2), and the tomb biography of the High Priest of Amun Amenemhat (*Urk.* IV, 1408 l.8–1411 l.16; Gardiner 1910). These 18th Dynasty examples are pseudo-literary or literarized commemorative texts (cf. **7.3**).

[15] The inscription describing the appointment of Useramen (n.14) is also known from a papyrus copy: Dziobek 1998: 1–21; see p. 258).

the literary corpus and throughout the body of written texts (Luft 1973; Schott 1990: 293–309 [1352–1422]). Their use is generically determined, and some genres, by their nature, have titles, and others such as tales do not. The colophon, though not restricted to literary texts, occurs with great consistency at the end of copies of them (*Wb.* I, 45.1–4). The best known Middle Kingdom form of the colophon is attested in mid- to late 12th Dynasty Theban manuscripts:

> It is come from beginning to end   (*jw:f-pw ḥȝt:f r-pḥwj:fj*
> as found in writing.   *mj-gmjjt m-sš*)

This concludes both tales and wisdom texts as does an abbreviated form: *jw:f-pw* (see Parkinson 1991b: 95 for details; see also L. Morenz 1996: 14–15 n.59). The *jw:f-pw* form appears from the second half of the 12th Dynasty, but the earliest attestations of colophons in slightly different forms are in the Coffin Texts, such as a coffin from el-Bersha (temp. Senwosret I: *CT* VII, 262j [B3C]; Willems 1988: 74). The relatively northern location of el-Bersha may be significant as the site might reflect practices at the Residence. The colophon could have arisen in the funerary context, whose influence pervades the written forms of literature, but it may have been normal in institutional scriptoria. While the colophon marks a wide range of texts as parts of the transmitted body of written literature, it also exemplifies the literary texts' uniquely verbal nature, and the reification of the performance text into a thing, a manuscript, that can be owned.

4.3 AUTHORS AND AUTHORSHIP

> He composed this writing with his own fingers
> when he came to inscribe the tomb . . .
> he was not (merely) a draughtsman; his heart alone guided him.
>
> Description of the Scribe of the Divine Book,
> Merire, in a tomb at el-Kab, *c.* 1128 BCE (PM V, 181 [4])

The identity of the authors of Middle Kingdom poetry is unknown. With one possible exception, the author-figures featuring in the literary texts are pseudonymous. The 'author-function' is differently constructed in the Middle Kingdom from modern Europe and 'does not operate in a uniform manner in all discourses, at all times, and in any given culture' (Foucault 1977: 130). Of the literary corpus, only the teachings and discourses are explicitly identified in their titles with a male protagonist who is their supposed creator. Wisdom is exemplified and validated by the experiences of individuals who possess it, so that the protagonist is easily presented as an author figure.[16] One teaching is made by 'a man for his son' (*A Man* 0.2), its anonymity presumably emphasizing its wisdom's universality. A similar disregard for authorial identity can be detected in the textual history of *The Loyalist Teaching*, the only surviving Middle Kingdom copy of which is the Abydos stela of Sehotepibre, which is entitled so as to make him the protagonist. This would have been a strikingly blatant plagiarism if identified authorship had been important in the literary tradition.

The supposed composers of teachings frequently are – or resemble – known prestigious historical figures, and three are royal, but they are not the actual authors. The 'author' Prince Hordedef also features in a tale as a protagonist; both 'authored' wisdom texts and tales use the same historical periods as settings. The pseudonymity of *The Teaching of Amenemhat* was explicitly acknowledged by Ramessid scribes – whether or not one believes their attribution to a historical author Khety (see pp. 90–1). None of the protagonists of other wisdom genres, such as *The Discourse of Sasobek*, is a certainly attested historical figure; this lack of historical fame may relate to those genres' embodying of troubled conditions, which it would be inappropriate to link with figures of established eminence. It cannot be known how far the audience regarded the claims to authorship as fictional, or how far they were intended to do so. Some protagonists were later sometimes presented as if historical (see **2.2.2**). It is, in any case, easy to blur the distinction between fiction and fact in literature, both for the audience (without intention) and for the author (deliberately).[17] Explicit signs of fictionalization that the modern reader cannot detect may well be present in many cases (see further **5.1.2**).

Ramessid exceptions show that the actual author and protagonist of a wisdom text could be the same individual. Deir el-Medina authors include the draughtsman Menna (Guglielmi 1983; McDowell 1999: 144–7; see J.J. Janssen 1992: 87 n.35), the Scribe of the Tomb Amennakht, and possibly the scribe Hori (Bickel and Mathieu 1993; McDowell 1999: 139–42). However, these texts are not known to have been circulated beyond the authors' immediate associates, and may well belong to a different, more 'proletarian' literary context (Loprieno 1996b: 55–8) where levels of literacy were higher than in the Middle Kingdom.

In general, the fictional author of Middle Kingdom poems is often

---

[16] The late New Kingdom *Onomasticon of Amenemope*, which is a teaching of classified items and categories, has a similarly personal title (Gardiner 1947: I, 24–6). The emphasis on individual experience sets them, together with autobiographies, apart from many types of text.

[17] See Olsen 1987: 192. One (fictional) example of such confusion is Max Beerbohm's Enoch Soames (*Seven Men*, 1919); events in his life have had (actual) official commemoration in the British Library, and American libraries have offered to buy fake copies of his non-existent poems (reported in *The Times*, March 17, 1997).

specified to be literate, although there is also a tradition of peasant (i.e., oral) wisdom, as with *The Eloquent Peasant*, while *The Discourse of The Fowler* may draw on attitudes to the primordial aspects of country life and wisdom as ancient simplicity. The speakers of teachings, for which social status was apparently important as a guarantee of efficacy, range from kings and princes, through revered viziers, to a scribe with no other title than 'a man of Sile', suggestive of a lowly position in a marginal town (*Khety* 1a). The title of *The Teaching of a Man for His Son*, although anonymous as if spoken by a literary 'everyman', alludes to the rank of 'gentleman' (literally, 'son of a man'), suggesting that the 'everyman' of literature was implicitly a gentleman and office-holder. The authors to whom the discourses and dialogues are attributed are of lower social status, as is appropriate for their often problematic circumstances. The highest in rank is apparently the lector priest of Bastet Neferti; others range through common w^cb-priests to an otherwise title-less scribe. The lowest is a title-less marginal man, a 'fowler of the Southern City' (*The Fowler* l.1). In the tales, the major tellers – and the fictional protagonists – display a more inclusive range: from the princes to an oasis dweller and a lowly herdsman (Parkinson 1996a: 143).

'The function of an author is to characterize the existence, circulation, and operation of certain discourses within a society' (Foucault 1977: 124), and this range of types of fictional author/protagonist acts as a literary signal. There are few indications of how closely they could correlate with actual composers of literature. It is impossible to determine whether the texts are the result of single or multiple – as redactional criticism tends to argue – authorship, but all present themselves with a single implied author. As Philippe Derchain (1996a: 94) remarks, someone must have written them. The fact that the high official Sehotepibre appropriated the 'authorship' of *The Loyalist Teaching* (whose protagonist seems to have been a vizier) for his stela, which also uses older high status forms (Posener 1976: 14–16; Simpson 1991: 332–5), associates literature with the very inner elite. Claims by works to be courtly documents or to come from the lowest levels of society may be courtly or pastoral 'travesties' respectively, in which the audience disguises itself by identifying with characters from a different level of society (cf. M. V. Fox 1985: 292–4).

The implied author usually shows access to esoteric and religious knowledge and fine style, suggestive of relatively elite circles; the texts themselves are mostly secular (Posener 1971: 251). Although oral poetry could have been very sophisticated in many contexts, the use of written forms suggests that the lowest social levels as presented are fictions. Kings, princes and viziers are also unlikely to have been the status of the actual authors. The centre of the fictional range lies with officials not necessarily of the highest rank: it is easy to imagine such officials enjoying both courtly travesties and description of the misfortunes of individuals from lower social levels. In addition, the rank of lector priest may correspond to a known owner of literary manuscripts (see above). The actual authors are likely to have been men associated with this social range.

The sophistication of the texts is such that their composition was surely a specialized activity, although it is unlikely to have formed an independent profession. The possibility of composers who earned revenue by their skill is suggested by the compositions' frequent mention of the rewards of eloquence (e.g., Derchain 1972; cf. Loprieno 1988: 89), although literary eloquence is not their primary profession.[18] Texts that were circulated throughout the country are likely to have been produced under elite patronage; the nature of such patronage, whether central or local, is unknown (cf. Roccati 2000: 12–14). The author and the protagonist/ actor are always ultimately 'loyalist', although often initially dissenting and ostensibly peripheral, which may point to composition being done under the direct patronage of the high elite. *Ipuur* mentions 'story-tellers ($sddw$)' (4.13; Parkinson 1996a: 144 n.57) in a context which suggests that such composer/performers attended the great and the wealthy, along with lyric 'musicians' (*Ipuur* 4.12–13). As depicted in *Neferti*, the literary laments at social disorder were probably recited in stable wealthy contexts. Perhaps literary works came in general from the royal court, from rather lower levels of its administration and bureaucracy, or from local courts, and some were circulated with official support within the elite and the subelite.[19] Nevertheless, the poems' themes imply some value attached to social and intellectual freedom among both the authors and audience: 'the dominant culture of a complex society is never a homogeneous structure. It is layered, reflecting different interests within the dominant class' (Clarke *et al.* 1976: 12).

4.4 AUDIENCE AND PERFORMANCE

> Les gens regardent toujours d'un livre la facette qui reflète leur propre vie.
>
> Marguerite Yourcenar, *Les Yeux ouverts: entretiens avec Matthieu Galey* (1980), 'Une malle et un empereur'

Literature's context is known only from its own self-representations within fictional frames, where it is '"performative utterance" which actually

---

[18] L. Morenz suggests that Djedi is a type of the 'man of letters' (1996: 107–23), but may overstate.

[19] The social standing of the later littérateurs of Deir el-Medina is broadly comparable with this model.

creates its object' (Iser 1989: 6); it remains uncertain when, where and how the compositions would be performed. The compositions seem designed for performance (Eyre 2000), an impression strengthened by modern adaptations and recitals (Parkinson 1999f: 11 n.11; 2000a). There are no independent textual or visual representations of readings; one representation of a possibly parallel situation is the 11th Dynasty scene of a seated 'scribe of the divine book' reciting a ritual text to a seated princess Ashayet on her sarcophagus (L. Morenz 1996: 71–4; photograph: Fischer 1996: pl. 14b). Literary self-representations include performances to groups (e.g., *Neferti* and *The Eloquent Peasant*; Chappaz 1986: 105–6), from which one may infer that the compositions could be read aloud at elite social gatherings; the epilogue of *Kagemni* (2.6) implies the possibility of a group reading a text to itself. Private reading should not be excluded. One word for these performances is *šdj* 'to recite' (Schott 1990: 521), also used of biographies, letters and spells, implying a formalized, declamatory method of delivery; funerary representational art uses various arm and hand gestures to indicate that people are reciting (Dominicus 1994: 77–130), and these may well correspond to actual performance practice. Singing (*ḥsj*) is reserved for specific types of spells, and for praise songs, harpists' lyrics, love-songs and funerary laments (Schott 1990: 489; L. Morenz 1996: 47–8). Its meaning may be close to that of *šdj*.[20] Fictional descriptions of literary performances do not mention instrumental accompanists, and the literary context must be considered separately from that of harpists who are often shown blind and thus unable to read (e.g., L. Morenz 1996: 75–7; Schlott 1996). *Neferkare and Sasenet* suggests an opposition between the two types of performance, in that the tale's protagonist is drowned out by court musicians when attempting to perform before the king (P. Chassinat I X+2.x+8–13). One literary protagonist, Ipuur, however, was later attributed with the title 'god's singer'.[21]

Accompanied lyrics are by nature performance-bound, but recitation can be private and personal. L. Morenz argues that reading in Egypt would have been reading – including murmuring – aloud, citing phrases such as 'Write with your hand, read with your mouth' (1996: 43–52, following other scholars). Overall, performance and reading of literary texts appear as a recitative art, in contrast with the manner of reading monumental texts and art, as described in an inscription from the Saite

---

[20] As suggested by *Herdsman* where a 'water-song' (*ḥsw-mw*) is 'recited' (13). In *Merikare*, 'writings' are 'sung' (18b), but in an educational context, and it is unclear whether these are literary texts such as were used in training scribes in later periods or ritual lyrics. This phrasing could also be a piece of poetic diction. In representations distinct gestures indicate singing and musical activity: Dominicus 1994: 167–78.

[21] See **A.1.2**. Men with this title, such as the New Kingdom Raia, chief singer of Ptah Lord of Truth, are shown in tomb reliefs singing with a harp: G. T. Martin 1985: pl. 22. L. Morenz suggests on this basis that *Ipuur* may be a *ḥsj* type of utterance (1999a: 131).

Period tomb of Ibi (*c.* 650 BCE), where the processes of 'seeing' and 'hearing' combine in a complex multi-medial process of 'comprehending' (ʿq) the tomb walls.[22] This may be reflected in literary texts' unusual unillustrated presentation (see above).

The internal audience described in some poems is part of the works' generic setting, comprising, for example, the children of the speaker of a teaching. The majority of such audiences are officials, many of higher rank than the speaker, and a number are from the royal court (Parkinson 1996a: 143). This fictional audience may not have corresponded with the actual intended audience, especially since the poems present a schematic picture of society. Thus, *Sinuhe* and *The Eloquent Peasant* avail themselves of settings at court, but finds show that they were read elsewhere in the Middle Kingdom. Comparable assessments of audiences for works of art in later cultures are able to draw upon sources lacking for the Middle Kingdom.[23]

Subject matter is perhaps a more reliable indication of the social environment than fictional settings. The vision of the poems extends beyond the royal court circle, but all still centre round the views and concerns of the official class: *The Eloquent Peasant* is not centred around the concerns of a peasant from the oases. The restrictions of literacy suggest that the 'implied readers' of a text must have been members of the elite or subelite (e.g., Baines 1990a: 57 n.9). Through recitation before a non-literate audience, the audience may have included a wider group than that of the written text. Similarly, funerary inscriptions refer to a wider audience than the literate (Eyre and Baines 1989: 109; Eyre 1993: 116), as on the stela of the Steward Montuwoser from the reign of Senwosret I:

> Now as for any people who shall hear (*sḏm*) this stela . . .
> Now as for any scribe who will recite (*šdj*) this stela,
> all people will come up to him.   (Sethe 1928a: 80, ll.1–4)

The extent to which literature permeated, or was restricted to, particular social levels is unknowable (Eyre 1993: 119). The multiple levels of meaning in tales such as *The Shipwrecked Sailor* and *Sinuhe*, which are both adventure tales and symbolic narratives, suggest that they were intended for audiences of varying levels of sophistication. Much in the corpus, such as the use of esoteric material in *The Shipwrecked Sailor* and the allusions to specifically written forms, could only be fully appreciated by the literate

---

[22] Kuhlmann 1973; Kuhlmann and Schenkel 1983: 71–2, pl. 23; see J. Assmann 1994b: 20–4 n.2. For the interrelationship see Bryan 1996; for a Middle Kingdom stela that conveys its message by visual means see Wildung 1997: 84–5, no. 92.

[23] For example, Beethoven's string quartets: see Kerman 1994 on their 'collegial and courtly' audiences; Botstein 1994 on reconstructing their social context.

elite, but this would not hamper some level of appreciation, for example, in a hypothetical village setting. However, a village audience's understanding of *The Eloquent Peasant* would be very different, through a difference in sympathy, with that of a courtly audience, and such an extended and lowly audience for the poems is ultimately implausible.

It remains difficult to imagine an actual reading of a work on the basis of the fictional descriptions: the fictional protagonist could correspond to an actual performer reciting from a manuscript or from memory, possibly a specialized performer, while the frequently attested role of the person who brings the protagonist to the scene of his performance may correspond to officials at the royal court with responsibility for entertaining the king (as is attested for other forms of recreation: see below). Outside the royal court, such organization would have been less institutionalized, while the nature and number of the audience remains uncertain and was probably diverse. It has been suggested that at least some literary works, including pessimistic discourses, were for recital at festivals (e.g., L. Morenz 1999a: 131–5). Ursula Verhoeven's suggestion (1996) that a specific royal ritual at Thebes was the occasion for the Late Egyptian *Story of Horus and Seth* is illuminating but ultimately problematic, underplaying the extent to which this text could have been circulated before and after the ritual and beyond that particular context – the copy was still part of a non-royal archive several generations later.[24] The fictional descriptions of literary events do not place them in a specific context, but only in a holiday mood, suggesting a specific atmosphere was the occasion.

4.5 THE LITERARY RESPONSE

> Art, if it doesn't start there, at least ends,
> Whether aesthetics like the thought or not,
> In an attempt to please our friends.
>
> W. H. Auden, *Letter to Lord Byron* iii (1991: 100)

The formal response to a performance and the inner response to a performance characterize literature as a social practice. Fictional texts evoke formal signs of appreciation for the fictional performer/composer.

---

[24] Pestman 1982. Performances of Shakespeare's *Twelfth Night* were not bound to the liturgical festival of that name. Bach's sacred music (cited by J. Assmann 1996b: 69) is not *situationsabstrakt*, but it is unlikely that all of its qualities are determined by its liturgical function, especially since (for example) the final version of the B Minor Mass (BWV 232) seems to have been composed without a specific performance in mind, and 'without regard to its use as a liturgical work' (Boyd 1990: 174).

In *Cheops' Court*, the king acknowledges the tales told to him with funerary offerings to the protagonists (though not the tellers who are his sons), while in the final stanza of *Neferti* the sage predicts that later readers will offer him a funerary offering of water (15g; see **9.1**). It seems likely that literary artists would have been greeted with acclaim and some recompense at the end (cf. Eyre 1993: 116–17). An audience would probably have shown signs of responsiveness throughout a performance.

In terms of inner response, the implied audience is not necessarily any single person, but the mode of address is personal (Loprieno 1988: 84–97). Descriptions of performances often include the audience's psychological response at the end. A favourable reaction is given to teachings and discourses, in which they are 'perfect (*nfr*) to the heart' (e.g., *Kagemni* 2.6–7, *Eloquent Peasant* B2 131; for 'perfect speech' see **6.4**). The same reaction is evoked by other genres, such as eulogies and hymns (e.g., *Urk.* IV, 685 ll.10–12), and in *Cheops' Court* a similar phrase describes king Sneferu's reaction to the sight of maidens rowing (5.14–15). Other genres describe different responses, including piety with the addresses to the living on funerary monuments, 'beatification' as the result of religious texts, and loyalism as a response to royal eulogies and proclamations.[25]

Literary responses are not inherent in an essential literature, but are part of a social contract between author and audience, and vary between different 'interpretive communities' (e.g., Fish 1980). There are some indications that the Egyptian response to literary works was distinctive: textual contradictions were not normally desirable, to judge by the manner in which the author of the Ramessid *Satiric Letter* denounces a writer of a letter, saying that

> Your utterance is not sweet, it is not bitter;
> all that comes from your mouth
> is [bitter almonds] and honey. (P. Anastasi I 5.2)

Such a comment could be made about *The Eloquent Peasant*'s third petition, where he addresses the High Steward with elevated eulogy and bitter derision. Despite this, the peasant's speeches are acknowledged in the text to be 'perfect' (B2 131–2), and are unified by their imagery and bound together by a single all-encompassing narrative with a concentric formal structure. It seems that the violent juxtapositions and the repeated frustration of expectations that are found in Middle Kingdom works were

---

[25] Such as the Semna stela and its accompanying statue which are designed 'so that you shall be firm for it, so that you fight for it' (Sethe 1928a: 84, ll.17–18; for the statue see Seidlmayer 2000). The appropriate response to royal eulogies is recounted in *Sinuhe*, where the praise of Senwosret I ends by urging the audience to communicate with the king and to be loyal (B 73–5).

seen as attaining a degree of unity. Critics have often isolated such features as signs of literariness, whereby discrepancies, blanks and gaps in literary texts stimulate the audience and 'induce and guide [their] constitutive activity' (Iser 1989: 29).

Other evidence for general interpretive practices can be found in the Coffin Texts. The spells in this funerary corpus exhibit textual variation, which is not an embracing of indeterminacy, but a desire to improve the text, including adapting it to local requirements. Coffin Text spell 335 has glosses that vary between manuscripts, and later redaction acknowledged the possibility of alternative interpretations, with the glossing phrase 'another way of saying it:' (*kjj-dd*; Osing 1977b; Rössler-Köhler 1979). They also show interpretation as a process of paraphrase. In the *Satiric Letter*, however, the scribe proclaims himself as one 'who can interpret (*lit.* untie) the difficulties of annals like the one who composed them' (*wh'-jtnw-gnnw mj-jrr-st*: P. Anastasi I 1.7), that is, reconstructing their original meaning. Literary texts also display an awareness of ambiguity (**2.4**); such ambiguity ranges from minor details, through amphibolistic readings to the irony of whole compositions.

The social role of literary response in Middle Kingdom Egypt is controversial (**1**); it is not just a matter of appreciating the affirmation of cultural norms (pace J. Assmann 1996b). For example, *The Eloquent Peasant* is not much more satisfactory as a cultural discourse on the unchallengeable value of elite values than it is as a practical model for petitioners to copy, in the absurd interpretation of G. D. Hornblower (1924). The tale is fissured through by an irony that is deeply disturbing, but is also an entertaining – if deadly serious – joke that can be a source of deep and perpetual delight. To emphasize literature's ability to delight modern readers is not to deny its cultural embeddedness or to suggest that the social is effaced in a work of art (Greenblatt 1990: 90). Scholars have argued that literature did not comprise 'entertainment' ('forgetting the heart', *shmh-jb*) before the New Kingdom, but such terms are attested already in the Middle Kingdom. The opening narrative of *Neferti*, perhaps the earliest extant literary text, describes literary production with a different term for 'enjoyment' (*dȝj-ḥr*; 1m) that occurs elsewhere parallel to *shmh-jb*.[26] In *Cheops' Court* (4.22 ff.) the pleasure of hearing tales is implicitly a parallel to the idle 'relief' (*qb*)[27] of voyeuristic amusement in pleasure pools. Perhaps significantly, references to 'entertainment' in Middle Kingdom courtly titles include 'Overseer of . . . the bird-pools of

---

[26] In *The Satiric Letter*, P. Anastasi I 8.7: Fischer-Elfert 1986a: 73 n.m; Guglielmi 1996a: 341. Also in an 18th Dynasty statue of an 'Overseer of the Bird-pools of Entertainment' describing royal recreation in the marshes (Marseille inv. no. 208; Charles 1960; Feucht 1992: 165; see **9.5.1**).

[27] *qb* can have derogatory connotations (Fischer-Elfert 1986b: 61 n.b; 115 n.a).

entertainment' on the Abydos stela of an official with known literary interests, Sehotepibre.[28] Such recreation, itself a literary theme in *The Sporting King* and *Fishing and Fowling*, is not only attested in connection with bird-pools in the Middle Kingdom: the Chief Treasurer of Kings Intef II and III, Tjetji, was one 'who entertained Horus (the king) with what he desires', and 'who followed him to all his fair places of entertainment' (Blumenthal 1970: 34 [A 3.14], 380 [G 7.18–19]). These officials may even have acted as masters of revels and have fulfilled the role of the courtiers in *Neferti* who supply literary entertainment: one 5th Dynasty example of an 'Overseer of the Entertainment of the King' was also in charge of performances as an 'Overseer of the Musicians of the Great House' (L. Morenz 1996: 109: n.485; PM III.1²: 145–6 [Sneferunefer]). In ideology, such entertaining of the king is culturally central (J. Assmann 1996b: 80), but, as with the production of literary texts (see above), the royal court is unlikely to have represented the exclusive extent of such activities in actuality.

Aesthetic pleasure is integral to the audience's response to cultural artefacts, since much official discourse is a celebration of elite culture; one early Ramessid tomb inscription alludes to its readers 'enjoying themselves' ($sd\underline{3}j$-$\underline{h}r$) in the tomb-chamber (Nefersekheru: Osing 1992b: 75, pl. 44, east wall, southern half l.3). However, such a response seems particulary prominent in literature. In general terms of reader-response, literature often evokes a playful use of practical documentary skills, in a manner similar to its playful use of practical types of writing. A remote but directly documented parallel is in fifteenth-century Italian painting, where Michael Baxandall speaks of Piero della Francesca's 'playful' use of his audience's commercial experience in geometry and mathematics (1988: 86–102). The elite audience of the literary teachings could have exercised its official skill in making moral choices in the safe context of fiction, that is, playfully and without suffering any consequences. For the audience of *The Eloquent Peasant*, the peasant's rhetoric may have been a playful demonstration of the skills that they used in their official lives.[29]

Literature presents itself as a flaunting of leisure. It is not only a conspicuous display of wealth, but a luxury item (L. Morenz 1996: 201). In part this status goes with writing's being a privilege of the elite who possessed leisure (cf. J. Assmann 1996d: 25–8), but it is also a matter of attitude, and not just economic wealth. In *Neferti* and *Cheops' Court* King Sneferu is wealthy and secure enough to be bored and in need of

---

[28] Sethe 1928a: 69, l.15. See Ward 1982: 45 (351). Similar titles were held by the 12th Dynasty officials Hetep and Ihy; also BM EA 614, l.2.

[29] In a Ramessid literary text from Deir el-Medina, the words of a Teaching are described by its recipient as 'sweeter than honey': pleasure is a response to didactic texts, even though in practice education was not always sweet (ODeM 1219, ll.3–4; Fischer-Elfert 1997: 10–11).

entertainment. His restless idleness that requires 'relief' contrasts with the equally positively characterized Senwosret I in the royal eulogy included in *Sinuhe* who 'allows no rest around his heart' (B 59; a passage reflecting official discourse). The same idleness is also embodied in the figure of Djedi who is presented to the reader as recumbent, and whose enjoyment of life is conspicuous (*Cheops' Court* 7.14–16; L. Morenz 1996: 115–16). In *The Shipwrecked Sailor*, a tale is told to relieve a count who is melancholy, though apparently for serious reasons. Entertainment, 'forgetting the heart', and 'following the heart (desire)', which are engendered by literature, should not be seen as dichotomously opposed to intellectual and cultural concerns. To describe the context of literature as entertainment or leisure does not mean that it is frivolous or trivial and not a serious intellectual concern or without public purposes. Many artefacts of *homo ludens* may entertain, but are also deeply serious.

5
Literature in culture

5.1 LITERATURE AND IDEOLOGY

> Culture once confronted with anarchy, must be no mere pious abstraction but a strenuous social force.
>
> Terry Eagleton, *The Function of Criticism* (1984: 62)

5.1.1 TEXTS AND IDEOLOGY

Texts are integral parts of the social webs of signification that can be termed culture (for example, in the sense of Geertz 1973: 3–30). As such, they do not reflect reality, but obey rules of decorum.[1] While decorum is a self-sustaining system, the court's probable influence in shaping it should not be underestimated. Texts embody the norms of Middle Kingdom ideology, that is, of a system of ideas propounded by the elite, the forms and ways in which meaning serves to sustain relations of dominance (see, e.g., R. Williams 1977: 55–71; Hawthorn 1996: 67–70). Ideology is manifest in what can be termed official discourse – not just in legal and moral texts, but also in religious and elite texts of commemoration and display ('monumental discourse').

Ideology, however, is not the same as 'reality', however one may attempt to define it. Ancient statements about the construction of society are contradicted by archaeological evidence (see **4.1**), and a similar dichotomy exists between the ideological religion of the state and the actuality of piety; a 'sweetness and light' view glossed over the probable harshness and complexity of life for the ancient population (e.g., Baines 1991a). Although ideology is never static or monolithic, Middle Kingdom official discourse presents a comparatively uniform view of reality. Thus, the Semna stela of Senwosret III claims that the 'Nubian hears to fall at a word' (Sethe 1928a: 84, l.5), but does not draw the reader's attention to the fact that this is at variance with the inscriptions' physical context in a heavily fortified building, built to monitor and control the same Nubians.

---

[1] An example of the extent of the difference between ancient and modern literary decorum is the modern western emphasis on romantic love as a means for understanding experience, whereas Middle Kingdom texts dwell on the social and ethical aspects of an individual's life in collective society (cf. Parkinson 1999f: 7–9).

Such gaps between reality and expression can be expected in most complex cultural products, since ideology 'typically legitimates the social order by representing it as a spurious unity, metaphysically ordained, and thereby forestalls knowledge of the contradictions which in fact constitute that order' (Dollimore 1989: 14). The relationship between Middle Kingdom ideology and literature is complex – as with so many other forms of cultural discourse – since literature is marked as entertainment, as supposedly influenced by the non-elite (**4.3**), and also by elements suggestive of dissent, which I discuss in this chapter. It also presents itself as 'fictional'.

5.1.2 LITERATURE AS IMAGINARY

Assertions of veracity are fundamental to ideological claims, although the assertions are themselves aesthetically shaped and in part fictional. All historical narratives are to some extent fictional accounts of events (see, e.g., Fay *et al.* 1998), and in many contexts fiction is 'not the other of truth but a way of shaping social and visible reality' (A. Assmann 1999: 85). In the Semna stela, the veracity of the king's claims is crucial for this monumental statement addressed to posterity:

> My Person has seen it; it is not an untruth (*jwms*) . . .
> I speak true.
> Here is no boastful phrase
> that has come forth from my mouth.
> (Sethe 1928a: 84, ll.9–12; cf. Blumenthal 1970: 434–5 [H1.5–8])

Veracity is also evoked in the private commemorative stela of the Steward Montuwoser (temp. Senwosret I), who describes the audience's reaction to his funerary biography's claim to personal worth:

> Now as for any people who will hear this stela . . .
> they will say 'It is the truth'.
> Their children will say to ⟨their⟩ children:
> 'It is the truth; there is no falsehood in it'. (Sethe 1928a: 80, ll.1–3)

The contemporaneous stela of general Montuhotep concludes the account of his campaign to Nubia with the words:

> I tell these things which have happened (*nn-ḫprw*) truthfully (*m-wn-mꜣꜥ*).
> (ll.22–3; Obsomer 1995: 321–5; 323)

The contemporaneous stela of Nesumontu asserts that its inscription

> is the explanation (wḥʿt) of what happened to me;
> it is what I did, truly;
> there is no boasting, no falsehood in it.
>
> (Sethe 1928a: 82, ll.11–12; Obsomer 1995: 546–52)

The First Intermediate Period witnessed the development of such protestations of veracity in biographies, seemingly in response to (understandable) scepticism about the claims of funerary inscriptions; some texts explicitly contrast 'speaking in truth' with speaking as 'the position/office of the necropolis' (j3wt-ḥrt-nṯr: Coulon 1997). Many later types of text express awareness that rhetoric is not always 'truthful' (Coulon 1999; esp. 103–17), but this awareness is particularly mobilized in literature's self-presentation. Whether derived from rhetorical practice or not, the denial of falsehood necessarily textualizes the possibility that what is being said is false. Significantly this formula occurs in the context of a genre that has strong affinities with both teachings and narratives. In contrast, Middle Kingdom literary texts do not make the same assertion of veracity, and the compositions often rupture the naturalism of the 'everyday world' with improbable or fantastic scenarios.

In *Possible Worlds in Literary Theory*, Ruth Ronen describes fictionality as 'a type of relationship between writer and reader reflected in the world the text projects' that differs from the modal structure of the actual world, constituting a world 'uncommitted to reality' (1994: 87, 143). Fictionality is often seen in a bipolar taxonomy as equivalent to literariness, and is connected with the idea of literary language as distinct from normal language; as Raymond Williams noted (1977: 191), this emphasis on language is over-specialized, since literariness is not just a matter of language but of more general cultural conventions and norms. Gerald Moers has dedicated an outstanding study on fictionality to Egyptian narrative tales (2001; see also 1999c). In general literary theory, fictionality has always been closely linked with narratology, while non-narrative compositions are less easily categorized.

To modern readers wisdom texts seem to take the norms of ideological values as their referential system 'complete and unbroken' into texts, much like official discourse (Moers 2001: 180); they seem 'committed to reality'. The frames of many teachings, however, use the same formal devices as narratives which act as 'transformative and distancing' elements. The suggestion that these are 'auxiliary' rather than true fictions (cf. A. Assmann 1980: 108) is unconvincing, since it divides two closely related genres. Ronen argues that fiction does not 'base itself on textually immanent features. The state of being fictional is identified with a complex of literary, cultural and institutional considerations' (1994: 10). Fictionality is a variable aspect between different types of fictional texts, and need not be marked consistently within a text. Fictionality is also a sign of a text's literariness rather than an immanent constituting factor. Here, the work of Wolfgang Iser (e.g., 1993) provides a useful reader-response based approach, distinguishing between fictive and fictionalized texts.

Historical fact is incorporated into fictionalized works such as *Sinuhe* without explicitly marking them as distinctly factual; modern examples include Marguerite Yourcenar's use of classical history in *Mémoires d'Hadrien* (Poignault 1995). Another example is Virginia Woolf's *Orlando* (1928), which is a mock historical biography of Vita Sackville-West based closely on fantastic-sounding but actual details of her private life and family estate (e.g., Gilbert 1993). Without inside knowledge such as provided by Sackville-West's children and her historical account of the estate, it is difficult to detect such features as historical or fictionalizing.

Egyptian narratives contain occasional explicit indicators of fictionality in narratives (see Moers 2001: 79–105). In *Cheops' Court*, Prince Hordedef remarks of the tales which were set in the past that such narrations are

> something that those who have passed away know;
> truth cannot be known from falsehood. (6.23–24)

For the Middle Kingdom audience, this would also be an implicit comment on the tale as a whole which concerns 'those who have passed away'. A frame setting the poem in the past is a fictionalizing sign in many texts, also often marking them as self-reflexive by recounting the production of the text itself. In *Kagemni*, the fictionalizing use of the past is signalled by a discrepancy between the text's statements about the vizier and what was known of a historical vizier of the same name. Many such historical discrepancies may have been clear fictionalizing signs for the original audience, but are now lost to us. Tales also signal fictionality by intertextual means that are now often difficult to detect: the choice of a voyaging sailor as a narrator in *The Shipwrecked Sailor* may imply that it is a traveller's tall story (Baines 1990a: 59 n.22): in the Ramessid *Satiric Letter*, for example, a travelling scribe is mocked with a prediction that his audience will 'pay no attention to your narratives ($s\underline{d}dw$)' (P. Anastasi I 26.3). The sailor's anonymity may also have signalled a move from basic referential reality (Loprieno 1996b: 44; Baines 1990a: 58).

The fictionality of the discourse genre is problematic for the modern reader, who may feel them to be rhetorical representations of actuality, rather than fully fictionalized or self-thematizing literary works (see **1.4**). The protagonist Neferti claims that his prophetic words will earn him respect by their veracity (*Neferti* 15g; echoed in subsequent reception, as in the 'Eulogy of Dead Writers': P. Chester Beatty IV vso 3.7–8). His prophecy is nevertheless marked as fictionalized by its past narrative: the long-dead Sneferu requests a discourse about 'what will come, for today has come, and is (already) passed by' (2n). Such framing devices, however, are not always present. Thus Khakheperreseneb says in his lament 'I have spoken these things as I have seen', in terms resembling official claims of Senwosret III, while dismissing matters that are formulated in terms of the past in a similar manner to official discourse and to Prince Hordedef: 'this is falsehood' (*Khakheperreseneb* rto 6). In this case, the poem may have an implied frame in its genre-label 'Words', which is necessarily associated with a period of disorder. Teachings, however, affirm that 'as for their truthfulness (*sp n-mȝʿt*), that is their value' (*Ptahhotep* 509; parallels, e.g., *The Loyalist Teaching* 9.2), but as Ronen notes (1994: 178):

> In the fictional world model the source of authority generating a modal structure is itself fictional, which means that there are no a priori criteria of validation for fictional facts. The norm for determining authenticity is internal to the fictional world.

The 'truth' a text voices is the (fictionalized) protagonist's subjective interpretation and experience of reality. Thus, the teacher of *Merikare* draws attention to the difference between the omniscience of the ideal king and his own partial knowledge (41a and 42d), and the ironic structure of *The Eloquent Peasant* relies on awareness of how the peasant speaks 'truth' to his fictional audience, but his speeches spring from his ignorance of his situation with regard to them. With most teachings the proclaimed speaker was known to have been dead at the time of composition and dissemination (see also Parkinson 1991b: 98). Pseudepigraphy in official discourse, such as the much later 'Shabaka Stone' and the 'Famine Stela', can also legitimize, drawing on the use of the past to authenticate records rather than to fictionalize. One can only tell the two apart by the relationship between the author and text.[2]

Three extant texts present apparent problems for this analysis of the teaching's pseudepigraphy as fictionalizing. *The Teaching of a Man* is not attributed to a dead sage, but its anonymity is probably a fictionalizing signal comparable with that of characters in *The Shipwrecked Sailor*. The author of *The Loyalist Teaching*, whose name is lost, has been suggested to be a contemporaneous vizier Montuhotep (**A.1.5**), but there is no specific evidence for this ascription. *The Teaching of Khety* is the third text. Although the reading of this name has been contested, the protagonist is probably the same Khety who is mentioned in the Ramessid 'Eulogy of

---

[2] Loprieno (1996c: 286) stresses pseudepigraphy's role as an explicit sign of literary creation.

Dead Writers' as having composed 'the papyrus with *The Teaching of Sehotepibre* (= *Amenemhat*) when he (Amenemhat I) was at rest (dead)' (P. Chester Beatty IV vso 6.13–14; **2.2.2**). He was treated as a historical figure of the early 12th Dynasty by Ramessid scribes, although their specific historical knowledge is debatable (McDowell 1992). One can thus propose that there was a historical figure who composed one teaching pseudonymously and another under his own name. However, Khety may be fictional (Loprieno 1996b: 53), since his name is typical of the preceding Intermediate Period, and his son's (Pepy) of the Old Kingdom; the Ramessid scribes could have attributed another much copied composition to the fictional sage of *The Teaching of Khety*, falsely regarding him as a historical figure. Even if he was a historical figure, as opposed to an intertextual one, it is unknown whether he actually composed the teaching or it was posthumously attributed to him. And even if he was both historical and contemporaneous with the text, he is still probably partly fictionalized in the teaching, since it is unlikely that the composer of *Amenemhat* was a title-less inhabitant of Sile who only came to the Residence to put his son into school.

Middle Kingdom fictionality is different in measure from modern concepts. Fictionality and non-referentiality appear to varying degrees, just as framing devices sporadically mark explicitly what was implicit in the institution of literature. Similarly, Vergil's eclogues are 'a work of art that thematizes art itself' (Iser 1993: 34), but they are such only sporadically (Martindale 1997c: 111), and are also highly political. The essence of literary texts was perhaps in their social and cultural contract as play, which enabled fictionality and thus neutralized the utilitarian effects of language, and allowed consequent divergences from ideological norms since it remained 'only' social play. The most accessible sign of literature is now the extent of its divergence from the cultural norms of official discourse.

5.2 THE DIFFERENTIATED NATURE OF LITERARY DECORUM

> There is a dark side even to perfection.
> I like that.
> M. Piper (and B. Britten), *Death in Venice* (1973), I.v

Divergences from social norms are often inherent in literature's intertextuality in various cultures, and in its disarranging of semantic contexts. Paul Hamilton (1996: 157) notes how, for example, Shakespeare's drama has a striking energy ... through its appropriation or symbolic acquisition of materials normally belonging to cultural stock-in-trade other than the theatre's. The novel, theatrical presentation of ceremony, dance, emblem, ritual and language stemming from a non-theatrical provenance amplifies and profits dramatically from the energy ordinarily concentrated around them. The theatrical shift, too, can imply a subversive disrespect for propriety.

Literary decorum is integral with general decorum, but one can analyse which rules of decorum are symptomatic of and distinctive to literary texts. Bruce Smith comments (1991: 22):

> To assume, as some modernist critics have done, that 'official' discourse – moral, legal, and medical – is always in control of poetic discourse is, surely, just as naive as to assume that poets are the unacknowledged legislators of mankind. Rather than dictating or being dictated to, poetic discourse often *mediates* between the ideal prescriptions of philosophy and the untidy facts of history.... The function of ideology, Marx argues, is to conceal contradictions and to present a falsely coherent account of how things are. Poetic discourse, I believe, can – under certain conditions, at least – address those contradictions.

Iser's analysis of reading foregrounds the extent to which literature is preoccupied with the gaps of ideology, 'those aspects that have been omitted, ignored, displaced, and the like in order that our world may be stabilized by its institutions', and 'deals with the inescapable residue that escapes the mastery of the systems concerned' (1989: 210, 212). Such approaches are relevant to the Egyptian case, especially since texts comment on literature's differentiation from official monumental discourse (P. Chester Beatty IV vso 2.13–3.1, cited on p. 74).

Questions of whether art is ideological or inherently a critique of ideology have been central in some literary critical debates (**2.4**), while Middle Kingdom literature has often been regarded as supremely ideological (**1.3–4**). However, just as the characters in literature represent a body of people who go beyond the literate oligarchy (L. Morenz 1996: 112), so the concerns of the literary corpus are broader and more socially inclusive, notably in such pervasive themes as the problematic meaning of life for an individual in a society hampered by human shortcomings. The literary corpus can be distinguished by the manner in which the genres treat their topoi, in terms of presentation of cultural faultlines, and the inclusion of voices otherwise excluded. I discuss five examples of the differences between literary and ideologically normative discourse; in each, literary discourse gives textual visibility to a wider range of categories of experience, and thus corresponds more closely to modern ideas of the social and political 'reality', as suggested by theoretical models, common experience and archaeology.

1. The heart and society

A recurrent theme of wisdom literature is the human heart, the organ of understanding and knowledge (e.g., Brunner 1977). Private commemorative texts and the funerary biographies of officials present hearts imbued with certainty, those whose hearts have made them successful, and whose knowledge has resolved or 'untied' all difficulties and obstacles (J. M. A. Janssen 1946: 56–7 [w], passim; Doxey 1998). Religious and royal commemorative texts acknowledge the evil potential of the human heart implicitly (see further **7.2**). In these contexts, the matter is relatively clearcut, whereas literary texts expound not only the human heart's virtue or evil, but also its uncertainty, so that its possessor may fail to embody social ideals:

It is the heart which makes its lord a hearer or a non-hearer.	(*Ptahhotep* 550–2)
It is the heart which makes its lord wretched.	(*Sasobek* Bi.16)
[It is] the heart which makes plentiful character, a brave teacher to fashion good qualities.	(*P. Ramesseum II* vso i.5)
It is the heart which fashions good character.	(*A Man* 11.6)

Similarly 'quietness' is a positive ethical quality according to official norms (e.g., J. M. A. Janssen 1946: 115 [Gd]), but in *The Eloquent Peasant* the High Steward remains silent to the peasant's poetic pleading: quietness becomes the problematic motor of the action, leading the peasant to question the High Steward's heart. He concludes twice that 'what is in the heart (*wnnt-m-jb*) is unknowable' (B1 287, 304). This unavoidable incomprehensibility is the opposite of the norm in biographies, where the speaker Intef claims that he was lenient towards the man who spontaneously 'told him what is in (his) heart' (*wnnt-m-jb*)' (Sethe 1928a: 80, ll.18–19); someone who 'knew the turning (*pḫr*) of what was in the heart (*wnnt-m-jb*)' (BM EA 572 l. 11; Simpson 1974: pl. 12); and someone who 'punished the hidden hearted (*jmn-jb* + enemy determinative) ... and made the heart spit out what it had swallowed' (BM EA 566, ll.1–3; Simpson 1974: pl. 8).

In *The Tale of Sinuhe*, the unaccountable actions of the narrator's heart motivate the whole plot, remaining problematic and incomprehensible almost throughout the poem (see **8.2**). A sense of unresolved internal confusion is also strong in *A Man and His Ba*, where the protagonist's own *ba* quarrels with him, and in *Khakheperreseneb*, where a sage addresses his own recalcitrant heart (compare the funerary Coffin Text spell 113 for 'not letting the heart of a man oppose him in the necropolis': *CT* II, 130). The heart and the 'soul' are the sources of these men's suffering and incomprehension rather than of the knowledge and comfort that they might expect from them. The teachings expound values closely comparable to those of the biographies, but in the former the choice of virtue or folly has still to be made. In the prologue of *Ptahhotep*, the ancient sage's opening words declare that his age means that his 'heart has stopped and cannot recall yesterday' (16). In official discourse, age need not have this result: the owner of a Middle Kingdom stela from Edfu was 'someone old of heart, who did not know any wretchedness because of it' (l.12: Kuentz 1923: 110). Ptahhotep's heart is the expected source of his wisdom, which is based on cultural memory, repeating 'the counsels of the ancestors' (31); for the Middle Kingdom audience 'yesterday' is the idealized setting of the teaching. The frame is thus clearly marked as not being intended to authorize, instead subverting an ostensible convention.[3] The king tells Ptahhotep to

> Teach (your son) according to the speech of the past,
> so that he will be a model for the officials' offspring! ...
> No one is born already knowledgable! (37–41)

The last statement contradicts the normative views of biographies, such as that of Sarenput I of Elephantine (*Urk.* VII, 6 1.6; Lichtheim 1997: 13–18; Franke 1994: 205; cf. Guglielmi 1984b: 356–7), and particularly of eulogies of kings. This subversion of norms is continued in the first maxim, which warns against trusting too much in the quality that the teaching will promote by 'teaching the ignorant (*ḫm*) to be wise (*rḫ*)' (47):

> Be not proud because you are wise (*rḫ*).
> Consult with the ignorant (*ḫm*) as with the wise (*rḫ*). (52–54)

This merging of the two character types counters the differentiation of fool and wise that runs through other didactic texts (Shupak 1993: 258–61; compare P. Chester Beatty IV vso 6.5–6), and is an exceptional statement that functions as an initial signal. The injunction also contrasts with the norms of social intercourse with the uneducated, as formulated

---

[3] The statement that 'the nose is blocked' from old age recalls hymns where such suffocation is caused by the lack of the inundation, and in *The Loyalist Teaching* (3.5), the king. Intertextual allusion increases the irony of the passage describing someone whom the king is favouring.

by the chamberlain Intef, who 'mingled with the ignorant (ḥm) for the sake of quelling aggression' (Sethe 1928a: 80, 1.16). While the maxim praises the 'perfect speech' of maids (ḥmwt), the nomarch Hapidjefai claims in his biography that he '[did not cause] a maid (ḥmt) to be valued above her mistress (ḥnwt)' (Urk. VII, 63 1.13). *Ipuur* presents a vision of this fear realized:

> Indeed, all maids (ḥmwt) are full of their own utterances;
> it is burdensome to the servants when their mistresses (ḥnwt) speak.   (4.13)

The bleak view of the lower orders in many poems is very different from the efficient and obedient servants in tomb scenes (e.g., Davies and Gardiner 1920). Fugitive dependents were a significant phenomenon (e.g., P. Brooklyn 35.1446: Hayes 1955), but are referred to in very few official texts, whereas they are treated at some length in *The Loyalist Teaching* (11.9–12).

2. Fools and Enemies
The teachings dwell on the active nature of evil and of the evil-doer far more than do the moralizing sections of biographies, where vice is simply shunned as being 'lacking' in the deceased, often reinforcing an immediately preceding assertion of virtue (Doxey 1998: 68–71). Stylistically this focus can be seen in the frequency of vetitive constructions in the teachings, which concentrate on the dangers facing the ideal life. The wisdom texts as a whole concern the actual embodiment of ethical ideals in individual behaviour and experience; this is attainable if problematic in the teachings, while it is deeply problematic in the discourses which are uttered in troubled individual and social circumstances. In both genres folly is inherent in kings as well as in enemies.

In the mid-12th Dynasty biography of Khusobek, the foreign country Retjenu is 'the vile' enemy (Sethe 1928a: 83, 1.10; Baines 1987), as against the substitute home in the roughly contemporaneous *Sinuhe* (the country also features in the fragmentary *Discourse of Renseneb*). In official discourse, travel abroad is presented as 'extending the boundaries' or acquiring tribute, whereas in literary tales boundaries are crossed and journeying takes on a more interior aspect (cf. Moers 1999b, 2001).

3. Gender and sexuality: women and 'homosexual' men
Women are presented in the official discourse of non-royal monuments as wives 'whom (the husband) loves', but in literary texts their role is more ambivalent (Moers 2001: 211–19). Literary women largely fall into a wider range of two schematic stereotypes: the good wife and the wicked temptress (Troy 1984). In *Ptahhotep*, they are 'fields good for their lords'

(330) but also potential 'storm-winds' (333). They are also to be avoided, because experience of them is 'the likeness of a dream' by which men die (287). In maxim 37, praise is given to a plump cheerful woman (499–506; Cannuyer 1986), suggesting a different decorum from that of representational art, which portrays women as slim.[4] *The Teaching of Ptahhotep*, in the one complete version of the text, starts and ends with women who diverge from the norms of the elite, signalling the variousness of the life that it considers. Women remain largely unempowered as protagonists: the wives of the eloquent peasant and Sinuhe scarcely appear, and do not speak.

In official representations and texts, few ambivalent qualities are attached to sexuality: it is displayed decorously within a controlled family context and is a force for producing children and regeneration, or in certain contexts, of conquest (Derchain 1975, 1976; Hare 1999: 106–48). In literary texts, sexual activity features more explicitly: in *Cheops' Court* adultery, although punished by death, features as the subject of an entertaining tale. Similarly, 'homosexual' desire features in a remarkably large number of extant compositions and only there, whereas in official texts, 'homosexual' activity is alluded to solely within a context of aggressive acts and does not disrupt normative gender roles (Parkinson 1995).

4. Responses to death and the divine

Death is acknowledged to be an enemy in official and religious texts and is referred to with a wide range of negative vocabulary, but almost invariably features as an enemy that was overcome or avoided (Zandee 1960: 5–7), whereas literary texts include pessimistic responses. It is inherently probable that such attitudes towards death were a feature of life in any period (e.g., Posener 1988: 12–18). Mourners are shown in tomb scenes from the Old Kingdom, but anomic expressions were not written beside them before the late 18th Dynasty (material gathered in Lüddeckens 1943); for example in the early 12th Dynasty tomb of Intefiqer's relative (Lüddeckens 1943: no. 2), the mourners' cry is positive 'you do not depart dead, you depart alive'. The anomalous event of death is here brought into conformity. In the late 18th Dynasty tomb of one Neferhotep, the mourners make a similar supremely ideological statement about death: 'How good is what has happened to him' (Lüddeckens 1943: no. 45). Pessimistic attitudes can only be paralleled in later texts, particularly harpists' songs on tomb walls (see **2.2.2**), where they are represented as being performed at banquets.[5] Thus, the first explicit appearance of the

---

[4] The exceptional fatness of the queen of Punt on the later funerary temple of Hatshepsut allies her with the foreign and the exotic (e.g., Bianchi 1997: 90–1).

[5] One New Kingdom example, the 3rd song in the tomb of Neferhotep, alludes to the festal context (Hari 1985: pl. 26 ll.6–9).

pessimistic voice is in literature; the extant contemporaneous songs on funerary monuments are uniformly positive in their descriptions of death (Lichtheim 1945), as in one of a mid-13th Dynasty official where the tomb is a home

> built for festival,
> planned for happiness.   (Sethe 1928a: 87, ll.1–2; date: Franke 1994: 71)[6]

Later New Kingdom songs incorporate pessimistic attitudes with glorifications of death that echo the mourners' positive cries or juxtapose them on tomb walls (e.g., Osing 1992c: 11–24; Kákosy and Fábián 1995), and thus are comparable to the 12th Dynasty literary formulation of both attitudes.

The gods also occupy a questionable status in literary texts both as objects of the theodic complaint (*Ipuur*) and of humour (*Horus and Seth*). Literary texts foreground personal and potentially problematic connections with gods, on both cosmic and personal levels, more than official discourse. This problematic is not just located in the past, when the gods had temporarily abandoned Egypt (a motif in official discourse), but is presented as a lived experience. Similar aspects are found in the presentation of kings, whose official infallibility and legitimation is challenged (*Merikare*) and mocked (*Cheops' Court*).

5. Generic and topical expectations

On a more formal level, literary texts tend to subvert expectations. *Neferti* works within the generic norm of a Royal Tale inscription providing a royal eulogy, to perform a dark prophecy. In *Cheops' Court*, Cheops' search for the 'number of the chambers of the sanctuary of Thoth' (7.5–6) is formally and thematically comparable with the official commemoration of King Neferhotep I's search for religious information recorded on a mid-13th Dynasty stela at Abydos (Helck 1983: 21–9); the tale and the stela are perhaps roughly contemporaneous. In the official Royal Tale scenario Neferhotep is 'seeking excellence for the future' (Helck 1983: 28, l.11) and is provided with the desired information from a library in an unproblematic manner (Helck 1983: 22, ll.10–16), whereas Cheops is 'seeking' information for his own pyramid (see **8.4**), and the more he asks for it, the more it recedes (9.1–18). Neferhotep is assured that

---

[6] A possible pre-New Kingdom example of a pessimistic song is the 'Song from the Chapel of King Intef', but an early New Kingdom date seems more likely (see **2.2.2**). Other possible examples may be implied in a song from the late 18th Dynasty tomb of Neferhotep which refers to 'those songs that are in the tombs of old' which 'belittled the necropolis' (Hari 1985: pl. 4, 1st song ll.3–4). This implies the existence of a written tradition of cynical songs before the late 18th Dynasty.

> What your spirit has ordained is what happens sovereign my lord!
> (Helck 1983: 22, l.11)

whereas one of Cheops' requests is met with

> Doing such a thing . . . is not ordained. (8.15)

Cheops' desired information is available only to others, whereas Neferhotep finds writings

> which no scribe in his Person's following had ever found.
> (Helck 1983: 25, l.14)

In *Cheops' Court* a serious search for religious information is enacted in a playful and subverted manner, and generates problems, continuing the tale into increasingly wonderful and fateful events (other examples of normative discoveries of esoteric information: Aufrère 1998: 21–5).[7] Thus, literature diverges from expected norms of discourse towards both pessimism and frivolity. These dark and light divergent features from official normative discourse are given a privileged position in literature. The apparently carefree tone of such phenomena also contrasts with the seriousness of official texts, in which authority 'passes over (i.e., ignores) what is light upon the heart' (stela of Intef: Sethe 1928a: 81, l.4; see also **7.3**).

5.3 PROGRAMMATIC AND OTHER MODELS FOR CONTEXTUALIZATION

> Behind your verse so masterfully made
> We hear the weeping of a muse betrayed.
> W. H. Auden, *Secondary Epic* (1991: 600)

Literary texts formulate attitudes that are in part discordant within the expectations of the written culture of which they are a part. Their intertextuality and the movement of semantic discourses are potentially divergent modes. How can these distinctive qualities be contextualized? The cultural function of much Middle Kingdom literature has often been described as 'propaganda' (see **1.3**), while pessimistic discourses have

---

[7] In a minor detail, an offer of royal bounty is rejected by the rower (5.20–6.7), whereas in official discourse bounty is accepted unquestioningly (e.g., Baines 1997b: 136–7 on an Old Kingdom biography).

conversely been interpreted as expressions of dissent (e.g., Goedicke 1977a; Cruz-Uribe 1987). Neither model can account for the interweaving and fusion of attitudes, such as the two contraries of the normal and anomalous – the 'propagandist' and the 'dissident' – whether within individual texts or in the total body of literature.

For the mixture of affirmative and subversive elements, one can compare a later and better documented highly 'propagandistic' elite work that also reveals a strong 'subversive' current. The *Aeneid* was written ostensibly as a glorification of Augustan Rome (R. D. Williams 1990: 21), but while some modern critics have viewed it as positive, upholding the values of its cultural context (e.g., Hardie 1986), others take it as a more 'pessimistic' work which includes 'further voices' which 'subvert the implications of the epic voice' (Lyne 1987: 2; Harrison 1990b). However, both elements can be considered integral to the whole (Martindale 1997b; Tarrant 1997b; Hardie 1997). The Augustan culture is presented equivocally and multivocally, and the work as a whole has 'no dogmatic lesson' (R. D. Williams 1990: 36). Similar political themes and 'further voices' are present in other ostensibly dogmatic epics, such as Milton's *Paradise Lost*, where they have played havoc with interpretation and reception (e.g., Hunter 1980; A. Patterson 1993: 244–75); they are also arguably integral to the reader's response to the poem (e.g., Fish 1971, esp. 38–48) and to its presentation of political themes.

Criticism derived from Marxist theory is particularly sensitive to such cultural features and to the relationship between texts and power. Stephen Greenblatt (1988: 21–65) discusses subversive elements in the records of a Renaissance colony in Virginia, which include 'the *testing* of a subversive interpretation of the dominant culture' and the '*recording* of alien voices' and interpretations. K. M. Newton (1990: 124–5) summarizes such approaches:

> the resistances and subversive elements, which on the surface undermine the ideological discourse of such texts, function rather to immunize that discourse against being seriously threatened since subversion is both generated and contained by the dominant ideology.

Thus, problematic elements are admitted for programmatic purposes. Only a limited degree of subversiveness is permissable, and it is experienced only vicariously by the audience; play is not unconstrained. Thus, the 'homosexual' desire thematized in Middle Kingdom literature is marginalized and bound within the norms of ideology even when being expressed. John Baines suggests that the 'ethical ambivalence' of the royal teachings may in part have been a legitimation for royal behaviour that had been pragmatic rather than ideologically ideal (1991a: 160–1), and that *Sinuhe*'s affirmation of Egyptian order is deepened by presenting the alternative so effectively (1982: 37); Jan Assmann (1990: 213–22) suggests a similar reading for the pessimistic descriptions of the discourses as justifying the power of absolute rulers as necessary to contain humanity's negative potential; Antonio Loprieno (1991b; 1996d) suggests that the loyalist teachings 'programmatically neutralized' the tensions between the elite and the state. In general terms, one may propose that literary discourse confronts the culture's fears and programmatically exorcises them. The metaphor of containment used by New Historicists is, in addition, appropriate for these texts in formal terms since framing devices and concentric structures, in which the 'subversive' elements are embodied, are so prominent.

Such a model of literature as neutralizing discourse can be traced in Middle Kingdom descriptions of how an official should listen to a petitioner, not to satisfy his plaints, but to calm him. In the early 12th Dynasty stela of the nomarch Montuhotep, he is:

> one calm until (a common man: *nds*) has spoken his wretchedness,
> until he has purged his belly's concerns,
> one who hears his words and drives off his wretchedness . . .
> I said: 'May your heart be well-disposed;
> do not be aggressive(?) against a petitioner until he has said what he came about'.
> (Schenkel 1964; Stewart 1979: pl. 18, ll.11–14; other examples: J. Assmann 1990: 74)

The 17th maxim of *The Teaching of Ptahhotep* (264–76) presents a petitioning as an opportunity for an official to satisfy discontent and regulate discourse,[8] while violent action is taken against 'talkers' in *Merikare* (e.g., 6d).

The strategies of other types of Egyptian writing offer parallels here, including religious and magico-medical texts, both of which categories have performative aspects (Eyre 1993: 118–19) and have been found grouped with literary texts in the 'Ramesseum library'. 'Magic' is a well-attested metaphor for artistic creativity (Ritner 1993: 31–2 n.142). Both spells and literature concern untoward situations, and both can confront an audience's fears. To confront and contain a subversive element or interpretation in literature might be compared with the motifs of encircling and binding that are integral to magical texts and to the treatment of enemies (for which see Ritner 1993: 57–67). To combat the element, a

---

[8] The topic features more briefly in *A Man* 12.5–7, and much later in the 'Installation of the Vizier' treatise (Shupak 1992: 14).

poison or hostile force must be identified in general terms or named (compare Vernus 1982: 321; Posener 1987a). The strategies are broadly similar; one can compare a late Middle Kingdom magical spell with a passage from *Ipuur*:

> Break out, o Asiatic woman who has come from the foreign country!
> O Nubian woman (*nḥsjjt*) who has come from the desert edge!
> Are you (*jnjw-ntt*) a servant? Come as ⟨his⟩ vomit!
> Are you a noblewoman? Come as his urine!
> (P. Berlin 3027 rto 2.6–10; text: Erman 1901: 14 (D); Borghouts 1978: 42, no. 66)

Interrogative constructions also occur in Execration Texts (Posener 1987a: 22), and in *Ipuur* they are used as the Lord to the Limit considers how to act against foreigners:

> Is it Nubians (*jnjw-nḥsjw*)? Then we shall make our protection . . .
> Is it Libyans (*jnjw:s m-tmḥw*)? Then we shall make a confrontation!
> (14.13–14)

The descriptions of chaos could be viewed as apotropaic representations.

5.4 COMPLEX MODELS: PLAY AND MEDIATION

> Héroique souci, royale inquiétude,
> Laissez-le respirer, et souffrez qu'un moment
> Son grand cœur s'abandonne au divertissement.
> Molière, *Les Fâcheux* (1661), prologue

Such a modern programmatic interpretive strategy, which makes literature's divergent decorum and problematic elements parts of a broadly culturally propagandist strategy, is however itself problematic and reductive in general theoretical terms and in specific readings. The extent to which literature's dissidence is contained is a point of contention in readings of early modern literature, and the identification of subversive elements is in itself a matter of interpretation: '*subversive* for us designates those elements of [a] culture that contemporary audiences tried to contain, or, when containment seemed impossible, to destroy and that now conform to our own sense of truth and reality' (Greenblatt 1988: 39). The principles of order and authority of much historical literature we would 'find subversive for ourselves' (1988: 39).

Middle Kingdom literary interpretation was apparently to some extent open. Since literature was restricted to the cultural elite and subelite, however, there would have been no possibility of misreading texts that included dissident elements as subversive to the elite's norms, and no need for literary critics who could ensure correct reading by lower classes. One should not overemphasize the private, unbounded and indeterminate nature of interpretation, since Middle Kingdom readers will have had 'inherited paradigms' of interpretation, against which to experience their 'fresh aesthetic response' (cf. Botstein 1994: 78). Nevertheless, the presence of ambiguity, irony and parody in many texts implies a tension between expected norms and divergent readings, and suggests that readings that were not purely programmatic were consciously envisaged. There is a tendency in literary studies to regard the audience as 'a unitary, unproblematic category' (Sinfield 1994: 53), whereas all works 'involve a multiplicity of interests, however well organized, for the crucial reason that art is social and hence presumes more than one consciousness' (Greenblatt 1990: 112). The 'power' evoked in programmatic readings is never a monolithic entity (Sinfield 1992: 45–6; cf. Brannigan 1998: 47–53), and the writer of a text cannot control its reading. Any text that opens up indeterminacy could be socially disruptive; as Alan Sinfield (1992: 48) notes:

> even a text that aspires to contain a subordinate perspective must first bring it into visibility; even to misrepresent, one must present . . . readers do not have to respect closes . . . We can insist on our sense that the middle of such a text arouses expectations that exceed the closure.

He dismisses the containment model as an '"entrapment model" of ideology and power' (1992: 39), asserting that whether the author sympathizes with or merely records the embedded subversive voices, they undermine the single coherency of the text, rendering it multivalent and equivocal. Stephen Greenblatt, in response, reasserts the extent to which the subversive elements remain unneutralized and are not co-opted by the dominant ideology in the containment model he proposes (1990: 165–6). Critics differ as to the extent they regard the text as an open site as opposed to a more self-sufficient (aesthetic) entity. New Historicists read for aesthetic coherence and balance, whereas Cultural Materialists read for incoherence, seeing discordant elements as inevitable remnants of dissidence in ideological works, which they seek to recover and rearticulate (Brannigan 1998: 114). Neither of these historicist schools fully admits the use of the potential within discourse to negotiate power relations to provide resistance (Brannigan 1998: 185), in which the literary text 'generates and multiplies meaning, and therefore must be accounted for as an active participant in the process of fashioning and interpreting society, culture, and history' (189).

An 'entrapment' model remains problematic for Middle Kingdom texts. A purely programmatic reading of anomalous elements can account for such features of the texts as entertainment, just as the licence of the European carnival can be read programmatically (Felperin 1992: 114–18; Mangan 1996: 37–41). The lightness and humour of *Cheops' Court* or of *Neferkare and Sasenet* might perhaps be explained as making these tales satires with programmatic points: that the kings of the 4th Dynasty with their improper actions should be scorned in favour of those of the 5th, or that kings who have homosexual liaisons should get denounced. The light tone, however, seems to exist beyond what is necessary for these supposed programmes – a point that has particular weight as the style of these tales becomes dominant in the following period of literary production (see **8.4**). *Neferti* is ostensibly suitable for a programmatic reading, but proves resistant. The sage's description of chaos seems to heighten the eulogy of the new king, but this interpretation cannot fully account for the elaboration and relishing of the dark side in the order-to-chaos scheme. In commemorative inscriptions, the chaos is typically described very briefly and assigned to the past. In many literary texts the central position of problematic elements in texts that 'contain' them can also formally privilege them by giving them centrality. Similarly, the eloquent peasant's speech remains unentrapped, powerful and prophetic.

Such complexity becomes clearer through an examination of the ostensibly similar rhetoric and strategies of literature and magical texts. One example of literature's inconclusiveness is the treatment of the 'enemy'. The Execration Texts list and catalogue enemies, including Egyptian rebels, in a systematic and reductive manner. In the Semna stela enemies are easily vincible (cited on p. 86), whereas in *Merikare* the foreigner has the role of an eternal thing of darkness:

He cannot prevail; he cannot be prevailed over. (34h)

Moreover, he is likened to the quintessentially Egyptian crocodile on the riverbank (35j–l). In *Sinuhe*, the protagonist's enemy from Retjenu is described with the same vocabulary as is used in the Execration Texts (Koenig 1990: 109–10; Fischer-Elfert 1996b), but once he is felled the conflict between foreign and Egyptian values embodied in the duel with him continues in an internal monologue (B 146–64). In other poems the enemy is either unknown or hidden within Egyptian society, as in *Amenemhat* where the rebels come unexpectedly from within the palace, and – most elusively of all – from 'subjects who do not really exist' (2a).

According to *Merikare*, the purpose of magic (and thus of magical texts) is to be a 'weapon to ward off the blow of what may happen (*ḥsf-ꜥ n-ḫprjjt*)' (47g); and 'what happens' is the subject of many literary texts. *The Discourse of Sasobek* is, according to its title, a speech 'according to what has happened (*ḫft-ḫprwt*)' (A 17). Enough survives to show that the discourse contained reflections on the complexity and incomprehensibility of such 'happenings':

> Behold! it cannot happen – (and) it happens! (Bi.10)

Ipuur's grief is 'because of what has happened in the land' (1.8) and *Khakheperreseneb* 'meditates on what has happened' (rto 10); the same word recurs in *Neferti*, and many times in *Ptahhotep*. One could almost say that magical texts are 'against' events while literary ones are 'in accordance with' them. They elaborate, comply with, and almost celebrate the unknown events that are in need of containment or must be warded off.

If literature in some sense complies with and integrates the problematic and the subversive, it also resists responding or repulsing directly. Although the texts reach harmonious resolutions, the problems, questions or complaints they raise tend not to receive a simple answer. Literary resolutions tend to be fragmented: aesthetic response provides emotional closure rather than any simple response. Simple answers seem to be deliberately undermined, as is the case of Sinuhe's motivation (**8.2**). The literary structure provides a resolution, as in *A Man and His Ba*, where a reconciliation of conflicting views is achieved through the imagery and rhetoric (**9.4**).

In *Neferti* the recitation of human woes apparently aims to elicit almost carefree enjoyment, suggesting a complex aesthetic response a little like that to a European tragedy. The prophecy faces, and urges the audience to face, the untoward reality of 'that which is before you' (4a), but without despair: Neferti tells his heart 'do not tire!' (4a). Through the protagonist's literary skills human and social woes that are 'undone' (4c, 10d) become 'perfect words and verses that are choice' (1l–m), and thus a source of satisfaction. Chaos is brought under the king's hand (literally: 2o) through the specifically literary nature in which it is prophesied and recorded. While literary structure provides containment, its tendency to suspensions and ambiguity highlights the absence of direct answers and suggests that the poem's complicity with the containing power is not absolute. What distinguishes the literary presentation is its consistent tendency, to use Robert Browning's phrase, to 'tell a truth obliquely' (*The Ring and the Book* XII, 855–6). This avoidance of simple answers may formulate the basic human experience that there are no simple satisfying solutions for such problems: literature's interpretation of problematic reality remains true to the experience of its audience. As Joseph Farrell notes for Vergil (1997: 228), 'the covert does not contradict but greatly enriches (and often complicates) the overt'. Subversive elements are part of cultural dialectic, and negotiating with them is a central cultural issue: 'culture is ... a vital nexus between politics and personal experience, mediating human needs and desires into publicly discussable form, teaching new modes of subjectivity and combating received representations' (Eagleton 1984: 118).

The question of authorization and how such discourse was allowed and enabled remains a complex issue. The poems retained a subversive potential with regard to the state, but, as Jonathan Arac observes of another culture's literary works (1995: 28), 'their critical authority depended on their limitation to elite audiences, esoteric subjects, and indirect means'. Why was such covert, but not overt, criticism permitted to exist in elite writing? Literary manuscripts provide no evidence for an institution of censorship in Middle Kingdom Egypt, although the practice of erasing names from inscriptions and administrative documents (*damnatio memoriae*)[9] shows that political 'censorship' of a radical nature could be envisaged. Alan Sinfield suggests that indirect dissident expression is allowed because 'dissidence is least threatening when it can be seen to be respecting boundaries' (1994: 64). Annabel Patterson provides evidence of an early-modern English conscious 'joint project, a cultural bargain, between writers and political leaders' with 'conventions that both sides accepted as to how far a writer could go in explicit address to the contentious issues of his day' (1984: 44–58).[10] The status of Middle Kingdom literary discourse as part of the system of decorum suggests a negotiated relationship with the dominant ideology and not a predominantly oppositional one or one in which it adopted a normative status. Two social models for a relationship between literature and power are possible: direct patronage by the state, or a more loosely defined status, such as the closely monitored theatre in Elizabethan England had, whose

> institutional position was complex. On the one hand, it was sometimes summoned to perform at Court and as such may seem a direct extension of royal power; on the other hand, it was the mode of cultural production in which market forces were strongest, and as such it was especially exposed to the influence of subordinate and emergent classes. (Sinfield 1992: 113)

---

[9] Brunner-Traut 1982; Nordh 1996: 94–6. Erasure from administrative records is mentioned in a 17th Dynasty Coptos decree: Sethe 1928a: 98, ll.15–16.

[10] Here one might compare Vergil and Propertius in the Roman world, where patrons were prepared to allow a degree of freedom and non-conformity in return for poetic excellence (Tarrant 1997b: 183).

Middle Kingdom literature's subversion was perhaps permissible since it is 'just' entertainment. The texts acted as a means of containment as well as expression, making the social and political consequences of such subversion now difficult to chart, and probably also unfulfilled in terms of state action: rhetorical strategies do not equal acts of political liberation (Greenblatt 1990: 166).

The dissident voices and gaps in Middle Kingdom literary texts are not merely faultlines due to inevitable jostling for power between dominance and dissidence in any text. Rather, they are carefully constructed integral features. The extent to which the resolution of literary meaning lies with the reader's aesthetic response is suggested by the ending of *The Shipwrecked Sailor*. This tale concerns the inescapability of unexpected disaster (Baines 1990a). This bleak message is contained in a nesting of tales within tales that is reassuring to the reader, but at the end the sailor's audience, his count, dismisses his tale as futile reassurance and mere 'cleverness' (183; cf. **8.4**). Yet the tale's significance continues in the concluding colophon; this, unusually, names the copyist and gives him the epithet 'clever-fingered' (l.188), taking up the count's dismissal of the sailor's 'cleverness'. The tale's audience can experience the uncertainty of reality and learn of the cataclysmic end of the earth, but at a safe distance: the scribe is distanced from all the cataclysms and is safely assured of his cleverness, although the narrator cannot be so assured, with the tale ending with a disruptive question and uncertainty in the narrator's voice. The pattern of 'beginning, middle and end, which is the essence of our explanatory fictions' about life (Kermode 1967: 35–6) is asserted in the poem's reception without denying its assertions of discord and disaster.

Middle Kingdom literature thus allows both a contextualization of the problematic and the playful, but on a level of individual response. Wolfgang Iser (1989: 29) argues the role of the reader is the key factor in such works:

> literature simulates life, not in order to portray it, but in order to allow the reader to share in it. He can step out of his own world and enter another, where he can experience extremes of pleasure and pain without being involved in any consequences whatsoever. It is this lack of consequence that enables him to experience things that would otherwise be inaccessible owing to the pressing demands of everyday reality. And precisely because the literary text makes no objectively real demands on its readers, it opens up a freedom that everyone can interpret in his own way. Thus with every text we learn not only about what we are reading but also about ourselves, and this process is all the more effective if what we are supposed to experience is not explicitly stated but has to be inferred.

Literary texts are often part of the display and fashioning of culture, as a complex and diverse entity; other practices, ritual and oral, have similar functions as symbolic cultural texts; a frequently cited example is the cockfight in Bali (Geertz 1973: 412–53). Literary mediation is differentiated from other textual forms through its playful unreality, and this feature can be associated with the social extension – to varying degrees – of discourse to textualize intellectual self-awareness in the Middle Kingdom. The potential of literature to destabilize the superficial unity of discourse with potential pluralism, together with the leisure of the elite in stability, allowed a 'dark side of perfection' to be formulated in written discourse. Potential 'things of darkness' (*The Tempest* V.i.278–9) appear and are acknowledged, accommodated and preserved as part of the cultural stream in the social practice of literature.

6
Literary form

6.1 FORMAL ASPECTS OF SOCIAL PRACTICE

> That was a way of putting it – not very satisfactory:
> A periphrastic study in a worn-out poetical fashion,
> Leaving one still with the intolerable wrestle
> With words and meanings.
>
> T. S. Eliot, *East Coker*, ii (1959: 23)

Literary discourse has a multivalent role in Middle Kingdom culture. In this chapter I examine ways in which this distinctive role is represented in formal terms. Much of the formal aspect of poetry is inaccessible, but the typological nature of the surviving poems is fairly consistent and can be analysed as a set of specifically literary genres. The style of the language of these genres also embodies literature as a differentiated social practice. Any analysis of the style of a past age is problematic, but is integral to any reading. I review the metrical nature of poetry and the indications of metrical form in the surviving manuscripts, before considering broader distinctive aspects of literary style.

6.2 LITERARY GENRES

> I believe in such cartography ... we are communal histories, communal books.
>
> M. Ondaatje, *The English Patient* (1992: ix)

In the absence of any ancient critical discourse, the inference of literary types draws on signals and indicators in the works themselves. The most explicit generic signal is a direct label, often presented as a title or incorporated into the work in other ways (A. Fowler 1982: 92–8, 130–48). Ancient terminology is crucial, but it is sparsely attested (listed by Schott 1990), as is the case with all types of Egyptian writing. No specific designation for a tale is known, while generic terms such as *mdt* 'discourse' can describe a wide range of texts, although they have a more specific genre reference in certain contexts (see n.3). The use of terms is often determined by the specific fictional context: the speeches of *The Eloquent Peasant* are variously referred to as 'a lament' (*nḥwt*, B1 60), 'this speech' (*mdt-tn*, B1 103), 'my plaint ... my wretchedness' (*ḥn:j ... m3r:j*, B1 311–2), 'this perfect speech' (*mdt-tn-nfrt*, B1 349–50), and 'your petitions' (*n3jj:k n-sprt*, B2 128). These cannot provide a typology for the poem as a whole.

Titles of compositions have a limited potential for the Middle Kingdom. Their frequent use is comparatively recent in literature; the opening formula of a text would give the audience as strong a generic signal as a title (A. Fowler 1982: 92, 98–105; Conte 1986: 76). Titling conventions vary from genre to genre; in the absence of any lists of literary works, one can only hypothesize that those without a title were referred to by their opening words, or 'incipit' (Parkinson 1996b: 302 n.47 with refs).

The range of features such as Alastair Fowler outlines (1982; see **2.3**) are sufficient to provide the following hypothetical schema of genres. Future discoveries of texts and analysis of relative chronology will alter this pattern, just as a new composition can reconfigure the genre system.

Genre	tale	teaching (*sb3jjt*)		reflective discourses	
Subgenre(s)	tale	royal teaching	private teaching	discourse (*mdt*) or verses (*tsw* etc.)	dialogue

This schema is not an attempt to classify the main literary genres, but to offer a map that will clarify the relationships among the various texts. It presents a synchronic overview of the whole Middle Kingdom (of necessity), and ignores diachronic and dynamic features which will have been influential. The genre system of the New Kingdom was radically different.

The tales are non-commemorative, non-functional, fictional narratives; a common word in *The Shipwrecked Sailor* is 'narrate' (*sdd*). In these works, the narrative relation of events dominates. The tale is formally the most open-ended genre (including complex sequences of tales, and incorporating other genres), and may well be the least well represented by surviving texts (see **3.2.2**). They display a wide range of tone, language and structure; they also display a variety of subject matter, but this is not a sufficient basis to propose any subgenres (pace J. Assmann 1992a: 380–2). All extant Middle Kingdom tales lack titles, apart from characteristic – but not invariable – introductory formulae: 'There was once...' and 'Now there was once a time when...' (Parkinson 1996b: 303).

The wisdom texts[1] are predominantly sapiential discourses; a key word is 'know' (rḫ). The coherence of this generic group is established by form, theme and style. The group can be divided into two: the didactic genre in which a key term is 'teach' (sbȝ; e.g., *Ptahhotep* 37, 47); and more reflective compositions with terms such as 'take thought for' (mhj) and 'meditate' (nkȝ; e.g., *Neferti* 3a; *A Man and His Ba* 32, 68, 78; *Khakheperreseneb* rto 10, vso 1).

The didactic genre is the most explicitly and strongly defined. Extant examples are entitled 'teaching' (sbȝjjt).[2] The formal structure varies from episodic aggregates of maxims dealing with distinct situations to longer, more interwoven thematic structures; these types are not mutually exclusive. The dominant tone in the teachings is didactic, although gnomic statements justifying the instructions are frequent, as are narrative sections that cite experience as an authority. Most teachings are centred around 'historical' individuals of high rank. The genre divides between royal and non-royal teachers. Content and tone vary accordingly, with the royal teachings having a higher proportion of gnomic and narrative elements.

Several of the reflective wisdom texts are entitled 'discourse' (mdt).[3] Two examples are known from a single papyrus, with rather extended titles 'Beginning of the Discourse...'; neither subsequent text survives (*Renseneb, The Fowler*). In *Sasobek* the title (without 'Beginning of...', A.17) is prefaced by an introductory narrative, whose beginning is lost (A.1–16); this could have been preceded by a title. *Neferti* has no title, but opens with a narrative prologue (1a–2q) and a descriptive introduction (2r–3e); *Khakheperreseneb* has a descriptive title (rto 1) which, like the introduction of *Neferti*, is not limited to a single designation. Both include the self-designation 'discourse' (mdt) or 'verses' (tsw). Introductions in this genre vary, and the choice between a title, narrative or prologue may have been determined by the complexity of the fictional context. Discourses seem to have required some sort of specific context; even those which open with titles have phrases implying a particular setting and circumstances (*Sasobek* A.17; *Renseneb* 1–2; *The Fowler* 1–3).

The most distinctive formal feature of the reflective wisdom texts, which are mainly pessimistic in tone and are often termed 'laments', is a syntactic verse-pattern 'then-now' (see **3.3.1**). As a whole, however, these texts are not 'laments'; *Neferti*, the only complete example, moves to a broadly positive resolution. The discourses also include more discursive passages that develop arguments.

---

[1] This term is problematic for Egyptology: e.g., Lichtheim 1997: 1–8.
[2] Schott 1990: 299–302 (1384–93), 345–7 (1552); the term is used of other types of text, such as an onomasticon (301–2 [1392]) and a calender of lucky and unlucky days (312 [1427d]).
[3] Schott 1990: 91–2 (159–61). For *mdt* in general see Schott 1990: 85–92 (153–61), discussed by Posener 1951a: 46–7; Brunner 1966a: 32–3.

Closely related to the discourses in style, tone and subject matter are *A Man and His Ba* and *Ipuur*, which are formally distinct in that the audience, passive in other discourses, assumes a significant speaking role. These two texts are structured as dialogues, in which the subject-matter is considered in a consistent series of exchanges, with individual speeches varying greatly in length. The argument has a rhetorically dramatic aspect. Both dialogues include 'then-now' formulations, as well as series of short stanzas patterned with refrains; both are fragmentary. The end of *A Man and His Ba* is reached without a narrative section (147–55), but this need not imply that the opening lacked a narrative (see p. 218 for possible reconstruction); one can, however, compare *Neferti*, which opens with narrative (1a–3e) and concludes with the monologue (15g). It is uncertain whether either dialogue would have included a title comparable to that in *Khakheperreseneb*.

Within individual texts there are indications of stylistic hierarchy, which may suggest that there was also a correlative hierarchy of genres and subgenres. A system of genres commonly involves hierarchy: 'not only are certain genres regarded *prima facie* as more canonical than others, but individual works or passages may be valued more or less according to their generic height' (A. Fowler 1982: 216). The principles of decorum that are related to hierarchy can govern many intrinsic features of genres such as appropriate subject-matter, as well as the mixing of genres. In the Middle Kingdom eulogy was apparently highly regarded – as in Latin literature, where it is a higher theme in Vergil's eclogues (e.g., Martindale 1997c: 113). In the argument of *A Man and His Ba* the lyrics with refrains seem to take precedence over narrative parables. To judge by the later reception (**3.2.2**) and the style of the teachings, they were perhaps the most elevated genre, while the tales were the least. Groups of compositions in a single genre can display differing degrees of elevation.

The majority of the 38 or so extant Middle Kingdom literary texts fall into the three groups mapped above. Additional fragments point to a wider range of possibilities, suggesting not only that the map is partial and affected by the chances of survival, but also that the system was inherently flexible and unschematic, open-ended both in formal terms and in the development of genres. These texts are absent from the Ramessid educational canon, although this is inconclusive for assessing their position in the Middle Kingdom. *P. Ramesseum II* does not match the principal genres: the papyrus contains a collection of short maxims, in which the word 'teach' occurs several times. They are not arranged systematically by subject, although several seem to be grouped thematically (Yoyotte 1961: 117–18; L. Morenz 1997a), and they mobilize diverse attitudes (Yoyotte 1961: 118). These short proverbs recall the style of oral wisdom of a kind alluded to in such compositions as *The Eloquent Peasant* (B1 50–51, 177;

Parkinson 1992: 169). The fact that these maxims use an exclusively proverbial form of presentation does not mean that they are more 'popular' or 'oral' than the other teachings: they contain phrases closely parallel to other 'canonical' texts (Barns 1956: 11–14). To judge by their context in the 'Ramesseum library' (**4.2**), they are not a copying exercise by an apprentice scribe. The structure is almost an extreme reduction of the maxim structure of *Ptahhotep* and *Khety*, and Blumenthal notes that the self-description of *Khakheperreseneb* as a 'collection of words' could apply to these maxims (1996a: 125); another possible parallel is the onomastica where each entry is laid out on a separate manuscript line (such as P. Ramesseum D) as some of the maxims are (for demotic monostichic texts see, e.g., Quack 1994: 19). The arrangement of the manuscript, in which the layout changed during copying, suggests a formally freer type of text that was perhaps adapted and excerpted by each copyist. This looser structure and composition might have been a more peripheral form than that of the more culturally central teachings or discourses. Such texts might have been composed and circulated within a more restricted circle, whereas the more central compositions were apparently disseminated through the country in a relatively standardized form.

Two more substantial compositions are *The Sporting King* and *The Pleasures of Fishing and Fowling* which have affinities with Late Egyptian literature, and have been dated to the 18th Dynasty (J. Assmann 1985: 48–9), although a fragmentary late Second Intermediate Period manuscript of a possibly related type of eulogy (Parkinson 1999d) suggests that such discourses were part of the Middle Kingdom literary canon.

All the literary genres, although distinctive, are not autonomous and cut off from other types of discourse. Most are canonical and in that reflect the concerns of central ideology, changing as it does (cf. R. Williams 1977: 180–5). The creation and use of genre is – like all writing – integral with the exercise of elite power (Brannigan 1998: 77–8), although the evolution of genres is not determined solely by 'power', but by a complex web of social practices. The same is true of metre and style, as is accessible in much later better documented works such as *Paradise Lost* (1667) where the choice of blank verse was informed by intertextual, cultural and political concerns (Lewalski 2000: 456–8).

6.3 METRICS

> Converted into dust and bookworm excreta,
> riddled lines with just the ghost of their metre.
>
> T. Harrison, *The Trackers of Oxyrhynchus* (1988),
> speech of Grenfell/Apollo

Metrical structure is often important in defining literary types, but is partly inaccessible for Egyptian, whose script does not record vowels or accentuation; the manuscript presentation is thus important. For Egyptian the definition of 'verse' (*versus* = written line) is problematic. Stichic writing is extremely rare, exceptions including a 26th Dynasty manuscript of *The Teaching of Amenemope* (P. BM EA 10474: Posener 1966: 59–62; Verhoeven 1999: 259), and a demotic funerary text of the early first century CE (P. BM EA 10507; M. Smith 1987). Stichic writing in Middle Kingdom manuscripts does not correspond to verses: the stanzas of the el-Lahun Hymns to Senwosret III are arranged in lines to avoid duplicating the refrains (e.g., Osing 1992a: 101–9), a practice that is common where elements of a text are repeated, as in the biographical stela of Intef where an initial word acts as a refrain (e.g., Grapow 1936: 30–2; Parkinson 1991a: 61–3). Stichic writing also occurs without repeated elements, marking some separate maxims in the late 12th Dynasty *P. Ramesseum II*. Similar graphic devices occur in administrative documents with tabulated information or lists in columns (Grapow 1936: 37–51), while in literary manuscripts these often reflect the incorporation of textual forms with particular layouts, such as the arrangement of the king's letter in *Sinuhe* (B 178–99) or the list of goods in *The Eloquent Peasant* (B1 1–14).

Metrical form has been studied by scholars from Adolf Erman onwards (see Fecht 1993: 70–5). Gerhard Fecht (1963, 1964, 1965, 1966, 1982, 1993) has proposed a system comparable with that of Coptic verse (for which see Junker 1908; Säve-Söderbergh 1949). Coptic verse does not rhyme, but is rhythmical. A verse is measured out with word clusters, each of which has a single stress; the number of accented syllables is fixed, while unaccented syllables do not count at all (producing apparently irregular verse lengths). The grammatical rules which allow these stresses to be identified were modified by the rhythm of the language, and in scanning one must allow for variations that cannot now be traced grammatically.[4] On the Coptic model, Egyptian metrics was not a 'quantitative metre' like Greek or Latin, which have a 'regulated alternation of long and short syllables', but was a stress metre, where the regular pattern is provided by counting cola, the 'components of sentence stress'. A colon is 'that component of the stream of speech [which is] divided by possible pauses for breath' (Fecht 1993: 76). A general development was from smaller word clusters to larger ones, as stress grew stronger (Fecht 1993: 82). The word for 'phrase' (*ts*) is used for a 'verse' (Fischer-Elfert 1986a: 96; Schott 1990: 398–401 [1715]) although its correlation with a

---

[4] Säve-Söderbergh 1949; thus *nto* is unstressed in Allbery 1938: 168 l.30, but stressed in 181 l.34.

single verse on Fecht's rules is imprecise: in *Khety* (2d–e) a *ts* is cited which is two metrical verse-pointed verses.

Fecht's analysis has not been universally accepted (Burkard 1983, 1993, 1996; Lichtheim 1971; Schenkel 1972; overview: Buchberger 1993: 21–5). An alternative analysis is proposed, for example by John L. Foster (e.g., 1975, 1977, 1980, 1994), based on verse-points and parallelism of members forming 'thought couplets'. This approach, however, is unconvincing for many texts: parallelism is not constant and is arguably a stylistic rather than a formal device (cf. J. Assmann 1982a). Scholars such as Irene Shirun-Grumach (1977) and Bernard Mathieu (1989, 1990, 1994, 1996a) have proposed modifications of Fecht's rules, arguing for a compromise between the two styles of analysis.

Fecht analyses all formal texts as verse (1993: 69). Some Middle Kingdom documents, such as letters, do not respond to metrical analysis, suggesting that 'prose', or unpatterned written language, also existed (Parkinson 1991a: 30). Verse thus seems to isolate patterned written culture – the high cultural stream of tradition – from more practical writings, including administrative and occasionally technical texts. All commemorative and religious texts, and all the literary corpus, are metrically patterned. *Cheops' Court* is metrical, although much less regular than such tales as *The Shipwrecked Sailor* (see Parkinson 1999f: 102–20 for a verse translation). This difference in metrical form parallels that of stylistic and topical register (cf. **7.3**). Other analyses focusing on parallelism, however, regard verse as a more restricted phenomenon: Lichtheim (1971) argues for a variation between verse and prose within commemorative and literary texts, with tales being predominantly prose; other scholars view tales such as *The Shipwrecked Sailor* as verse, but *Cheops' Court* as prose (L. Morenz 1996: 107 n.471; Burkard 1996).

Verses are grouped into stanzas, which were termed *ḥwt*, 'mansions'. Sections of the mortuary Pyramid Texts inscribed from the 6th Dynasty were carved in *ḥwt*-sign shaped columns, but the word is not attested separately until the New Kingdom, when it is used of sections of such compositions as the Chester Beatty love-songs and *Amenemope* (Schott 1990: 289–91 [1349]). The word is etymologically parallel to 'stanza' (Gardiner 1931: 27; Blackman 1938). In New Kingdom manuscripts 'stanzas' are marked off from one another by rubrics of some or all words of the first verse; red ink is a practice for highlighting sections of cursive texts found from the Old Kingdom (Posener 1951b). Also, a sign reading 'pause (*grḥ*)'[5] marks the end of a stanza, indicating its role in performance. The sign is first attested in the Coffin Texts.

---

[5] The sign probably derives from the shape of the *ḥwt*-marker (as in *PT* 533e; see Grapow 1936: 53; Blackman 1938: 65), but the occurrence of (*jr-grḥ*, 'make a pause') in

The importance of stanza divisions in the New Kingdom is explicit in the *Satiric Letter* (P. Anastasi I 11.1–2), in which a scribe is mocked for his ignorance about the stanzas of *The Teaching of Hordedef* (quoted on pp. 51–2). The *Letter* also mentions a practice of referring to a stanza by its first verse (Fischer-Elfert 1986a: 94–6), which is attested in New Kingdom ostraca listing first verses.[6] A standardized marking of stanzas is not found in Middle Kingdom manuscripts, suggesting that the attested divisions might result from later codification and education practices. Nevertheless, such divisions as that of *Sinuhe* into 40 stanzas, attested in Ramessid educational manuscripts, reflect a structural division in the original composition (J. Assmann 1983b).

The use of red ink is less consistent in Middle Kingdom manuscripts, although it occurs fairly regularly for the incipit or title of a text. Rubrics are applied variously by different contemporaneous scribes, as can be seen by the 'Berlin' and 'Ramesseum libraries' (**4.2**). The scribe who wrote both the *Sinuhe* B manuscript and *The Eloquent Peasant* B1 manuscript tended to mark rubrics indicating new stanzas almost only in horizontal lines, while the scribe of *The Eloquent Peasant* B2 manuscript consistently rubricized the start of new petitions (Parkinson 1991c: xviii–xx); by contrast the scribe of *A Man and His Ba* papyrus used only black ink. Manuscripts from the slightly later Ramesseum archive show a similar variety: in *Sasobek* the start of sections of text seem consistently rubricized, whereas the scribe of the *Sinuhe* and *The Eloquent Peasant* papyrus (R) rubricized only the incipit and date (R 5) in the former, but in the latter he consistently rubricized the narrative formula 'And then X said' (Parkinson 1991c: xxiv). Such variation suggests practice was not standardized.

Red dots or 'verse-points' punctuate New Kingdom hieratic literary manuscripts written in horizontal lines, but scholars have questioned whether they are primarily indications of verses or of units that often coincide with verses (e.g., Buchberger 1993: 22–3; see also Tacke 2001). From the New Kingdom they occur in apprentice copies of Middle Egyptian literature and in non-apprentice copies of Middle and Late Egyptian texts of various types. It is improbable that they mark dictated units of text, since most copies show no evidence of having been written from dictation (Burkard 1977). Sometimes verse-points mark off phrases of a stichically written stanza, such as in a eulogy in a Ramessid Miscellany (P. Lansing 13b–15: Gardiner 1937: 112–15). Much later, in the Roman Period demotic 'Song of the Harpist', each stichically written line consists

---

P. Harris 500 shows that it was more than a graphic shape. Occasionally it marks off a group of stanzas (see Römer 1987).

[6] E.g., sequences of the opening words of stanzas of *Khety* (Posener 1938: no. 1017), and of *Amenemhat* (Sn 143: Hayes 1942: pl. 25). For numbered stanzas see, e.g., van der Walle 1985.

of two verse-pointed clauses, with the line-ends seemingly marking a stronger division of the text than the verse-points (Thissen 1992); a similar practice is found in Coptic manuscripts (e.g., Till 1961: 302; Kuhn and Tait 1996: 8–9). Post-Ramessid copies of some texts show that verse-pointed units were equivalent to a single stichically written 'verse': one copy of *The Teaching of Amenemope* is stichic while another is verse-pointed instead (P. BM EA 10474 and Tablet Moscow I 1.8324: Posener 1966: 53–4; Grumach 1972).

While the verse-pointed units seem in general to correspond to lines of verse, they do not invariably correspond to metrical structures identified by applying Fecht's rules. Some divergences can be explained by scribal error and corrupt textual traditions: for example, in an unlikely division a verse-point interrupts a direct genitive in several manuscripts of *Sinuhe*: *s3b-ʿd-mr-d3twt-ʿjtj-ʿ.w.s. m-t3w-stjw* 'Governor of the Sovereign's (l.p.h.) • Domains in the Syrian lands' (AOS, G, C 1: Koch 1990: 1). The misplacing of verse-points would have been easy when they were added almost mechanically after the main text was written (e.g., Condon 1978: 50; Tacke 2001: 136–41). Although the verse divisions of the stichically written *Amenemope* do not exactly match Fecht's rules, in which a verse should be of two or three cola, the divergence (8 per cent) is too small to challenge his principles. This divergence may suggest that the number of cola in each line is more flexible than Fecht would accept, or it could be due to the influence of speech patterns that are lost to us, as with Coptic. Generic considerations are also probably relevant.

The evolution of the standardized New Kingdom punctuation is uncertain. The late Second Intermediate Period papyrus of *The Tale of the House of Life* has verse-points in its later standard usage, and they are attested earlier in some late Middle Kingdom literary manuscripts from Thebes and el-Lahun. In *P. Ramesseum II*, they divide the text into sections in the same way as stichic writing: the scribe seems to have moved from stichic writing to verse-pointing system as the manuscript progressed. The points, however, do not mark single verses but larger units. *The Ramesseum Wisdom Fragment* has red verse-points placed to the right of vertical lines of hieratic. Verse-points are also known from late 12th Dynasty el-Lahun papyri (unpublished); none of these is certainly literary. P. UCL 32110G from el-Lahun is a liturgical text written in vertical lines with red verse-points placed to the right of the line, marking off short, verse-like phrases, perhaps units for liturgical recitation. These would correspond to Fecht's groups of cola, which are components of speech 'divided up by possible pauses for breath' (Fecht 1993: 76). It is thus possible that verse-points were developed for copying liturgical texts for recitation and adapted later for literary texts.

Georges Posener suggested that accounts, which are laid out in lines with check marks, provided the model for marking off lines of verse (1951b: 77). Another possible ancestor is the single or double line in red or black which separates spells written on Middle Kingdom coffins, or occasionally, sections of a spell (Spell 336 in B1L: *CT* IV, 327). These texts are written in linear heiroglyphs in vertical lines, between ruled lines, with the horizontal line spanning the column. The lines correspond to the 'pause' sign in other manuscripts of the same spells. The lines occur on coffins from most major sites from the 11th Dynasty on (e.g., Coffins B2–4Bo from el-Bersha: Willems 1988: 70–1). Ramessid ostraca of the educational text *Kemit* are written in a similar style, with horizontal lines marking off units of text equivalent to metrical verses, while some manuscripts use verse-points instead of lines (e.g., O. IFAO 1116–7). Two Ramessid manuscripts of *The Teaching of Amenemhat* written in this style (see p. 73) also use red horizontal lines instead of verse-points. This suggests that the two styles of punctuation were equivalent, and that verse-points may thus have developed as an abbreviated form of the lines used in funerary and liturgical texts written in linear hieroglyphs. The abbreviation evolved due to the more cursive nature of the hieratic script and the lack of ruled lines,[7] and the accountancy check marks would have provided a suitable model for the points. There may have been influences other than religious manuscripts: horizontal lines also mark sections of letters, as in a model letter on a First Intermediate Period jar stand (Simpson 1981).

The standardized system of verse-points was established by the late Second Intermediate Period. It is probable that 'from no later than the New Kingdom, metre ceased to coincide with the sentence intonation of living speech so that writing and reading metrical texts increasingly became an acquired skill' (Fecht 1993: 82), and this was when the pointing system was gradually and inconsistently introduced to literary texts, sometimes in a partially evolved form. Idiosyncratic usages are attested even in the Ramessid period, as in P. Chester Beatty II (*The Tale of Truth and Falsehood*), where points mark off single cola, rather than verses. The punctuation and metre of literary manuscripts is thus a distinctive feature, but not a signal exclusive to literary works; it indicates the texts as intended for recitation and part of the written stream of tradition.

---

[7] Their presence on the vertically written hieratic manuscripts such as P. UCL 32110G shows that direction of writing was not the sole factor.

6.4 STYLE

> What is the phrase for the moon? and the phrase for love? By what name are we to call death?
>
> Virginia Woolf, *The Waves* (1992: 227)

Ancient style can act as a barrier to modern readers of many literatures, as Paul Veyne notes in an essay entitled 'Our intense style, or why ancient poetry bores us' (1988: 180–8). That of Egyptian writing has to be assessed within an awareness of the original oral arena, and of its culturally distinct conventions (e.g., R. Williams 1977: 173–9). Studies of rhetoric (e.g., Fecht 1970; Guglielmi 1984a–c, 1986a–c, 1987, 1996b; Junge 1984a; Coulon 1999) continue to illuminate the stylistic variety, which will become more apparent as the genre-system and the intertext are more fully understood. For the modern reader the general tone still often can seem remote even to the point of monotony, despite growing awareness of increasingly varied tones: the bizarre, baroque, satiric, elegaic, impassioned, didactic, reflective; familiar types such as comic and tragic are lacking. Style is not an autonomous phenomenon: 'form' and 'content' are inseparable. Here I review several aspects that are fundamental to literary reading.

Literature is described in *Neferti* as comprising 'perfect words, choice verses' (2j). The phrase 'perfect words/speech' (*mdt-nfrt*) was used to describe style in various types of text (Schott 1990: 88–9 [157]). A Coffin Text spell describes an otherworldly scribe who is 'a lector priest and scribe of perfect speech, an attendant of (the god) Perception' (spell 533; *CT* VI, 127e–g). 'Perfect speech' was also an important skill in official life. Rhetoric was a basic constituent of culture and civilization, as it was in the European Renaissance (see, e.g., Greenblatt 1990: 118), and Gerald Moers (2000: 59–80) suggests that 'perfect speech' denotes the *Kultursprache* of the Middle Kingdom. Such 'perfect discourse' included both official monumental and literary rhetoric, which has often hampered the identification of specifically poetic speech in Egyptian discourse (Baines in press). Modern readers often regard poetry and rhetoric as distinct, if not opposed, in contrast to medieval and Renaissance discourse theory (Payne 1973: 9–59).

The perfection of speech has social and aesthetic aspects. The importance of such speech in official cultural life cannot be overestimated (see Doxey 1998: 52–8; Franke 1994: 19 n.56). Biographies speak of their protagonists as 'one who speaks well (*nfr*) before his lord' and 'one who says what is good (*nfrt*)' (J. M. A. Janssen 1946: 69 [Bb.4], 122–5 [Hc]). The Chamberlain of Senwosret I, Intef, claimed to be 'one who taught a man what would be excellent for him' (Sethe 1928a: 81, 1.2), a phrase that is evoked in Ptahhotep's instruction to 'teach the great according to what is excellent for him' (399). On a Theban stela of the First Intermediate Period (Fischer 1996: 83–90; earlier treatment Roccati 1993: 255) a man on a diplomatic mission says that the people involved

> rejoiced on meeting me
> because I was perfect of speech (*nfr n-dd*).
> I was one open of mouth, effective of plans,
> commanding of voice on the day of assembly, who spoke a phrase (*ts*).
>
> (ll.5–7)

The idea of discourse as a negotiation of social power, and of language as 'contiguous with the power structures that sustain the social order' (Sinfield 1992: 35) runs through Egyptian writings (e.g., Derchain 1987, 1989; Eyre 1990; Coulon 1999). For example, in the Hymns to Senwosret III, the eulogist declares:

> The tongue of his Person restrains Nubia,
> his phrases (*tsw*) have made the Asiatics flee . . .
> his commands have made his boundaries, his words (*mdww*) have gathered
>   together the Two Banks.
>
> (Sethe 1928a: 66, ll.8–9, 12–13)

In *Merikare*, the new king is told that:

> The strong arm of the king is his tongue.
> Words (*mdt*) are stronger than any weapon (9b–c)

In *The Eloquent Peasant*, the implications of speech in relation to power are presented explicitly when Nemtinakht cites as a generally acknowledged proverb that:

> 'A wretch's name is uttered (only) because of his master'

that is, 'a poor man exists/is acknowledged only insofar as he has a master' (B1 51: Parkinson 1988: 60–1; Loprieno 1988: 14–17, 88–9). This occurs in a scene which turns on the fact that the peasant has no clearly defined master, and it is noticeable that the peasant's name is not 'uttered' by anyone, except in the narration at the very start of the tale (R 1.1).

A distinction was made between formal, official and literary language on the one hand and common speech on the other (L. Morenz 1996: 32–6; **3.2.1**). The most explicit description of 'perfect speech' in social terms is in the stela of Montuwoser (temp. Senwosret I), where the Steward describes himself as

> someone who spoke in the manner of the officials,
> someone free from saying *p3*.[8]

The article *p3* is characteristic of colloquial Late Middle Egyptian (Loprieno 1995: 68–9). A hierarchy of language and style is evident in texts (e.g., Junge 1984b), as are distinct registers (e.g., Goldwasser 1990). Although such variety has diachronic aspects, the selection of registers is synchronic and intertextual. One example is the greeting between Hordedef and Djedi in *Cheops' Court* when the language assumes a more stately register which the tale states explicitly befits the salutations of two such men (Goedicke 1986b). Parallelism of members is a sign of a high stylistic register, as are couplets and refrains, redolent of the style of prestigious eulogies such as the el-Lahun Hymns to Senwosret III. Although it is possible to characterize some items of grammar and lexis as literary in the broadest sense, we cannot chart fully the differing registers of diction or gauge the resonances of words and assess if they are lofty or humble diction (compare O'Hara 1997: 254–6 on Vergilian diction). For example, many of the terms to do with fishing which occur in the fifth petition of *The Eloquent Peasant* are rare (Parkinson 1988: 222–3), and may have struck the original audience as unusual; but they could have been intended to sound like either vulgar working language or impressively recherché diction.

The sense of speech's being 'perfected' involves imagery of it as 'craft' (*ḥmwt*), a metaphor also used of wisdom and magical utterances (Schott 1990: 312–3 [1428a–b]) and of speech that is particularly 'choice'.[9] The 'perfection' of speech ensures that cultural values and wisdom are remembered (*Ptahhotep* 507–11). The 'craftsman' features in *Sasobek*, apparently as a metaphor for the wise man. Artistic perfection is expressed in the first maxim of *Ptahhotep*:

> The limits of art (*ḥmwt*) have not been attained;
> no artist is (fully) equipped with his excellence (*ʿpr-ȝḥw:f*).
> Perfect speech is more hidden than malachite;
> (yet) it is found with the maids at millstones. (52–9)

---

[8] Sethe 1928a: 79, ll.17–18; see J. P. Allen 1994: 1–2; L. Morenz 1996: 34–6.
[9] In a Ramessid magical spell, a man in a festive state has his mouth 'open with perfect speech (*mdwt-nfrwt*) and choice verses (*tsw-stpw*)' (P. Chester Beatty IX vso B 12.13–13.1: Gardiner 1935a: 110), while in the Ramessid P. Chester Beatty IV, the author Khety is someone 'whose verses are choice' (vso 6.13).

Ptahhotep presents craft as an ideal, unlike the 'limits of physical strength' which *Amenemhat* states can be 'attained' (10c). The second verse of the cited passage (56) can be paralleled in the Coffin Texts where the deceased is said to have 'become equipped with all excellence', here meaning magical powers (exs. in Schott 1990: 1–4, 142). Literature and magic are often associated (L. Morenz 1996: 144, cf. n.627). The language of culture and literature can be presented as sacred and secret, a theme perhaps deriving from the esoteric nature of sacred texts (e.g., L. Morenz 1996: 78–106). The opening of *Khakheperreseneb* describes the sage's desired speech as

> unknown utterances
> and extraordinary phrases,
> in a new language that does not pass away. (rto 2)

The speaker wishes to 'know what others ignored – what is not repeated' (rto 7). Just as the magic of words is dulled by being 'laid bare', and being 'recalled by men'[10] (*Ipuur* 6.6–7), so literary art is something remote. It is achieved after 'searching',[11] and is something rare, rather than original in the modern sense (Parkinson 1996d).

Perfect speech embodies social prestige:

> May you say distinguished things, so that the officials who shall hear may say:
> 'How perfect (*nfr*) is the outcome of his mouth (*prw n-r₃:f*)!'.
> (*Ptahhotep* 625–7)

Nevertheless, 'perfect speech' is not isomorphic with the social structure, since it is found with maidservants and oasis-dwellers. While this presentation of 'perfect speech' as coming from marginal social figures may reflect the unrealistic inclusive aspirations of Egyptian high culture (Moers 2000: 59–80), it is also a literary travesty, and embodies a topos of such speech as being rare, unexpected and potentially divergent from social norms. The peasant claims his 'perfect speech' is something 'that comes from the mouth (*prrt m-r₃*) of Re' (349–50), echoing a phrase in the funerary 'Abydos formula' (verse 13; e.g., Lichtheim 1988: 87). He thus claims the highest possible register for his own art, allying it with the creative power of divine speech (e.g., J. Assmann 1984c: 684; Bickel 1994: 100–11), regardless of the social alignment of 'perfect speech' with the social elite (cf. Coulon 1999: 114–15).

The introduction to *Khakheperreseneb* (rto 1–9; **9.2**) is in part a medita-

---

[10] However, *sḫȝ* may be *s⟨w⟩ḫ* 'to garble': Borghouts 1980: 1141; L. Morenz 1996: 91–100.
[11] *ḥḥj*: *Khakheperreseneb* 2.1; *Cheops' Court* 4.22, 25, 7.7; *ḏʿr. Neferti* 1k.

tion on the difference between literary speech and the official speech of the 'ancestors' manifested in tomb-inscriptions. Tomb-inscriptions were noted for their self-aggrandizing discourse (Coulon 1999: 122), and the early Ramessid biography of Nefersekheru asserts its truthfulness while warning its readers to avoid the common assumption that

> every man boasts about himself in his own writings.
> (Osing 1992b: 47, pl. 35, ll.15–16)

Sinuhe, by contrast, mobilizes this awareness, subverting the conventions of the biography to describe human fallibility through its variety and richness of style.

Literary discourse thus thematizes style more explicitly than other genres, suggesting a degree of autoreflexivity, regarded by Russian formalists as a criterion for literariness (**2.2.1**). *Khakheperreseneb* is not unique in its self-concern, although it is particularly explicit (Parkinson 1996d; compare Moers in press). Ptahhotep speaks a great deal about speech (e.g., 48, 58, 129–30, 159, 370–1, 624–5), and his teaching is self-referential, not only about the topic of teaching (e.g., 399, 566) but also about how it is to be received and retold to future generations (e.g., 507–634). The structures of many tales show the same concern with their own style and form: *Cheops' Court* consists chiefly of a tale about the telling of various tales, and *The Shipwrecked Sailor* is a tale of a tale told by a sailor of a tale told to him. The sailor survives his shipwreck and prospers by his speech (cf. Loprieno 1991a: 217), and many literary protagonists are distinctive and characterized by their artful language. Literary diction, however, displays a difference of degree rather than a cleavage from official style.

Antonio Loprieno characterizes literary language as systematic as against episodic, as a forerunner of the later distinction of metaphoric versus referential language (1996e: 519–20, drawing on the ideas of Roman Jakobson). It remains uncertain, however, whether literary language tends towards connotative rather than denotative words, as for example James O'Hara has suggested for Vergil (1997: 255). Middle Kingdom literature is a poetry of syntax rather than metaphor, and does not conform to modern expectations of poetic language as metaphoric, and is often no more metaphoric than some contemporaneous inscriptions. *The Sporting King*, however, may be an instance of the relevance of imagery (in general see Osing 1977b) for literary description, since the central speech is commissioned with the question 'Like what [is that which you say] you have [seen]?' (A2.2). The use of imagery is fully functional, and not just decorative, and the metaphoric distance is sometimes so great that it verges on the surreal, notably in some striking metaphors in *The Eloquent Peasant* (Parkinson 1992: 173). A comparison of the definitions of the social and ethical ideal of Maat ('Truth') in a commemorative inscription and in literary texts shows a higher level of imagery in the latter. The king's speech in the mid-13th Dynasty Stela of Neferhotep I concludes:

> The reward[12] of one who acts is that which he has done:
> this is Maat upon the heart of god.   (Helck 1983: 29, ll.14–15)

In *The Loyalist Teaching*, the same principle is expounded in the more concrete, individualized terms of an example, relating to themes of provision and the audience's responsibilities developed elsewhere in the poem:

> He who fixes the taxes in proportion to the grain/barley
> is [a just] man (*mȝʿtj*) in god's eyes.   (12.1–2)

In *The Teaching of a Man*, the definition is given in a metaphor:

> [. . .] Maat is a dyke.   (13.5)

This resonates with other sections of the poem, where the king is 'a dyke for him who pleases him' (2.6), and the official 'is a [dyke] ⟨for⟩ him who petitions him' (13.9). The motif of 'action results in action' that is integral to Maat is elaborated in *The Eloquent Peasant* into an allusive sequence:

> This is an ordinance: Act for the man who acts, to cause him to act.
> This is thanking him for what he does;
> this is parrying a thing before shooting;
> this is commissioning something from a master craftsman.   (B1 140–42)

A possible model for literary style as differentiated is provided by the peasant's first petition, which transposes the actual audience from the episodic, referential narration of what has happened to 'this' protagonist, onto the more systematic and allusive plane of 'As if', in a world of metaphor and simile. The petition is made when the peasant meets Rensi 'going down' (B1 66) to his official boat at Heracleopolis, where there was a sacred lake called 'the Sea of Maat (*mȝʿt*)' (Gessler-Löhr 1983: 147–50). He transposes this context into a grand metaphor:

> If you go down to the Sea of Maat (*mȝʿt*).   (B1 85–6)

---

[12] Blumenthal 1970: 85 (B4.15).

This is then developed into an extravagant and culturally resonant image of prosperity and hunting in a boat, followed by a parody of a royal titulary (Parkinson 1988: 78–91; Coulon 1999: 106).

A related aspect is the superfluity of literary style, which is both more 'artificial' than natural speech and more extended than other forms of discourse. The speeches of *The Eloquent Peasant* are numerous and wisdom discourses such as *Ipuur* exuberantly extended, and such qualities are claimed by the protagonist of the Ramessid *Satiric Letter* (P. Anastasi I 7.8–8.1, cited on pp. 59–60). Interpretive layers are also presented in abundance, and allusions are made to more than one contextual sphere (e.g., Loprieno 1991a). Such features accord with the concept that literary language can be a form of discourse that 'means one thing, at the same time means *another*, and yet at the same time does not cease to mean the first thing' (Paul Ricoeur, cited by Iser 1989: 119). In the descriptions of Sinuhe's prosperity abroad, no less than with Rosalind in *As You Like It*, ostensibly descriptive language becomes the medium of a hidden desire. Multiple meanings decentre the audience, as in *The Shipwrecked Sailor*, producing an awareness of the multifariousness of a poem's meaning. Similarly, the phrase 'I shall show you what is before you' in wisdom discourses (see p. 196) articulates both the didactic and mimetic role of the poet's art and literature's claim to describe reality, but it also establishes a pact between author and audience and announces the subjectivity of its imagined reality.

Structural irony, parody and humour consistently complicate and elaborate the message of texts; such features were probably more pervasive than can now be assessed (e.g., Eyre 1999: 237). Constellations of vocabulary cluster around certain themes (e.g., '*nḏ* 'lessening' is used of the land in distress, often with the theodic metaphor of a bad shepherd: *Neferti* 11b, *Ipuur* 12.1; *Loyalist* 13.8), and within poems key words are repeated with differing nuances, resonating with intertextual associations, but also continually fashioning 'an intensely reflexive system' within a poem (to borrow Durling 1976: ix–x on Petrarch). Wordplay in literary texts complicates rather than explains, as it does in aetiological myths such as *The Book of the Heavenly Cow* (Hornung 1997), or in the elucidation of dreams in the Ramessid Dream Interpretation Manual from Deir el-Medina (P. Chester Beatty III: Gardiner 1935a: 9–22). Wordplay often expresses the complexities surrounding literature's concerns. For example, telling absolute goodness from apparent goodness in *The Eloquent Peasant* is expressed in a densely punning verse:

Only the goodness of the good man is good beyond him (*nfr-nfrt-nfr-r:f*).

(B1 337; see **7.2**)

as is finding a valid expression of reality in *Khakheperreseneb*:

> No speaker has now spoken yet – may one who will speak now speak (*n-ḏd-ḏd(w) ḏd-ḏd.tj.fj*).
>
> (rto 5)

Formally wordplay provides sequences in structure, as in *The Eloquent Peasant* (Eyre 2000), *Cheops' Court* (Eyre 1992) or *Ipuur*, where ostensibly isolated, even contradictory, descriptive stanzas are subtly linked into a coherent whole. The verbal art provides a sense of unity in diversity.

The colophon to literary manuscripts (**4.2**) implies that the compositions were perceived as unities. An absolute organic unity is a fallacy of aesthetic integration, rejected by recent historicist criticism (e.g., Greenblatt 1990: 168). The ideal of unified composition is implied by the Ramessid *Satiric Letter* where an un-unified letter is ridiculed as if from the hands of seven scribes, and contrasted with the writer's own letter which

> I alone have created, by myself, with no one else with me.
> (P. Anastasi I 5.5–6.2, 7.5–6: Fischer-Elfert 1986a: 59, 71)

A mixture of discordant elements in a scribal composition is denounced as incompetent, as it is 'mixed up', and the rival scribe is criticized for writing 'neither praises nor vilifications' (4.7–8; Fischer-Elfert 1986a: 50). Many Middle Kingdom poems display a tension between unity and diversity (see **4.5**).

Characterization is an instance of how expectations of organic unity can be anachronistic and inappropriate. The generally 'objective' style of Egyptian narration means that literary characterization is often expressed through the character's own words rather than the author's voice. Few comments are offered, with exceptions such as when Cheops and Rudjdjedet are said to fall into a 'bad mood' (*Cheops' Court* 9.12, 12.21) and when the eloquent peasant is said to be afraid of what was about to happen (B2 117–18). There is none of the 'free indirect discourse' of later and modern narrations in which the author's voice is modified to express the characters' own feelings (Laird 1997: 286), but the characterization is subtle and complex, if radically different from that of a modern novel. The impact would have been different in performance from how it appears to a modern reader (e.g., Parkinson 2000a).

Literary personages are not essential psychological unities but simulated persons who are creations of a text's conventions. The discontinuous nature of Shakespearean characterization, for example, has often been underplayed in interpretation (Sinfield 1992: 52–79). Characters act not because of psychological motivation – as in modern European expectations of reality – but due to the requirements of the text; a classic study of this phenomenon is Arthur Mizener's of Chaucer's Cressida (1959). Characterization is never a process of describing real people, but of mobilizing rhetorical and cultural (stereo)types within an intertextual field of references (such as Lavinia's blush in Vergil's *Aeneid*: Laird 1997: 290). Such intertextual signals are now largely obscured, and can easily be misread (as with Sneferu's characterization in *Cheops' Court*: **8.4**). Characterization must be assessed within cultural and social aspects rather than psychologistic readings (Hardie 1997: 321); thus John Baines' criticism of Sinuhe's characterization as flawed (1982) is largely irrelevant, and the supposed inconsistencies result from a modern viewpoint.[13]

Poststructuralist criticism has emphasized the role of gaps and indeterminacies in language as opposed to unity. For critics such as Iser such features are a 'basic element for the aesthetic response' of filling them (1989: 9), as well as creating a poem's multivalency in ideological terms (cf. D. Fowler 1997: 266 on the *Aeneid*). The importance of indeterminacy is also seen in the poem's concern for expressing the inexpressible, or in T. S. Eliot's words 'a raid on the inarticulate' (*East Coker* l.179; 1959: 26): *Sinuhe* centres around something 'like an unrepeatably great matter' (B 215–6), while *A Man and His Ba* is about something 'too great for exaggeration' (6); the opening of *Khakheperreseneb* laments the speaker's inability to express his woe (Parkinson 1996d).

The plot of *The Eloquent Peasant*, where even silence is a mistaken communication, questions to what extent speech and meaning can be determined or controlled by the audience. The generic fusion of narrative and discursive modes in this poem articulates the instability of interpretation, as do the intensely reflexive uses of language and the pervasive employment of irony. The tale is not the only Middle Kingdom composition with these features, but its fissured complexity is a strongly marked instance. The tale concerns a difficult and problematic conversation between a speaker and his audience. The contradictions of its supremely neat and simple plot remain inexhaustible; despite its narrative resolution, it grows more deeply unsettling the more one examines the implications about communication, as if suggesting that 'poetic language . . . (is) a problematic of ordinary language, a making explicit, indeed conspicuous, of the undeclared difficulty of everyday speech' (Felperin 1992: 54–5 on Shakespeare's romances). *The Eloquent Peasant* systematically neutralizes or problematizes the utilitarian outcomes of rhetoric (Parkinson 2000b): 'poetry makes nothing happen' (Auden 1991: 248). The treatment reflects the ambivalence of rhetoric in cultural and social life, but it is formulated deliberately and self-consciously rather than unintentionally expressing flaws in ideology. Such gaps are thus to be interpreted in part as aesthetic

---

[13] Bryan's analysis of the protagonist in *The Shipwrecked Sailor* (1980) is an example of judging a character as a real individual or by expectations of contemporary literature.

features, not exclusively as cultural faultlines. The delicate and unstable resolutions in Middle Kingdom compositions can perhaps be compared with what Paul Alpers (1979: 103) terms the 'suspensions' in Vergil's *Eclogues*, a term that 'suggests a poised and secure contemplation of things disparate or ironically related, and yet at the same time does not imply that disparities and conflicts are fully resolved'.

The semantic complication of much literary discourse is complemented by largely inaccessible aesthetic and stylistic features, such as the cantabile qualities of alliteration and assonance, the emotional impact of which cannot be assessed adequately, as with metrical structure. James O'Hara has suggested that the first audiences of Vergil may have 'paid more attention to the sound and beauty of the language than to what was being said' (1997: 246). The original impact of the Middle Kingdom poems was probably more diverse than a modern reader can appreciate.

Thus aesthetic and emotional considerations must inform any cognitive approach to the poems, although close readings of entire works have rarely been attempted (e.g., Fecht 1965; Broze 1996). I present one short example of a moderately close reading, in order to suggest what could be undertaken for the whole corpus. In *The Eloquent Peasant* the peasant's final words are brief but resonant:

ḏd.jn-sḫtj-pnḥsfw	And this peasant said, 'The thirsty man's	
n-jb m-mww	approaching water,	
dʒt-rʒ n-ḥrd n-sbnt	the nurseling's reaching of a mouth	
m-jrtt ntf-mt	for milk – he dies,	
nḥjj-mʒ:f n-jj:f	while for him who prays to see it come,	
jj wdf-mt:f-r:f	death comes slowly.'	(B2 118–22)

While the sound of this cannot be recovered, the consonants suggest assonance between *n*s and *m*s in many verses, and also with *jj* and *f* in the final couplet. These elaborate verses occur in a plain narration, adding to their effect, and they open with wordplay: the statement about the 'thirsty man (*jb*)' 'approaching (*ḥsfw*)' water is inspired by the fact that the peasant is, according to the narrator, expecting (*jb*) to be punished (*ḥsf*: B2 117–18). The evocation of water alludes to the gift of essential 'water to the thirsty' as an ethical act expressed in biographical formulae, alluded to earlier in the poem (B1 277–8), while thirst is elsewhere associated with death (Zandee 1960: 67–70; *Sinuhe* B 22–3; *Loyalist* 10.8–9). Although the peasant stresses the irony and poignancy of these imagined deaths, his images also associate death with pleasant relief.[14] The reference to a child

---

[14] For a nurseling's as an especially poignant death cf. *CT* I, 167g–8b; *A Man and His Ba* 78–80.

recalls the situation at the start of the poem, where the peasant sets off to acquire provisions for his children (R 1.3).

The sheer change from the peasant's earlier utterances marks this one out as charged with impact. The syntax itself operates on an emotional level: *ntf* (B2 121) refers to both the 'the thirsty man' and the 'nursling', who die within reach of life. The asyndeton, in which the subject of *ntf-mt* is the shifting genitive phrase of the previous clauses, emphasizes the passion of the outcry,[15] also evoking the abruptness of a death that overtakes both the syntax and the attempts to reach succour. The metrical enjambment adds to the impression of speed and desperation. In contrast, death's 'coming slowly' (*jj wdf*) is expressed as two verbs with a single subject, enacting the slowness by postponing the subject. The repetition of *jj* acts in a similar manner, and mobilizes the paradox of the situation, alluding also to the fatal associations this verb can have (Zandee 1960: 47, 52; S. Morenz 1975) and the earlier descriptions of 'evil happenings' (*jjt*, B1 88). The verb 'delay' (*wdf*) ironically recalls not only the stereotypical hopes – here reversed – that death will 'delay' in legal inscriptions (e.g., *Urk.* I, 162 l.12), but also the king's command to 'delay' the peasant from completing his case which sets the whole ironic plot in motion (B1 109; Parkinson 2000b). The paradox of his being denied what he seeks is more complex for him than for the thirsty man or the child. Having been given nothing and threatened with death when he demanded justice, he is now even denied the death. In his sixth petition similar images of food and water referred to the arrival of Maat (B1 273–4, 277–8). Here, however, they are turned from expressing the desirability of life to reflect his desire for death, which he now associates with Maat. This highly patterned paradox encapsulates the paradox of the situation underlying all the petitions, which also evokes images of extreme suffering in order to touch the audience. The pathos and sympathy evoked by such passages are crucial in shaping the reading of the tale.

Any analysis of literary form is inevitably reductive, but should be attempted in order to acknowledge the emotional impact of style, metrics and genre to model the social role of such discourse. An aesthetic response is evoked in many high cultural products and is not exclusive to literature (e.g., M. Müller 1998); nevertheless, it is a characterizing feature of the way in which the poems were staged and how they present themselves, and is integral to their social role and significance.

In a late 18th Dynasty graffito, a child's feeding expresses the sweetness of a god's name (Gardiner 1928: pl. 5 l.13).

[15] *ntf-mt* has often been mistranslated 'such is death' (e.g., Gardiner 1923: 21), but this requires 'death' to be the predicate (i.e., **mt-pw* or **ntf-pw mt*), so it is probably a participial statement (or possibly a statement of possession).

7
The cultural themes of literature

7.1 THE THEMATIC RANGE

> According to his powers, each may give;
> Only on varied diet can we live.
> The pious fable and the dirty story
> Share in the total literary glory.
>
> W. H. Auden, *Letter to Lord Byron* iii (1991: 98)

Literature was integral to the Egyptian stream of tradition and discourse about central cultural values, especially Maat – justice, truth, order, right (J. Assmann 1989b, 1990). As with many central values, there was an absence of explicit 'theological' or 'philosophical' statements about Maat itself, but while it remained an underlying concern of official discourse, it is particularly explicit and prominent in many literary texts, where it is expressed in a complex and often questioning manner. The high seriousness of subject matter and exploration of its problematic aspects that is distinctive for Middle Kingdom literature is not present in all literary texts, which include a variety of themes as well as of styles and linguistic registers. Genres such as teachings were closer to the ideological formulation of values, while others were more ideologically peripheral in their concerns (J. Assmann 1990: 40–51). This spread corresponds to a hierarchy of 'high' and 'low' registers of literary tradition, with central cultural themes corresponding to high linguistic and stylistic registers. Higher and lower registers accord with the hierarchy of decorum, the diverse experiences of high- and low-ranking characters, and their movements between centre and periphery. The poems, however, are varied and each contains higher and lower positionings, and their ranking in registers may be counter-intuitive for modern readers: the apparently simple *The Shipwrecked Sailor* is a darkly questioning theodicy (e.g., Baines 1990a; Loprieno 1991a). The diversity is attested primarily in low and high tales; such diversity may be in part a feature of that genre, but the phenomenon is relevant to other genres, including wisdom texts: *The Teaching of Khety* shows a variety in audience and tone within the most canonical genre (**10.6**), while *The Maxims of P. Ramesseum II* reveal a formal diversity

(**6.2**). The chances of preservation may favour a vision of a bipolar opposition of high and low literary traditions, but in fact this range forms a continuum. This range is attested not only between but also within genres, suggesting that variety of expression is a fundamental part of Egyptian literature.

7.2 THEODICY: THE GREAT ARGUMENT

> That to the highth of this great Argument
> I may assert Eternal Providence
> and justifie the wayes of God to men.
>
> Milton, *Paradise Lost* (1667), I ll.24–6

Many literary works formulate how the absolute ideal of Maat is enacted in the imperfections of life. Maat is wide-ranging, including the world order established at creation and the social order as a microcosm of the created cosmos (cf. J. Assmann 1990; 1991: 259–87). The king as the ultimate social authority had a cosmic role (e.g., J. Assmann 1970: 58–65), an aspect that was asserted by Senwosret I at the start of the 12th Dynasty (Franke 1996: 294). The social realization of Maat relied on royal and official personal action. Maat was, however, not merely the actual social order of the created world, but a generative principle. On both a cosmic and social level, however, Maat was faced with perpetual opposition from human dissent in society and from cosmic forces. Jan Assmann (e.g., 1990: 201–22) has used the terms 'negative cosmology' and 'negative anthropology', in which the creation and maintenance of order is a struggle against 'a constant counterforce or gravitation towards standstill and disintegration' (1989a: 63–6). Order is thus required to be continually imposed and sustained by god and his deputy the king, whom he appointed, according to 'The King as Sunpriest' treatise,

> for judging men, for making the gods content,
> for creating Maat, for destroying Evil (*jsft*). (J. Assmann 1970: 88)

Implicit in this characterization is an awareness of the imperfection of existence (J. Assmann 1994a; alternative view: Lichtheim 1992: 45–7; see Frandsen 2000: 9–12). This awareness is formulated in narrative terms in the myth of a golden age, a version of which is narrated in the royal funerary *Book of the Heavenly Cow* (Hornung 1997; Guilhou 1989) from the late 18th Dynasty. The text centres around the preparation of a funerary icon of a cow (vv 166–201), but also explains how the present state of the world came about through humanity's rebellion (vv 1–100), formulating what Erik Hornung terms 'an aetiology of imperfection'.

The rebellion of humanity results in the separation of the sky and earth, the withdrawal of the creator god, and the sundered world. The separation is generally presented as a positive and early phase of creation in the Coffin Texts (Bickel 1994: 176–98), although the Coffin Texts also refer to the angry withdrawal of the creator god (*CT* V, 151a), and related ideas about the past as a golden age can be traced back to the 4th Dynasty (Baines 1989; cf. Otto 1969). The rebellion of humanity is alluded to in *The Teaching of Merikare* (46h–i, 47i; Bickel 1994: 218, 227; cf. Bickel 1994: 225–8), although some scholars interpret this as referring to a primordial rebellion among divine beings (e.g., Lorton 1993a: 139–40; Meeks and Favard-Meeks 1996: 22–7). The initial rebellion of humanity is the archetype of all social dissent, and provides the aetiology of all later conflicts: 'slaughtering (šʿt) among men' (v. 139) exists since the just 'slaughtered' the rebels against the creator god (vv 133–9).

Official discourse presents the elite and the state as without dissent in itself. All disorder is allied with external forces, as in the Tod inscription of Senwosret I, where rebels within Egypt are associated with foreigners and the 'outsider' (cf. Franke 1994: 166–7 n.10). The source of internal dissent is distanced from the state itself by placing it within individuals whose nature is fundamentally negative: 'malcontents' are literally 'those scheming(?) of heart'. While such a cosmology legitimizes the state's action by allying rebellion with cosmic forces of chaos which require regulation at all costs, it also articulates a distinction between the ideal world and the actual state.

Theodicy is a concern of Middle Kingdom written culture (e.g., Otto 1951; Barta 1974a, 1990; Herrmann 1977; J. Assmann 1984a: 198–221; Sitzler 1995; Blumenthal 1996a: 114–16). The most explicit declaration of the creator god's justice is that of Coffin Text spell 1130 (*CT* VII, 461–71; Hermsen 1991: 227–34; Sitzler 1995: 3–19; translation: Parkinson 1991a: 32–4). The earliest coffins with the 'Book of the Two Ways', of which this spell forms the conclusion, date to the late 11th Dynasty.[1] The spell, which is a speech by the creator, may represent a funerary adaptation of another document, since it has an unusually reflective tone (Otto 1977: 17), and its formulation as a deity's speech may suggest an origin in cult ritual (J. Assmann 1975b, esp. 427 no. 20; Otto 1977: 2–4). It is highly intertextual, drawing on formulae from funerary biographies – non-divine first person speeches – and implying that the creator is to be judged by

---

[1] B6C, B1Bo (Willems 1988: 70–4), attested from el-Bersha and the western Delta (Silverman 1988, 1990, 1996: 133–7; Hoffmeier 1996: 49–50).

the standards of human ethics. His own heart is thematized in the opening speech, where he voices his benevolence by repeating

> the four good deeds
> that my own heart made for me
> within the serpent's coils, for love of silencing Evil. (*sgr-jsft*). (*CT* VII, 462b–c)

The third of his 'good deeds' is an absolute denial of responsibility for evil, alluding to the rebellion of humanity, although the opposition of humanity is stated in general, ahistorical terms:

> I have made every man like his fellow;
> I did not ordain them to do Evil (*jsft*); it was their own hearts which
>   destroyed that which I pronounced. (*CT* VII, 464a–b)

The order 'pronounced' by the creator evokes the ideas of creation through utterance and also of speech as embodying Maat. The human heart caused the divine to withdraw from the world, resulting in god's being 'hidden', an aspect that is alluded to in the spell by naming the speaker as 'He whose Names are Hidden'. This aspect is foregrounded in literary texts. In *Merikare*

> Generation passes generation of humanity,
> while god, who knows their character, has hidden himself. (43a–b)

and in *Sasobek*

> The counsels of god are hidden. (B1.11)

The withdrawal of the creator god's presence and manifestations articulates the imperfect state of the world in literary and official discourse. Thus, in the early 12th Dynasty inscriptions of Sarenput I, god's withdrawal is a sign of the imperfect state of the chapel of the saint Heqaib, which is a result of human inability to be dutiful. The ruined chapel

> was not planned for eternity;
> its work was like what an outsider makes
> who does not think of eternal things that last. (Franke 1994: 154–5, 166–7)

The king and his deputies act as intermediaries, but as part of the sundered world they realize Maat in the world only to a limited extent. The issue of the king's divinity permeates much discourse about royalty (e.g., Loprieno 1996c; in preparation).

Absolute Maat is thus an ideal that is manifested imperfectly in the present sundered world. Gerhard Fecht has termed this tension the 'relativization' of Maat (1975: 642). It is often implied in official discourse, but is explicit in such literary works as *The Eloquent Peasant*, where an official is eulogized as 'the greatest of the great', as in biographies (J. M. A. Janssen 1946: 16 [R.25]; Fischer 1985: 16–17 [716a–b]), while the relativity of this greatness is elaborately expounded:

> Whose great ones have one greater!
> whose rich, one richer! (B1 120–1)

This formulation parallels the later eulogy of the divine 'Lord of Truth (*mꜣꜥt*)'

> whose truth has truth! (B1 335; Fecht 1975: 641; Parkinson 1988: 288–9)

Later in the petitions, the human embodiment of greatness is compromised by the negative qualities of his heart:

> A selfish (*lit.* grasping-of-heart) great one is not great! (B1 196)

The relativization of qualities is expressed in a positive sense in *The Teaching for Kagemni* in an injunction against greed:

> A cup of water quenches thirst.
> A mouthful of herbs makes the heart firm.
> A good thing (*nfrt*) serves for (*jdn*) goodness (*bw-nfr*).
> A few little things serve for greatness. (1.5–6)

Although the passage is positive, it remains distinct from the more absolute bipolar presentations of official discourse. The idea of 'serving for' or 'deputizing' (*jdn*) runs through treatments of authority and responsibility for Maat, as where the king in *The Eloquent Peasant* deputizes to Rensi, who commissions further deputies to deal with the peasant (B1 109–18).

While partial embodiments can 'serve for' ideals, a distinction is drawn between, for example, the ideal of 'goodness' and a good man:

> The goodness (*nfrt*) of the good man (*nfr*) is good (*nfr*) beyond him.
> (*Eloquent Peasant* B1 337; Parkinson 1988: 288–9; cf. Fecht 1975: 641–2)

Ideal virtue can thus be debased in a hypocritical manner, as in *Ipuur*:

> O, but [Maat] is throughout the land in its very name,
> but what they do while founded (*grg*) on it is Evil (*jsft*).　　　(5.3–4)

These verses play on the usually positive connotation of *grg* 'to found, to establish' (e.g., Blumenthal 1970: 176–7 [E1.18–21]; *Merikare* 17b), and also evokes the homonymous *grg* 'falsehood' (Coulon 1999: 109–10). A similar statement occurs in *Khakheperreseneb*:

> everyone is founded (*grg*) on crookedness,
> and honest speech is abandoned.　　　(vso 5)

The world of eulogistic official discourse is acknowledged as being idealized or restricted, often in time. In a 10th Dynasty inscription of the nomarch Khety II of Asyut, contemporaneous with the historical king Merikare, his world is a limited kingdom surrounded by disorder, in which there is no 'strife' (*ꜥḥꜣ*: Griffith 1889: pl. 13 [Siut IV] ll.31–4; Franke 1990: 123), recalling descriptions of the ideal first creation and Otherworld. References to the 'first occasion' (e.g., Vernus 1995a: 36–9) can imply the subsequent rebellion, while the Otherworld is described in idealized terms, although both this world and the Other are parts of a single cosmos (J. Assmann 1990: 196–8). In the sundered cosmos, absolute Maat is suprasocial and otherworldly. In a Coffin Text spell, the deceased claims:

> I will be caused to ascend to the place in which Maat is.　　(*CT* III, 143f–144a)

In the mid-18th Dynasty biography of the Vizier Rekhmire, the tomb is 'the town of Maat, the city of Igeret (the necropolis)' (*Urk.* IV, 1085 l.1), while a Ramessid harpist's song extols the 'land of eternity' as 'righteous and just', elevated from all 'disturbance' and rebellion (Hari 1985: pl. 4, 1st song ll.4–5). In the Late Egyptian *Story of Horus and Seth* the idea is formulated more negatively, when Osiris claims that misdeeds have made Maat sink into the Otherworld (15.4).

In *The Teaching of Ptahhotep*, although the supremacy of Maat is asserted unambiguously, it is significantly associated with the god of the dead:

> (Maat) is undisturbed since the Time of Osiris.[2]　　　(89 [P])

In the sundered cosmos, the dead are empowered beings and intermediaries between humanity and the gods (e.g., Baines 1991a: 147–61) and death is as an interface of actual and ideal. The existence of death can

---

[2] Burkard 1977: 11; cf. Bickel 1994: 175.

justify suffering in this world by allowing the promise that all will be made good after death. The world of the dead is synonymous with perfection and the divine, so that 'remembering the West', the realm of the dead, is an idiom for virtue and duty to the gods (*CT* VII, 18x–y; Mathieu 1991). The fourth deed of the creator god in Coffin Text spell 1130 describes humanity's awareness of death as intended to inspire respect for the gods:

> I made that their hearts should refrain from forgetting the West
> for love of their making offerings to the gods of the nomes.
>
> (*CT* VII, 464d–e)

Maat is the standard by which humanity is judged after death, when unjust suffering will be made good, and in *The Eloquent Peasant* (B1 338–41) Maat is able to guarantee a man's survival and will 'descend with him into the necropolis'.[3] This passage follows an injunction to embody the ideal and the description of the relativization of goodness quoted above, and such goodness is contrasted with the absolute ideal:

> But Maat is for eternity (*nḥḥ*). (B1 338)[4]

Maat can transcend the state and society, and perhaps the cosmos. Just as Maat survives an individual's death, as in *Ptahhotep*'s assertion that 'When the end comes, Maat endures' (97), so Maat in this reading continues as 'eternal', though this need not mean beyond the eventual end of the created cosmos (see J. Assmann 1975a: 23–5). An allusion to this cataclysm (see Bickel 1994: 228–31) is made in Coffin Text spell 1130, when the creator declares:

> I have made millions of years
> between me and that Weary-hearted one, the son of Geb (= Osiris);
> then I shall dwell with him in one place. (*CT* VII, 467e–468b)

A more explicit presentation of the theme occurs in the 18th Dynasty Book of the Dead spell 175,[5] which enacts an explanation of the theodic problem of death, to enable the dead man to 'not die again'. The spell opens with a lament of the creator Atum to Thoth about the tumult caused by his creatures ('What is this which happens with the Children of

---

[3] As in *Ptahhotep*, 'a man will last when he uses Truth aright' (338–40).
[4] Elsewhere in the poem, 'eternity ' is the beyond (B1 126, 178). On 'eternity' see J. Assmann 1975a.
[5] Hornung 1979: 365–71, 517–18; T. G. Allen 1974: 183–5. The spell is attested by the reign of Amenhotep III: Hornung 1997: 92. See also Otto 1962: 252–3; Bickel 1994: 229 n.13. The text is cited after the Papyrus of Ani, frame 29 (Budge 1913: pl. 29).

Nut?': l. 2). There follows a dialogue between Atum and Osiris, who asks about his state in the Otherworld 'What is this?' (l.10). As part of his justification, Atum describes how life after death is not simply deprivation, paralleling statements in the Coffin Texts (spell 184) that the gods have given the dead 'blessedness instead of sex'.[6] Atum recounts how Horus is enthroned and Osiris has been provided with a 'lifetime of millions (of years)' (l.16). To demonstrate 'how good is that which I have done for Osiris' (l.19), he describes how he will eventually

> destroy everything I have made.
> This land will return into Primeval waters (Nun),
> into the Boundless waters, like its original state.
> I am the one who will remain with Osiris,
> having made my form as another serpent
> unknown to humanity, unseen by the gods. (ll.17–19)

The creator survives in his primordial state, as does time, since these two gods are 'today and tomorrow' (Coffin Text spell 335: *CT* IV, 192a–193c). The continuity of Maat is perhaps implicit since it is an attribute of the creator. The survival of Maat seems to be alluded to more directly in *The Shipwrecked Sailor* in the form of the serpent's daughter, who survives a cataclysm with him (see **7.3**).

The ideal of Maat is sited in the distant past or in the Otherworld, while the actual of this world and more recent human history is partial and imperfect. This dichotomy permeates Middle Kingdom discourse, and questions the creator's justice in allowing this state to come about. Suffering and imperfection are universals of human experience, and theodicy is a general category of religious thought (e.g., Berger 1973: 60–87; Crenshaw 1983). As Clifford Geertz (1973: 100–8) notes, the theodic problem of suffering can be phrased more generally as the problem of meaning. Theodic discourse is common to Egyptian and Mesopotamian texts.[7] Any theodic justification of god entails considering the social order in relation to the divine, since statements about divine justice towards man are necessarily made through the medium of social reality and many theodic resolutions involve either an assimilation of divine and human action or an embodiment of divine will through human agency (e.g.,

---

[6] *CT* III, 82d–83a; cf. Otto 1962: 250–1; Baines 1990a: 66.
[7] J. Assmann 1984a: 198–200; Baines 1991a: 161–4; Sitzler 1995; compare R. J. Williams 1983. According to Giorgio Buccellati, the treatment of the theodic problem in Mesopotamian wisdom texts can be analysed in broad terms as 'the ultimate validity of the absolute, both in the divine . . . and in the human . . . sphere' (1981: 36), and is focused on human fallibility rather than divine justice (cf. von Soden 1965; Schmid 1966: 131–41). In Egypt, by contrast, the gods, especially the creator, remain the central reference point.

Miller 1982: 138; Brueggemann 1985). The theodic answer – that humanity's rebellion, rather than god's will, caused imperfection – articulates the social aspect, presenting dissent in terms of rebellion against a king.

Theodic themes can be related in part to writing's role as state apparatus. Similarly, in early modern English literature there is an alignment between the comparable Christian concept of the 'fall' and the coercive state (Sinfield 1992: 167). Such a socio-functionalist reading accords with negative characterization of humanity but not fully with that of the cosmos. Humanity, and not the creator and his deputies, is answerable for the sundered world, but the creator remains responsible for the nature of man. Humanity's hearts create disorder, but their origin is 'tears of my (the creator's) Eye' (*CT* VII, 465a), evoking a more primeval dissent (Bickel 1994: 93–4) and suggesting that imperfection already existed before humanity could create it. Erik Hornung takes the concept of negative cosmology back further than the beginning of the sundered world, by suggesting that 'the Egyptian gods are unable to transcend the boundary of the existent' (1982: 212). The gods' nature does not remove from them the responsibility to oppose evil even though it is pre-existent (cf. also Westendorf 1986a: 473–4 n.2), and the ontology that Hornung detects (1982: 143–96) is itself a response to the problem of evil's existence, in which the theodic problem is primarily one of a lack of divine response to negative forces.

There is no theodic questioning in Middle Kingdom official discourse. The Coffin Text spell presents a divine answer, asserting the creator's benevolence not in response to complaint or questioning, while the setting only implies a moment of opposition in the solar cycle, since the speech is uttered 'before those who silence the storm (*nšn*), at the sailing of the entourage' (*CT* VII, 461d–e). A passage in the Ramessid P. Chester Beatty IV suggests that such questioning was considered inappropriate:

> May you not question (*ndnd*) god; god loves not one who approaches him, since he is one into whose dealings one should not pry.
> (vso 5.1–2, after Gardiner 1935a: 42)

More restricted injunctions not to question divine oracles occur in other Late Egyptian works such as *The Teaching of Ani* (B20.12–14; Quack 1994: 108–9), and *Amenemope* (21.13–14; Grumach 1972: 134–9). The latter also warns against 'destroying the plans of the gods' (21.14), setting the questioning of god's justice in the same context as the chaos-ridden land of the laments, where 'the plans of the gods are thrown into tumult' (*Khakheperreseneb* rto 11).

The complaint-and-answer character of theodicy is particularly suited to the form of a dispute (cf. Herrmann 1977: 260), and theodic themes are most fully articulated in the discourse and dialogue genres, although the narratives often embody the issue of divine justice through anomic experiences, and the teachings assert Maat by guiding the audience through pragmatic problems of social behaviour. The decorum of Middle Kingdom poems allows the complaint to god to be voiced, so that theodicy is among possible, even alternative, explanations of meaning. The unusual nature of the Coffin Text theodicy is significant here: although it precedes the emergence of written fictional literature, it draws on the same intertext. Its concise absolute statements of the creator god's intentions contrast with the elaborate and oblique literary presentation of the same issues, where the 'counsels of god' remain 'hidden'.

7.3 THE LOW TRADITION

> he wolde never ete
> Upon such a dere day – er hym devised were
> Of som aventurus thing – an uncouthe tale
> Of some main mervayle.
>
> *Sir Gawayne and the Grene Knight* (c. 1375), ll.91–4

While theodicy is a central theme at the highest levels of literary expression, literary texts also express less elevated themes. The themes are not mutually exclusive: all are integral to literature's decorum. The clearest examples of the range of literary expression are in tales. The differences between *Cheops' Court* and *The Shipwrecked Sailor* parallel the general variation between Middle Kingdom and the Ramessid Period narratives, and some scholars (e.g., J. Assmann 1996a: 307–10) have suggested that the two groups belong to distinct and consecutive traditions of discourse that are 'functionally' different. In place of this diachronic model, I present a synchronic reading, identifying such diversity within the Middle Kingdom practice of literary entertainment in terms of intertext and technique.

The poems that articulate the theodic theme, such as *Sinuhe* and *The Shipwrecked Sailor*, are structurally symmetrical on all levels from individual verses to the structure of major divisions, and are concentrically patterned, like some official inscriptions (e.g., Franke 1996: 285). They tend to be thematically unified and coherent, and avoid the Late Middle Egyptianisms that permeate less culturally high compositions. *Cheops' Court*, by contrast, is more episodic and has a more repetitive style of narration; its linguistic register is lower. The intertext also varies: the higher tales incorporate other, more prestigious genres, such as the pessimistic discourses included in *The Eloquent Peasant*, and the biography and liturgical lyric in *Sinuhe*; *Cheops' Court* is stylistically more bound to the narrative genre.

Allusions to esoteric knowledge place the audience of both higher and lower traditions within the elite, but are mobilizing differently. In *The Shipwrecked Sailor*, allusions establish the serpent as a metaphor for the creator (Baines 1990a: 62–3, 65–7), and include a reference to the 74 forms of the Sungod which are listed in the New Kingdom funerary *Litany of Re* (Hornung 1975–6), Maat as the daughter of the creator (whom the serpent 'carried away in foresight' [128–9] from a fatal cataclysm: Derchain-Urtel 1974), and the myth of the end of the world as recorded in the Book of the Dead. In the last of these, the Sungod appears as 'a serpent (*ḥ f3w*) unknown to humanity' (Budge 1913: pl. 29 l.19), while the tale's serpent is like a god who is 'in a far land, unknown to humanity' (147–8). The description of the island's bounty and its disappearance also show close similarities to the cosmos, although the motif may also recall that of the otherworldly Field of Reeds (Baines 1990a: 67). These allusions were probably very esoteric in the Middle Kingdom, since the *Litany of Re* is an 18th Dynasty composition that is only found in very restricted contexts (Hornung 1975–6: 9–20, 23); its source material is unlikely to have been more widely accessible in the 12th Dynasty. *Cheops' Court* mobilizes esoteric information, including the royal birth cycle (9.21–11.3; see, e.g., Blumenthal 1999 with refs.), which is again known only from New Kingdom royal sources, but whose existence in Middle Kingdom iconography is suggested by a reference to a 'birth shrine' in the Annals of Amenemhat II (H. Altenmüller 1996). Thus, esoteric information was available to the author and audience of this tale, but it is mobilized in an apparent mood of parody. Its esoteric character is more directly presented than in the subtle allusions of *The Shipwrecked Sailor*. For example, Cheops has been continually seeking 'the number of the Chambers of the sanctuary of Thoth' (9.2) which he is eventually informed are accessible only:

> in a casket,
> of flint, in a room,
> called Sipti, in Heliopolis.   (9.4–5)

The 'number of the Chambers' has proved a crux (e.g., Gardiner 1925). Erik Hornung (1974) has connected the 'chambers' with a passage in the Coffin Texts and identified them as 'shrines', but his linking of the two passages is unconvincing.[8] In the Coffin Texts, enigmatic 'caskets' are

---

[8] The word *jpwt* in a caption over a diagram of the 'field of the gods' (spell 652: *CT* VI, 273i) simply refers to the following 'inventory' of the features of the field, rather than 'chambers'.

connected with the Sungod, as is flint, a fiery stone;[9] the name Sipti means 'investigation', and may denote a room of 'inventories' (*sjpt*) such as occur in King Neferhotep I's inscription where a 'great inventory' or 'investigation' is made (Helck 1983: 21 l.7), but it may also allude to the 'investigation' of the soul after death. The information is not fully mobilized in the subsequent narrative, but merely initiates the next episode, since it is accessible only to the as yet unborn High Priest of Memphis (9.11–12). It probably did not feature again in the tale, remaining as inaccessible to the ancient audience as to the modern scholar. The chambers exist not to generate meaning, but simply to be mysterious, and they may be completely fictional.[10] A sign of the scenario's fictionality may be the ideologically implausible assumption that a temple room should be inaccessible to the king.

The stagings of entertainment in the two traditions are also distinct. *Cheops' Court* is patterned after monumental Royal Tales, and continually frustrates the expectations of the genre, as *Neferti* does (**5.2**). In both the tone is less grandiose and formal than that of, for example, the Building Inscription of Senwosret I (cf. Blumenthal 1982: 18–19): in *Neferti* King Sneferu refers to his courtiers as 'mates' (*rhw*: cf. Posener 1956: 30) and to the relatively lowly Neferti as his 'friend'. Nevertheless the Royal Tale is mobilized differently with regard to King Sneferu in *Cheops' Court* and in the prologue to *Neferti*. In the former his boredom is stated more bluntly than in *Neferti*, where it is merely implicit in his desire for entertainment (compare 4.22–5.1 with 1f–m), and it is dispelled with diverse effects in the two poems. In *Cheops' Court* the king views fantastic 'prodigies which happen' (e.g., 4.18), while in *Neferti* the king is instructed to behold future events, and 'what happens' (3a) is problematic and deeply significant.

The 'perfect (*nfr*) speech', that is 'perfect to the heart' (see **4.5**) embodies a full range of meaning that includes ethical goodness, aesthetic beauty, and anything attractive and enjoyable; the low and high traditions draw on this range variously. The general atmosphere of *Cheops' Court* is relaxed, not ethically charged, and the avowed aim is to provide 'relief'. *Cheops' Court* includes such subject matter as voyeurism in the marsh landscape, adultery, and 'having a good time (*hrw-nfr*)' that is in part sexual. *Cheops' Court*'s treatment of such good times contrast with that of *Neferti*, where the king is entertained with a description of how

---

[9] For caskets see Borghouts 1975; for the relevant associations of 'flint' see Midant-Reynes 1981: 40–3. For shrines of flint see Hornung 1974: 34.

[10] The interior of the royal pyramid, for which Cheops apparently intends to make the like of the Chambers (7.6–8), is an archetypally hidden place (as in *Ipuur*'s reference to 'what the pyramid hid': 7.2), yet the Chambers are inaccessible even to the pyramid's builder.

Destroyed indeed are those things of goodness – the fishpools,
which were full of people gutting fish,
which overflowed full of fish and fowl.
All goodness has fled . . . (7a–c)

The marsh landscape here is a source of basic sustenance and cultural significance, and not just entertainment, while 'goodness' has ethical overtones as well as describing happy pursuits. Instead of the high tradition's theodic concern with the relationship of god and humanity, kings and gods in *Cheops' Court* are actors in creating events rather than as subjects analysed through narrative. Similarly, magic features not as an ethical force to 'ward off the blow of what may happen' (*Merikare* 47g), but principally as a means of creating a prodigious tale. The prominence and direct presentation of human sexual desire and fulfilment recalls less formal registers of visual art, as against the more discreet coding in more formal contexts (e.g., Derchain 1975, 1976; Robins 1996; cf. Patanè 1989). In high register poems, sexual acts are generally fraught with ethical and social significance and choice, as in *The Teaching of Ptahhotep* (e.g., 277–97, 325–38). In *Cheops' Court*, however, sex is presented inconsequentially as 'holiday', even when it has fatal consequences for the adulterous protagonists, as it is in the Late Egyptian stories and love-songs.

Cheops' Court, which probably dates to the mid-13th Dynasty, is the main evidence for the full diversity of literary texts. Linguistic and other differences between it and such high tales as *The Shipwrecked Sailor* can be related to their dates: the manuscripts, and possibly their dates of composition, are at least 200 years apart. Despite the later date of the tale such diversity is likely to be synchronic as well as diachronic, just as a variety of registers is to be expected in the language and material culture at any one given period. Writing is itself often a differentiating criterion in a culture, creating a dichotomy between high (literate/written) and low (non-literate/oral) culture (e.g., Goody 1987: 161–4; **3.2.1**). Many features of the style of *Cheops' Court* are attested in earlier compositions, and linguistic features of the lower tradition occur in less formal early Middle Kingdom texts, gradually penetrating more formal writings (e.g., Junge 1984b). *The Eloquent Peasant* (perhaps reign of Senwosret II) has an episodically structured narrative section like *Cheops' Court* rather than *The Shipwrecked Sailor*, although like the latter it belongs to a high tradition and its stylistic simplicity is studied. The narrative prologue of *Neferti* (probably reign of Amenemhat I) recalls the style of *Cheops' Court*, albeit to different effect. These narratives use an established style of tale-telling to contrast inconsequential events and ethical wisdom discourse. The opening formula in *Neferti*, 'Now there was once a time when . . .' (1a), is characteristic of later low Middle Kingdom tales, and occurs in literarized 18th Dynasty monumental inscriptions and Late Egyptian tales (cf. L. Morenz 1996: 111–12). All these high poems presuppose the contemporaneous existence of a lower tradition of narratives that is directly attested later in *Cheops' Court*.

Such a lower tradition could be exclusively oral. *Cheops' Court* has increased the number of 'folktale' motifs which are presented at face value, rather than subtly adapted as in *The Eloquent Peasant* or *The Shipwrecked Sailor* (Parkinson 1992: 168–9; Baines 1990a: 57–8). Oral influence could thus have permeated written literature increasingly as the dynasty progressed, with the lower tradition developing in independent written form only towards the end of the Middle Kingdom. Although the written tradition may have been moved closer to oral poetics, a direct oral influence is perhaps unlikely. Evidence of a low written tradition contemporaneous with the high tradition is provided by fragmentary manuscripts of tales, often overlooked in analysis. Many of these are problematic in dating, or are too fragmentary for their register to be assessed. Thus, *The Tale of the Herdsman*, from a mid-12th Dynasty manuscript, includes the folktale-like motif of a herdsman and a goddess. The language, however, is formal and the motif of the lowly pastoral wise man is well attested in the high tradition (Parkinson 1996a: 148–9). The tale draws on esoteric texts of limited accessibility, including a water-spell also known from a single attestation in the Coffin Texts, and the incident of the predatory goddess in the form of a 'woman' with long hair may allude to another spell (154) which mentions how the Sungod 'set a snare against him (an enemy) as a woman with braids (*st-ḥmt ḥnsktt*)' (*CT* II, 282a; L. Morenz 1996: 133). The tale thus implies familiarity with religious texts, although the water-spell might have been accessible to herdsmen (Ritner 1993: 207 n.956, 229–30; L. Morenz 1996: 132 n.566). The tale itself seems to belong to the high tradition.

Tales apparently belonging to the low tradition include *The Tale of Neferkare and Sasenet*, which cannot be dated precisely, but contains incidents that are suggestive of a humorous parody of religious texts (van Dijk 1994; Parkinson 1995: 72). The tale also contains an ironic treatment of an unwelcome speaker being brought to perform before a king, an incident that is almost a parody of the royal reception of other littérateurs. The fragmentary late 12th Dynasty manuscript of *The Tale of P. Lythgoe* is from the Residence's cemetery, and seems compatible in style with *Cheops' Court*, including episodes of making 'holiday' (rto 6–7), physical violence (vso 5–7), and a narrative formula describing the passage of time (vso 9–10). The roughly contemporaneous *Tale of Hay* from el-Lahun also includes dramatic and violent events. *The Cairo Mythological Tale* on a late 12th Dynasty papyrus contains an episode between the creator god(?) and the divine council. The style seems similar to *Cheops' Court*, and one of the god's commands gets the reply:

This is not what is done, sovereign . . . (7)

This contradiction recalls Djedi's reply to Cheops (8.16–17). From el-Lahun comes a small but coherent fragment of *Horus and Seth*, probably of the mid-12th Dynasty, and thus among the earlier literary manuscripts. The narrative style is repetitive like *The Shipwrecked Sailor* or *Cheops' Court*, and is linguistically perhaps closer to the former. The tone in which the preserved incident is narrated is paralleled in the Late Egyptian Story of *Horus and Seth* (Broze 1996), where the god Seth tries to seduce Horus in order to discredit him. Both versions describe sexual activity in detail. The chat-up line of Seth – 'How fair is thy backside' (X+2.1) – probably parodies the ritual greeting 'How fair is thy face!' (Parkinson 1995: 70). The wordplay between 'backside' (*phwj*) and '(sexual) strength' (*phtj*) is inconsequential apart from providing Horus with a neatly phrased excuse to refuse, rather than the aetiology common in mythic narratives included in magical spells. The fragment is thus allied by various features with the lower tradition of *Cheops' Court*. The manuscript of *Horus and Seth* is probably only a century later than the composition of *Sinuhe*, showing that the high and low traditions were contemporaneous by this date, if not before.

The diversity of literature could result from social changes, as elite practice extended into the lower classes, rather than being an integral part of literary practice. Plastic arts show a range of styles belonging to the spheres of the central court and local centres, diachronically and synchronically (e.g., Bourriau 1988; Franke 1994: 105–17 on Elephantine). Nothing, however, suggests radically different social contexts for literary compositions, or suggests that *Cheops' Court* represents a rejection of official language in favour of unofficial language in the evolution of a new self-consciously 'proletarian' form of literature (Loprieno 1996e: 522). The fictional court context of the literary production in *Cheops' Court* is the same as that of the high works of *Neferti*, *Kagemni* or *The Eloquent Peasant*. The provenanced *Tale of Horus and Seth* does not derive from a radically different social context from that proposed for other works: it derives from a medium-sized house at el-Lahun containing the vestige of an official archive. Both context and date argue against Jan Assmann's view that 'entertainment' in Middle Kingdom literature is restricted to the ritual context of propitiating the king (1996b: 78–81), and against earlier scholars' assumption that anything that seemed 'low' and 'vulgar' to a modern reader must have been composed for 'fellaheen' (Gardiner 1931: 11; Lefebvre 1949: 72).

One can hardly propose a 'two world' model to explain the range of Middle Kingdom literature, with a low tradition similar to the medieval world of carnival analysed by Mikhail Bakhtin (see, e.g., Rose 1993: 125–70). The lower tradition has many carnivalesque features, such as a tendency to 'turn its subject into flesh' (quoted Rose 1993: 167), but it is not a simple inversion of the higher tradition; rather they are parts of a single continuum. The 'vulgarity' of *Cheops' Court* lies in its appeal not to the lower classes, but to the inconsequentialities of everyday life, as against the concerns of official life, often evoking humour through incongruity. While *Horus and Seth* could be a local composition (see **4.2**), it is unlikely that all the low works were merely local productions from the geographical periphery, since *Neferkare and Sasenet* was transmitted over many centuries, and *The Teaching of Khety*, which is allied with the low tradition, was part of the central canon in the Ramessid Period.

The more prominent role of women and sexuality in the lower tales is perhaps suggestive of a more 'domestic' context, as opposed to a 'courtly' setting dominated by male office-holders; Egyptian discourse acknowledges a distinction between the 'front rooms' and the 'back rooms' of the palace (*Merikare* 15g). In contrast, the concerns of the '"intimate" sphere of family and household' (Eagleton 1984: 115–56) are in general very subdued in the higher registers of literature. Nevertheless, the written transmission of the texts allies them all with the male world of officialdom. The low and high poems could arise in the same general social context, but for less and more stately or official occasions, governed by broader and narrower decorum as suited to the audience's mood, like the different fictional audiences in *Cheops' Court* or *Neferti*. The 'holiday' (*hrw–nfr*) that is a common motif in Middle Kingdom literature, and integral to its cultural function, can range from ritual acts to adulterous sex. This diversity in literature parallels not only social decorum, but also the registers of speech from official diction to something close to 'sermo quotidianus' that were available to an individual in different contexts, as is attested in letters of different degrees of formality from the early 12th Dynasty priest Heqanakht (J. P. Allen 1994: 11; see also Vernus 1996a; on later Egyptian: Goldwasser 1999).

Both the high and low traditions have similar cultural roles. Both are potentially subversive, one through its pessimistic other voices, and the other through its humour. Laughter is mentioned in Egyptian discourse as a sign of rejoicing, as when the Nile rises (*Nileflood Hymn* 3.7–8), and is integral to ideology (Guglielmi 1980: 69–86; L. Morenz 1999b). Inappropriate laughter, however, is subversive in *Neferti*, where 'one laughs aloud at death' (9b) in the chaos-ridden land. *The Teaching of a Man* enjoins 'Do not laugh' in inappropriate circumstances (14.1), while *Ptahhotep* advises that one should laugh only when (the great) laugh.   (131; L2 only)[11]

Laughter at kings and gods can be disruptive, since it can be directed negatively at its targets, but it can also be empathetic, just as parody is with textual targets. Biographies sometimes envisage inclusive humour, as when the tomb-owner proclaims himself not only to have a 'smiling face' (J. M. A. Janssen 1946: 92 [Cp. 1–3]) but also to be a cause of laughter for both inferiors and fellow officials (J. M. A. Janssen 1946: 93 [Cp. 4–5]). How far laughter was satiric and aggressive is difficult to assess, as with later visual humour (J. Assmann 1993; Parkinson 1999a: 171), but this is a problem in interpreting much humour (Guglielmi 1979). Humour and high seriousness are neither opposed, nor mutually exclusive, categories (e.g., Wilson Knight 1930): elements of humour are present in *The Eloquent Peasant* and serious ones in *Cheops' Court*. Although the lower tradition is less highly decorous, it is not necessarily more countercultural; the frivolity of such texts may negate their humour's power to articulate dissent by rendering its message 'light upon the heart', a quality eschewed in official discourse (see further **5.2**). While royalty is presented in a less respectful fashion than in high texts, the fantastic and inconsequential staging means that this will hardly impact on the audience's perceptions of the state.

The influence of the lower tradition on literary production seems to have increased with time. The next period, the early New Kingdom, was one of literary transition, seemingly dominated by official commemorative texts, while older literary texts were largely recopied, and few new ones were composed. Official discourse became highly literized, with compositions modelled on fictional literary classics; for example the biography of an 18th Dynasty High Priest of Amun is phrased as a teaching (*Urk.* IV, 1408 1.8–1411 1.16; Gardiner 1910; Gnirs 1996: 209). By the Ramessid Period, new literary texts were composed (Baines 1996a; see **9.5.2** on the absence of some Middle Kingdom genres). At the same time, new genres seem to have entered the transmitted canon, including performance genres such as lyrics, which have been preserved from the Middle Kingdom only when inscribed in tomb scenes; among such new genres are love-songs (Mathieu 1996a). More proletarian narratives were composed in the more colloquial Late Egyptian (e.g., A. Assmann 1983; Hollis 1990). The emergence of the low tradition as dominant in Late Egyptian literature does not embody a hitherto unrecorded subculture of laughter emerging into written culture, nor the creation of literature as a new aesthetic free space for entertainment (e.g., J. Assmann 1996a: 307–10), but rather

---

[11] The textual tradition of the New Kingdom ms L2 is already attested in the 12th Dynasty ms L1 (lost at this point).

represents a privileging of an existing strand of literary discourse. The lower Middle Kingdom tales were more or less direct models for the Late Egyptian Stories, while *The Teaching of Khety* is a model for some of the Late Egyptian Miscellanies (Guglielmi 1994; **10.6**). The Miscellanies are anthologies of a group of central and canonical texts that occur in apprentice manuscripts from different parts of the country, but with local and personal variations in the selection from the repertory (e.g., Quirke 1996b: 382–3; McDowell 1999: 130–1); some are closely contemporaneous with the composition of some of the included texts. Their creation seems to be more closely associated with advanced educational contexts than the Middle Kingdom poems were. Their production and the usage of the classical texts in education may relate to an increased importance for institutionalized education in the scribal profession. The comparative frequency of texts with a more open transmission in later periods (Quack 1994: 19–21) probably reflects a later ascendency of the lower registers of literary decorum as represented by *Khety* and *The Maxims of P. Ramesseum II* (**6.2**): monostichic arrangement, as in *P. Ramesseum II*, occurs in wisdom texts from the Ramessid Period on (see Lichtheim 1983: 1–12). The Miscellanies' selections also include lyric and religious genres that lay outside the Middle Kingdom literary range, although several types, such as eulogies and hymns, descriptions of professions and localities, recall motifs included in *The Sporting King* and *Fishing and Fowling* (**9.5.1**). At the same time, the higher register of teachings also acted as a model for renewed literary production in the later New Kingdom. The temporal progression from high seriousness to something once considered more peripheral can be paralleled, for example, in English literature, where in the evolution of epic and romance things of high seriousness become 'fabulous', and romance appears as the 'diaspora of ritual' (cf. Conrad 1985: 18).

While texts in the higher tradition were canonized to be copied and/or quoted, the lower tradition survived and acted in part as productive models for new literary compositions.[12] This bifurcation of roles for Middle Kingdom texts is part of the literary diglossia of the Ramessid Period between ancient and modern writers (Loprieno 1996e: 522–3). Much of the low tradition was not used in education (**3.2.2**): humorous works are everywhere underprivileged in academic discourse and in the critical formation of literary canons, and early Egyptologists were surprised to read the 'futilités' of the Late Egyptian *Tale of the Two Brothers* (Maspero 1911: v).

---

[12] Mathieu (1999: 38–9) even argues for a transmission of *Cheops' Court* into the Greco-Roman Period.

PART THREE

Readings

8
Tales

8.1 HIGH AND LOW NARRATIVES

> That is not the whole story, but that is the way with stories . . . It's a way of explaining the universe while leaving the universe unexplained.
>
> J. Winterson, *Oranges Are Not the Only Fruit* (1985), 'Deuteronomy'

A small group of fully preserved high register tales are the best known and studied poems and hence can be analysed in greater depth than is possible than for other texts. Both *Sinuhe* and *The Eloquent Peasant* seem to have been central to the surviving Middle Kingdom canon, being preserved in four manuscripts each from the period. Two of these finds group them together, and these tales are not only related by genre, but can also be regarded as thematically complementary: Sinuhe presents himself as an innocent wrongdoer, while the peasant proclaims himself an innocent sufferer. Although a narrative mode cannot address intellectual themes as abstractly as discourses can, neither of these two tales is a simple relation of events. Their emplotment also reveals that the sequence of events is subordinate to other concerns and generates faultlines. *The Tale of King Cheops' Court* and that of *The Shipwrecked Sailor* are relatively complete unitary compositions[1] that have the superficial appearance of simple folktales, different from the rhetorical elaboration of varied styles in the other tales. The contrast of these two from the same social context allow one to chart the range of literary entertainment in terms of response (outlined in **7.3**).

8.2 *THE TALE OF SINUHE*: THE SEARCH FOR A VOICE

> Ce qui compte est ce qui ne figurera pas dans les biographies officielles, ce qu'on n'inscrit pas sur les tombes.
>
> Marguerite Yourcenar, *Mémoires d'Hadrien* (1982: 500)

---

[1] For *Cheops' Court* as a unitary composition, rather than an 'anthology of folktales', see Goedicke 1992b: 23–4.

Sinuhe is one of the few Middle Kingdom compositions to have had a significant modern reception, although this is largely due to its coincidental resemblances with the Biblical narration of the exodus, the modern *Bildungsroman*, and travel novels (see further **11.3**). Its self-conscious concern with distinctively Egyptian practices and institutions (including concerns such as the king, the country's borders, funerary practices and language) have increased its appeal to modern readers. The wide-ranging narrative is tightly structured: rubrics preserved in Ramessid manuscripts divide the text into 40 stanzas, which can be grouped in a fivefold structure (J. Assmann 1983b) presenting a concentric pattern of passage and return (Baines 1982). Sinuhe's passage through the course of his narrated life is marked in terms of geography, motif and genre.

The tale is introduced as a tomb biography, presenting it as an idealized narration of past experience. The opening titulary includes the fictional title of 'Governor of the Domains of the Sovereign in the Lands of the Asiatics' (R 1; Blumenthal 1995: 887; Moers 2001: 70 n.230), which is an official resumé of the stay abroad which is about to be narrated. In terms of narrative analysis, the ostensible genre provides the 'story', an idealized sequence of events, but the emplotment imbues them with a potentially very different significance. The eventual closure implicit in the start is opened out and rendered ambiguous by what follows: from the beginning there is a potential tension between the story and the emplotment, and they run increasingly counter to each other. The start presents the biography as a work from the past. This genre implies that Sinuhe addresses the audience from an Egyptian tomb, and the opening of the tale thus contains the answer to any questions which the narrative might subsequently provoke as to whether the protagonist returns to Egypt. In his self-introduction Sinuhe associates himself with Queen Nefru, who is set in relation to two generations of kings and their pyramid temples (R 3–5);[2] these locations begin the narration *sub specie aeternitatis*, an impression heightened by her epithet 'lady of blessedness' (cf. J. Assmann 1984d: 695; Doxey 1998: 94–102). Sinuhe begins his speech by describing himself as 'a follower who followed his lord' (R 2–3), a formulaic assertion that will sound increasingly ironic as the narrative develops, although it is ultimately reaffirmed.

The narrative style includes the 'annalistic infinitive', characteristic of a commemorative inscription, such as were left by expedition leaders, and a genre close to the biography.[3] After the calm and elevated opening of the biography, however, the audience is increasingly confronted with a

---

[2] For these locations see Gomaà 1987: 41–4; H. Altenmüller 1992: 37.
[3] Spalinger (1998: 315–26) argues unconvincingly that it gives the effect of journal jottings. Cf. Baines 1987: 58–9.

complex shattering of the expectations derived from the genre. The central sections of the tale provide a varied multiplicity of genres, beyond those normally included in biographies. Throughout the tale, the biographical style occurs sporadically, as if an attempt was being made to reassert it. However, these attempts fail, just as Sinuhe's attempts to fashion a meaningful life abroad fail[4] until the end of the poem when generically anomic features vanish, and the tale concludes as it began. The generic tension enacts the tensions of Sinuhe's life.

What breaks the pattern of the biography is the characterization of the protagonist, as displayed in his 'flight' (wʿrt: Parant 1982: 34, 11–38) which is the semantic cause of the formal complexity of the poem. The suddenness of this event has startled the modern reader, as is witnessed in the Egyptological concern with the so-called 'riddle' of the flight, which has made Sinuhe the Hamlet of ancient Egyptian literature (e.g., Wessetzky 1963; Goedicke 1984b; Tobin 1995; Obsomer 1999). Sinuhe relates how in a moment he moved from being in attendance on the king,[5] to lurking between two bushes, a position that occurs elsewhere in literary texts as the hiding place of thieves (*Ipuur* 5.11–12). Sinuhe himself experiences this transformation as startling: throughout the poem there is a repeated searching for a rational explanation for this event.

Despite the author's presentation of the flight as problematic, many critics have sought a single rational motivation (cf. Spalinger 1998: 312). For example, it has been assumed that the narrative covertly alludes to an alarming 'conspiracy' among rival princes which the prince Senwosret later overcomes, and the text has been emended to support this reading.[6] However, the passage is coherent as it stands:[7] the messengers from the court meet Senwosret to tell him of the old king's death, and he immediately leaves for the palace 'without informing his expedition'. Subsequently a message is sent to 'the (other) royal children who were / accompanying him' and 'one (i.e., the new king, Senwosret) summoned one of them', implicitly to aid him. Sinuhe then narrates:

Now, when I was standing (on duty)
I heard his[8] voice as he spoke,

---

[4] For example, the inclusion of a royal letter is a well-attested biographical motif from the Old Kingdom (e.g., Eichler 1991), but it is followed by a reply, which is atypical.
[5] For a literalistic assessment of Sinuhe's possible rank see Obsomer 1999: 239–41.
[6] Initially Gardiner 1916: 13, without emendation; text emended by Koch 1990: 11a n.11a, after W. V. Davies 1975: 45; see Foster 1982: 82–3.
[7] Shirun-Grumach 1984. Other commentaries not already mentioned include: Parant 1982: 1–10; Foster 1982: 82–3; Théodoridès 1984: 84–7.
[8] 'His' might refer to 'one of them' (Gardiner 1916: 13), but it more probably refers to 'one', the king speaking through his messenger (Shirun-Grumach 1984).

as I was in the near distance.⁹
My heart was distraught, and my arms spread out ...   (R 19–26, B 1–3)

The overheard communication of the unexpected death of Amenemhat I to the royal children is the cause of Sinuhe's flight. The death is initially narrated in *Sinuhe* in the annalistic style of official discourse, as a calm, divine, cosmically harmonious event – the natural setting of the king in his 'horizon' (R 6) – although it produced 'grief' in human hearts (R 8–11).¹⁰ This objective narration will have contrasted with the elite audience's knowledge that he was assassinated – perhaps derived from *The Teaching of Amenemhat* rather than from general knowledge – and the dichotomy between official discourse and knowledge is opened out when the 'people's grief' is re-enacted in Sinuhe's more intense personal reaction.

Other rationalizations that implicate Sinuhe in the death have also been proposed.¹¹ The presentation of the circumstances in *Amenemhat* (9a) suggests that the attack was believed to have originated in the women's quarters of the palace, and this is implicitly part of the overheard communiqué. Since Sinuhe introduced himself as a 'servant of the Royal Chambers (*jpt*)' (R 3), and his office was related to Queen Nefru (Obsomer 1999: 240–1), the audience could consider that he might have reason to feel threatened: he would lose his mistress if she also had been attacked or if she were implicated in the plot (Posener 1956: 68; Obsomer 1999: 230–1). Later he states that he had not been accused of anything before fleeing, and that he 'was not high-of-back previously' (B 230), which is possibly an allusive denial of involvement in the assassination (Parant 1982: 101–3). Likewise, the new king is later eager to assure him that Nefru is alive and still in power (B 185–7). However, if these allusions to the origin of the assassination imply the possibility of a rational personal fear, this is a 'reason' that is raised only to be dismissed, further problematizing Sinuhe's motivation.

The modern reader is perhaps tempted to go further and suspect that Sinuhe's narration is disingenuous, that he knew more about the assassination than he says. However, his account of overhearing the conversation was probably not as self-consciously mysterious to the original audience as

---

⁹ This is a necessary statement (pace Colin 1995: 204) since he overhears the secret news, and to allow this he must be suitably placed unseen, but hearing – 'in the near distance'. For the emendation 'in the vicinity of a *conspiracy*' see n.6.
¹⁰ The narrative is not anomic in generic terms: an allusion to the death of a king – either Amenemhat I or Senwosret I – occurs in the opening lines of the biography of Samonth (e.g., Obsomer 1995: 539–42, no. 32). On royal deaths see Blumenthal 1970: 53–5 (A8).
¹¹ The suggestion that it was death for an official to hear of a king's death is a superfluous rationalization for his fearful reaction (e.g., Gardiner 1916: 13–14); this reading fails to account for the new king's subsequent incomprehension of his motivation.

it has seemed to some modern readers (e.g., Tobin 1995). Sinuhe signals the only significant juncture at which he speaks in 'half-truths' to the audience (B 37). The reader's temptation is due not to an intention of the author, but to modern expectations of psychological complexity and unified presentation (**6.4**).[12]

Sinuhe's narration enacts a theme implicit in contemporary biographies, that a man's character determines his career (Doxey 1998: 29–79); the heart is elsewhere presented as determining humanity's state, making character a theodic issue. By comparison with the self-descriptions in non-fictional biographies, Sinuhe is not marked by explicit descriptions of ethical characteristics, while the narrative instead shares his immediate experiences with the audience. This is often done in a present tense with soliloquies, making him an empathetic everyman. The use of an autobiographical narration prevents any detached comment by the author, and the tale, which continually returns to the problems of speaking, conversing and of expression, instead provides a 'portrait of a voice' (in Yourcenar's phrase: 1982: 527): the narration of events creates a distinctive voice, beyond the norms of official discourse, and a self-fashioning process rather than the self-eulogy typical of biographies. Sinuhe's expected character as an ideal 'follower' is undermined and challenged by the emplotment of his life, raising questions of the nature of social and individual identity; the choice of biography as a framing genre embodies and shapes these concerns as does the poem's concern with Egyptianness. It is unlikely that these questions are specifically part of an intellectual crisis of the early 12th Dynasty, and they are probably general cultural concerns. The nature of Sinuhe's identity (as Egyptian or outsider) and his ethical character provides a continual 'game' for the audience, rendering the poem in part a playful exercise in character assessment, which was an important skill in official social life. Modern (mis)readings of his characterization show the extent to which character-assessment is opened out in the poem.

If characterization cannot be judged by modern conventions, different conventions do not imply less aesthetic complexity. In literature, as in life, actions often lack an explicit rational explanation,[13] as Lionel Trilling remarked: 'certain kinds of unmotivated events in fiction represent what happens in life. Life is not only a matter of logic and motivation but of chance' (1942: 56). The uncertainty of life is articulated in the discourse

---

[12] The idea that Sinuhe flees because of a hidden inner life, never vouchsafed to the reader, is developed in Tobin's reading of the tale as a modern 'who-done-it' mystery novel (1995). Such psychological readings are relevant to characters in (post)-Freudian modern novels – such as Charlotte Bartlett in E. M. Forster's *A Room with a View* (1908) – but can be inappropriate strategies for a different genre.

[13] In Henry James's *The Turn of the Screw* ambiguity fissures readers' responses (Hawthorn 1996: 201–25), and in *A Passage to India*, the key event is left problematic as a 'trick' (E. M. Forster in a letter of 1924: Stallybrass 1979: 26).

genre – often in contradictory statements such as in *Sasobek* (Bi.10, quoted on p. 104) – and arguably underlies the emplotment in *Sinuhe*. The protagonist initially describes his flight in terms of blind panic: the allusiveness of his narration of the message heightens the unspeakable import of the affair. His description of his reaction is intensely physical, evoking a bodily disintegration that is reminiscent of the dispersion of the body feared in the funerary texts (cf. Meskell 1999: 119–22). His heart is not a fixed certain entity as in most biographies (see **5.2**), and the great Egyptian emphasis on bodily wholeness means that the dispersal of his body – 'my arms spread out' (B 2) – casts his identity into doubt. This motif of bodily dissolution runs throughout the poem. He describes his flight as inspired by his personal fear of a chaotic of interregnum:

> expecting strife to arise;
> I did not think to live after him (Amenemhat I). (B 7)

Such panic would not have surprised the original elite audience, for whom the unexpected death of a king was of immediate significance. Allusions to 'strife' in the Tod inscription of Senwosret I (l.29) show that such expectations were well founded (Obsomer 1999: 265–6). A passage in the much later *Teaching of Amenemope* suggests that the ancient interpretive community envisaged flight without obvious rational motivation more easily than do some modern critics:

> Do not cry 'wrong!' against a man, when the circumstances (*sḫrw*) of (his) flight (*wꜥr*) are hidden.
> (11.6–7; Blumenthal 1998b: 231)

The flight is presented in broad terms. It embraces elements of geographical confusion, as the direction of his flight across the Nile is determined by a 'rudderless barge' (B 15), rather than being planned. Elsewhere the rudder is used as a metaphor for government,[14] and as Sinuhe's position is lost, his social role is reversed (B 10–11) in an incident that recalls the inversions of social roles in the discourses. The resonant place-names mentioned here create a sense of an Egyptian abandoning his cultural identity: Sinuhe, 'The Son of the Sycomore', flees past the sanctuary of the sycomore (B 9: see Parkinson 1999f: 44 n.9; for the flight see Obsomer 1999: 243, 245).

The frequent allusions to night time in this passage create a sense of

---

[14] E.g., *The Eloquent Peasant* B 157–8; general discussion: Herrmann 1954. The direction of the wind is also infelicitous, to judge by a Coffin Text spell for 'not crossing to the east' (*CT* VI, 144a–46f): Moers 2001: 254–5 in general.

disorder as an external force: the messengers reached the new king 'at night-time' (R 20), and another incident on the flight – possibly including the crossing of the Nile – happens at 'supper-time' (B 11–12). These geographical and cosmological references suggest that the ultimate *primum mobile* of the tale can be traced beyond Sinuhe to Amenemhat's death, which is presented in cosmological terms in *Amenemhat*. This cosmological aspect is also mobilized later when Sinuhe's period away is later described as 'like the state of a dream' (B 224–5) – an extended episode of night-time chaos (see further **11.2**).

In the later dialogue between Sinuhe and his foreign patron Amunenshi, ruler of Retjenu Sinuhe is asked for the first time to justify his presence abroad, and is questioned about the state of Egypt. He replies that

'it is not known how this (the death of Amenemhat) happened'.[15]
But I spoke in untruth.[16] (B 37)

This reverses the claims of veracity of official discourse, such as the Semna stela where there king declares 'there is no untruth in this' (Sethe 1928a: 84 l.9; **5.1.2**). This is an 'untruth', since the message he overheard implicitly included such information. The aside creates a bond of complicity between Sinuhe and the audience against Amunenshi. What follows is a largely truthful account, except for the detail that 'it was reported to me' (B 38). The death was not 'reported' to Sinuhe, but overheard (see Lichtheim 1973: 234 n.5; Théodoridès 1984: 97); Sinuhe's retelling at this point seems designed in part to increase his importance in Amunenshi's eyes. The heart is here described as the source of the flight (as in B 202, 229: Parant 1982: 129–37), and as a force separate from him. The following verses, however, offer another alternative formulation of the motive:

I do not know what brought me to this country – it is like a plan (*sḫr*) of god.
(B 42–3)

The phrase alludes to the imperfect state of the sundered cosmos in which 'the plans of god are hidden' (*Sasobek* Bi.11). The descriptions distance the cause of the flight from Sinuhe – it was not him, but his heart, or an unknown force (cf. Parant 1982: 137) – and the flight is always alluded to in circumlocutions: the narration never uses the verb 'flee' (*wʿr*) directly of Sinuhe (Parant 1982: 27). This formulation presents the flight as a dilemma

---

[15] The phrase recalls *Ipuur* 2.3, where it is said of the land's social chaos: 'We know not what has happened through the land'.
[16] Gardiner 1916: 24–9, who rendered: 'but then I said falsely' (26 n.1); contra Barns 1952: 5 n.23. For *jwms* see, e.g., Parant 1982: 41; Théodoridès 1984: 95–6.

of human responsibility – when he acted irrationally, was his heart or god responsible? – and thus represents the flight as a theodic problem: how could the gods be so unjust as to lead a worthy follower astray, or allow him unintentionally to lead himself astray (see further Blumenthal 1998b; Spalinger 1998: 333–4)? The 'plans (*sḫrw*) of god' are usually synonymous with order, and neglect of them is a sign of chaos (as in *Khakheperreseneb* rto 11); but here the 'plan' is an ambivalent force.

The staging of the conversation between Sinuhe and Amunenshi signals to the theodic aspect: Amunenshi refers to the state of Egypt 'without that excellent god' (B 44), and elsewhere the state of the land 'without' god is an embodiment of the theodic problem. The fact that Sinuhe talks about the events in Egypt with an Asiatic may itself be a sign of such a state: in *Ipuur* the sage laments:

> what has happened to (the land) through this (chaos) – causing the Asiatics to
>   know the state of the land! (15.1)

This troubling conversation opens out the implications of the act of flight, turning the narration of unmeditated impulsive action into a questioning of character and destiny. It is followed by Sinuhe's eulogy of Senwosret I, which reaffirms the state's power in the face of Asiatic questioning in standard terms for the actual Egyptian audience. Although this section returns the poem to the world of official discourse, as well as having the apparent aim of encouraging Amunenshi's loyalty to Egypt (B 73–5), the context abroad subverts its character. The eulogy addresses both the state of interregnum referred to by Amunenshi and the latter's status as a ruler of lands the king subjugates, but it is also relevant to Sinuhe's unauthorized movement out of Egypt, since he asserts that 'coming and going (into Egypt) are at his (the king's) order. It is he who smites countries' (B 49–50). The king's awesomeness recalls Sinuhe's fear: thus, the verse 'He is one who curbs the horn, weakens hands' (B 54) looks back to the physical infirmity of Sinuhe's panic (B 2–3). The king can

> destroy the fugitive;
> for the one who turns his back to him there is no end. (B 56–7)

The undertone of personal relevance renders the eulogy potentially ambivalent and enacts Sinuhe's own emotions. Even the third stanza affirming the king's grace in positive terms[17] is ironically relevant since this grace is described in the geographically specific terms of an Egyptian 'city' (B 66) and 'this land' of Egypt (B 70), which Sinuhe has left.

---

[17] For this motif in official discourse see Franke 1996: 281–2.

In his reply Amunenshi ironically remarks that while Egypt is 'happy' (*nfr*: B 76) as Sinuhe claimed (B 70), Sinuhe is 'here' with him. Philippe Derchain detects a ferocious tone (1985), but I consider that it is more gentle and humorous than fierce. This reply laconically expresses how inappropriate Sinuhe's language was for his interlocutor (cf. Eyre 1999: 238–9 on *Wenamun*) and opens up a gap between official ideological language and experience. It draws attention to the dichotomy between the eulogy and its speaker's voice, effectively undercutting the return to official discourse and preventing any closure. This response dismisses the propagandistic potential of such loyalistic discourse (B 73–5), reinforcing the ironic subversion within the speech itself. The whole conversation conveys a sense of meaning as residing in the subtext, producing an uncertain edgy and guarded quality to the exchange, provoking the audience to examine the motive and significance behind the words. The alternative state of happiness that Amunenshi has promised, in terms of Sinuhe's hearing 'the speech of Egypt' (B 31–2), is likewise rendered ironical by the dichotomy that has just been mobilized.

Amunenshi's promise is developed as his actions to ensure Sinuhe's happiness with him are narrated (B 77 ff.), concluding with a description of the 'happy (*nfr*) land', called Iaa (B 81).[18] Although this is an abundant paradise, described in similar terms to the island of *The Shipwrecked Sailor* (47–52), its un-Egyptian nature is indicated by there being 'milk in everything cooked' (B 91–2; Fischer 1976: 97–8), and by its liminal location 'on his boundary with another country' (B 80–1). The motif of boundary crossing in the poem (Moers 2001: 251–63) reverses the usual aim of official discourse, which is to protect or extend the boundaries of Egypt (Blumenthal 1970: 185–9 [E 2]). The country is a substitute for Egypt, just as the superficially Egyptianized Amunenshi is for Senwosret: the place and its ruler are correlatives for Sinuhe's uncertain status (cf. Loprieno 1988: 41–59, 83).

The central section of the poem describes Sinuhe's prosperity abroad in formulae drawn from funerary biographies, evoking a comparison with Egypt, as does the reference to the royal messengers of the Residence (B 94–5). The opening passage is a loyalistic biography but without the king, just as the previous speech was a loyalist eulogy spoken by a fugitive. These stylistically ironic sections embody the plot's central paradox of Sinuhe's status. At the formal centre of this section, and of the whole poem, the incident of Sinuhe's duel with a 'hero of Retjenu' embodies this paradox in action. The underlying thematic tension is made explicit in Sinuhe's axiomatic meditation before the event:

---

[18] See Görg 1987. The name might also recall, less auspiciously, the name of a negative divine being known from the Coffin Texts, Iaau (for whom see Frandsen 2000).

> There is no foreigner who allies with a Delta-man;
> what can establish the papyrus on the (foreign)-mountain? (B 121–3)

The 'hero' (*nḫt* B 109) of Retjenu is introduced as a figure from the ritual Execration Texts which enacted the overthrow of enemies (Fischer-Elfert 1996b): his presentation also parodies the 'hero'-treatment (*nḫt* B 51) of the king earlier extolled by Sinuhe. Conversely, the same epithets are used here of Sinuhe as were used by him of the king (48–9 and 106: 'excellent plans'); both conquer with a bow and arrow (ʿḥ₃: B 62–3, 138–9; cf. Obsomer 1999: 248–52). These allusions suggest that Sinuhe here proves himself a true hero, fulfilling a quasi-royal role (cf. Fecht 1984), ousting his rival.

Sinuhe's efficacy here contrasts with his initial weakness in fleeing, consciously heightening the tensions, and may redeem him in the eyes of the audience for his earlier flight. The quasi-royal nature of his military prowess is rendered ambivalent by the ironic context in which this motif was first expressed earlier in the poem. Also, is Sinuhe a 'bowman' like the king or a 'Bowman' meaning a 'barbarian' whom the king attacks (cf. B 63)? The allusion to the enemy as an 'execration figure' also potentially recalls Sinuhe's own status since such figures include disloyal Egyptians living abroad (e.g., Posener 1987a: 35–44, 55–6; possibly alluded to in *Sinuhe* B 33–4). Sinuhe is now himself a 'hero of Retjenu' so that the duel is a combat not only between two cultures but also between their competing claims on Sinuhe's identity. His victory is both over an aggressor and over himself.

The fluctuating quasi-dramatic nature of the characterization is presented by the duel being flanked by speeches and soliloquies (as opposed to biographical narrations of past events). Sinuhe's highly figurative self-reflective speech before the duel evokes the theodic aspect of his position, asserting divine control over events with a rhetorical question:

> Does god not know what he has fated? (B 126)

The successful outcome of the duel produces a soliloquy of dramatic exultation, including a self-assessment of his past actions:

> For god acted to be gracious to one with whom he was angry,
> whom he led astray to another country.[19]
> Today, is he not appeased?
> A fugitive flees for his surroundings;
> (but) my reputation is in the Residence . . . (B 147–50)

---

[19] Compare *A Man and His Ba* 11: 'my soul is leading me astray'.

This language implies a reproach to god, who feels 'anger' and 'leads astray' (Parant 1982: 143–58). Sinuhe's guilt or shame is assuaged and transferred to an external force (god), providing a sense of an inner identity that can be separated from his actions, which runs counter to the mobilization of actions and achievements in official biographies, when character is integral. The sequence of couplets (B 149–54) moves the text into a higher stylistic register. The antitheses allow Sinuhe to distance himself from the fugitive that he actually is, using the third person and present tense in the first verse of each couplet, and the first person in the second verse (Parant 1982: 28–30). The antitheses, however, recall the 'then-now' formulations of laments (Schenkel 1984; Westendorf 1986b), rendering this lyric of rejoicing intertextually ironic.

This joyful paean suddenly breaks down and the concise antithetical affirmations of prosperity give way to convoluted questioning clauses. The pattern of syntax here reverses the duel narrative where the syntax moves from complex clauses to simple as Sinuhe achieved his victory (B 134–41).

> Goodly is my house, wide my dwelling-place,
> and memory of me is in the palace.[20]
> Whatever god ordained this flight – be gracious,
> and bring me home (r-ẖnw)!
> Surely you will let me see the place where my heart stays! . . .   (B 155–8)

This passage ironically echoes the preceding assertion that god is pacified and mobilizes the language of personal piety to enact a realization by Sinuhe of himself and his situation (cf. Goedicke 1990). He expresses what he really desires, which has been unstated up to now, in such a manner as to suggest that he has not consciously realized it. This enactment of changing thoughts and emotions will have been quasi-dramatic in performance. His realization is achieved not only by his having faced death (J. Assmann 1996a: 159), but also by the stark confrontation of Egyptian and alien values in the duel; the mention of the king's 'palace' (B 154) triggers the change in tone, as if memory of the king has a transforming effect. The responsibility for his present situation, however, is now assigned to god and god's heart rather than Sinuhe's; the flight was fixed in advance (Parant 1982: 169–96). His heart has always been in Egypt, even though earlier it had 'carried' him off on 'the paths of flight' (B 39–40); his present prosperity is being 'afflicted' (B 161). In the next stanza Sinuhe's heart is 'weary' (B 170), a word suggestive of death: the human heart on its own is helpless and unstable. Such contrasts and reversals continually undermine the stability of discourse and character.

---

[20] Dramatically ambiguous: it could be 'my memory', i.e., my thoughts.

The final stanza of this section marks a sudden change, with a short and concise introduction to the arrival of the royal letter, which opens the next section, as an epistolary divine intervention. The letter's opening statements echo Sinuhe's wish that was privately articulated to the audience, suggesting the king's suprahuman perception of his subject's state (this capacity is later acclaimed as godlike; B 214–17). The king responds to Sinuhe's implied rebuke to god, telling him that his flight was 'the counsel of your own heart' (B 182–3), and his panic sprang from Sinuhe's heart not his:

> This idea (*sḫr*)[21] carried off your heart –
> was it in my heart against you?   (B 185)

As a representative of the divine, the king denies that he willed the flight. The letter then rehearses the funeral that embodies an eternal homecoming, and reunites his body with the earth of the homeland, transforming Sinuhe's night-time panic and disintegration in the flight into a night vigil (B 191) that will ensure his rebirth. Thus he will be 'saved from the west' (B 214). This motif is echoed in Sinuhe's response to the letter – as a gesture of abasement he scatters earth on himself in a minor union or 'landfall' that is also a gesture of mourning.

In reply, Sinuhe admits that it was his heart and not god that caused his panic:

> How can this be done for a servant
> whom his heart led astray to alien countries?   (B 202, in part recalling B 162)

He thus takes the responsibility on himself, while also abandoning himself into the hands of the king in his full panoply of cosmic divinity. The universal gods listed in the epistolary greetings have particular reference to foreign lands (Yoyotte 1964), as if formulating the king's world-wide influence, implying that there is no alternative reality 'altogether elsewhere', free from responsibilities or the problems of cultural identity.

His reply provides the fullest description of his 'flight' as inexplicable panic:

> I did not plan it, it was not in my heart;
> I did not conceive it, I know not what took me from my place;

---

[21] The 'idea' – a significantly vague term (Gardiner 1916: 66) – is either the thought of punishment referred to in the preceding verses or the idea of fear (Parant 1982: 60–8). The 'idea/plan' is not god's (as Sinuhe claimed in B 42–3) but Sinuhe's own.

> it was like the state of a dream, like a Delta-man seeing himself in
>   Elephantine,
> a man of the marshes in Upper Egypt; I had no cause to be afraid.
> No one ran after me; I heard no reproaches;
> my name was not heard in the herald's mouth;
> nevertheless, that trembling of my limbs – my feet hastening,
> my heart driving me,
> the god who ordained this flight dragging me away! (B 223–30)

This dream metaphor echoes the earlier landscape metaphor of the papyrus and the mountain (B 121–3); the 'state' recalls the earlier description of Amenemhat's death as 'the state that had happened in the Council Chamber' (R 18–19). The metaphor also echoes the language of dream interpretation manuals – attested later, but probably existing in the Middle Kingdom (Gardiner 1935a: 9) – providing an image of self-analysis. This intertextual allusion reflects Sinuhe's search for the meaning of his flight, by suggesting that his experiences are in need of interpretation (**11.2**). It also domesticates the flight in terms of Egyptian geography, as if internalizing the flight. Here the hitherto alternating agents of heart and god are brought together into a single explanation. The idea of the heart being a 'god within' may be alluded to, in order to prevent the paradox from becoming unsustainable (cf. Baines 1982: 40).

This ambiguous and paradoxical explanation is not prevarication but an accurate assessment in comparison with the initial narration of the flight, modifying the king's explanation as the 'counsel of your heart'. It was both Sinuhe and another, external force – it was his fault but not his intention. The rhetorical strategy of admitting a fault, regretting it, and thus in part justifying oneself recalls that of the royal protagonists in *Amenemhat* and *Merikare*, who recount similarly fatal errors.

The letter goes on to further neutralize the literal sense of his travels:

> Whether I am home (i.e., Egypt), whether I am in this place –
> it is you who veils this horizon of mine (B 232–3)

This description of the king's ability to control the light and dark evokes the language of burial and the image of the 'horizon' as the tomb (e.g., *Cheops' Court* 7.26, 7.8). It also implies that the individual has a 'horizon' separate from his physical placement, in either of the poem's two distinct worlds. The formal symmetry of letter and answer provides a sense of imminent closure, while the exchange between Sinuhe and Senwosret is more balanced than that between Sinuhe and Amunenshi, producing a sense of communication and reconciliation.

Sinuhe's subsequent geographical progress to the palace is described in a swift and continuous narration, with the division between the sections of stanzas occurring as Sinuhe reaches the boundary of Egypt (J. Assmann 1983b: 32, 38). Sinuhe's letter provided the king with political information about local rulers, but this is downplayed: the rulers that he specified in his letter become unnamed accompanying 'Asiatics' (B 245). This bringing of foreigners into Egypt restores the normal ideological pattern of boundary-crossing, in which they come to Egypt with 'tribute' (e.g., Kamrin 1999: 93–6). The progress finally halts with a description of Sinuhe prostrate before the enthroned king:

> unconscious of myself before him,
> while this god was addressing me in a friendly manner.
> I was like a man seized in the dusk,
> my soul faint, my limbs trembling,
> my heart not in my body.
> I did not know life from death. (B 253–6)

Modern readers who interpret Sinuhe's fear at this point as a sign of some secret guilt (e.g., Tobin 1995: 176) underestimate the awesomeness of such a context. Sinuhe's reaction is intertextually normal compared with that of the protagonist of *The Shipwrecked Sailor* before another god (67–76). His detailed self-description enacts a second panic and bodily disintegration and quasi-death on leaving Egypt (B 21–4),[22] with the statement about his heart echoing B 39–40 (Parant 1982: 129–35). The image of 'dusk' recalls the night-time associations of the flight, when his heart carried him off (death can 'seize': Zandee 1960: 85–7). Earlier, his heart and an unknown god 'dragged him away' (*sṯꜣ*: B 230), but here he has been 'ushered in' to the king (*sṯꜣ*: B 249, 251). The unknown god who ordained the flight is replaced with 'this god', the king who veils and unveils the horizon (B 232–3), and the darkness is dispelled. Sinuhe is surprised in the dusk not by the lack of, but by the presence of, a king.

The king's subsequent speech considerably distances the consequences of the flight from Sinuhe, describing Sinuhe as a victim of wrong rather than as a wrongdoer – 'flight has made its attack on you' – also declaring that Sinuhe has been 'acting against himself' (B 259), but without distancing him from the motivation or blame. Significantly the scene turns about Sinuhe's inability to find his voice when he is addressed (B 259–60). When he is asked why he 'does not speak though your name is pronounced' (B 259–60) his reply explicitly expresses this meeting's parallelism with the initial panic:

---

[22] E.g., in each episode he is 'raised up' (B 23 and 256–7: *ṯs*).

For it (my behaviour or silence) is not disrespect (*lit.* shortcoming) to god
  (i.e., you, the king),
but it is a terror, which is in my body,
like that which created the ordained flight.   (B 261–2; Barns 1952: 30–2)

The word 'ordained' externalizes the flight implicitly, but acknowledges that it was created and realized through his own fear, and the terror is here contrasted with any offence towards 'god'. Sinuhe's behaviour displays a resignation to the anomaly, but also an admittance and expression of responsibility 'in my body' (B 262).

The circumstances of the original terror are re-enacted with great symmetry, resulting in a sense of resonant closure: as in the first instance, royal children are summoned by Senwosret. Modern readers who find the arrival of the queen and princesses charming (e.g., Gardiner 1916: 164–5) trivialize its significance at least in part. Their shriek is a humorous touch, but it also voices the central question of identity and demonstrates how dramatically Sinuhe has changed physically. His earlier claims to have attained an Egyptian-like prosperity and possess white linen (B 153) are revealed as delusory here. He appears like a treacherous deserter such as the one described in the Ramessid *Satiric Letter* as having 'taken the form of an Asiatic' (P. Anastasi I 20.3–4).

The princesses enact a rite of rebirth (B 269–79) of a type known from tomb scenes and stelae,[23] in which Sinuhe is renamed as 'Northwind's Son', presumably evoking a practice of Asiatics adopting new names in Egypt.[24] The renaming expresses the paradox of a 'Bowman (i.e., barbarian) born in the Homeland (*tꜣ-mrj*)' (B 276), summarizing the poem's entire paradox. The transformation also evokes the concern of pessimistic literature with the invasion of Egypt by such Asiatics. The song renders the incident as almost an epiphany – lyric, erotic, and sacred (cf. Loprieno 1988: 95–6) – modulating the hitherto naturalistic mode.[25] The gods are suddenly present in person in the form of the king and the 'Lady of All', providing a sense of immediate reality against which the past exile is dismissed as a 'dream', elsewhere an image of fallibility of human life (see **11.2**). The geographical disunity of Egypt that Sinuhe used as an image of his confusion (B 225–6) is now reintegrated in the person of the crowned king of Upper and Lower Egypt (B 271–2). In terms of royal discourse, this scene, in which the king is 'embraced' (*ḥnm*: B 272) by the goddess

---

[23] E.g., Parkinson 1991a: 78–81; Franke 1994: 24 n.83; L. Morenz 1997b.
[24] Samehyt, instead of Sanehet (Sinuhe): B 276. Coincidentally, this is paralleled in the colonization of the New World: Columbus renamed himself and his king also rhetorically renamed him (Greenblatt 1991: 83).
[25] The discrepancy of the apparently ageless children detected by several critics underlines this (Purdy 1977: 117–18; Baines 1982: 44 n.52).

of the night sky, structurally balances the scene at the beginning where the old king was united (*ẖnm*: R 7) with the sun in death: in between royalty has been absent in person. The scene also balances the earlier eulogy to Senwosret, but is performed to a present king and is more intense in its allusions.[26]

In the song the princesses offer a final explanation of Sinuhe's flight:

> For fear of you he took flight,
> through dread of you he fled the land.   (B 277–8; Parant 1982: 249–62)

This echoes Amunenshi's earlier eulogistic statements about the king's fearfulness (B 45). In this formulation the panic – the symptom of chaos – is accommodated within the order of the court (Parant 1982: 261); the king is now the god who controls Sinuhe's life. In terms of specific details, however, this explanation differs slightly from Sinuhe's original account, in which fear of the interregnum – rather than of 'this god' – inspired the flight. The symmetry of emplotment induces awareness of this discrepancy, that is then swept away as the king responds more broadly:

> He shall not fear!
> He shall not gibber[27] for dread!   (B 279–80)

This resonant statement, which is a concluding climax to the princesses' *coup de théâtre*, moves the action forward by reassuring the fearful supplicant, but it also dismisses the tale's entire panic-driven plot and Sinuhe's narration, which the king earlier urged and enabled ('Raise him up and let him speak': B 256–7), as no more than incoherent gibbering. The two worlds of his experience remain irreconcilable, and later he is physically separated from the 'years' that he has narrated (B 290). The two aspects of the king – his fearfulness and his love – which were juxtaposed uneasily in Sinuhe's eulogy, are here fused into a predominantly benevolent whole (cf. Posener 1956: 103). The incident dismisses any idea of the unjust fearfulness of the royal or divine order.

Part of this incident's power derives from a sense of loss being made good: his loss of life at court is reciprocated in the princesses' loss of him, his gibbering by their cry, and an outsider placed at the centre in a scene of unity and reintegration. However, closure is resisted, and minor elements of the plot are unresolved: Sinuhe's new name establishes a tension between his name as given in the opening titles: which is now his

---

[26] Brunner 1955; Derchain 1970; Westendorf 1977a; Goedicke 1988a; L. Morenz 1997b.
[27] So Sander-Hansen 1957: 148–9; see Parant 1982: 286–9; Goedicke 1998a: 36 n.36. The word 'gibber' (*ꜥj*) occurs earlier with derogatory overtones describing the worried people of Retjenu: B 132.

true name? The punning new name, 'Northwind's Son' turns the allusion of his original name ('Sycomore's Son') to Hathor as the goddess of that tree into an allusion to her as goddess of the northwind ($s3$-nht > $s3$-$mḥ$ jjt) who presides at once over his rebirth as an Egyptian (through the queen) and over his travels in the north. The new name thus does not completely negate Sinuhe's experiences, even though the rebirth distances him from the preceding narrative.

Another faultline is the manner in which he abandons Iaa and his children (cf. Purdy 1977: 120). In his letter, he promises to leave them (B 234–5) – reversing the usual associations of 'handing over' offices to heirs after a successful life (B 234, 239) – in terms that suggest a conflict of emotion. The word used of the children – 'chicks' (B 235) – implies unusual tenderness.[28] Such hard losses may have thrown the significance of his return to Egypt into relief, but they also heighten the tensions. While the plurality of aspects are brought triumphantly within the patten of the whole, just as the disruptive events are, their continuing existence provides the composition's formal centre and thematic substance.

The final stanzas of the poem form a retreat from this climactic scene in the palace. The narrative moves Sinuhe from the palace to a royal house and finally to his tomb, in a sweep similar to that which brought him back to Egypt. His establishment in the beyond implies a wisdom that makes good his earlier misunderstandings and errors, as attested in the idea of the dead man as a sage (e.g., *A Man and His Ba* 145–6). He achieves physical unity and centrality 'in the midst of' (B 300–301) his culture and society: his tomb is centrally located, as opposed to his earlier position in the 'near distance' (B 2) or in another land; this is apparently to be imagined as one of the nine secondary pyramids in the outer enclosure of the king's pyramid at el-Lisht (see Dieter Arnold 1992: 19, 34). The description of his material prosperity recalls earlier descriptions of often fallacious material achievements, and concludes the motif of how an identity is embodied in material terms.

In formal terms, the description of the house- and tomb-building completes a generic progress back towards the biographical genre (compare the inscriptions in el-Bersha tomb 8 and that of Sarenput I).[29] Sinuhe's identity is now defined not by his unstable heart and character,

---

[28] $ṯ3t$; contra Gardiner, who emended to read 'viziership' (1916: 89); see Barns 1967: 12. The same metaphor of children as young birds occurs in, e.g., magic spells to protect children (e.g., Parkinson 1991a: 129–30). Gardiner suggested that a later phrase describing Sinuhe's eldest son (1916: 90, B 239) was of a lowly origin, and thus potentially dismissive, but this is unlikely given the use of the same phrase in B 242.

[29] (Griffith and Newberry 1895: pl. 21 ll.12–13; 2) see Obsomer 1995: 480, no. 3; Franke 1994: 192–203. See in general Doxey 1998: 36–7. The preceding description of the king's gift of food is also part of this generic movement: a similar description occurs in Sarenput I's biography: Franke 1994: 204.

but by the physicality of his rejuvenated body, here represented as a statue. His earlier physical decay of panic and loss of identity is made good not only by his regeneration (B 290–95), but also as his tomb 'image' with royal attributes in imperishable metal, like a divine image (B 307–8).[30] The statue is the focus of the funerary cult, of which the biography is also integral; the final verses, recounting Sinuhe's death ('landing' B 309–10), reaffirm the framing genre.

The audience is in a sense back where it started, listening to a tomb biography. In objective terms, Sinuhe has not changed (Baines 1982: 43); the convention of presenting the titles that one attains at the end of a career at the start of a biography further neutralizes any sense of simple transformation. Since his identity is also the artefact of his tomb and its biography, the description of the tomb becomes a correlative for a self-description of the poem's fashioning (ecphrasis: see, e.g., Barchiesi 1997), making it equivalent to the descriptions of reception at the end of many poems (such as *Neferti*: **9.1**). In the Ramessid 'Eulogy of Dead Writers', the tomb-chapel and pyramid are metaphors for the cultural endurance of the writers' texts, and this motif of a literary text as enduring monument is here presented literally. The monument's normal status as a symbol of ideology is transformed at the very end of the poem, since it is implicitly inscribed with the divergent record of his experiences. The verse in which Sinuhe describes his favours from the king as exceptional (B 309) signals this.[31]

The suffering Sinuhe experiences is mitigated not only by the conclusion which is implicit in the opening verses, but also by touches of humour, while the whole plot has an ironic edge in that the exile is self-imposed and mistaken. In line with official ideology, the problematic flight is justified by allusions to negative cosmology, as are the actions of Sinuhe's fallible heart. The tale has thus been read as an assertion of the king's power and a call to loyalism (e.g., Posener 1956; Obsomer 1999, esp. 266–8). Although the tale concludes with a rationalization of the flight, the various different explanations of which combine in the dramatic context, the plurality of explanations and voices forecloses a single overview. A multiplicity of hearts, and of their locations, produces a sense of continuous self-fashioning that is not limited by Sinuhe's location or rank, or even by his officially recognized 'character' and 'wisdom', which were known to Amunenshi (B 32–3). Sinuhe's physical struggles and his crossings of boundaries are complemented by his internal conflicts and

---

[30] A motif in *The Shipwrecked Sailor* and *Cheops' Court*: see, e.g., Aufrère 1991: 311–13. The questions raised by Sinuhe's identity exhibit analogies with those aroused by the Renaissance French case of Martin Guerre, the doubts about whose identity were resolved only by physical presence (cf. Greenblatt 1990: 131–45; Davis 1983).

[31] His self-description as a 'lowly man' (šwȝw) evokes descriptions of chaos and unrest, such as the Tod inscription of Senwosret I (l.29; see Barbotin and Clère 1991: 21 n.97).

crossing of more than geographical boundaries (Moers 2001: 251–63), providing a complex staging of the relationship between individual and society. In its concern with the motivation for an action, the tale is remarkably explicit about emotions and physical results, producing a sense of subjective personalities projecting their interpretations upon a single event. Gaps in the text are foregrounded and left for the reader to fill. Such unresolved questions do not concern the mechanics of the plot (e.g., Tobin 1995: 176–7), but address cultural issues on a broad basis. The tensions in the poem are, however, resolved on an emotional level, with the resonant account of Sinuhe's reintegration into Egyptian society, mobilizing the distinctive monumental aspects of Egyptian culture (cf. Baines and Lacovara 2002). The emplotment provides a sense of gaining or regaining something, of 'arriv(ing) where we started / and know(ing) the place for the first time' (Eliot 1959: 48). Nothing has happened, but everything has happened (just as the aria at the end of the *Goldberg Variations* (BWV 988) is the same as the opening aria, but does not sound the same after 30 variations).

The sympathy of the audience has been evoked by intimate descriptions of the very features that make Sinuhe culturally flawed, and the power of the closure depends on the three stylistically and formally marked emotional episodes in the poem that are sited at the moments of confusion: his panic, the duel and its aftermath, and his collapse before the king. The resolution of the last of these is staged significantly as a performative utterance before a courtly audience, evoking the poem's status as a literary recitation. The kaleidoscopic range of genres in the poem gives a sense that no domain of discourse is of restricted access to individual personality. The densely allusive texture, full of ironic self-echoes, heightens the tensions inherent in a search for meaning, and all forms of Egyptian discourse seem centred around the uncertain impulses of the reader's own heart: 'literature confronts people with themselves' (Iser 1989: 208). The tale's multiplicity of voices are all reported by Sinuhe himself; the central questioning of motivation, which generates doubt about the value of culture in character, is thus located not in voices such as Amunenshi's, but in Sinuhe's own soliloquies. The treatment of the biography genre seems designed to suggest the limitations of official discourse to present human experience: the formulaic phrases enclose the tumult of an individual's life, which in Virginia Woolf's phrase remains unbounded (*The Waves*: 1992: 199). In contrast to the framing genre, which normally advocates the values of self-control and silence, the emotional centres of the tale are those that voice emotional, physical and cultural uncertainty: 'Is it him in truth/Maat (*m-mꜣʿt*)?' (B267). The status of the individual's voice is rendered problematic. Sinuhe's voice utters not an official narration of events, but a struggle to find and define itself, to articulate:

what your humble servant was afraid to say –
it is like an unrepeatably great matter. (B 215–16)

8.3 *THE ELOQUENT PEASANT*: ELOQUENCE'S ANSWER

> Your tears have value if they make us gay;
> O *Happy Grief!* is all sad verse can say.
> W. H. Auden, *The Truest Poetry Is the Most Feigning* (1991: 620)

The overall structural pattern of *The Eloquent Peasant* is, like *Sinuhe*'s, centralizing, with a pattern of narrative introducing a series of discourses followed by a concluding narrative.[32] A narrative formula introduces the tale,[33] and each petition is then introduced by a narrative formula, not by a title as in *Sasobek* (A.17). As in *Sinuhe*, the relationship between the dominant and included genres is complex.

The protagonist is introduced as 'a peasant of the Wadi Natrun' (Gomaà 1987: 284–5) – socially and geographically on the edge of Egyptian culture.[34] His progress in the tale follows a geographical pattern towards the royal Residence, from the periphery to the centre. The action of the narrative is restricted to material theft on a petty scale: after the protagonist is robbed of his donkeys and exotic produce, he petitions Rensi, a deputy of the king, to reassert justice. In contrast, the petitions display a high level of rhetoric, and their motivation turns the plot from a simple sequence of events into something more elaborate and ironic. The profusion of the peasant's discourse is enforced by the fictional audience's admiration, which is presented to him as a neglect that is both the motivation and the subject of his petitions. Through literary expression and generic structure, the petitions go beyond the fate of the individual protagonist (e.g., Herrmann 1977: 265; Brunner 1986a: 24) and address the question of theodicy. The resolution, however, is subtle and indirect.

The avoidance of all extraordinary circumstances in the narrative initially encourages the audience to understand it without reference to any framework other than that immediately provided: such a reading is also supported by such 'naturalistic' details as the description of the path where the peasant is robbed (B1 24–7). Like the magical 'potent image' which the villain Nemtinakht wished for in his villainy, but did not have

---

[32] Fully referenced discussion of these issues: Parkinson 2000b.
[33] Fecht 1975: 37; cf. *Neferti* 13a; *Tale of Nefer*[. . .] 1; *Urk.* IV, 1089 l.7; Vernus 1978: 115–19, 138–9.
[34] The 'peasant' is not a farmer, but his designation *sḫtj* defies exact translation (Fecht 1975: 638). For an alternative identification of the location see Devauchelle 1995.

(B1 23), the numinous is often alluded to, but remains absent from the action. The incident on which the plot turns is plausible enough, and the theft of donkeys may have been commonplace in villagers' lives; a Ptolemaic document describes a complaint which parallels the peasant's situation (Turner and Cockle 1982).

The principal value which the peasant affirms in the discourses is Maat (cf. J. Assmann 1990: 58–91). Maat is enjoined and its efficacy is described in gnomic statements, as are the results of its presence and absence (e.g., 'Look, Maat flees . . .', B1 128–9). The eulogistic sections allude similarly to Maat as the basis for the ideal official they acclaim. His articulation of Maat draws on cosmic, social and ethical aspects, progressively emphasizing their interrelationship. The peasant's first evocation of Maat's power moves from the context of speaking into a navigational image with personal and potentially social overtones (B1 85–6; pp. 123–4).

The second petition emphasizes the cosmic aspect in its opening invocation (B1 121–2) and the social in a lament with less cosmic associations (B1 128–39). Throughout the petition, the absence of Maat is presented in almost purely social terms. The third petition's opening eulogy returns to a cosmic level, acclaiming Rensi as 'Sungod, lord of heaven, with your entourage' (B1 171–2), and in the first direct description of Maat unites the social and the cosmic aspects in the image of air:

'Doing Maat is breath of the nose' (B1 177)

Maat is here juxtaposed with 'eternity' (B1 177) and with the divine, implying a suprasocial aspect. Rensi's personal responsibility for Maat is also foregrounded, and is contrasted with his role in an evil society. This responsibility is mobilized in the second half of the petition when Rensi is denounced in sharp contrast to the opening.

The fourth petition continues this presentation, but emphasizes the personal psychological level. After the fifth petition's condensed statement of the tale's social aspect, the sixth petition alludes to the universal and cosmic, where 'creating Maat' is 'like the sky's calm after high wind, which warms all cold' (B1 275), and paradoxically evokes the distinction between absolute Maat and its imperfect realization:

Making defects makes Maat less:
(so) measure well!
Maat (itself) has not been damaged, nor has overflown. (B1 281–3)

Inherent in this is Rensi's personal responsibility to embody Maat and his failure to do so: 'Your surroundings are awry, you who should be right!' (B1 293).

The seventh petition continues this fusion of the universal and the personal. Its opening invocation, like that of the third petition, highlights the social and cosmic aspects of Rensi's role, with an allusion to the divine:

> You are the helm of the whole land.
> According to your command the land sails.
> You are the fellow of Thoth.   (B1 298–9)

Personal and social faults are contrasted with Maat (B1 301–2 versus B1 305), which is manifested in the peasant's own actions. This fusion of all three levels is emphasized towards the end, where Rensi's power is defined in terms of its effect on others, and the official's duty is formulated in terms of universal creation and re-creation, alluding to the sixth petition's characterization of Maat as restoration:

> The officials are repellers of evil, they are lords of goodness,
> they are craftsmen of creating what is, joiners of the severed head.
>   (B1 318–20)

In the eighth petition, Rensi's role is presented in purely social terms and his failure is contrasted with an abstract description of Maat in relation to the creator and to the Otherworld, explicitly concerning the relativization of the ideal (B1 334–8; see **7.2**). The ninth petition continues the description in still more abstract terms with a definition of the relationship of Maat and its contrary:

> (Even) when its portion exists, Falsehood [sallies forth(?)].
> Against it Maat turns itself back;
> Maat is the goods of Falsehood,
> is making it flourish; (yet) it (Falsehood) has not been gathered in(?).
>   (B2 95–7)

The second half of the petition applies this understanding on a personal and social level, while retaining an otherworldly reference point that is emphasized in the peasant's final words when Rensi apparently still does not hear him. These stress the relativization of Maat in this world once more, by expressing the peasant's need to turn to an otherworldly judge:

> Look, I am pleading to you, and you do not hear –
> I will go to plead about you to Anubis.   (B2 113–15)

While the social aspect of Maat is foregrounded by the specific setting (Herrmann 1957: 82–3), the tale engages the totality of Maat and concerns the relationship of the abstract ideal order originally embodied in creation with the fallible social order of the sundered world. The action Rensi himself must take to support Maat is the nexus through which these issues are presented.

The petitions repeatedly return to the problem of unjust suffering and can be seen as moving towards an increasingly theodic discourse. Rensi's (apparent) refusal to help the peasant forces him to go beyond a social definition of Maat. The peasant's central complaint is that a principle of reciprocity inherent in Maat, whereby virtue is rewarded and vice punished, is being ignored. His inability to explain the violation of this principle in exclusively social terms leads him to formulate Maat in suprasocial terms, according to which virtue's reward is neither immediate nor earthly. Increasingly he enjoins virtue without regard for its earthly consequences, and so throws the otherworldly aspect of Maat into relief. By making the distinction between the actual and the ideal, the peasant is able to reconcile social injustice with Maat, whose validity it might otherwise deny. The specific social setting articulates both the inherency of these universal concerns in all matters and their interrelationship.

The discourses grow progressively more abstract. This movement alludes to an ultimate reference point in the universal and absolute, not the specific. This balance and breadth of reference – universal : specific; ideal : actual – parallels the tale's social range, which includes both the lowly, marginal peasant and the king, while its hierarchical 'deputizing' structure (e.g., B1 158) presents a correlative to the discourses' presentation of absolute ideals embodied in relativized actuality. The peasant, however, never directly calls the validity of Maat or the justice of the creator into question. However, while the hierarchical world presented by the narrative does not directly include the divine, even in the presentation of the king, the discourses make constant reference to the divine and the suprasocial. Rensi is acclaimed with metaphoric divine epithets that establish him as a representative of the ultimate authority within the hierarchy of deputies.

Thus the complaints to Rensi are in some sense a complaint to god. However, one cannot propose a purely allegorical reading of the tale in which Rensi would represent the creator, since his role is also presented in simple social terms as that of a human official (cf. Herrmann 1957: 85–7), and he is also likened to lowly professions. The secular setting sets up an opposition, as well as a similitude, between the divine and human spheres. This dichotomy may be reflected in the siting of the tale in the historical Heracleopolitan Period, which probably highlights the potential ambivalence of authority (**3.1.2**). This polarity is integral to the tale's structure as well as its imagery (cf. Parkinson 1992: 172–3).

The peasant's first and only direct appeal to the divine is not only rhetorical, but also characterises the divine as being silent:

> O Lord of Silence, may you give me back my goods!   (B1 60–1)

Rensi subsequently is silent, which motivates the subsequent petitions and the body of the tale. Silence is associated with Rensi's power: he uses silence, not speech, as a device to force the peasant to speak. Significantly, Rensi's silence is first introduced when he fails to respond to the officials and to the peasant (B1 80–2). Silence to an appeal can be an appropriate response,[35] but Rensi's silence here also implies ambiguity as to what will happen next. When he denounces Nemtinakht to the officials, they reject his view; this is presumably part of the reason for his delay in passing judgement despite his immediate and correct appraisal of the peasant's case (cf. B1 73–4) and his apparent ability at the end to judge the case himself without recourse to any higher authority (B2 133). Rensi's silent behaviour is then reaffirmed by the higher authority of the king, who also remains aloof from the peasant. The tactics of Rensi and the king are thematically allied with the 'hidden' nature of divine providence, which is alluded to by the peasant in the third petition when he refers to the 'mystery of Maat' (B1 213).[36] To the actual audience, it characterizes him as the ideal 'silent man' (*gr*).[37] Significantly, Nemtinakht's disregard for the peasant was expressed differently: 'he paid him no attention' (B1 63).

Silence, however, is potentially ambivalent: it could be taken as indifference to evil. Lack of hearing is an established motif in laments over the state of the land:

> See how the hearer is now deaf.   (*Neferti* 8d)

> Silence against what is heard is a disease.   (*Khakheperreseneb* vso 4)

> You have not heard what you (should) have heard!   (*Sasobek* Bii.15)

The tale also mobilizes this aspect, and the peasant develops the theme of negative silence intensively, in explicit and implicit forms. Silence is a

---

[35] *Ptahhotep* 265–6. Silence as a means of gaining more information about a case is also attested in the statement by Ramses IV in a literary encomium, where he describes his conduct in the council: 'I was silent in order to gain perception of affairs, to turn crying out(?) into joy' (2.10–3.1; text: Gardiner 1955b, 1956).

[36] Gardiner 1923: 14; Herrmann 1977: 271; Parkinson 1988: 184–5.

[37] Alluded to in B1 57; see J. Assmann 1984b; Brunner-Traut 1984, and, e.g., *Kagemni* 1.1.

failure or inability, almost helplessness, compared to the peasant's activity: Rensi does not 'speak Maat' like the peasant. His silence is foregrounded by the large number of unanswered questions the peasant addresses to him, and is such that he disappears from the poem between the third and ninth petitions except in the introductions to the peasant's speeches. His silence transforms him into the topic of the discourse, and thus the object of the audience's attention and critical examination, rather than any uncritical sympathy. He ceases to be a main actor, and the audience can perceive him only through his presentation by the peasant; empathy is thus created with the peasant, not with Rensi. Rensi's behaviour embodies conflicting attitudes: a caring action to alleviate the peasant's want (by provisioning him), and ironic detachment.

Together with this subversion of the thematic alliance between Rensi and the divine, there is a metaphorical subversion. The alliance is proclaimed in the eulogies of the opening petitions, which are formulated with inalienable predications (B1 171–3), but thereafter the peasant emphatically rejects Rensi as a true image of god. He presents him progressively as more and more debased, affirming in the eighth and ninth petitions a hierarchy of god > Maat > peasant > Rensi, in contrast to the earlier god > Maat > king > Rensi > peasant. Finally, Anubis is appealed to as an authority above the fallible Rensi (B2 114–15). The gods play a significant figurative role: many of those mentioned in the peasant's descriptions of Rensi have a noticeably ambivalent character, including the crocodile Khenty (B1 150), Sekhmet the 'Lady of Plague' (B1 151), and even the Nileflood (B1 173; for this god's negative aspects see, e.g., B. Altenmüller 1975: 126). Others are imagined as possibly capable of injustice: 'So is Thoth really lenient? If so, then you may do wrong!' (B1 180 1). This divine ambivalence involves Rensi and conversely suggests that his injustice may be a token of theirs. This possibility is raised only to be rejected together with Rensi's role as a divine exemplar. After the third petition the gods are invoked as unambivalent upholders of Maat – one can compare the ambivalent role of Thoth in B1 180–1 with the positive acclamation in B1 299–300 – as the peasant becomes gradually more explicit in presenting Maat's relationship with the actual world. The progressively explicit emphasis on the 'transcendent' aspect of the ideal which the peasant's theodicy involves can be seen in the theme of retribution, which he presents increasingly not as divine intervention but as a consequence inherent in the potentially evil nature of actuality and its fallibility (B2 95–7). This development is articulated stylistically in antithetical statements that climax towards the end in paradoxical formulations of the relationship of Maat and Falsehood (B2 96–7).

In this way, the peasant affirms an implicit theodicy by distinguishing between the ideal and relativized actuality so as not to compromise the ideal and the divine, but to cast the responsibility onto Rensi, the human embodier of Maat. Rensi's heart and will are a central concern of the petitions (e.g., 'one cannot know what is the heart', B1 287) just as in the narrative Nemtinakht's heart is the initial source of evil ('And then this Nemtinakht, seeing this peasant's asses / which pleased his *heart*, spoke saying...', B1 22). The tale presupposes choice, while the heart's role recalls the negative anthropology of official and religious texts. The frequent figurative definition of evil in negative formulations, as deviations from the ideal, reflects this approach.

Other ambivalent attitudes in the petitions do not pattern into a single progression, but display the complexity of the problem of distinguishing Maat from 'apparent Maat' (Fecht 1975: 642). The progression is a desperately fluctuating struggle. While a sense of the transcendence of Maat emerges, so does a sense of growing exasperation and despair. The peasant's words are 'what comes out of the mouth of the Sungod' (B1 350; see p. 121), in an official phrase that reverses his earlier image of Rensi as 'a Sungod' (B1 171), and the peasant later implies that he is Maat itself:

Has Maat not addressed him (Rensi)? (B1 306)

Nevertheless, he also presents the tongue and language as something dangerous – a 'bane(?)' (*ṯmw*: B1 162–3; cf. Fecht 1996: 235, 256–7), 'a weed' (B1 184–5), a 'floodburst' (B1 308), and even allusively excrement (B1 309–10), suggesting that a theodic reading is not totalizing.

The petitions, with their theodic concern, do not constitute the whole tale, but they are placed in a narrative setting and presented ironically. This irony is staged in the scene where King Nebkaure requests that the petitions be made to continue through the device of Rensi's silence. Unlike the similar scene in *Neferti*, there is no simple request by the king to 'bring his speeches for our entertainment'. His desire for entertainment has to be inferred by the audience/reader, and this would be done fairly automatically, given the scenario of the king requesting speech and the mention of 'a peasant whose speech is truly perfect' (B1 106–7) by Rensi, who acts as the bringer of the littérateur. The scenario relates more to the topos of the production of literary or rhetorical texts than to any legal procedures for written appeals brought to the king by intermediaries.[38]

The elaborate arrangements to keep the peasant speaking are described, not the king's expectation of pleasure (as in *Neferti*). Any description of

---

[38] Contra Shupak 1992: 10; see, however, the treatise on 'The Duties of the Vizier', section 11, where the petitioner must have his petition put in writing before the Vizier takes it to the king (van den Boorn 1988: 193–201, 330–1). I assume that in the tale the writing down is unnecessary in legal terms since the king refers the complaint back to the High Steward.

the discourses' reception is delayed until the very end of the tale, when they are presented to the king in a swift narrative passage (B2 130–1). This treatment foregrounds the peculiarly indirect relationship between the entertainer and the entertained. King Nebkaure's commissioning of the discourses is made through an oath, 'As you wish to see me in health (*snb*) . . .' (B1 109), which presents the affair in the explicitly serious terms of the king's well-being. This serious staging prevents the king from appearing as a sadistic joker or trickster, while the following instruction about provisioning the peasant and his family – very generously (Parkinson 1988: 100–101) – creates an impression of benevolence. However, the staging also establishes that the king's 'health' depends on the peasant's mental and physical suffering, in a very different manner from the presentation of the mutually beneficial interdependence of the elite and its underlings made in *The Loyalist Teaching*. Similarly, the king, who is remote from the protagonist and yet directly responsible for his predicament, both perceives his plight sympathetically and inflicts suffering on him (B1 109–15). This opposition, like others, becomes increasingly problematic as the peasant's expressions of suffering increase.[39]

The ironical emplotment problematizes the meaning of the petitions on every level, a complexity that is also mobilized in the sheer improbability of the peasant's speeches, which is integral to the emplotment as well as structurally and thematically central. The theodic subject matter is unlikely to reflect what any actual peasant could have spoken about. In sociocultural terms, this discrepancy could render the tale a 'democratizing' ideological statement, in which the voicing of Maat by a marginal figure affirms the cultural unity of society and the fair distribution of justice regardless of rank. However, such a reading is rendered problematic by the ironic staging of the peasant's speeches and their style. None of the original actual audience can have believed his petitions to have been in a style that was naturalistic for such a person. The tale implicitly acknowledges this by presenting the peasant as exceptional, an awareness he himself voices (B1 314). The stylistic choice of a low narrative to introduce the tale articulates the peasant's cultural position: the peasant's first speeches to his wife (R 1.3–4) show that he does not speak in 'the manner of the officials'.[40] In the dialogue with Nemtinakht he initially maintains the speech-code appropriate to underlings, using the stereotyped response 'I will do as you wish' (B1 34; compare, e.g., Davies and Gardiner 1920: pls. 9, 11, 12). The peasant's initial speeches as they are repeated to the actual audience become more rhetorically striking, but

---

[39] The version of the R manuscript makes the opposition less explicit when first introduced by omitting the paradoxical pairing of Rensi's silence and the peasant's speaking.

[40] See pp. 119–20; Loprieno 1996e: 520. *p3* occurs in the early speeches at R 1.4, 1.6, B1 50, and in narrative at B1 29 = Bt 33–4 (not in R).

although the dialogue with Nemtinakht is a skilful verbal sparring match, transitional between the narrative and the rhetoric of the petitions, his speeches remain short (see also Parkinson 1992: 166). His subsequent ten-day – that is week-long – petitioning of Nemtinakht is reported rather than restaged for the audience (B1 62–3). These petitions exactly parallel the length of the later series of nine, presumably occupying nine days followed by a single recitation of the series on a tenth day (B2 62–3).

Once the peasant starts to petition Rensi, he is obviously speaking 'fairly', that is he speaks 'in the manner of the officials, free from saying *pɜs*'.[41] His first exchange with Rensi, which prefaces the first petition (B1 67–70), is transitional in style; being simply phrased, with a degree of formality and measured repetition (cf. Parkinson 1988: 67–8). Although 'poetry and recital have always been important in Egyptian village society' (Eyre 1993: 119–20, with references), the style seems meant to be seen to cross the boundaries of what was plausible in the initial narrative setting of such society.

The audience's awareness of the plot's irony is increased by the realization that the fictional or actual impact and success of the peasant's speech on its audience cannot be measured by its achieving his aims within the narrative, despite the fact that petitioning (*spr*) is by its nature contextually determined speech, having the rhetorical aim of 'touching' and persuading someone that is integral to the plot. One can assess the peasant's communication by the 'conversational conventions' of petitioning in 12th Dynasty society, in terms of modern discourse analysis and Grice's 'cooperation principle'.[42] Petitions could address two levels: the human sphere and the divine, including the dead. The latter is attested in a few Middle Kingdom sources,[43] and more numerous New Kingdom ones (e.g., Pinch 1993: 333–5). Evidence for the conventions of petitioning within the human sphere in the Middle Kingdom is slight (cf. Shupak 1992), unlike Elizabethan England, which literary critics can analyse as 'a petitioning Society' (A. Patterson 1993: 57–79). The New Kingdom treatise on 'Duties of the Vizier' suggests the importance of 'petitioning' in contacts between high officials and the populace (van den Boorn 1988: 330–1). Middle Kingdom texts present petitioning as a means of calming and regulating discourse (**5.3**); *Ptahhotep* urges a 'calm' hearing (265),

---

[41] *pɜ* occurs only once in the petitions, as an emphasized demonstrative (B1 229; Parkinson 1988: 201).

[42] 'Make your conversational contribution such as is required, at the stage at which it occurs, by the accepted purpose or direction of the talk exchange in which you are engaged': Grice 1975: 45; see Brown and Yule 1983: 31–3.

[43] For example, a harpist's song 'petitioning' Hathor (Parkinson 1991a: 126–8; L. Morenz 1996: 65–9). In *A Man and His Ba* a dead man can 'petition' the Sungod without hindrance (145–7). Petitioning the dead occurs in an early Middle Kingdom letter to the dead, P. Berlin 10482 (e.g., Franke 1994: 138).

implying that petitioners had some licence to try the temper of their hearers, although in *The Tale of Neferkare and Sasenet* an unwelcome petitioner is drowned out by court musicians (P. Chassinat I X+2.x+7–13). The social aspects of petitioning may have made it a suitable vehicle for the licensed complaining voices of literature, just as Shakespearean fools, such as Thersites who is 'a privileged man' to speak unsavoury observations (*Troilus and Cressida*, 2.3) and the 'all-licens'd Fool' of *King Lear* (1.4), were literary creations based on actual figures (e.g., Mangan 1996: 50–73). Despite this licence, the peasant's strategies after the first petition, notably his lack of restraint and offensiveness, are likely to contradict those actually expected of petitioners (cf. M. V. Fox 1983: 12–15; Parkinson 1992: 169–70).

Aspects of the peasant's petitions – their length and acrimony – may well represent aspects of villagers' reality of dealing with officialdom and of legal cases in general, which are normally omitted from official descriptions.[44] Several earlier scholars remarked that the peasant's hyperbole was natural for a petitioning fellah (Maspero 1911: 48; Lefebvre 1949: 43 n.3), but while the tale's rhetorical profusion may relate to some reality, the representation of discourse is different from the concise way in which the 'petitioning' (*spr*) is recorded in the 17th Dynasty Karnak Juridical stela (Helck 1983: 67 ll.16–18) and in royal letters copied on the late 12th Dynasty administrative Papyrus Brooklyn (Insertions B and C: Hayes 1955: 71–85 pl. 5–6; Quirke 1990b: 140–6). The peasant's speeches are differentiated from normal petitioning discourse in their effect as well as in their style. *Ptahhotep* relates how a pleader should grow calm by speaking, even if his appeal is not granted, but the peasant's self-expression ends not in 'soothing the heart' (*Ptahhotep* 276), but in a desire for death (B2 119–22). He understands that he has not persuaded the fictional audience, and is unreconciled with his continuing plight. Rensi does not provide a 'good hearing' (*Ptahhotep* 276), nor react in any way (e.g., B1 211), and at the end the peasant expects that he will act in order 'to punish him for the speech he had made' (B2 117–18). The style and context of the discourses are continually problematized.

This differentiation and problematization determines the reading of the whole poem. The two parts – narrative and discourse – cannot be considered separately: the peasant's speeches are not self-contained as a theodicy any more than they are as pragmatic petitions, since they do not reconcile him to his situation despite its positive conclusion on an abstract level. Instead the course of events and of his discourse leads him to plan suicide, and the resolution is reached in the concluding narrative. Drawing

---

[44] Bontty 2000; discussion of the tensions between the central state and village society, drawing on the tale: Eyre 1996b.

on the 'entrapment' model of Egyptian discourse, one might argue that the ironic narrative simply confirms the peasant's theodicy by showing his initial complaint to be groundless, so that its ironic staging of the discourses would integrate the social order with the ideal order he articulates. However, the poem resists such a reading: for example, in the petitions Rensi's human fallibility is central to the peasant's justification of ultimate authority, but the narrative presents Rensi as not acting fallibly and as allied with the divine on a thematic level. Similarly, the distinction between the human and divine and the ideal and actual, on which the peasant's discussion rests, is lessened in the narrative, which concludes by implying that the social order can on occasion embody the ideal. Thus, the narrative at once undermines both the peasant's ground for complaint and his way of justifying authority. This contrasting relationship of the two parts and their different modes which justify authority on different levels and by different methods, is foregrounded by the continuous ironic awareness of the discrepancy between the situation as narrated and as perceived by the peasant in his discourses.

The structure avoids a simple structural pattern of complaint and answer in social and theodic terms. The self-justification of authority is never stated in answer but remains implicit in the dramatic situation, so that it is the irony itself which answers the complaint. One effect of this is to acknowledge the possibility of evil triumphing: appropriately, Nemtinakht, the original source of evil in the tale, reappears in the conclusion. Similarly, the actual situation narrated is not the exact opposite of the peasant's subjective view: Rensi's officials side with Nemtinakht (B1 74–80), showing that some of the peasant's denunciations are justified. The narrative thus supports his complaint as well as negating it. While providing a reassuring ending, the plot continually raises questions: What if the officials had triumphed, or if Nemtinakht had; what if the peasant had given up earlier? This tension is not diminished when the ideal and actual are integrated in the resolution, since the extraordinary nature of the peasant's eloquence keeps the audience aware of the improbability of a happy ending.

The tale stages an indirect conflict of protagonists – one of whom is inactive – creating a conflict between ideas and attitudes in a debate. The audience witnesses the dramatic formulation of ideas. The physical recital of the tale will have placed the original actual audience in a position parallel to the fictional audience of Rensi and his attendants. The alliance of the audience and Rensi will have been strengthened by social alignment, since the original audience ranked above the peasant, although perhaps below Rensi, and possibly even below his attendant officials at the capital. The dramatic irony will have further allied the audience with Rensi in an 'amiable community' aware of the true situation. For the audience the beating and suffering of a peasant, which is frequently depicted on elite tomb walls, is unlikely to have been a major event that created sympathy and outrage.[45] But while this ironic situation excludes the peasant, it does not make him into an unsympathetic victim (Booth 1974: 27–30: communities created by irony). The biography of the 11th Dynasty Steward Rediukhnum describes him as 'someone with smiling face for the petitioner until he has said what is in his heart' (l.5; J. M. A. Janssen 1946: 92 [Cp2]; Lichtheim 1988: 42–6). Despite the peasant's status as a subordinate outsider, the petitions seem designed to evoke empathy with him through their intense rhetorical presentation of subjectivity and his eloquent formulation of central values. The narrative also may represent a movement in sympathy: the negatively characterized Nemtinakht beats the peasant (B1 53–4), and during his petitions Rensi threatens him with being seized by a follower in a detail that recalls Nemtinakht's abuse (B1 134–5, cf. B1 31–2), and then has him beaten in terms which echo Nemtinakht's attack (B1 217–18). These echoes increase sympathy for him at Rensi's expense and highlight the irony: Nemtinakht beat the peasant in connection with an attempt to stifle his complaint, whereas Rensi has him beaten to inspire him to continue the complaint.[46]

While the conclusion presents the peasant as rewarded in the capital, rather than as poor on the edge of Egypt, this progression does not negate the suffering involved in the realization of Maat. In social terms, the peasant gains by speaking, but for Rensi the matter of restitution seems settled before the first petition (implicit in B1 73–4, 107). The length and passion of the monologues, and their address to the audience, ensure that their denunciations of the fallible world are not forgotten at the conclusion. The justification of cultural values is achieved at a cost that balances the detached irony of the narrative. Suffering results in 'perfect speech', but the peasant's continual urging of an empathetic response, as expressed in the rebuke 'You do not pity, nor suffer, nor yet destroy!' (B1 348–9), forestalls any distanced appreciation. The audience cannot escape the poem's emotional impact, just as the involved Rensi cannot escape from the peasant's denunciations. The beating and suffering prevent the peasant from reconciling himself with adversity, unlike other speakers of wisdom discourses. The question remains why can the order of Maat not be embodied in perfect speech without the generation of so much

---

[45] E.g., Fischer 1976: 9–11, fig. 3. On audience sympathy in general, see Brown and Yule 1983: 248.

[46] Rensi's interventions are necessary to maintain his official credibility after the peasant's direct abuse, and are almost inevitable parts of the plot to keep the peasant talking (cf. Parkinson 1988: 121, 191–6).

suffering and anxiety,[47] as it is in the literary teachings, and why must his eloquence have such an ambivalent role? The uncontained suffering is central to problematic of the poem, like 'the apple itself in the middle of the blessed garden' in *Paradise Lost* (Hunter 1980: 177). The ideal of Maat triumphant and the suffering involved are associated at the end in a paradoxical balance of opposing moods, momentarily uniting the two poles of ideal and actual.

The poem resolves these tensions in a profound manner, articulating the complexity of things through its thematic and stylistic richness. Irony is sustained throughout, being evident not only in the first narrative interlude (B1 102–18) and recurrent ironies in the petitions, but also in the resolution, particularly in the peasant's final words:

So, shall I live on your bread,
and drink your beer for ever? (B2 125–6)

Whether one takes these clauses as sarcastic rhetoric or as a negative exclamation – 'I will not live on your bread, / and drink your beer for ever!' (Kammerzell 1993: 21) – the couplet is deeply ambiguous. On one level the peasant is simply responding to Rensi's proposal that the peasant should 'deal with him' (B2 124), but it could also imply that he knows of Rensi's covert material support for him – whereas his ignorance is what has enabled the plot to support the discourses (B1 114–18). The speech gains in resonance from the fact that in his petitions he has used grain and provisions as metaphors for Maat (e.g., B1 282–3). Such local ambiguities and uncertainties help involve the audience in the peasant's anxiety, as well as generally evoking sympathy for him. The tale is staged in such a way that no absolute closure is possible. The audience must make evaluative inferences about the production of speech (for judgements required when reading stable ironies, see Booth 1974: 39–43). Thus it is appropriate that when the king has heard the petitions, he tells Rensi 'Judge yourself, Meru's son' (B2 133): like Rensi the actual audience is left to judge the tale itself.

The narrative presents the 'perfect speeches' as the aesthetic high-point and centre of the tale. They fulfil expectations, being densely and allusively unified despite the rapid changes in tone and trains of thought. Speech is, however, also ambivalent: it is what judges people themselves:

The tongue of men is their balance (B2 92–3)

---

[47] Compare Greenblatt on the staging of anxiety in Elizabethan institutional and literary culture (1988: 128–63).

– that is, the balance they use, but also the balance for weighing them, in which they can be found wanting. The balance is an appropriate metaphor for the balancing of tensions and judgements throughout the tale (thus in B1 196–8 – 'your tongue is the plummet...' – the audience is the balance, as well as Rensi). Another relevant analogy is the context of a legal case, in which a consensual resolution is required. Writing is similarly ambivalent: it contains and neutralizes the peasant's discourse, but given its cultural prestige, it also validates and empowers – a reading that is supported by the use of writing as a metaphor for authority's embodiment of the ideal in the eighth petition (B1 336–7).

The plot's ironic structure creates an instability of sympathies. Although the tale mobilizes social, political and religious values, it is staged in terms of literary production, and the peasant's final empowerment is made not only in social terms of justice, but also of the well-attested literary motif of a commoner triumphing over authority and being rewarded for literary production (B1 133–4; Derchain 1972). The direct and combative presentation of suffering is made within the framework of suffering itself as a Middle Kingdom literary topos; otherwise the agony and the offensiveness of the poetry would be uncomfortable for even an elite audience. In terms of emplotment, the resolution is delayed until the petitions are finally recited to the peasant and then presented as a manuscript to the king. The petitions are rehearsed, and their reception is restaged for the king in the final narrative. This is broadly similar to the narrative conclusion of *Kagemni* (2.3–7), but differences significantly articulate the problematic staging: the petitions are presented and read to the author, then presented to the royal audience, and only then is the response given. The conflict between the protagonists and the various tensions in the tale are resolved through the existence of this mobile manuscript and the intellectual and aesthetic response of finding it 'more perfect to his heart (*nfr-ḥr-jb*) than anything in this entire land' (B2 131–2; see **4.5**). This performative moment of recitation, and the 'new roll' on which they are written, mirror the experiences of the audience who are hearing (or reading) the petitions from just such a manuscript.

This manuscript, almost the archetype of the manuscripts of the tale owned by people such as the owner of the 'Berlin' and 'Ramesseum libraries', embodies the transfer of control over the social energies, tensions, and anxieties generated by the preceding tale from the fictional protagonists to the actual audience, generating a powerful aesthetic frisson that one might compare with the familiar moment of transference in the epilogue to *The Tempest*, when authority is passed from the performer to the audience (Greenblatt 1988: 57). And at this moment, all the tale's ambiguities about silence are subsumed in the peasant's final silence, which is his response to the manuscript. The fissured, suspended nature of the text reaches its summation in the wonder of the unexpected written manuscript. The deferral of the legal case, the empathetic ambiguity of social tensions, and the uncertainties of the theodic questionings are suspended and resolved in a specifically literary moment of reception.

8.4 THE RANGE OF RESPONSES: FROM *CHEOPS' COURT* TO *THE SHIPWRECKED SAILOR*'S ISLAND

'Like an old tale still . . .

Shakespeare, *The Winter's Tale* (c. 1610), V.ii

Cheops' Court has a sequential structure of tale after tale. It presumably opened with an introduction in which King Cheops was bored and requested his sons to amuse him with tales of prodigies (Parkinson 1999f: 102–3). The first tale concerned the reign of Djoser (1.14) and a lector and chief (probably Imhotep: 1.16[48]), and was presumably told by a prince. The second tale concerns adultery involving the lector Ubainer in the reign of Nebka,[49] and is told by prince Chephren (1.17–4.17). The third tale is an episode from the reign of Sneferu, involving the lector Djadjae-mankh, narrated by prince Bauefre (4.17–6.22). The self-references or echoes within these tales are sequential, and counter-pointing devices provide a sense of continuity and progression. For example, the third tale of Sneferu with a wonder involving water is echoed in the later promised crossing of Cheops to Sakhebu through a sage's power (9.17–18). In the final episode there are other echoes of the second and third tale (see also Derchain 1986: 20–1).

There is also a broader underlying thematic unity: royalty is common to all parts of the poem. Thus a core theme is the exercise and assumption of kingship, the happening of events between the past and the future. The tales concern 'prodigies' or 'signs' (*bjзjt*: Graefe 1971: 130–6), such as feature in official commemorative inscriptions at the Wadi Hammamat, where in the late 11th Dynasty 'the prodigies (*bjзjt*) which happened for his Person' Montuhotep III are presented as omens showing divine favour for the king and involvement in his activities (Shirun-Grumach 1993: 1–48; cf. Jenni 1998: 137–8). The official significance of such omens as royal legitimation is parodied into tales of wonder, although the growing association of the prodigies with the royal figures of the tale may mobilize

---

[48] No traces survive: Blackman 1988: pl. 1.16; the title is an anachronism (Goedicke 1992b: 25 n.17).

[49] This order contradicts that of the Turin Canon, where Nebka precedes Djoser. This probably reflects ancient historical uncertainty (cf. McDowell 1992). Ubainer's name ('Stone-opener') may be a chronologically discordant allusion to Imhotep: Jenni 1998: 119–20.

its significance as the tale progresses. In *Cheops' Court*, intertextual allusion gives way to humorous and direct parody – 'the comic refunctioning of preformed linguistic or artistic material', in which the frustrations of anticipations is humourously staged through disruptive discongruity (Rose 1993: 5–53). This stylistic device relating the tale to official discourse is more light-hearted than the intertextual probing of the biography genre in *Sinuhe*. For example, the granting of offerings for the dead kings and wonder-workers at the end of each tale, which creates a fundamental structural pattern, recalls such texts as the decree on a stela of Senwosret III from Deir el-Bahri establishing the offerings for the cult of Montuhotep I (Naville and Hall 1907: pl. 24; PM II², 391)). These offerings become humorous when they are offered to the still living Djedi (9.20–21), who has a more than healthy appetite (7.2–4). In assigning these offerings, Cheops says how he has 'seen' the wonders that he has just heard, apparently alluding to the 'seeing' of omens and the might of god that occurs in the Wadi Hammamat inscriptions (Shirun-Grumach 1993: 40–1; Jenni 1998: 137), or the viewing and restoring of ruined monuments in royal inscriptions in the genre of the Royal Tale, such as the Tod inscription of Senwosret I (l. 26).[50] This motif itself is further parodied in the third tale within the tale, when Sneferu 'sees' beautiful semi-nude rowers. Each episode ends with the official phrase 'And it was done exactly as his Person had commanded' (compare, e.g., Helck 1983: 110 ll.3–4). These intertextual movements and sematic transformations seem designed to create humour.

The theme of royal legitimation underlies the contrast that structures much of the tale, between Sneferu and Cheops. The assessment of their characters remains problematic. Philippe Derchain (1969) interprets the Hathoric epithets describing the rowers who have not borne a child in the tale about Sneferu as suggesting that his rowing expedition is slightly sacrilegious, and that Sneferu is a king who enacts 'le rêve solaire' which is later fully embodied in the divine birth: 'authentiques fils du soleil, (ils) auraient évincé ceux qui se contentaient d'une parodie' (1969: 23). This negative reading, however, may underestimate the role of genre and judge Sneferu's characterization by modern expectations. Henry G. Fischer has established iconographic parallels for the episode which suggest that the trappings of the activity were part of a well-attested courtly ritual rather than being usurped aspects of divinity.[51] This more positive reading of Sneferu's character accords with such texts as *Neferti*, where he is a friendly merry king (Graefe 1990). Such allusions to religious ritual are probably not

---

[50] In the Semna stela the king declares he has 'seen' his own achievements (Sethe 1928a: 84, ll. 8–9).
[51] Fischer 1977: 161–5, 169–70. Even the Fish-pendant is potentially a symbol of rebirth (Jenni 1998: 121). For the nets as dresses see Knigge 1997.

to be read so seriously as Derchain suggests: they may be witty allusions that increase both the wonder of the incident and the renown of Sneferu. Here, the king (*snfrw*) presides over courtly 'holiday' (*hrw-nfr*: 6.13–14; L. Morenz 1996: 109), and carefree entertainment is a sign of leisurely glory not of its opposite, just as Bakhtinian carnival does not necessarily deride specific targets in a negative manner (Rose 1993: 168). The other princes' tales similarly allude to religious imagery and ceremony: the crocodile created by Ubainer in the second tale is associated with resurrection (Eyre 1992). The tale of Sneferu mobilizes other such cultural material both more directly and more frivolously than earlier tales: fatal adultery by a pool becomes ceremonial enjoyment of women on a lake, and the fatal crocodile in the depths becomes an inconsequential fish pendant that is simply lost in the water (Goedicke 1992b: 26). The potential for significance is directly related to the degree of inconsequentiality. By contrast, in *Sinuhe* the goddess Hathor acts as Sinuhe's patroness, presiding over his home, his travels and eventual return, and his symbolic rebirth through the figure of Queen Nefru (e.g., L. Morenz 1997b: 17), thus articulating a unity through his diverse experiences. In the episode of Sneferu's expedition in *Cheops' Court*, Hathoric allusions do not deepen the significance but only the cleavages of the young women presented for the king's entertainment.

By contrast, Cheops' speeches and actions suggest that he is to be viewed as a bad king, or at best a bad-tempered one; significantly, he is the only king for whom no major wonder is done. These characterizations of the two kings are not based on historical information from the Old Kingdom, but on Middle Kingdom interpretations of the kings' pyramids and titularies (survey: Baud 1998). Here it is significant that the 12th Dynasty kings dedicated statues of royal ancestors including Djoser, Sneferu and the 5th Dynasty king Sahure who feature in the tale (e.g., Vandersleyen 1995: 58 n.4, 85 n.1). Despite this mobilization of historical attitudes, the narration seems to focus on the wonders themselves, and not their role as signs, or the moral appraisal of the royal protagonists (pace Mathieu 1999: 37). A detailed assessment of character and motivation, as in *Sinuhe*, is not a concern. The wonders enact a contrasting assessment of the two salient kings, but the overall moral dimension lies rather in the contrast between past 'fictions' and present verifiable truth, which is itself subverted by the general past setting of the tale as a whole.

While the structure is more episodic than other high tales, it shows the same concern with centrality. The central episode brings the sequential pattern of past tales to a climax with a supposedly 'real' anecdote, forming a pattern of fable leading to reality: Cheops is offered a wonder 'in his own time' (6.24), just as the past kings were. The action is placed centrally between three past kings, who feature in the related tales, and three future kings, who are born in the final extant episode (Barocas 1988: 124–5).

This focus partly breaks the pattern of tale-telling, but it is also an inevitable transformation: the tales have been moving historically closer to the setting of the Court, and are in a sense challenges for Cheops to show his own reign to be as wonderful as the preceding ones. The matter is introduced by Hordedef, who is intertextually the wisest and most famous of the princes (Wildung 1969: 217–21). Sneferu as the best-known king is thus followed by the best-known prince. Other details link this episode with the preceding: the fantastically described aged Djedi is a survivor from Sneferu's reign, and the location of his residence at *Djed*-Sneferu (7.1)[52] reinforces this association. His great age contrasts with his status as a 'little man' (*nds*) which can mean a 'young man' (Żába 1974: 101). The motif that wisdom will result in an old age with healthy limbs is here exaggerated with his leisurely pose and healthy appetite (7.2–4; 7.14–16; compare *Ptahhotep* 637), all with apparently humorous intent. Djedi is also a typical lettered man, embodying the role of the reader and the time-range of the tale itself, since he spans times past and time present (L. Morenz 1996: 107–23). The elaborate greetings between him and Hordedef when they meet, which include more explicit religious allusions than are in the earlier tales, heighten the elevation of the context. References to eternity and blessedness establish the two participants as ethical sages. Although the allusions are delivered respectfully, the greetings also include touches of sly wit, suggesting a competition in courtesy.[53]

Djedi is introduced as knowing three things, just as there were three previous tales of wonder (7.4–6). When he meets Cheops, two wonders are initially accomplished, enacting the first of these three promised things: 'how to join a severed head', an action that ironically alludes to royal creative powers (*Loyalist* 5.7; see also L. Morenz 1996: 120). The potential for an extreme example of this ability, when Cheops requests a man to be decapitated (see also Derchain 1996c), is frustrated, as Djedi answers that:

Look, doing (*jr*) such a thing to the noble flock is not commanded (*n-wd̠.tw*)!
(8.17)

This probably parodies the theodic statement of the creator in Coffin Text spell 1130:

I did not command them to do (*n-wd̠:j-jr:sn*) evil.   (*CT* VII, 464a)

---

[52] See Gomaà 1986: 374 (noting that the pyramid city was still functioning in the later Middle Kingdom); L. Morenz 1996: 118. Barocas (1988: 125–6) suggested that Djedi is not a lector priest for reasons of the plot: he should be unknown to Cheops.
[53] Meltzer (1994: 170) interprets these as showing 'sarcasm and oneupmanship' between the two sages.

A commoner, not the king, mobilizes the metaphor of the king as a good shepherd of the human flock, reversing the ideological power of discourse. The actual wonder is then performed on various animals. A comparison with preceding tales is invited by the involvement of animals which are, like the crocodile, 'typically symbolic of uncontrolled or uncontrollable natural or royal power' (Eyre 1992: 281; L. Morenz 1996: 120), but these deeds are narrated more briefly than preceding tales, and thus can be interpreted as less spectacular. As the episode proceeds Cheops' character is increasingly revealed as flawed, and his conversation with Djedi is curt (Meltzer 1994: 170–1). He apparently ignores the second promised ability of Djedi (the tame walking lion),[54] and rushes impatiently to the third thing, 'the number of the Secret Chambers of the sanctuary of Thoth' which the audience already knows that he has been seeking for his pyramid complex (his 'horizon': 7.6–8; contra Goedicke 1992b: 26–9). The wonder of the chambers, which is the most prestigiously esoteric yet (see pp. 139–40), is also left unachieved. This parody of a central type of discourse, the Royal Tale (see **5.2**), has the effect of making Cheops look potentially ridiculous, as he fails to discover esoteric religious information,[55] and his goal continually recedes as he pursues it. Unlike Sneferu, Cheops is not satisfied, but instead receives a prophecy of the end of his dynasty. As one issue is suspended, the narrative moves on. Djedi offers consolation and the episode ends with a rewarding response, like the preceding tales, that ironically points to the fictionality of the supposedly 'real' wonder, alluding to the reference to fictionality with which it opened: 9.19–21, 6.23–5). However, the plot has to proceed further for a full resolution in these future events. The solar associations of the uncompleted prodigy are developed in what follows, creating a sense of suspense, in particular, about Cheops' desire to journey to now 'see' the temple of Sakhebu (a solar city: Gomaà 1987: 72), and implicitly to see the Sungod's children who will be born there (9.15–8). The characterization is laconic, but creates an impression that Cheops thinks more than he says, suggesting an intention to dispose of the children.[56]

The subsequent major shift in the narrative includes time, place, and

---

[54] If the text is correct as it stands: Derchain 1986: 15–17. On this reading, a verbal echo of the second thing promised will remind the audience that Cheops is forgetting this. The alternative reading (e.g., Blackman 1988: 11a n.6b) is that the manuscript omits the narration of the second thing.

[55] Later tradition ascribed this role in particular to Hordedef rather than Cheops (Wildung 1969: 217–21; Aufrère 1998: 23–5), a fact the tale probably mobilized ironically.

[56] Perhaps the portrayal of King Herod in the New Testament influences the modern reader's expectations too much here, but the audience has seen Cheops already suggesting a man should be killed and later the maidservant's threat to 'go and tell this / to the Person of the Dual King Cheops!' (12.12) implies some kind of plot. See Blumenthal 1999, esp. 36–41.

protagonists who suddenly include the court of the Sungod (9.21–2).[57] The general tenor of the lost ending of the whole tale is known from the historical accession of the children of divine descent, and it is likely that Djedi dissuaded Cheops from resisting the fated succession. The tone of the final episode is slightly darker, with domestic squabbling and treachery (Meltzer 1994: 172). The highly repetitive narration of the birth of the future kings, although a feature of the tale as whole, probably represents a stylistic heightening. The humorous potential is less pointed in the birth of the divine children, which is modelled on the royal birth cycle (see p. 139). The humour here springs from mingling divine and human spheres. In the birth cycle, a god manifests himself as the king, but here deities disguise themselves as relatively humble musicians who walk with a porter, in contrast to the royal litter and boats elsewhere in the tale. In this case, mockery and laughter are significantly channelled through performing arts to create a mood of celebration. Contrasting echoes of earlier tales are significant (cf. Derchain 1986: 20–1), and Rudjdjedet's name (Rudj*djed*et) associates her with *Djed*i, allying her with Sneferu rather than with Cheops.

The narrative as a whole can be read as literary enactment of a pattern of doubt – about the kingship of Cheops – and reaffirmation – represented by the divine children who will be kings – although the active role of the kings is minimized as against the wise and the divine, establishing a 'corrélation entre sagesse, sages et culte solaire' (Barocas 1988: 127–8). The laughter that is directed against the centres of society and culturally central textual genres is central to this reaffirmation. The bathos of Cheops' interview with Djedi suggests a carnivalesque intent, as well as an almost inversionary laughter that moves the audience's approval away from the ridiculed figure of the king in contrast to the empathetic joy aroused by Sneferu's frivolity.

The tale's humour can be contrasted with that of *The Shipwrecked Sailor*, which is more tightly and concentrically patterned not only in the centralizing sequence of narrators, but also on the level of detail. One can detect a contrast between the uses of wordplay: in *Cheops' Court*, it is an incidental structuring device and explicit (as in the naming of the divine children, and less explicit in the incident of the crocodile: Eyre 1992), while in *The Shipwrecked Sailor* there is a significant ambiguity in the phrase describing the location as an 'island of the *ka* (*jw n-k₃*)' (Loprieno 1991a: 214). Similar linguistic ambiguity attends the uses of the word *ḥnw* which refers to two places: the Residence and the land of Egypt, and the

---

[57] The transition to a higher sphere was prepared for by the elevated dialogue of Hordedef and Djedi, while the latter's presence prepared the audience for a low-life episode taking place outside the court. Hordedef's visit to the relatively lowly Djedi likewise foreshadows the visit of the goddesses and of divine offspring to the home of Reuser.

'interior' of the island, embodying the contrasting worlds of the tale, and formulating the travelling between home and the island which, in turn, patterns the whole tale (see also Rendsburg 2000).

Conversely, in *The Shipwrecked Sailor* humour is more incidental than in *Cheops' Court*, although both serpent and sailor may be presented with touches of humour (e.g., Foster and Brock 1998: 6). The only explicit mirth that is mentioned is the serpent's laughing at the sailor's folly in misunderstanding his mystical nature and promising offerings (149); this laughter alludes to pessimistic doubts about the efficacy of offerings to the gods (Baines 1990a: 64–5). The most fantastic elements ironically express the tale's grimmest side, and the fantastic serpent forms an analogue of the divine which is threatened by chaos along with humanity (Baines 1990a). The events of *Cheops' Court* are presented in a more literal manner. In *The Shipwrecked Sailor*, as in *Sinuhe*, a journey ultimately provides no escape from the problematic of life; there is no world elsewhere. In both, the structurally central reality collapses: Sinuhe's experiences abroad are shown to be dreamlike, while the sailor's island will literally become nonexistent (153–4): the problematic continually intrudes. In *Cheops' Court*, fresh fantastic events continually happen, taking the place of those that happen or almost happen. *Cheops' Court* parodies high generic registers for comic effect, whereas in a sense *The Shipwrecked Sailor* parodies low registers of narrative for serious effect.

While allusions to esoteric knowledge in *Cheops' Court* are parodic and intermittent, in *The Shipwrecked Sailor* they occupy a central structural position (see **7.3**). The tale's presentation of this information is metaphorical and allusive on varying levels and denies the possibility of an exact allegory between serpent and creator god – the serpent himself refers to 'god', implying that he himself is not identical with 'god' (113–4: alternative reading: Baines 1990a: 68). The allusions to the divine are central to the meaning as well as to the formal structure, embodying the theodic issue of how a man can face catastrophe. The necessity to endure catastrophe through narrating is transported onto a cosmic level in the central episode, which implies a justification of the god's responsibility for suffering in which even the deities must face catastrophe, since even the cosmos will end. This motif of 'likeness' gives a sense of the whole universe's being bound together in patient endurance, while also creating the expectation of hearing a lesson that is not conveyed directly, but through analogy.[58] *The Shipwrecked Sailor* creates a universe of analogy, repeatedly referring to 'something similar' to explicate events (22, 125). The namelessness of the protagonists, and the ambiguities surrounding the

---

[58] This organization has favoured modern allegorical interpretations: Goedicke 1974, 1980; Manuelian 1992.

location of the island, increase this allusive atmosphere. Amid such uncertainty, the reader latches onto specific points: the description of the mysterious island as 'the island of the spirit', a reference to the number 75, and the 'serpent's little daughter' (128–9), all of which further expand the meaning beyond the surface significance of what is being narrated. Whereas part of the appeal of the tales is the desire to know what will happen next, *Cheops' Court* creates suspense by telling what will happen, while *The Shipwrecked Sailor* creates suspense more subtly by withholding information: the setting is indicated only in the opening speech of the narrator (1–21) to his 'Count', arousing the audience's curiosity as to why the unnamed Count is in need of the tale. Similarly, before the serpent appears, the island is subtly indicated to be inhabited by allusions to 'notched sycamore figs' and 'vegetables as if cultivated' (49–50; Parkinson 1999f: 98 n.8), foreshadowed by the mention of a 'shelter of wood' (43), which may not be a natural construction. In *Cheops' Court*, the narrative of events does not have the extra layer of evoking 'something similar', and even the mysterious and the inaccessible is precisely located in a room in Heliopolis (9.4–5).

The reaction of the fictional audiences and tale-tellers provides a frame within which to assess the poem's intended reception. To judge by the fictional audience, the overall aim of *Cheops' Court* is amusement, rather than having the more serious implications of the high narratives (cf. Otto 1966) or offering a subversive vision of a second world outside officialdom. Instead, humour is presented as entertainment through being staged in a specifically literary scenario that structures the first section of the poem and sets the context for the remainder. In the later parts, where the comic episodes concern the potentially serious matter of a change of dynasty, the political implications are partly neutralized by the distant setting, and by concentrating on the royal births, which is a matter for rejoicing and carefree 'holiday' (12.8). The tales of wonder of *Cheops' Court* are followed by the tale itself, which is no less fantastic despite being supposedly more 'real'. The lofty introductions to the tales reinforce their fictionality (see **5.1.2**), as opposed to the technique of *The Shipwrecked Sailor*, where the awareness of fictionality seems to increase the intensity of the message. *The Sailor* thematizes tale-telling, but the emplotment traces back a retold tale to its source with a sustained ethical dimension:

> Listen to my [speech]!
> Look, it is good to listen to men. (181–2)

The last verse also occurs in *A Man and His Ba* (67). Narration is here synonymous with the transmission of wisdom, rather than the repeating of prodigies as in *Cheops' Court*, and the telling itself embodies wisdom: the ones who know how to endure suffering tell of their past suffering. Analogy rather than sequentiality is the main pattern:

> I shall tell you something similar,
> which happened to me myself . . . (21–3)

says the sailor and the serpent-god says:

> How joyful is he who tells of what he has tasted (i.e., his experience), so that the calamity passes.[59]
> I shall tell you something similar . . . (124–5)

In return for this the sailor promises to 'relate your power to the sovereign' (139). The sailor's quick response to the serpent is what initially saves him (Loprieno 1991a: 217) and speech is presented to the audience as wisdom, as art:

> A man's utterance saves him.
> His speech makes the face (of anger) be veiled for him. (17–9)

Speech controls action and happiness, whereas in *Cheops' Court* it simply generates the following action. The act of telling is wisdom and endurance: the ability to tell of anomalous events brings them under control. This ethical point is echoed through enclosing narratives, until the sailor urges the Count to learn from his example with a phrase that correlates 'landfall', making the dramatic setting itself a metaphor for successful life, with an (objective) view of experience:

> Look at me, after I have reached land, and have seen what I had tasted (i.e., my past experience). (179–81)

This is true wisdom, perhaps as opposed to the un-foolish and 'vigilant' seamen (96–101; Cannuyer 1994) whose ability to 'foresee' storms proves ineffectual[60] and is an ironic allusion to the official's prized ability to foresee the future (e.g., Franke 1994: 168–9); these sailors are expendable, vanishing from the tale without causing the reader any regret. In *Cheops' Court* wonders are continually being 'seen', but in *The Shipwrecked Sailor*,

---

[59] The form of *snj* is uncertain (cf. Baines 1990a: 60): one could read 'while the calamity passes', or 'when the calamity has (*snj.⟨n⟩*) passed. A similar phrase occurs in *Ptahhotep* 557: 'How joyful is he of whom this is said . . .'.

[60] One can compare the effectiveness of the Serpent's 'foreseeing' and the futility of the sailor's (see Cannuyer 1990 on *sr* in the tale).

the various uses of the word 'see' combine to suggest an aim of attaining a degree of self-realization and self-control, and of resisting despair.

At the start of the tale the Count is facing a problematic interview with his king (14–17), but the sailor's tale rewrites this prospect with his account of adventures that earned reward from the king. But then the containment of calamity is disrupted, as is the formal structure (Baines 1990a: 68–9), when the sailor's words meet a refusal from the tale's audience:

> Then he said to me: 'Don't act the clever man, my friend!
> Who pours water [to] a goose,
> when the day dawns for its slaughter on the morrow?' (183–6)

These much-debated lines (Spalinger 1984; Devauchelle 1989; Baines 1990a: 61) echo earlier passages. The opening speech of the 'excellent follower' (13–14) used 'pouring water' as a positive gesture; and the sacrifice of fowl was mentioned as a gesture of gratitude(?) in 145–6. Thus, the prince's reply draws on the sailor's expressions to refuse his suggested remedies, reformulating them into an expression of despair. The formulation may also be doubly ironic, since birds could well be given water just before being sacrificed or butchered (Devauchelle 1989). The question thus forms a supreme suspension in terms of moral and narrative plot. This uncertain atmosphere is reinforced by the timeless anonymous nature of the characters, who lack the historical references which in *Cheops' Court* provide the audience with a known ending that is still effective now, even though the manuscript is incomplete. The Count's refusal has been prepared for from the start by the sailor's remark that 'speaking to you is wearisome' (20–1), and travellers' tales may have been notoriously unreliable (p. 89). Nevertheless, the final speech marks a brutal change in the formal structure. Throughout the tale the pattern of reassuring tale within tale has been countered by the repeated motif of expectation and disappointment; here the attempts at reassurance receive a final shocking twist and the pattern is shattered; the echoes of earlier passages make this ending more bleak. The instability of the tale's 'similarities' is repeatedly foregrounded, and this instability is complemented by the sequences of unanswered questions and of incomplete actions that assert the prevalence of the untoward. The reader follows a journey in a search for meaning that is continually thwarted, except in terms of the audience's literary response (see **5.4**); this subversion of expectations of closure is integral to the tale's meaning, whereas the frustration of expectations and of Cheops' intentions in *Cheops' Court* is an entertaining strategy to generate the need for the tale to continue.

The Shipwrecked Sailor is from a different literary register from *Cheops' Court*, but it does not necessarily embody a radically different cultural role. Both draw on a similar intertext and use similar techniques. Rather, in each the literary event of narration is staged to pass the time in such a way as in part to suggest different aspects of literature's wide-ranging role. In *The Shipwrecked Sailor* narration provides consolation for the flawed universe, while in *Cheops' Court* it provides entertainment; in one, it is a force against calamity, in the other against boredom. *The Shipwrecked Sailor* is in a sense more potentially 'dissident' literature than *Cheops' Court*, raising doubts about the nature of existence and the utility of cultural values in the face of calamity. *Cheops' Court* raises questions about good and bad kings, but for less challenging ends: in *The Shipwrecked Sailor* the king's interaction with his subject, the Count, is left ominously open.

The tension between the norms of official discourse and the literary articulation of divergent experience generates meaning in the high tradition precisely because the two discourses are closely related. The relationship of official discourse with the low, more colloquial, tradition is less close, and when a lower register of narrative style is more independent of official discourse than in *Neferti* or *The Eloquent Peasant*, it can seem more spontaneous to a modern reader and thus closer to modern expectations. But it is also more inconsequential in terms of shaping and testing cultural values.

9
Discourses and dialogues

9.1 DISCOURSES: THE WORLD'S RECREATION

> Love cools, friendship falls off, brothers divide: in cities, mutinies; in countries, discord; in palaces, treason; and the bond cracked 'twixt son and father.
>
> Shakespeare, *The Tragedy of King Lear* (*c.* 1608), I.ii

The extant discourses display a wide range of subject matter, as well as varying degrees of abstraction from the situation presented by their settings. They are also tonally distinct in degree of pessimism. The discourses are dominated by lament formulations, reflecting the reversals of the Nile, death, and the pattern of the transfer of rulership. The association of the king with the Nileflood occurs in Senwosret I's self-presentation as an agent of recreation and renaissance (Franke 1996: 290), and the discourses exist against this official presentation of the pattern of loss and renewal, and the general importance of the non-existent and inchoate in Egyptian thought (Hornung 1982: 172–85). However, the social role-reversals of the discourses also invert the descriptions of the ordered behaviour of servants and the professions in official discourse such as First Intermediate Period biographies (L. Morenz 1999a: 125–30).

The Words of Neferti is the only completely preserved discourse, and is thus the most significant exemplar of the genre. It is also the most explicit text articulating literary activity and charts the differentiation between official eulogy and a more mediated, entertaining, form of discourse. This treatment may be in part an artefact of the poem's early date, when written literature was comparatively new, and required a more explicit identification than later.[1] The composition's conciseness may also be conditioned in part by this date; longer and more elaborate compositions come later. Although *Neferti* engages with specific political themes from the recent past (Posener 1956: 21–60), its construction may be intended to prevent the poetry from being 'simply a vehicle for political comment'

---

[1] It need not reflect a programmatic intention to proclaim the introduction of written literature either as propaganda or as re-creation (cf. Eyre 1993).

(Tarrant 1997b: 173 on Vergil): Neferti's discourse is introduced by substantial, frivolous-toned, narrative prologue.

The narrative setting has two ostensibly programmatic effects. One is to guarantee through royal authority the prophetic discourse in honour of the future king Ameny, which follows the prologue: the renowned Sneferu himself (Graefe 1990) is the person who transcribes it – although the original audience can hardly have believed that the eulogy was a genuine prophecy. Sneferu's renown also enhances the glory of Ameny, since the poem associates the two of them by presenting the royal succession as passing from Sneferu's idealized reign to that of Ameny. The conflict between order and chaos revealed as the passage from rule, through interregnum, to rule is well attested in official discourse, and is the poem's major structuring theme. Royal inscriptions describing the restoration of monuments were presumably one official prototype for the description of chaos (e.g., the Tod and Elephantine inscriptions of Senwosret I). Similar descriptions of ruin and restoration also occur in the contemporaneous non-royal inscriptions of Sarenput I in the chapel of Heqaib in Elephantine (stela nos 9; Franke 1994: 160–1). In *Neferti*, however, Sneferu's frivolity marks him as the fictional king par excellence; although he authorizes the prophecy, he also fictionalizes it.

The second effect of the setting is to counter and contain the prophecy's negative aspects before it begins. In the face of the lament, Sneferu's renown acts as a reassurance that all will be made well, which is reinforced by the semantic similarity of his name with the name of the protagonist – 'He who makes good' (*snfrw*: Graefe 1990: 259) and 'May you be good' (*nfr.tj*) – as well as with Neferti's 'perfect speech' (*mdt-nfrt*) and 'good deed' (*sp-nfr*: 1l; L. Morenz 1996: 5–6). He also contains, and thus counters, the lament by recording it in writing, but this simultaneously signals the event's literary nature: he is producing the archetype of the poem's manuscript (compare the roll at the end of *The Eloquent Peasant*). The containment is staged in terms of enjoyment; since he requests 'entertainment' (1m, 2k), he moves the text's reception from one of indoctrination to one of amusement.

The antiquity of the setting provides a reassuring frame for the discourse, but also transforms the prophecy for the actual Middle Kingdom audience. The lament is in the future tense, doubly neutralizing the lament's impact: the chaos is in the past for the actual audience who view it through the fictional audience, for whom it is in the future. This framing, however, also distances the positive resolution of the prophecy (as Blumenthal notes 1996a: 119), and the intricate temporal perspective provides an oblique angle on the political concerns (as with the *Aeneid*: Tarrant 1997b: 177). The transfer of discourse into a non-functional context is signalled, as in *The Eloquent Peasant*, by the juxtaposition of two contrasting modes and by a sharp contrast in style between the simple and repetitive narrative, in two long stanzas, and the more concise, elevated style of the shorter stanzas of the lament. The scenario of the Royal Tale would create expectations of a eulogy, but instead a brief introduction describing Neferti's discourse (3a–e) prepares the audience for a change in tone, and an agonized cry follows:

> Stir my heart,
> and beweep this land, in which you began! (3f)

Although this is an extemporary performance before the king, the sage addresses his own heart. The monologue is ostensibly an interior meditation, and this device moves the discourse into a subjective personal world since the fictional and the actual audiences are identified with the sage's heart.

The contrast in tone with the narrative might be considered a humorous touch, in which a commoner gives the king a shock, as in the central episode of *Cheops' Court*, but the text provides no indication that Sneferu does not get what he wants. The lament is explicitly presented as a source of pleasure for the fictional audience, paralleling the role of such discourses as literature in the Middle Kingdom corpus. The style of the narrative is marked as verging on entertaining parody, and the changes in expectations are integral to literary discourse (**5.2**). The lament's basic pattern of 'then-now' inversions itself thematizes sudden changes. The comic tone of the narrative and the amiable role-reversal that is produced by the poem's being written down by the king neutralizes the disruptive implications of such inversions, transforming the pattern of inversion into delight. The sage is associated with the joyful goddess Bastet (2r), as against the baleful Sekhmet with whom she is often paired, which may be significant in characterizing his utterances as positive rather than negative. The inversions of the lament and the humour of the narrative diversely inhabit common ground: social role-reversal, with 'the lowermost uppermost' (12c), can evoke laments for the dead (L. Morenz 1999a: 115 n.29; **3.3.1**), but also is potentially humorous in many cultures, where comedy concerns 'the master supposed for the servant, the servant for the master' (G. Gascoigne, *Supposes* [1566], cited by A. Fox 1997: 187). Both the light-hearted role-reversals of later 'satiric papyri',[2] and the intertext of the lament genre suggest that such comic potential is relevant to Egyptian texts. Thematically, the two sections of the poem become unified as the

---

[2] See, e.g., Parkinson 1999a: 171 with references; J. Assmann (1993) restricts the high cultural expressions of such humour to the Ramessid Period.

audience realizes that both the narrative and the lament are concerned with ideal rulers.

Neferti's lament, which is presented as imagined reality, includes wide-ranging descriptions of chaos. Although the chaos is recounted as in the future, it is presented as immediate to his own heart:

> Do not tire! Look, it is in front of you!
> May you attend to what is before you! (4a)

This looking at chaos recalls inscriptions in which the king views destroyed temples before restoring them, as in the Tod inscription: 'A disaster is what I have seen' (1.28). That inscription also shares the poem's concern with enemies throughout the land (1.30; cf. 7d), and poor men becoming robbers (1.29). A phrase in Neferti's lament occurs in a later stela of Ahmose I (rto 18: Helck 1983: 109; *Neferti* 4c), where the restoration is prompted by the king's memory of the disaster, an inner awareness similar to that evoked by Neferti here. The presentation of chaos in *Neferti* is, however, more elaborate than in official discourse. Elke Blumenthal (1982: 6) identifies a sequence of themes concerning cosmic matters (4–7), Asiatics (6–8), and internal chaos (8–11, including personal chaos resulting from failures in communication), and concluding with a return to the cosmic theme (11). This is not a simple ordered progression. The themes are densely interwoven and run across stanza boundaries, while elements acting as refrains, such as 'Destroyed is . . .' and 'I shall show you' (*dj:j-n:k*), run counterpoint both to the stanzas and to the motifs. The phrase 'I shall show you', although addressed to the sage's heart and not directly to the king, ironically echoes scenes in temple relief, where the gods give to the king, and the performative captions read 'I have given to you (*dj.n:j n:k*) all life and power'. There also is an element of contradiction in the chaotic world: the 'river of Egypt is dry' (6a), but two stanzas later foreign flocks come to drink at the river (8a).

Throughout, the lament encompasses cosmology. The chaos is enough to provoke the injunction 'May the Sungod begin to (re)create!' (4c, echoing 3f), foreshadowing the theodic complaint to the creator that is elaborated in the later *Ipuur* (Blumenthal 1996a: 115). The concluding stanza encapsulates and summarizes the whole lament in the loss of the sage's and god's birthplace:

> The land will have no Heliopolitan nome –
> the birthplace of every god.[3] (12g)

---

[3] A 'birthplace of the god' features in Coffin Text maps of the otherworldly 'Field of Hetep' (*CT* V, 358, xxi).

The mention of the nome marks the climax of the lament, and recalls its origin since it is spoken by a man from there (2s). Egypt is abandoned by all the gods (a theme in later writings: J. Assmann 1991: 276–87). The lament presents 'a powerful rendering of life as the Egyptians most deeply do not want it', to paraphrase Northrop Frye on *King Lear* (1964: 99).

Neferti offers no direct explanation for the cause of the chaos, although the Sungod's withdrawal is implicitly a reaction to the social wrongs. The assertion that 'The Sungod separates himself from mankind' (11d), however, alludes to the myth of the sundered world and mankind's rebellion against the creator. The discourse as a whole does not need to discuss the origin of chaos, since the lament is countered with the prophecy of the arrival of a king Ameny (13a), who fulfils Neferti's wish for a re-creation of the land (4c). The contrast between the withdrawal of the gods and the arrival of the king is counterpointed geographically by the loss of the god's (and Neferti's) birthplace in the northern Heliopolitan nome (12g) and Ameny's arrival from the south (13a–b), and the parallel is reinforced by wordplay between the 'birthplace (*msḫnt*) of the gods' and the 'child (*ms*) of Southern Egypt' (12g–13b). The topographical change suggests that the future will be different from, and will surpass, the past, just as the new order will neutralize the chaos.

The name of king Ameny is a short form of Amenemhat, which to an early 12th Dynasty audience meant Amenemhat I, and the mention of a fortress named 'Walls of the Ruler' confirms this identification with a specific detail (Posener 1956: 22–8). Ameny's arrival from the south and the orientation of the lament towards the north and east of the country may have legitimized Amenemhat's expansion from Thebes and his suppression of internal dissent in the north (cf. Do. Arnold 1991: 18–19). However, the southern origin of Ameny also alludes to the myth of the distant goddess Sekhmet (Franke 1994: 8 n.1), which belongs with that of the sundered world and the rebellion of mankind. Ameny's descent as the son of a 'woman of Bowland'[4] may be a discordant historical allusion, contradicting what the audience knew of Amenemhat I's actual ancestry, and reinforcing the fictionalized nature of the prophecy.[5] While the allusiveness of naming Ameny – literally 'The Hidden One' (13a) – rather than Amenemhat might be appropriate for a prophecy, it also reverses the aim of panegyrical identification: commemorative texts aim to record the name of the restorer of order. Although the name allies him with the creator god,[6] who in other texts has 'hidden himself' after the sundering

---

[4] 13b; Gomaà 1986: 9–11. See Franke 1996: 280 n.17 for similar expression of southern descent in a roughly contemporaneous official biography, possibly modelled on *Neferti*.
[5] See Zetzel 1997: 197–8 on the ambivalent effect of such allusions in a prophecy in the *Aeneid*.
[6] It may also associate him with Menes (*jmnjj: mnj*), the mythical founder of Egypt (e.g., J. Assmann 1991: 275).

of the world (**7.2**) but who here returns to Egypt, it also blurs his historical identity. The obliqueness of the naming is striking in a setting that generates expectations of a direct eulogy.

Through Ameny, all will be well 'for all time and eternity', relegating chaos to a temporary disruption (14b). The physical correlative of this is the fortress 'Walls of the Ruler' – a royal rampart against chaos (15a) which reverses the earlier image in the lament that likened society to a defenceless fortress (7f–i). It is a defence, together with the king's fearfulness, against the north-eastern Asiatics, who run through two final stanzas as a reprise of the theme of invading chaos. The language of the final stanzas is an unmodified version of that of monumental inscriptions, and is less diverse than the descriptions of the chaos. It probably represents a third and final, heightened, stylistic register in the poem. The differences in style between the frivolous prologue and these more elevated final stanzas may present Ameny as in some sense surpassing Sneferu. The introduction of the king's arrival with a nominal sentence makes the resolution an interpretive gloss – such as occurs in medical, liturgical and funerary texts (Osing 1977c) – on what precedes: it is not just 'The fact is that a king will come', but also 'This chaos means that a king will come . . .'. This introduction might suggest that chaos exists only so that it can be set right, programmatically demonstrating the value of kingship, but it also implies verbally – as the concentric form of prologue-lament-resolution does structurally – that the centre of the poem is the chaos. The number of stanzas that voice chaos (4–12) is three times that of those articulating the resolution (13–15); the symbolic numbers, nine and three, respectively reinforce the impression of totality (e.g., Fecht 1975: 639). Chaos and order are thus bound together, and the prominence of chaos is the reverse of the pattern in official discourse.

This structuring might be read programmatically as a strategy to associate the king with times of suffering in order to prevent an audience from interpreting the text as an unjustified eulogy of a despot. Similarly, the oblique naming of Amenemhat might be a strategy to soften the text's propagandistic aim, just as the prologue might sweeten it with entertainment. Such strategies, however, are lacking in official discourse, where eulogies require no justification or sweetening. The poem's distinctive features do not strengthen eulogistic aims; rather the specifically political assertions are qualified and placed in an antique and fictionalized context.

In the final verses, the sage moves from the official language describing Ameny's achievements to his own personal one. He moves from an abstract summary of the restoration:

Maat will return to its (proper) place,
with chaos driven outside (15e)

through an implicit injunction for the actual audience to be loyal to the king:

He who will witness, he who will follow the king, will rejoice! (15f)

to a personal reflection on the prophecy's reception:

The sage will pour water for me,
when he sees that what I have said has happened. (15g)

The horror of 'what happens' in the land is made good through the poet's words 'happening', even though 'what I have said' has been predominantly a description of chaos. This prophecy also contrasts Neferti's ordered 'perfect words' and those of the country's enemies, which are chaotic and self-destroying when faced with the king (14d): while the enemies will have to 'beg water' (15c–d), the sage will have water poured out for him by a later sage who has read the poem with his prophecy (15g). 'Pouring water' is a funerary activity, such as are attested in the Ramessid P. Chester Beatty IV as a literary response in honour of an ancient writer.[7] These verses return the audience to the fictional setting of the utterance, and the success of the prophecy is linked to the actual audience's response to the poem (cf. L. Morenz 1996: 156–7, 201).

This conclusion forms a suspension in which the poem's setting is not renewed, as if the audience has to complete the hermeneutic circle by their reception and appreciation. The consolation offered by the prophesied renewal of order and the authority to enable this are thus passed to the Middle Kingdom audience – the poem's art is immediate, whereas the historicity of the prophecy is negated by being left free-floating. Ideological comment is subordinated to the literary event. The perfection of the poet's speech not only describes the arrival of order, but also itself redresses the failure of speech and communication which was symptomatic of the chaotic land (5a, 10h–i, 11a); art both summons up and restores the nightmare of history. The lament's descriptions express the concern for the state of the land which was lacking, and thus reasserts right. In this respect the fictional poet – and by extension the actual one – assumes the royal role as a god who restores order and recreates the world (L. Morenz 1996: 4 n.11). This transformation was staged in the narrative prologue, where the roles of royal master (dictating) and servant/scribe (copying) were strikingly reversed: the motif of the king writing is quite rare even

---

[7] Vso 6.11–7.2; see also Donker van Heel 1992: 21–2. Literary occurrences include *Ipuur* 7.4–5; *A Man* 7.5; *Amenemhat* 4d. Pouring water also occurs at the conclusion of *The Shipwrecked Sailor*, which may be in part an ironic allusion to this literary practice.

in normal circumstances (L. Morenz 1996: 25). This staging of the poet's role shows literary composition dominating the state: non-royal poetic description is presented as a cosmos-constituting pronouncement, not just a means employed by the royal court to control the populace (cf. **5.3**). The end of the laments and of the world's re-creation is rejoicing (15f), which is also 'entertainment' at a literary event.

9.2 *THE WORDS OF KHAKHEPERRESENEB*: STRUGGLING WITH SILENCE

> For last year's words belong to last year's language
> And next year's words await another voice.
> T. S. Eliot, *Little Gidding*, ii (1959: 44)

Interpretations of *The Words of Khakheperreseneb* have been hindered by the assumptions that the poem is exceptional and that only extracts are preserved in the surviving apprentice manuscripts, even though the text may be complete (Parkinson 1997b); critics have also tended to discuss the opening stanzas in isolation. The poem is an internal dialogue between a man and his heart, and it seems to follow the pattern of monologues such as *Sasobek* or *The Eloquent Peasant*, where the addressee remains silent, rather than that of *A Man and His Ba*. There is no narrative prologue, but the title naming the protagonist sets the scene, implying that the speech is a personal soliloquy, as opposed to public communication: the literary utterance stands alone. The choice of the name Khakheperreseneb, including the throne-name of Senwosret II, evokes a time of untroubled rule; as Bernard Mathieu notes, there is a contradiction between the tone of the laments and the substance of his name (1996b: 13; see Cruz-Uribe 1987: 109 for a historicist explanation, suggesting that Khakheperreseneb speaks for contemporaneous disenfranchised nomarchs). His second name 'Ankhu' ('Living one') is also a potentially positive sign, and may make him a representative of the living (Parkinson 1999f: 148 n.1). His role as a priest at Heliopolis is probably an intertextual allusion to the Heliopolitan literary sage, Neferti.

The poem's title implies a struggle to speak, and the much discussed introduction develops the problems of speaking meaningfully about an unprecedented experience of suffering (Mathieu 1996b; Parkinson 1996d; Moers in press). A 'new language' is needed to express this since 'changes are happening – it is not like last year' (rto 10). In the second section the protagonist states 'I have said these things as I have seen' (rto 6), a claim that is made in the future tense in *Neferti* (5e, 15g). Moers (in press) argues that the protagonist is thus confronting literary tradition as embodied by

Neferti, criticizing rhetorical discourse's use of repetition as an expression of cultural identity. However, such intertextual allusions to the tradition, setting one's experience in a non-identical relationship with other works, may be part of standard literary discourse rather than representing an 'individual discovery of the historicity of the literary word'. The monologue does not stage the speaker's confrontation of literary conventions, but self-consciously deploys and revives established forms, making worn-out modes of speech effective.

As well as being 'new', the verses are described as 'straining out what is in my body' (rto 3); the idea of speech as excretion is paralleled in *The Eloquent Peasant* (B1 306–7, 310), and as 'distilling' in *Merikare* (9i), where the metaphor suggests selectivity as well as self-expression (Ockinga 1983: 90–1). In the second stanza, the subject matter moves from dissatisfaction with ways of expression to the speaker's suffering. His speech is now revealed to be directed at his heart in order to bring relief, as an acknowledged speech does also in *Ptahhotep* (264–76; cf. p. 100):

> I would speak this and then my heart would answer me.
> I would enlighten it about my anguish.   (rto 7–8)

The role of the heart suggests a 'philosophical' purpose to the poem,[8] but the specific situation, which is implicit in the title's mention of 'heart-searching', is also the common literary theme of psychological isolation. In *The Shipwrecked Sailor*, the sailor spends three days 'with my heart as my fellow' (42). Similarly, Neferti addresses his heart and urges it to respond (3f–4a).

In the next stanza 'the state of things which have happened throughout the land' (rto 10) is articulated in well-attested terms, similar to those of *Neferti*; while this does not contradict the aims asserted in the first two stanzas, it marks a movement to a less self-consciously troubled mode of speech. Discussing this apparent change, Bernard Mathieu (1996b: 15) suggests a reading of the poem as political propaganda that protests against traditional forms but then subsumes it in traditional forms in order to reassert the status quo. The unfolding of the discourse does not, however, require such a narrowly historicist reading. The lament implies that the grievous state of the land is not the responsibility of the gods, since 'the plans (*sḫrw*) of the gods are thrown into tumult, their directives neglected' (rto 11). The ancestors, whose speech is now worn out, are reduced to 'Lords of Silence', who are violated (rto 12). The lament describes distress

---

[8] Loprieno 1996b: 46. The phrase 'to be searching of heart' is also used of interpreting inscriptions in the early Ramessid tomb inscriptions of Nefersekheru (Osing 1992b; pl. 35 ll. 4–5).

in cosmic terms, as a struggle between 'Maat' and 'Evil', and as an external force overwhelming the sage, being 'what destroys him' (Parkinson 1997b: 66–7).

Nevertheless, the poem is rendered ambiguous through its presentation of its own subjective status in the previous stanza. The protagonist's suffering is the result of

> the load which is on my back,
> (namely) the utterances that are what make me helpless.
> I would tell it (my heart) what I suffer because of it.
> I would say 'Ah!' on account of my relief (?). (rto 7–9)

In *A Man and His Ba* the man talks of 'my heavy need' as 'a [load] which (my soul) has placed on me' (28–9). The opening stanzas have expressed the aim of language as internal, to seek out the heart, and they raise an issue inherent in the genre: how far are the expressions of woe formulations of actual distress, and how far are they fictional or conventional literary expressions? The positive allusions in the sage's name imply that he is speaking in a good time. His woe is also initially identified directly with the 'utterances' which he must communicate, that is, unburden onto his heart in order to escape from them. The words themselves are suffering and a burden (an image repeated in rto 10, 13, vso 6), not just an expression of it. He goes on to imply that his distress is due to an unresponsive heart:

> As for a brave heart amid pain,
> it is a companion for its lord.
> If only I had a heart which knew suffering!
> Then I should alight on it,[9]
> load it with words of misery,
> and drive away my anguish onto it. (rto 13–14)

The idea of the 'brave heart' also occurs in *P. Ramesseum II*, where the heart as the enricher of character is described as a 'brave teacher to fashion good qualities' (vso i.5). The motif of the heart is related to a theodic theme, implying that a man's suffering in an imperfect world may be due to his own heart rather than the 'painful situation' in the land imposed by external forces. Although this shift heightens the ambiguity, it paradoxically marks a progress towards possible resolution, since the sage moves

---

[9] This image also occurs at the resolution of *A Man and His Ba*: 'I shall alight when you are weary' (153, recalling earlier passages: 37, 50–1).

from describing his inability to speak to an expressive description of the land in chaos.

The section preserved on the verso begins formally as a prayer, addressed not to a god or external force to rescue the protagonist from the situation, but to his own heart:

> O come my heart, that I may speak to you!
> and you shall answer me my verses,
> explain to me what is throughout the land . . . (vso 1)

The heart's fault is that it will not respond with an explanation or interpretation (wh^c: see **11.2** for this idiom). In the subsequent descriptive lament, 'hearts' feature prominently: the hearts of two people whose roles are reversed are 'calm' at this (vso 3); hearts find it impossible to 'put aside' these things (vso 3):

> The heart cannot accept Maat/Truth.
> They have had no patience ($wḫd$) with the reply to a speech. (vso 5)

This recalls the ideal heart, which was described as 'knowing suffering' ($wḫd$: rto 13–14). Woe is articulated as a failure in communication, and as the loss of honest speech. No attempt is made at knowledge or communication, just as in *Neferti* 'what comes from the mouth cannot be suffered ($wḫd$)' (11a). The speaker cannot speak because speech is impossible. Although the causes of misery that are described in ostensibly objective terms are external, such as the 'strangers' who persist (vso 2), there is a sense in which the sage's heart makes its own place. Other hearts, not just his own, are defective, so that the uncertainty and ambiguity are maintained. The final verses summarize Khakheperreseneb's situation:

> I speak to you, my heart, so that you shall answer me.
> A heart which is touched ($pḥ$) cannot be silent.
> Look, the servant's portion is like the lord's;
> and many things are burdensome for you. (vso 5–6)

The 'servant' is the heart, and the 'lord' Khakheperreseneb, echoing the earlier commendation of a brave heart's relationship with its 'lord' (rto 13). Although it is uncertain whether this is merely a final extract or the end of the original composition, the phrase suggests a reconciliation between the two that acknowledges their similarities in suffering. The heart has now been 'touched' (Ockinga 1983: 92–3 n.38), just as the eloquent peasant says (albeit ironically) to his interlocutor 'Look, you are touched!' (B1 250). The heart too can feel suffering now, being burdened, and this is a paradoxically positive note.[10]

The interdependence of the protagonist and his heart is unambiguously asserted, and is almost a sign of social solidarity and reciprocity, rather than being a role-reversal in which the servants now possess as much as their lords. The language echoes an earlier passage which lamented that 'yesterday's portion (ḥrt) thereof (i.e., of woe) is like today's' (vso 3). The heart, of course, does not reply, but this need not undermine the sage's confidence that he is reaching a resolution. Implicit in this silent conclusion is the knowledge that speaking to the heart is a literary convention, and the heart, as in *Neferti*, will not necessarily answer.

The opening stanzas foreground both the intertextual position of Khakheperreseneb and the internal nature of his conversation. This allows the subsequent expression of his distress to acquire a triumphant character and thus to explain his lament. Since self-expression becomes possible as he addresses his heart, the lack of communication in the land is implicitly overcome. The fictional and entertaining nature of speech, which was set in a distant time in *Neferti*, is here marked by being set within the protagonist's psyche, and thus also removed from pragmatic ends of discourse. From its opening on, *Khakheperreseneb* presents its own internal, subjective status, subverting the referential aspect of the descriptions of 'what has happened'. The chaos and suffering in the poem are neutralized by being expressed and recorded in exuberantly virtuosic verses. The inexpressible becomes unproblematic by being formulated in the traditional style of literature, which itself is renewed in this manner.

9.3 *THE DIALOGUE OF IPUUR AND THE LORD TO THE LIMIT*: THE ARCHITECTURE OF THE GREAT ARGUMENT

tantaene animis caelestibus irae

Vergil, *Aeneid* (19 BCE), I l.11

The differentiated nature of literary discourse often involves a tension between different attitudes and discourses. The subgenre of dialogue stages this unfolding directly as a discussion between two speakers, showing how far the attitudes in question are incorporated within literary discourse. In the subgenre, two voices are explicitly in conflict, but the exchange of

---

[10] The dialogue is not fully resolved, however, since the final verse is ambiguous: since 'many things' might be 'burdensome for' the heart (Gardiner 1909a: 108), or 'because of' it and its intransigence (Kadish 1973: 79).

king and courtiers as it occurs in official Royal Tales in a simple pattern of question and answer, doubt and affirmation, is resisted.

The analysis of both surviving dialogues has been problematic. The text of *Ipuur* is unstable, due to the state of the manuscript and its publication history, and interpretation is uncertain. Although the poem is comparatively well-known among modern readers, including Bertolt Brecht (e.g., Wenig 1969; J. Assmann 1996a: 127–8), its style has had little sympathetic reception (Renaud 1988) and it has attracted controversy concerning the possible 'historical' basis of its descriptions of chaos (see Lichtheim 1973: 149–50; L. Morenz 1999a: 113–18). In contrast to historicist approaches that assign the text to an intermediate period, Gerhard Fecht (1972; see now Sitzler 1995: 33–6) has examined part of the poem as a theodic complaint, although his approach is overly redactionalist.

Ipuur is named once in the surviving manuscript without a title (15.13), although he is an 'Overseer of Singers' in the 'Daressy fragment' (**2.2.2**). He appears to be addressed in the plural at least once (16.12: Fecht 1972: 195), suggesting that he is a representative of a larger group, or of humanity. It is difficult to deduce his rank from the context. The identity of his interlocutor has been much debated. Historicist critics, following Alan H. Gardiner (1909a), have regarded the interlocutor as a king, while Eberhard Otto and others have identified him as the creator god (Quack 1997: 349–51 with refs.; Fecht 1972: 35–7, 44–8). If the interlocutor is divine, Ipuur may be imagined as being dead (Fecht 1972: 47–8); such a situation is alluded to in other literary texts, where a dead man is described as appealing to a god (*A Man and His Ba* 145–7). The interlocutor is described as 'the Person of the Lord to the Limit' (*ḥm n-nb-r-ḏr*: 15.13, 16.11 [Fecht 1972: 194]). 'Person' (*ḥm*) is used of the king and can be applied to gods (as in *Horus and Seth*), while 'Lord to the Limit' is used of the creator god in the Coffin Texts in a theodic context,[11] and of the king in the Middle Kingdom in *Amenemhat* only.[12] Various considerations make an identification of the Lord as the king the most likely. The text seems to allude to the creator god in the third person as 'the All-Lord' (*nb-tm*).[13] The general character of the passages addressed to the interlocutor in the

---

[11] Spell 1130: *CT* VII, 461d; *CT* VI, 376d; as an epithet of various gods including Atum, Re, Osiris, and Thoth: B. Altenmüller 1975: 272–3.

[12] Commoner in the New Kingdom: Blumenthal 1970: 103. The rare female equivalent *nbt-r-ḏr* is used of the queen in *Sinuhe* B 172, 274, and of the goddess Hathor in various texts including: the Coffin Texts: B. Altenmüller 1975: 277; P. Ramesseum VIII 11.7: Gardiner 1955a: pl. 38; a funerary harpist's song: Parkinson 1991a: 127.

[13] 12.11; read differently by Helck 1995: 56–7. In the Coffin Texts *nb-tm* has a similar range of application to gods to that of *nb-r-ḏr*. B. Altenmüller 1975: 275–6. If the Lord to the Limit and the creator are the same, Ipuur must address his interlocutor in both the second and the third person. Although this variety of address is possible, certain phrases suggest that 'he' and 'you' are distinct individuals (e.g., 12.12).

second person as a whole is suggestive of a human addressee,[14] and one verse places the interlocutor in the position of someone who offers to a god (5.9; see Fecht 1974), while a couplet draws a parallel between the addressee and a mortal 'man' (8.5–6). Ipuur uses variously both second person singular and plural (e.g., 12.5–6: m̱tn and ṯw), showing that the interlocutor is imagined as being accompanied by an entourage.

The social aspect of the speeches' subject matter and the prominence of royal motifs are suggestive of a king, whom the title 'Lord to the Limit' marks as a representative of the creator. He is a theodic figure rather than a historical or political one. The universalized nature of this terminology suggests that the setting may have been timeless like that of *Khakheperreseneb*, rather than a specific reign as in *The Eloquent Peasant*.

The nature of the composition is better assessed from a view of the whole than from detailed analysis of imagery or motif (see Parkinson 1999f: 170–99 for some developments in the dialogue on a level of detail). The text seems to be organized in a pattern of lament/complaint and answer, but it is uncertain how much is lost at the beginning. The surviving text opens with a speech of Ipuur (1.1–6.14) that describes the misbehaviour of various professions (1.1–1.5; L. Morenz 1999a: 119–30). It is addressed to the (plural) entourage (1.7–8), and is full of images that reverse official descriptions of the professions at work. The speech then becomes a lament, structured by refrains ('O, but . . .'), of some 67 stanzas (Lament I: 1.9–6.14). The basic theme is 'This is the destruction of the land' (2.12). Egypt is described as being without Maat, and abandoned by god (5.3–4). The refrain implies a contrast ('but') with the ideal state of affairs. The actual state of affairs inspires doubt as to efficacy of offerings, and a theodic complaint is explicitly sounded:

> Is it libations for Ptah, taking [materials(?)]?
> Why do you give to him? It does not reach him,
> and your giving to him is misery! (5.7–9; Fecht 1974)

This motif of an unsuccessful appeal recalls the setting, in which Ipuur is speaking to the king. Such is this misery that there is a desire for oblivion:

> If only this were the end of mankind! (5.14)

The lament details social rather than cosmic chaos, concentrating on the immediacy of suffering in specific detail.

Immediately after this lament comes a second, slightly shorter, one of 50 stanzas with refrains starting 'Look . . .' (Lament II 7.1–9.8). These

---

[14] 1.7–8; this recalls a phrase in *The Fowler* (P. Butler l.15), where the addressee is human.

refrains are perhaps more blunt and direct than those of the preceding. The first part of Lament II is very concerned with the state of the kingship and the uraeus, signalling what Odette Renaud (1988: 73) termed the 'source-theme' which has been implicit in the preceding stanzas, the ruin of royal power as the origin of woe. The lament then moves to more general social concerns:

> For, look, these things – the transformations of mankind!
> (7.8; see Buchberger 1993: 209 n.89)

Both laments are very long, and full of violent actions and contrasts, as if providing a comprehensive account of all possible social ills. They are more elaborate than the descriptions of *Neferti* and more extensively and evidently self-contradictory (Lichtheim 1973: 149–50; Renaud 1988). They are, however, even in this, highly coherent in producing the effect of an onrush of chaos and reversal. 'Pour décrire un univers anormal, [l'auteur] a utilisé un discours lui aussi anormal', making it dramatic, excessive and terrible.[15] The contradictions that express chaos also signal the fictional nature of the text, while the elaborate use of wordplay foregrounds its character as a rhetorical tour de force. The laments utilize a great diversity of terms for evil and misfortune, and the impact of the stanzas is increased by their being linked together by recollections of words and themes (examples in Parkinson 1999f: 191–9). The frequent repetition of phrases and patterns of reversals presents the dominance of evil. By creating the opposite of official descriptions of good governance, the laments create an awareness of the continuing lack of any saviour to restore order.

Ipuur's speech continues with a largely hortative section (Injunction I; 9.8–10.12). This seems to begin with two stanzas urging the plural fictional audience to 'destroy' those who cause evil (9.8–10.2),[16] followed by a descriptive lament about what is 'destroyed' (10.2) easing the transition from mediation to hortation. This is followed by six(?) short stanzas with the refrain 'Destroy the enemies of that fine Residence, splendid of courtiers!' (10.6; see Fecht 1972: 31–2). There follows a second hortative section, similarly structured with refrains urging the audience to 'Remember . . .' good events, in particular cultic actions (Injunction II = 10.12–11.10; Fecht 1972: 27–31). This section echoes descriptions of temples in festal hymns, as in a Ramessid hymn to the

---

[15] Renaud 1988: 74; interpreting differently as revealing the speaker's exasperation (1988: 72).
[16] For alternative reading of ḥḏ as 'Destroyed are . . .' throughout this passage see, e.g., Quack 1992: 88; 1997: 346 n.7. This section may relate to official battle lyrics, such as that in the tomb of Khety II at Asyut (Griffith 1889: pl. 13 [Siut IV] ll.11–15; Franke 1990: 125–6), which displays similarities in phrasing to other passages of *Ipuur*.

Nileflood (ODeM 1105, rto 20–vso 1; text: Fischer-Elfert 1986b: 46–7), and relates to official injunctions to priests to 'remember' the cult, such as in the inscription of Sarenput I in the Heqaib chapel (temp. Senwosret I; stela 10 l. x+4: Franke 1994: 178, 182).[17] This is not just an injunction to be mindful of the present cult, as in *Merikare* (23e–24b), but develops the theme of lost good mentioned in a previous stanza (10.4–5), explicitly locating such things in the past, mobilizing the past:present pattern of the laments for hortative effect. In the earlier laments, religious affairs were described as neglected; remembrance, piety, wisdom and social good are synonymous.

The pair of laments and the pair of injunctions are bound together by the use of refrains. One pair presents the situation and the other desired responses, while the description of wrongs links the first injunction to the preceding lyrics. As in *Neferti*, an imbalance is created: the negative laments are longer and more forceful than the injunctions, and the positive consolations that are described are temporally distant and less secure. In particular, laments are elsewhere used to throw the glory of a future king into relief, and here could introduce a representation of royal authority who will set the cosmos to right, as in official discourse and in *Neferti*. Alternately they could describe programmatically the state of a land without royal authority. These laments, however, gain much of their force from the fact that the potential saviour is in control and presiding over the chaos. Ipuur moves from the laments not to reaffirm authority but to question the basic assumption of authority that the present social order reflects the intent of a just and benign creator.

After a fragmentary passage, in which the Sungod is mentioned (11.11), comes a passage that opens as if returning to the 'look . . .' lament but is a more reflective complaint about the nature of creation (11.11–13.8; Fecht 1972):

> Look, why was He seeking to shape (*lit.* build) ⟨humanity (?)⟩,[18]
> when the meek were not distinguished from the savage,
> so that he might have brought coolness upon the heat?[19]
> One says 'He is the shepherd of all;
> there is no evil in his heart.'
> (But) small is his herd, even though he has made the day to care for them,
> and fire belongs to their hearts!

---

[17] In P. Chester Beatty IX (= P. BM EA 10689) vso B 13.1–2 (a magical text), a magician is urged 'Remembered for you is the holiday; forgotten for you is the evil on the holiday' (Gardiner 1935a: pl. 60, 110).

[18] The scribe's omission is supplied thus by Gardiner 1909a: 79. On the metaphor of building as creation see, e.g., Franke 1994: 286 n.37.

[19] Possibly echoing an earlier fragmentary passage (9.9).

> If only he had realized their character in the first generation![20]
> Then he would have struck down opposition, and stretched out his arm against them,
> and destroyed the flock of them and their heirs.   (11.1–12.3)

The passage can be elucidated by comparison with the final stanzas of *Merikare*, where similar language is employed in a eulogy of, rather than a complaint about, the creator (46–7). The verse about making the day for humanity reveals an anthropocentric ethos, similar to that of *Merikare* (47a), which is different from the view of the cosmos presented in Middle Kingdom funerary literature (Bickel 1994: 178–9, 215–23). The shepherd/herdsman metaphor is commonly applied to the figure of the creator and king (e.g., D. Müller 1961; Blumenthal 1970: 323 [G 4.36–8]); here, however, the smallness and nature of the herd implies that the divine shepherd has failed in his duty: in *Loyalist* it is said that 'the bad shepherd – his herd is small' (13.8). The metaphor also alludes to royal responsibility. In *Merikare*, the language of 'smiting' articulates the fact that the creator is victorious over rebellious men (47i–j), while here such action is lacking, even though desired by men. It develops the observed despair of people – who wished they had not been born (4.2–3) – into a sustained, extreme questioning complaint. Although the 'character' of men is presented as the original source of evil in the mythical rebellion of mankind, Ipuur voices the creator's responsibility for humanity's fiery hearts that gave rise to this 'opposition'. The density and allusiveness of the argument contrasts sharply with what precedes: clause and imagery are more extended and densely interwoven here, as they are in *The Eloquent Peasant*'s petitions, than in the series of stanzas with refrains. The passage gains additional force by being addressed to the Lord himself, not to him and his entourage.

After further descriptions of human wickedness that implicitly justify this questioning, Ipuur complains that god takes no action to rectify or constrain humanity's flawed nature. The lack of god is stated through the metaphor of a pilot:

> There is no pilot in their hour[21] . . .   (12.5–6)

The metaphor of shepherd/herdsman is also reintroduced:

> He who tends his [herd], he sees the day, and [his her]d is small.

---

[20] Compare the Coffin Texts: 'before the first generation had been born' (*CT* II, 34d). The phrase also features in the Tod inscription of Senwosret I, where the king's renown is decreed to him from 'the first generation' (l.40, Barbotin and Clère 1991: 25, n.132).

[21] Gilula 1981: 395–6. A similar sentiment is found in 5.3.

This verse echoes the opening of the complaint, but here the herdsman is not the creator of the day, but someone who simply views it, and the description is an instance of social chaos, enacting the withdrawal of god within the metaphors. Together these metaphors, which elsewhere can refer to the king, form a transition from the complaint against the absent god to that against his representative:

> The All-Lord (*nb-tm*) has made that the sky be separate from the earth,[22]
> and fear is in every face when he comes –
> (but) if he does these things as one who attacks you,
> who will enter (protest) against this, if you refuse to?
> Surely, Utterance, Perception, and Maat are with you –
> but it is confusion which you have put throughout the land,
> and the noise of tumult. (12.11–13)

The passage mobilizes the myth of the sundered earth, which was itself a reaction to the rebellion of mankind: the separation of earth and sky recalls the reasons for the creator's absence. The Lord is here directly accused of responsibility for the chaos in the land: Ipuur moves from the effects to the cause of the distress. The god Utterance should fell the enemies of the cosmos, as in the statement by the creator where it fells his enemy (*CT* VII, 466b), but here only tumultuous noise is created. The subsequent verses contain bitter denunciations, interwoven with descriptions of the violent state of the land, that articulate the irony implicit in the preceding images and their relevance to the Lord:

> Does a herdsman (really) love death?[23]
> If so, you should command that assent (*wšb*) be given to this! (12.14)

Similarly Ipuur rebukes the Lord for 'creating' this chaos and 'speaking Falsehood!' (13.1–2), when it is the divine attributes of Utterance and Maat (12.12) that should be spoken, and the king should create love and order (e.g., Blumenthal 1970: 432–4 [H1.2–4]).

The fragmentary state of the manuscript makes it uncertain who speaks the next section (13.9–14.5). In 15.13 Ipuur begins to 'answer' the Lord (Fecht 1972: 187–9), who therefore speaks the immediately preceding lines, but the point at which he starts to speak is uncertain (see below n.24).

---

[22] See n.13.
[23] Similar bitter rhetorical questions occur in the complaints of *The Eloquent Peasant* (e.g., B1 179–81; Parkinson 1988: 163–4). In the light of these parallels I differ from Gilula 1981 and read *jn-jw-rf-mnjw mrj:0-mwt*. Alternatively, one could render with a similar general import: 'Is a loving shepherd (as good as) dead? If so . . .'. Other comments on the phrase include: Fecht 1972: 83–6; Lichtheim 1973: 162 n.28.

Ipuur's speech probably includes the following descriptive section (13.9–14.5) which echoes Injunction II ('Remember . . .') in form and tone. The new section comprises a series of descriptive stanzas, with the refrain 'It is so good . . .', asserting a vision of an ideal ordered society in a festivity that is not limited to the cultic. This complements the sage's laments and is both a moment of release and a bitter contrast, the refrains reversing the preceding expressions of desperation and implying an alternative world to that described in the two laments. The final stanza describes the New Year – a dangerous period potentially full of reversals – as a happy feast.

The complaint about the creator and king is thus flanked by two descriptive sections of lost happiness. The stanzas with refrains move from descriptions of evil, through injunctions to react, to remembrance, and then after the discursive complaint, to a description of happiness that is not specifically located in a different time-frame and which provides a sense of an alternative reality. There is a similar progression in the lyrics of *A Man and His Ba*, in which they prepare for the final resolution of the complaint.

The next section is a very fragmentary '"Kriegerischer" Abschnitt' (Fecht 1972: 35). This is apparently spoken by the Lord and may be the first time that he answers Ipuur in the original whole composition. Once again, the identity of the speaker is uncertain; Fecht places the start of the Lord's reply in the lacuna of 15.5–10 (1972: 33–5), making this section balance Ipuur's earlier injunctions to 'destroy' (Injunction I), so that the whole of Ipuur's speech after the laments would be concentrically structured around the discursive complaint. Such a short reply by the Lord as Fecht proposes (15.5/10–15.13) is perhaps unlikely, and the start of the Lord's speech can also be placed in the four-line lacuna of 14.6–9.[24] The speech apparently balances the preceding discursive complaint of Ipuur, and takes up the theme of enemies from Injunction I (9.8–10.11). This passage includes rhetorical questions, similar to Ipuur's, evoking how Egypt should protect itself against foreigners (see p. 101), but juxtaposed with this is the question:

> But how – when every man is killing his brother,
> and the Youth we raised for ourselves have become Bowmen (*pḏtjw*,
>   barbarians),
> fallen to destruction? (14.14–15.1)[25]

---

[24] The speaker refers to himself as 'we' in 14.14–15.1, unlike Ipuur's general use of the singular elsewhere to refer to himself. The speaker addresses his audience as 'you (plural)' both in 15.3 and 15.11; the Lord addresses Ipuur in the plural in 16.12 (as restored by Fecht 1972: 194–201). One cannot easily restore a change of speaker any earlier than 14.6–9; the lacuna of 13.8 is scarcely large enough to restore '[What the Lord to the Limit said, / when he answered Ipuur:]' as in 15.13.

[25] See also Buchberger 1993: 363–5, with different reading.

Here the 'we' is apparently the Lord and his entourage, and their troops have themselves become the enemies. This transformation of the people into barbarians recalls the fluctuating identity of Sinuhe who became 'a Bowman (*pdtj*) born in Egypt' (*Sinuhe* B 276).[26] The Lord uses the transformations of mankind, which were earlier a manifestation of his responsibility, to imply that the defenceless and disordered state of the land is the responsibility of humanity, apparently suggesting that it is something 'that you (plural) have made happen' (15.4, broken context). Violent conflict is characteristic of the earlier laments aimed at the Lord (14.14 echoes earlier 9.3). The Lord also indicates that the threat derives from outside Egypt, as if foreigners represent the ever-present chaos, while Egyptians can unleash this on themselves. The motif of invasion is attested in *Neferti* and *Merikare*, and also in royal monumental texts such as the Tod inscription of Senwosret I, which mentions Nubians, Asiatics, and Medjai of the Eastern desert in connection with the restoration of a temple (ll.35–8). The Lord appeals here both to a negative anthropology of the Egyptians, and to a negative cosmology in which the state is threatened by external forces that are represented by foreigners. He thus mobilizes human conflict to defend his responsibility. The description of conflict, however, serves to render the title 'Lord to the Limit' ambiguous, by suggesting not limitless power, but a limit to the ruler's sway, since the Egyptians are becoming enemy peoples from beyond the limits of order. The Lord's reply apparently concludes with a list of good things (15.10–13), which recalls and presumably 'answers' the list that was cited against him earlier (10.12–11.9; 13.9–14.5).

Ipuur's response (15.13–16.10) rejects the Lord's speech directly on behalf of mankind:

> So you (sing.) have done what seems perfect to their hearts, and have made
>   people live[27] by this:
> (But) they (still) cover their faces for fear of the next morning![28]
>
> (15.13–16.1; Fecht 1972: 187–9)

The sarcastic contrast between what is claimed and what is the case recalls the technique used earlier (12.1–2). Ipuur then begins a parable (16.1), which may have taken up motifs in the previous fragmentary speech, concerning a man who dies leaving an immature son who laments his

---

[26] See **8.2**. There are other intertextual allusions here. The irony of royal soldiers acting as enemies of the king is central to *Amenemhat*, which is specifically alluded to elsewhere in *Ipuur* (6.12–14).
[27] This echoes other official eulogies: Blumenthal 1970: 350 (G6.16–18).
[28] Compare *Khakheperreseneb*: 'each day one must wake to it (wrong)' (vso 3); 'every day one wakes to suffering' (vso 4).

death, and apparently describes how the innocent can suffer, despite the Lord's rebuke that mankind is responsible for its own wrongs. The protagonist seems to allude to the responsibility of the king and court as protectors of the poor, apparently arguing that ultimately they are responsible for the death (16.2). The earlier brief vignettes of woeful situations here become a fuller and more detailed narration that may have had a correspondingly greater impact on the audience.

Enough remains of the following section to show that it was a reply by the Lord to the Limit, seemingly a renewed rebuke of humanity's wrong and irresponsibility (16.11–17.2; Fecht 1972: 194–201):

If one calls upon[29] them, [they do not hear].   (16.13; Fecht 1972: 196)

The weeping of the innocent child (16.2) is here replaced with an injunction to the gods themselves to weep as men destroy the temples and tombs[30] that were earlier described by Ipuur as images of social order. Humanity – 'their followers' – has rejected the gods rather than being abandoned by them. The penultimate extant line reads:

How evil is the beginning ⟨blank⟩   (17.1)

One can perhaps restore 'of rebellion' (cf. *Merikare* 1f) or 'of humanity' (since one other blank left by the scribe can be restored thus: 11.13). Beyond this point, the text is lost; the copy as preserved did not continue much further, but since the manuscript was reused, the original composition may have contained further speeches before a resolution was reached.

The structure can be summarized as follows:
[title/introduction]

[. . .]

Ipuur: Introduction to lament
      Lament I ('O, but . . .')
      Lament II ('Look . . .')
      Injunction I ('Destroy . . .')
      Injunction II ('Remember . . .')
      Discursive Complaint
      Meditation ('It is so good . . .')

---

[29] This may echo the earlier rebuke to the Lord to remember leaving the temple for '[a man] who has called upon (*jȝš*) you' (11.7).

[30] Recalling the language of royal restoration texts, such as the Tod inscription of Senwosret I, ll.27–30.

Lord: Rebuke I

Ipuur: Reply and parable

Lord: Rebuke II

[...]

The refrained laments contrast sharply with the more densely articulated discursive sections, although there are transitional passages between the formally distinct sections. On the reconstruction just given, the initial(?) speech of Ipuur dominates the whole in both length and formal variety. Thematically, the two long laments were perhaps flanked by an introduction and an injunction (I), with the speech culminating in a discursive complaint, flanked by two sections on lost ideals (Injunction II and Meditation). The speech can also be read sequentially as two laments followed by two injunctions, ending with the complaint and the final meditation. The additive style of short stanzas gives way to a desperately questioning complaint, in which the speaker offers answers only for them to be rejected and lead into further questioning, before the final section where the resumption of stanzas reinforces the sense of despair by contrasting the complaint with a vision of an alternate and unattained reality.

The nature of the whole dialogue's resolution remains problematic, as does the manner of the argument, but the conclusion was probably positive in some sense (e.g., Quack 1997: 351–3). In the only similar work whose ending is preserved, *A Man and His Ba*, the resolution is articulated in a short speech by one of the protagonists. The use of parables in an argumentative dialogue can be seen more clearly in *A Man and His Ba*, where they are a final manoeuvre by one speaker, so that these fragmentary speeches may have been close to the end. *A Man and His Ba*'s conclusion seems abrupt to a modern reader, and the same could have been true of *Ipuur*, but it remains difficult to imagine how this poem could be resolved within a short space after Rebuke II. There is nothing to suggest that the composition would have contained a direct theodic declaration in reply to the central complaint similar to the creator's declaration in Coffin Text spell 1130 (cf. Fecht 1972: 120–7). The dialogue operates with literary and rhetorical effect, with refrains – apparently a prestigious form – being a prerogative of Ipuur. The Lord's extant replies seem limited to addressing the issues that have been immediately raised, and are rebukes against the source of the wrongs, suggestive of an allusive answer, as opposed to the concise, non-specific statement in the Coffin Text spell. The speeches and sections seem to grow shorter as the dialogue progresses, perhaps producing a positive movement towards dialogue after the long monologue of Ipuur.

The Lord's replies seem to be increasingly pessimistic in tone, perhaps suggesting a movement towards a shared stance of the two protagonists, and some sort of a reconciliation.

The overall tone of the text and its possible effect on the audience is less difficult to assess, but is nevertheless problematic. Both the laments and the more discursive complaints uttered by Ipuur are types of text elsewhere presented for the entertainment of a fictional audience, but that is not the case here, even though the laments order the chaos of a meaningless world aesthetically into formal poetry of a high register.[31] The dialogue structure presents a more combative attitude involving the fictional audience, and thus implicitly the actual audience. In presenting a vision of the woes caused by a lack of effective royal power, the dialogue is in part a reflection on the central importance of kingship (Renaud 1988). The audience's sympathies, however, seem to be evoked for Ipuur rather than for the representative of kingship. Part of the overall effect may also have been to encourage the audience to 'expose thyself to feel what wretches feel' (*The Tragedy of King Lear*, III.4 l.34). The last fully preserved verse of the central 'complaint' section is an urgently expressed desire that the Lord should feel sympathy with humanity who suffer under chaos: 'If only you would taste (*dp*) a little of the misery of this!' (13.5–6). Similarly, in *The Eloquent Peasant* (B1 142–4) the peasant wishes misfortune on his interlocutor, so that he will experience suffering similar to that being presented to him. Since the actual audience will have been members of the elite who are described as having been overthrown and usurped, the reversals will have been specifically relevant, rather than simply evoking a life-in-death state for the whole land that draws upon the imagery of generalized funerary laments. Although Ipuur voices the elite's concerns, potential empathy with the oppressed is present. The actual elite audience – in a period characterized by some degree of social mobility – could have identified itself either with the fictional former elite who are now oppressed or with the fictional new elite who had once been oppressed. No simple identification is allowed, and society is bound together into a unity, if an unhappy one.

The issues of audience identification are thus complex, as in *The Eloquent Peasant*, through the mobilization of social ranks and sympathies as well as through the fictional audience. If Ipuur acts as a representative of humanity, the whole is in some sense a dialogue about responsibility for culture and society. Both Ipuur and the Lord include detailed assessments of human political conduct, rather than generalized laments, and the poem's pessimism appears much more direct than that of *Neferti*,

---

[31] L. Morenz (1999a: 134) suggests there are elements of humour in the poem, but I do not detect any such, beyond the general concerns of literature with entertainment.

where a sage's lament is distanced from present political authority. Ipuur argues in favour of elite intervention and responsibility, while the Lord apparently argues that responsibility is with the governed as well as with the governors. Both mobilize a negative Egyptian concept of human nature, but for contrasting ends. The questioning includes the authority of the creator, and his withdrawal is presented as a sign both of his and of humanity's responsibility for wrong. This exploration opens up and mobilizes gaps in the ideology. The discussion is staged as a virtuosic performance and the skilfully constructed and self-contradictory rhetoric that presents its pessimistic vision also in part characterizes it as a fictional literary performance similar to Neferti's. The aesthetic aspects, however, also involve the audience in the debate of ideas, as well as distancing them through its fictional character: Ipuur sarcastically acclaims the Lord's actions in terms reminiscent of literary reception as being 'perfect to the heart' (15.13, quoted above; cf. **4.5**). Given the architecture of the extant composition, it is hard to imagine a resolution that could have contained the full force of this discourse to the extent that it entrapped it.

9.4 *THE DIALOGUE OF A MAN AND HIS BA*: REPRESENTING DEATH

> A man awaits his end
> Dreading and hoping all. . . .
> He knows death to the bone –
> Man has created death.
>
> W. B. Yeats, 'Death' (1929)

The Dialogue of a Man and His Ba, which is the best preserved example of the dialogue genre, has been problematic for interpretation. There has been discussion as to whether the poem is based on specific individual experience – reading it as a sort of suicide note – or on an analytical argument. The latter approach has predominated, and the poem has been read as a 'theological' duel between differing attitudes to burial, the efficacy of funeral rites (R. J. Williams 1962), or to the nature of the *ba*, the principle of existence and movement for a person after death, often loosely translated as 'soul' (Barta 1969; overview: Lohmann 1998: 207–10). The nature of the *ba*, however, is not at stake; it is simply one of the speakers (Renaud 1991; Tobin 1991: 355–6). Some parts of the text, such as the *ba*'s parables, are not susceptible to a 'theological' line of interpretation, and this possible discrepancy has given rise to allegorical readings of certain sections, and ultimately of the whole text. In such approaches the two speakers represent idealistic and materialistic philosophies (Goedicke 1970a: 38–59; Tobin 1991: 359).

This strategy is problematic in its analysis of the dynamics by which the discussion proceeds. The protagonists restate their positions in various metaphorical ways (Barta 1969: 99) and the text ends as the *ba* abruptly agrees with the man, on no evident rational basis. Moreover, for an argumentative treatise the audience has to decide between the speakers' arguments, whereas the dialogue does not contain a clearly argued dismissal of either side's case. A view of the dialogue in terms not of content but of its literary structure suggests a more coherent analysis. The poem is dominated by figurative and subjective imagery ('to me', 'like'). Various motifs are interwoven increasingly, and each speaker employs imagery and literary form to persuade his opponent and the audience.[32] The dialogue is not a logical argument about an aspect of belief but a discourse about a broad subject. The composition has been thought to be abnormal because of its cynicism (e.g., Renaud 1991), but it has clear affinities with other Middle Kingdom compositions: the phraseology, subject matter and included genres recall those of *Ipuur*, while the personal focus recalls *Khakheperreseneb*. The man of the dialogue is probably meant to be considered a sage (see Parkinson 1996c). A bleak view of death, similar to the *ba*'s, also features in *Sasobek*:

> Death is a *qj*-canker;
> it is the destruction(?) of life;
> it is consuming the heart (i.e., oblivion or regret?) [. . .]   (A.24)

Death, presented in terms of burial, is a common motif as a stimulus to virtue; the injunctions to 'remember the West', are a *memento mori* and inspiration to piety, as in *Sinuhe* ('Remember the day of burial', B 190–1; cf. p. 135). Here, however, 'remembering burial' (56) is problematic. The dialogue's subject matter is not just burial customs, but the nature of mortality and death. The laments about the suffering of life are voiced as justifications of the man's attitude to death, rather than death being presented as a justification of life's imperfection. A later dialogue on the problem of death is in Book of the Dead spell 175 (**7.2**), and the same subject matter features in the New Kingdom harpist's songs (**2.2.2**). In particular the 'Song from the Chapel of Intef' juxtaposes different and discordant responses to death and seeks to reconcile the audience to its horror and blessing 'on the level of aesthetics, as a blending of tones' (M. V. Fox 1977: 420). Similarly, the dialogue takes the theme of death and

---

[32] This approach is similar to Renaud's (1991), but her analysis is based on rhetorical patterns rather than on imagery.

moves forward through transformations of literary form, imagery and tone to a reconciliation of the protagonists, and hence the audience, with the prospect of death. It is an internal dispute about individual suffering, almost a monologue (Tobin 1991: 343, 354–6).

Throughout the poem, the man is weary of life and eager to prepare for death now, while his *ba* threatens to abandon him if he proceeds like this.[33] Variation has been detected in the man's attitudes, but this relies on uncertain lexical detail, especially the transitive verb *jhm*, which can however be understood as to 'constrain (towards)' in all occurrences, making the man's various statements all parallel.[34] Until the resolution, there is thus no vacillation in either speaker's opinions. Both articulate similar world-views, assuming that there is life after death (1–3: *ba*; 23–7: man); both assume that 'life is a transitory state' in which things decay (20–1: man; *ba*: passim). The difference is in their attitudes rather than their beliefs. The man dwells on the blessing of death, the *ba* on its horror; the man's attitudes are close to those of official discourse, while the *ba* presents a counter-discourse.

I here present an analysis in terms of the developing impact of the imagery on the audience. The first preserved lines of the Berlin papyrus belong to a speech of the *ba*, which was probably preceded by some sort of introductory heading and a speech by the man. The man's statement in 5–6 that 'my *ba* does not agree with me' implies an earlier statement by himself (see, however, Tobin 1991: 343–4 n.13). Part of the first speeches are preserved on the Amherst fragments, including the phrase '[Com]e(?), I shall teach you' (see **A.1.2**). I assume a symmetrical pattern to the dialogue of

[Opening: man + b]*a* + man (interrupted by *ba*) + *ba* + man + *ba*.

The poem may well have begun with a title similar to that in the Late Egyptian dialogue where parts of the body dispute their roles (Turin 58004; López 1984: pl. 184; trans: Kammerzell 1995a):

> Contending (*wpt*) of the belly and the head, to solve what they did;
> a loud relation(?) before the Court-of-Thirty,
> as to who was their chief.   (l.1)

---

[33] So Lichtheim 1973: 163; on the question of suicide see Tobin 1991: 342–3. A *ba* that abandons its owner can be paralleled in *Sinuhe* B 255, where 'my *ba* perished'.

[34] 12, 18–19, 49–50. The relationship to *jhm* 'to tarry', with a transitive causative *sjhm* 'to delay' in *The Eloquent Peasant* R 17.6, is uncertain. R. J. Williams (1962: 53–4) compared *sjn* (*Wb*. IV, 384–8, 9ff) which has two opposite meanings (1962: 54); *jhm* in the dialogue might derive from the same stem as the verb of motion, with a similar, but transitive sense 'to confine, restrict' with *r* introducing to what, rather than from what, the man is 'confined'. This would suit the meaning of *jhmt* in 131 suggested by Smither (1939; although *jhmt* may be derived from *jhm* 'grief': Williams 1962: 54 n.4). Compare also Lohmann 1998: 227–8.

The fictional context is uncertain, and the dialogue may be an inner dialogue with the *ba* being chosen as the most appropriate interlocutor for the subject matter (Menu 2000: 20–2). From the way the man speaks about the beyond, he seems to be alive (cf. Lohmann 1998: 209), and it is possible that he is aged, like the protagonists of the teachings, or is preparing to die in despair (J. Assmann 1996a: 199), as the peasant attempts to do towards the end of *The Eloquent Peasant*. An audience is imagined, but it is not clear who they are. They may be simply a projection of the actual audience with no real role in the fictional setting, or perhaps a court of judges as in the example cited;[35] the protagonists reach their own conclusion through their conversation without any intervention by the fictional audience, as in a court of law where reconciliation was the goal.

The man laments the fact that his *ba* will abandon him because he is seeking the West due to the 'suffering of life' (18). He challenges the *ba* to 'make sweet the West', with the comment 'is this a pain' in which 'pain' (*qsnt*) relates to the fatal 'day of pain' (*hrw-qsnt*, 10, 15), implying that the suffering of death is due to the *ba*'s desertion. The man initially uses the term 'West' for the death that he desires, and death (*mt*) for the 'second', ultimate death to which the *ba* is hastening him by its disobedience; the *ba* also uses *mt*. The man reflects on what will happen to them at the hands of the gods of judgement, including the Sungod, who will help him as the *ba* does not (28–9). Much of the speech alludes to funerary discourse, recalling passages such as:

> This tomb-chapel which I have made to be a shade for my *ba*, to be an
>   alighting place for my shade.[36]

At this point the *ba* interrupts with a sarcastic comment, and urges the man to value life rather than dismissing it because it is 'transitory' (20–1; so Tobin 1991: 346–7 n.32):

> You should ponder (i.e., care for) life, like a lord of wealth![37]   (32–3)

---

[35] Another possible parallel is Coffin Text spell 149, where the deceased says 'I speak with/in (? *m*) my heart to them who are in the Council (*ḏꜣḏꜣt*) in the Mansion of the Foremost of the Westerners' (*CT* II, 243c–244a).

[36] Sethe 1928a: 88 l.20 (funerary stela with an address to the living); see Lohmann 1998: 230 for a parallel in *CT* I, 362d–364a.

[37] 'Ponder' (*mhj*) is an ironic touch, since the man actually 'ponders' death too much (cf. 68: 'Forget care (*mhj*)!'). Compare *The Teaching of a Man* 'The thoughtful (*mhj*) man rests in his pyramid' (7.6); in *Sinuhe*, the protagonist is ordered to 'ponder your corpse and return!' (B 199). The 'lord of wealth' is clearly a positive figure (pace Letellier 1991), as in *A Man*: 'And one without portion is a lord of wealth; / one poor of land is a lord of a family' (4.5–6). Compare Lohmann 1998: 229–30.

The speech is colloquial and rapid, and the meaning is reinforced by wordplay on 'wealth' (ʿḥʿw) and the homophonous 'lifetime', linking lifetime and prosperity. In what is initially an equally biting response, the man warns the *ba* of the consequences of its attitude. The language is terse and the syntax elliptical like the *ba*'s; the effect is perhaps suggestive of an intimate discussion (33–6). The man then adopts his opponent's imagery, reversing the 'man of wealth' with an allusion to a 'desperado' (ḫnrj: 35). The man resumes his original theme and proceeds to eulogize the West in more stately language, promising the *ba* that it will benefit there (36–49). But if it abandons the man and 'constrains him to (utter) death in *this* manner', it will suffer (49–51). The paradox is that by urging him to shun the West the *ba* will lead him to absolute death. The man concludes with an image of fine funerary rites (51–5), attractively described: the day is one of 'burial' not 'pain'; the corpse's resting place, the bier, is a homely 'bed'.

The *ba* takes up this description of burial and echoes it point for point in a brutal reversal of the man's official-style discourse (J. Assmann 1996a: 201). The offerings brought then (53) are now 'tears' (57), the dead have no 'bier' as before (54–5) but are 'cast on the high ground' (58–9). The syntax points up the allusions, since the *ba* employs the same nominal constructions as the man's eulogy (cf. 56–9 and 20–1, 38). The re-description reverses the meaning of the man's description, and the image is further developed, with more rapid, convoluted syntax. The *ba* echoes the man's promise of being like 'one who is in a pyramid' (41–2), and evokes 'fair pyramids' (61) intended to make men into gods, but undercuts the image with its exact antithesis: a corpse on the river bank for whom only fish talk (63–7), in an image known from laments such as *Ipuur* 2.6–7. A single sentence thus places two extremes of burial in symmetrical contrast. The climactic image of the corpse echoes ironically the man's vision of the *ba* drinking from the river bank (46–7), as well as moving the social setting from the elite who have heirs (42–3, 52) to the solitary and the poverty-stricken, who 'die on the shore for lack of a survivor' (64). This section, with its transformations, is the structural centre of the poem and the epitome of the dialogue: it presents two opposing attitudes to death, following a pattern of 'then-now' that is characteristic of laments. The *ba* then tells two parables that exemplify the introductory injunction to 'Follow the happy day! Forget care!' (67–8). The details of these narratives are unclear, but the tone is apparent. Their style is once again rapid and elliptical, and the social context they evoke is that of 'little men' (nḏs), rather than the elite.

The first little man takes great care as he travels – a familiar metaphor for life – just as the dialogue's protagonist has shown concern for burial. Nevertheless, his care is in vain and he ends up with his family perishing on the shore amid the crocodiles, a creature associated with predatory and anti-social emotions as well as an archetypal aggressive animal. This is a narrative version of the *ba*'s image of a man marooned 'on a bank' without any 'survivors' (64–5), and it expresses the same horror of death. The little man's concluding lament for the loss of his children's life stresses that life, however transitory, is precious (68–80); this is the opposite attitude from that expressed in *Ipuur*, where children wish they had never been born (4.2–3). The parable argues both that taking care against disaster is useless, and that one should care for life, making the little man echo the *ba*'s earlier injunction (32–3: 'ponder', *mhj*).

The second parable tells of an impatient man who, when his impatience is thwarted by his wife, leaves the house to relieve himself and returns alienated.[38] The domestic quarrel, with its lack of patience and hearing (80–5), parallels the dispute between the man and the *ba*, although there is no need for an allegorical reading in which the little man is the *ba*, and the wife the man. Rather, the little man's impatience in 'demanding' (*dbḥ*, a word used of invoking funerary meals) dinner provides an analogue for the man's eagerness for death which, according to the *ba*, leads him astray and demeans him as the little man is demeaned. Throughout this whole speech the *ba* has lowered the tone drastically, from 'gods' in their pyramids (60–3) to a urinating man in a lowly setting of domestic strife (84–5).

The man's response retains this tone, but reformulates it as a clearly structured, highly patterned lyric with the refrain: 'Look, my name reeks, look. . . .' (86–103).[39] This reference to the man's name echoes the man's earlier contrasting statement that the *ba*'s 'name will live' in the West if he agrees with the man (36–7). The lyric presents a sequence of extravagant images, stylistically and formally remote from the comparatively simple narratives of the parables. All the images express the wretchedness of life, due to the *ba*'s dissent, an aspect that is possibly intensified by the orthographic ambiguity of the refrain, since 'reeks, look' can read 'reeks because of you' (cf. Goedicke 1970a: 146–7; J. Assmann 1996a: 203–4). Instead of swift action upon action, and images of death as a hasty 'casting forth' (58–9) or as being shipwrecked amid a storm (71–5), the audience hears a series of essentially static images. The measured cadences rise above the language of the previous speeches, while the motifs remain lowly. The imagery is dominated by stench, taking up what was implicit in the little

---

[38] The man goes outside to relieve himself, according to Badawy 1961 taking *sst* in 82, 84 as a causative of *stj* 'pour'. Additional support for this interpretation is in the imagery of lament as excretion in *The Eloquent Peasant* (B1 309–10).

[39] For the motif of stench see J. Assmann 1996a: 204; P. Anastasi I 28.7 (Fischer-Elfert 1986a: 238); Fischer-Elfert 1999: 195 (*A Man* 19.7). For the contrary of a 'perfumed name' see Franke 1994: 178, 183.

man's incontinence (refrain and 82, 84): the smell is of crocodiles, fishing and shores (74–5). The references to labouring fishermen mobilize a low social context similarly to that of the previous speech, as well as the same landscape of the shoreline. The images, however, now articulate not the man's folly in longing for death, but his weariness of life. Just as the *ba* presented a parody of a funeral, the man here produces a parody of the marsh landscape of re-creation and rebirth (see further **9.5.1**) that is transformed into an image of the horror of living. Almost all the images refer back to earlier parts of the composition; even the allusions to adultery and unwanted offspring (97–101) take up the parables' motifs of family loss and dissention (68–85, including comprehensively both horizontal and vertical family relationships). The last stanza's reference to a seditious 'port of the sovereign' (102–3) transform the riverbank landscape into a broader social context and a still more personal expression.

The second poem continues this broadening movement, while it retains a personal concern in its refrain: 'Whom can I speak to today?'. The poem moves from an individual's 'name' to a lament about the state of society, using 'then-now' formulations that echo the *ba*'s earlier formulation of the fate of the dead. Its pessimism does not imply that the man is in a psychotically depressed state, as in Odette Renaud's reading (1991), where the man is a 'nervous depressive' who regains serenity through poetry (the refrain occurs elsewhere as the utterance of a sage: Parkinson 1996c). In the dialogue a wise man feels alienated from society by his perception of the horror of death, and by his resulting internal conflict. The use of 'today' (*mjn*) in the refrain intensifies an earlier passage where the man said:

This is too much for me today –
ba has not agreed with me! (5–6)

The refrain is also a direct rebuttal of the *ba*'s speeches – for the man there is no one worth talking to. All communication – which is vital to Maat – is ended. This is the longest and the most forceful of the lyrics. It echoes earlier statements[40] and it echoes itself: this degree of repetition articulates the pervasiveness of horror. The bleakness of the *ba*'s images and narratives now becomes an implicit justification of death, since life is not worth living. For all the predatory motion evoked, the man's vision is again static: only wrong roams the earth (129).

The third lyric (130–42) resumes the subject of death as it appears to

---

[40] For example, 'mercy has perished' (107) echoes the 'perishing' (74) of the family; good is 'thrown down everywhere' (109), just as a dead man was 'cast out' onto the high ground (58–9); 'a man who should enrage a man with his bad deed' (110) recalls the misdeed in front of the household in the second parable (85); 'wrongdoer' (113) echoes 'wrong' (40).

the man – a release and a consolation for a painful life. It is a direct answer to the *ba*'s challenge to 'think about burial' (56), made with a dramatic change of tone. The refrain is full of murmuring assonance: 'Death is in my sight, today, like . . .' (*jw-mt m-ḥr:j mjn mj . . .*). Immediate, vivid and fresh imagery articulates a sense of release after the preceding speeches (e.g., Fecht 1993: 92–3), and this has prompted a strong modern reception.[41] This intense lyric takes the preceding strings of images and transforms them. It is not only an exact reversal of the imagery of the *ba*'s tirades against death, but also the converse of that used by the man himself earlier. The stenches of the first lyric are now the 'smell of myrrh' and 'lotuses' (132–3, 135); the weather is 'windy' (134) not 'burning' (88, 90) or dark and stormy (71–2); people now sit 'on the shore of Drunkenness' (135–6) rather than dead on a 'shore' (64), or lamenting by 'a lake infested with a swarm of crocodiles' (74–5), or 'sitting on the river-edges with a swarm of crocodiles' (97). The motif of travel has a similar summation: travelling is evoked not as a river journey by night to disaster (70–5), but as 'a well-trodden path' as a man returns home from an expedition (136–7); death is not 'going forth (*prj*) outside' to misfortune like the man in the first parable (73, 77) or the man in the second parable who rushes out of and into his house in a fury, but a release, a 'going forth' from confinement or service and a return home. The sky now gives a revelation, in contrast with the world where even friends were 'expressionless' (138–9, 118–20); and the man is no longer surrounded by unknown strangers but is about to 'see home' (141). After the earlier claustrophobic stasis the stanzas enact the stages of a journey – leaving a confined space, sailing, feasting on the far bank, and re-entering home – such as are enacted at the joyous end of *Sinuhe*. This is not only an antithesis of the journey of the first parable, but it parallels the progress of a funeral across the Nile (as in the *ba*'s hostile description) as a celebration. Death is presented as the ultimate positive: it makes good what was lacking in life, reversing the 'then-now' pattern of the laments. The man's present life, not death, is the negation: life is now 'being taken into captivity'.[42] These similes reconcile the audience to life as well as death – the images are drawn from an idealized human life that is now presented as potentially serene and even glorious, not only as a 'transitory state', or a cause of 'suffering' (20–1, 18).

The sequence of lyrics forms a thematic progression from a lament about individual reputation and social horror 'today' to an equally personal and immediate vision of death 'today' as a release and a return home. The

---

[41] For example, there is a version as 'une cantilène de Pentaour' by Marguerite Yourcenar (1984: 16).
[42] 'Taken' is added as a correction between the lines (141–2).

sequence ends with a description of the 'beyond', moving from the egocentric 'here' and 'now' to a 'there' and 'future' state. Although, as J. Assmann stresses (1996a: 196–200), the 'here' and 'there' are parts of the same cosmos, the contrast between the otherworldly ideal and the present imperfection is concisely expressed. Its succinctness contrasts sharply with the never-ending repetition of the preceding laments, but it is also densely allusive and resonant with the whole weight of the dialogue behind it.

> Yet one There is a living god,
> punishing the wrongdoer's deed.

These *living* gods rebut the *ba*'s worry about the otherworldly judges of the dead (1–3), and the wrongdoings of the second lyric (103–29) find in them a vanquisher. Death is the true life, marking a return to official discourse (e.g., Coffin Text spell 76 [*CT* II, 1i]; Franke 1994: 136–8). This is implicitly a summation of the 'then-now' lament motif.

> Yet one There stands in the (Sun)-barque,
> distributing choice offerings thence to the temples.

The piety which was implicitly lacking in the plundering society described in the second lyric here finds a supporter, with an image of distributing offerings (105–6) that also occurs in the theodicy of Coffin Text spell 1130 (*CT* VII, 464e). The barque recalls the boat of the first parable, and elevates the motif of travel to a divine and cosmic level. The food recalls the demands for sustenance in the second parable, and the 'standing' in the Sun-barque the stand of the survivor at the funeral (42), as well as the injunctions for the *ba* to 'stand' with man in the next life.[43]

> Yet one There is a sage
> who cannot when he speaks be prevented from appealing to the Sungod.

Such conversation is invoked in funerary texts (Silverman 1988: 69 [A ll. 228–9]). The audience is no longer in the presence of 'unknown' men who err (124–5), or a 'stupid' *ba*, but a 'sage'. The Sungod is evoked, no longer as a fierce sun (65) or as a judge to be feared, but as one who hears the man who is petitioning. He is now the guarantor of justice in the Otherworld whom the man invoked in his first answer (25–6). He is also the interlocutor whom the man has lacked, and who will make good the complaints.

---

[43] 7, 16; for which compare *CT* II, 110i–j: 'Go my *ba* so that that man may see you; stand opposite him in any place he is'; similarly *CT* II, 111j–k.

As with the preceding lyric, the stanzas refer to this life, expressing the capacity of the dead to help the living, as if this vision of death redeems the earlier views of life as an isolated state. In the progression of the lyrics, the man reclaims the imagery of the whole dialogue, and elevates the tone and literary register: rather than sarcastic, rapid, elliptical speeches, the man concludes with verses suggestive of serene calm. The man thus surpasses the *ba*'s speeches, responding to its two parables with four lyrics, and drawing on a hierarchy of literary genre and stylistic registers. Nevertheless, the man assimilates the previous imagery: his final speech incorporates and does not exclude what has gone before. The two contrasting tones and attitudes to death are reconciled within the lyrics by use of common imagery, the earlier occurrences of which remain in the audience's mind during the final lyric: its 'there' implies a 'here'.

The poem concludes with a short speech of the *ba*, whose acquiesence articulates this union of opposing attitudes more explicitly. The speech is introduced briefly like his earlier sarcastic interruption (30–1), and is not a capitulation or a final unresolved attempt at persuasion. The *ba* does not retract, but has been won over to a reconciliation by the poetic resolution of the lyrics; such a conclusion accords with the possible setting in a lawcourt, where the aim was to have the two contestants leaving reconciled and content. As in the man's lyrics, the imagery in each of the final verses alludes to earlier speeches, with the *ba* drawing on that of his opponent, just as the man has done. Thus, the *ba* now urges the man to 'throw lament over the fence'[44] and describes itself as the 'partner and brother' (148–9) who was found lacking in the lyric lament (e.g., 114–15), using the word 'West' (151–2). Its injunction to 'make offering on the censer' (149) alludes both to the man's descriptions of funerary preparations (51) and to his complaint that the *ba* was then 'casting him on the fire' (13). In this manner, the *ba* now advocates a paradoxical balance between the two attitudes:

> May you cling[45] to (eternal) life by the means you describe (i.e., burial)!
> Love (*mrj*) me here, having thrust aside the West!
> and also still desire (*mrj*) to reach the West, your body making landfall.
> (150–2)

The 'West' has been the man's way of referring to death and the *ba* uses vocabulary he employed in his eulogy of that realm (37–9: 'port' and

---

[44] *ḥr-ḥȝȝ* (148) can be elucidated by comparison with *ḥȝjt* 'palisade' (P. Chester Beatty IV vso 6.4: Gardiner 1935a: 43 n.2, pl. 20; see also AL 77.3224), suggesting a meaning 'put upon, i.e., over, the fence, i.e., discard'. Pace Goedicke 1970a: 182; Tobin 1991: 352; Lohmann 1998: 225 n.96.

[45] See Blumenthal 1970: 72 (B1.25).

'alighting'). The dialogue ends with the two facing death together (153 echoing 37, 50–1), in a final harmonious allusion to the imagery of the riverbank and voyaging:

> so shall we make harbour together.

This is the only occurrence of the first person plural in the poem, and perhaps recalls the declaration of the creator in Coffin Text spell 1130 that, when the world ends,

> then I shall dwell with (Osiris) in one place.   (CT VII, 468b)

The speakers interweave the two aspects of death metaphorically, and interweave them with life. The positive aspects of death are an answer to life's imperfection, which is itself an answer to the problem of death, as in other theodicies. In the final lyrics, the man implicitly justifies the creator for condoning the suffering of mortality by describing the transcendence which is attained through mortality. Even in the Otherworld, however, man still has to 'appeal' (146), and the man is only one side of a dialogue. This is no simple solution in which the audience can judge one of the speakers to be right and the other wrong; in intertextual terms neither is a unique voice. The man wins his *ba* over to agreement through his transformations of literary form and imagery, but the unity which this produces articulates both speakers' views simultaneously. The conflict is suspended not through argument but through performative 'perfect speech' before an audience, and the acceptance of the diverse aspects of death is staged as a literary event.

9.5 *THE SPORTING KING* AND *FISHING AND FOWLING*: RECREATIONAL DISCOURSES

> And though this Discourse may be liable to some *Exceptions*, yet I cannot doubt but that most Readers may receive so much *pleasure* or *profit* by it . . . if they be not too grave or busie men. . . . In writing of it, I have made myself a recreation of a *recreation*.
>
> Isaak Walton, *The Compleat Angler, or The Contemplative Man's Recreation* (1676), introductory letter 'to all readers'

9.5.1 COMPOUND GENRES

In addition to the group of discourses discussed above, whose protagonists were regarded as central to the Middle Kingdom corpus, two discursive poems from a single source are comparable in nature (see **6.2**). They display features often associated with post-Middle Kingdom compositions and are comparatively long, but it is uncertain whether their different character is to be explained exclusively by a later date. Analysis and interpretation are hampered by the fragmentary state of the manuscripts, but some sense of their form can be recovered (for a possible third example of the genre see Parkinson 1999d). They indicate how fragmentary and partial modern knowledge of the corpus is.

The Sporting King seems to describe the court at play in the form of eulogies to the king within a framing narrative. The main protagonist is playfully described as 'Two Ladies: Fisher/Fowler' (C 1.12). There are parallels for the subject matter, including monumental inscriptions such as the Annals of Amenemhat II at Memphis (x+23–5; Baines in preparation). The discourse is introduced as follows:

> The King's Sealbearer, the Royal Document Scribe of the Presence,
> Sehotepibreankh [said]:
> 'I have seen, Sovereign (l.p.h.), my lord!'
> And then his Person said: 'Like what [is that which you say] you have [seen]?'
> And then the Royal Document Scribe of the Presence said:
> 'I have seen the eating of birds, [. . .],
> a storm before a great wind . . .' (A2.1–4)

The narrative reads like an adaptation of the Royal Tales, comparable with that of *Neferti* and *Cheops' Court*. The questions introducing the speeches in particular recall the dialogue between Djedji and Cheops, though without the latter's pointed tone. The riddling introduction gives an extemporary air to the speech, which is not immediately recognizable as a narrative or a wisdom discourse, although its loyalist elements are common to these. The concern with 'seeing' may recall the 'seeing of prodigies' in *Cheops' Court*, which is a parody of official discourse (p. 183). It may also relate to official eulogies with refrains in which the king was 'seen like' various metaphors, as expressed much later in Tuthmosis III's much-imitated poetical stela (e.g., Mathieu 1994). The following speech about the phenomenon is – like the subsequent ones – full of imagery: 'It is like . . .' (*jw:s-mj-* . . .: A2.10).[46]

As a result of this speech describing the prodigious sight and Sehotepibreankh's urging that the king's 'concern be in the meadow' (B1.5), the court then proceeds, not to cultic or building activity, but to a sporting

---

[46] The formulation also occurs in Late Egyptian love-songs describing the beloved (e.g., *sw mj-*, Cairo vase ll.3–6: M. V. Fox 1985: 31, 383; Mathieu 1996a: 97, pl. 17).

trip. Another speech by Sehotepibre follows, spoken 'at the foot of the throne': 'Take unto yourself this your red shaft, . . .' (B2.4–6).

The introduction to this speech and the phrase 'Take unto yourself' are stately and liturgical (*Wb.* II, 60.1–4, e.g., Erman 1911: 40–5), and set the tone for the long speech extolling the king's hunting paraphernalia with elaborate and wide-ranging imagery. In terms of rhetorical techniques, a close parallel is the Ramessid literary *Eulogy of the Chariot of Amun* (Schulman 1986).

Other fragments preserve further incidents of travel, followed by other speeches, including another starting 'Take unto yourself . . .' (C1.12). There seem also to be perhaps two speeches in praise of the Marsh-goddess, the first of which is presented as 'Words spoken by the lect[or . . .]' (E2.3). An unplaced fragment shows that a courtier ('Friend') is also a speaking protagonist in the narrative (Frag. 1.6).

The composition includes non-narrative sections whose topics and tone are unusual in the discourse genre. It adopts a fusion of genres, similar to that of *The Eloquent Peasant* and *Sasobek*, but uniting narrative with eulogy rather than with ethical discourses. The composition draws heavily on formal literature and is of a consistently high register, but while it is episodic like *The Eloquent Peasant*, it apparently lacks any high intellectual dialogue or pessimistic tone. The nature of the speeches suggests that the poem expands a literary form out of ceremonial hymns, with the narrative frame placing the eulogy in a fictional context (cf. Parkinson 1999d). Just as *The Eloquent Peasant* makes petitioning speeches into literature, so these compositions transfer eulogistic speeches and annalistic narratives into a less ideologically programmatic mode of presentation. The ceremonial language suggests that the intended audience must have been familiar with such procedures, and was possibly sited in the courtly elite.

Fishing and Fowling is almost a non-royal version of *The Sporting King*. Non-royal involvement in such activities is well attested in tomb decoration (see n.48) and texts, where it is presented as entertainment. A mid-18th Dynasty statue inscription records how an 'Overseer of the Birdpools of Entertainment (*sḥmḫ-jb*)' accompanied the king on such a sporting expedition to the Fayyum:

> when his Person spent a moment in enjoying himself (*sḏꜣj-ḥr:f*) and
>   entertaining himself (*sḥmḫ-⟨jb⟩:f*) in his tarrying time,
> in traversing the birdpools of the Lake-land . . .
>   (Charles 1960:18–19; Feucht 1992: 165)

A Miscellany text also deals with the same subject matter (Gardiner 1937: 35–6; Caminos 1954: 126–31).

The extant text contains no third-person narrative, but comprises a speech addressed to a superior with narrative sections in the first person. A possible narrative parallel is *The Tale of the Shipwrecked Sailor*, which is also an account of an expedition addressed to a superior. The present account, however, is more discursive and reflective than narrative, describing a sequence of actions in general terms, as the speaker urges his 'lord' Inseni to return to country pursuits:

> My lord! My lord!
> Spend the night at the screen! (B2.9–10)

In *The Sporting King* the narrative and discourse aspects are juxtaposed, whereas in *Fishing and Fowling* they are more fully melded together. The extant manuscript opens with a question:

> What is [the craft of] my beloved (i.e., the Marsh-goddess) like?[47]
> A great matter has begun from it, of [which(?)] one has said: '[. . .]' (A1.1)

This question is similar to that introducing the first speech in *The Sporting King* (A2.2–3).

It is possible to identify elements of the poem's intertext. The mention of a 'great matter' recalls a phrase in *The Loyalist Teaching*: 'I shall speak a great matter' (1.3; see p. 237). The composition seems to describe the nature of the ideal life, which celebrates 'A holiday, as we go down to the water-meadow' (A2.1).

The phrase 'holiday' (*hrw-nfr*) occurs as a refrain (A2.4, A2.5, B3.10); it has ethical and other connotations (e.g., Lorton 1975; J. Assmann 1991: 200–15), and occurs, for example, as an incipit in a later love-song (Mathieu 1996a: 114, pl. 22–4 [O. Borchardt 1.1]). A relationship with ethical discourse can also be detected in the encouragements to go fishing and fowling, whose descriptions of the pastoral life as the ideal profession recall the illustrations of the ideal and unideal professions in *The Teaching of Khety*:

> As for a fisherman who does not go to town,
> he lives on fat. (B4.1–2)

This speech is not pessimistic or mocking in tone, but the extent to which it diverges from the normal range of literary discourses is suggested, for example, by the use of the verb 'to take thought for' (*nk3*), an activity that is central to the pessimistic *Khakheperreseneb* (rto 10, vso 1): here 'there is no one who (has to) take thought (*nk3*) for provisions' (A2.8). The poem

---
[47] For 'the craft of Sokhet' (the Marsh-goddess) see Guglielmi 1973–4: 210–11, 216–17.

includes more directly didactic elements than *The Sporting King*, such as when the speaker encourages his lord to return to the marshes, with the words:

> I shall teach (*sbꜣ*) you the Lake-land of Sobek. (C3.11)

followed by a list of Fayyum and Delta toponyms (C3.11–15). Although lists are a common rhetorical device (e.g., Derchain 1996b: 360), this suggests a link with onomastica, which are allied with technical or religious texts. Other details relate to liturgical texts: for example, 'How fair is your face (*nfr.wj-ḥr:k*) Inseni' (B1.6) is a ritual greeting for gods and kings (parodied in *Horus and Seth*; Parkinson 1995: 70 n.101). The celebration of the happy day includes invocations to Sobek, Lord of Lake-land (e.g., A2.4), and offerings and rituals are enacted. Similarly ceremonial precedents may be present in what is apparently an invocation to the Marsh-goddess Sokhet: 'Come with [me], [. . .] my [. . . (woman)] to the encampment of the northern region!' (C2.12–13). Like *The Sporting King*, the poem evokes a leisured ethos, though it is less courtly in atmosphere.

One can only speculate on the intended effect of these poems. It is easy for a modern reader to assume that such – very substantial – poems are patchworks of didactic and descriptive modes (e.g., Caminos 1956: 25), very different from poetic genres that are now current. The subtlety of Vergil's *Georgics* might, however, suggest otherwise. The poems show clear affinities with canonical genres, but divergences from the expectations of the three principle genres are striking, and in terms of form, motif and intertext the compositions are reminiscent of the Late Egyptian Miscellanies, which include poems describing and extolling the Residence of the king (Lichtheim 1980). Such compositions are unlikely to be an innovation of the Ramessid Period, as was once thought, since an early 18th Dynasty example is now known of a personal piety text with the motif of longing for a city (Guksch 1994; Baines 1996a: 165).

It is not clear whether the poems centre around any theme other than courtly recreation. This absence can be detected in a comparison of the treatment of the landscape here as against texts such as *Sinuhe* and *The Shipwrecked Sailor*. There the landscape is an 'altogether elsewhere' (in Auden's phrase: 1991: 33) and the motif of travel embodies a debate on cultural values. In contrast, the landscape of *The Sporting King* is the background to a trip, rather than a sign of an interior journey; it provides ambience and confirmation for the values of the court. The marshland is the setting for other works, but in these it is usually in a problematic context as in *The Fowler* and *The Herdsman*. In *Fishing and Fowling* the marsh landscape represents an alternative world in part, reminiscent of the values attached to the pastoral world of western literature, and seems to exist for the pleasure of the elite, as opposed to the grim and challenging metaphors of marshland in the laments of *A Man and His Ba* (86–103). This landscape is described as being unused to such anguish, in vocabulary familiar from literary laments:

> small are the sufferings (*mnt*) of it. . . .
> the fisher- and fowler-man cannot bear (*wḫd*) to see suffering (*ȝhw*).
>
> (C3.15–16)

In terms of motif, *Fishing and Fowling* evokes a retreat into a more personal, private countryside atmosphere, as in a section expressing pastoral longing which draws a contrast between the 'town' and the 'country' (B4.2–9; e.g., Parkinson 1999f: 294). The same contrast also occurs, but to different effect, in the lament of *The Fowler* (P. Butler 16–21). Fishing and fowling is the elite entertainment par excellence, and the subject matter of sport in the marshes can have weighty symbolic overtones as in tomb-scenes where the tomb-owner enjoys and 'sees' the marsh landscape;[48] this can be mobilized in literary texts such as in the first petition of *The Eloquent Peasant* (B1 85–93). The Annals of Amenemhat II indicates how much such sport is part of official ideology, rather than the private relaxation of western pastoral, although such events are not without aesthetic and pleasurable elements even when performed by royalty (e.g., Baines in preparation). Here, the presentation is remarkably descriptive, and *Fishing and Fowling* contains little trace of the activity's symbolic aspects, despite the references to ritual. Its aim is apparently 'carefreeness' (ʿ*m-jb* B4.9), and it recalls the ethos of Sneferu's boating trip in *Cheops' Court*, as if it were narrating how:

> you'll see the beautiful pools of your lake.
> And you'll see its countryside and its beautiful banks.
> Your heart will gain relief by this.   (*Cheops' Court* 5.5–7)

The religious aspects of sport are mobilized in *The Sporting King*, but to virtuosic and decorative effect. Both the compositions seem to belong to a leisured poetry, a playful adaptation of courtly liturgies, almost foreshadowing the ethos of the Ramessid love-songs. While the language is courtly, the serious tone which is peculiar to much of the central canon is lacking, suggesting that these compositions might lie in some sense on the periphery of the high literary tradition, and also exemplifying the versatile

---

[48] For interpretation see K. Martin 1986; Eaton-Krauss and Graefe 1985: 36–8; Feucht 1992; Kamrin 1999: 105–15.

capacity of poetry to absorb other genres. This expansion of subject matter and tone, the length, and the presumed structure of the poems all may suggest a late date and a transitional status between the Middle Kingdom canon and later literature.

9.5.2 THE END OF DISCOURSE

Despite problems of dating and context, it is possible to ask why the pessimistic discourse is so characteristic of the Middle Kingdom. Its emergence has been regarded as a natural consequence of the Kingdom's use of literature as a vehicle for political propaganda, but this approach is problematic. New Historicist critics argue that 'as soon as a genre of representations begins to ask troubling questions, power finds a new way in which to represent its interests' (Brannigan 1998: 78). This point may be relevant for the Middle Kingdom, where the most directly questioning discourses, such as *Ipuur*, seem to date from late in the period. One might thus suggest that the lament genre which expressed and contextualized the problematic earlier in the Middle Kingdom gradually became too threatening, as its increasingly direct complaints and questions threatened the ability of the court poets to secure a resolution. However, this reading may underestimate the complexity of the earlier works, in which the strategies of containment are in part subverted, and may impose an overly programmatic 'entrapment' model.

Since entertainment was central to literary reception, other, less programmatic, factors are relevant to the disappearance of a genre. The ability of high cultural participants to enjoy 'pessimistic' poems imagining distress and poverty may have diminished as the court and government became less prosperous and stable in the late 13th Dynasty and beyond (e.g., Bourriau 1988: 53–4):

> Only the young and the rich
> Have the nerve or the figure to strike
> The lacrimae rerum note.
>
> (W. H. Auden, 'A Walk after Dark', 1991: 346)

The apparent absence of new pessimistic discourses from the period of renewed prosperity in the New Kingdom may also have been due to a canonization of existing wisdom literature, that made the creation of new writings in the discourse genre inappropriate (e.g., Baines 1996a: 157–65). This attitude was perhaps part of the trend towards lower forms of literature, including more peripheral forms and topics. Extant evidence suggests a hiatus in the production of the three classical genres in the early New Kingdom, with official texts, eulogy, and lyric becoming the principal genres of early New Kingdom literary activity. These genres are prominent in the intertext of these compound genres, suggesting that they had a transitional status in the gradual dispersal or evolution of the discourse genre.

Nevertheless, the teaching and tale genres were revived in the later New Kingdom, in a diversification in cultural decorum. The new teachings were a consciously classical re-creation, to judge by their not being composed in full Late Egyptian (Baines 1996a: 168), while the Late Egyptian narratives were a development of the 'low' tradition of Middle Kingdom tales. In New Kingdom writings, the basic human need to express pessimism and the untoward seems to have found expression in genres other than discourses, such as harpist's songs, personal piety texts and the satiric Miscellanies. Although these changes are unlikely to have been the result of a conscious policy, but are rather the result of a gradual evolution, the question remains: if the classical genre of teachings could be revived, why not the discourses?

The abandonment of the high theodic tradition, and the completeness with which it was supplanted, may embody a decision not to raise potential 'things of darkness' continually in a culturally central medium and canonical genre. The fact that the protagonists of the dark discourses were listed with other less threatening literary sages, and were represented in the Ramessid 'Daressy fragment' (**2.2.2**) interspersed with ancestral holders of state offices, might also suggest that the awareness of any distinctly dark note in these texts had lessened. The discourses were still circulated and read, but their canonization into classic texts and educational exercises may well have formed an appropriation and partial neutralization of their original potential subversiveness. Such a phenomenon can be observed in other literary traditions: Shakespeare's transformation into a canonical school-author has resulted in the need to re-politicize the plays (e.g., Dollimore and Sinfield 1994; Dollimore 1989). But if canonization lessened the ambivalence of the discourses, their potential as productive models for new composition remained, as is shown by the revival of many aspects of the genre in much later periods (see, e.g., Depauw 1997: 97–9; Frankfurter 1998: 241–8; Bresciani 1999).

The neglect of the darker genres of the Middle Kingdom's literary heritage in the New Kingdom can perhaps be elucidated by suggesting that the closeness of Middle Kingdom literature to official discourse was paradoxically what allowed it to be subversive, since it could simultaneously contain and provoke subversion. In the late New Kingdom, by contrast, literature had become a more distinct form of discourse, as seen in the diglossia between Ramessid literary Late Egyptian as opposed to the Middle Egyptian employed for official and monumental texts. In the process literature became less able to generate subversion in a maintainable or acceptable (i.e., entertaining) form. The discourse genre did not 'begin to ask troubling questions' (Brannigan 1998: 78), but the context that enabled those questions changed, so the ending of the discourses may not reflect the political exhaustion or suppression of a genre but a shift in the ever-changing relationship between literary and official discourse.

10
Teachings

10.1 LEARNING NOTHING: THE PROBLEM OF CONTEXT

> The good ended happily, and the bad unhappily. That is what Fiction means.
>
> Oscar Wilde, *The Importance of Being Earnest* (1895), II

The genre of teachings is well attested in Middle Kingdom manuscripts, and was central to the corpus in the Ramessid Period, but its modern reception has been problematic. It is the most alien genre for modern readers, and some of the most sophisticated analyses of Egyptian literature make it almost peripheral compared to tales (**1.4**). Much study by Egyptologists has assumed a literal interpretation of the genre-term 'teaching', and the poems are generally agreed to have been part of the Middle Kingdom educational syllabus and a vehicle for teaching rules of conduct (e.g., Shupak 1993: 2–3), although there has been little discussion about their precise context (in general, see Brunner 1991a). This assumption underlies Jan Assmann's analysis of all Middle Kingdom literature as 'cultural texts'. I here argue that Teachings belong to the same literary context of entertainment as the tales and discourses.

The literal meaning of the term 'teaching' (*sbȝyt*) cannot be doubted, nor its relationship to scribal training with attendant corporal punishment (Shupak 1993: 31–3), but the narrowly functionalist approach to the genre is not necessarily compelling. Numerous copies of Middle Kingdom teachings were made during scribal training in the Ramessid Period (**3.2.2**), but the functioning of the texts' content in teaching practices is problematic, because the state of many copies, which are corrupt to the state of unintelligibility, suggests that they were exercises in writing out texts rather than in absorbing the wisdom they contained; in manuscript cultures verbatim memorizing and copying are often important for their own sakes (Goody 1987: 167–90).

The extant Middle Kingdom manuscripts of teachings span the second half of the 12th Dynasty. All lack contextual provenance, except for P. Prisse containing *Ptahhotep* and *Kagemni*, which may come from a non-royal tomb at Thebes, possibly together with *The Tale of the Shipwrecked*

Sailor (**4.2**). No Middle Kingdom copies show any evidence of having been made by apprentice scribes. Although there are no Middle Kingdom educational ostraca, several writing boards survive; the temporary nature of their surface suggests that these were educational copies (Vernus 1984). These writing boards, however, contain no teachings, but only model letters, funerary formulae, name lists, and the educational composition *Kemit*. Literary texts do occur on ostraca and writing boards in the late 17th to early 18th Dynasty.[1] The earliest board with a teaching is Carnarvon Tablet I from the start of the 18th Dynasty, which contains *Ptahhotep* and part of the commemorative text inscribed on King Kamose's stela; the writing board with *The Oxford Wisdom Text* is from the same period. Thus, although there are some educational manuscripts from the Middle Kingdom, the educational usage of literary genres – as opposed to *Kemit* – is unattested before the end of the Second Intermediate Period. Teachings appear in educational copies at the same time as other genres, including tales (*Sinuhe*), discourses (*Khakheperreseneb*), and commemorative texts (Kamose). Only two pieces of evidence can be cited for literary texts being used in Middle Kingdom educational practice, and both are indirect and speculative. 1) *The Teaching for Merikare* refers to the king 'singing the writings' (18b) while young, but the type of writings and level of education are not specified. 2) Pascal Vernus (1996b: 121) suggests that one text tradition of *Ptahhotep* (represented by L1, L2, and C) was a redactional variant on the original text (that of P. Prisse) to provide a more comprehensible text for students and that this tradition is first attested in a mid-12th Dynasty manuscript (L1). Nothing suggests, however, that L1 is an apprentice manuscript, or that the variations between the two manuscripts had this purpose.

The case of the Kamose inscription shows that the New Kingdom educational practice included a secondary usage of some texts, and the prominence of teachings in this corpus need not therefore indicate their primary function. The secondary educational usage of a text is not a reliable indicator of its primary function: even the Ramessid love-songs, generally considered to be, in part, entertainment literature, are found in an educational copy (McDowell 1999: 152; Posener 1977–80: no. 1635). As a modern example, one can cite the *Collected Works of Shakespeare*, which are taught in schools, of which copies are common in middle-class houses although they are not always understood in detail and are often preserved in textually corrupt and highly redacted versions, and which are closely associated in most people's minds both with schooling and with definitions of national culture and heritage. Following the Egyptological

---

[1] Ostraca include copies of *Sinuhe* in the 17th–18th Dynasty at Deir el-Ballas, and *Amenemhat* and *Khety* from Deir el-Bahri: Quirke 1996b: 392–3.

model, they could be analysed as primarily educational texts, but there is convincing evidence that they were not originally written or published to be school texts or cultural icons (cf., e.g., Sinfield 1994; Greenblatt 1988: 160–1).

The teachings state the explicit aim 'to teach' throughout past, present and future:

> I shall speak a great matter, and shall cause you to hear,
> cause you to know the counsels of eternity,
> the way of living truly,
> the passing into blessedness. (*Loyalist* 1.3–8)

The first verse also occurs in King Neferhotep I's inscription, where it introduces the king's plan to erect cultic monuments (Helck 1983: 23 l. 6). The teachings are injunctions to perfection (e.g., *Amenemhat* 1e) and as such the protagonists 'speak Maat' as exemplars, whereas the protagonists of the other genres are situated in less ideal contexts. The teachers urge obedience to ideology and for that reason seem to have been at the centre of the stream of tradition; the texts' aim to turn ignorance into wisdom (*Ptahhotep* 47) is integral to divine and royal creation:

> He (the king) creates the ignorant to be wise.
> (*A Man* 4.1; Fischer-Elfert 1999: 68–70)

They enact the dissolution into chaos of the discourses exactly in reverse, acclaiming the powers of loyalty and wisdom to effect transformations. Teaching also concerns self-fashioning:

> [It is] the heart that enriches character –
> a brave teacher to fashion good qualities. (*P. Ramesseum II* vso i.5)

The world that they present is ostensibly unproblematic, and their discourse is often considered 'authorative' rather than 'authorial' (Loprieno 1996b: 46).

However, even in these poems there is a tension between the ideology and its individual embodiment. Although the compositions deal with the ideal of wisdom, and have appropriate settings in the past or in the reign of an unspecified king, they formulate the interplay of ideal and actual in terms of personal conduct and ethical choices, and the settings act as fictionalizing devices (**5.1.2**).

The nature of the original audience and response of the teaching genre is difficult to induce as it is with other genres. The very number of the ostensible addressees changes from singular to plural in both *Amenemhat* and *Loyalist*, while there is no indication that the intended actual audience – as opposed to the fictional audience – is young, any more than that *The Eloquent Peasant*'s actual audience were High Stewards. The teachings are marked by their vibrancy of thought and density of utterance as being intended for a sophisticated audience (as Vernus notes with different conclusions: 1996b: 121). The genre's setting in which the teacher leaves his position and hands over to a successor need not indicate a concern with actual induction into office, since it fits within the fictional frame. The same applies to teachings as 'testaments' spoken by the dead. Induction and testament are markers of broad cultural themes, not of a specifically educational context (cf. Perdue 1981 on liminality).

The response of learning as declared in the settings is problematic. The royal teachings in particular are not as exclusively didactic as they claim. *Amenemhat* states it will teach how to be king (1d): no specific information is provided, and the intended audience was not limited to royal princes, as this statement implies if taken literally. Since kingship was an ideological centre to the whole culture, the topics would be relevant to a wider audience, and humanity itself is addressed directly (5a–c). *Amenemhat*, however, provides description rather than directly didactic information, and only the first three stanzas have any substantial didactic content or form; it is probably one of the earliest examples of the genre. The most instruction that *Amenemhat* gives is that kings should not trust people, and should be morally good. Likewise, the claim of *The Teaching for Merikare* to 'give all the laws about the kingship' (48b) cannot be taken literally. In tone, the royal teachings are reflective as well as didactic, and in many places are didactic by example, through implication, and by extension rather than directly: in *Merikare*, the king giving the teaching urges Merikare to learn 'the virtue of my generation' (50a). In both these teachings the king is not an ideal exemplar of wisdom for the audience, although a maxim in *P. Ramesseum II* suggests that education was thematically compatible with a description of fallibility such as occurs in the royal teachings:

> A clean man(?) . . . he[2] is foolish and God causes that he put the fault right,
>   like a teach[er].   (rto iv.2)

In both royal teachings, the explicitly didactic elements cluster at the start and end of the text, at the framing points.

In contrast, a few Ramessid Period teachings attested at Deir el-Medina were written by contemporaneous historical individuals, such as the *Letter*

---

[2] One might emend to read 'the king is foolish ($\langle nj \rangle sw \langle t \rangle$)' (Brunner 1991b: 194; Buchberger 1993: 352); compare 'The king cannot be foolish' (*Merikare* 41b).

of Menna written by a draughtsman for his son which addresses a specific and possibly 'real' situation in a literary manner, and *The Instruction of Amennakht* which was copied by the Scribe of the Tomb Amennakht's apprentices (p. 76). These examples, however, embody later decorum and literary practices, higher rates of literacy, and a different attitude to text compilation. Such 'historical' teachings are also attested only as local productions, and are conscious imitations of the then classic Middle Kingdom poems. They thus provide little evidence for the role of the central high cultural works of the earlier period.

As Paul Veyne (1988: 103) comments on Roman poetry, 'what reader would think of taking a poetic fiction for some moralist's guidebook?'. One can draw a general parallel between the modern reception of Middle Kingdom teachings and that of Classical poems such as Vergil's *Georgics*, which is, if anything, more didactic in terms of specific information. This has often been regarded as a treatise on rural practices ornamented with poetic language, but recent critics such as William Batstone stress that

> rather than create security, clarity, univocity, the poem complicates our feelings and confounds our paradigms. It offers an excess of thought and feeling which, while true to the life of the mind, exceeds both the propositions by which we try to secure our understanding and the determinations upon which we must act and do . . . The poem offers a place where we can experience what we are and what we can be, as well as what we are not, where we can know that truth is always also its opposite, and feel the pressure of things in our lives, both our intellectual and emotional lives, and our practical lives. The Georgics most assuredly does not tell us what to do.   (1997: 142–3)

Increasing understanding of the intertext suggests that the teachings' world is differentiated from the ideological norm in a manner similar to other fictional genres. Teachings signal their cultural role as literary texts by placing wisdom at issue, rendering it problematic, non-pragmatic and fictionalized. The teachings often refer to an external ideal authority which they set apart from purely social authority of etiquette and obligation, providing a sense of questioning and defining the values as they can be formed in the audience. Moreover, they do this to varying degrees within the genre. Such divergence and diversity is compatible with their later adoption as educational texts: in modern European culture originally disturbing and political texts such as *The Tragedy of King Lear* are used to educate schoolchildren.

The idea of literature as play as well as education permeates many teachings. *Ptahhotep* celebrates 'following the heart' (186), as does *Merikare* (30a–d). *The Loyalist Teaching* concerns the proper enjoyment of life and rewards, and even *Amenemhat* is concerned in part with regaining the 'happy hour' (*wnwt nt-nfr-jb*: 6f, 14f), a phrase that echoes descriptions of literary response (**4.5**). In broad terms entertainment and cultural education are not incompatible: playing with something is a way of learning (cf. Iser 1989: 260–1), and most of the world's literature is didactic in some sense, including Jane Austen's didactically entitled novels or Racine's *Phèdre*. Edmund Spenser stated that 'the generall end' of his *The Fairie Queene* was 'to fashion a gentleman or noble person in vertuous and gentle discipline' by describing 'doctrine by ensample' ('A Letter of the Authors', 1589). That poem 'affirm(s) the existence and inescapable moral power of ideology as that principle of truth towards which art forever yearns' (Greenblatt 1980: 192). Nevertheless, despite this general aim of transmitting cultural norms and despite the poet's affirmation of ideological values, the poem remains unlike contemporaneous manuals of courtly etiquette, and is instead fissured with faultlines, fraught with ethical play.

The royal teachings relate to royal eulogistic self-descriptions that are themselves ultimately modelled on non-royal biographies, just as the tales concerning kings are modelled on monumental Royal Tales. Perhaps the oldest preserved of such self-descriptions are the funerary inscriptions of the 11th Dynasty Intef II from his tomb-chapel at Thebes (Clère and Vandier 1948: 10–12 [§16]; Schenkel 1965: 92–6; Dieter Arnold 1976: 50–6, pls. 52–3), which combines eulogistic statements and narrations of achievements. The royal teachings, however, include non-specific formulation of historical incidents, which embody the nature of the ideal and actual. These represent potentially sensitive doctrine relating to the human and divine sides of kingship. The political aspects are viewed ideologically *sub specie aeternitatis* as in official discourse, but the king's morality is in part subjected to the same scrutiny as a normal mortal (cf. Baines 1991a: 160–1). The cynical meditations of Amenemhat and the harsh policies advocated to Merikare create an impression very far from the idealized kings of eulogies (Derchain 1989: 42), although they are not opposed to royalty (Quack 1992: 89–90). The teachings exemplify the need for rulership and highlight the burdens of responsibility as a political justification, as in European Renaissance drama:

> We are invited to understand these costs in order to ratify the power ... The rulers earn, or at least pay for, their exalted position through suffering, and this suffering ennobles, if it does not exactly cleanse, the lies and betrayals upon which this position depends. (Greenblatt 1988: 54)

The inequality of power will not have troubled the elite audience of the royal teachings, but this audience will have been relatively close witness to the king and thus a source of potential dissent for individual rulers. Royal power is not presented as based on 'lies', but the cynicism of the manipulation of the masses in *Merikare* in particular is counter-ideologically prominent. Even the specifically personal flaws can be read programmatically, since 'such arbitrary and general "human" failings obscure the kind of instability in the ruling faction' (Sinfield 1992: 121, on rebels in *Henry V* comparing the concurrent career of Essex). Amenemhat's fallible humanity is presented as if to exonerate the kingship from the assassination. Literature thus 'reveal[s] not only the rulers' strategies of power, but also the anxieties informing both them and their ideological representation' (Sinfield 1992: 127). The poems, however, resist an exclusively programmatic reading.

The non-royal teachings are concerned with individual improvement and the permanence of wisdom. Like the tales, they often concern the fate of the individual and his place in society, which is presented in generalized and largely non-narrative terms as a largely unproblematic context. The teachings are often set in idealized unproblematic times, and the key intertextual comparison is with ecomiastic, as opposed to narrative, biographies (cf. Gnirs 1996; Doxey 1998: 7–18). As in many biographies, non-royal teachings express the impact of the king on humanity, and the interdependence of the individual and society. They also deal with more specific subject matter and life-situations, tending to use techniques of expansion and amphibole. Even 'eating bread' – a basic activity, although one that is a sign of social dependence – 'is according to the counsel of god' (*Ptahhotep* 142), and although 'all behaviour is by measure' (228), the ideals of behaviour are enacted with contrasting pragmatic considerations in mind. These teachings are thus more diverse in their propounding of cultural values than they at first appear.

10.2 *THE TEACHING OF AMENEMHAT*: REWRITING HISTORY

> There needs no ghost, my lord, come from the grave
> To tell us this.
>
> Shakespeare, *The Tragedy of Hamlet* (c. 1600), I.5

Scholars have argued about how far *Amenemhat* is a politically specific composition. For example, Elke Blumenthal (1984b, 1985) sees it as a work commissioned by Senwosret I, which would justify a vendetta on his father's assassins as well as legitimising him as the new king, while Hans Goedicke (1988b) argues for a literal reading as an address to the new king warning him of the dangers of his accession (see **1.1**, **1.3**). *Amenemhat* is a dense and concise work, as is *Neferti*, the discourse which concerns the same king. It opens and closes with a specific and highly dramatic situation of speaking, in which the king is imagined as dead and addressing his son in a 'revelation', a dream (1c–e).³ Although such communication between the dead and the living was considered normal, as shown in roughly contemporary letters to the dead (e.g., Parkinson 1999la: 142–5), the fictional nature of the text is thus signalled in this setting. Such dreams feature in monumental discourse such as perhaps the Elephantine inscriptions of Senwosret I (Schenkel 1975b: 116–18; reading disputed: Quack 1992: 131). There they provide divine omens assuring the royal succession in an unproblematic manner. The son to whom he speaks is not identified, except by the designation the 'Lord to the Limit', since the king's successor would be known to the audience (differing interpretation: Thériault 1993: 154–6). His name is withheld until the end, presumably for rhetorical effect, producing a sense of a sudden appearance as the restorer of order, just as in *Neferti* the restorer appears at the last moment.

The poem consists of 15 stanzas which form three thematic sections (1–5, 6–9, 10–15). It opens as a royal proclamation, comparable with the Elephantine inscription:

> Look, I speak to you (pl.) that [you] may [. . .]   (x+5b–6b)

This opening address asserts the ostensible didactic purpose and sets the general theme of the whole:

> Rise as a god!
> Listen to what I tell you,
>   that you may be king of the land . . .⁴   (1d)

This articulates a king's becoming divine at accession; throughout the poem, the 'son' is to 'rise' and 'stand' (1d, 15f; see Blumenthal 1970: 41–5 [A5.13–18]), while the father 'descends' in the Sun-barque (15e). The first section of *Amenemhat* continues to warn against trusting unreliable people, and it moves from positive injunctions to warnings and negative injunctions. Phrases reminiscent of non-royal biographies articulate the king's virtue as in many royal inscriptions (e.g., Blumenthal 1970: 352 [G6.25]). There follow antithetical phrases, reminiscent of laments that present the treachery of the people who abused his beneficence (4). The generic movements between official discourse and lament that formed a progression from doubt to resolution in *Neferti* here generate doubt. The

---

³ See, however, Posener 1956: 71; Blumenthal 1970: 103 (B6.29), 435 (H1.19). The question whether the king is presented as living or dead has been much discussed: e.g., Posener 1956: 69; Foster 1981; Burkard 1999.
⁴ 1d–e; see Goedicke 1988b: 61–76; Burkard 1999: 155–6.

genres of funerary biography and lament evoked here are also grimly appropriate to the fictional context of the king's speech.

The lament is developed into an injunction to wider humanity – the king's 'living images' (5a)[5] – to make revenge for him, implying that the fictional setting is soon after Amenemhat's death, during the new king's accession. Although there may have been purges and executions following Amenemhat's assassination, the 'mourning' (5b)[6] that he urges is also the teaching itself: the poem and the audience's response form a self-creating redress and restitution. Like other literary self-characterizations, this thematizes expressing the inexpressible: the mourning will be 'such as was never heard before' (5b). The king urges that a response to his misfortune, and memory of it, is essential for the future, since:

When one fights in the arena, forgetful of the past,
the goodness of someone who ignores what should be known is of no avail.
(5d–e)

This observation is proved by the king's fate, since it was his lack of awareness of his subject's failings that led to his death. The fighting here has the dual sense of avenging the king (as in the previous verse: 5c), and of struggling, fighting to maintain the state (as in the Semna stela: Sethe 1928a: 84, 1.18; Blumenthal 1970: 186–7 [E2.6–8]). The reciprocity that is central to Maat concerns knowledge and memory (J. Assmann 1990: 60–4), and is here represented as specific personal knowledge and empathy. This stanza introduces the personal recollections of the king that occupy the following central stanzas, in which he 'teaches' through shared experience, not through command and instruction.

The central section of the teaching opens with a description of the moment of the attack (Burkard 1999: 156–62). This narrates the 'yesterday' of the king, which must be remembered: 'It was after supper, when night had fallen . . .' (6a). This specification of time evokes intimacy, and the passage implies that the king is old. His mortal need to sleep is presented (6c), in contrast to the royal vigilance eulogized in official discourse (Blumenthal 1970: 76 [B2.13–14], 324 [G4.40]). Sleep as a lack of vigilance is attested in *Ipuur*, where the sage asks 'Is he (god) asleep?' (12.5; cf. *The Eloquent Peasant* B1 232). Sleep's positive potential was suggested earlier, when security was emphasized – 'May you sleep, your own heart watching out for you' (3a) – but here it is ambivalent.

These contrasting associations are mobilized in the description of how the king's 'heart had begun to follow sleep (*ḥȝtj:j šms-qd*)' (6d), an idiom

---

[5] Cf. *Merikare* 46e; Westendorf 1981; Ockinga 1984: 52–6; Bickel 1994: 216.
[6] Westendorf 1981: 39–40; Ockinga 1984: 56; Dominicus 1994: 60–1.

that may recall hedonistically 'following the heart (šms-jb)' in the non-royal teachings, while the mention of a 'happy hour' suggests that the king has retired after sexual pleasure (Burkard 1999: 157–8). Sleep is central to the dramatic setting, in which the king is speaking to his son in a dream. Neither he nor his son can 'sleep until dawn' in a sign of their responsibility that reverses a standard phrasing to indicate the sleeper's prosperity earned through virtue (Blumenthal 1970: 348 [G6.12]; Posener 1976: 39). While the time of the attack displays the king's individual humanity, it also associates it with darkness, and the cosmic cycle. The king describes his half-asleep state as being a 'worm' (*lit.* 'son-of-the-earth', 6f), and this image may evoke the potential crises of the solar cycle: in the later Book of the Dead spell 87, the deceased wishes to identify himself with a 'worm' which 'sleeps and is (re)born daily', like the Sungod.[7] The simile also alludes to burial, since the worm belongs to 'the necropolis': the ruler of the land of the living is now a son of the land of the dead.

The king's capacity to repel his attackers is narrated in hypothetical terms (Burkard 1999: 159–61):

If I had quickly taken weapons in my hand,
I would have made the back-turners retreat with a charge. (7c–d)

The description of the assassination concludes with three gnomic phrases, in which the king implicitly justifies his inaction and weakness by the negative cosmology in which 'no one is strong in the night . . .' (7e). The next stanza follows with more specific extenuating circumstances, that the king was isolated from help, lacked his co-regent, and 'had not thought of servants' negligence' (8e). The passage describes an event that should have been unthinkable, and then turns to desperate questions that are stylistically reminiscent of petitions. These justify the king by demonstrating that the evil was unforeseeable in his personal experience and involving the audience in his assumption that such things are impossible. That assumption, however, ignores the human and cosmic tendency to disorder (**7.2**) which is part of ideology's legitimation of kingship. This argument that the king was unaware of something so universal has been prepared for by allusions to the attack's uniqueness: the lament too must be unique 'such as was never heard before' (5b). The mention here of a 'woman commanding troops' probably relates to the origin of the attack among the royal women (9a; Posener 1956: 85; Obsomer 1999: 230–1), but it also signifies that attack's inexplicability since the gender of the attackers' leader, who were earlier described with the sexually pejorative term 'back-turners' (Parkinson 1995: 66–7), sets them apart from normal patrilineal

---

[7] In the Coffin Texts, however, the *s3-t3* worm is presented only as an enemy (*CT* VII, 98i).

succession. Mentions of 'tumult' and 'water' in this passage again evoke cosmic chaos. The king claims to have neglected evil because of his reign's very success:

> Since my birth, evil had not come near me;
> my deeds as a strong hero were inimitable. (9e–f)

The historical veracity of such statements is doubtful, especially since Amenemhat may have virtually usurped the throne (e.g., Vandersleyen 1995: 38–9, 43–4). Nevertheless, the assassination is thus cast as a moment of failure that is almost a consequence of success.

The following final third of the composition opens with a description of the order that was undermined and that had provided the expectation of security. The king describes his achievements in grandiose, absolute terms in relation to the whole of humanity and to divinity (10–11). This passage returns to the style of official inscriptions presenting an idealized version of the king's life that moves beyond the lament-like descriptions of the ingratitude which precipitated the assassination (4). Imperfection (such as 'hunger') was banished, and the king vaunts his control over animals and foreigners who symbolize both the active opponents and the negative cosmology. The king's actions involve standing on 'boundaries' (10b) and 'reaching the limits' (10c), fulfilling potential in spatial terms that echo his successor's role as 'Lord to the Limit' (1c).

The motif of control climaxes in a description of his funerary complex (13; cf. *Sinuhe* B 300–8). The Tod inscription of Senwosret I describes the building of a temple in similar terms, including the stonework and the doors (l.49), and the teaching's description is appropriately funerary, with strong ethical overtones of the embodiment of virtue; it is 'made for all time / prepared for eternity' (13c). These verses are dominated by stately parallelism: all is now immutable. The final claim that 'I know, for I was the lord of it, to the limit!' (13d) resumes the theme of knowledge in an assertion of the truth of the account, such as are attested in royal inscriptions (**5.1.1**). It also recalls the epithet 'Lord to the Limit' applied to the new king in the opening of the teaching (1c). As a monumental funerary summation of the reign, the building becomes associated with the king's address to his son. The thematization of its artistry (cf. M. Müller 1998) creates an image of the poem itself (ecphrasis).

The closure that this stanza offers, however, is left unresolved, since a sudden collapse follows, reversing and contradicting the imposition of order that was evoked earlier: 'But now the children of the masses are in the street' (14a). The scene changes from inside the stately mansion to the common street outside, from the 'lord' to the 'many', from ordered centre to chaotic periphery. There follows an evocation of dispute and opposition, part of which recurs in a royal context in the later *Ipuur* (6.13):

> the wise is saying 'It is so!',
> the fool saying 'It is not!' (14b)[8]

Fools exist and the order of wisdom meets opposition, as royal power does. The dispute in the street is ironically equivalent to the 'fight' the king enjoined on humanity in the address of the fifth stanza (5c), but becomes a paradoxically positive sign, since it is due to the people's temporary 'lack' of Senwosret. In this way the turbulence is associated with the assassination, which also occurred in Senwosret's absence. This separation of father and son is then re-enacted (from 8a) as the king resumes his place in the barque of the Sungod passing through the Otherworld at night. With the mention of Senwosret by name in the centre of the stanza, the children of the masses (14a) become the 'children of a happy hour (*wnwt nt-nfr-jb*)' (14f), and the disputes become praises of the new king. This passage also echoes the description of the assassination before which the king 'had spent a happy hour' (6b). The lost time of pleasure is regained, and the separation of father and son leads to an affirmation of the son's inheritance.

The final statements and injunctions of the teaching represent Senwosret as the fulfiller of 'what was in the heart' of Amenemhat, namely his son as 'my likeness, wearing the White crown, divine progeny!' (15b–c). Awareness of human fallibility is central to attaining the potential of divinity. The final lines of the poem urge conflict once again (cf. 5c, 7a):

> May you fight for the wisdom of the wise-hearted,
> for you loved him beside your Person (l.p.h.)! (15h–j)

The final line of the Semna stela declares that it was erected 'in order that you shall fight for it (the border/king's statue)' (cf. Barta 1974b; Seidlmayer 2000: 236–7), and the same language occurs in *The Loyalist Teaching* (6.1): 'Fight for his (the King's) name!'. Although the ending resumes the style of official discourse, here the fighting is not tied to a functional context as on a stela set up in a fortress (cf. Van Siclen 1982; Seidlmayer 2000), but to a fictionalized personal force. The wisdom comes from another world, and from the past. Although fighting is here synonymous with mourning and revenge (5c) and echoes the description of the assassination when the king woke 'to fighting' (7a), it is also enacted in

---

[8] The text of the final stanza(s) is problematic and corrupt: see Burkard 1999: 163 for alternative reading.

the literary teaching, which instantiates the awareness and the struggle that the fallible yet 'wise-hearted' king demands.

The assertion of the king's role is placed in question not only by the assassination, but also by the dead king's cynicism, which he passes on to his son. Kingship's singularity is both 'unique' (like the creator god) and 'lonely' (like a man: 2c–e), terms that can suggest anti-social isolation.[9] The king's human failings are rendered 'tragic' and not simply reprehensible; they paradoxically ally him with the Sungod who also has to struggle against chaos. This ambivalence contrasts with the presentation, for example, in the Hymns to Senwosret III, where kingship is straightforwardly 'unique' and a refuge for humanity, and with the doctrinal presentation of the king's knowledge in the 'King as Sunpriest' treatise (J. Assmann 1970).

The question of how far *Amenemhat* presents kingship or associated cultural values in an educational manner is problematic. The fact that the king was assassinated is unlikely to have been new information to the original elite audience at the time of its composition. More generalized propaganda about the nature of kingship would scarcely be necessary, since, if the teaching of high officials was partly done in the Residence – as in the biographical epithet 'Pupil of Horus' (*sb3-ḥr*; Doxey 1998: 121) – such indoctrination would have been conveyed in many other ways. As in *Sinuhe*, the poem fluctuates between monumental style and personally experienced anguish, perhaps programmatically fulfilling the ideological aim of showing the burdens of responsibility. The vividly charted nightmare aspects are, however, thematically and formally central, and go beyond the needs of such a purpose.

If one attempts, however speculatively, to imagine the situation of the first recital, one may gain some sense of the work's potential emotional impact. The poem was presumably composed in the royal court, probably early in Senwosret I's sole reign. One might envisage Senwosret sitting surrounded by courtiers, like Sneferu in *Neferti*. The courtiers might be a significantly different group after the purges and executions following the old king's death. The poem would make a short but highly virtuosic performance, providing a lament of the sort to which the court was probably accustomed since the previous reign when *Neferti* was composed, but it would also confront the king with a man speaking in the voice of his father's ghost. Although the monologue ends with sublime assurance, the description of the old king's murder would be shockingly vivid and personally relevant for the king and other audience: everyone would have

---

[9] *Merikare* 41f, where the 'goodly office' of kingship has 'no son, no brother'. The word 'unique, only' (*wʿ*) occurs in both *Amenemhat* 2c and *Merikare* 41g. See Parkinson 1996a: 146–50 on the ambivalence of such individuality.

known the old king and the conspirators. Even in performances away from the court, the poem would have retained its immediacy because the elite was so small. While one cannot imagine what the audience might have thought during the performance, this hypothetical scenario suggests something of the poem's complexity. For each member of this audience the poem would have a different significance: those who might have suspected that Senwosret was implicated in his father's murder could even have heard it as a device to catch the conscience of the king (cf. Volten 1945: 125–8; Obsomer 1999: 232–3). The poem denies that the old and new king had ruled jointly for ten years, a fact that would be known to the audience and that legitimized the new king as designated successor (**1.1**). The denial presents the succession in ideologically normative terms, but also enables a bleaker, more strongly paradoxical vision. The suppression of the co-regency would also have signalled the poem as fictional; in a charged atmosphere, the fictionality was perhaps integral to such a daring performance.[10] In other literary traditions, dreams are often evoked to excuse the potentially offensive aspects of fictional texts (e.g., examples in Holland 1994: 3–5, 17–18). The poem, considered as a performance, does not provide the audience with an educational process, but a display of emotion and problematic experience.

10.3 *THE TEACHING FOR MERIKARE*: SHEPHERDING REBELLION

> Il y a sur cette terre des fléaux et des victimes et . . . il faut, autant qu'il est possible, refuser d'être avec le fléau . . . Tout le malheur des hommes venait de ce qu'ils ne tentaient pas un langage clair . . . J'essaie d'être un meurtrier innocent.
>
> A. Camus, *La Peste* (1947), Part 4, chap. [6]

The Teaching for Merikare is more discursive than *Amenemhat*, and reviews a whole reign rather than explaining a single catastrophe, discussing the king's realization of Maat (e.g., J. Assmann 1984a: 201–2). The identity of Merikare's teacher is problematic (see **A.1.5**), but his characterization is broadly similar to that of the king in *Amenemhat*,[11] although he is more strongly marked as a representative of embattled monarchy. The beginning

---

[10] Describing royal fallibility to a court audience always risks disapproval: Benjamin Britten's *Gloriana* (1953) was officially commissioned to celebrate the 'new Elizabethan age' of Elizabeth II, but was denounced for its depiction of the old age and death of Elizabeth I as 'unfit' for the young queen and her people (Mitchell 1993).
[11] It is thus not necessarily 12th Dynasty propaganda against the preceding Heracleopolitan Dynasty: cf. Parkinson 1991e: 172–3 on the Heracleopolitan setting of *The Eloquent Peasant*.

is fragmentary, and the context was not explicitly described (to judge by the size of the lacuna). King Khety is, however, apparently on the point of death like the vizier in *Ptahhotep*, since the phrase 'may you reach (*pḥ*) me' (48d) seems to imply that the teacher is already on the threshold of the next world.[12] A narrative setting or an extensive frame were probably not needed, since the king's name will have been sufficient to signal the context and indicate the work's fictionality for the 12th Dynasty audience. The reign that provides the setting evokes a troubled period, as is evident in a later reference to this time as 'a reign of ill' (49h). The misfortunes of the king's reign, which seem to have included his end, are presented in the text as a given, drawing on the audience's general knowledge.

The teaching opens ominously with injunctions on how to govern and to avoid being 'lenient' (1d). These actions are enjoined as a response to deeds that are introduced as 'the beginning of [rebellion(?)]' (1f). The teaching is, however, more explicit about the internal nature of the conflict than inscriptions such as the Tod inscription of Senwosret I, which phrases it primarily with reference to the 'enemy' and foreigners (Helck 1985; Barbotin and Clère 1991: 31; on rebels in the land see Blumenthal 1970: 248–56 [F8]). The teaching subverts the ideological presentation of Egypt as a united country with references to its being internally divided (e.g., 26g–i), mobilizing the potential of the Heracleopolitan setting more specifically than *The Eloquent Peasant*; specific toponyms are prominent in the poem. The opening stanzas concern words as a means of restraint (cf. Derchain 1989): 'your words exist against e[vil]' (2b). This concern with rhetoric may be in part a self-reflexive prelude to the poem, as in the opening stanzas of *Khakheperreseneb* and of *Ptahhotep*. Formally it recalls the sequences of maxims in *Ptahhotep* that are introduced with 'If you find . . .' (Blumenthal 1980a: 6; Fischer-Elfert 1999: 405–6).

The teaching starts with pragmatic advice for a new king, describing specific instances of potentially troublesome underlings (3a–6f), and then diverges more and more into historical narration and generalized reflection. Increasingly within each stanza the material moves between specific and general, with themes crossing the stanza boundaries. The style enacts the protagonist's statement that 'all that is done is bound together' (42k), which underlies the presentation and emplotment of the events that it narrates. This is a central ideological assertion, and is integral to the reciprocity of Maat, but the poetry enacts a complex search for meaning in the patterns of historical experience and events, and the 'binding

---

[12] See 20e, where *pḥ* is to 'reach' the Otherworld and become godlike (20f). The same imagery of fulfilment and landing occurs in *Ptahhotep* 637 ('As you reach me . . .'). See the discussion by Quack 1992: 90, as an 'Abschiedsrede'.

together' forms an unideological presentation of reality and society's relationships. Although this sequence of maxims leads to an injunction to be skilful in words since 'words are stronger than any weapon' (9c), rhetoric also gives voice to subversive actions (e.g., 5k–6f) and calls forth the necessity to punish.

There follows a sequence of stanzas which concern the appropriate treatment of less troublesome groups, including the ancestors (10a–11g), the officials (12a–13h), the great (14a–15g), distressed underlings (16a–18g), the military youth (21a–22d), associates (22e–23b), and the gods (23c–25b). The first of these stanzas interweaves the ideas of reading, virtue and endurance through Maat, asserting that god as well as society will ensure that goodness is repaid (9a–e, 10a–g). Words and wisdom are presented as the key to order and continuity (9i–j). The focus moves from the specific to the general, and from this world to the Otherworld, but there is also a complementary and subversive juxtaposition. The articulations of reciprocity and retribution are interwoven with brutally pragmatic observation, such as instructions to increase wealth, because a poor man cannot afford to speak truth (14d–e). This statement runs counter to the idealizing presentation of lowly dispossessed men who speak truth, such as the Heracleopolitan eloquent peasant, marking this assertion as intertextually ambiguous. This pragmatism serves to reinforce the responsibility of wealth.

The Otherworld's justification of actions on earth is affirmed in a paradoxical manner:

> [life] upon earth passes – it is not long.
> To be remembered because of it is success.
> Even a million men cannot benefit the Lord of the Two Lands.   (13c–e)

The statement about the million men reverses the official position that the king is worth a multitude of common men (e.g., Blumenthal 1970: 264–5 [G1.1–3]), a motif taken up later in the poem (41d). Reciprocity and retribution – the means by which the king can impose order – are expressed not only through divine intervention, but with the more personal imagery of an individual *ba* coming back to take vengeance on someone (18e–g),[13] as inexorably as fate after death. Implicit in this is a warning to the royal pupil not to trust in his own power. In contrast to earlier passages, the teacher advocates lenience with the more idealistic assurance that

---

[13] See Fecht 1991: 119–20. The subject matter relates to personal experience as manifested in letters to the dead (Baines 1991a: 151–5).

> God knows the malcontent.
> God will impose his doom with blood.
> Only the lenient man will increase his (own) lifetime. (17d–f)

Assertions like this suggest that society tends ineluctably and undetectably towards tumult.

The next stanza continues this motif in a discussion of judgement after death, and retribution in the next life:

> A man who reaches them (the gods) without doing wrong,
> he is There like a god,
> free-striding like the Lords of Eternity. (20e–g: cf. J. Assmann 1990: 131)

After this, the old king pronounces on how to treat the military youth on the one hand and the gods on the other (21a–25b), with injunctions to cultic observance, since 'god knows the man who acts for him' (24g). Cult is represented as an investment in the future, since chaos is an ever-present threat; the statement that 'the enemy cannot be cool within Egypt' (25a–b) is an indirect affirmation that Egypt is not a stable unity: the enemy is 'within'.

A sequence of stanzas then narrates a conflict that happened within Egypt, a destruction of a necropolis in battle. The 'destroying of tomb-chambers' (25e–f) implies that the silent land, the port of Maat (**7.2**) was ravaged by the conflict. In laments, 'men live in the necropolis' (*Neferti* 12d), but here the generalized complaint is made specific by the turmoil. It is uncertain how far this narrative is based on historical events (e.g., Vandersleyen 1995: 7–8), although the necropolis at Abydos was deliberately desecrated (Janet Richards, pers. comm.). Given that monuments are synonymous with the achievements of reign (see later 29b, d), it is possible, as Quack argues, that the event may not have been an accident of warfare (1992: 42–5, 85–6), but the presentation nevertheless makes it into a metaphor of conflict. The passage contains a mingling of future and past tenses (similar to that in *Neferti*), making the struggle into something almost perpetual that was predicted by the ancestors and by the Residence:

> As such things happen, these happened.
> Those things cannot go otherwise, even as they (the ancestors) said it. (26e–f)

The old king mentions his involvement as an aside, interweaving it with injunctions to treat the south – which the audience subsequently learns (42a–b) included the scene of his 'vile deed' – well:

> I did the like, and the like happened,
> as is done to someone who goes against god in this way. (26a–b)

The inevitability of this retribution is expressed in a proverbial-sounding metaphor:

> There is no pure water which lets itself be concealed. (27c)

This takes up the image of the king's conquest of Thinis as a potentially ambivalent 'cloud-burst' (26h; see Darnell 1997a on clouds as 'typhonic' display).

This description is followed by a more historically specific section reviewing the achievements of the reign (28a–39c) and describing the prosperous state of the land which Merikare can now inherit ('All is now well for you . . .'). As in *Amenemhat* this justifies the old king's actions:

> Follow your heart, for this is what I have done!
> There is now no enemy in the midst of your borders. (30c–d)

Despite the old king's involvement in the brutal sacrilege, Egypt is happy as a result of his actions. The king describes himself in normative terms as a restorer of order and political unity, recreating 'the land they have destroyed' (32a), but the passage is ironically interwoven with references to the destruction of monuments. This reverses the intertextual connection of this motif with the king's restoration of buildings and alludes to the destruction of tomb-chambers mentioned earlier. Against this stability are set the possibility of a 'vile heir' (33c) and the image of the Asiatic who

> has been fighting since the Time of Horus.
> He cannot prevail; he cannot be prevailed over. (34h)

These two motifs also derive from official discourse, but here the vile heir is potentially the son to whom the teaching is addressed, as opposed to being a non-specific future possibility in the Semna stela (Sethe 1928a: 84, ll.15–16). The Asiatic's crime is 'fighting' – which is also the sacrilege in the necropolis mentioned earlier (25e). Related words for containment occur in the subsequent stanzas – fortresses, monuments, boundaries, numbers of fighters – suggesting a world full of conflict and requiring restraint.

The threat of disorder forms an injunction constantly to remember the principle of reciprocity: one evil deed and the enemy will rush in, since 'no one is free from enemies' (40f). Opposed to this threat is the royal 'Lord of the Two Banks' who is a 'sage' (41a). The power he must protect is that of wisdom, the wisdom that the teaching presents.

The specific review of the reign moves to increasingly generalized statements about kingship, and the fourth and final sequence of stanzas reflects on the nature of the 'perfect office' of kingship (41e ff.). However, the perfect office is formulated as an individual responsibility, and is bound up with the imperfection of the old king's actions. As with *Amenemhat*, it is a lonely business (41f–i), and the king's responsibility for 'the vile[14] deed which happened in my time' (42a), which was previously alluded to, is here narrated:

> It happened, but not as my action,
> and I knew of it (only) after it had been done.
> See my shortcoming, which is preeminent in what I did.[15]   (42c–e)

This action further allies him with the destructive forces represented by the enemy who loves vileness. The death or misfortune of a king is a potential crisis, as *Sinuhe* demonstrates, to challenge the justice of the gods, as the absence of royal effective power does in *Ipuur*. The old king transgressed in ignorance, but he still earned retribution. What was stated earlier is enacted here: there is no escape from the consequences of a destructive act (42f). His example reveals how:

> with its like is a blow repaid:
> all that is done is bound together.   (42j–k)

Maat is impersonal, and no god personally intervenes to save the king. This reflects what J. Assmann (e.g., 1989a) has termed 'indirect causation', as opposed to a theology of volition which he assigns to later periods. The king is as prey to dangers as the poor man who can only present his good character to the gods, despite being set apart from a million others and born with understanding (41a–d).

The next stanza moves from a personal level to a more universal appraisal of the world, and the fluctuating pattern of the topic gives way to a more consecutive presentation of a grand theme:

> Generation passes generation of men,
> while god, who knows their character, has hidden himself (*jmn.n-sw*).
>   (43a–b)

The ultimate controller of men has withdrawn in the sundered cosmos, but Maat is operative and unavoidable. The idea of god as nevertheless

---

[14] This word allies the king's action with those of enemies: cf. 34b, 38g, 40a.
[15] Compare Quack 1992: 70–1, 85–6.

irresistible is developed in the next verses with the image of the god's cult image on earth being compared to a flood of water:[16]

> no river lets itself be concealed,
> but it opens the dyke in which it hid itself (*jmn.n:f-sw*). (43h–i)

The divinely ordained power of Maat may not be manifest, but it endures. This principle is applied on a personal level with a repetition of the *ba* verses from earlier (18e), providing a summation of previous advice and of the preceding narration of misfortune, and moving to an injunction to Merikare to prepare for eternity through virtue: 'Act for god, and he will do the like for you' (45a).

The next two stanzas are the culmination of the text (Lichtheim 1973: 98), with universalized assertions:

> Humanity is cared for, the flock of god.
> For their sakes (*jbw*, lit. hearts) he made heaven and earth. (46a–47k)

Man is here both the 'image' and offspring of the creator (46e, i), and human 'hearts' are the focus of the created world (46b, 46f, 47a). Susanne Bickel notes how untypical these themes are for Middle Kingdom religious discourse (1994: 216–19; cf. 1998). The passage is, however, similar in subject matter to the Creator's declaration in Coffin Text spell 1130: both describe the cosmos and the creator's responsibility for it, and both are theodic statements with men's hearts at their centres. But whereas the declaration has a dogmatic assertive directness, the old king's description operates on more levels and is more allusive. The literary text addresses personal concerns that do not emerge in religious texts until a later date. Humanity as the subjects of king and god and humanity's troubled heart are central here, whereas in the Coffin Texts the transfigured dead form the audience of the creator god's self-justification, while he remains the subject.

Even *Merikare*'s ostensibly positive affirmation has a dark side. The creation of heaven and earth alludes to the sundered world. Rebellion is even evoked as a primeval force, when the creator 'drove off the rapacity of the waters' (46c; possibly a metaphor rather than an allusion to myth). At the end of the stanza the old king describes how the creator

> has killed his enemies and has destroyed (*ḥḏ*) his children,
> for thinking to make rebellion (*sbjt*). (46h–i; cf. Quack 1992: 96–7)

---

[16] Compare Posener 1962–6: 343; Loprieno 1993c: 17.

The next stanza continues the anthropocentric description of the cosmos, and describes the institution of rulers, providing an aetiology of kingship:

> He has raised (*ṯs*) for himself a shrine[17] around them.
> They weep and he is listening.
> He has made for them rulers from birth,
> commanders (*ṯsw*) to sustain (*ṯs*)
> the back of the weak.[18] (47c–f)

The world is a shrine similar to those erected by the king in official discourse (the temple being an image of the cosmos: e.g., J. Assmann 1984a: 43–50). Awareness of humanity's propensity towards disorder implies that containment and restraint are necessary to 'sustain' humanity, in addition to the creation of joy. Parallel to the imposition of rulers is the institution of magic, which is associated with the elite and royalty in *Ipuur* (6.6–7; cf. L. Morenz 1996: 91–100). It is a power that enables people 'to ward off the blow of what may happen' (47g) exactly as kingship is; nevertheless, this phrasing echoes the earlier statement that no magic was strong enough to ward off agents of retribution that implicitly overtook the king (18e–g). The presentation of god echoes that of the king: the creator's hostile action against rebels parallels that earlier enjoined on the king (5i). God's punishment of humanity's rebellion legitimizes the use of royal force against the king's enemies (recurring key words are *sbj* and *ḥꜣkw-jb*, e.g., 2a, 47i), but it also justifies the misfortune that overcame the old king himself, and thus legitimizes his fallibility by mobilizing the concept of the sundered world. The very failing which might be thought to cast doubt on the benevolence of god – the imperfection and misfortune of the shepherd king – demonstrates the fact that humanity is 'cared for' by the shepherd-creator. Nevertheless, the underlying tension between the king's role as god's deputy and his own human fallibility and suffering differentiates the poem from official presentations of the king's role.

The image used for god's hostile action against the 'malcontents among humanity' is one of domestic strife: it is 'like a man striking his son for the sake of his brother' (47j). Thus the violence of god against the old king, earlier related as a disaster, is here transfigured into an action of caring. The old king's suffering has become an indication that 'god knows every name' (47k), not just that of the king. The king himself is a 'sage' (41a), and in this respect a god, as Middle Kingdom discourse affirmed (e.g., Blumenthal 1970: 105; Franke 1996), but the old king reveals that his

---

[17] Compare the epithet of the creator 'He who is in his shrine' in Coffin Text spell 1130 (*CT* VII, 468f).
[18] Blumenthal 1970: 356–7 (G6.33). See, e.g., J. Assmann 1989a: 60–3.

knowledge was imperfect, so that the king, like humanity, is a partial image of god.

This grand metaphor of king, god and shepherd provides a paradigm of kingship and gives meaning to the untoward. The final stanza returns to the didactic setting. The eulogy of creation is undercut with the potential of ignorance and dissent, as the king enjoins restraint from killing courtiers – which would have an obvious appeal to the elite audience – and virtue towards the 'whole population' (49e). The teaching concludes:

> You are (to be) called 'Destroyer of the time/reign of ill',
> by those who are posterity in the House of Khety,
> with the prayer 'May he come (again) today!'
> Look, I have told you the excellence of my generation.
> May you act by what is set down (*grg*) before you! (49h–50b)

This passage affirms the value of personal experience, as does the conclusion of *Amenemhat*, and provides an ironic reference to the frame, since the audience will have known that the 'posterity' of the Heracleopolitan Dynasty was supplanted by the 11th and 12th Dynasties, especially if Merikare was the last king of the dynasty (Vandersleyen 1995: 8). The 'time of ill' is implicitly identified with Khety's reign, in a reversal of the usual official descriptions of a king's own reign as succeeding such a time. This allusion may be reinforced by wordplay with the king's name Khety (*ḥtj*: L. Morenz 1997c) which makes him a sort of everyman of his time, but also recalls that 'generation (*ḥt*) passes generation' (43a), displaying the transitoriness of all experience. The king appeals to his own generation, rather than to the usual primordial 'first generation' of official discourse (e.g., Barbotin and Clère 1991: 25 n.132). The phrase 'what is set down before you' relates the poem to the whole state of the land, which is 'set down' or 'established' (*grg*) by the king (e.g., Blumenthal 1970: 176–7 [E1.18–21]), while its being placed 'before you' recalls the immediacy of laments such as *Neferti*.

The state's strategies of repression are legitimized by an ideology of the benevolent creator and his deputy and representative, the good shepherd. The teaching is interwoven stylistically within stanzas, but also throughout the whole, which moves from specific instances of dealing with potential rebels to the creator's primordial restraint of rebellion. While this progression asserts the ideological line that 'all is bound together', the creator's care is demonstrated through a stark vision of a divided state and a remorseless world, in which even conflict and destruction within Egypt are imbued with eternal laws of truth. The fusion of the ideal and the actual which this achieves is taken to the limit, producing a continually fluctuating sense of fissures that is distinct from the sequence of order-disorder-order of official discourse. The anomalies of history are made to reflect the justice of god, but in a process that also voices the problematic.

10.4 *THE TEACHING OF PTAHHOTEP*: FRAGMENTING THE IDEAL LIFE

> The smug philosophers lie who say the world is one;
> World is other and other, world is here and there . . .
>
> Louis MacNeice, *Plurality* (1979: 243)

The Teaching of Ptahhotep presents a vision of elite social experience, spoken by a vizier in an idealized world of the Old Kingdom in which virtue is rewarded. This aspect has often been implausibly assumed to reflect a hypothesized untroubled Old Kingdom ethos. The teaching is bipartite: a sequence of maxims with a lengthy epilogue of a more reflective nature. The maxims have a partly list-like structure that can be compared with encyclopaedic texts such as the onomastica and technical treatises, but they lack the specific information expounded by those. The sequence of maxims also poses a textual problem, since they vary between different Middle Kingdom manuscripts, suggesting that there was some fluidity in composition and transmission (see **3.2.1**).

Although in some texts 'teaching' (*sb3*) can be associated specifically with training for office, the subject matter here is not related to a specific office, and a multitude of mutually exclusive career possibilities is envisaged for the vizier's son who is being appointed. Although the teaching is addressed to this individual of high rank, the topics covered depart ostentatiously from the ideological ideal of the son succeeding his father. The 10th maxim evokes the hypothetical situation 'If you are base . . .' (175) which would be unlikely for a vizier's son, while elsewhere the setting is expanded on a more metaphorical level, as in a mention of the son 'ploughing' in the 9th maxim (161).[19] In this respect the teaching differs from the 18th Dynasty treatise 'The Duties of the Vizier' (van den Boorn 1988), which deals with the same ostensible subject matter of official conduct but is more literally conceived.

Courtly etiquette and training were integral to achieving an official position. A high proportion of biographical epithets connect the individual in specific and generalized ways with the king, as opposed to either gods or other officials (Doxey 1998: 109–28), suggesting that the court was an arena of ritualized etiquette with power determined by one's

---

[19] Vernus (1999: 143) reads these features literally as showing that the teaching's audience had 'un large éventail sociologique'.

standing in relationship to the king, and by rhetorical performance and self-presentation. *Ptahhotep* refers little to the king, drawing more on the biographical theme of an individual's self-fashioning rather than that of royal advancement. Despite this subject matter, the teaching is not a convincing manual about courtly etiquette of the kind attested from early modern Europe, although it is possible to argue that the poem teaches correct behaviour attitudes and fine style by means of examples, modelled on the sequence of problems or cases in mathematical and medical technical treatises, where instances are introduced, as here, by the phrase 'If you find . . .'. However, the specific instructions on ethical etiquette are often the given points of departure of the maxims, rather than what they propound, and in ethical terms it teaches generalized banalities. The injunctions to act become instead means for meditation. The prominence of hypothetical situations creates a world of 'as if', while the medical terminology suggests not that the teachings were technical texts, but one that provided relief.[20] The instructive aim is fissured with faultlines, and fraught with ethical play.

The narrative prologue establishes the idealized setting, in which King Isesi immediately grants the ideally aged vizier's request for a 'staff of old age' who requires teaching, but it also signals the poem's divergence from the ideological norm. The description of Ptahhotep's infirmity is distinct from the allusions in biographies to a long life as a happy result of virtue; the one comparison known to me is with the inscription of the Vizier Useramen, installed under Tuthmose III when his father was old (Theban Tomb 131), but this Royal Tale-style inscription, like others of the period, is modelled on classical literary texts.[21] Ptahhotep ostensibly urges conformity to the traditional ideals of society, but his self-description reveals a striking ambivalence to the past, which implies that old age embodies moral failing as well as authority (cf. J. Assmann 1990: 61–2; see pp. 94–5 for an attempt to chart this passage's gradual divergence from the norms with regard to the heart). The pseudepigraphic frame thus subverts both the official use of pseudepigraphy and the wisdom handed down.

The ostensible aim of the teaching is to promote 'knowledge' (*rḫ*). Nili Shupak describes *rḫ* as 'knowledge obtained by learning and intended for a practical purpose' (1993: 229), and Miriam Lichtheim has argued that it does not mean 'wisdom' (1997: 5–6). In biographies of the period the word usually denotes knowledge of a specific matter (e.g., Doxey 1998: 46–8, 332–6), but in the teaching the learning process is so generalized

---

[20] Like the tale of Pericles, of which Shakespeare's Gower asserts 'Lords and ladies in their lives / Have read it for restoratives' (*Pericles*, Scene 1).
[21] The introduction recalls *Neferti* as well as *Ptahhotep*; part of the text is also known from a papyrus copy: Helck 1955. Text: *Urk.* IV, 1380–4; Dziobek 1998: 3–21, pl. 1. The inscription is accompanied by a 'Teaching' by the vizier's father (see p. 74).

and intangible that a sense of 'wisdom' is inevitable. Is the value of the poem in the norms it teaches, in the rhetoric it teaches, or in the words with which it supposedly teaches?

The first maxim (52–9) concerns the dangers of wisdom, forming an ironic opening to the sequence. The praise accorded to the 'perfect speech' of maidservants runs counter to normal representations of social practices and of attitudes to the speech of illiterates (see p. 95). It produces a sense of a cultural union that goes beyond the normal hierarchy (cf. Greenblatt 1988: 49), but this is unlikely to correspond to any social reality, actual or intended, of inclusive high culture (cf. Moers 2000: 59–80). Instead, this sense qualifies the stereotype that wisdom brings social advancement. Perfect speech may be rarer than precious 'malachite' and be found with serving maids (58–9), but they are not rich, except in words, and the stanza that ostensibly asserts the inclusiveness of culture embodies social fissures.

The main body of the maxims includes indications of further voices. There is not simply a difference between the outward voice of the author and the subtext of an inner voice, but also a feature similar to what is seen in *The Eloquent Peasant* and *Amenemhat*, where violent shifts occur between two aspects of the single authorial voice, between eulogy and denunciation, and between self-eulogy and self-lament. While *Ptahhotep* urges conformity to authority (e.g., 441–9), it also gives voice to contradictory elements, stimulating a complex and questioning reading. Specific evidence that doubt could attend ideological assurances of happy endings occurs in the biography of the nomarch Montuhotep from the start of the 12th Dynasty (Schenkel 1964; Stewart 1979: pl. 18), in which he is made to say:

> Repute (*sḏm*) is in the speech of men,
> as that verse which is upon the mouths of the great ones:
> 'The goodness of a man is his monument;
> the man of evil character is forgotten'.
> If it will come to pass as is said,
> my good name will last in my city. (l.16)

The 'if' shows that paradigmatic sayings about the triumph of virtue were not infallible certainties even in official discourse. The teaching is likewise full of hypothetical instances that are here mobilized to create a sense of complexity rather than merely of comprehensiveness as in technical treatises. Overall, *Ptahhotep* creates a different impression, for example, from the Chamberlain Intef's economastic biography (temp. Senwosret I: Sethe 1928a: 80–1; Parkinson 1991a: 61–3; cf. Lichtheim 1988: 106–11); although this is closely related in expression to the teachings (Doxey 1998:

208), its epigrammatic statements that wisdom leads to promotion are secure and unqualified in comparison.

The maxims expressing diverse attitudes might seem to be a partly random anthology of sayings for which an assumption of thematic unity is inappropriate, but the setting presents them as part of a single continuous utterance. A loose structure is evident in the maxim's order in the complete version of P. Prisse, for example at the start with the 2nd to 4th maxims, and the 18th to 19th and 26th to 27th maxims. The form of the maxims is a stylistic choice: one can compare *Kagemni* which has a content comparable with Ptahhotep's maxims, but is more closely interwoven thematically with epigrammatic verses formed into long passages, whereas the maxims assemble them into shorter passages with an explicit single topic. The distinctive form of the maxims can be observed within *The Teaching of Ptahhotep* itself: their stanzas are shorter and more epigrammatically dense than the more elaborate and extensive stanzas of the epilogue (507–644). The form of the maxims allows an encyclopaedic treatment of situations in elite life but also a variety of approaches to the same topics that surface in different situations. This diversified structure can juxtapose abstract themes, relating to general ethical matters and to 'god', with specific everyday matters. I discuss here the treatment of some attitudes.

Throughout the maxims the triumph of Maat is repeatedly affirmed through mentioning the reverse possibility that wrong might prevail. Such negative formulations of right occur in official biographies (e.g., J. M. A. Janssen 1946: 152–8 [A–L]), but more absolutely. In the fifth maxim:

> baseness can carry off riches,
> but wrong has never yet brought its deed to land. (92–3)

There is a muted allusion to judgement after death – which is itself a response to a theodic problem (Fecht 1958: 18–20). The formulation 'When the end comes, Maat endures' (97) accommodates both perspectives on the triumph of Maat: it endures, but only finally. The social hierarchy is also presented in a positive manner as the direct consequence of god's will and reward:

> It is god who advances position. (229)

This recalls – and generalizes – the statements in biographies that a man's king and his own character advance his position (J. M. A. Janssen 1946: 105–6 [Ev]). Elsewhere, however, the social suffering of the virtuous is also admitted:

> There is many a father who suffers ... (171)

>   It is the solitary whom god brings up. (173)

The description of 'what happens' in the world is likewise complex in relation to divine or royal responsibility:

>   what happens (ḫprwt) is what god commands. (116)

unlike the 'stratagems of men' (115). God rewards virtue with prosperity and security (181–5), but nevertheless the audience which is being enjoined to virtue may be 'base' (175; compare 428 where the audience could have once been 'little (nḏs)'). The poem mentions falling from prosperity and fluctuations in fortune, reversing the description of a stable and unquestioned meritocracy in official biographies.

The theme of wealth is characteristic of early 12th Dynasty biographies (Doxey 1998: 33–6), the most plausible date of *Ptahhotep*'s composition (**A.1.5**), but it is not a common motif in them, and is associated with the use of wealth in provisioning the poor, whereas the poem makes it a separate theme, and renders it problematic. In the 11th maxim, the concern with wealth is qualified; instead of urging the audience to 'follow an excellent man' (as in 175), it advises 'follow the heart' (186):

>   Property will exist – (so) follow your heart!
>   Property is of no avail when it (the heart) is disaffected. (192–3)

The teaching is as concerned with doubts over the meaning of 'what happens' as other non-didactic literary texts (see **5.2**). The 22nd maxim articulates the social consequences of a man's behaviour in a qualified manner: wealth 'happens for you (ḫprwt-n:k)' as 'that which has happened (ḫpr) to one favoured by god' (339–40; cf. 116 quoted above). But although this favour is a reward for virtue, 'what will happen (ḫpr) cannot be known, when thinking of tomorrow' (343). Similarly, in the 30th maxim the vizier warns:

>   Do not trust in your riches,
>   which came to you (ḫpr-n:k) as a gift of god. (433–4)

These statements imply that both the wealth and god's favour may disappear: the audience may be rich and happy or poor and suffering at different times. The teaching envisages changes in the social hierarchy and the presence of parvenus (Vernus 1999: 149–51), although this is not presented as a unified 'political' theory of human society as Vernus suggests, but as a literary description of the mutability of humanity comparable with that of the discourses. As in the first maxim, one cannot rely on wisdom bringing good fortune; this is a warning not merely against pride in being newly rich, but against the notion that virtue is inevitably rewarded. The 35th maxim is explicit on this point, developing the motif of friends as a wealth 'greater than riches' (491). Good character is its own reward in this world, and its benefits are viewed in more transcendent terms than those of prosperity:

> The property of one man can belong to another;
> a gentleman's qualities are excellent for him (alone).
> Good character will be a memory. (492–4)

A similarly varied approach to the ambivalence of society is found in the 29th maxim (422–7), which appears to acknowledge that a righteous man can commit a 'misdeed', while the fallibility of others prompts clemency and pardon:

> Pass over this; do not remember this! (424)

The role of the heart is also described ambivalently: in the 11th maxim one should 'follow the heart' (186), whereas in the 25th maxim:

> The man who listens to his heart will feel 'If only!' (387)

The 19th maxim (298–315), which is numerically the central one in the complete version of P. Prisse, concerns the vice of being 'grasping of heart', specifically 'greed' but also more generally 'selfishness' and 'egotism' (J. Assmann 1990: 87–8). This is the central fault, the 'sum of every ill' (310). The maxim starts with correlation of being happy and abstaining from 'every evil' (298–9), and the final verses assimilate doing Maat and behaving according to convention and hierarchy:

> A man will last when he uses Maat aright.
> The man who goes according to his position makes a legacy by this;
> there is no tomb-chamber for the selfish. (312–15)

The presentation of the heart as what determines a man's ability to be wise (550–2) makes the whole teaching almost reflexive: the sense of experiencing and acquiring wisdom is a natural extension of the self-fashioning theme of commemorative texts. Biographies concern individuals 'whose heart taught me to be calm', and a 'wise man who taught himself wisdom', as well as people taught by royal authority.[22]

---

[22] J. M. A. Janssen 1946: 98–9 (Dr.3). The heart can also act as the father/teacher, as in the

In the central maxim, the god-given rules of society are implicitly just, and the generalized character of what is wrong is foregrounded, as against the specific problems of its being manifested in society. The maxim is preceded by one on adultery (277–97): selfishness is sited within society, with domestic and social consequences. The central maxim is followed by another (the 20th) on the wider social aspects of greed 'in the division' of wealth (316).

The maxims thus display an inclusive range of paradigmatic and pragmatic pronouncements. The final maxims, which concern the treatment of others and the themes of friends, generosity and marriage, contain several divergent social figures, such as social parvenus (428–40), the boy-prostitute (457–62), and the plump wife (499–506), presenting a diversified view of society. It is unlikely that these were specifically contemporaneous social dangers, against which the reader had to be educated; rather they articulate the extended range of literary discourse's concerns. The setting of the idealized past may heighten the problematic character of these figures: if there was such social mutability in the good old Old Kingdom, what does this imply about the present? The 36th maxim about 'teaching absolutely' (495) offers a sense of closure which is immediately undermined by the 37th maxim extolling the plump woman who is 'light-hearted' (500), a quality that was earlier condemned (382).

The epilogue makes the teaching's transcendence from social norms and concerns more explicit. This increased abstraction from social situations is paralleled in the style, which becomes more highly wrought and uses wordplay more extensively. Wisdom here is potentially its own reward:

The wise man shall be satisfied on account of his wisdom. (526)

This section resumes the prologue's topic of old age as a metaphor for wisdom's success. Wisdom is presented not just in terms of social position but in physical, that is individual and personal, terms, with the virtuous official being described as someone whose

lips are righteous while he is speaking,
his eyes see,
and both his ears hear what is excellent for his son –
a doer of Maat, free from Falsehood.[23] (529–32)

---

description of 'one whom his character taught, like a child grows up through his father' (98 [Dr.2]).
[23] See Fecht 1991: 115–17. For this passage compare the Wadi Hammamat inscription of Ameny (no. 3024, temp. Senwosret I: Vernus 1995b: 106–7).

This is a directly antithetical allusion to the opening description of Ptahhotep's infirmity (11–13). Several verses later the same image of physical well-being is applied more directly to the obedient son who

> has splendid body,
> and is blessed before his father. (560–1)

The son's 'blessedness' plays on the usual funereal associations of this word. The teaching and the continuity of wisdom thus provide a metaphorical answer to Ptahhotep's lament on the imperfection of old age, which is made good through the transmission of virtue to his son, and now he voices his longevity in terms of a desirable favour. Similarly, the assertion that the teacher's son will be acclaimed as 'having come out of (his father's) flesh' possessing his teaching (629–30) contrasts with the opening assertion that 'no one is born wise', moving the poem closer to the positive attitudes of official discourse.

This positive reading can, however, be reversed, so that the contrasting description of physical weakness undermines this presentation of his virtue. In this perspective, this theme is not simply resolved, but suspended in the poem's final stanzas. The epilogue develops the idea of hearing as obedience to social norms (e.g., J. Assmann 1990: 73–6), but this is also a structural irony, when one recalls Ptahhotep's original lament that 'the ears are deaf' (14). Wordplay and irony create a sense of the complexity of actions, and a discussion of the heart's role in hearing foregrounds the issue of intention:

> Someone who hears is loved by god. Someone hated by god does not hear.
> It is the heart which makes its lord
> a hearer or a non-hearer –
> the life, prosperity, and health of a man! (545–52)

Implicit in these verses are the two contrasting aspects of the heart which were previously juxtaposed in several maxims about the heart's responsibility for social behaviour. The antithetical first verse of the quoted passage articulates a tension between two possible implications of the relationship between people who are obedient and disobedient to social norms: god loves the obedient man, but is the disobedient man such because he is already hated by god (cf. Miosi 1982: 81)? The ambiguity is immediately resolved by the assertion that a man's heart is the sole determining factor for his prosperity, ascribing to it a quasi-royal role with the epithet 'life, prosperity, health'.[24]

---

[24] The epithet may derive from epistolary formulae, where a letter's recipient is termed 'the

The poem never challenges society and its norms directly, but a questioning of their validity is implicit in such ambiguities. While there are allusions to the absolute dependence of the social structure and events on god's will (e.g., 116, 229), they are presented as the activities of humanity; the extent of both royal and divine influence on society remains unresolved. This formulation accommodates a questioning of the justice of society within the rules of decorum without presenting it as a direct challenge to the legitimacy of kingship. The epilogue seems to fuse social and transcendent aspects of the teaching. The good son is of 'god's giving' and also 'someone who gives increase to what he was told before his lord' (634). The potential dichotomy between the ideal and both social and individual actuality is abrogated, as the two are (momentarily) reconciled:

(The good son) shall do Maat, his heart having acted according to his
    position. (635–6)

While the epilogue addresses a wider audience, moving from a single man with a single son to a multitude of children and their descendants, the 'hearing' that it extols provides a resolution, not only as obedience to cultural norms, but also as the response to a literary event. The children are, in one sense, the response to the text, and almost the text itself, being the embodiment of the sage's wisdom. The same constellation of ideas is found in *Kagemni*, *Neferti* and most explicitly in the imagery of the Ramessid 'Eulogy of Dead Writers', where the teachings act as children for their authors. The reception of the teaching is expressed as the audience's ability to perform:

You should say distinguished things, so that the officials who hear will say,
'How good is what comes out of his mouth!'. (626–7)

In the epilogue virtue traverses time in ever-increasing robustness and plenitude, but a purely positive reading is continually problematized. The optimistic sequence of stanzas describing the son is interrupted by a description of the fool. The fool has no 'years of life', but has 'a living death every day!' (585: J. Assmann 1990: 76–7). This description of the intractable fool, who

will see wisdom (*rḫ*) as ignorance (*ḫm*),
good (*ȝḫt*) as harm (*mnt*)' (577–8)

---

lord – life, prosperity, health!' (cf. James 1962: 129), rather than directly from its application to kings.

echoes the teaching's opening sub-title, which describes its aim as

> teaching the ignorant (*ḥmw*) to be wise (*rḫ*) . . .
> good (*ꜣḫt*) to him who shall listen. (47, 49)

In the final verses the epilogue is anchored back in the present of the setting with a description of Ptahhotep's age as a sign of his rewarded virtue:

> I have achieved a hundred and ten years of life
> as a gift of the king,
> with favours beyond[25] the ancestors',
> through doing Maat for the king, until the state of blessedness.[26]   (641–4)

Ptahhotep is now speaking from the threshold of death, having reached the ultimate ideal age of 110, which is now a favoured state and not decrepitude. The son is told that 'you shall reach me, with your limbs sound' (637), echoing the earlier description of physical well-being as a result of virtue. There is also an allusion to the fictionalized setting in the ancient past, since Ptahhotep associates himself with 'the ancestors'. And this allusion recalls that, although Ptahhotep promises that Maat will bring longevity (also in 590) as 'a gift of the king', the prologue asserted that the results of age were 'evil in every aspect' (20–1), making this longevity also potentially an indictment of doing Maat and of the king's gift.

10.5 *THE LOYALIST TEACHING(S)*: IMAGINING SOCIAL SOLIDARITY

> In the prison of his days,
> Teach the free man how to praise.
>
> W. H. Auden, *In Memory of W. B. Yeats* (1991: 249)

The Loyalist Teaching has a sequentially bipartite structure that is evident in the manuscript tradition. A historical setting was probably implied by the missing name and titles of the protagonist (now lost), but the unnamed king to whom loyalty is urged is presented in general terms. The 'loyalism' which has given the work its modern title, and which relates primarily to its first part, reaffirms the civilization's pivotal formulation of the king as

---

[25] So P (*lit.* 'in front of'); L1 has 'like the ancestors'.
[26] A similar sentiment occurs in *A Man*, 6.22.

the embodier of Maat in the world. In terms of decorum, the general loyalism can be related to the absence of any strongly marked elements of dissent in the text: a poem can be ambivalent about deceased royal individuals, as in the tales and royal teachings, but it cannot question the office itself or the reigning king.

The king is 'in his palace' (5.6) and perpetually assimilated with those cosmic gods who define the conditions of human life, the Sungod and the Nileflood (2.7–3.7). He is presented in terms of the ideal office rather than as an individual embodier of the office. He is assimilated with the creator of individual bodies (5.7, 5.9–10), the protector of the state (5.11, 5.13–14), and with attributes of intimate perception (2.5–6), comparable with those mobilized in narrative terms in *Sinuhe* (Posener 1956: 124). As in the commemorative graffito of Hor at Wadi el-Hudi (temp. Senwosret I; Seyfried 1984; Obsomer 1995: 630–5), his power is acclaimed as absolute and universal. The characterization of the king, however, is strongly dual: he is both a gentle goddess Bastet and a fierce Sekhmet (5.11-14); even the other gods to whom he is assimilated are potentially hostile, as is shown by the ambivalent mobilization of the Sungod and the Nileflood in *The Eloquent Peasant's* third petition (B1 171-4; Parkinson 1988: 157–60, 187).

This metaphorical presentation, which occurs in non-royal biographies (Blumenthal 1970: 94–105 [B6]; Posener 1976: 20–1; Ockinga 1984: 128–30; Doxey 1998: 76–8), makes the king the representative of the gods and of their involvement with human affairs. In turn,

> They strike his opponents for him. (5.5)

The 'favour' of the undifferentiated 'god' in *Ptahhotep* — as opposed to the specific king Isesi — is here presented as the actions of an unspecified king who embodies the divine on earth. No man exists of himself; all men are shaped by the king. The king is the creator of humanity (5.7-10), while in more literal terms,

> The man he favours will be a lord of provisions;
> his adversary will be a nobody. (3.9-10)

This couplet encapsulates the reversals of the pessimistic laments, but in 'he manner of official discourse. There is an unquestioned correlation between loyal virtue and reward, more so even than in the largely idealized World of *Ptahhotep*, and this atmosphere is embodied in the symmetry of style. Whereas in the latter virtue leads to blessedness and a good memory (590, cf. 314–15), here that is more directly and concretely dependent on the king:

> Enter into the earth which the king gives! (7.1)

The idea of the king as the successor and deputy of the gods is matched by the succession of wisdom and loyalty, because

> speech has taught, since the time of the god. (8.2)

In contrast with the world of *Merikare*, no dissenting speech is envisaged. The final verses, however, also present warnings and the first half ends on a rhetorical question:

> The son who hears will be a faultless man.
> Can any plan of his not succeed? (8.7–8)

The second half of the teaching is introduced as

> Another method for developing your hearts,
> – which is better than anything – concerning your servants. (9.3–4)

The discourse here derives from medical texts (Fischer-Elfert 1999: 408), presenting wisdom and order as a restorative for society and developing the themes of the king as the creator and sustainer of humanity's bodies on a less cosmic scale. The metaphors expressing the king's role are here applied to humanity, articulating a more complex patterning of society than in official discourse. The audience's responsibility as individuals in charge of social groups is defined in relation to the higher authority of 'god' (11.7, 12.2), rather than loyalistically to the king. This part deals with the role of the lower levels of society, a theme that is prominent in tomb scenes of the owner's workers, but is unusual in the written record:

> It is humanity who create what exists (*shpr-ntj*) (9.7)

'Creating what exists', which usually designates a divine function, can be metaphorically exercised by officials, as in *The Eloquent Peasant*, where 'the officials' are 'the craftsmen of creating what is' (B1 320). Social solidarity is integral to the value of Maat (J. Assmann 1990) and the presentation of society here is broadly in terms of official ideology, but opens out its implications. For example, the eulogy of the king as creator of bounty runs counter to this eulogy of the underlings as 'creators'. Perhaps significantly, this part was omitted from Sehotepibre's adaptation of the poem for his monument (see **4.2**).

The imagery of cattle articulates the thematic unity of this part (in 10–11, 13). Other strands of imagery and phraseology, such as the reference to the Nileflood in 11.1, echoing 3.3, sustain continuity with the first part. The less elevated subject matter accommodates the possibility of divergence from the ideal more fully, and the possibility that loyalism will be wanting in individuals is more fully stated than before. A vivid image of the anti-social man articulates the alternative to loyalistic solidarity:

> There will be no sleep for the solitary man.
> No one sends a lion on a mission.
> No herd can isolate itself from the walled enclosure;
> its voice is like the thirsty creature's outside the well,
> with [decay] around it, and the wailing of birds.[27]   (10.5–9)

This presents an image of society as a created environment: the animal is excluded from a 'well' (*šdjjt*) which has been dug, and from an artificial 'enclosure' (*jnbt*). These images embody an awareness of the need for order to be imposed on humanity, which is presented as a self-destructive beast. The self-isolated man's nature deprives him of satisfaction, like a solitary, prowling, sleepless lion. He is here the basest form of life, virtually a carcass, just as in *Ptahhotep* the fool had a 'living death' (581). As there, failure is due to 'selfishness', here in terms of failing to acknowledge a generalized role in society. Such a vivid embodiment of the negative sides of life is lacking – if implicit – in official discourse, except for the descriptions of rebels slain by the king.

The image of society as a flock or herd articulates humanity's need for a shepherd, as in the final stanzas of *Merikare*. Here, the potential for evil is formulated in terms of humanity, avoiding explicit theodic questioning: the image of the 'bad shepherd' (13.8) applies to an official rather than to a higher figure of authority as in *The Eloquent Peasant* (B1 208–9) and *Ipuur* (12.1), and is a metaphor for potential failing, rather than an actual situation. The office of the shepherd itself is acclaimed without qualification:

> To god [these are exc]ellent offi[ces].   (11.7)

The 'office' has a multivalent role here: it acts as a metaphor for the duty of the elite and recalls descriptions of kingship as the 'excellent office' (D. Müller 1961; Blumenthal 1970: 27 [A2]) but also continues the descriptions of lowly professions that benefit society. The image both presents the role of the lowly and alludes to that of the elite who watch over

---

[27] The image of death from thirst can be compared with the near-death of another self-exile from society, Sinuhe (cf. Parkinson 1996a: 147–8).

humanity as their flock. All belong in a social continuum. The prominence of the deputizing motif and the imagery of the flock suggests that theodic concerns are relevant here.

The second part ends, like the first, by considering burial. Here a man's eternity is guaranteed by his being loved by the people, as well as by his royal favour. There should be social and temporal solidarity throughout all levels. The final stanza articulates a movement from the low levels of society towards the excellence of eternity:

> [Honour] the blessed dead; bring food-offer[ings]!
> [This is more excellent for] the doer than for him for whom it is done –
> the cared one protects him who is still on earth. (14.10–12)

It is not just the king who protects: the symmetry of social responsibility is such that it creates a potential faultline, as well as evoking the ideological norms of reciprocity. In this conclusion the text's unity is reinforced by the repetition of 'fight for' (14.1, 4.1, 6.1). By moving from the servants of the dead towards the audience's duty to its elders and ancestors, the teaching completes a thematic circle by returning to the theme of how to behave to superiors, including those touched with divinity. In this way, the poem's thematic unity enacts the solidarity of society. The final stanzas convey a sense of joy and release, as the language moves to a high funerary register, resuming the formality of the opening eulogy. However, in contrast to the call to loyalism in Hor's graffito or Sehotepibre's monument, the poem's presentation of society's interests and responsibilities is bipolar and multivocal.

The Teaching of a Man shows close similarities in theme and phraseology with *The Loyalist Teaching*, but largely concerns speech whereas *The Loyalist* concerns action. Their close relationship suggests that they may have been composed as a complementary pair, although this may be an intertextual relationship rather than the functional one proposed by Hans-Werner Fischer-Elfert (1999). Like *The Loyalist*, the teaching also has an unspecific setting, even to the point of having a generalized protagonist (see **4.3**, **5.1.2**). It opens with a eulogy both of the divine and of the king, who is 'your god' (5.5), a formulation known from *The Oxford Wisdom Text* (A.3), from inscriptions and hymns (Blumenthal 1970: 95 [B6.3, 6.6], 367–8 [G6.69–70]). These powers control what happens to a man.

Fate, however, is mentioned in a difficult passage (3.1–4), suggesting another method of accommodating the theodic problem (see Baines 1994b: 40–1; Fischer-Elfert 1999: 58–67). Related to this motif is a relativization of divine power, which is manifested in a mixing of phraseology associated with the divine and the royal. The assimilation is made more explicit:

what you have is great for you,
since you have spent your lifetime within the counsels of your god. (5.4–5)

The divine is presented progressively more in terms of its representative the king, while a clear distinction is none the less drawn between king and 'god'. Although the king's power is universal – it 'crosses the Sea' (8.3) – it remains threatened by society's response:

God binds them (foreigners) for him.
Someone who does not attack him is someone who has reached land.
Someone who does not dispute with him rests in a pyramid. (8.6–8)

Such verses raise the possibility of dissent.

The panegyric on the king is repeatedly darkened by emphasis on the disorder that is destroyed, which is not situated paradigmatically outside Egyptian society or in the past as in official inscriptions, but is within the audience, like the 'fool' in the epilogue of *Ptahhotep*. The statement that 'A man causes his own enemies to flourish' (24.8) embodies the negative view of humanity that legitimizes absolute rule, but it can also imply royal responsibility for dissent. The dichotomies of many other literary texts are here formulated in terms of an individual's dual relationship with the king:

great is the favour of god;
great is his punishing, entirely.
Great is his power – I have seen his fame. (3.5–7)

This polarity is close to the sentiment, for example in *Kagemni*, that

what will happen,
what God does when he punishes, is unknowable. (2.2)

This in turn is close to the discourses' statements about the hidden, invisible nature of god, although the king's fame is here visible. The aim of official discourse 'to place dread of the king through foreign lands' is transformed here into an internalized comprehension: 'Praise the king within your bodies' (*Loyalist* 2.1; Posener 1976: 20), a quality that is only occasionally attested in such commemorative inscriptions as on the statue of the Theban official Tjutji:

I placed fear of my god in my heart,
the king in my breast,
and the awe of my lord throughout my limbs
(J. M. A. Janssen 1946: 81 [Bm.84])

The prominence of this aspect in teachings is such that one might compare Louis Althusser's comments on literary works as 'making us "perceive" ... in some sense from *the inside*, by an *internal distance*, the very ideology in which they are held' (1971: 222–3). The divine king is the centre of *The Teaching of a Man*'s stated aim:

> He causes the little to surpass the great,
> and the last is the first;
> one without portion is a lord of wealth;
> one poor of land is the lord of a family.
> He causes one who lacks a landing to land;
> the homeless is the lord of a port.
> He teaches one who desires speech,
> that he shall open the ears of the deaf. (4.3–10)

This superficially propagandist reference is intertextually ambiguous. Although it formulates education as manifesting the king's constitutive role for culture, the last-shall-be-first pattern is elsewhere something to be dreaded. This ambivalent use of eulogies occurs also in the eloquent peasant's petitions (e.g., B1 316–8; Parkinson 1992: 173).

The loyalist teachings tend to foreground gaps and suspensions, often using metaphors to bring together such disparate elements as the imagery of a shepherd or a dyke. The social solidarity that the king ensures runs counter to his pre-eminence. The fusion and tension between the particular and the general is characteristic of Egyptian literary discourse. Antonio Loprieno (1996d: 405) has discussed these differentiations as neutralizing tensions, making them conform with Jan Assmann's model of the texts as normative. The process of differentiation, however, is more active: these gaps are not so much neutralized as articulated and fashioned by the poems, and the resolutions are suspended rather than closed.

The aesthetics of texts that assert central ideological and political values of their period are alien to a modern aesthetic of innovation and divergence. What can be termed an aesthetic of identity as opposed to innovation[28] is visible throughout Egyptian elite culture and is very prominent in these poems, but its presence does not run counter to the differentiated role of literary discourse. Even when literary discourse is closest to official discourse, as in the loyalist teachings, it is still distinctive, and is not a single-voiced assertion of cultural identity, but a meditation on it.

---

[28] 'The *aesthetic of identity* ... is based on the total identification of depicted phenomenon of life with model-clichés (i.e., topoi) that are known beforehand to the audience and operate according to a system of rules': Lotman 1977: 290.

10.6 *THE TEACHING OF KHETY*: LEARNING LAUGHTER?

> et c'est une étrange entreprise que celle de faire rire les honnêtes gens.
>
> Molière, *La Critique de l'École des femmes* (1663), vi

The Teaching of Khety belongs to the central group of genres, but is distinctive in its themes and subject matter from the other non-royal teachings. In this respect it is comparable with the royal teachings, but is allied with the lower registers of literary discourse. Though single and simple in its subject matter, the poem has a wide range of vocabulary and expression. It is potentially problematic for the non-functionalist analysis of the teaching genre that I have proposed, since it is particularly concerned with its framing situation. Among Ramessid manuscripts of Middle Kingdom works, it is the most characteristically educational teaching, so that for example Nili Shupak allies it with the 'school texts' rather than literary teachings (1993: 26).

Khety concerns scribal education, but it may be a poem about it rather than an educational composition. The teaching is made for Khety's son:

> while journeying south to the Residence
> to place him in the scribal school.   (1c–d)

It thus opens with a journey, which is the fictionalized motif par excellence (Moers 1999b, 2001), and the ascribed authorship may also mark it as at least partly fictionalized (see **5.1.2**). The mention of the school in the frame is revealing, since it implies that the theme of institutional educational was not already implicit in the genre-label; mentions of the 'school' cluster significantly at the framing points (1c, 22e, 26a). The setting is echoed in the opening verses, in which writings are compared to a boat (2c) such as the one on which the teaching is apparently taking place (1c).

After the introduction, the poem has a bipartite form, with vignettes describing a life without education instead of didactic maxims in the first part. Despite reservations by some critics, the tone of these stanzas is one of savage humour.[29] *The Loyalist* stresses the integration of society, while *Khety* stresses the opposite, denigrating the 'professions' that were acclaimed in *The Loyalist* and are shown on tomb walls in an idealized, though often humorous, manner (e.g., Parkinson 1991a: 81–3). The

---

[29] Lichtheim 1973: 184; contra Helck 1970a: 161–2, who reads it as a serious propaganda text. Similarly Foster 1999 reads the vignettes as designed to create sympathy.

teaching accords with official ideology in affirming absolute divisions in society that were probably not so clear-cut in reality (see **4.1**), while diverging from presentations of it as a happily divided whole. Although *Khety* is not a central part of the 'great tradition' of discourse about Maat as a cultural concern, it displays thematic similarity with this tradition. Its intertext is not limited to the educational treatise *Kemit* that it quotes (2d–e). For example, the vignettes recall the laments of *Ipuur* which list irregularly-behaved professions, inverting biographical descriptions of people at work (1.1–1.5; cf. L. Morenz 1999a: 119–30). The ritual-sounding phrase 'I will show you' that acts as a refrain in *Khety* also occurs in *Neferti* (p. 196); here it is not a ritual induction of the pupil (pace Fischer-Elfert 1999: 393), but an intertextual allusion to the lament genre or to rituals. Similarly the introductory phrase 'I have seen' (e.g., 2a, 3b, 4a–b) echoes official inscriptions, discourses and compound genres (pp. 183, 227).

In Hans-Werner Fischer-Elfert's analysis (1999), these differences from other high writings are explained by the hypothesis that *Khety* is the introductory text in a tripartite course for the scribe's induction, comprising *Khety*, *A Man* and *The Loyalist Teaching* (1999: 366–99). These poems are closely related and one Ramessid ostracon (OG 347/DeM 105) contains the final lines of *A Man* followed by the opening of *The Loyalist Teaching* (Fischer-Elfert 1999: 382). The similarities he notes, however, may be intertextual rather than functional. He suggests that the extreme corruption of the text in the New Kingdom may be the result of its being used in oral pre-training before being written down. However, the corruption is not unparalleled (Hoch 1992), and has been exaggerated by modern editors' tendency to emend (e.g., Helck 1970a). The state of the extant text does not prove that it was originally intended for and transmitted through the lower levels of institutional education.

These differences can perhaps be explained not as reflecting a different level of education, but by *Khety*'s being in some sense more peripheral in terms of elite high culture, that is, being composed within either a lower social level or a lower literary occasion. The subject matter and the level of the fictional audience's aspiration seem to embody a lower level of audience than other high register teachings. The scornful attitude towards the workers in *Khety* might reflect a culture of scribedom rather than officialdom, while the distinct style might suit an intended audience from a distinctly lower social level than other teachings. *Khety* also concerns acquiring skills that pass without comment in the noble *sprezzatura* of the Middle Kingdom high teachings, that is, it focuses on literacy rather than courtly rhetoric. However, the pupil in *Ptahhotep* is said to be 'a model for the officials' offspring', while Khety's pupil is to be educated 'among' this same group, so the fictional audiences of these two texts are broadly compatible. If the Ramessid tradition that *Khety* was by the same author cas *Amenemhat* has some historical basis, they both would also originate in the same social level. There is no reason why the monumental and dramatic *Amenemhat* could not have been written by the same man who composed the vulgar *Khety*: Shakespeare wrote comedy as well as tragedy, and the early 12th Dynasty funerary priest Heqanakht wrote letters to different addressees in different styles.

I suggest that *Khety*, *Amenemhat* and *Ptahhotep* probably had the same actual audience, with *Khety* embodying a less formal occasion within broadly the same social sphere. The teaching opens with a potential joke, as the teacher says 'I have seen beatings' (2a). The declaration 'I have seen' may imply an inappropriately high register for what follows (cf. p. 183), and in the context of a journey to school the audience is led to expect a description of the beatings suffered there, like those later standard in Ramessid descriptions of education (e.g., Caminos 1954: 83; cf. Foster 1999: 121–2). Instead, it is the illiterate workers who are beaten. There may be a similar subversion of expectations in the allusion to the 'profession greater than any other' (e.g., 3d), which recalls the description of the 'profession' of kingship and officialdom in teachings, but here is that of the scribe. What the teaching describes, however, is primarily other professions, its exact antitheses.

The vignettes of workers have no ethical aspect or high seriousness. The form is a parody of a lament about the state of society, but here the social horrors are not placed in the past or in an imagined period of chaos, but within the normal state of affairs of society, and are turned into a source of laughter. Peter Seibert's analysis of the formulaic descriptions suggested that they drew on oral standardizations of the topics; just as *The Shipwrecked Sailor* evokes oral folktales but is not one, so *Khety* draws on oral characterization, but is part of the written tradition. The apparently lowly style may deliberately match a lowly subject matter that was normally outside official diction, rather as the metaphors in *The Loyalist* match the topics to which they are applied (Posener 1976: 13).

Although one can argue with Waltraud Guglielmi (1994) that the purpose of the descriptions in *Khety* is to define the social role of scribes in a manner to encourage apprentices, its humour and style could also relate to the textual aspects of entertainment and intertextual parody. In this reading, the exaggerated humour is in part because the subject matter lay outside normal literary decorum, whose boundaries – rather than those of the scribe's social position – needed reinforcement, just as in Sidney's *Arcadia* the poet 'carefully reinforces the boundaries of the honor code by means of cruel laughter' in the incident of a clownish rebellion (Greenblatt 1990: 116). Wit and humour can be an aesthetic quality of literature as entertainment, and need not be only a disguise for the social and political function of a text.

The one reference to god's relationship with man in the presentations of the trades is distinct from the serious theodicy of other high literary texts. The concerns of lowly men were not incompatible with theodicy, as is seen in *The Eloquent Peasant*, and the partially preserved *Discourse of the Fowler* may also address such issues. Here, however

> The fowl-catcher is made very feeble
> by watching the flying birds.
> If a flock of water-birds passes over him,
> he says 'If only I had a net!'
> God does not let this happen to him,
> so that he is made feeble by his own plans. (20a–c)

The theme of humanity determining its state by its own plans is theodic, but here god is far removed from the illiterate underlings, and this is made into a source of amusement. The sight of birds is elsewhere a prompting to courtly pastime (e.g., *The Sporting King* A2.3), but here causes enfeeblement.

Only when the poem turns to scribedom, which 'is for eternity, its works are (like) stone' (22f) and which is associated with the Residence (1e, 2e, 22d, 30c[30]), does the divine intrude:

> Look, I have placed (*rdj*) you on the path of god. (30a)

Although the final stanzas appear serious, touches of wit may also be applied to the descriptions of scribedom. They are introduced with 'I will tell you' (23a), a phrase introducing some descriptions of labourers (10a, 21a). The image of the scribe being sent on missions as a child (3f) recalls official eulogies of the king, who ruled as a child or 'in the egg', as well as official careers described in biographies (Blumenthal 1970: 35–7 [A4], 223–4 [F2.29–31], 268–9 [G1.14]). This hyperbole recalls the exaggeration applied with humorous effect to the workers. In an obscure maxim about judgement, a 'brick' is mentioned as being grabbed (23c), suggesting a humorous description of an unseemly squabble in which the junior scribe is involved.[31] Another maxim opens with the universal injunction to 'speak no falsehood with your mouth' (28a)[32] and goes on to advise not filling that mouth with food (28d–f), as if juxtaposing great and little matters. One can compare the treatment of etiquette at table with *The Teaching for Kagemni*, where injunctions to behave modestly are couched

---

[30] Reading based on an unpublished manuscript: see Roccati 1994b: 87.
[31] In *Neferkare and Sasenet* a brick is wielded in a context of undignified behaviour (P. Chassinat I X+3.x+7).
[32] Reading after ODeM 1579; other manuscripts read 'against your mother'.

in universal principles; the emphasis on the comparatively trivial here may have humorous and playful implications.

The Ramessid *Satiric Letter* poses similar problems of interpretation to *Khety*: it can be read as a programmatic satiric commentary on the educational system (Fischer-Elfert 1986a: 289–90), but also as a self-mockery and a learned joke among equals.[33] The letter is intended to be

> a letter like an enjoyment (*sḏꜣj-ḥr*)
> that will become an entertainment (*sḥmḥ-jb*) for everyone.   (P. Anastasi I 8.7)

Drawing on this passage, one can perhaps imagine an audience of official and qualified scribes enjoying a performance of *Khety*, rather than apprentices learning from it. Such enjoyment might include descriptions of scribal experiences that recalled their apprenticeships; on a less speculative note, Khety flaunts literacy not only as social power, but also as leisure since it removes its practitioners from hard manual labour (e.g., 2b). It is not just satire of a particular social group but also a parody of the teaching genre (on parody versus satire see Rose 1993: 80–6). It is not a counter-discourse against the genre, but a light-hearted variation on its more serious exemplars. A modern reader, who cannot be well acquainted with the registers of genre and language, finds it difficult to recognize the humorous distance between the poem and the generic norms.

In other teachings the answer to the problem of meaning is problematically asserted as wisdom and the heart, but here the solution to the world's imperfection is simply the literacy that allows one to escape from wittily described drudgery. The discourses render chaos into aesthetic 'perfect speech', and the onomastica pattern the world into an ordered list (Kemp 1989: 29), while *Khety* records the irregular and distasteful realities of life in ordered forms and makes the audience smile at them. The entertainment offered by writing is in some sense itself theodic, providing a response to life's imperfection. *Khety* was perhaps written by a courtly author as a literary entertainment, and was, like other poems, subsequently adopted by scribal educators, when it was also an influential literary model for Ramessid literature (see **7.3**).

---

[33] Both *Khety* and the *Satiric Letter* were present in Qenherkhepshef's library at Deir el-Medina (**4.2**; Pestman 1982; McDowell 1999: 134–5).

11
Reading the poems

11.1 INTRODUCTION

> As long as our ignorance is so great, our attitude towards the criticism of these ancient literatures must be one of extreme humility.
>
> T. E. Peet, *A Comparative Study of the Literature of Egypt, Palestine and Mesopotamia* (1931: 6)

In this book I have attempted to anchor my readings of the poems in the (inter)textual world of the original audience, and to provide a slightly thicker description that recontextualizes the compositions. This is a historicist interpretive strategy that foregrounds the differentiated nature of literary texts, which is defined by genre and reception and distinguished by such features as fictionality and decorum. Literature in the Middle Kingdom was not what it is now, but we can usefully exploit what common ground there is between ancient and modern literary sensibilities and practices. Although 'there is no disinterested reading' (Sinfield 1994: 4), some strategies of reading are more appropriate than others for ancient texts. Despite the survival of sites such as the chapel of Heqaib, one cannot undertake an archaeology of specific occasions or individuals in relation to Middle Kingdom literary texts either for authors or for audience, but one can attempt to embed the texts in generalized hypothetical reconstructions of the pragmatic act of reading or listening,[1] acknowledging the importance of the material contexts of this act of communication.

11.2 IMAGES FOR READING

> We ... assume that permanence is a property of pyramids and suffering. But true permanence is a state of multiplication and division ... thought and experience are bequeathed.
>
> Patrick White, *The Aunt's Story* (1948), chap. 12

---

[1] Cf. Meskell 1999. For a review of the dangers inherent in the split between analysis of texts and other forms of material culture in the ancient Near East see, e.g., Zettler 1996.

I have examined ways of contextualizing these texts within the surviving system of Egyptian writings and asked what role these texts had in written culture in a period of significant social change, notably in increasing access to writing and expression of individual experience. In defining the function of 'literature' one can induce a cultural context by comparing the decorum of the literary corpus with that of contemporaneous official writings. Literary and official writings belonged broadly together; both present themselves as circulated by the state, or with the state's approval, but this does not mean that the two spheres of discourse were undifferentiated. Literary expression is never autonomous or abstract, but is an integral part of its culture, which it fashions (cf. Greenblatt 1990: 89–90).

Middle Kingdom writings offer a paradigm of the state's construction of reality. In commemorative texts expectations are invariably fulfilled in a unified vision of order, sweetness and light, despite the generally pessimistic underlying Egyptian world-view. Literary decorum, however, extends to embrace the anomalous or untoward, including the frivolous, the fully fictionalized, and the unexpected.

Rather than trying to translate the allegiance of these texts from conformity with the dominant ideology into dissident discourse by emphasizing their subversive aspects, I have proposed possible models for how their expression attains a harmonious unity within the culture, so that these (potentially 'subversive') texts could be a central part of the stream of tradition. Close readings suggest that, despite the poems' centrality, they were not fully complicit with or co-opted by the ruling power, and programmatic models of their purpose, such as 'propaganda', are inappropriate. They evoke a potential distance between their audience(s) and ideological norms, even when extolling these norms: Sinuhe's return to Egypt reaffirms the state's meaningfulness, but the experiences he narrates also relativize cultural norms. The poems thus resist closure and remain, if not open, at least suspended. In the absence of any ancient analysis of literature, I draw from the poems two possible metaphors for the characterizing features of literature.

Literary decorum includes unreality and indeterminacy. In *Cheops' Court*, the uncertain reality of tales is mobilized very explicitly, over and above their being concerned with 'prodigies'. The official claim to truthful commemoration is reversed in *Sinuhe*, which is indeed a fictional commemorative inscription. The supposedly reliable narrator and autobiographer draws attention to his potential duplicity (B 37), thus reminding the audience that this fictional inscription – unlike a real one – does not claim to be made 'in truth'. While all narrative inscriptions are in some sense fictionalizing and celebratory (cf. Baines 1999b), this is more fully and explicitly the case in fictionalizing literature. This self-conscious fictionality can also be seen in *Sinuhe*'s concern with the potential chaos after the death of Amenemhat I; in Sinuhe's account, his life is made chaotic not by an actual disruptive succession, but by his 'thinking that this strife would arise' (B 7). This fear itself turns out to have been imaginary, as Sinuhe implicitly acknowledges some 50 verses later, when he assures Amunenshi of Senwosret I's easy succession (B 46–7). Sinuhe later assigns to his flight – and thus to the subsequent events – the status of 'a dream' (B1 224; Loprieno 1988: 58–9). This is an ambiguous status, as dreams could be revelations, nightmares or delusions.[2] In *The Teaching of Ptahhotep* they are fallacious pleasures or nightmares (287, 358–60), while in a later harpist's song the 'occasion of a dream' is an image of the unreal and transitory pleasures of 'what is done upon earth' (Hari 1985: pl. 4, l.6). Dreams required interpretation and implicitly could elude it.[3] In *Sinuhe*, the metaphor of the dream is 'like a Delta-man seeing himself in Elephantine' (B 224–6; see p. 161).

This geographical image is recalled in the later *Satiric Letter*, where the protagonist sarcastically accuses a rival littérateur's speeches as being:

> mixed up when heard, so no interpreter can untie them;
> they are like the speech of a Delta-man with a man of Elephantine.
>
> (P. Anastasi I 28.6)

In keeping with this parallel, *Sinuhe*'s imagery shows that the narration deliberately diverges from the expectations of its framing genre of a 'true' official account of a real life, and also is divergent within itself: Sinuhe's memoirs are 'mixed up' and self-contradictory. Such confusion paradoxically provides an intimate perception of reality, as against the unified representations of official discourse. Comparable features, such as ambiguity, paradox and irony, can be extensively documented in the poems, which are semantically multifarious works whose 'meaning' cannot be neatly 'untied'.

The dream can be a useful metaphor for the (modern) understanding of Middle Kingdom literary texts as imaginative and ambiguous works. Dreaming is a general human experience that is mobilized as a metaphor in European literature (see, e.g., Holland 1994: 3–21). The dream expresses how the decorum of fictional literature articulates and explores imaginary alternative experiences of reality, such as the other worlds of Sinuhe's life abroad, the nightmare descriptions of the land in the discourses, and the varied possibilities of social destiny in the teachings.

---

[2] See, e.g., Donadoni 1986b; Vernus 1986; Szpakowska 2000.
[3] Compare the description of a revelatory dream in the much later stela of King Tanutamun: 'The dream is true: it is good to one who places it in his heart, and damaging to one who ignores it' (l.7; Grimal 1981: 8). This recalls the dual description of *The Teaching of Ptahhotep* as 'good for him who will hear / woeful for him who will transgress it' (49–50).

The 'commemorative inscription' of *Sinuhe* even renders his identity and name of uncertain reality ('Is it him in truth, sovereign my lord?' B 267). These divergent and self-contradictory elements propose other, more problematic, constructs of reality than those of ideology. The language of Sinuhe's metaphor recalls that of dream interpretation manuals in which a man's 'seeing himself' as something can be analysed for prophetic meaning: the dream is an image of not only divine revelation, but also of stepping back from oneself. The poems often mobilize these alternatives introspectively, as if to encourage the audience's reflections.

A second metaphor for literature can be drawn from texts of the early 12th Dynasty, in which officials claim to have 'solved problems', literally 'untied what is knotted (*wḥʿ-tsswt*)' (J. M. A. Janssen 1946: 56–7 [W]). The word for a metrical verse is also a 'knot' (*tsw*; see **6.3**). Although this primarily refers to its succinct 'knot' of syntax, it is as if literature were concerned with 'knotting' what official norms try to untie. The appropriateness of this metaphor is indicated by the fact that to 'untie' (*wḥʿ*) is a word for textual interpretation, as in the *Satiric Letter* (P. Anastasi I 1.7, 28.7).

Literary texts do not concern exclusively what is problematic, and are integral with official culture. 'Verses' can be magical or funerary texts, while physical knots were features of magical practice, operating as 'acts of creation and as protection from threatened dissolution' (Ritner 1993: 143–4). The knot of verse is complex and ambivalent, like the dream, not just an obstacle that resists untying, but also something that gives unity. In the *Satiric Letter*, the scribe scornfully writes to his rival, using unifying wordplay, that:

your verses (*tsw*) mix 'this' and 'that';
all your words are upside down without being knotted together (*ts*).

(P. Anastasi I 4.8)

In literature the 'knotty' difficulties and choices of life become 'choice verses' or 'knots' of 'perfect speech', a sort of spell of unity, and for the audience the nightmares of troubled experience become a multivalent entertaining reverie or revelation of grace without losing their untoward, disturbing qualities.

Through its acknowledgement of life's anomalies, randomness and complexities, Middle Kingdom literature allowed its privileged audience to explore or enact – that is, to contain within themselves – various complementary realities, as the poet 'taught' (*sbꜣ*), 'meditated on' (*mhj*), or narrated (*sḏd*) their interpretations of the 'counsels/nature' (*sḫr*) both of humanity and of the divine. *Sasobek* concerns the 'counsels of god' (B11), *Ptahhotep* expounds the 'counsels of the ancestors' (31), *The Loyalist*

Teaching tells of 'the counsels of eternity' (1.6), and *Kagemni* is spoken 'after (the sage) had comprehended the counsels of humanity' (2.3–4). As the audience listened to the poetry of imagined princes and peasants, they expanded their own experiences and lived out those of others from other social worlds. The travesties of these fictional individuals distanced the narrated experiences from the audience, who both experienced and stepped away from the difficulties of life, gaining 'relief' (*qb*), a sense of transcending them in something that was 'perfect to their hearts'. By offering a context in which to face the problematic and the incomprehensible, literature both examined central values and offered a space for personal entertainment. As Michael Baxandall remarks in his study of the social context of painting in fifteenth century Italy, successful works of art 'often express their culture not just directly but complementarily, because it is by complementing it that they are best designed to serve public needs: the public does not need what it has already got' (1988: 102).

The Middle Kingdom saw a general extension of written discourse that drew on earlier performative practices. It is uncertain whether that extension prompted the creation of written literature, or whether its creation was a deliberate expansion of writing for cultural ends. Gerald Moers (2000: 59–80), for example, regards literary texts as part of a unified elite *Kultursprache* introduced to assert cultural unity as part of the Middle Kingdom's renaissance. Whichever is the case, potential 'things of darkness' (*The Tempest*, 5.1.278–9) and light-hearted attitudes eschewed in much official discourse were expressed and interpreted in literature. Literature was one institutionalized form of imaginative cultural self-interpretation. Without distancing devices and fictionality, it would presumably have been impossible to do this within official decorum: peasants were almost certainly not so eloquent, and their complaints no doubt passed unrecorded by officials. Dissident voices were recorded in literature, since they were 'no more yielding than a dream' (*A Midsummer Night's Dream*, 5.1.419). It thus allowed a space to realize an interplay between the ideals asserted by ideology and the untoward events of actuality, between ideal life dreamt of by the audience and the vagaries of actual experience.

In a period of constant drive towards recentralization, the Middle Kingdom poems continually speak of little men and the dark side of ideological perfection. Even if social changes in the 12th Dynasty were well documented, these poems could hardly be read as direct reflections of them or as ideological pronouncements designed to assist them. The institution of literature no doubt responded to particular social and historical circumstances, but also to a common human need, what Wolfgang Iser calls 'the staging of the human condition in a welter of unforeseeable patterns' and 'a panorama of what is possible' for homo ludens (1993: xviii). For critics who ask why any society needs literature, its universally accessible distinctive qualities often lie in its playfulness, multivalency and variety, as well as what Seamus Heaney has termed the 'redress of poetry' (1996: 1–16). It is a conceptualization that does not deny the unknowable. The simultaneity of mutually exclusives together with 'the split signifier and the inverted schemata open up the play-space of the text'.[4] Middle Kingdom poems fit the idea that reading literature is 'a means whereby we may extend ourselves'.

11.3 THE MODERN READER: RESPONSES AND EVALUATION

We know the *Mozart* of our fathers' time
Was gay, rococo, sweet, but not sublime
A Viennese Italian: that is changed
Since music-critics learned to feel 'estranged'.

W. H. Auden, *Metalogue for the Magic Flute* (1991: 579)

I now address our role as readers of this literature, entering the circle binding us to the text, the author and the dead audience, joining ancient Egyptian and modern interpretive communities. The problems of this hermeneutic circle are foregrounded in the political self-awareness and commitment of some modern critics, especially with issues of gender and sexuality (e.g., Sinfield 1992, 1994). Scholars often downplay the political and social relevance of reading ancient texts, while the aims of historical 'anthropology' are themselves socially determined and can be problematic (e.g., Gumbrecht 1996: 16–17). A total fusion of horizons is impossible, but a process of negotiation and dialogue can be envisaged.

Literature forms cultural paradigms that have meaning and can be approached only within and through their context. Literature represents its culture deliberately, and often reflexively addresses a posterity such as the modern reader, although 'the whole bias of the readers' attention varies with time and place in ways that the author could not foresee' (A. Fowler 1982: 264). An audience's attitudes change with each generation, but works that possessed some autonomy can communicate after the culture of composition is past. Since Egyptian literature has no continuous history of reception, its survival remains more tenuous and it can often seem little more than an incomprehensible ghost in many discussions; Baron Textor de Ravisi's 'Belle au bois dormant' (1878: 554) remains unwoken.

---

[4] Citations from Iser 1989: 257, 261.

It seems clear that Egyptian literature was a privileged mode of discourse and social institution. Its sudden flourishing in the Middle Kingdom suggests that the state placed a particular value on its high and low registers and made a major investment in it. Since the survival of any manuscript implies that some members of the literate elite valued its text, all surviving texts were probably of considerable prestige. The praise of Khety in the Ramessid 'Eulogy of Dead Writers' shows that there was comparative evaluation of 'authors', while within the poems themselves, the fictional Neferti and the peasant are esteemed because their words are outstanding. Criteria of value that can be induced from the texts include features which produce aesthetic and stylistic complexity, moral, ethical and cultural relevance and correctness, density, elaboration, inclusiveness and unity. Aspects such as humour and irony were probably also important in audience expectation, although humour, so far as it can be identified, is often incidental rather than pervasive. The sheer cantabile qualities of literature are almost unrecoverable. Value judgements are integral to interpretation and understanding (e.g., Olsen 1987: 138–55), but concepts of value vary between cultures, and esteemed features can cause confusion for a reader with a different world-view. I have not attempted a critique of Egyptian cultural expression. Since the ancient copyists were better informed judges of value than the modern scholar can be, I have aimed to interpret unfamiliar features as virtues rather than faults: to paraphrase the 1623 editors of Shakespeare, 'if then you doe not like (it) surely you are in some manifest danger not to understand it'.

Although the original meaning is distinct from the modern appropriation of the text, the two are for us essential constituents of each other (as Kennedy remarks of Vergil: 1997: 53–5). Because of the gap between them and the original, readers of ancient texts are particularly aware of the dangers of unbounded interpretation. My own interpretation of *The Eloquent Peasant* is valid for me, but parallels and contextual evidence may subsequently show that the original audience is unlikely to have envisaged such an interpretation. They certainly understood it more fully than I ever shall. Egyptologists have mostly addressed the question of what a text means or meant, as opposed to what it means for the individual reader, in the historicist terms of extracting correct historical information; on this basis they have often provided an evolutionary critique of Egyptian civilization. But 'meaning' is a more elusive goal. The conventions of interpretation in the Middle Kingdom, which must have existed, are not extant, but the necessary minimum can be intuited. Like Egyptology, modern criticism is itself a historical and institutional practice, the result of specific changes in a century marked by an increase in analytic discourse often abstracting art from cultural and social concerns (see, e.g., Eagleton 1984; Gumbrecht 1996: 6–10).

While admitting that theoretical movements do not transcend their context, critics such as Terry Eagleton defend the institution of theory as championing awareness of the symbolic processes of social life. Reading literature and reading literary theory are thus both relevant to the life of any audience, since humanity, like literature, is a cultural artefact (Eagleton 1984: 124; Geertz 1973: 33–54). Similarly, 'archaeology becomes a relevant social science that says something about culture, selves and difference both in antiquity and in a contemporary setting'.[5] Middle Kingdom poems invite such approaches since they are aesthetic artefacts that generate and reveal their own subjectivity, fashioning and displaying culture.[6]

The modern reader's attitude towards the values that a text mobilizes is potentially problematic. Here some critics take an absolute line: 'where one cannot accept the ethics of the text, one cannot accept the aesthetics' (Donovan 1977: 157). If one cannot accept the cultural values, can one reconstruct the original audience's delight in their articulation, and can one interpret that articulation? Can an atheist reader fully interpret *Paradise Lost*, a post-holocaust reader *The Merchant of Venice*, or a modern liberal reader the works of the 12th Dynasty royal court? Most readers now find the ideology and the authoritarian nature of Egyptian loyalism, which are mobilized in literary texts, deeply rebarbative from their contemporary context.

Sinuhe is one of the few Middle Kingdom texts with a modern reception, and is more generally paradigmatic since the work itself thematizes Egyptian culture. Even after major misreadings of its language and form were clarified, its western twentieth-century reception can be seen as reshapings of the tale to fit modern concerns and stereotypes, under the influence of the Biblical presentation of Egypt, most drastically in Mika Waltari's novel *Sinuhe the Egyptian* and subsequently in the 1954 Hollywood film version (Parkinson 1999a: 167; 1999b). Academic studies have also unthinkingly rewritten the text with similar concerns. Enough survives of the original context to indicate that such reshapings are inappropriate for the original context. Such episodes may question the validity of modern interpretations. In turn, readings that foreground the dark or subversive side of the texts may be anachronistic products of a modern reader who resists envisaging a poetry that eulogizes despots and so reads against the grain:

---

[5] Meskell 1999: 224; compare Liverani 1996. As Paul Hamilton remarks, 'there is perhaps inherent virtue in historicizing because it sharpens our contrary awareness of the past which our interpretations play in "the construction and reconstruction of our own world" [Hawkes 1992: 139]' (1996: 165).
[6] That is, they are 'cultural texts' in the original sense of the phrase: Geertz 1973: 447–51.

> The recent privileging of the 'private' over the 'public' (voices of Latin literature) is a symptom of the liberal humanist's interest in the individual subject and his or her responsibility for exercising personal choice in the face of vast supra-personal forces or institutions. The consequence for readings of the *Aeneid* is to locate true value in the interior experiences of an Aeneas, a Dido, a Turnus, of suffering parents and children, exposed to the impersonal and inhuman structures of militarism and absolutism. (Hardie 1997: 314)

Aspects of Middle Kingdom literature are appealing to recent pessimistic times, and it is easy now to privilege the significance of 'little men' in the corpus over the mainstream ideology. The elements that accord with most modern readers' sense of reality are those which we identify as subversive when they do not accord with the earlier culture's values, while 'propaganda' is used to designate any form of discourse that propounds values that readers find unsympathetic, and all the while modern ideology is accorded a self-evident truth. New Historicist approaches accommodate this conflict by likening the processes of modern reading to the original strategies of the text. Many principles of authority in earlier cultures subvert modern ideas of personal and social order, but modern reading and analysis replicates the containment of certain elements in the ancient texts.

Stephen Greenblatt's bleak conclusion that 'there is subversion, no end of subversion, only not for us' (1988: 39) is not the only possible reaction to this issue (see Brannigan 1998: 56–127). One should not denigrate the relevance of 'subversive' voices in an attempt to overcompensate for being modern outsiders. Subversion and containment denote positions that shift constantly with the contexts of their articulation (Montrose 1992). These issues are clear in politically committed queer readings of modern canonical texts: as Alan Sinfield remarks 'members of subordinated groups are prone to assume that subcultural work is all very well, but (that) the mainstream is what counts. This is self-oppressed' (1994: 81). Whatever degree of privileging is involved in modern readings of ancient texts, the debate over the various voices in literature bears witness to the poems' ambivalence (for Vergil, see, e.g., Tarrant 1997b: 182–6), while formal features demonstrate that this tension is present in the original ancient texts, suggesting that the debate is a valid response.

Egyptian literature, once an elite form of discourse, is now being studied by an academic minority, but aspects of modern study might not seem alien to the ancient scribes, since the Middle Kingdom classics were used in later education and archives. Yet the poems' original centrality to their living culture cannot now be paralleled. Literary theory and the study of Egyptian texts have developed separately, but these texts – like those of the Middle Ages (Middleton 1992: 30–1) – should contribute to the theoretical debate, from which they have been marginalized (cf. A. Assmann 1999). There is, of course, a danger of imposing inappropriate theoretical models and categories. One insight of post-paradigm thinking is that theory is not everything and is not exclusive; to distinguish between flexible reading and a rigid schema of critical theory is not to argue against theory itself. Moreover, the insights of different schools with opposed principles and details can contribute to the study of ancient texts (cf. Michalowski 1996: 179–81). The texts should be given an appropriate response: 'the first requisite, it seems to me, is to proceed more inductively than we are currently used to doing, to avoid the imposition of a prior set of theory isms on complicated historical data' (Perloff 1995: 61). Rather than the provincializing approach of seeking for 'reductive formulas professing to account for them' (Geertz 1973: 453), the poems require aesthetically, pragmatically and theoretically informed responses.[7]

Behind these problems is a broader question, often not explicitly posed: what function does reading ancient Egyptian literature have, since it is not obviously a central site of cultural contest or consideration? Does its study by academics exhaust its potential? Any reading, whether contemporaneous or subsequent, is a movement away from the original intended meaning, since it is a reconstruction, a transformation, a translation. While the academic historicist practice of interpretation tries to eschew subjectivity, interpretations are inevitably subjective. All understanding of historical periods is formed from the present, as postmodern criticism has stressed (e.g., Bagnall 1995: 5 for antiquity; in general, Fay et al. 1998).

The reader's subjectivity is inevitable and integral to any approach, while philology and literary theory provide frameworks within which responses can be shaped, and the interplay of interpretation and significance is profitable. Different ages have engaged with different aspects of different works of art, and appropriated them in different ways (e.g., Taylor 1990). In particular, academic discourse can be only a partial response to the texts. In the late twentieth century, reading texts became difficult to justify and instead theory became dominant ('really hunky': Sinfield 1992: 279). Such superficially scientific approaches risk neglecting the actors' perspectives and assuming that the ancients were as scholarly and serious as oneself; the impersonal, 'objectivizing' context of reading texts risks distorting our analysis. As Philippe Derchain remarks, 'le lecteur-modèle d'aucun Égyptien n'est un égyptologue' (1987: 1). The scholar can imagine a 'self-identical past' (Hamilton 1996: 81), and over-objectify past subjective experience, forgetting that the ancient words were

---

[7] An overly historicist approach can become a process of cracking the code to gain access to 'the historical context', which is itself a modern construction (Felperin 1992: 79–81). No literary text exists as an entity that can be 'decoded' from its cultural signs (R. Williams 1977: 168–9).

once not only a means of power and cultural negotiation, but perhaps also exuberant, witty, even frivolous. They were intended to be experienced subjectively in a dialogue of author and audience. As the comte de Caylus noted 'les Anciens n'ont pas toujours été grands, austères, nobles & sérieux' (1756: 104). W. B. Yeats expressed the possible dichotomy between the circumstances of a text's composition and the serious-minded life of its editor more forcefully in his mocking poem *The Scholars* (1915):

> What would they say,
> Did their Catullus walk that way?
> (ll.11–12; text: Albright 1992: 190, with Auden's defence of editing scholars: 1992: 563–4)

Louis MacNeice (1979: 118–19) also attacked the way in which scholars 'chop the ancient world' in a 'simple' manner, regardless of its 'unimaginably different' full life, while among modern critics, Greenblatt has commented that he is

> frequently baffled by the tendency especially in those explicitly concerned with historical or ideological functions of art to ignore the analysis of pleasure or, for that matter, of play. . . . Literature may do important work in the world, but each sentence is not hard labour, and the effectiveness of this work depends upon the ability to delight. (1990:9)

Academic discourse cannot colonize or entrap the complex energies of Egyptian literature and is not an end in itself. The fictional audiences of the poems can provide a model: like Rensi in *The Eloquent Peasant*, the reader should be entrapped by the protagonist's eloquence. Surprisingly few scholars mention that they read Middle Kingdom texts with pleasure,[8] although the poems' aesthetic nature is central to interpretation, as is their historicity and cultural specificity. Equally central is empathy.

11.4 ANSWERING VOICES

> There is a land of the living and a land of the dead, and the bridge is love, the only survival, the only meaning.
> Thornton Wilder, *The Bridge of San Luis Rey* (1927), part 5

---

[8] Works of Derchain and Baines are exceptions. See Baines 1997a: 218 on the celebratory quality of Egyptian rituals and architecture. On approaching ancient subjective experience see, e.g., Meskell 1997. As Susan Sontag remarked: 'in place of hermeneutics we need an erotics of art' (1994: 14).

> Comment pouvez-vous lire à présent? Il fait nuit.
>
> Edmond Rostand, *Cyrano de Bergerac* (1897), V.v

Any engagement of a modern literary sensibility with an ancient work from before the era of modern literature risks anachronism. However, while it is often noted that some societies have no 'literature' (Sinfield 1994: 28), any judgement of a culture as pre-literary runs other risks. If we withhold our privileged terms 'literature' and 'art', we risk denigrating a culture, and relegating its artefacts to socio-functional practices and its 'poems' to 'texts', in a way that might be unethical if done to a living contemporaneous culture: 'chacun apelle barbarie ce qui n'est pas de son usage' (Montaigne, *Essais* I [1580], xxxi). The poems were created in a different culture in a different land. While the basic human substance and condition may be what it was in the Middle Kingdom, humanity is now fashioned differently, and a sense of otherness is integral to the response of a traveller to this antique land, as evoked for modern Egypt by Amitav Ghosh (1992). We cannot make ourselves contemporaries of the texts, nor make the texts contemporaneous. No hermeneutic contiguity or complete 'fusion of horizons' between the texts and the modern reader can be claimed, but one can make connections through literary engagement, as well as exploring cultural differences, in order to restore a sense of the actors' perspective. No ancient voice can speak for itself, and this lack cannot be made good by, or even strategically avoided through, academic discourse. The inevitable failure to regain a clear-speaking ancient Egyptian Eurydice does not, however, mean that the literary project fails, since complete interpretation is always impossible: translations are always failures to some extent; 'cultural analysis is essentially incomplete' (Geertz 1973: 29).

Reading creates a personal significance for the poems; the lack of such would frustrate the self-proclaimed aim of Middle Kingdom literature to be an enduring communication and to 'speak to the future', trusting that it would 'listen' (*Ptahhotep* 519). 'Hearing' involves an active aesthetic response as well as a correct assessment of cultural values. The former is often necessary if a reader is to resolve a poem's diverse formal and thematic tensions, and help imaginatively in interpretation. The fact that all interpretations are personal can enable the reader, in Stephen Greenblatt's phrase, to 'renew the marvelous at the heart of the resonant', that is of an object or text's ability to evoke the 'complex dynamic cultural forces' which it represents and in which it is embedded, while 'wonder' at the marvellous is the power 'to stop the viewer in his tracks, to convey an arresting sense of uniqueness, to evoke an exalted attention' (1990: 161–83). Wonder is surely an appropriate response to the Middle Kingdom poems, with their virtuosic language and sudden changes in the tone as well as of the prodigies of *Cheops' Court*. Yet, as Paul Veyne ironically remarked 'rare is the ancient work that will not disappoint modern taste' (1988: 183). Such factors underlie my drawing comparisons with early modern English literature: the modern reader's reaction to Shakespeare is (comparatively) unmediated and spontaneous, and can serve as a reminder of how spontaneous, complex, sensuous, passionate, wonderful, visceral and cerebral a Middle Kingdom audience's response to the poems might have been.

To emphasize ancient literature's ability to engage modern readers is not to deny its cultural embeddedness or to suggest the 'effacement of the social' in a work of art (Greenblatt 1990: 89–90), but is to evoke its original cultural role. My own engagement with Middle Kingdom poems mirrors my reading of the literature produced by my own European world; my readings are shaped by my culture, training, the place and time of writing, sexuality, personal relationships and political sympathies, none of which can claim absolute validity. They are nevertheless the only ones directly available to me, and one must use what one can. A first person approach is not a surrender to unbounded subjectivity, nor is it only a profitable academic strategy; it is 'an intellectual necessity . . . a matter of choosing the most directly accessible reference point' (Zumthor 1986: 3–4).

Much recent historical literary criticism has moved from travel to the past toward a more mediated dialogue with the past (Hawthorn 1996: 75–81), while Stephen Greenblatt (1988: 1–20) describes his motivation for studying *Shakespearean Negotiations* as a desire to speak with the dead. Like all conversations this can increase understanding both of the other person and of oneself. Reading should seek a balance between the reconstruction of a text's original cultural meaning and the modern appropriation of this; an awareness of an unimaginably different world and of a common human condition; the other and the self; strangeness and familiarity; resonance and wonder; the competing voices of dead writers and of living readers. Such pairs can only suggest the framework of a dialectic process of negotiation and dialogue, elegantly evoked in Marguerite Yourcenar's *Carnets de notes de 'Mémoires d'Hadrien'* (1982: 519–41), where she described her position as 'un pied dans l'érudition, l'autre dans la magie, ou plus exactement, et sans métaphore, dans cette *magie sympathique* qui consiste à se transformer en pensée à l'intérieur de quelqu'un' (1982: 526). Such a description of the interpretive process accords well with Egyptian ideas of literary art as compatible with the artistry of magic, and with the communication between the dead and the living that was integral to their culture.[9]

---

[9] 'Literature professors are salaried, middle-class shamans' as Greenblatt remarks (1988: 6).

My readings do not 'analyse' the texts; there is a sense in which 'every work constitutes its own best description' (Todorov 1981: 4). I attempt to contextualize them and to suggest ways in which we – who are often from a modern western culture – can 'listen', sympathetically, with self-awareness and self-effacement, and without imposing our own voices more than is appropriate for a dialogue, so that we can engage significantly with these compositions. In other words, we should attempt to fully read the poems, as King Merikare was (fictionally) enjoined:

> Look, their words endure in writings.
> Open, and read! (*Merikare* 10c–d)

This injunction was configured with radically different attitudes to the past, of reading and of literary writings. We cannot reconstruct what a Middle Kingdom Egyptian person experienced or imagined, but in reading a copy of one of these poems, carefully inducing, intuiting and imagining what we cannot directly know, we are in effect reading it over the shoulders of the dead. We thus draw a little closer to conceiving that experience, since reading enables us to engage in a dialogue with the ancient author, as the ancient audience did. That is as far as we can go and it is, perhaps, enough.

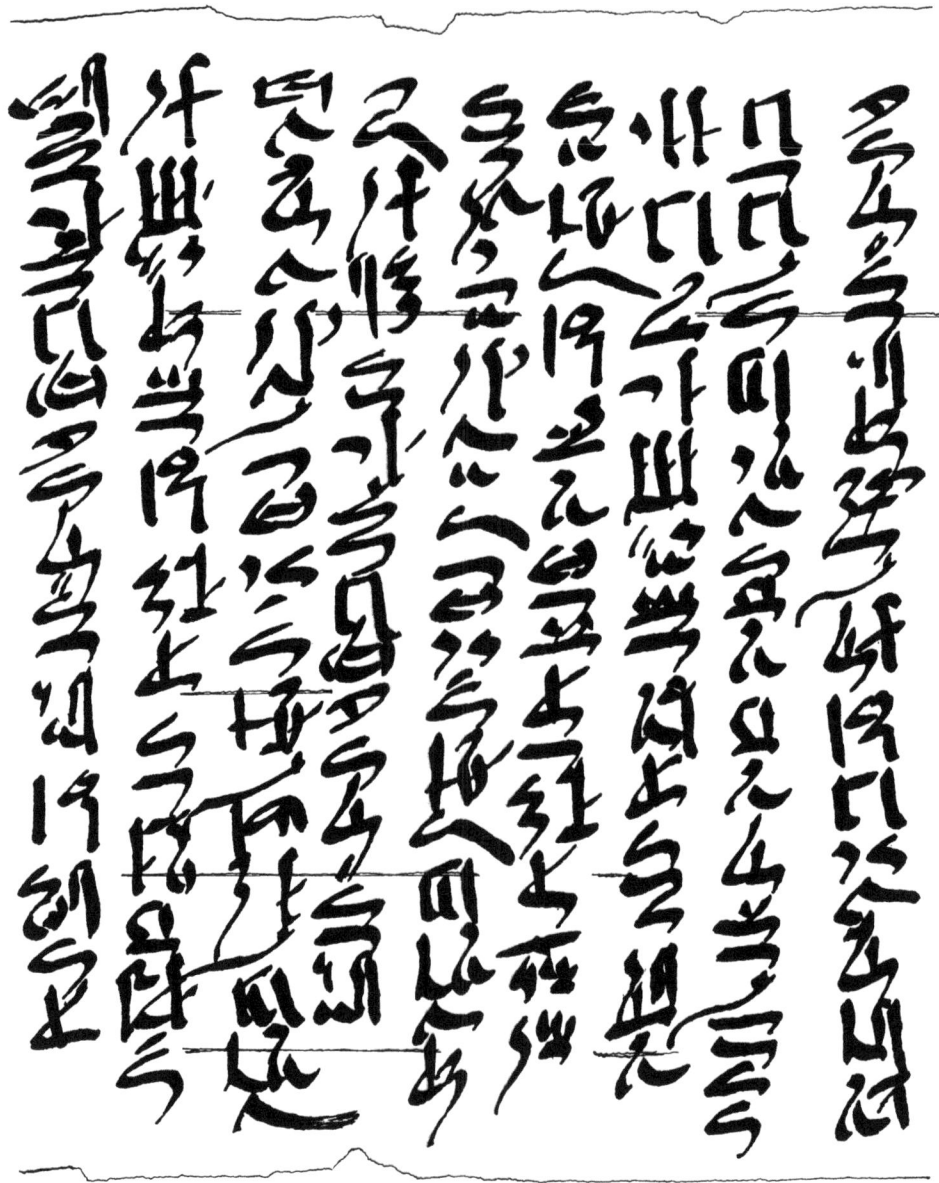

A passage from a Middle Kingdom literary manuscript: *The Eloquent Peasant* B1 65–73. Drawing by R. B. Parkinson.

Appendix 1: Survey of the Middle Kingdom literary corpus

A.1 THE EXTANT CORPUS

> Nor is there singing school but studying
> Monuments of its own magnificence.
> W. B. Yeats, *Sailing to Byzantium* (1928)

This list is arranged by genre rather than by date, in the order: tales, discourses and dialogues (including compound genres), and teachings. Within each genre the texts are arranged by the date of their fictional setting (in the order: divine history, human history, general or unspecified). Each entry provides brief information about the manuscripts, of the form and completeness of the preserved text, and of the date of the setting and of composition. For texts preserved in a single manuscript, fuller details are given, while indications of the earliest extant manuscript are given if more than one is preserved. Provenances are often noted in general terms – Thebes and Memphis, rather than Deir el-Medina or Saqqara (for a listing of the texts by manuscripts see Quirke 1996b). More detailed descriptions are given for texts that are unpublished or untranslated.[1] An indication of the length of the extant text is given in metrical verses (estimates are often approximate, and include estimates of lacunae where appropriate; all figures have been rounded up).

References are given to a primary text publication and a recent translation; studies are listed including the relevant entries in W. Helck et al. (eds) *Lexikon der Ägyptologie* (7 vols.; Wiesbaden: Harrassowitz, 1975–92), subsequent important articles, and references to the previous published surveys (Posener 1951a; Parkinson 1991b). I have passed over the many New Kingdom ostraca with unidentified literary texts,

---

[1] I am grateful to Dr R. Janssen for permission to collate the unpublished el-Lahun material with the originals in the Petrie Museum, University College London (listed in Quirke 1996b, from whom I occasionally differ), and to the Griffith Institute for access to Gardiner's unpublished transcriptions of P. Cairo CG 58040. Publication of the el-Lahun papyri is underway by Stephen Quirke and Mark Collier.

of which not enough is preserved to establish a dating to the Middle Kingdom.

A.1.1 TALES

The Tale of Horus and Seth and other tales of gods from el-Lahun

P. Lahun VI.12 (= P. UCL 32158) dates from the late 12th Dynasty, and is from a house in Rank N el-Lahun (Gallorini 1998). On the verso is an administrative fragment, and the papyrus belongs to an excavation lot containing a medical text, letters and accounts, that were apparently the vestige of an official archive (Lot VI: Quirke 1990b: 166). The orthography of many of the el-Lahun papyri is dated before that of *The Shipwrecked Sailor* by Eugène Dévaud (1924). Fragments of two columns and two lines survive (*c.* 40 verses), narrating Seth's attempted seduction of Horus. The position of tales about the gods within Middle Kingdom literary genres is disputed.[2] Jan Assmann (e.g., 1977c: 33 n.52) has suggested that this and *The Cairo Mythological Tale* were parts of magical texts rather than tales, but fictional tales with at least one divine character are attested, and they are more likely to be tales (e.g., Baines 1996b: 366, 1999a: 34–5; Quirke 1996a: 266–7).

Other possible literary manuscripts mentioning gods from el-Lahun (unpublished) include the small fragment P. UCL 32110D, with 2 horizontal lines on recto and verso, mentioning Geb on the recto; this, however, is more probably an incantatory text, since the verso includes the phrase 'I am the father' and 'I am Anubis'. Another fragment is 32149D (4 vertical lines on the recto, while the verso is blank) which also mentions Geb. Fragment 32116A has 7 lines on the recto, a narrative text mentioning Nephthys and Setekh, including the phrase 'And Nephthys said to Setekh'; on the verso is an incantatory text.

Text: Griffith 1898: I, 4, II, pl. 3; *translation*: Parkinson 1991a: 120–1.
Studies: Parkinson 1991b: no. xxxi, 1995: 70–1; Posener 1951a: no. 19.

The Cairo Mythological Tale

The recto of a late Middle Kingdom manuscript, said to be from the Theban necropolis at el-Qurna ('Gurnah'; P. Cairo CG 58040), comprises a column of 10 lines, and a fragment with the remains of a further 4 lines of another column. It narrates an episode in which a man called Ukhekhiu(? *Wḫḫjjw*) is being discussed by the gods:

---

[2] The third example listed in Parkinson 1991b: 120 no. xxxiii – *The Mythological Tale of the Sun's Eye* (Caminos 1956: 40–50, pl. 17–23; Korostovtsev 1960) – is to be dated to the New Kingdom in view of Late-Egyptianisms in the text.

Then the Person of this god said
'He has [. . .] him to(?) go and investigate his land-plot
in the middle of the night'.
Then he met a serpent; then it bit him –
an evil that had been fashioned in his land-plot.
Then he died immediately.
And the Person of this god said to Perception
'Let one say to the Council in Thinis(?)
"Let Ukhekhiu be saved . . ."'
And the [Coun]cil said [to] the Person of this god
'This is not what is done, sovereign . . .'. (1–7)

On the verso are 13 vertical lines (with ruled guiding lines) of a text that Gardiner tentatively suggested was 'philosophical', but which is probably magical.[3]
Text: unpublished; Alan Gardiner's transcription is in the Griffith Institute, Oxford, Ms AHG 29.9–12.
Studies: Gardiner 1931: 9; Parkinson 1991b: no. xxxii; Posener 1951a: 18.

The Tale of the Court of King Cheops

The tale is preserved on the fragmentary P. Westcar (= P. Berlin 3033; Burkard and Fischer-Elfert 1994: 114–15 no. 171), of unrecorded provenance (Dawson and Uphill 1995: 438). The date of the papyrus is disputed: it is generally assumed to be of the 15th/17th Dynasties (Möller 1909: 18–19), but the early New Kingdom has also been suggested (e.g., Barocas 1988: 129; Mathieu 1999: 37). Twelve columns survive (= *c.* 535 verses), and these open with a series of tales set in various Old Kingdom courts (Djoser, Nebka, Sneferu), which are told to King Cheops (*c.* 2551–28 BCE) by his sons. The first tale is lost apart from Cheops' response, and it seems that at least two columns are missing. That tale was probably introduced by a narrative prologue similar to that of *The Words of Neferti*. Instead of a fourth tale, there is a narrative about a wonder done by the wise man Djedi in the presence of Cheops himself. After this comes a third person narrative describing the birth of the first three kings of the 5th Dynasty (*c.* 2465–26 BCE). The end is lost, and the manuscript breaks off in the middle of an incident, but only a few short episodes may be missing. The royal characters are historical (although Prince Bauefre is slightly problematic:

---

[3] I am grateful for H.-W. Fischer-Elfert for advice on this issue. Mention is made of 'the enclosure that is behind you' (2) and 'the departure (*p3-šmt*) of those who act' (6–7); one of the few comprehensible sentences is the wish 'May your (sing.) heart be well at this' (8).

296   *Appendix 1: Survey of the Middle Kingdom literary corpus*

von Beckerath 1975a). The non-royal characters are not otherwise known and are presumably fictional; some feature in the list of P. Athens (L. Morenz suggests a possible historical original for Djedi: 1996: 122 n.541). The actual mother of the first two 5th Dynasty kings was Khentkaus, while in the tale the mother is the wife of a priest, Rudjdjedet.[4] The Late Middle Egyptian language suggests a later date of composition than that of other early or mid-12th Dynasty tales. H. Jenni (1998) has argued for an early 12th Dynasty date, reading the tale as propaganda for Senwosret I, but this is unconvincing. Ludwig Morenz (1996: 107–10) and others assign it to the Second Intermediate Period on its general atmosphere and presentation of kingship. Some favour an early New Kingdom date partly on similar grounds (e.g., Goedicke 1992b: 35–6). Detlef Franke has noted that the tale's presentation of three brothers as kings recalls the sequence of kings at the height of the 13th Dynasty (Neferhotep I, Sahathor, Sobekhotep IV: 1994: 69–70). Whether or not this is a coincidence, a dating to this general period is the most plausible.

Text: Blackman 1988; *translation*: Parkinson 1999f: 106–27.
Studies: el-Aguizy 1997; Barocas 1988; Derchain 1969, 1986, 1996c; Edel 1990: 31–3; Eyre 1976, 1992; Fischer 1977; Goedicke 1972, 1985b, 1986b, 1992b; Hornung 1974; Jenni 1998; Knigge 1997; Mathieu 1999; Meltzer 1994; L. Morenz 1996: 107–23; Parkinson 1991b: no. xxv; Posener 1951a: no. 17; Simpson 1982; Staehelin 1970.

The Tale of King Neferkare and General Sasenet

Three short episodes of this tale are preserved on fragments of a 25th Dynasty papyrus from Thebes (P. Chassinat I = Louvre 25351), a stone writing board from Deir el-Medina, and a 19th Dynasty writing board (totalling *c.* 73 extant verses). The tale is set in Memphis and concerns an affair between a king and his military commander; a 'pleader of Memphis' attempts to denounce the commander, and the king, probably the historical Neferkare Pepy II (*c.* 2246–2152 BCE), is tracked by a courtier(?) Hent's son Tjeti. The beginning is preserved:

> Now there was once a time when the Person of the Dual King, [Nefer]ka[re],
> Son of Re, [Pepy], true of voice,
> was [the worthy] king [in this entire land].
> Now . . .   (T. OIC 1–2 + T. IFAO 1)

---

[4] H. Altenmüller (1970) sees Rudjdjedet as a disguised name in a *roman à clef* reflecting events at the end of the 4th Dynasty closely, but this approach is problematic (Goedicke 1992b: 32–5).

Appendix 1: Survey of the Middle Kingdom literary corpus 297

The language, names and titles are suggestive of a Middle Kingdom date. In style and tone the tale is reminiscent of *The Tale of Cheops' Court*, and may date from the same general period or later.
Text: Posener 1957; *translation:* Parkinson 1991a: 54–6.
Studies: van Dijk 1994; Kammerzell 1995b; Parkinson 1991b: no. xxvi, 1995: 71–4; Posener 1951a: no. 21; Richter-Aeroe 1984; Verhoeven 1999: 260–1.

The Tale of the Eloquent Peasant

The almost complete text is known from four Middle Kingdom manuscripts from Thebes (*c.* 610 verses), of which one also contained *The Tale of Sinuhe* (P. Ramesseum A = P. Berlin 10499; Burkard and Fischer-Elfert 1994: 116–17 no. 173). The earliest are the two partial copies from 'Berlin library' (see **4.2**) of the second half of the 12th Dynasty, which present slightly different versions (B1 and B2 = P. Berlin 3023, 3025; Burkard and Fischer-Elfert 1994: 112 no. 168, 114 no. 170). The tale is set in the reign of Nebkaure Khety of the Heracleopolitan Dynasties, and begins:

> There was once a man
> called Khunanup . . . (R 1.1)

Within an ironic narrative are set nine discursive petitions on the nature of Maat, which occupy most of the composition. The narrative, however, is the mode which determines the meaning of the whole as an allusive theodicy. Various factors suggest that the tale was composed in the mid-12th Dynasty; a more precise date of composition may be provided by B1 65–8, which is a mock titulary similar to that of Senwosret II (Parkinson 1992).
Text: Parkinson 1991c; *translation:* Parkinson 1999f: 92–101.
Studies: Allam 2000; Ayad 1996; Berlev 1987; Bontty 1997: 219–35, 2000; Dakin 1998; Devauchelle 1995; Eyre 2000; Fecht 1975, 1996; Foster 1989–90; Gardiner 1923; Gilula 1978b; Gnirs 2000a; Goedicke 1998b; Hare 2000; Herrmann 1955, 1958, 1977; Junge 2000; Kuhlmann 1992; Leprohon 1975; Light 2000; Loprieno 2000; L. Morenz 1998, 2000; Pamminger 1993; Parkinson 1988, 1991b: no. xx; 1991e, 1992, 2000b; Posener 1951a: no. 11; Ranke 1954; Roccati 1993; Shupak 1992; Simpson 1990; Théodoridès 1990; Vernus 1990a; Westendorf 1977b.

The Tale of Sinuhe

The composition is preserved in five Middle Kingdom manuscripts (with variants) from Thebes and the necropolis of Haraga in Middle Egypt near el-Lahun (L. Morenz 1996: 155–6), and over twenty New Kingdom copies (provenances including Thebes, the tomb of Sennedjem at Deir el-Medina, and Deir el-Ballas). The earliest manuscript is P. Berlin 3022 (Burkard and Fischer-Elfert 1994: 110–11 no. 167), from the 'Berlin library' (see **4.2**) from the second half of the 12th Dynasty; Obsomer (1999: 208) suggests a date in the reign of an Amenemhat, perhaps III, based on a scribal error in the manuscript. The tale of voluntary exile and return under Senwosret I is complete (c. 575 verses), and has been much analysed. The narrative is introduced as the biography of a courtier whose service began under Amenemhat I:

> The Patrician and Count,
> Governor of the Sovereign's Domains in the Syrian lands,
> the True Acquaintance of the king, whom he loves,
> the Follower, Sinuhe says: (R 1–2)

The first-person narrative incorporates a rich variety of genres. The setting and the eulogistic elements may suggest that it was composed shortly after the reign of Senwosret I: R 4–5 implies that both kings Amenemhat I, Senwosret I and Queen Nefru are imagined as already dead.[5] Vernus' linguistic analysis (1990b: 185) supports an early Middle Kingdom date.

Text: Blackman 1932: 1–41; Koch 1990; *translation:* Parkinson 1999f: 27–53.
Studies: Allam 1986; J. Assmann 1983b; Baines 1982; Barns 1952, 1967, 1972; Barta 1990; Behrens 1981; Berg 1984; Blumenthal 1983, 1995, 1998b; Brunner 1955; Cannuyer 1985; Colin 1995; W. V. Davies 1975; Derchain 1970, 1985; Donadoni 1986b; Fecht 1984; Fischer 1976: 97–9; Foster 1980, 1982, 1983, 1993; Galán 1998; Gardiner 1916; Goedicke 1957, 1984a, 1984b, 1984–5, 1985a, 1986a, 1988a, 1990, 1992a, 1998a; Grapow 1952; Green 1983, 1984; Greig 1990; Jasnow 1999: 204–5; Kahl 1998; Kitchen 1994, 1996; Koyama 1982; Loprieno 1988: 41–59; Malaise 1974; Moers 2001: 251–63; L. Morenz 1997b, d; Obsomer 1999; Otto 1966; Parant 1982; Parkinson 1991b: no. xix; Patanè 1989; Posener 1951a: no. 14, 1956: 87–115; Purdy 1977; Sander-Hansen 1957; Schenkel 1973, 1984; Shirun-Grumach 1984; Simpson 1984b; Spalinger 1998; Théodoridès 1984; Tobin 1995; Westendorf 1977a, 1986b; Yoyotte 1964.

The Tale of the Shipwrecked Sailor

This tale is preserved in one manuscript (P. St Petersburg 1115), which may have been written by the same scribe as P. Prisse (Hodjash and Berlev

---

[5] Compare the Annals of Amenemhat II, where offerings are given 'to the Dual King Kheperkare in Khnumsut' (l.6); the mention of 'Nefru true of voice, lady of blessedness' on a statue base dated to year 11 of Amenemhat II (Gardiner and Peet 1952: no. 71, pl. 21). See Blumenthal 1995: 884 n.a.

Appendix 1: Survey of the Middle Kingdom literary corpus 299

1997: 285, n.9; von Bomhard 1999; **4.2**), and thus may also have come from Thebes. The dating of these manuscripts is uncertain (see below, *Kagemni*), but they probably come from the mid- to late 12th Dynasty. Vernus' linguistic analysis (1990b: 185) places the composition in the first half of the 12th Dynasty, while Sergei Ignatov (1994: 197–8) places it at the very start. The tale is a first-person narrative, ostensibly a simple tale of adventure, which is introduced thus:

> Speech by a clever follower: (1)

Although the preceding margin is unusually narrow, nothing is lost before this (*c.* 210 verses), and the manuscript is complete.[6] The structure involves a tale within a tale, told by a serpent about the problem of suffering. The tale ends as the follower relates his lord's laconic and dismissive reply.
Text: Blackman 1932: 41–8; *translation*: Parkinson 1999f: 89–101.
Studies: H. Altenmüller 1989; Baines 1990a; Berg 1990; Bolshakov 1993; von Bomhard 1999; Bradbury 1988: 139–40; Bryan 1980; Burkard 1993; Cannuyer 1990, 1994; Desroches Noblecourt 1998; Devauchelle 1989; Dévaud 1916–17; Foster 1988; Foster and Brock 1998; Gilula 1977; Gnirs 1998; Goedicke 1974, 1980; Helck 1992; Ignatov 1994; Kurth 1987; Loprieno 1991a; Manuelian 1992; Moers 2001: 245–51; L. Morenz 1994; Otto 1966; Parkinson 1991b: no. xxi; Posener 1951a: no. 15; Rendsburg 2000; Simpson 1984a; Spalinger 1984; Vandersleyen 1990; Westendorf 1990.

The Tale of P. Lythgoe

This fragmentary manuscript comes from the necropolis at el Lisht (P. MMA 09.180.535), from the cemetery south west of the pyramid of Amenemhat I near the tomb of Senebtisi (Simpson 1960: 65–6, 1980: 1059; for the date of Senebtisi see, e.g., Ryholt 1997: 84). It can be dated by the hand to the second half of the 12th Dynasty. Recto and verso each contain 11 lines of narrative text, and presumably form part of a single composition (totalling *c.* 30 verses). On the recto there is mention of 'the Vizier Djefa's son Ne[. . .]' and a 'field of the vizier Wehau', and the verso includes an episode of violence, reminiscent of the Osiris myth (J. P. Allen, pers. comm.). Neither vizier is historically attested, although

---

[6] Bolshakov (1993) argues from examination of the manuscript that a sheet was cut off from the start, and that the opening words imply previous matter now lost. The join that he discusses is probably the remains of a sheet acting as a blank protective margin. The opening words ('Speech by . . .') can be an initial phrase (Baines 1990a: 58), even if taken as a narrative verb (*sḏm.jn.f*: 'And a clever follower said': Loprieno 1991a: 215; contra Bolshakov 1993: 255). A letter to the dead opens with the phrase 'Speech by . . .' (Sethe 1928a: 99, 1.6).

a Vizier Wehau is mentioned in a New Kingdom list of otherwise unknown and possibly fictitious officials (Simpson 1963b). A mention of the Residence (rto 3) suggests the setting is the 12th Dynasty; the date of composition is uncertain.
Text and translation: Simpson 1960.
Studies: Helck 1982; Parkinson 1991b: no. xiii.

The Tale of the Herdsman

This fragmentary tale is preserved in the same manuscript as *The Dialogue of a Man and His Ba*, from the Theban 'Berlin library', on a sheet that was partially cleaned and then added to that roll from another manuscript. The hand is from the second half of the 12th Dynasty, but in an older style than that of the dialogue (cf. L. Morenz 1996: 136–7). Traces show that four lines were erased at the start and four at the end; it is uncertain how much has been lost before and after these. Twenty-five lines remain (= 35 verses), describing in the third person an incident apparently featuring a herdsman,[7] who tells his colleagues of his meeting with a goddess in the marshes.[8] It includes a 'water-spell' known also in Coffin Text spell 836; the relationship between the two texts is unclear.[9] Vernus' linguistic analysis assigns the composition to the early 12th Dynasty (1990b: 185).
Text: Gardiner 1909b: 6, 15, pl. 16–17; *translation:* Parkinson 1999f: 287–8 (inc. new readings of palimpsest traces).
Studies: Drenkhahn 1977; Gilula 1978a; Goedicke 1970b; L. Morenz 1996: 124–35; Ogdon 1982, 1987; Parkinson 1991b: no. xxii; Posener 1951a: no. 16.

The Tale of Hay/Khenemsu

The conclusion to a third person narrative survives on the fragment of a late 12th Dynasty papyrus from a house in rank N at el-Lahun, the recto

---

[7] L. Morenz (1996: 135) suggests on the basis of a detail of the spell recited by the protagonist that the speaker is a god, but this interprets the spell-recitation too literally.
[8] The goddess seems to be Hathor, although Morenz suggests the goddess Seret (1996: 126–8 n.E, 132–5).
[9] *CT* VII, 36i–s, attested only on Theban Coffin of the Steward Buau, dated to the late 11th, or start of the 12th, Dynasty (see **4.2**). Study: L. Morenz 1996: 130–41. The spell has a concluding narrative (36r–s) that is similar – but not identical – to *The Herdsman* 17–22: 'At dawn, very early, he crossed over; / and thousand joined with thousand(?)'. The similarity may be due to the context inherent in the water-spell rather than to the Coffin Text spell's being directly adapted from *The Herdsman* (pace Ogdon 1987; L. Morenz 1996: 131–2). As Gilula (1978a) suggests, the spell was probably incorporated independently into both the Coffin Text corpus and the literary tale. The spell does not imply that *The Herdsman* predates the Coffin.

of which contains an apparently liturgical (e.g., Parkinson 1999d: 187–8) copy of hymns to Senwosret III (P. Lahun LV.1 vso = P. UCL 32157; see Gallorini 1998). This group of papyri included a veterinary text, mathematical texts, and accounts of people associated with the priestly sphere (Lot LV: Quirke 1990b: 165). Parts of one and a half columns are preserved (c. 40 verses), including the colophon. In these, the name Hay occurs twice, but he may not have been the main protagonist, and a man called Khenemsu(?) also plays a prominent role. The fragment starts with an episode of violence:

> [they finished?] this [speech], and they did things against him.
> And they put him in the street. (1–2)

and continues with Hay's burial, which is probably the work of the main protagonist:

> Then he slaughtered [. . .] and he made a burial [for] Hay;
> he caused Khenemsu to enter the [Enclosure(?)];
> he placed him at the burial of Hay,
> [. . .] to Lower Egypt bearing his rope.
> And he placed him over the [pyram]id of Neferka[re], the justified
> and said 'May you be well, Khenemsu . . .' (19–24)

The tale seems to conclude with the resolution of a conflict:

> and Khenemsu, who went(?), was well, he having driven off the anger. (26)

The mention of the monument of Neferkare, probably Neferkare Pepy II (c. 2246–2152 BCE), might suggest a setting in late Old Kingdom Memphis, similar to that of *The Tale of Neferkare and Sasenet*.
Text and translation: Griffith 1898: I, 4, II, pl. 4. An unpublished transcription by A. M. Blackman is in the School of Archaeology and Oriental Studies, University of Liverpool, with some readings suggested by B. Gunn.
Studies: Parkinson 1991b: no. xxiv; Posener 1951a: no. 20.

The Tale of a King and the Ghost of Snefer

Four fragments of a Late Period papyrus – possibly 25th Dynasty – comprise pieces of 22 lines (P. Chassinat II = P. Louvre E 25352; c. 45 verses). The papyrus comes from the Theban area (Posener 1957: 120). There is mention of a king and an 'excellent spirit' who identifies himself as 'Khentyka's son Snefer', both of which names are attested in the Old

and Middle Kingdoms. The tale is composed in late Middle Egyptian, similar to that of *The Tale of Neferkare and Sasenet*.
Text and translation: Posener 1960; other (unpublished) fragments of P. Chassinat II are now in the Louvre (E 32548a, b, c).
Studies: Posener 1952a: no. 64; Verhoeven 1999: 261.

The Tale of the House of Life

Fragments of a tale occur in five columns of a manuscript (P. BM EA 10475 vso) in a hand very similar to that of P. Westcar from the 17th Dynasty(?). The provenance is unknown, but may be Thebes. The verso contains a verse-pointed narrative in Middle Egyptian, mentioning the palace, a woman with 'the enti[re] Royal Apartments under her hand' (X + 5.1), and the House of Life. There is a high proportion of dialogue in what survives; the fifth column describing a 'period of 40 days as a fair festival' (X + 5.3) seems to have been the end of the text.
Partial text and translation: Parkinson 1999d: 190–3.

The Tale of Nefer[pesdet]

P. UCL 32156A is a late 12th Dynasty papyrus from el-Lahun. On the recto 7 vertical lines comprise the beginning of a tale, with a rubric:

> There was once a man,
> called Nefer[pesdet]
> He was a commoner, stro[ng of arm[10] . . .]
> And these workers (*kjwtjw*) said to him
> '[. . .] what you have done is good . . .' (1—5)

The text continues with the complaint of a group of workmen to their commander, presumably Nefer[. . .]. There are traces of a further two lines, deliberately erased (on the verso is an account). The text could also be the narrative introduction to a wisdom text (Quirke 1996b: 387). Unpublished.

The Tale of Nemay

A group of four fragments from el-Lahun (P. UCL 32105A and B), written in vertical (A) and horizontal (B) lines on the recto only (remains of 7, 5, 4, 7 lines), belong to a tale. One phrase reads '"[. . . Nema]y, my friend." Then Nemay said' (it is also possible that two men called Nemay

---
[10] Restored from *Neferti 2c*.

and Khenemsu are speaking in turns: Quirke 1996a: 270). Another clause reads: 'And his Person said', and mention is elsewhere made of luxury cloth.
Unpublished.

Other Tales from el-Lahun

P. UCL 32271B recto is a magico-medical text; the verso comprises 5 vertical lines of a literary narrative, including the phrase 'those who eat lotuses'. It is recorded as being from Lot XLI, which also included a list of performers at festivals (Griffith 1898: pl. 24–5).
Unpublished

P. UCL 32150A comprises small fragments with horizontal and vertical lines in black ink on the recto (there are accounts on the verso). These are perhaps a narrative; the preserved fragments contain parts of dialogue (e.g., 'with you' and 'with me').
Unpublished

Other possibly literary fragments from el-Lahun include: P. UCL 32095D vso (4 vertical lines of unidentified text); 32107B (2 fragments with 2 horizontal lines on recto, and 2 horizontal lines on both recto and verso: unlikely); 32217G (1 vertical line, perhaps ritual); 32149A (7 fragments).

A.1.2 DISCOURSES AND DIALOGUES

The Words of Neferti

The text is completely preserved (c. 190 verses), in New Kingdom copies only, of which the earliest is from the first half of the 18th Dynasty (recent list: Mathieu 1993: 343 n.43). Provenances include Memphis (Quirke 1996b: 390) and Thebes. There is a narrative introduction set in the court of Sneferu (2575–51 BCE), which begins:

> Now there was once a time when the Person of the Dual King, Sneferu, true of voice,
> was the worthy king in this entire land.
> On one of these days . . . (1a–c)

The great lector priest of Bastet, Neferti is asked for 'a few perfect words, and choice verses' (1l–m). He responds with a lament for a chaotic period, and 'takes concern for the events in the land; / he recalls the state of the east' (3a–b). This chaos will be ended by the arrival of a king called Ameny, who can be identified with Amenemhat I. There is no epilogue, although the last lines allude to Neferti's future fame, and this is indeed attested in the Ramessid 'Eulogy of Dead Writers' (P. Chester Beatty IV vso 3.6), and P. Athens. On the basis of the eulogy of Ameny / Amenemhat I, the composition has often been assigned to his reign or shortly afterwards (e.g., Eyre 1993: 115), although such a eulogy could have been composed later in the 12th Dynasty, in part glorifying him as a dynastic ancestor rather than as a contemporaneous ruler. Ludwig Morenz (1996: 109–10), however, suggests a date in the Second Intermediate Period on the basis of the prologue's similarity with the style of *Cheops' Court*; on balance, this seems unlikely.

Text: Helck 1970b (see also Posener 1977–80: no. 1407); *translation:* Parkinson 1999f: 134–43.

Studies: Blumenthal 1982, 1984a; Derchain 1972; Eyre 1991, 1993; Foti 1976; Goedicke 1977a; Graefe 1990; Kammerzell 1986; Parkinson 1991b: no. xv; Posener 1951a: no. 24, 1956: 21–60, 145–57; Quack 1993.

The Words of Khakheperreseneb

The text is known from an early 18th Dynasty writing board from Thebes (BM EA 5645) and an ostracon (Cairo JdE 50249).[11] The protagonist is acclaimed in the Ramessid 'Eulogy of Dead Writers' (P. Chester Beatty IV vso 3.7) and is also depicted with the title 'lector-priest' on the 'Daressy Fragment'. His name incorporates the prenomen of Khakheperre Senwosret II, and shows that the poem must be of his reign or later; Vernus' linguistic analysis (1990b: 188) places it in the 13th Dynasty. The text on the board is arranged into three paragraphs, which were apparently copied at different times, on the front of the board, and one on the back (ic. 90 verses). It may thus be either a selection or a complete version of the text (Parkinson 1997b: 65–6). Perhaps significantly, it lacks a colophon. The title is:

> The collection of words, the gathering of verses,
> the seeking of utterances with heart-searching,
> made by the priest of Heliopolis,
> Seny's son Khakheperreseneb,
> called Ankhu. (rto 1)

It is a reflective lament about 'what is throughout the land' (vso 1), addressed to the protagonist's unresponsive heart.

---

[11] Another New Kingdom ostracon that preserves fragments of a literary text which also addresses the heart (Parkinson 1997b: 64 n.28) is probably a love-song (compare with M. V. Fox 1985: 22: 'I say to my heart. . .').

Text: Gardiner 1909a: 95–110, pl. 17–18; Parkinson 1997b; *translation:* Parkinson 1999f: 146–50.
Studies: Chappaz 1979; Colin 1996; Helck 1980; Kadish 1973; Mathieu 1996b; Moers in press; Ockinga 1983; Otto 1975; Parkinson 1991b: no. xiv, 1996d; Posener 1951a: no. 25; Vernus 1995a: 1–33.

The Discourse of Sasobek

This discourse is preserved in a fragmentary manuscript from the 'Ramesseum library' at Thebes (P. Ramesseum I = P. BM EA 10754; see **4.2**), copied in the second half of the 12th Dynasty. The bottom half of the roll is particularly damaged. It is unknown how much is lost, but parts of at least 162 lines remain (= *c.* 350 verses). There are 16 lines of an introductory narrative of which a large proportion may be missing; it spans several periods of time (A.11). The narrative tells how Sasobek is apparently imprisoned, but is 'released on the petition of this dancer' (A.9) of 'the Count Nefer's son Ineni' (A.8). This seems not to be a full restitution, and he continues to insist on absolute justice by speaking a lament, entitled:

> Discourse spoken by the scribe
> Hathorhotep's son Sasobek,
> his mouth moving according to what had happened,
> and what was presented to mankind(?). (A.17)

His subsequent speech is broadly reflective, and seems similar in tone and subject to the petitions of the eloquent peasant. The uncertainty of life is described in general terms:

> This life of a span, it is not known what happens in it. (A.18)

> Yesterday has perished [. . .] from him(?);
> tomorrow exists for all time, (but) there is no knowing its state –
> what to it are perishing and becoming?
> [. . .]
> [There is no] knowing his state when he plans the morrow. (Bi.5–7)

The audience of his discourse is referred to in the second person both in the singular and in the plural; it was probably Ineni (or his representative, a 'Sealbearer': A.12–14) and members of his entourage. The discourse is partly didactic, urging the addressee, who has 'not heard what you should have heard' (Bii.15), to realize in action the wisdom that Sasobek has gained and now voices. The desired action would presumably be the vindication of Sasobek:

Set your hands to good! (Bi.13)

There was at least one narrative interlude in the discourse (Cii.1). The date of composition is uncertain.
Text: Barns 1956: 1–10, pl. 1–16.
Studies: Parkinson 1991b: no. xi; Posener 1951a: no. 29.

The Discourse of Renseneb

This is known only from an incomplete manuscript of three lines and an additional fragment from the second half of the 12th Dynasty, provenance unrecorded (P. Moscow – Pushkin Museum of Fine Arts – 1695), which begins:

> Beginning of the discourse
> spoken by the priest of Sekhmet, Renseneb.
> [. . .] in Retjenu,
> in the following of the Overseer of Sealbearers, Senebtifi. (1)

At this point the manuscript breaks off (= *c*. 10 verses). The date of composition is uncertain.
Text and translation: Posener 1969.
Studies: Parkinson 1991b: no. xii; Posener 1951a: no. 30.

The Discourse of the Fowler

The start of this text is preserved on the verso of the same manuscript as *Renseneb*, and comprises four lines, of which the last has been partially erased like the subsequent lines. A title and traces of an introductory prologue are preserved:

> Beginning of the discourse spoken by Hori's son,
> – he is a fowler (*ḥȝmw*) of the Southern City,
> called Iuru,[12]
> who was summoned after he had been in the palace. (1–2)

He seems to be complaining 'about his state' (3).
The verso of the mid- to late 12th Dynasty P. Butler (= P. BM EA 10274) from Thebes (Parkinson 1991c: xi, xxvi) contains 39 lines of a discourse. The manuscript lines of P. Butler are numbered and indicate that nine are missing from its start. The discourse is spoken by a fowler to his superior:

[12] The name Iuru is attested in the 12th Dynasty: Ranke, *PN* I, 18.11.

O [for] your hand on your fowlers (wḥ'w)! Do not let [. . .]
for I have surpassed the others who have not attacked for us!
You (pl.) are ready of arm since the time of Horus,
when Sokhet (the marsh goddess) came into being for us.
May you renew action, according to what you know!
Look, our state is before you
– the water-meadow has flown away into the land, but there is no leaving it.
Its margins and districts are now under the herdsmen of the foreign countries;
the stillness now under the byres of the bulls;
the huts of hiding now under the town-dwellers' grain.
The face looks askance at action.
No-one can find the advance of [. . .], for lack of an exact man,
– the officials drive him off from his father's property,
an attacker has occupied his seat,
and his son has abandoned him on account of the lawcourt. (12–25)

Later he urges his audience to

pity me, until my good fortune comes, until you know [our] state.
O may you protect me [from him who . . .] my birds!
O then I shall be weighty through waiting! (38–42)

This subject matter seems to have had overtones of questioning both good governance and the nature of the ideal life, implying that wisdom is not confined to the established oligarchy. This is probably the same composition as the discourse of P. Moscow; a total of c. 50 verses is preserved between the two manuscripts. The style of the discourse resembles that of the petitions of *The Eloquent Peasant*.
Text: Griffith 1892: 458, pl. 3-[5] (P. Butler); Posener 1969: 101–6 (P. Moscow); *partial translation*: Parkinson 1999f: 290. An unpublished transcription by A. M. Blackman is in the School of Archaeology and Oriental Studies, University of Liverpool.
Studies: Fischer-Elfert 1989: 23–6; Parkinson 1991b: no. xiii; Posener 1951a: no. 31 + 12.

The Abydos Discourse

A New Kingdom(?) ostracon from Abydos contains the opening of a discourse in five lines, of which only the beginning 30 per cent is legible:

[1] Beginning of the discou[rse . . .] [2] verses [. . .] [3] [. . .] [4] Horus [. . .] [5] know [. . .]
Text and translation: Simpson 1995: 13, 15 (A4).

The Dialogue of Ipuur and the Lord to the Limit

This dialogue is known from a fragmentary 19th Dynasty manuscript (P. Leiden I.344 rto) from Saqqara, containing 17 columns, of *c.* 14 lines each (*c.* 660 verses). On the verso is a hymn to Amun (Zandee 1992). Only the top left hand part of column 1 is preserved, but the extant text opens *in media res*, suggesting that at least one further is probably lost (i.e., 40–50 verses). The first extant column of the verso text is apparently the start of that composition (Zandee 1992: 6), however, suggesting that not much of the start of the roll is missing (i.e., only one column from the start of the recto: cf. Fecht 1972: 42). There was presumably either a brief narrative introduction, similar to that of *Neferti* and *Sasobek*, or an extended title, as in *Fowler* and *Renseneb*. It is uncertain how many lines of the poem are lost at the end. After the final extant lines (17.1–3), there is a lacuna of about ten manuscript lines followed by traces in the verso hand (three lines: Zandee 1992: 1083–4, pl. 37–8), so there cannot be much of this copy of the poem lost in the lacuna (at most 25 verses). J. Zandee suggests that the lacuna may have contained the continuation and conclusion of the verso text and that not much of the original roll is lost, but the verso text is too fragmentary to estimate exactly what length of roll is missing at the end.[13] It is possible that this copy of the poem originally ended shortly after 17.3, but it is also possible that the roll contained an incomplete copy of *Ipuur*, or that it originally contained a complete copy of *Ipuur* on the recto that was partially erased when the papyrus was reused to copy a hymn to Amun which began on the verso but extended onto the recto.

The text is a lament about the state of the land: Ipuur (or 'Ipu the elder'), who is given no title, is addressing the 'Lord to the Limit', who replies with at least two speeches (15.13, 16.11). The Dialogue takes place before an audience – perhaps the Lord's entourage – that is also addressed (e.g., 7.1). The Lord is apparently the king, rather than a god, although the text's concerns are theodic.

The date of composition is disputed. As the text stands, internal evidence points to the late Middle Kingdom (e.g., Vernus 1990b: 189–90), but many critics (e.g., Fecht 1972) have made redactionalist studies and dated parts of the composition earlier. Wolfgang Helck (1995: 72–7) has suggested, without any concrete evidence, that the text is not a unity (cf. Quack 1997: 347). The sage is mentioned on the 'Daressy Fragment' as 'the Overseer of Singers, Ipuur' (cf. L. Morenz 1999a: 131), and he may be included in the list of P. Athens.

---

[13] Even if the three lines are the direct continuation of the verso text, the papyrus could have been much longer when *Ipuur* was copied on the recto, and may have been cut down before the verso text was copied.

Text: Gardiner 1909a: 1–95, pl. 1–16; many new readings are supplied by Fecht 1972; Helck 1995 (unreliable); *translation*: Parkinson 1999f: 155–65.
Studies: Barta 1974a; Faulkner 1964; Fecht 1972, 1974; Franke 1998b; Gilula 1981; L. Morenz 1996: 87–106, 1999a; Otto 1951; Parkinson 1991b: no. xvi; Posener 1951a: no. 8, 1946; Quack 1997; Renaud 1988; Roccati 1994a; Schorr 1974; Spiegel 1975.

The Dialogue of a Man and His Ba

The dialogue is preserved in a papyrus from the second half of the 12th Dynasty 'Berlin library' at Thebes (P. Berlin 3024; Burkard and Fischer-Elfert 1994: 113 no. 169; see **4.2**). It may have been composed around the middle of the dynasty, not long before the group of manuscripts were written, since colloquialisms and an unusual interrogative nominal construction (20) might suggest a later Middle Kingdom date (cf. Silverman 1980: 85–6), although Vernus' linguistic analysis (1990b: 185) associates the dialogue with the texts of the early Middle Kingdom. At the beginning of the manuscript, at least half a sheet is lost – perhaps one and a half sheets, which would have contained around 35 lines. 155 lines remain, including the end of the composition (*c.* 200 verses).

The poem is a dialogue in various literary styles, between a man (the 'Lebensmüder' or 'man tired of life' of Adolf Erman's original edition) and his *ba* on the nature of death, which is recounted by the man who is not named in the extant text. It seems to take place before an audience of accessors (addressed in the plural in 1). The composition may have opened with a brief statement as in the New Kingdom dialogue *The Contending of the Belly and the Head* (see p. 218).

The Amherst Papyri included five small fragments (H–L; P. Amherst III) in a hand very similar to those from the 'Berlin library', and probably coming from the same source (Newberry 1899: pl.1). Georges Posener judged them to be from a different text from the other Berlin manuscripts,[14] but as Percy Newberry suggested (1899: 9) they are parts of the lost start of *A Man and His Ba*, and not part of an otherwise lost fifth roll in the 'library'. The fragments preserve parts of at least nine lines (*c.* 15 verses), some of which (J–K) read '[Com]e(?), I shall teach you [. . .] the form (?) of the West [. . .] A man is [. . .]', another (L) 'it is the hour'.
Text: Faulkner 1956 (P. Berlin 3024 only); *translation*: Parkinson 1999f: 151–65.
Studies: J. Assmann 1996: 199–210; Barta 1969; Bolshakov 1985; Brunner-Traut 1967; Depuydt 1993; Fecht 1991; Goedicke 1970a; Hannig 1991;

---

[14] 1951a: no. 32; followed by Parkinson 1991b: no. ix ('The Amherst Wisdom Text'), 1991c: x–xi.

Letellier 1991; Lohmann 1998; Menu 2000; Osing 1977a; Parkinson 1991b: no. xvii, 1991d, 1996c; Posener 1951a: no. 7; Renaud 1991; Schenkel 1973; Tobin 1991; Welsh 1978; R. J. Williams 1962.

A.1.3 OTHER WISDOM TEXTS

The Oxford Wisdom Text

A fragmentary writing board in the Ashmolean Museum, Oxford (1964.489a,b), probably from Thebes, has seven lines of text on each side (*c.* 50 verses). The hand is possibly the same as that of Tablets Carnarvon I and II from Deir el-Bahri and dates to the start of the 18th Dynasty (Vernus 1984: 706, no. 8). One side concerns the relationship of the 'god' (king) with the duties of an official, to whom the text is addressed; the lines on the other side are more didactic and less reflective. Both sides were written by the same hand, and both presumably contain the same text, which seems to be either a discourse or a teaching. The language is classical Middle Egyptian. The date of composition is uncertain.
Text and translation: Barns 1968.
Studies: Parkinson 1991b: no. x.

The Maxims of P. Ramesseum II

P. Ramesseum II (= P. BM EA 10755), from the late Middle Kingdom 'Ramesseum library' at Thebes (see **4.2**), comprises two fragments containing six columns which seem from the hand to have been copied at different times (*c.* 115 verses). The text is a loose collection of reflective maxims of a generally pessimistic nature; it is unlikely to be an abstract of a single unitary text. On the recto, each maxim is written on a separate line, while from the second column of the verso onward the writing is continuous. On the verso, the divisions between maxims (not metrical verses) are marked by red verse-points (see **6.3**).
Text: Barns 1956: 11–14, pl. 7–9.
Studies: L. Morenz 1997a; Parkinson 1991b: no. xviii; Posener 1951a: no. 59.

The Ramesseum Wisdom Fragment

A small fragment now mounted together with *The Discourse of Sasobek* (P. BM EA 10754.'Frags.D') seems to be in a distinct, though similar, hand. This is presumably from the 'Ramesseum library', and is apparently part of an otherwise unknown text, not mentioned by Barns (1956) or Gardiner (1955a). Parts of three lines are preserved, with rubrics and verse-points; l.x+1 mentions 'officials' (in a rubric) and x+3 reads '[he

who makes] an end for himself — he is an ignoramus'. This phrase suggests that it is part of a discourse or teaching.
Unpublished; Parkinson 1991b: no. xib; mentioned by Quirke as a teaching (1996b: 387 [M10]; number misquoted as EA 10770).

Excursus: *The el-Lahun Wisdom Text*

P. UCL 32106C rto contains 7 vertical lines in black with red verse-points to the lower right of each section of text; on the verso are 6 partly erased vertical lines. One line on the recto (6) has a line number (60), suggesting that this is the end of a roll of some length. Other fragments that Stephen Quirke considers to be parts of the same manuscript are P. UCL 32107H (2 vertical lines with verse-points; 32107E may belong to this fragment), 3211 OF (2 fragments, with 3 horizontal lines with verse-points); 32117E (ends of 3 vertical lines with no surviving verse-points; a medical text (?) on the verso). It is uncertain what type of text this is: the proposed identification as a wisdom text (Quirke 1996b: 387) rests in part on the literary-sounding word *3jr* 'oppress' in 32110F, but this word occurs in other types of text (e.g., *CT* III, 358c, VI 293k, 406t), and an identification as a ritual text is more likely.[15]
Unpublished.

A.1.4 COMPOUND GENRES

The Account of the Sporting King[16]

A late 18th Dynasty manuscript contains parts of 18 columns; it is uncertain how much is lost at each end (P. Moscow, unnumbered; *c.* 455 verses). The papyrus was purchased at Thebes (Caminos 1956: vii), and may derive from a Theban library of manuscripts comprising copies of *Ptahhotep* (L2), *Sinuhe* (G), *Merikare* (M), *Fishing and Fowling* and the New Kingdom *Mythological Tale* (Quirke 1996b: 390 suggests Saqqara as the findspot for unstated reasons). The fragments reveal a narrative interspersed with long eulogizing speeches made by the King's Sealbearer Sehotepibreankh, an official otherwise unknown, to a king who is playfully titled 'Two Ladies: Fisher and Fowler (B1.3, CI.12). There is mention of Amenemhat II (E2.10), who is presumably the king who requests these speeches during a court hunting trip (A2.1-3). The text

---

[15] Other possibly related el-Lahun fragments with verse-points are: 32152D (2 vertical lines with a verse-point on the recto, with one vertical line on the verso); 32110G (3 vertical lines; epistolary formula on verso).

[16] Since the relationship between narrative and discourse in the genre of the text as a whole is not certain, I have used the neutral term 'account'.

therefore dates no earlier than the second half of the 12th Dynasty. The Annals of Amenemhat II include an account of a fishing and fowling trip.[17]
Text: Caminos 1956: 22–39, pl. 8–16; *partial translation:* Decker 1975: 38–44.
Studies: Parkinson 1991b: no. xxix.

The Account of the Pleasures of Fishing and Fowling

This text is likewise known only from a late 18th Dynasty papyrus (P. Moscow, unnumbered), which provides fragments of 12 columns occupied by a monologue in praise of pastoral activities (totalling *c.* 570 verses).[18] The provenance is the same as that of *The Sporting King*. The first column begins 'Like what is the [craft of] my [belov]ed?' (Sokhet, the goddess of the marsh; A1.1). This is paralleled in *The Sporting King*, where the speeches are requested with a similar question (A2.2). Since it is likely that there was some introductory statement, at least one column is probably missing, and the fact that a 'lord Inseni' is addressed suggests that a narrative prologue or frame has been lost. It is uncertain whether the text as a whole was a narrative or some form of discourse: the closest extant parallel is *The Sporting King*.

Vernus' linguistic analysis (1990b: 186) assigns the composition to the second half of the 12th Dynasty.
Text: Caminos 1956: 1–21, pl. 1–7; *partial translation:* Decker 1975: 31–38.
Studies: Parkinson 1991b: no. xxx; Posener 1951a: no. 35.

The Royal Eulogy of P. BM EA 10475

Fragments of seven columns on the recto of a manuscript, in a hand very similar to that of P. Westcar, contain a royal eulogy; on the verso is *The Tale of the House of Life*. The provenance is unknown, but may be Thebes. The eulogy refers to an unnamed king in the third person. One rubric (X+2.x+5) suggests that the discourses were contained within a narrative frame, similar to *The Sporting King* or to the commemorative Royal Tales.
Partial text and translation: Parkinson 1999d: 181–90.

---

[17] ll.x+23–x+25; Baines in preparation. The Account might draw on this tradition of Amenemhat's activities (Quirke 1996a: 271), although such activities were probably standard royal pursuits.
[18] Quirke's suggestion (1996a: 271; 1996b: 388) that this and *The Sporting King* are parts of a single composition is unfounded.

A.1.5 TEACHINGS

The Teaching for Kagemni

The final section of this teaching (*c.* 45 verses) is preserved on two columns at the start of the 12th Dynasty P. Prisse (= P. Bibliothèque Nationale Paris, 183–94) which was said to be from the necropolis at Dra Abu el-Naga at Thebes (Dewachter 1988; see **4.2**). The dating of P. Prisse, which may have been written by the same scribe who copied *The Shipwrecked Sailor*, is controversial;[19] both can be dated to the mid- to late 12th Dynasty. Both the teachings it contains are set in the Old Kingdom and are apparently written in an archaistic style of hieratic, while *The Shipwrecked Sailor* manuscript exhibits the more modern convention of both horizontal and vertical lines, and a less formal and slightly less archaic style of script. It is uncertain how much is lost from the start of the manuscript. The end of the Teaching is preserved together with a narrative conclusion in which a Kagemni becomes vizier under the new king, Sneferu (*c.* 2575–2551 BCE). Kagemni is almost certainly the pupil rather than the teacher, and was perhaps based on the historical vizier Kagemni of the 6th Dynasty (*c.* 2300 BCE) who was revered in the late Old Kingdom and early Middle Kingdom.[20] The father was probably a vizier, and may perhaps be identified with the Kaires mentioned in the Ramessid 'Eulogy of Dead Writers' (**A.2**).

The date of composition is very uncertain. The use of the demonstrative *p3* in 2.5 might suggest a date of composition later in the 12th Dynasty rather than earlier.

Text: Gardiner 1946; *translation:* Parkinson 1999f: 291–2.
Studies: Barta 1980; Gardiner 1951; Morschauer 1994; Parkinson 1991b: no. i; Posener 1951a: no. 2.

The Teaching of Hordedef

Only copies from the Ramessid Period survive; provenances include Deir el-Medina. These provide an incomplete text (*c.* 75 verses), despite the

---

[19] Identification of Hodjash and Berlev 1997: 285 n.9; von Bomhard 1999. Möller initially dated the palaeography of P. Prisse to the early 12 Dynasty (1909: 12), but Dévaud's analysis of its orthography placed it, with Möller's agreement, in the later 12th Dynasty, after the Berlin library from the period of Amenemhat III (1924: 11; cf. Parkinson 1991c: xxv–xxvi). This has not been universally accepted (e.g., Seibert 1967: 68 n.77; Burkard 1977: 337), and Hodjash and Berlev (1997) attempt to redate P. Prisse to Möller's earlier estimate (see also von Bomhard 1999: 55–6). The palaeography favours an earlier date than the orthography, but a date earlier than mid-12th Dynasty is hard to envisage.

[20] For the possible institutional practices of such reverence see Leclant and Berger 1996.

composition's recorded fame.[21] The teaching is attributed to an attested historical figure of the 4th Dynasty (c. 2540 BCE), who was revered from the late Old Kingdom on (Wildung 1969: 217–21; von Beckerath 1975b; Ritter 1999: 44), and was later renowned for wisdom apart from this teaching. The son for whom he makes the teaching is otherwise unknown:

> Beginning of the teaching
> made by the Patrician and Count,
> the King's son, Hordedef
> for his son, whom he nurtured,
> called Au[t]ibre. (1a–b)

The date of composition is uncertain, perhaps early in the Middle Kingdom since the language appears early (e.g., Lichtheim 1973: 6; Ritter 1999: 46, suggesting end of the 11th Dynasty). The 'Harpist's Song from the Chapel of King Intef', which cites Hordedef, has been used to date the teaching. The song is stated to have originated in the chapel of an 11th (or 17th?) Dynasty king Intef, and so might support a pre-12th Dynasty date for the teaching, but that attribution of the song is probably fictional.

Text: Helck 1984: 1–24 (see also Posener 1977–80: nos. 1396, 1604); *translations*: Brunner 1991b: 101–3; Roccati 1994b: 25–7.
Studies: Parkinson 1991b: no. ii; Posener 1951a: no. 3, 1952b, 1966, 1980b; Ritter 1999; Roccati 1982b.

The Teaching of Ptahhotep

Two distinct versions of this composition are attested from the second half of the 12th Dynasty in P. Prisse probably from Thebes (see above, *Kagemni*) and L1 (= P. BM EA 10371/10435), perhaps also from Thebes (Quirke 1990b: 210). The dating of P. Prisse is disputed, and Eugène Dévaud considered that L1 was the earlier manuscript (1924). Only the version preserved in P. Prisse (P) is complete, while the other (L1) is essentially that found in a late 18th Dynasty papyrus perhaps from Thebes (L2; see above, *The Sporting King*). The existence of two versions need not imply that there was a long period of transmission before the mid-12th Dynasty, and that the text originated in the Old Kingdom. Pascal Vernus' linguistic analysis would place the composition early in the Middle Kingdom (1990b: 185 n.77), and an intertextual relationship with the graffito of Ameny at Wadi Hammamat (temp. Senwosret I) also suggests

---

[21] See **2.2.2**. P. Anastasi I 11.1–2; P. Harris 500 6.6–7; P. Chester Beatty IV vso 3.5; ODeM 1734 l. 5; P. Athens. See Mathieu 1993: 345 n.50.

Appendix 1: Survey of the Middle Kingdom literary corpus 315

an early 12th Dynasty date. Ramessid copies are known from Deir el-Medina (Vernus 1996b; Fischer-Elfert 1997: 18–23).

The teaching is set in the old age of Ptahhotep during the reign of Isesi (c. 2388–56 BCE). Two historical viziers Ptahhotep (I and II) are known from that time; the career of the first would fit the setting more exactly, and he may have been the basis for the character here.[22] In the complete copy (c. 495 verses), there is a narrative prologue, followed by 37 maxims and a reflective epilogue. The text begins:

> The teaching of the Overseer of the City and Vizier Ptahhotep (1–4 [P])

and after the scene-setting prologue the maxims are entitled:

> Beginning of the verses of perfect speech
> spoken by the Patrician and Count,
> the God's father, whom the god loves,
> the eldest King's Own Son,
> the Overseer of the City and Vizier Ptahhotep,
> in teaching the ignorant to be wise,
> and to be the standard of perfect speech,
> good for him who will hear it,
> woeful for him who will transgress it. (42–50 [P])

Text: Žába 1956; *translation*: Parkinson 1999f: 250–72.
Studies: Blumenthal 1987; Brunner, 1980b; Burkard 1977, 1988; Cannuyer 1986; Fecht 1958, 1981, 1986; Fischer-Elfert 1994: 45–7, 1997: 18–23; Goedicke 1967; Lacombe-Unal 1999; Parkinson 1991b: no. iii; Polaček 1974; Posener 1951a: no. 4; Troy 1984; Vernus 1995b, 1996b, 1997, 1999.

The Teaching for Merikare

The body of this text, which is known only from New Kingdom copies, is complete, although the start is extremely fragmentary (c. 390 verses). Provenances include Memphis and Thebes; the earliest manuscript is from the mid-18th Dynasty. The king Merikare named in the title is attested as a historical figure, although his position in the Heracleopolitan dynasties

---

[22] Both of their tombs at Saqqara may show signs of later reverence: PM III², 596–8, 600–5; see, however, Martin-Pardey 1982: 1181; Vernus 1997: 437–8. The actual reign of Isesi produced royal letters inscribed on tombs (e.g., Baines 1997b: 141–2 with refs), perhaps indicating a historical change in writing practices (Posener-Kriéger 1972: 33) that might underlie the presentation of the reign as a literary setting here.

(2080–1987 BCE) is unsure (Vandersleyen 1995: 6–8). The identity of the teacher is uncertain (see López 1973):

> [Beginning of the teaching
> made by the Dual King(?), Khet]y
> for his son, Merikare. (1a–b)

The reading '[Khet]y' is defensible, but an identification with Nebkaure Khety is no more than a plausible hypothesis. The text implies that the author is a successor of a king 'Meri[ib(?)]re' (25i). The date of composition is uncertain: Vernus' linguistic analysis (1990b: 185) assigns it to the 11th or the early 12th Dynasty, while Joachim Quack (1992: 114–36) favours an early 12th Dynasty date. Susanne Bickel (1994: 178–9, 219), by contrast, has suggested a New Kingdom date from a comparison of cosmology with the Coffin Texts; I agree with her observations but suggest that the difference is one of discourses rather than chronology. The poem's stylistically interwoven quality might suggest a date later in the 12th Dynasty than *Amenemhat*.
Text: Helck 1977 and Quack 1992 (cf. Leitz 1996: 134–6); *translation*: Parkinson 1999f: 216–34.
Studies: Aufrère 2000; Blumenthal 1980a; Demedchik 1993; Derchain 1989; Donadoni 1986a; Goedicke 1993; Kammerzell 1997; López 1973; Lorton 1993a, 1993b, 1993c; L. Morenz 1997c; Parkinson 1991b: no. iv; Posener 1950b, 1951a: no. 10, 1962–6, 1980e; Quack 1990, 1992; Rathke-Konrad 1997; Rowinska and Winnicki 1992.

The Teaching of Amenemhat I

The text is complete (*c.* 95 verses), but preserved only in New Kingdom copies from Thebes and Memphis, of which the earliest is from the start of the 18th Dynasty (Gardiner 1935b; Grimal 1995b: 276–7; Guksch 1998). It is entitled:

> Beginning of the teaching
> made by the Person of the Dual King, Sehotepibre,
> Son of Re, Amenemhat, true of voice,
> when he spoke in a revelation
> to his son, the Lord to the Limit. (1a–c)

According to a prayer for the scribe Khety in the Ramessid P. Chester Beatty IV, the teaching was composed by him 'when he (the king) was at rest' (vso 6.14), and therefore has been assigned to the reign of Senwosret I or later. Vernus' linguistic analysis (1990b: 185) places it in the early

12th Dynasty, but Nicolas Grimal (1995b) unconvincingly suggests a date in the 18th Dynasty. Khety is also listed among other sages in the 'Eulogy of Dead Writers' (P. Chester Beatty IV vso 3.6), and P. Athens; he probably does not figure on the 'Daressy Fragment'.
Text: Helck 1969 (see also Goedicke 1988b; López 1978: nos. 57048, 57066, 1980: no. 57126, 1982: no. 57363; Posener 1977–80: nos. 1267–1395); *translation:* Parkinson 1999f: 206–11.
Studies: Blumenthal 1980b, 1984b, 1985; Fischer-Elfert 1984; Foster 1981; Goedicke 1988b; Grimal 1995a, 1995b; Guksch 1998; Konrad 1999; Obsomer 1995: 112–33; Parkinson 1991b: no. v, 2000c; Posener 1951a: no. 23, 1956: 61–86; Thériault 1993; Westendorf 1981.

The Teaching of Duaf's Son Khety

Although the text is complete (*c.* 190 verses), the predominantly Ramessid copies are corrupt, making its interpretation, including that of the protagonist's name, problematic. The earliest copy is from the early 18th Dynasty; provenances include Thebes and Memphis. If the name is read as 'Duaf's son Khety' (Posener 1980a), he may be the same Khety who is acclaimed as the author of *The Teaching of Amenemhat* in P. Chester Beatty IV. Thus, he could have been a historical figure and the actual author of this teaching, which would then date to the early 12th Dynasty (in accordance with Vernus' linguistic analysis: 1990b: 185). Khety, however, could also have been a fictional sage, to whom *Amenemhat* was pseudonymously attributed (see **4.3**, **5.1.2**). He is described simply as 'a man of Sile' (if read thus),[23] a place in the north-eastern frontier of Egypt; this designation is more reminiscent of the later 12th Dynasty (Quirke, pers. comm.). The dating is thus uncertain. The teaching is spoken as Khety takes his son to the school in the Residence:

> Beginning of the teaching
> made by the man of Sile
> called Duaf's son Khety,
> for his son, called Pepy. (1a–b)

The first part comprises a series of mocking descriptions of various professions which advocates the scribal profession, while more general injunctions form a shorter concluding section. Posener's analysis as early 12th Dynasty propaganda to recruit scribes is problematic in terms of method (**1.3**). Hans-Werner Fischer-Elfert also favours an early 12th

---

[23] Burkard 1977: 44–5; for the location of Sile (*ṯrnw*) see Gomaà 1987: 222–4; Vandersleyen 1993. 'A man of the cabin (*ṯrt*)' has also been suggested: Fischer-Elfert 1999: 370 n.8.

Dynasty date (1999: 417–8); it cannot predate the founding of the new capital by Amenemhat I, since the 'Residence' is mentioned (1c and 2e).
Text: Helck 1970a (see also López 1978: nos. 57023, 57082, 1980: no. 57298; Posener 1977–80: nos. 1442–1590). The translation of Roccati (1994b: 79–87) takes into account an important unpublished copy in the Museo Egizio, Turin (see also Roccati 2000). *Translation:* Parkinson 1999f: 275–83.
Studies: von Beckerath, 1983 (esp. 63 n.2); Brunner 1980d; Burkard 1977; Foster 1999; Hoch 1992; Parkinson 1991b: no. vi, 1999e: 49–51; Posener 1951a: no. 22, 1980a; Quack 1990; Seibert 1967; Théodoridès 1958–60; Westendorf 1973.

The 'Loyalist' Teaching

The complete text (*c.* 145 verses) is known only from New Kingdom copies; the earliest dates from the start of the 18th Dynasty. Provenances include Thebes and Deir Rifa. An edited version of the first half occurs on the biographical stela of the King's Sealbearer Sehotepibre from Abydos, of the reign of Amenemhat III (Cairo CG 20538; Lange and Schäfer 1902: pl. 40; Sethe 1928a: 68–9). This part enjoins praise of, and loyalty to, the king from officials, while the second half concerns the individual's responsibility to the rest of society. The name of the protagonist was edited out by Sehotepibre, and is lost in the later copies:

> Beginning of the teaching
> made by the Patrician and Count,
> the God's Father, whom the god loves,
> the Privy Counsellor of the Palace,
> the Head of the Entire Land,
> the Sem-priest and Controller of Every Kilt
> [. . .]
> He speaks a teaching before his children. (1.1–2)

These surviving titles in the later copies are suggestive of a vizier as protagonist. The stela of Sehotepibre was modelled on that of the Vizier Montuhotep (temp. Senwosret I: see Obsomer 1995: 172–89, 225–9), and the teaching Sehotepibre used might have been of a similar date – Montuhotep has even been suggested as the author (Berlev 1976: 325; Posener 1976: 14; Simpson 1991: 337; Fischer-Elfert 1999: 418–20), but there is no specific evidence for this hypothesis. Vernus' linguistic analysis (1990b: 185) favours the earlier date. Oleg Berlev (1981: 15) has suggested an allusion in 5.7 to the name of Senwosret I (*ts-wsrt* = *sn-wsrt*), and compares the text with the graffito of Hor in the Wadi el-Hudi (temp.

Senwosret I; Seyfreid 1984; Obsomer 1995: 630–5; Fischer-Elfert 1999: 399–401, 420). B. U. Schipper (1998) argues that the original text was the short version found on the stela, and that the longer version is a New Kingdom reworking and expansion of the Middle Kingdom original; her redactionalist approach, however, relies on questionable assumptions.
Text: Posener 1976 (see also López 1984: no. 57547); *translation*: Parkinson 1999f: 238–45.
Studies: Berlev 1976, 1981; Chappaz 1982; Fischer-Elfert 1994: 41–4; Parkinson 1991b: no. vii; Posener 1951a: nos 27, 33–4, 1980c; Schipper 1998.

The Teaching of a Man for His Son

The Teaching of a Man is preserved in New Kingdom copies only, and remains incomplete (*c.* 215 verses survive); the earliest manuscript is Second Intermediate Period: provenances include Thebes and Medinet Ghurob. Hans-Werner Fischer-Elfert (1999) has reassembled the text into 24 stanzas, but there is a lacuna of unknown length at the start of stanza 14, and the section his edition terms 'Anhang I' is now known to be part of the teaching, somewhere before stanza 17 (Fischer-Elfert 1998: 91). The title is universalized, alluding to the phrase 'son of a man', that is, 'gentleman':

> Beginning of the teaching
> made by a man for his son. (0.1–2)

The teaching has three major themes: loyalism (1–8); rhetoric and correct behaviour in judicial activities (9–19); and the role of rhetoric in handling underlings and domestic matters (20–4).

The date of composition is uncertain. The early 12th Dynasty has been suggested on the basis of a dubious historical allusion to the death of Senwosret I (3.7; Brunner 1978). Fischer-Elfert (1999: 417–21) associates it with *The Loyalist Teaching* and *Khety*, whereas Vernus (1990b: 186–7) assigns it to the second half of the 12th Dynasty on linguistic grounds.
Text: Fischer-Elfert 1998; 1999.
Studies: Burkard 1977; Fischer-Elfert 1988, 1991; Foster 1986; Gaál 1984; Helck 1984: 25–72; Parkinson 1991b: no. viii; Posener 1951a: nos 6, 26, 1980d, 1985, 1987b.

A.2 LOST WORKS AND ATTRIBUTIONS

> Papyri! Insects gnaw them. Time corrodes . . .
> T. Harrison, *The Trackers of Oxyrhynchus* (1988),
> Grenfell's opening speech

The sources for Middle Kingdom literature are partial and fragmentary: only 21 of the 38 texts listed here are known from Middle Kingdom manuscripts, and only nine texts are substantially complete. New investigations on sites and in museums reveal new manuscripts, and catalogues of Ramessid ostraca produce significant numbers of unidentified literary fragments. Only an infinitesimal proportion of the papyri that once existed have survived (e.g., Posener 1962: 633–4; L. Morenz 1996: 13). In addition to these largely fragmentary preserved texts, further apparently lost works and unknown protagonists are alluded to in other sources (see **2.2.2** for details). The sages listed in P. Athens may include protagonists and 'authors' of lost texts. Eight 'sages' (*rḫ-ḫt*) are mentioned in the Ramessid 'Eulogy of Dead Writers' of P. Chester Beatty IV, who are the fictional authors of wisdom texts (both didactic and reflective). Although these works are the best preserved genres, three names, whose compositions are unattested, feature in the list. Thus nearly 40 per cent of the supposed literature alluded to in this eulogy has not survived. I discuss these names below:

1. Imhotep (Posener 1951a: no. 1)

Imhotep is paired with Hordedef (vso 3.5). He was perhaps of sufficient cultural fame for his wisdom to be included without being the 'author' of a specific text (Fischer-Elfert 1996a: 509). The same factor is sufficient to explain his presence on the 'Daressy Fragment', but in the 'Harpist's Song from the Chapel of King Intef' and the song in the tomb of Amenpahapy there are more specific-sounding references. He is also included in the list of P. Athens.

2. Kaires (Posener 1951a: no. 5)

Kaires (*k3-jr-s(w)*) is paired with Ptahhotep (vso 3.7), and his name has an Old Kingdom form. He is presumably identical with the Vizier Kaires(u) shown on the 'Daressy Fragment'. The suggestion that Kaires is the 'author' of *The Teaching for Kagemni* is plausible (Posener 1951a: no. 5). No historical vizier Kaires is known from the Old Kingdom, although the title Vizier may be a later fictional attribution. Elmar Edel noted the possibility of identifying Kaires with the Vizier *k3jj* from the end of the 5th Dynasty (1953: 224–5; cf. PM III², 479). A tomb at Saqqara belongs to a 5th/6th Dynasty *k3-jr* of unknown rank (PM III², 631–2), and a 5th–

Appendix 1: Survey of the Middle Kingdom literary corpus 321

6th Dynasty false door with the name *k3-jr-s(w)* survives from Mit–Rahina (Malek 1992: 61, 64) whose fragmentary titles seem unlikely to belong to a vizier.

3. Ptahemdjehuti (Posener 1951a: no. 28)
Ptahemdjehuti is paired with Khakheperreseneb (vso 3.6), which might imply that he was considered to be a figure from the Middle Kingdom. Dietrich Wildung (1977: 29) suggests that he may correspond to a Nakhtdjehuty in the 'Daressy Fragment'. Nothing else is known about him, although he might be associated with one of the surviving wisdom texts which lack the name of a protagonist; Posener (1976: 14 n.11) tentatively suggested *The Loyalist Teaching* as a possibility. The name is otherwise unattested, although its form can be paralleled in the Middle Kingdom (e.g., *wsjr-m-rˁ*: Ranke, *PN* I, 84 no. 25). He may be a Ramessid fiction.

In addition, *The Teaching for Merikare* states that 'King Khety ordained as a teacher (*sb3w*) that . . .' (39a). A reference to a lost work or works has been seen in this and in an earlier reference to a 'prophecy (*sr*) of the Residence' (26d; Posener 1951a: no. 9; Fecht 1972: 172–86; Fischer-Elfert 1996a: 510). Gerhard Fecht proposes that these were incorporated into *Ipuur* (see Quack 1992: 87–8), but it is unlikely that these are references to actual literary compositions.

Appendix 2: Kemit

Kemit is a letter used in scribal training during the New Kingdom that has been problematic for modern classification.[1] The complete text (*c.* 65 verses) is preserved largely in hundreds of copies from Deir el-Medina. Middle Kingdom manuscripts include a fragmentary papyrus from el-Lahun from the second half of the 12th Dynasty (P. UCL 32271B rto), and possibly two writing boards. Other writing boards date from the late Second Intermediate Period and start of the 18th Dynasty.[2]

The introductory formulae of the letter are similar to those of the Heqanakht letters from the beginning of the 12th Dynasty – as against the different formulae of the later el-Lahun letters. Mention is also made of the 'Residence' (17.3), suggesting a 12th Dynasty date, as does Vernus' linguistic analysis (1990b: 185). A date at the end of Amenemhat I's reign or during that of Senwosret I is most likely. The designation *Kemit* is known from a citation in *The Teaching of Khety* (2d–e); the term can be translated 'Compendium'.[3] The designation may also occur in a scribal eulogy of P. Chester Beatty IV:

> they have all made my name blessed beside *Kemi⟨t⟩*.[4]   (vso 6.11)

Kemit may be: 1) a Middle Kingdom teaching text about teaching; 2) a Middle Kingdom literary text that was taken over for use in teaching; 3) a Middle Kingdom non-literary text that was taken over for use in teaching

---

[1] E.g., Parkinson 1996b: 307–8. *Text:* Posener 1951c: pl. 1–21 (see also López 1978: nos. 57054, 57060, 1980: nos. 57286, 57307–8, 1982: no. 57448, 1984: nos. 57545–6, 57549, 57551–4; Posener 1977–80: nos. 1428, 1639); *translation:* Wente 1990: 15–16. *Studies:* Barbotin 1997; Barta 1978; Brunner 1980a; Chappaz 1989; Dakin 1992: 465–71; Kaplony 1974; Parkinson 1991b: no. xxviii; Posener 1951a: no. 13.

[2] P UCL 32271B rto: unpublished (Quirke 1996b: 381). Middle Kingdom writing boards: 1) CG 25367 (Vernus 1984: 706 no. 5), temp. Senwosret I–II (cf. Obsomer 1995: 212–4); the identification as *Kemit* is not certain, since only epistolary formulae survive, to judge by the published photograph. 2) Fragments from the New Kingdom tomb of Puiemre (TT 39), in an apparently Middle Kingdom hand (Posener 1948: 42; N. Davies 1923: pl. lxxixa; not in Vernus 1984); the date is uncertain. Later writing boards include: Louvre AF 497 (Barbotin 1997); Tablet Carnarvon III (Vernus 1984: 706 no. 9; Carnarvon and Carter 1912: 90–3).

[3] Kaplony 1974: 186–90. Or 'Fulfilment' referring to a theme of the composition; however, thematic titles of literary texts are otherwise unattested.

[4] Schott 1990: 378; Posener 1948: 49; alternate reading: Gardiner 1935a: 43 n.7.

in the Middle and New Kingdom. Jean-Luc Chappaz's survey of the text (1989) reveals how suitable it would be for training in signs, words and grammar. The extant copies on writing boards show that it was used as a scribal exercise by the start of the New Kingdom, while the citation of *Kemit* in *Khety* suggests a use in education by the early 12th Dynasty, provided that *Khety* is dated thus. The title 'Compendium' is also suggestive of this, although it could have been added when the text was adapted. The late 12th Dynasty copy on papyrus (P. UCL 32271B) is not necessarily one made during training, but could be an advanced scribe's copy or a master-copy.

The script used in copies ranges from a Middle Kingdom style hieratic, through linear hieroglyphs suitable for religious texts (see **4.2**), to fully drawn hieroglyphs. The ruled lines flanking the lines of text are typical of manuscripts in linear hieroglyphs and in hieratic imitations of inscriptional forms (as in a hieratic stela, temp. Senwosret I; Simpson 1958b, 1961). Other texts, including model letters, are copied on ostraca in this script (Quirke 1996b: 381). The script embodies a continuous textual tradition going back to a period when its forms were very close to the cursive hieratic of literary manuscripts and letters. A possible explanation for this continuity is that the text was employed as a training text when the linear script was still in wide use; Hans-Werner Fischer-Elfert notes that such old-fashioned hands were used for administrative documents in provincial centres such as Elephantine well into the late 12th Dynasty (pers. comm.). All these factors suggest that classification (1) above is the most plausible analysis.

Although the letter consists of a selection of epistolary and didactic formulae, it also coheres into a first-person narrative concerning an errant son called Au. The name of the sender is not given. The formulae conclude with the statement that:

> As for these documents, I have sent a messenger to your Person about it.
> Au will act as you wish (?). (5.2–4)

The writer then urges his lord to:

> Sweeten this heart of mine, (and) make Au return! (6.2–3)

From this indirect narration the audience can gather that the writer is a servant who has been sent to find a runaway son, Au. This motif is paralleled in the Ramessid *Letter of Menna* from Deir el-Medina (see **4.3**), which alludes to several Middle Kingdom texts. The narrator tells how he has found Au enjoying a luxurious lifestyle (6.4–7.4), describing him as 'a youth to whom the musician/harem woman looks' (7.4). Even she is urging him to return to his weeping wife (8): she may feature as an indication of his irresponsible luxury. The rest of this section (9–12) is addressed not to the lord, but to a woman who is presumably Au's wife (Wente, however, interprets this section as Au's letter to his wife: 1990: 16). The woman is urged to 'come north' with a 'narration' (9.1) of a similar situation experienced by the writer: his friends once found him in a reverie (10.1–3), having 'returned from the city of my sister (i.e., lover)' (11.1). This section seems to be an anecdote of how, after the sender had renounced pleasure, he returned to his own city and family life (11.2–4, 12.1–5). It is presumably an encouragement to the wife to reclaim the errant Au.

A second more discursive narration begins at 13.1:

I shall repeat what my Overseer said, for the sake of restraining desire.
(13.1–2)

What follows is a self-eulogy and injunctions in favour of wisdom and scribedom. This is perhaps the advice that the addressee will repeat to Au. A son, possibly a metaphor for a pupil, is the ideal means of transmitting learning:

O open your book! Make yourself a son who is taught according to books!
(15.1; repeated in 17.2)

The text concludes with the verses about the advantages of being a scribe that are cited in *Khety*.

The text is difficult to assess because of obscurities and corruptions, but it gives an impression of general disjunction between sections, suggesting that literary coherence was not a prime aim in composition (e.g., Hayes 1948: 10), while the indirectness of the narrative recalls the techniques found in actual letters, where the background is implied rather than a subject for exposition.

The text exemplifies and advocates the advantages of being a wise literate man, constituting an epistolary narrative with discursive and didactic elements. The epistolary form occurs in much later tales such as *The Tale of Woe* (Caminos 1977, 1980; Moers 1995), which is an anonymous letter like *Kemit*. Another later parallel is provided by the Ramessid Late Egyptian Miscellanies, often entitled 'Letter-teachings' (*sbȝjjt-šʿt*: Schott 1990: 303–4 nos 1398–1400), a description that would match *Kemit* closely. The most important example of this genre is *The Satiric Letter* of P. Anastasi I, which incorporates various 'scholastic' genres (Fischer-Elfert 1986a: 271–6; 289–90), and which Orly Goldwasser (1991) views as the climax of a canonization of letter-writing into literature.

Appendix 2: Kemit

The closest contemporaneous parallels are model letters which are known from the early Middle Kingdom[5] and from el-Lahun. P. Lahun III.2 (= P. UCL 32196) is a roll on which nine letters were copied one after the other (Griffith 1898: pl. 27–8; Wente 1990: 69–70). At least some were composed as models rather than actual letters: the personal names are stereotypical. *Kemit* is distinctive and a clearly separate composition, but it could have been written as an elaborate model letter intended to teach scribes a range of writing's aspects (literacy and literature), since it also includes non-epistolary formulae from biographies (particulary in the concluding sections: 11.1, 12.1–3) and features common to the literary corpus.

---

[5] Cairo CG 25367 (Vernus 1984: 706 no. 5), MMA 28.9.4 (James 1962: 98–101, pl. 30; Wente 1990: 66–7), MMA 26.3.277 AB (James 1962: 97–8, pl. 29). A model letter on an ostracon is Cairo JE 49911 (James 1962: 78–9, pl. 20). A letter on a jar stand from Nag el-Deir may be a model letter or a letter to the dead (Simpson 1981).

References

EGYPTIAN COMPOSITIONS

In references, short titles are used for major literary compositions and frequently cited texts; they are listed alphabetically here by short title, with full titles and references to the standard text editions. Citations of the texts are according to the conventions of the editions listed here. Fuller bibliographies for literary texts are supplied in Appendix 1.

Amenemhat	*The Teaching of Amenemhat*: Helck 1969; some additional manuscripts in Goedicke 1988b
Annals of Amenemhat II	Altenmüller and Moussa 1991: folding plate
Building Inscription of Senwosret I	de Buck 1938b: 49–51. See also Shirun-Grumach 1993: 149–53
Cairo Mythological Tale	Unpublished: see **A.1.1**
Cheops' Court	*The Tale of King Cheops' Court*: Blackman 1988
'Daressy Fragment'	Wildung 1984: 14, fig. 4
Elephantine inscription of Senwosret I	Schenkel 1975b: 111–22; new arrangement of fragments with line numbering: 1999
Eloquent Peasant	*The Tale of the Eloquent Peasant*: Parkinson 1991c (new line numbering)
'Eulogy of Dead Writers'	Gardiner 1935a: pl. 18–20
Fishing and Fowling	*The Account of the Pleasures of Fishing and Fowling*: Caminos 1956: pl. 1–7
Fowler	*The Discourse of the Fowler*: Posener 1969: 103 (and unpublished; see **A.1.2**)
'Harpist's Song from the Chapel of Intef'	M. V. Fox 1985: 378–80
Hay	*The Tale of Hay*: Griffith 1898: pl. 4

Herdsman	*The Tale of the Herdsman*: Gardiner 1909b: pl. 16–17
Hordedef	*The Teaching of Hordedef*: Helck 1984: 1–24
Horus and Seth	*The Tale of Horus and Seth*: Griffiths 1889: pl. 3
Hymns to Senwosret III	Griffiths 1889: pl. 1–2
Ipuur	*The Dialogue of Ipuur and the Lord to the Limit*: Gardiner 1909a: pl. 1–16; new readings in Fecht 1972
Kagemni	*The Teaching for Kagemni*: Gardiner 1946: pl. 14
Kemit	Posener 1951c: pl. 1–21. (Cited by phrase number)
Khakheperreseneb	*The Words of Khakheperreseneb*: Parkinson 1997b: 56–60
Khety	*The Teaching of Khety*: Helck 1970a
Loyalist	*The Loyalist Teaching*: Posener 1976: 53–139
A Man	*The Teaching of a Man*: Fischer-Elfert 1999
A Man and His Ba	*The Dialogue of a Man and His Ba*: Faulkner 1956: 22–6 (photographs: Goedicke 1970a: pl. 1–10)
Merikare	*The Teaching for King Merikare*: Helck 1977; also Quack 1992. Concordance to line numbers: Blumenthal 1983: 238–9
Neferkare and Sasenet	*The Tale of King Neferkare and General Sasenet*: Posener 1957
Neferti	*The Words of Neferti*: Helck 1970b
Nefer[. . .]	*The Tale of Nefer[. . .]*: unpublished; see **A.1.1**
Nileflood Hymn	van der Plas 1986
Oxford Wisdom Text	Barns 1968: pl. 10–11
P. Lythgoe	*The Tale of P. Lythgoe*: Simpson 1960: pl. 15a
Ptahhotep	*The Teaching of Ptahhotep*: Žába 1956
Renseneb	*The Discourse of Renseneb*: Posener 1969: 103

Sasobek	*The Discourse of Sasobek*: Barns 1956: pl. 1–6
Satiric Letter	*The Satiric Letter* of P. Anastari I: Fischer-Elfert 1992a
Sinuhe	*The Tale of Sinuhe*: Koch 1990
Sporting King	*The Account of the Sporting King*: Caminos 1956: pl. 8–16
The Shipwrecked Sailor	*The Tale of the Shipwrecked Sailor*: Blackman 1932: 41–8
Tod inscription of Senwosret I	Barbotin and Clère 1991: fig. 3

BIBLIOGRAPHY

Adams, W. Y. 1997, 'Anthropology and Egyptology: Divorce and Remarriage?' In Lustig 1997: 25–32.

el-Adly, Sanaa Abd El-Azim 1984, 'Die Berliner Lederhandschrift (pBerlin 3029)', *WdO* 15, 6–18.

el-Aguizy, O. 1997, 'The Particle k_3 and Other Related Problematic Passages in Papyrus Westcar', *BIFAO* 97, 157–63.

Albright, D. 1992, *W. B. Yeats: The Poems*. Everyman's Library. London: J. M. Dent and Sons.

Allam, S. 1986, 'Sinuhe's Foreign Wife (Reconsidered)', *Discussions in Egyptology* 4, 15–16.

——, 2000, 'Social and Legal Aspects Regarding the "Trader from the Oasis"'. In Gnirs 2000a: 83–92.

Allberry, C. R. C. 1938, *A Manichaean Psalm-Book* 2. Stuttgart: Kohlhammer.

Allen, J. P. 1994, 'Colloquial Middle Egyptian: Some Observations on the Language of Heqa-nakht', *LingAeg* 4, 1–12.

——, forthcoming, 'The High Officials of the Early Middle Kingdom'.

Allen, T. G. 1974, *The Book of the Dead or Going Forth by Day: Ideas of the Ancient Egyptians Concerning the Hereafter as Expressed in Their Own Terms*. SAOC 37.

Alpers, P. 1979, *The Singer of the Eclogues: A Study of Virgilian Pastoral*. Berkeley: University of California Press.

Altenmüller, B. 1975, *Synkretismus in der Sargtexten*. GOF IV. 7.

Altenmüller, H. 1970, 'Die Stellung der Königsmutter Chentkaus beim Übergang von der 4. zur 5. Dynastie', *CdE* 45/89, 223–35.

——, 1980, 'Illustration', *LÄ* III, 137–40.
——, 1989, 'Die "Geschichte des Schiffbrüchigen" – ein Aufruf zum Loyalismus?' In H. Altenmüller and R. Germer (eds), *Miscellanea Aegyptologica: Wolfgang Helck zum 75. Geburtstag*, 7–21. Hamburg: Archäologisches Institut der Universität.
——, 1992, 'Die Pyramidennamen der frühen 12. Dynastie'. In U. Luft (ed.), *The Intellectual Heritage of Egypt: Studies Presented to László Kákosy by Friends and Colleagues on the Occasion of His 60th Birthday*, 33–42. StudAeg 14.
——, 1996, 'Geburtsschrein und Geburtshaus'. In Manuelian 1996: 27–37.
Altenmüller, H., and Moussa, A. M. 1991, 'Die Inschrift Amenemhets II. aus dem Ptah-Tempel von Memphis: Ein Vorbericht', *SAK* 18, 1–48.
Althusser, L. 1971, *Lenin and Philosophy and Other Essays* (B. Brewster, trans.). London: New Left Books.
Altieri, C. 1978, 'The Hermeneutics of Literary Indeterminacy: A Dissent from the New Orthodoxy', *New Literary History* 10, 71–99.
Andrássy, P. 1998, 'Überlegungen zur Bezeichnung *s n niwt tn* "Mann dieser Stadt" und zur Sozialstruktur des Mittleren Reiches'. In Eyre 1998: 49–58.
Arac, J. 1995, 'What Is the History of Literature?' In Brown 1995: 23–33.
Arnold, Dieter 1976, *Gräber des Alten und Mittleren Reiches in El-Tarif*. AV 17.
——, 1992, *The Pyramid Complex of Senwosret I: The South Cemeteries of Lisht* III. Metropolitan Museum of Art Egyptian Expedition 25. New York: Metropolitan Museum of Art.
Arnold, Dorothea 1991, 'Amenemhat I and the Early Twelfth Dynasty at Thebes', *Metropolitan Museum Journal* 26, 5–48.
Arnold, F. 1989, 'A Study of Egyptian Domestic Buildings', *VA* 5, 75–93.
——, 1990, *The Control Notes and Team Marks: The South Cemeteries of Lisht* II. Metropolitan Museum of Art Egyptian Expedition 23. New York: Metropolitan Museum of Art.
——, 1991, 'The High Stewards of the Early Middle Kingdom', *GM* 122, 7–14.
Assmann, A. 1980, *Die Legitimität der Fiktion: Ein Beitrag zur Geschichte der literarischen Kommunikation*. Theorie und Geschichte der Literatur und der schönen Künste 55. Munich: Wilhelm Fink.
——, 1983, 'Schriftliche Folklore: Zur Entstehung und Funktion eines Überlieferungstyps'. In A. Assmann *et al.* 1983: 175–93.
——, 1996, 'The Curse and Blessing of Babel: Or, Looking Back on Universalisms'. In Budick and Iser 1996: 85–100.
——, 1999, 'The History of the Text before the Era of Literature: Three Comments'. In Moers 1999a: 83–90.

Assmann, A. et al. (eds) 1983, *Schrift und Gedächtnis: Beiträge zur Archäologie der literarischen Kommunikation*. Munich: Wilhelm Fink.

Assmann, J. 1970, *Der König als Sonnenpriester: Ein kosmographischer Begleittext zur kultischen Sonnenhymnik in thebanischen Tempeln und Gräbern*. ADAIK 7.

——, 1974, 'Der literarische Text im alten Ägypten: Versuch einer Begriffbestimmung', *OLZ* 69, 117–26.

——, 1975a, *Zeit und Ewigkeit im alten Ägypten: Ein Beitrag zur Geschichte der Ewigkeit*. AHAW, 1.

——, 1975b, 'Aretalogien', *LÄ* I, 425–34.

——, 1977a, 'Eulogie, Königs-', *LÄ* II, 40–6.

——, 1977b, 'Harfnerlieder', *LÄ* II, 972–82.

——, 1977c, 'Die Verborgenheit des Mythos in Ägypten', *GM* 25, 7–43.

——, 1977d, 'Fest des Augenblicks – Verheissung der Dauer. Die Kontroverse der ägyptischen Harfnerlieder'. In J. Assmann *et al.* 1977: 55–84.

——, 1982a, 'Parallelismus membrorum', *LÄ* IV, 900–10.

——, 1982b, 'Persönlichkeitsbegriff und -bewusstsein', *LÄ* IV, 963–78.

——, 1983a, 'Königsdogma und Heilserwartung: Politische und kultische Chaosbeschreibungen in ägyptischen Texten'. In D. Hellholm (ed.), *Apocalypticism in the Mediterranean World and the Near East*, 345–77. Tübingen: J. C. B. Mohr (Paul Siebeck).

——, 1983b, 'Die Rubren in der Überlieferung der Sinuhe-Erzählung'. In M. Görg (ed.), *Fontes atque Pontes: Eine Festgabe für Hellmut Brunner*, 18–41. ÄAT 5.

——, 1983c, 'Schrift, Tod und Identität: Das Grab als Vorschule der Literatur im alten Ägypten'. In Aleida Assmann *et al.* 1983: 64–93.

——, 1984a, *Ägypten: Theologie und Frömmigkeit einer frühen Hochkultur*. Stuttgart: W. Kohlhammer.

——, 1984b, 'Reden und Schweigen', *LÄ* V, 195–201.

——, 1984c, 'Schöpfung', *LÄ* V, 677–90.

——, 1984d, 'Vergeltung und Erinnerung'. In Junge 1984c: 687–701.

——, 1985, 'Gibt es eine "Klassik" in der ägyptischen Literaturgeschichte? Ein Beitrag zur Geistesgeschichte der Ramessidenzeit', *ZDMG Suppl.* 6, 35–52.

——, 1989a, 'State and Religion in the New Kingdom'. In J. P. Allen *et al.*, *Religion and Philosophy in Ancient Egypt*, 55–88. Yale Egyptological Studies 3. New Haven: Yale Seminar.

——, 1989b, *Maât: L'Égypte pharaonique et l'idée de justice sociale*. Conférences, essais et leçons du Collège de France. Paris: Juillard.

——, 1990, *Ma'at: Gerechtigkeit und Unsterblichkeit im Alten Ägypten*. Munich: C. H. Beck.

——, 1991, *Stein und Zeit: Mensch und Gesellschaft im Alten Ägypten*. Munich: Wilhelm Fink.
——, 1992a, 'Egyptian Literature'. In D. N. Freedman *et al.* (eds), *The Anchor Bible Dictionary* II, 378–90. New York and London: Doubleday.
——, 1992b, *Das kulturelle Gedächtnis: Schrift, Erinnerung und politische Identität in frühen Hochkulturen*. Munich: C. H. Beck.
——, 1993, 'Literatur und Karneval im Alten Ägypten'. In S. Döpp (ed.), *Karnevaleske Phänomene in antiken und nachantiken Kulturen und Literaturen*, 31–57. Stätten und Formen der Kommunikation im Altertum 1. Trier: WVT Wissenschaftlicher Verlag.
——, 1994a, 'Maat und die gespaltene Welt oder: Ägyptertum und Pessimismus', *GM* 140, 93–100.
——, 1994b, 'Ancient Egypt and the Materiality of the Sign'. In H. U. Gumbrecht and K. L. Pfeiffer, *Materialities of Communication*, 15–31. Stanford: Stanford University Press.
——, 1995, *Egyptian Solar Religion in The New Kingdom: Re, Amun and the Crisis of Polytheism* (A. Alcock, trans.). Studies in Egyptology. London and New York: Kegan Paul International.
——, 1996a, *Ägypten: Eine Sinngeschichte*. München, Wien: Carl Hanser Verlag.
——, 1996b, 'Kulturelle und literarische Texte'. In Loprieno 1996a: 59–82.
——, 1996c, 'Der literarische Aspekt des Ägyptischen Grabes und seine Funktion im Rahmen des "monumentalen Diskurses"'. In Loprieno 1996a: 97–104.
——, 1996d, 'Spruch 62 der Sargtexte und die ägyptischen Totenliturgien'. In Willems 1996a: 17–30.
——, 1996e, 'Preservation and Presentation of Self in Ancient Egyptian Portraiture'. In Manuelian 1996: 55–81.
——, 1999a, 'Cultural and Literary Texts'. In Moers 1999a: 1–15.
——, 1999b, 'Literatur zwischen Kult und Politik: Zur Geschichte des Textes vor dem Zeitalter der Literatur'. In J. Assmann and Blumenthal 1999: 3–22.
——, 1999c [1975], *Ägyptische Hymnen und Gebete*. OBO.
Assmann, J., and Assmann, A. 1983, 'Schrift und Gedächtnis'. In A. Assmann *et al.* 1983: 265–84.
Assmann, J., and Blumenthal, E. (eds) 1999, *Literatur und Politik im pharaonischen und ptolemäischen Ägypten: Vorträge der Tagung zum Gedenken an Georges Posener 5.–10. September 1996 in Leipzig*. BdE 127.
Assmann, J., Feucht, E. and Grieshammer, R. (eds) 1977, *Fragen an die altägyptische Literatur: Studien zum Gedenken an Eberhard Otto*. Wiesbaden: Dr. Ludwig Reichert.

Auden, W. H. (E. Mendelson, ed.) 1991, *Collected Poems*. London: Faber and Faber.

Aufrère, S. 1991, *L'Univers minéral dans la pensée égyptienne* I: *Le Monde des déserts, des mines et des carrières. L'Offrande des métaux et des pierres et le remplissage de l'Oeil-Oudjat. Les Divinités de l'univers minéral dans la mentalité et la religion des anciens Égyptiens*. BdE 105/1.

———, 1998, 'Les Anciens Égyptiens et leur notion de l'antiquité: Une quête archéologique et historiographique du passé', *Méditerranées* 17, 11–55.

———, 2000, 'Une vision en filigrane de la Première Période Intermédiaire: À travers l'*Enseignement à Mérykarê*', *Égypte, Afrique et Orient* 19, 3–7.

Ayad, M. 1996 'Nemty-Nakht's Warning to the Peasant', *GM* 152, 9–10.

Badawy, A. 1961, 'Two Passages from Ancient Egyptian Literary Texts Reinterpreted', *ZÄS* 86, 144–5.

Bagnall, R. S. 1995, *Reading Papyri, Writing Ancient History. Approaching the Ancient World*. London and New York: Routledge.

Baines, J. 1982, 'Interpreting Sinuhe', *JEA* 68, 31–44.

———, 1983, 'Literacy and Ancient Egyptian Society', *Man* (n.s.) 18, 572–99.

———, 1984, 'Schreiben', *LÄ* V, 693–8.

———, 1985, *Fecundity Figures: Egyptian Personification and the Iconology of a Genre*. Warminster: Aris and Phillips. Chicago: Bolchazy-Carducci.

———, 1986, 'The Stela of Emhab: Innovation, Tradition, Hierarchy', *JEA* 72, 41–53.

———, 1987, 'The Stela of Khusobek: Private and Royal Military Narrative and Values'. In Osing and Dreyer 1987: 43–61.

———, 1988, 'An Abydos List of Gods and an Old Kingdom Use of Texts'. In J. Baines *et al.* (eds), *Pyramid Studies and Other Essays Presented to I. E. S. Edwards*, 124–33. Occasional Publications 7. London: Egypt Exploration Society.

———, 1989, 'Ancient Egyptian Concepts and Uses of the Past: 3rd–2nd Millennium Evidence BC'. In R. Layton (ed.), *Who Needs the Past? Indigenous Values and Archaeology*, 131–49. London: Unwin Hyman.

———, 1990a, 'Interpreting the Story of the Shipwrecked Sailor', *JEA* 76, 55–72.

———, 1990b, 'Restricted Knowledge, Hierarchy, and Decorum: Modern Perceptions and Ancient Institutions', *JARCE* 27, 1–23.

———, 1991a, 'Society, Morality, and Religious Practice'. In B. E. Shafer (ed.), *Religion in Ancient Egypt: Gods, Myths and Personal Practice*, 123–200. Ithaca and London: Cornell University Press.

———, 1991b, 'Egyptian Myth and Discourse: Myth, Gods, and the Early Written and Iconographic Record', *JNES* 50, 81–105.

——, 1994a, 'On the Status and Purposes of Ancient Egyptian Art', *Cambridge Archaeological Journal* 4, 67–94.
——, 1994b, 'Contexts of Fate: Literature and Practical Religion'. In C. J. Eyre *et al.* (eds), *The Unbroken Reed: Studies in the Culture and Heritage of Ancient Egypt in Honour of A. F. Shore*, 35–52. Occasional Publications 11. London: Egypt Exploration Society.
——, 1996a, 'Classicism and Modernism in the Literature of the New Kingdom'. In Loprieno 1996a: 157–74.
——, 1996b, 'Myth and Literature'. In Loprieno 1996a: 361–77.
——, 1996c, 'Contextualizing Egyptian Representations of Society and Ethnicity'. In Cooper and Schwartz 1996: 339–84.
——, 1997a, 'Temples as Symbols, Guarantors, and Participants in Egyptian Civilisation'. In S. Quirke (ed.), *The Temple in Ancient Egypt: New Discoveries and Recent Research*, 216–41. London: British Museum Press.
——, 1997b, 'Kingship Before Literature: The World of the King in the Old Kingdom'. In R. Gundlach and C. Raedler (eds), *Selbstverständnis und Realität: Akten des Symposiums zur ägyptischen Königsideologie in Mainz 15. – 17.6.1995*, 125–74. ÄAT 36,1.
——, 1999a, 'Prehistories of Literature: Performance, Fiction, Myth'. In Moers 1999a: 17–41.
——, 1999b, 'Forerunners of Narrative Biographies'. In A. Leahy and J. Tait (eds), *Studies on Ancient Egypt in Honour of H. S. Smith*, 23–37. Occasional Publications 13. London: Egypt Exploration Society.
——, in press, 'Research on Egyptian Literature: Background, Definitions, Prospects'. In Proceedings of the 8th International Congress of Egyptologists. Cairo: American University in Cairo Press.
——, in preparation, 'A Hunting Party under Amenemhat II: On the Evolution, Purpose, and Form of Annals'.
Baines, J., and Eyre, C. J. 1983, 'Four Notes on Literacy', *GM* 61, 65–96.
Baines, J., and Lacovara, P. 2002, 'Burial and the Dead in Ancient Egyptian Society: Respect, Formalism, Neglect', *Journal of Social Archaeology* 2, 5–36.
Bakhtin, M. M., and Medvedev, P. N. 1978, *The Formal Method in Literary Scholarship*. Baltimore: Johns Hopkins University Press.
Barbotin, C. 1997, 'Une nouvelle attestation de *Kémit*', *RdE* 48, 247–50.
Barbotin, C., and Clère, J.-J. 1991, 'L'Inscription de Sésostris Ier à Tôd', *BIFAO* 91, 1–32.
Barchiesi, A. 1997, 'Virgilian Narrative: Ecphrasis'. In Martindale 1997a: 271–81.
Barns, J. W. B. 1952, *The Ashmolean Ostracon of Sinuhe*. London: Oxford University Press for Griffith Institute.
——, 1956, *Five Ramesseum Papyri*. Oxford: Oxford University Press.

Barns, J. W. B. 1967, 'Sinuhe's Message to the King: A Reply to a Recent Article', *JEA* 53, 6–14.
——, 1968, 'A New Wisdom Text from a Writing Board in Oxford', *JEA* 54, 71–6.
——, 1972, 'Some Readings and Interpretations in Sundry Egyptian Texts', *JEA* 58, 159–66.
Barocas, C. 1978, *L'antico Egitto: ideologia e lavoro nella terra dei faraoni*. Rome: Newton Compton.
——, 1988, 'Les Contes du papyrus Westcar', *SAK Beiheft* 3, 122–9.
Barta, W. 1969, *Das Gespräch eines Mannes mit seinem BA (Papyrus Berlin 3024)*. MÄS 18.
——, 1974a, 'Das Gespräch des Ipuwer mit dem Schöpfergott', *SAK* 1, 19–33.
——, 1974b, 'Der Terminus *twt* auf den Grenzstelen Sesostris' III in Nubien'. In W. Müller (ed.), *Festschrift zum 150jährigen Bestehen des Berliner Ägyptischen Museums*, 51–4. Staatliche Museen zu Berlin, Mitteilungen aus der ägyptischen Sammlung 8. Berlin: Akademie.
——, 1978, 'Das Schulbuch Kemit', *ZÄS* 105, 6–14.
——, 1980, 'Lehre für Kagemni', *LÄ* III, 980–2.
——, 1990, 'Der "Vorwurf an Gott" in der Lebensgeschichte des Sinuhe'. In B. Schmitz and A. Eggebrecht (eds), *Festschrift Jürgen von Beckerath: Zum 70. Geburtstag am 19. Februar 1990*, 21–7. HÄB 30.
Barthes, R. 1975 [1970], *S/Z* (R. Miller, trans.). London: Jonathan Cape.
Batstone, W. 1997, 'Virgilian Didaxis: Value and Meaning in the *Georgics*'. In Martindale 1997a: 125–44.
Baud, M. 1998, 'Une épithète de Rêdjedef et la prétendue tyrannie de Chéops: Études sur la statuaire de Rêdjedef, II', *BIFAO* 98, 15–30.
Baud, M., and Dobrev, V. 1995, 'De nouvelles annales de l'Ancien Empire égyptien: Une "Pierre de Palerme" pour la VIᵉ dynastie', *BIFAO* 95, 23–92.
——, 1997, 'Le Verso des annales de la VIᵉ dynastie: Pierre de Saqqara-Sud', *BIFAO* 97, 35–42.
Baxandall, M. 1988 [1972], *Painting and Experience in Fifteenth-Century Italy: A Primer in the Social History of Pictorial Style*. Oxford and New York: Oxford University Press.
Beardsley, M. C. 1958, *Aesthetics: Problems in the Philosophy of Criticism*. New York: Harcourt, Brace and Co.
Beckerath, J. von 1975a, 'Baef-Re', *LÄ* I, 600.
——, 1975b, 'Djedefhor', *LÄ* I, 1099.
——, 1983, 'Ostrakon München AS 396', *SAK* 10, 63–9.
——, 1992, 'Zur Geschichte von Chonsuemḥab und dem Geist', *ZÄS* 119, 90–107.

Behrens, P. 1981, 'Sinuhe B 134 ff oder die Psychologie eines Zweikampfes', *GM* 44, 7–11.
Berg, D. 1984, 'Note on Sinuhe B 5–7', *GM* 79, 11–13.
——, 1990, 'Syntax, Semantics and Physics: The Shipwrecked Sailor's Fire', *JEA* 76, 168–70.
Berger, Peter L. 1973, *The Social Reality of Religion*. Harmondsworth: Penguin [1967: *The Sacred Canopy*].
Berlev, O. D. 1976, review of Simpson 1974, *BiOr* 33, 324–6.
——, 1981, review of Posener 1976, *OLZ* 76, 14–15.
——, 1987, 'The Date of the "Eloquent Peasant"'. In Osing and Dreyer 1987: 78–83.
Berlin, A. 1996, 'A Search for a New Biblical Hermeneutics: Preliminary Observations'. In Cooper and Schwartz 1996: 195–207.
Bianchi, R. S. 1997, 'The Theban Landscape of Rameses II'. In J. Phillips (ed.), *Ancient Egypt, The Aegean, and the Near East: Studies in Honour of Martha Rhoads Bell*, 87–94. San Antonio: Van Siclen Books.
Bickel, S. 1994, *La Cosmogonie égyptienne avant le Nouvel Empire*. OBO 134.
——, 1998, 'Changes in the Image of the Creator God During the Middle and New Kingdoms'. In Eyre 1998: 165–72.
Bickel, S., and Mathieu, B. 1993, 'L'Écrivain Amennakht et son *Enseignement*', *BIFAO* 93, 31–52.
Birch, D. 1989, *Language, Literature and Critical Practice: Ways of Analysing Text*. Interface Series. London and New York: Routledge.
Birch, S. 1857, *Introduction to the Study of the Egyptian Hieroglyphs*. In J. Gardiner Wilkinson, *The Egyptians in the Time of the Pharaohs: Being a Companion to the Crystal Palace Egyptian Collections*, 175–282. London: Bradbury and Evans.
Björkman, G. 1964, 'Egyptology and Historical Method', *OrSu* 13, 9–23.
Blackman, A. M. 1932, *Middle-Egyptian Stories*. BAe 2.
——, 1938, 'The Use of the Egyptian Word $ḥt$ "House" in the Sense of "Stanza"', *Or* 7, 64–6.
——, 1988 (ed. W. V. Davies), *The Story of King Cheops and the Magicians: Transcribed from Papyrus Westcar, Berlin Papyrus 3033*. Reading: JV Books.
Blumenthal, E. 1970, *Untersuchungen zum ägyptischen Königtum des Mittleren Reiches* I: *Die Phraseologie*. ASAW 61:1.
——, 1977a, 'Die Textgattung Expeditionsbericht in Ägypten'. In J. Assmann *et al.* 1977: 85–118.
——, 1977b, 'Expeditionsberichte', *LÄ* II, 59–61.
——, 1980a, 'Die Lehre für König Merikare', *ZÄS* 107, 5–41.
——, 1980b, 'Lehre Amenemhets I.', *LÄ* III, 968–71.

Blumenthal, E. 1982, 'Die Prophezeiung des Neferti', *ZÄS* 109, 1–27.
——, 1983, 'Zu Sinuhes Zweikampf mit dem Starken von Retjenu'. In M. Görg (ed.), *Fontes atque Pontes: Eine Festgabe für Hellmut Brunner*, 42–6. ÄAT 5.
——, 1984a, 'Neferti, Prophezeiung des', *LÄ* IV, 380–1.
——, 1984b, 'Die Lehre des Königs Amenemhet (Teil I)', *ZÄS* 111, 85–107.
——, 1985, 'Die Lehre des Königs Amenemhet (Teil II)', *ZÄS* 112, 104–15.
——, 1987, 'Ptahhotep und der "Stab des Alters"'. In Osing and Dreyer 1987: 84–97.
——, 1995, 'Die Erzählung des Sinuhe'. In E. Blumenthal *et al.*, *Mythen und Epen* III, 884–911. TUAT III:5.
——, 1996a, 'Die literarische Verarbeitung der Übergangszeit zwischen Altem und Mittlerem Reich'. In Loprieno 1996a: 105–35.
——, 1996b, 'Die altägyptische Literatur im Kulturkontext'. In V. Hertel *et al.* (eds), *Sprache und Kommunikation im Kulturkontext: Beiträge zum Ehrenkolloquium aus Anlass des 60. Geburtstages von Gotthard Lerchner*, 17–31. Frankfurt am Main and New York: Peter Lang.
——, 1998a, 'Prolegomena zu einer Klassifizierung der ägyptischen Literatur'. In Eyre 1998: 173–83.
——, 1998b, 'Sinuhes persönliche Frömmigkeit'. In I. Shirun-Grumach (ed.), *Jerusalem Studies in Egyptology*, 213–31. ÄAT 40.
——, 1999, *Die biblische Weihnachtsgeschichte und das alte Ägypten*. Bayerische Akademie der Wissenschaften, philosophisch-historische Klasse, Sitzungsberichte 1999:1. Munich: Bayerische Akademie der Wissenschaften.
Bolshakov, A. O. 1985, 'O dialogizme "spora cheloveka i ba"'. In *Kulturnoe Nasledie Vostoka: problemi, poski, suzhdeniya*, 17–29. Leningrad: Nauka [not seen].
——, 1993, 'Some *de visu* Observations on P. Hermitage 1115', *JEA* 79, 254–9.
Bomhard A. S. von 1999, 'Le Conte du Naufragé et le Papyrus Prisse', *RdE* 50, 51–65.
Bontty, M. 1997, *Conflict Management in Ancient Egypt: Law as a Social Phenomenon*. Doctorate dissertation, University of California at Los Angeles. Ann Arbor: UMI.
——, 2000, 'Images of Law and the Disputing Process in the Tale of The Eloquent Peasant'. In Gnirs 2000a: 93–107.
Booth, W. C. 1974, *A Rhetoric of Irony*. Chicago: Chicago University Press.
Borghouts, J. F. 1975, 'Enigmatic Chests', *JEOL* 23, 35–64.
——, 1978, *Ancient Egyptian Magical Texts*. NISABA, Religious Texts Translation Series 9. Leiden: E. J. Brill.

——, 1980, 'Magie', *LÄ* III, 1137–51.
——, 1989, 'A New Middle Kingdom Netherworld Guide', *SAK Beiheft* 3, 131–9.
Botstein, L. 1994, 'The Patrons and Publics of the Quartets: Music, Culture, and Society in Beethoven's Vienna'. In R. Winter and R. Martin (eds), *The Beethoven Quartet Companion*, 77–109. Berkeley and London: University of California Press.
Bourriau, J. 1988, *Pharaohs and Mortals: Egyptian Art in the Middle Kingdom*. Exhibition catalogue. Fitzwilliam Museum, Cambridge: Cambridge University Press.
——, 1991, 'Patterns of Change in Burial Customs during the Middle Kingdom'. In Quirke 1991a: 3–20.
Bowman, A. K., and Woolf, G. (eds) 1994, *Literacy and Power in the Ancient World*. Cambridge: Cambridge University Press.
Boyd, M. 1990 [1983], *Bach*. The Master Musicians. Oxford: Oxford University Press.
Bradbury, L. 1988, 'Reflections on Traveling to "God's Land" and Punt in the Middle Kingdom', *JARCE* 25, 127–56.
Brannigan, J. 1998, *New Historicism and Cultural Materialism*. Transitions. Basingstoke and London: Macmillan.
Bresciani, E. 1999, '"Il pleut sur la pierre": Prophéties politiques dans la littérature démotique'. In J. Assmann and Blumenthal 1999: 279–84.
Brooks, C. 1949, *The Well Wrought Urn: Studies in the Structure of Poetry*. London: Dennis Dobson.
Brown, G., and Yule, G. 1983, *Discourse Analysis*. Cambridge Textbooks in Linguistics. Cambridge: Cambridge University Press.
Brown, M. (ed.) 1995, *The Uses of Literary History*. Durham NC and London: Duke University Press.
Broze, M. 1996, *Les Aventures d'Horus et Seth dans le papyrus Chester Beatty I: Mythe et roman en Égypte ancienne*. OLA 76.
Brueggemann, W. 1985, 'Theodicy in a Social Dimension', *Journal for the Study of the Old Testament* 33, 3–25.
Brunner, H. 1955, 'Das Besänftigungslied im Sinuhe (B 269–279)', *ZÄS* 80, 5–11.
——, 1966a, 'Die "Weisen", ihre "Lehren" und "Prophezeiungen" in ägyptischer Sicht', *ZÄS* 93, 29–35.
——, 1966b, 'Wiederum die ägyptischen "Make Merry" Lieder', *JNES* 25, 130–1.
——, 1977, 'Herz', *LÄ* II, 1158–68.
——, 1978, 'Zur Datierung der "Lehre eines Mannes an seinen Sohn"', *JEA* 64, 142–3.
——, 1979, 'Zitate aus Lebenslehren'. In Hornung and Keel 1979: 105–71.

Brunner, H. 1980a, 'Kemit', *LÄ* III, 383–4.
——, 1980b, 'Lehre des Ptahhotep', *LÄ* III, 989–91.
——, 1980c, 'Lehren', *LÄ* III, 964–8.
——, 1980d, 'Lehre des Cheti', *LÄ* III, 977–8.
——, 1986a [1966], *Grundzüge einer Geschichte der altägyptischen Literatur.* Darmstadt: Wissenschaftliche Buchgesellschaft.
——, 1986b, 'Willensfreiheit', *LÄ* VI, 1265–6.
——, 1991a [1957], *Altägyptische Erziehung.* Wiesbaden: Harrassowitz.
——, 1991b, *Die Weisheitsbücher der Ägypter: Lehren für das Leben.* Zurich and Munich: Artemis.
Brunner-Traut, E. 1967, 'Der Lebensmüder und sein Ba', *ZÄS* 94, 6–15.
——, 1982, 'Namenstilgung und -verfolgung', *LÄ* IV, 338–41.
——, 1984, 'Schweiger', *LÄ* V, 759–62.
Bryan, B. 1980, 'The Hero of the "Shipwrecked Sailor"', *Serapis* 5, 3–13.
——, 1996, 'The Disjunction of Text and Image in Egyptian Art'. In Manuelian 1996: 161–8.
Buccellati, G. 1981, 'Wisdom and Not: the Case of Mesopotamia', *JAOS* 101, 35–47.
Buchberger, H. 1989/90, 'Zum Ausländer in der altägyptischen Literatur: eine Kritik', *WdO* 20/21, 5–34.
——, 1993, *Transformation und Transformat: Sargtextstudien* I. ÄA 52.
de Buck, A. 1932, 'Some New Interpretations in Sinuhe'. In S. R. K. Glanville (ed.), *Studies Presented to F. Ll. Griffith*, 56–60. London: Oxford University Press for Egypt Exploration Society.
——, 1938a, 'The Instruction of Amenemmes'. In P. Jouguet (ed.), *Mélanges Maspero* I, 847–52. MIFAO 66.
——, 1938b, 'The Building Inscription of the Berlin Leather Roll'. In *Studia Aegyptiaca* I, 48–57. Analecta Orientalia 17. Rome: Pontificium Institutum Biblicum.
Budge, E. A. W. 1913, *The Book of the Dead: The Papyrus of Ani, the Scribe and Treasurer of the Temples of Egypt, about B.C. 1450.* London and New York: The Medici Society and G. P. Putnam's Sons.
Budick, S., and Iser, W. 1996, *The Translatability of Cultures: Figurations of the Space Between.* Irvine Studies in the Humanities. Stanford: Stanford University Press.
Burkard, G. 1977, *Textkritische Untersuchungen zu altägyptischen Weisheitslehren des Alten und Mittleren Reiches.* ÄA 34.
——, 1980, 'Bibliotheken im alten Ägypten', *Bibliothek: Forschung und Praxis* 4, 78–115.
——, 1983, 'Der formale Aufbau altägyptischer Literatur: Zur Problematik der Entschliessung seiner Grundstrukturen', *SAK* 10, 79–118.
——, 1988, 'Ptahhotep und das Alter', *ZÄS* 115, 19–30.

——, 1993, *Überlegungen zur Form der ägyptischen Literatur: Die Geschichte des Schiffbrüchigen als literarisches Kunstwerk*. ÄAT 22.

——, 1996, 'Metrik, Prosodie und formaler Aufbau ägyptischer literarischer Texte'. In Loprieno 1996a: 447–63.

——, 1999, '"Als Gott erschienen spricht er": Die Lehre des Amenemhet als postumes Vermächtnis'. In J. Assmann and Blumenthal 1999: 153–73.

Burkard, G., and Fischer-Elfert, H.-W. 1994, *Ägyptische Handschriften* 4. Verzeichnis der orientalischen Handschriften in Deutschland XIX.4. Stuttgart: Franz Steiner.

Burrow, C. 1997, 'Virgils, from Dante to Milton'. In Martindale 1997a: 79–90.

Caminos, R. A. 1954, *Late-Egyptian Miscellanies*. Brown Egyptological Studies 1. London: Oxford University Press.

——, 1956, *Literary Fragments in the Hieratic Script*. Oxford: University Press for Griffith Institute.

——, 1977, *A Tale of Woe: Papyrus Pushkin 127*. Oxford: University Press for Griffith Institute.

——, 1980, 'Literarischer Brief', *LÄ* III, 1066–7.

Cannuyer, C. 1985, 'Note à propos de *Sinouhé B 133–4*', *GM* 88, 11–13.

——, 1986, 'L'Obèse de Ptaḥḥotep et de Samuel', *ZÄS* 113, 92–103.

——, 1990, 'Encore le naufrage du *Naufragé*', *BSEG* 14, 15–21.

——, 1994, 'Humanisme et humilité en Égypte: Le Sens de [mꜥk3] (*Naufragé* 29, 96 et 99)'. In P. Naster *et al.* (eds), *Humanisme, science et religion: In memoriam Aristide Théodoridès*, 15–23. Acta Orientalia Belgica 8. Brussels, Leuven: Société Belge d'Études Orientales.

Carnarvon, Earl of, and Carter, H. *et al.* 1912, *Five Years' Explorations at Thebes*. London: Oxford University Press.

Caylus, comte de 1756, *Recueil d'antiquités égyptiennes, étrusques, grecques, romaines et gauloises* IV. Paris: N. M. Tilliard.

Chabas, F. 1858, 'Le Plus Ancien Livre du monde: Étude sur le Papyrus Prisse'. In *Œuvres Diverses* I (BdE 9, 1899), 183–214.

——, 1859, 'Note sur la littérature des anciens égyptiens', previously unpublished, dated 1859. In *Œuvres Diverses* I (BdE 9, 1899), 317.

——, 1865, *Les Papyrus hiératiques de Berlin: Récits d'il y a quatre mille ans*. In *Œuvres Diverses* II (BdE 10, 1902), 289–364.

Champollion, J.-F. le jeune 1868, *Lettres écrites d'Egypte et de Nubie en 1828 et 1829*. Paris: Firmin Didot.

Chappaz, J.-L. 1979, 'Un manifeste littéraire du Moyen Empire – les lamentations de Kha-khéper-ré-seneb', *BSEG* 2, 3–12.

Chappaz, J.-L. 1982, 'Un nouvel ostracon de l'*Enseignement loyaliste*', *BSEG* 7, 3–9.

——, 1986, 'Quelques reflexions sur les conteurs dans la littérature égyptienne ancienne'. In A. Guillaumont (ed.), *Hommages à François Daumas* I, 103–8. Publications de recherche, Université de Montpellier: Montpellier.

——, 1989, 'Remarques sur un exercice scolaire', *BSEG* 13, 33–43.

Charles, R.-P. 1960, 'La Statue-cube de Sobek-hotep gouverneur du Fayoum', *RdE* 12, 1–26.

Clarke, J., Hall, S., Jefferson, T., and Roberts, B. 1976, 'Subcultures, Cultures and Class: A Theoretical Overview'. In S. Hall and T. Jefferson (eds), *Resistance through Rituals: Youth Subcultures in Post-war Britain*, 9–74. London and Birmingham: Hutchinson and Centre for Contemporary Cultural Studies.

Clère, J. J., and Vandier, J. 1948, *Textes de la Première Période Intermédiaire et de la XIème Dynastie*. BAe 10.

Colin, G. 1995, ' "Dans une proximité lointaine" ou "En allant et venant"? (Sinouhé B 2 [R 25])', *RdE* 46, 203–5.

——, 1996, 'Khâkheperrêseneb et la conscience de l'Histoire', *GM* 150, 43–6.

Condon, V. 1978, *Seven Royal Hymns of the Ramesside Period: Papyrus Turin CG 54031*. MÄS 37.

Conrad, P. 1985, *The Everyman History of English Literature*. London: J. M. Dent.

Conte, G. B. 1986 [1974, 1980], *The Rhetoric of Imitation: Genre and Poetic Memory in Virgil and Other Latin Poets* (C. Segal, trans.). Cornell Studies in Classical Philology 44. Ithaca NY and London: Cornell University Press.

——, 1994 [1987], *Latin Literature: A History*. Baltimore and London: Johns Hopkins University Press.

Cooper, J. S., and Schwartz, G. (eds) 1996, *The Study of the Ancient Near East in the Twenty-first Century: The William Foxwell Albright Centennial Conference*. Winona Lake IN: Eisenbrauns.

Coulon, L. 1997, 'Véracité et rhétorique dans les autobiographies égyptiennes de la Première Période Intermédiaire', *BIFAO* 97, 109–38.

——, 1999, 'Le Rhétorique et ses fictions: Pouvoirs et duplicités du discours à travers la littérature égyptienne du Moyen et du Nouvel Empire', *BIFAO* 99, 103–32.

Cox, J. N., and Reynolds, L. J. 1993, *New Historical Literary Study: Essays on Reproducing Texts, Representing History*. Princeton: Princeton University Press.

Crenshaw, J. L. 1983, 'Introduction: The Shift from Theodicy to Anthropodicy'. In Crenshaw (ed.), *Theodicy in the Old Testament*, 1–16. Issues in Religion and Theology 4. London: SPCK.

Cruz-Uribe, E. 1987, 'The Fall of the Middle Kingdom', *VA* 3, 107–11.

Dakin, A. N. 1992, 'Kemit: A Revised Translation with Material for a Commentary'. In *Sesto congresso internazionale di Egittologia: Atti*, 465–71. Turin: Congress.

——, 1998, 'On the Untranslatability of Maat and Some Questions about the *Tale of the Eloquent Peasant*'. In Eyre 1998: 295–301.

Darnell. J. C. 1997a, 'The Message of King Wahankh Antef II to Khety, Ruler of Heracleopolis', *ZÄS* 124, 101–8.

——, 1997b, 'A New Middle Kingdom Literary Text from the Wadi el-Hôl', *JARCE* 34, 85–100.

Darnell, J. C., and Darnell, D. 1996, 'The Theban Desert Road Survey (The Luxor-Farshût Desert Road Survey)', *Oriental Institute 1995–1996 Annual Report*, 62–70.

d'Athanasi, G. 1837, *Catalogue of the Very Magnificent and Extraordinary Collection of Egyptian Antiquities, the Property of Giovanni d'Athanasi*. London: Leigh Sotherby.

Dautong, G. 1999, 'The Inscription of Amenemhet II from Memphis: Transliteration, Translation, and Commentary', *Journal of Ancient Civilizations* 14, 45–66.

Davies, N. de G. 1923, *The Tomb of Puyemrê at Thebes* II: *The Chapels of Hope*. Robb de Peyster Tytus Memorial Series III. New York: Metropolitan Museum of Art.

——, 1933, *The Tomb of Nefer-hotep at Thebes* I. The Metropolitan Museum of Art Egyptian Expedition 9. New York: Metropolitan Museum of Art.

Davies, N. de G., and Gardiner, A. H. 1920, *The Tomb of Antefoker, Vizier of Sesostris I, and of his Wife, Senet (No. 60)*. TTS 2.

Davies, W. V. 1975, 'Readings in the Story of Sinuhe and other Egyptian Texts', *JEA* 61, 45–53.

Davis, N. Z. 1983, *The Return of Martin Guerre*. Cambridge: Harvard University Press.

Dawson, W. R., and Uphill, E. P., revised by M. L. Bierbrier 1995 [1951], *Who Was Who in Egyptology*. London: Egypt Exploration Society.

de Rougé, E. 1852, 'Notice sur un manuscript égyptien en écriture hiératique . . .'. In *Œuvres Diverses* 2 (BdE 22, 1908), 303–19.

de Tolnay, C. 1975, *Michelangelo: Sculptor, Painter, Poet* (G. Woodhouse, trans.). Princeton: Princeton University Press.

Decker, W. 1975, *Quellentexte zu Sport und Körperkultur im alten Ägypten*. Sankt Augustin: Richarz.

Delia, R. D. 1979, 'A New Look at Some Old Dates: A Reexamination of Twelfth Dynasty Double Dated Inscriptions', *BES* 1, 15–28.

——, 1980, review of Murnane 1977, *Serapis* 5, 51–4.

——, 1982, 'Doubts about Double Dates and Coregencies', *BES* 4, 55–69.

Dellamora, R. 1995, 'Textual Politics/Sexual Politics'. In Brown 1995: 143–57.

Demarée, R. J., and Egberts, A. (eds) 1992, *Village Voices: Proceedings of the Symposium 'Texts from Deir el-Medina and Their Interpretation' Leiden, May 31–June 1, 1919*. Leiden: Centre of Non-Western Studies, Leiden University.

Demedchik, A. 1993, 'A Note to §141 of Sir A. H. Gardiner's "Egyptian Grammar"', *GM* 134, 29–30.

——, 1998, 'The "Region of the Northern Residence" in Middle Egyptian Literature'. In Eyre 1998: 325–30.

Depauw, M. 1997, *A Companion to Demotic Studies*. Papyrologica Bruxellensia 28. Brussels: Fondation égyptologique Reine Élisabeth.

Depuydt, L. 1993, '"Wisdom Made a Weapon": On Manichaeism in Egypt', *CdE* 68/135–6, 301–15.

Derchain, P. 1969, 'Snéferou et les rameuses', *RdE* 21, 19–25.

——, 1970, 'La Réception de Sinouhé à la cour de Sésostris Ier', *RdE* 22, 79–83.

——, 1972, 'Intelligenz als Karriere (*Neferti*, 10–11)', *GM* 3, 9–14.

——, 1975, 'La Perruque et le cristal', *SAK* 2, 55–74.

——, 1976, 'Symbols and Metaphors in Literature and Representations of Private Life', *Royal Anthropological Institute News* 15, 8–10.

——, 1985, 'Sinouhé et Ammounech', *GM* 87, 7–13.

——, 1986, 'Deux notules à propos du Papyrus Westcar', *GM* 89, 15–21.

——, 1987, *Le Dernier Obélisque*. Brussels: Fondation égyptologique Reine Élisabeth.

——, 1989, 'Éloquence et politique: L'Opinion d'Akhtoy', *RdE* 40, 37–47.

——, 1992, 'Les Débuts de l'histoire [rouleau de cuir Berlin 3029]', *RdE* 43, 35–47.

——, 1994, 'Allusion, citation, intertextualité'. In M. Minas and J. Zeidler (eds), *Aspekte spätägyptischer Kultur: Festschrift für Erich Winter zum 65. Geburtstag*, 69–76. Aegyptiaca Treverensia 7. Mainz: Philipp von Zabern.

——, 1996a, 'Auteur et société'. In Loprieno 1996a: 83–94.

——, 1996b, 'Théologie et littérature'. In Loprieno 1996a: 351–60.

——, 1996c, 'La Clémence de Khéops déjouée', *BSEG* 20, 17–18.

Derchain-Urtel, M.-Th. 1974, 'Die Schlange des "Schiffbrüchigen"', *SAK* 1, 83–104.

Desroches Noblecourt, C. 1998, 'Le Périple du "Naufragé" et le calendrier du Ramesseum', *Memnonia* 9, 59–66.
Devauchelle, D. 1989, 'Naufragé 184–186', *GM* 101, 21–5.
——, 1995, 'Le *Paysan* déraciné', *CdE* 70/139–40, 34–40.
Dévaud, E. 1916–17, 'Le Conte du naufragé: Remarques grammatiques, lexicographiques, paléographiques, etc', *Recueil de Travaux* 38, 188–210.
——, 1924 *L'Âge des papyrus égyptiens hiératiques d'après les graphies de certains mots (de la XII*e *dynastie à la fin de la XVIII*e *dynastie)*. Paris: Paul Geuthner.
Dewachter, M. 1988, 'L'Apparition du Papyrus Prisse (pBN 183–194)', *RdE* 39, 209–10.
Dollimore, J. 1989 [1984], *Radical Tragedy: Religion, Ideology, and Power in the Drama of Shakespeare and His Contemporaries*. New York and London: Harvester Wheatsheaf.
Dollimore, J. and Sinfield, A. (eds) 1994 [1985], *Political Shakespeare: Essays in Cultural Materialism*. Manchester: Manchester University Press.
Dominicus, B. 1994, *Gesten und Gebärden in Darstellungen des Alten und Mittleren Reiches*, SAGA 10.
Donadoni, S. F. 1986a [1957], 'Àpropos de l'histoire du texte de "Merikare"'. In *Cultura dell'antico Egitto: Scritti di Sergio F. Donadoni*, 129–36. Rome: Università di Roma 'La Sapienza', Dipartimento de scienze storiche archeologiche e antropologiche dell'antichità.
——, 1986b, 'L'"ispirazione divina" di Sinuhe', *ibid.*, 289–91.
Donker van Heel, K. 1992, 'Use and Meaning of the Egyptian Term *W3ḥ Mw*'. In Demarée and Egberts 1992: 19–30.
Donovan, J. 1977, 'Feminism and Aesthetics', *Critical Inquiry* 3, 605–8.
Doxey, D. M. 1998, *Egyptian Non-royal Epithets in the Middle Kingdom: A Social and Historical Analysis*. PÄ 12.
Drenkhahn, R. 1977, 'Hirtengeschichte', *LÄ* II, 1223–4.
Dubrow, H. 1982, *Genre*. The Critical Idiom 42. London: Methuen.
Durling, R. M. 1976, *Petrarch's Lyric Poems: The* Rime sparse *and Other Lyrics*. Cambridge MA: Harvard University Press.
Dziobek, E. 1998, *Denkmäler des Vezirs User-Amun*. SAGA 18.

Eagleton, T. 1983, *Literary Theory: An Introduction*. Oxford: Blackwell.
——, 1984, *The Function of Criticism: From the Spectator to Post-Structuralism*. London: Verso Editions and NLB.
Eaton-Krauss, M., 1980, 'Zur Koregenz Amenemhets I. und Sesostris' I', *MDOG* 112, 35–51.
Eaton-Krauss, M., and Graefe, E. 1985, *The Small Golden Shrine from the Tomb of Tutankhamun*. Oxford: Griffith Institute.
Edel, E. 1953, 'Inschriften des Alten Reiches: II Die Biographie des *K3j-gmj-nj*", *MIO* I, 211–26.

Edel, E. 1990, 'Der Kanal der Beiden Fische', *Discussions in Egyptology* 16, 31–3.
Eichler, E. 1991, 'Untersuchungen zu den Königsbriefen des Alten Reiches', *SAK* 18, 141–71.
——, 1994, 'Zur kultischen Bedeutung von Expeditionschriften'. In B. Bryan and D. Lorton (eds), *Essays in Egyptology in Honor of Hans Goedicke*, 69–80. San Antonio: Van Siclen Books.
Eliot, T. S. 1959 [1944], *Four Quartets*. London and Boston: Faber and Faber.
Ellul, J. 1973, *Propaganda: The Formation of Men's Attitudes* (K. Kellen and J. Lerner, trans.). New York, Vintage books.
Erman, A. 1901, *Zaubersprüche für Mutter und Kind*. APAW, Ph.-H. Klasse, 1901:1.
——, 1911, *Hymnen an das Diadem der Pharaonen, aus einem Papyrus der Sammlung Golenischeff*. APAW 1911.
——, 1923, *Die Literatur der Aegypter*. Leipzig: J. C. Hinrichs.
——, 1927, *The Literature of the Ancient Egyptians: Poems, Narratives, and Manuals of Instruction, from the Third and Second Millennia B.C.* (A. M. Blackman, trans.). New York: Harper and Row.
Eyre, C. J. 1976, 'Fate, Crocodiles and Judgement of the Dead: Some Mythological Allusions in Egyptian Literature', *SAK* 4, 103–14.
——, 1990, 'The Semna Stelae: Quotation, Genre and Functions of Literature'. In Groll 1990: 134–65.
——, 1991, 'Why Was Egyptian Literature?' In *Sixth International Congress of Egyptology: Abstracts of Papers*, 164–5. Turin: Organizing Secretariat.
——, 1992, 'Yet Again the Wax Crocodile: P. Westcar 3, 12ff.', *JEA* 78, 280–1.
——, 1993, 'Why Was Egyptian Literature?'. In *Sesto Congresso Internazionale di Egittologia: Atti* II, 115–27. Turin: Congress.
——, 1996a, 'Is Egyptian Historical Literature "Historical" or "Literary"?' In Loprieno 1996a: 415–33.
——, 1996b, 'Ordre et désordre dans la campagne égyptienne'. In B. Menu (ed.), *Egypte pharaonique: Pouvoir, société*, 179–93, = *Méditerranées* 6/7.
——, (ed.), 1998, *Proceedings of the Seventh International Congress of Egyptologists: Cambridge, 3–9 September 1995*. OLA 82.
——, 1999, 'Irony in the Story of Wenamun: The Politics of Religion in the 21st Dynasty'. In J. Assmann and Blumenthal 1999: 235–52.
——, 2000, 'The Performance of the Peasant'. In Gnirs 2000a: 9–25.
Eyre, C. J., and Baines, J. 1989, 'Interactions between Orality and Literacy in Ancient Egypt'. In K. Schousboe and M. T. Larsen (eds), *Literacy and Society*, 91–119. Copenhagen: Akademisk Forlag.

Farrell, J. 1997, 'The Virgilian Intertext'. In Martindale 1997a: 222–38.
Faulkner, R. O. 1956, 'The Man Who Was Tired of Life', *JEA* 42, 21–40.
——, 1964, 'Notes on "The Admonitions of an Egyptian Sage"', *JEA* 50, 24–36.
Fay, B. *et al.* (eds), 1998, *History and Theory: Contemporary Readings*. Oxford: Blackwell.
Fecht, G. 1958, *Der Habgierige und die Maat in der Lehre des Ptahhotep (5. und 19. Maxime)*. ADAIK 1.
——, 1963, 'Die Wiedergewinnung der altägyptischen Verskunst', *MDAIK* 19, 54–96.
——, 1964, 'Die Form der altägyptischen Literatur: Metrische und stilistische Analyse', *ZÄS* 91, 11–63.
——, 1965, *Literarische Zeugnisse zur "persönlichen Frömmigkeit" in Ägypten: Analyse der Beispiele aus den ramessidischen Schulpapyri*. AHAW 1965:1.
——, 1966, 'Die Form der altägyptischen Literatur: Metrische und stilistische Analyse', *ZÄS* 92, 10–32.
——, 1970, 'Stilistische Kunst'. In H. Altenmüller *et al.*, *Handbuch der Orientalistik* I: *Ägyptologie 2 Literatur*, 19–51. Leiden: E. J. Brill.
——, 1972, *Der Vorwurf an Gott in den "Mahnworten des Ipu-wer"*. AHAW 1972:1.
——, 1974, 'Ägyptische Zweifel am Sinn des Opfers: Admonitions 5, 7–9', *ZÄS* 100, 6–16.
——, 1975, 'Bauerngeschichte', *LÄ* I, 638–51.
——, 1981, 'Ptahhotep und die Disputierer (Lehre des Ptahhotep nach Pap. Prisse, Max. 2–4, Dév. 60–83)', *MDAIK* 37, 143–50; corrections on sheet in *MDAIK* 38 (1982).
——, 1982, 'Prosodie', *LÄ* IV, 1127 54.
——, 1984, 'Sinuhes Zweikampf als Handlungskern des dritten Kapitels des Sinuhe-"Romans"'. In Junge 1984c: 465–84.
——, 1986, '*Cruces Interpretum* in der Lehre des Ptahhotep (Maximen 7, 9, 13, 14) und das Alter der Lehre'. In A. Guillaumont (ed.), *Hommages à François Daumas* I, 227–51. Montpellier: Université de Montpellier.
——, 1991, 'Die Belehrung des Ba und der "Lebensmüde"', *MDAIK* 47, 113–26.
——, 1993, 'The Structural Principle of Ancient Egyptian Elevated Language'. In J. C. de Moor and W. G. E. Watson, *Verse in Ancient Near Eastern Prose*, 69–94. Alter Orient und Altes Testament 42. Neukirchen-Vluyn.
——, 1996, 'Der beredte Bauer: Die zweite Klage'. In Manuelian 1996: 227–66.
Felperin, H. 1992 [1990], *The Uses of the Canon: Elizabethan Literature and Contemporary Theory*. Oxford: Clarendon Press.

Feucht, E. 1992, 'Fishing and Fowling with the Spear and the Throwstick Reconsidered'. In U. Luft (ed.), *The Intellectual Heritage of Egypt: Studies Presented to László Kákosy by Friends and Colleagues on the Occasion of His 60th Birthday*, 157–69. StudAeg 14. Budapest: La Chaire d'Égyptologie.

Fischer, H. G. 1976, *Varia*. Egyptian Studies 1. New York: Metropolitan Musuem of Art.

——, 1977, 'Some Iconographic and Literary Comparisons'. In J. Assmann *et al.* 1977: 155–70.

——, 1982, 'A Didactic Text of the Late Middle Kingdom', *JEA* 68, 45–50.

——, 1985, *Egyptian Titles of the Middle Kingdom: A Supplement to Wm. Ward's INDEX*. New York: Metropolitan Museum of Art.

——, 1996, *Varia Nova*. Egyptian Studies 3. New York: Metropolitan Museum of Art.

Fischer-Elfert, H.-W. 1984, 'Textkritische Kleinigkeiten zur "Lehre des Amenemhet"', *GM* 70, 89–90.

——, 1986a, *Die satirische Streitschrift des Papyrus Anastasi I.: Übersetzung und Kommentar*. ÄA 44.

——, 1986b, *Literarische Ostraka der Ramessidenzeit in Übersetzung*. KÄT.

——, 1988, 'Zum bisherigen Textbestand der "Lehre eines Mannes an seinen Sohn": Eine Zwischenbilanz', *Oriens Antiquus* 27, 173–209.

——, 1989, 'Der ehebrecherische Sohn (P. Deir el-Medineh 27, Stele UC 14.430 und P. Butler verso)', *GM* 112, 23–6.

——, 1991, '"Die Lehre eines Mannes für seinen Sohn": Eine Lehre für den kleinen Mann?' In *Sixth International Congress of Egyptology: Abstracts of Papers*, 172–3. Turin: Organizing Secretariat.

——, 1992a [1983], *Die satirische Streitschrift des Papyrus Anastasi I: Textzusammenstellung*. KÄT.

——, 1992b, 'Synchrone und diachrone Interferenzen in literarischen Werken des Mittleren und Neuen Reiches', *Or* 61, 354–72.

——, 1994, 'Vermischtes III', *GM* 143, 41–9.

——, 1996a, 'Die Arbeit am Text: Altägyptische Literaturwerke aus philologischer Perspektive'. In Loprieno 1996a: 499–513.

——, 1996b, 'The Hero of Retjenu – an Execration Figure (*Sinuhe* B 109–113)', *JEA* 82, 198–9.

——, 1997, *Lesefunde im literarischen Steinbruch von Deir el-Medineh*. KÄT 12.

——, 1998, 'Neue Fragmente zur *Lehre eines Mannes für seinen Sohn* (P. BM EA 10775 und P. BM EA 10778)', *JEA* 84, 85–92.

——, 1999, *Die Lehre eines Mannes für seinen Sohn: Eine Etappe auf dem 'Gottesweg' des loyalen und solidarischen Beamten der frühen 12. Dynastie*. 2 vols, ÄA 60.

Fischer-Elfert, H.-W., and Hoffmann, F., in preparation, *Die magischen*

Texte und Vignetten des Papyrus Nr. 1826 der Nationalbibliothek Griechenlands. Beihefte zu den Würzburger Medizinhistorischen Beiträgen.

Fish, S. 1971 [1967], *Surprised by Sin: The Reader in Paradise Lost*. Berkeley: University of California Press.

——, 1980, *Is There a Text in This Class? The Authority of Interpretive Communities*. Cambridge MA: Harvard University Press.

Fitzenreiter, M. 1995, 'Totenverehrung und soziale Repräsentation im thebanischen Beamtengrab der 18. Dynastie', *SAK* 22, 95–130.

Fokkema, D., and Ibsch, E. 1986, *Theories of Literature in the Twentieth Century*. London: C. Hurst.

Forgacs, D. 1986, 'Marxist Literary Theories'. In Jefferson and Robey 1986: 166–203.

Forster, E. M. 1927, *Aspects of the Novel*. London: E. Arnold and Co.

——, 1965 [1951], *Two Cheers for Democracy*. Harmondsworth: Penguin.

Foster, J. L. 1975, 'Thought Couplets in Khety's "Hymn to the Inundation"', *JNES* 34, 1–29.

——, 1977, *Thought Couplets and Clause Sequences in a Literary Text: The Maxims of Ptahhotep*. SSEA Publication 5. Toronto: SSEA.

——, 1980, '*Sinuhe*: The Ancient Egyptian Genre of Narrative Verse', *JNES* 39, 89–117.

——, 1981, 'The Conclusion to *The Testament of Ammenemes, King of Egypt*', *JEA* 67, 35–47.

——, 1982, 'Cleaning up *Sinuhe*', *JSSEA* 12, 81–5.

——, 1983, 'The *sḏm.f* and the *sḏm.n.f* Forms in The Tale of Sinuhe', *RdE* 34, 27–52.

——, 1986, 'Texts of the Egyptian Composition "The Instruction of a Man for His Son" in the Oriental Institute Museum', *JNES* 45, 197–211.

——, 1988, 'The Shipwrecked Sailor: Prose or Verse? (Postponing Clauses and Tense-neutral Clauses)', *SAK* 15, 69–109.

——, 1989–90, 'Wordplay in *The Eloquent Peasant*: The Eighth Complaint', *BES* 10, 61–76.

——, 1993, *Thought Couplets in* The Tale of Sinuhe: *Verse Text and Translation. With an Outline of Grammatical Forms and Clause Sequences and an Essay on the Tale as Literature*. MÄU 3.

——, 1994, 'Thought Couplets and the Standard Theory: A Brief Overview', *LingAeg* 4, 139–63.

——, 1999, 'Some Comments on Khety's Instruction for Little Pepi on His Way to School (Satire on the Trades)'. In E. Teeter and J. A. Larson, *Gold of Praise: Studies on Ancient Egypt in Honor of Edward F. Wente*, 121–9. SAOC 58.

Foster, J. L., and Brock, L. P. 1998, *The Shipwrecked Sailor: A Tale from Ancient Egypt*. Cairo: The American University in Cairo Press.

Fóti, L. 1976, 'The History in the Prophecies of Noferti: Relationship between the Egyptian Wisdom and Prophecy Literatures', *StudAeg* 2, 3–18.

Foucault, M. 1977, *Language, Counter-Memory, Practice: Selected Essays and Interviews* (P. Kamuf, trans.). Oxford: Blackwell.

——, 1981 [1976], *The History of Sexuality*. I: *An Introduction* (R. Hurley, trans.). Harmondsworth: Penguin.

Foulkes, A. P. 1983, *Literature and Propaganda*. New Accents. London: Methuen.

Fowler, A. 1971, 'The Life and Death of Literary Forms', *New Literary History* 2, 199–216.

——, 1982, *Kinds of Literature: An Introduction to the Theory of Genres and Modes*. Oxford: Clarendon Press.

Fowler, D. 1997, 'Virgilian Narrative'. In Martindale 1997a: 259–70.

Fox, A. 1997, *The English Renaissance: Identity and Representation in Elizabethan England*. Oxford: Blackwell.

Fox, M. V. 1977, 'A Study of Antef', *Or* 46, 393–423.

——, 1982, 'The Entertainment Song Genre in Egyptian Literature'. In S. Israelit-Groll (ed.), *Egyptological Studies*, 268–316. Scripta Hierosolymitana 28. Jerusalem: Magnes Press.

——, 1983, 'Ancient Egyptian Rhetoric', *Rhetorica* 1, 9–22.

——, 1985, *The Song of Songs and the Ancient Egyptian Love Songs*. Madison and London: University of Wisconsin Press.

Frandsen, P. J. 2000, 'On the Origin of the Notion of Evil in Ancient Egypt', *GM* 179, 9–34.

Franke, D. 1988, 'Zur Chronologie des Mittleren Reichs (12.–18. Dynastie), Teil 1: Die 12. Dynastie', *Or* 57, 113–38.

——, 1990, 'Erste und Zweite Zwischenzeit: Ein Vergleich', *ZÄS* 117, 119–29.

——, 1991, 'The Career of Khnumhotep III of Beni Hasan and the So-called "Decline of the Nomarchs"'. In Quirke 1991a: 51–67.

——, 1993, review of Parkinson 1991a, *BiOr* 50, 347–53.

——, 1994, *Das Heiligtum des Heqaib auf Elephantine: Geschichte eines Provinzheiligtums im Mittleren Reich*. SAGA 9.

——, 1995, 'The Middle Kingdom in Egypt'. In J. M. Sasson *et al.* (eds), *Civilizations of the Ancient Near East* II, 725–48. New York: Charles Scribner's.

——, 1996, 'Sesostris I., "König der beiden Länder" und Demiurg in Elephantine'. In Manuelian 1996: 275–95.

——, 1998a, 'Kleiner Mann (*nḏs*): Was bist Du?', *GM* 167, 33–48.

——, 1998b, '*qrḥt*: Geschöpf des "Ersten Tages". Eine Assoziationstechnik zur Statuserhöhung in der 10. und 11. Dynastie', *GM* 164, 63–70.

Frankfurter, D. 1998, *Religion in Roman Egypt: Assimilation and Resistance*. Princeton: Princeton University Press.

Fry, P. H. 1995, *A Defense of Poetry: Reflections on the Occasion of Writing*. Stanford: Stanford University Press.

Frye, N. 1964, *The Educated Imagination*. Bloomington: Indiana University Press.

Gáal, E. 1984, 'Ein neues Ostracon zur "Lehre eines Mannes für seinen Sohn"', *MDAIK* 40, 13–25.

Gabolde, L. 1998, *Le "Grand Château d'Amon" de Sésostris Ier à Karnak: La Décoration du temple d'Amon-Rê au Moyen Empire*. Mémoires de l'Academie des Inscriptions et Belles Lettres n.s. 17. Paris: Institut de France, Boccard.

Gadamer, H.-G. 1979 [1965], *Truth and Method* (trans. W. Glen-Doepel). London: Sheed and Ward.

Galán, J. M. 1998, 'Two Passages of Sinuhe Reconsidered', *SAK* 25, 72–81.

Gallorini, C. 1998, 'A Reconstruction of Petrie's Excavation at the Middle Kingdom Settlement of Kahun'. In Quirke 1999: 42–59 (with errata).

Gardiner, A. H. 1909a, *The Admonitions of an Ancient Egyptian Sage, from a Hieratic Papyrus in Leiden*. Leipzig: Hinrichs.

——, 1909b, *Die Erzählung des Sinuhe und die Hirtengeschichte*. Literarische Texte des Mittleren Reiches II. Leipzig: Hinrichs.

——, 1910, 'The Tomb of Amenemhet, High-priest of Amon', *ZÄS* 47, 87–99.

——, 1916, *Notes on the Story of Sinuhe*. Paris: H. Champion.

——, 1923, 'The Eloquent Peasant', *JEA* 9, 5–25.

——, 1925, 'The Secret Chambers of the Sanctuary of Thoth', *JEA* 11, 2–8.

——, 1928, 'The Graffito from the Tomb of Pere', *JEA* 14, 10–11.

——, 1931, *The Library of A. Chester Beatty: Description of a Hieratic Papyrus with a Mythological Story, Love-Songs, and Other Miscellaneous Texts*. The Chester Beatty Papyri I. London: Emery Walker.

——, 1932, *Late-Egyptian Stories*. BAe 1.

——, 1935a, *Chester Beatty Gift*. Hieratic Papyri in the British Museum: 3rd series. London: British Museum.

——, 1935b, 'The Earliest Manuscripts of the Instruction of Amenemmes I'. In P. Jouguet (ed.), *Mélanges Maspero* I, 479–96. MIFAO 66.

——, 1937, *Late-Egyptian Miscellanies*. BAe 7.

——, 1942, 'Writing and Literature'. In S. R. K. Glanville (ed.), *The Legacy of Egypt*, 53–79. Oxford: Clarendon Press.

Gardiner, A. H. 1946, 'The Instruction Addressed to Kagemni and His Brethren', *JEA* 32, 71–4.
——, 1947, *Ancient Egyptian Onomastica*. London: Oxford University Press.
——, 1951, 'Kagemni Once Again', *JEA* 37, 109–10.
——, 1955a, *The Ramesseum Papyri*. Oxford: University Press for Griffith Institute.
——, 1955b, 'A Pharaonic Encomium', *JEA* 41, 30, pl. 7–11.
——, 1956, 'A Pharaonic Encomium (II)', *JEA* 42, 8–20.
——, 1957, 'Hymns to Sobk in a Ramesseum Papyrus', *RdE* 11, 43–56.
Gardiner, A. H., and Peet, T. E. 1952 [1917], *The Inscriptions of Sinai* I. London: Egypt Exploration Society.
Gasse, A. 1992, 'Les Ostraca hiératiques littéraires de Deir el-Medina: Nouvelles orientations de la publication'. In Demarée and Egberts 1992: 51–70.
Geertz, C. 1973, *The Interpretation of Cultures*. New York: Basic Books.
Gessler-Löhr, B. 1983, *Die heiligen Seen ägyptischer Tempel: Ein Beitrag zur Deutung sakraler Baukunst im alten Ägypten*. HÄB 21.
Gestermann, L. 1987, *Kontinuität und Wandel in Politik und Verwaltung des frühen Mittleren Reiches in Ägypten*. GOF IV.18.
——, 1995, 'Der politische und kulturelle Wandel unter Sesostris III.'. In L. Gestermann and H. Sternberg-el Hotabi (eds), *Per Aspera ad Astra: Wolfgang Schenkel zum neunundfünfzigsten Geburtstag*, 31–50. Kassel: published by editor.
——, 1997, 'Sesostris III.: König und Nomarch'. In R. Gundlach and C. Raedler (eds), *Selbstverständnis und Realität: Akten des Symposiums zur ägyptischen Königsideologie in Mainz 15.–17.6.1995*. 37–47, ÄAT 36,1.
Ghosh, A. 1992, *In an Antique Land*. London: Granta Books.
Gilbert, S. M. 1993, 'Introduction' and 'Notes'. In B. Lyons (ed.), *Virginia Woolf: Orlando*. London: Penguin Books.
Gilula, M. 1977, 'Shipwrecked Sailor, Lines 184–85'. In J. Johnson and E. F. Wente (eds), *Studies in Honor of George R. Hughes*, 75–82. SAOC 39.
——, 1978a, '*Hirtengeschichte* 17–22 = *CT* VII 36m–r', *GM* 26, 21–2.
——, 1978b, 'Peasant B 141–145', *JEA* 64, 129–30.
——, 1981, 'Does God Exist?' In D. W. Young (ed.), *Studies Presented to Hans Jakob Polotsky*, 390–400. Beacon Hill, MA [Boston]: Pirtle and Polson.
Gnirs, A. 1996, 'Die ägyptische Autobiographie'. In Loprieno 1996a: 191–241.
——, 1998, 'Die levantinische Herkunft des Schlangengottes'. In H. Guksch and D. Polz (eds), *Stationen: Beiträge zur Kulturgeschichte*

Ägyptens, Rainer Stadelmann gewidmet, 197–209. Mainz: Philipp von Zabern.
——, 2000a (ed.), *Reading the Eloquent Peasant: Proceedings of the International Conference Held at the University of California, Los Angeles, March 27–30, 1997*, = LingAeg 8.
——, 2000b, 'The Language of Corruption: On Rich and Poor in The Eloquent Peasant'. In Gnirs 2000a: 125–55.
Goedicke, H. 1957, 'The Route of Sinuhe's Flight', *JEA* 43, 77–85.
——, 1962, 'A Neglected Wisdom Text', *JEA* 48, 25–35.
——, 1967, 'Unrecognized Sportings', *JARCE* 6, 97–102.
——, 1970a, *The Report about the Dispute of a Man and His Ba (P Berlin 3024)*. Baltimore: Johns Hopkins University Press.
——, 1970b, 'The Story of the Herdsman', *CdE* 45/89, 244–66.
——, 1972, 'Zu zwei Stellen im Papyrus Westcar', *WZKM* 63/4, 1–5.
——, 1974, *Die Geschichte des Schiffbrüchigen*. ÄA 30.
——, 1977a, *The Protocol of Neferyt*. Baltimore: Johns Hopkins University Press.
——, 1977b, 'The Date of the "Antef Song"'. In J. Assmann *et al.* 1977: 185–96.
——, 1980, 'The Snake in the Story of the Shipwrecked Sailor', *GM* 39, 27–31.
——, 1984a, 'Sinuhe's Duel', *JARCE* 21, 197–201.
——, 1984b, 'The Riddle of Sinuhe's Flight', *RdE* 35, 95–103.
——, 1984–5, 'Sinuhe's Foreign Wife', *BSEG* 9/10, 103–7.
——, 1985a, 'The Encomium of Sesostris I', *SAK* 12, 5–28.
——, 1985b, 'Rudjedet's Delivery', *VA* 1, 19–26.
——, 1986a, 'Three Passages in the *Story of Sinuhe*', *JARCE* 23, 167–74.
——, 1986b, 'Gentlemen's Salutations', *VA* 2, 161–70.
——, 1988a, 'Readings V: Sinuhe B 10', *VA* 4, 201–6.
——, 1988b, *Studies in 'The Instruction of King Amenemhet I for His Son'*. Varia Aegyptiaca Supplement 2. San Antonio: van Siclen Books.
——, 1988c, *Old Hieratic Paleography*. Baltimore: Halgo.
——, 1990, 'Sinuhe's Self-Realization (Sinuhe B 113–27)', *ZÄS* 117, 129–39.
——, 1992a, 'Where Did Sinuhe Stay in "Asia"? (Sinuhe B 29–31)', *CdE* 67/133, 28–40.
——, 1992b, 'Thoughts about the Papyrus Westcar', *ZÄS* 120, 23–36.
——, 1993, 'The Living Image', *GM* 134, 41–54.
——, 1998a, 'The Song of the Princesses (*Sinuhe* B 269–279)', *BSEG* 22, 29–36.
——, 1998b, 'Comments Concerning the "Story of the Eloquent Peasant"', *ZÄS* 125, 109–25.

Goedicke, H., and Wente, E. F. 1962, *Ostraka Michaelides*. Wiesbaden: Harrassowitz.

Goldwasser, O. 1990, 'On the Choice of Registers: Studies on the Grammar of Papyrus Anastasi I'. In Israelit-Groll 1990: 200–40.

——, 1991, 'On Dynamic Canonicity in Late-Egyptian: The Literary Letter and the Personal Prayer', *LingAeg* 1, 129–41.

——, 1999, '"Low" and "High" Dialects in Ramesside Egyptian'. In S. Grunert and I. Hafemann (eds), *Textcorpus und Wörterbuch: Aspekte zur ägyptischen Lexikographie*, 311–28. PÄ 14.

Gomaà, F. 1986, *Die Besiedlung Ägyptens während des Mittleren Reiches* I: *Oberägypten und das Fayum*. TAVO Beiheft B 66/1.

——, 1987, *Die Besiedlung Ägyptens während des Mittleren Reiches* II: *Unterägypten und die angrenzenden Gebiete*. TAVO Beiheft B 66/2.

Goodwin, C. W. 1866, *The Story of Saneha, an Egyptian Tale of Four Thousand Years Ago*. London: Williams and Norgate. (Reprinted from *Frasers Magazine* 1865 v.6, 131–50).

Goody, J. 1987, *The Interface Between the Written and Oral*. Studies in Literacy, Family, Culture and the State. Cambridge: Cambridge University Press.

Görg, M. 1987, 'Das Land *Jȝȝ* (Sin B 81.238)'. In Osing and Dreyer 1987: 142–53.

Graefe, E. 1971, *Untersuchungen zur Wortfamilie* bjȝ-. Dissertation, University of Cologne.

——, 1990, 'Die gute Reputation des Königs "Snofru"'. In Israelit-Groll 1990: 257–63.

Grajetzki, W. 2001, *Die höchsten Beamten der ägyptischen Zentralverwaltung zur Zeit des Mittleren Reiches: Prosopographie, Titel und Titelreihen*. Achet Schriften zur Ägyptologie 2. Berlin: Achet Verlag.

Grapow, H. 1936, *Sprachliche und schriftliche Formung ägyptischer Texte*. LÄS 7.

——, 1952, *Untersuchungen zur ägyptischen Stilistik* I: *Der stilistische Bau der Geschichte des Sinuhe*. VIO 10.

Green, M. 1983, 'The Syrian and Lebanese Topographical Data in the Story of Sinuhe', *CdE* 58/115–16, 38–59.

——, 1984, 'The Word *ḫgȝw* in Sinuhe B 13', *GM* 70 (1984), 27–9.

Greenblatt, S. 1980, *Renaissance Self-fashioning: From More to Shakespeare*. Chicago: University of Chicago Press.

——, 1988, *Shakespearean Negotiations: The Circulation of Social Energy in Renaissance England*. Oxford: Clarendon Press.

——, 1990, *Learning to Curse: Essays in Early Modern Culture*. New York and London: Routledge.

——, 1991, *Marvelous Possessions: The Wonder of the New World*. Oxford: Clarendon Press.

Greenblatt, S., and Gunn, G. (eds), 1992, *Redrawing the Boundaries: The Transformation of English and American Literary Studies*. New York: Modern Language Association of America.

Greig, G. S. 1990, 'The *sḏm:f* and *sḏm.n:f* in the Story of Sinuhe and the Theory of Nominal (emphatic) Verbs'. In Israelit-Groll 1990: 264–348.

Grice, H. P. 1975, 'Logic and Conversation'. In P. Cole and J. Morgan (eds), *Syntax and Semantics* III: *Speech Acts*. New York: Academic Press.

Griffith, F. Ll. 1889, *The Inscriptions of Siût and Dêr Rîfeh*. London: Trübner.

——, 1892, 'Fragments of Old Egyptian Stories from the BM and Amherst Collections', *PSBA* 14, 451–72.

——, 1898, *The Petrie Papyri: Hieratic Papyri from Kahun and Gurob*. London: Quaritch.

Griffith, F. Ll., and Newberry, P. E. 1895, *El-Bersheh* II. ASE 4.

Grimal, N.-C., 1981, *Quatre Stèles napatéennes au Musée du Caire JE 48863–48866*. MIFAO 106.

——, 1995a, 'Le Sage, l'eau et le roi'. In B. Menu (ed.), *Les Problèmes institutionnels de l'eau en Égypte ancienne et dans l'antiquité méditerranéenne*, 195–203. Colloque Aidea Vogüé 1992, BdE 110.

——, 1995b, 'Corégence et association au trône: L'*Enseignement d'Amenemhat I*ᵉʳ', *BIFAO* 95, 273–80.

Grumach, I. 1972, *Untersuchungen zur Lebenslehre des Amenope*. MÄS 23.

Guglielmi, W. 1973–4, 'Die Feldgöttin *sḫ.t*', *WdO* 7, 206–27.

——, 1979, 'Probleme bei der Anwendung der Begriffe "Komik", "Ironie" und "Humor" auf die altägyptische Literatur', *GM* 36, 69–85.

——, 1980, 'Lachen und Weinen in Ethik, Kult und Mythos der Ägypter', *CdE* 55/109–10, 69–86.

——, 1983, 'Eine "Lehre" für einen reiselustigen Sohn', *WdO* 14, 147–66.

——, 1984a, 'Sprichwort', *LÄ* V, 1219–22.

——, 1984b, 'Zur Adaption und Function von Zitaten', *SAK* 11, 347–64.

——, 1984c, 'Zu einigen literarischen Funktionen des Wortspiels'. In Junge 1984c: 491–506.

——, 1986a, 'Stilmittel', *LÄ* VI, 22–41.

——, 1986b, 'Vergleich', *LÄ* VI, 986–9.

——, 1986c, 'Wortspiel', *LÄ* VI, 1287–91.

——, 1987, 'Beiträge zur Stilistik: Die Litotes und das Priamel'. In Osing and Dreyer 1987: 167–79.

——, 1994, 'Berufssatiren in der Tradition des Cheti'. In M. Bietak *et al.* (eds), *Zwischen den beiden Ewigkeiten: Festschrift Gertrud Thausing*, 44–72. Vienna: Institut für Ägyptologie.

——, 1996a, 'Die ägyptische Liebespoesie'. In Loprieno 1996a: 335–47.

Guglielmi, W. 1996b, 'Der Gebrauch rhetorischer Stilmittel in der ägyptischen Literatur'. In Loprieno 1996a: 465–97.
Guilhou, N. 1989, *La Vieillesse des dieux*. Publications de la recherche, Université de Montpellier. Montpellier: Université Paul-Valéry.
Guksch, H. 1994, '"Sehnsucht nach der Heimatstadt": Ein ramessidisches Thema?', *MDAIK* 50, 101–06.
——, 1998, 'Grabherstellung und Ostraka-Produktion'. In H. Guksch and D. Polz (eds), *Stationen: Beiträge zur Kulturgeschichte Ägyptens, Rainer Stadelmann gewidmet*, 281–90. Mainz: Philipp von Zabern.
Gumbrecht, H.-U. 1996, 'Does Egyptology Need a "Theory of Literature?"' In Loprieno 1996a: 3–18.
Gunn, B. 1906, *The Instruction of Ptah-hotep and the Instruction of Ke'gemni: The Oldest Books in the World*. The Wisdom of the East. London: J. Murray.

Hamilton, P. 1996, *Historicism*. The New Critical Idiom. London and New York: Routledge.
Hannig, R. 1991, 'Die erste Parabel des "Lebensmüden" (LM 68–80)', *Journal of Ancient Civilizations* 6, 23–31.
Hardie, P. 1986, *Virgil's* Aeneid: Cosmos *and* Imperium. Oxford: Clarendon Press.
——, 1997, 'Virgil and Tragedy'. In Martindale 1997a: 312–26.
Hare, T. 1999, *ReMembering Osiris: Number, Gender, and the Word in Ancient Egyptian Representational Systems*. Stanford: Stanford University Press.
——, 2000, 'The Supplementarity of Agency in *The Eloquent Peasant*'. In Gnirs 2000a: 1–7.
Hari, R. 1985, *La Tombe thébaine du père divin Neferhotep (TT 50)*. Epigraphica. Geneva: Editions de Belles-Lettres.
Harrison, S. J. (ed.), 1990a, *Oxford Readings in Vergil's* Aeneid. Oxford: Oxford University Press.
——, 1990b, 'Some Views of the *Aeneid* in the Twentieth Century'. In Harrison 1990a: 1–20.
Hawkes, T. 1992, *Meaning by Shakespeare*. London and New York: Routledge.
Hawthorn, J. 1996, *Cunning Passages: New Historicism, Cultural Materialism and Marxism in Contemporary Literary Debate*. Interrogating Texts. London and New York: Arnold.
Hayes, W. C. 1942, *Ostraka and Name Stones from the Tomb of Sen-mūt (no. 71) at Thebes*. The Metropolitan Museum of Art Egyptian Expedition 15. New York: Metropolitan Museum of Art.
——, 1948, 'A Much-copied Letter of the Early Middle Kingdom', *JNES* 7, 1–10.

——, 1955, *A Papyrus of the Late Middle Kingdom in the Brooklyn Museum*. Brooklyn: Brooklyn Museum.
Heaney, S. 1996 [1995], *The Redress of Poetry: Oxford Lectures*. London, Boston: Faber and Faber.
Helck, W. 1955, 'Die Berufung des Vezirs *Wśr*'. In O. Firchow (ed.), *Aegyptologische Studien* [Fs. H. Grapow], 107–17. VIO 29.
——, 1963, 'Entwicklung der Verwaltung als Spiegelbild historischer und soziologischer Faktoren'. In S. Donadoni (ed.), *Le fonti indirette della storia egiziana*, 59–80. Studi Semitici 7. Rome: Università di Roma, Centro di Studi Semitici.
——, 1969, *Der Text der "Lehre Amenemhets I. für seinen Sohn"*. KÄT.
——, 1970a, *Die Lehre des Dw3-Ḥtjj*, 2 vols. KÄT.
——, 1970b, *Die Prophezeiung der Nfr.tj*. KÄT.
——, 1972, 'Zur Frage der Entstehung der ägyptischen Literatur', *WZKM* 63/64, 6–26.
——, 1977, *Die Lehre für König Merikare*. KÄT.
——, 1980, 'Lehre des Cha-cheper-Re-seneb', *LÄ* III, 977.
——, 1982, 'Papyrus Lythgoe', *LÄ* IV, 722.
——, 1983 [1975], *Historisch-Biographische Texte der 2. Zwischenzeit und neue Texte der 18. Dynastie*. KÄT.
——, 1984, *Die Lehre des Djedefhor und die Lehre eines Vaters an seinen Sohn*. KÄT.
——, 1985 'Politische Spannungen zu Beginn des Mittleren Reiches'. In *Ägypten: Dauer und Wandel*, 45–52. DAK Sonderschrift 18.
——, 1992, 'Die "Geschichte des Schiffbrüchigen" – eine Stimme der Opposition?'. In J. Osing and E. Rand Nielsen (eds), *The Heritage of Ancient Egypt: Studies in Honour of Erik Iversen*, 73–6. Carsten Niebuhr Institute Publications 13. Copenhagen: Museum Tusculanum Press.
——, 1995, *Die "Admonitions": Pap. Leiden I 344 recto*. KÄT 11.
Hermsen, E. 1991, *Die zwei Wege des Jenseits: das altägyptische Zweiwegebuch und seine Topographie*. OBO 112.
Herrmann, S. 1954, 'Steuerruder, Waage, Herz und Zunge in ägyptischen Bildreden', *ZÄS* 79, 106–15.
——, 1955, 'Bemerkungen zu Sprüchen aus den "Klagen des Bauern"', *ZÄS* 80, 34–9.
——, 1957, *Untersuchungen zur Überlieferungsgestalt mittelägyptischer Literaturwerke*. Berlin: Akademie Verlag.
——, 1958, 'Zum Verständnis der "Klagen des Bauern" als Rechtsforderungen', *ZÄS* 82, 55–7.
——, 1977, 'Die Auseinandersetzung mit dem Schöpfergott'. In J. Assmann *et al.* 1977: 257–73.
Hibbard, G. R. 1987, *William Shakespeare: Hamlet*. The Oxford Shakespeare. Oxford: Clarendon Press.

Hirsch, E. D. 1967, *Validity in Interpretation*. New Haven and London: Yale University Press.

Hoch, J. E. 1992, 'The Teaching of Dua-Kheti: A New Look at the Satire of the Trades', *JSSEA* 21/22, 88–100.

Hodjash, S., and Berlev, O. 1997, 'An Early Dynasty XII Offering Service from Meir (Moscow and London)'. In J. Aksamit *et al.* (eds), *Essays in Honour of Prof. Dr. Jadwiga Lipinska*, 283–90. Warsaw Egyptological Studies 1. Warsaw: National Museum in Warsaw "Pro-Egipt".

Hoffmeier, J. K. 1996, 'Are There Regionally-based Theological Differences in the Coffin Texts?' In Willems 1996a: 45–54.

Holland, P. 1994, *William Shakespeare: A Midsummer Night's Dream*. The Oxford Shakespeare. Oxford: Oxford University Press.

Hollis, S. 1990, *The Ancient Egyptian "Tale of the Two Brothers": The Oldest Fairy Tale in the World*. Oklahoma Series in Classical Culture. Norman and London: University of Oklahoma Press.

Hornblower, G. D. 1924, 'The Story of the Eloquent Peasant: A Suggestion', *JEA* 10, 44–5.

Hornung, E. 1967, *Das Amduat: Die Schrift des verborgenen Raumes* III: *Die Kurzfassung*. ÄA 7.

——, 1974, 'Die "Kammern" des Thot-Heiligtumes', *ZÄS* 100, 33–5.

——, 1975–6, *Das Buch der Anbetung des Re im Westen (Sonnenlitanei) nach den Versionen des Neuen Reiches*. Aegyptiaca Helvetica 2–3.

——, 1979, *Das Totenbuch der Ägypter*. Zurich and Munich: Artemis.

——, 1982, *Conceptions of God in Ancient Egypt: The One and the Many* (J. Baines, trans.). Ithaca, NY: Cornell University Press.

——, 1997 [1982], *Der ägyptische Mythos von der Himmelskuh: Eine Ätiologie des Unvollkommenen*. OBO 46.

——, 1999 [1997], *The Ancient Egyptian Books of the Afterlife* (D. Lorton, trans.). Ithaca and London: Cornell University Press.

Hornung, E., and Keel, O. (eds) 1979, *Studien zu altägyptischen Lebenslehren*. OBO 28.

Howard, J. E. 1986, 'The New Historicism in Renaissance Studies', *English Literary Renaissance* 16 (Winter), 13–43.

Hunter, G. K. 1980, *Paradise Lost*. Unwin Critical Library. London: Allen and Unwin.

Ignatov, S. 1994, 'Some Notes on the *Story of the Shipwrecked Sailor*', *JEA* 80, 195–8.

Iser, W. 1989, *Prospecting: From Reader Response to Literary Anthropology*. Baltimore and London: Johns Hopkins University Press.

——, 1993, *The Fictive and the Imaginary: Charting Literary Anthropology*. Baltimore and London: Johns Hopkins University Press.

——, 1996, 'Coda to the Discussion'. In Budick and Iser 1996: 294–302.

Israelit-Groll, S. (ed.) 1990, *Studies in Egyptology Presented to Miriam Lichtheim*. Jerusalem: Hebrew University.

Iversen, E. 1979, 'The Chester Beatty Papyrus, No. 1, Recto XVI, 9–XVII, 13', *JEA* 65, 78–88.

Jakobson, R. 1960, 'Linguistics and Poetics'. In T. A. Sebeok (ed.), *Style and Language*, 350–77. New York and London: John Wiley and Sons; Boston: Technology Press of Massachusetts Institute of Technology.

James, T. G. H. 1962, *The Hekanakhte Papers and Other Early Middle Kingdom Documents*. The Metropolitan Museum of Art Egyptian Expedition 19. New York: Metropolitan Museum of Art.

Jansen-Winkeln, K. 1991, 'Das Attentat auf Amenemhat I. und die erste ägyptische Koregentschaft', *SAK* 18, 241–64.

——, 1997, 'Zu den Koregenzen der 12. Dynastie', *SAK* 24, 115–35.

Janssen, J. J. 1992, 'Literacy and Letters at Deir el-Medina'. In Demarée and Egberts 1992: 80–94.

Janssen, J. M. A. 1946, *De traditioneele egyptische autobiografie vóór het Nieuwe Rijk*. Leiden: E. J. Brill.

Jasnow, R. 1999, 'Remarks on Continuity in Egyptian Literary Tradition'. In E. Teeter and J. A. Larson, *Gold of Praise: Studies on Ancient Egypt in Honor of Edward F. Wente*, 193–210. SAOC 58.

Jauss, H. R. 1982, *Towards an Aesthetic of Reception* (T. Bahti, trans.). Brighton: Harvester Press.

Jefferson, A. 1986a, 'Russian Formalism'. In Jefferson and Robey 1986: 24–45.

——, 1986b, 'Structuralism and Post-Structuralism'. In Jefferson and Robey 1986: 92–121.

Jefferson, A., and Robey, D. (eds) 1986 [1982], *Modern Literary Theory: A Comparative Introduction*. London: Batsford Ltd.

Jenni, H. 1998, 'Das Papyrus Westcar', *SAK* 25, 113–41.

Johnson, B. 1980, *The Critical Difference: Essays in the Contemporary Rhetoric of Reading*. Baltimore: Johns Hopkins University Press.

Junge, F. 1977, 'Die Welt der Klagen'. In J. Assmann *et al.* 1977: 276–84.

——, 1984a, 'Rhetorik', *LÄ* V, 250–3.

——, 1984b, 'Sprache', *LÄ* V, 1176–1211.

——, 1984c (ed.), *Studien zu Sprache und Religion Ägyptens zu Ehren von Wolfhart Westendorf*. Göttingen: Seminar für Ägyptologie und Koptologie.

——, 1994, 'Mythos und Literarizität: Die Geschichte vom Streit der Götter Horus und Seth'. In H. Behlmer (ed.), . . . *Quaerentes Scientiam: Festgabe für Wolfhart Westendorf zu seinem 70. Geburtstag überreicht von seinen Schülern*, 83–101. Gottingen: Seminar füxr Ägyptologie und Koptologie.

Junge, F. 2000, 'Die Rahmenerzählung des "Beredten Bauern": Innenansichten einer Gesellschaft'. In Gnirs 2000a: 157–81.

Junker, H. 1908, *Koptische Poesie des zehnten Jahrhunderts* I. Sonderabdruck aus Oriens Christianus 6. Berlin: Karl Curtius.

Kadish, G. E. 1973, 'British Museum Writing Board 5645: The Complaints of Kha-kheper-Rēʿ-senebu', *JEA* 59, 77–90.

Kahl, J. 1998, ' "Es ist vom Anfang bis zum Ende so gekommen, wie es in der Schrift gefunden worden war": Zur Überlieferung der Erzählung des Sinuhe'. In M. Dietrich and I. Kottsieper (eds), *"Und Moses schrieb dieses Lied auf": Studien zum Alten Testament und zum Alten Orient. Festschrift für Oswald Loretz zur Vollendung seines 70. Lebensjahres*, 383–400. Münster: Ugarit-Verlag.

——, 1999, *Siut-Theben: Zur Wertschätzung von Traditionen im alten Ägypten.* PÄ 13.

Kákosy, L. 1964, 'Ideas about the Fallen State of the World in Egyptian Religion: Decline of the Golden Age', *Acta Orientalia* (Hung.) 17, 205–16.

Kákosy, L., and Fábián, Z. I. 1995, 'Harper's Song in the Tomb of Djehutimes (TT 32)', *SAK* 22, 211–25.

Kalos, M., Nelson, M., and Leblanc, C. 1996, 'L'Ensemble monumental dit "Chapelle de la Reine Blanche" ', *Memnonia* 7, 69–82.

Kammerzell, F. 1986, 'Die Prophezeiung des Neferti'. In M. Dietrich *et al.*, *Deutungen der Zukunft in Briefen, Orakeln und Omina*, 102–10. TUAT II:1.

——, 1993, 'Die altägyptische Negation w: Versuch einer Annäherung', *LingAeg* 3, 17–32.

——, 1995a, 'Von Streit zwischen Leib und Kopf'. In E. Blumenthal *et al.*, *Mythen und Epen* III, 951–4. TUAT III:5.

——, 1995b, 'Von der Affäre um König Nafirku'ri'a und seinen General'. In E. Blumenthal *et al.*, *Mythen und Epen* III, 965–9. TUAT III:5.

——, 1997, 'Merikare E 30–31: Ein Fall von indirekter Rede mit Einaktantenanpassung im Mittelägyptischen', *GM* 161, 97–101.

Kamrin, J. 1999, *The Cosmos of Khnumhotep II at Beni Hasan*. Studies in Egyptology. London and New York: Kegan Paul International.

Kaplony, P. 1970, 'Hirtenlied, Harfnerlieder und Sargtext-Spruch 671 als verwandte Gattungen der ägyptischen Literatur', *CdE* 45/81, 240–3.

——, 1974, 'Das Büchlein Kemit'. In *Akten des XIII. internationalen Papyrologenkongresses*, 179–97. MBP 66.

Kemp, B. J. 1984, 'In the Shadow of Texts: Archaeology in Egypt', *Archaeological Review from Cambridge* 3:2, 19–28.

——, 1989, *Ancient Egypt: Anatomy of a Civilization*. London and New York: Routledge.

Kennedy, D. 1997, 'Modern Receptions and Their Interpretative Implications'. In Martindale 1997a: 38–55.
Kerman, J. 1994, 'Beethoven Quartet Audiences: Actual, Potential, Ideal'. In R. Winter and R. Martin (eds), *The Beethoven Quartet Companion*, 7–27. Berkeley and London: University of California Press.
Kermode, F. 1967, *The Sense of an Ending: Studies in the Theory of Fiction*. London and Oxford: Oxford University Press.
——, 1971 [1957], *Romantic Image*. London: Collins, Fontana Books.
——, 1975, *The Classic*. London: Faber and Faber.
Kerrigan, W. 1992, 'Seventeenth-Century Studies'. In Greenblatt and Gunn 1992: 64–78.
Kessler, D. 1988, 'Der satirisch-erotische Papyrus Turin 55001 und das "Verbringen des schönen Tages"', *SAK* 15, 171–96.
Kitchen, K. A. 1988, review of von der Way 1984, *JEA* 74, 279–81.
——, 1994, '*Sinuhe* B.219–223', in 'Sinuhe's Foreign Friends, and Papyri (Coptic) Greenhill 1–4'. In C. Eyre *et al.* (eds), *The Unbroken Reed: Studies in the Culture and Heritage of Ancient Egypt in Honour of A. F. Shore*, 161–4. Occasional Publications 11. London: Egypt Exploration Society.
——, 1996, 'Sinuhe: Scholarly Method Versus Trendy Fashion', *Bulletin of the Australian Centre of Egyptology* 7, 55–63.
Knigge, C. 1997, 'Die Bekleidung der Ruderinnen in der Geschichte des Papyrus Westcar', *GM* 161, 103–5.
Koch, R. 1990, *Die Erzählung des Sinuhe*. BAe 17.
Koenig, Y. 1990, 'Les Textes d'envoûtement de Mirgissa', *RdE* 41, 101–25.
Konrad, K. 1999, 'Wortverzeichnis und lexikostatistische Untersuchung der Lehre Amenemhets I.', *GM* 169, 87–100.
Korostovtsev, M. A. 1960, 'Egipetskii ieraticheskii papirus no. 167 gosudarstvennogo muzeya izobazitel'nykh iskusstv im. A. S. Pushkina v Moskve'. In V. V. Struve *et al.* (eds), *Drevnii Egipet: sbornik statei* [Golenishchev memorial volume], 119–33. Moscow: izdatel'stvo vostochnoi lityeratury.
Koyama, M. 1982, 'Essai de réconstitution de la composition de l'Histoire de Sinouhé', *Orient* (Tokyo) 18, 41–64.
Kuentz, C. 1923, 'Deux stèles d'Edfou', *BIFAO* 21, 107–11.
Kuhlmann, K. P. 1973, 'Eine Beschreibung der Grabdekoration mit der Aufforderung zu kopieren und zum Hinterlassen von Besucherinschriften aus saitischer Zeit', *MDAIK* 29, 205–13.
Kuhlmann, K. P. 1992, 'Bauernweisheiten'. In I. Gamer-Wallert and W. Helck (eds), *Gegengabe: Festschrift für Emma Brunner-Traut*, 191–209. Tübingen: Attempto.
Kuhlmann, K. P., and Schenkel, W. 1983, *Das Grab des Ibi, Obergutsver-*

walters der Gottesgemahlin des Amun (Thebanisches Grab Nr. 36) I: *Beschreibung der unterirdischen Kult- und Besstattungsanlage.* AV 15.

Kuhn, K. H., and Tait, W. J. 1996, *Thirteen Coptic Acrostic Hymns from Manuscript M574 of the Pierpont Morgan Library*. Oxford: Griffith Institute.

Kurth, D. 1987, 'Zur Interpretation der Geschichte des Schiffbrüchigen', *SAK* 14, 167–79.

Lacombe-Unal, F. 1999, 'Le Prologue de Ptahhotep: Interrogations et propositions', *BIFAO* 99, 283–97.

Laird, A. 1997, 'Approaching Characterisation in Virgil'. In Martindale 1997a: 282–93.

Lange, H. O., and Schäfer, H. 1902, *Grab- und Denksteine des Mittleren Reichs im Museum von Kairo no. 20001–20780* IV: *Tafeln*. Catalogue Général . . . Berlin: Reichsdruckerei.

Lapp G. 1988, 'Die Papyrusvorlagen der Sargtexte', *SAK* 16, 171–202.

Leclant, J., and Berger, C. 1996, 'Des confréries religieuses à Saqqara, à la fin de la XIIe dynastie?' In Manuelian 1996: 499–506.

Lefebvre, G. 1949, *Romans et contes égyptiens de l'époque pharaonique*. Paris: Adrien-Maisonneuve.

Leitz, C. 1996, review of Quack 1992, *WdO* 27, 133–40.

Leprohon, R. J. 1975, 'The Wages of the Eloquent Peasant', *JARCE* 12, 97–8.

Lepsius, C. R. 1849, *Die Chronologie der Aegypter: Einleitung und erster Theil, Kritik der Quellen*. Berlin: Nicolaische Buchhandlung.

——, 1859, *Denkmaeler aus Aegypten und Aethiopien* Abt IV. Berlin: Nicolaische Buchhandlung.

Lesko, B. S. 1986, 'True Art in Ancient Egypt'. In L. H. Lesko (ed.), *Egyptological Studies in Honor of Richard A. Parker*, 85–97. Hanover, NH: University Press of New England for Brown University Press.

Lesko, L. H. 1990, 'Some Comments on Ancient Egyptian Literacy and Literati'. In Israelit-Groll 1990: 656–67.

Letellier, B. 1991, 'De la vanité des biens de ce monde: L'Évocation d'un personnage de fable dans le "Désespéré" (P. Berlin 3024, col. 30–39)', *CRIPEL* 13, 99–105.

Lewalski, B. K. 2000, *The Life of John Milton*. Blackwell Critical Biographies. Oxford: Blackwell.

Lichtheim, M. 1945, 'The Songs of the Harpers', *JNES* 4, 178–212.

——, 1971, 'Have the Principles of Ancient Egyptian Metrics Been Discovered?', *JARCE* 9, 103–10.

——, 1973, *Ancient Egyptian Literature: A Book of Readings*. I: *The Old and Middle Kingdoms*. Berkeley: University of California Press.

——, 1980, 'The Praise of Cities in the Literature of the Egyptian New Kingdom'. In S. M. Burstein and L. A. Okin (eds), *Panhellenica: Essays* in *Ancient History and Historiography in Honor of Truesdell S. Brown*, 15–23. Lawrence KA: Coronado.

——, 1983, *Late Egyptian Wisdom Literature in the International Context: A Study of Demotic Instructions*. OBO 52.

——, 1988, *Ancient Egyptian Autobiographies Chiefly of the Middle Kingdom: A Study and an Anthology*. OBO 84.

——, 1992, *Maat in Egyptian Autobiographies and Related Studies*. OBO 120.

——, 1996, 'Didactic Literature'. In Loprieno 1996a: 243–62.

——, 1997, *Moral Values in Ancient Egypt*. OBO 155.

Light, M. A. 2000, 'The Power of Law: Procedure as Justice in The Eloquent Peasant'. In Gnirs 2000a: 109–24.

Lipking, L. 1995, 'A Trout in the Milk'. In Brown 1995: 1–12.

Liverani, M. 1990, *Prestige and Interest: International Relations in the Near East ca. 1600–1100 B.C.* History of the Ancient Near East Studies 1. Padua: Sargon.

——, 1996, '2084: Ancient Propaganda and Historical Criticism'. In Cooper and Schwartz 1996: 283–9.

Lohmann, K. 1998, 'Das Gespräch eines Mannes mit seinem Ba', *SAK* 25, 207–36.

Longman III, T. 1991, *Fictional Akkadian Autobiography: A Generic and Comparative Study*. Winona Lake IN: Eisenbrauns.

López, J. 1973, 'L'Auteur de l'Enseignement pour Mérikare', *RdE* 25, 178–91.

——, 1978, *Catalogo del Museo Egizio di Torino*, III:1 (2nd ser.), *Ostraca ieratici N.57001–57092*. Milan: La Goliardica.

——, 1980, *Catalogo del Museo Egizio di Torino*, III:2 (2nd ser.), *Ostraca ieratici N.57093–57319*. Milan: La Goliardica.

——, 1982, *Catalogo del Museo Egizio di Torino*, III:3 (2nd ser.), *Ostraca ieratici N.57320–57449*. Milan: La Goliardica.

——, 1984, *Catalogo del Museo Egizio di Torino*, III:4 (2nd ser.), *Ostraca ieratici N.57450–57568, tabelle lignee N.58001–58007*. Milan: La Goliardica.

Loprieno, A. 1988, *Topos und Mimesis: Zum Ausländer in der ägyptischen Literatur*. ÄA 48.

——, 1991a, 'The Sign of Literature in the Shipwrecked Sailor'. In U. Verhoeven and E. Graefe (eds), *Religion und Philosophie im alten Ägypten: Festgabe für Philippe Derchain zu seinem 65. Geburtstag am 24. Juli 1991*, 209–18. OLA 39.

——, 1991b, 'Middle Kingdom Loyalistic Literature between Topos and Mimesis'. In *Sixth International Congress of Egyptology: Abstracts of Papers*, 49. Turin: Organizing Secretariat.

——, 1995, *Ancient Egyptian: A Linguistic Introduction*. Cambridge: Cambridge University Press.

Loprieno, A. (ed.), 1996a, *Ancient Egyptian Literature: History and Forms*. PÄ 10.
——, 1996b, 'Defining Egyptian Literature: Ancient Texts and Modern Theories'. In Loprieno 1996a: 39–58.
——, 1996c, 'The "King's Novel"'. In Loprieno 1996a: 277–95.
——, 1996d, 'Loyalistic Instructions'. In Loprieno 1996a: 403–14.
——, 1996e, 'Linguistic Variety and Egyptian Literature'. In Loprieno 1996a: 515–29.
——, 1996f, 'Loyalty to the King, to God, to Oneself'. In Manuelian 1996: 533–52.
——, 2000, 'The Eloquent Peasant between Literature and Social History'. In Gnirs 2000a: 183–98.
——, in preparation, *History as Story: The Ancient Egyptian Royal Tale*. Athlone Publications in Egyptology and Ancient Near Eastern Studies. London: Athlone.
Lorton, D. 1970, 'A Note on the Expression *šms-íb*', *JARCE* 8, 55–7.
——, 1975, 'The Expression *írí hrw nfr*', *JARCE* 12, 23–33.
——, 1993a, 'God's Beneficent Creation: Coffin Text Spell 1130, the Instructions for Merikare, and the Great Hymn to the Aten', *SAK* 20, 125–55.
——, 1993b, 'The Instruction for Merikare and Amarna Ideology', *GM* 134, 69–83.
——, 1993c, 'The Instruction for Merikare, P 123–130', *Discussions in Egyptology* 26, 13–23.
Lotman, J. 1977 [1970], *The Structure of the Artistic Text* (R. Vroon, trans.). Michigan Slavic Contributions 7. Ann Arbor: University of Michigan.
Loyrette, A.-M., Nasr, M., and Basiouni, S. B. 1994, 'Une tombe en bordure des greniers nord du Ramesseum', *Memnonia* 4/5, 115–27.
Lüddeckens, E. 1943, 'Untersuchungen über religiösen Gehalt, Sprache und Form der ägyptischen Totenklagen', *MDAIK* 11.
Luft, U. 1973, 'Zur Einleitung der Liebesgedichte auf Papyrus Chester Beatty I ro XVI 9ff.', *ZÄS* 99, 108–16.
Luria, S. 1929, 'Die Ersten werden die Letzten sein (zur "Sozialen Revolution" im Altertum)', *Klio* 22, 405–31.
Lustig, J. (ed.) 1997, *Anthropology and Egyptology: A Developing Dialogue*. Monographs in Mediterranean Archaeology 8. Sheffield: Sheffield Academic Press.
Lützeller, P. M. 1990, 'Der postmoderne Neohistorismus in den amerikanischen *Humanities*'. In H. Eggert *et al.*, *Geschichte als Literatur: Formen und Grenzen der Repräsentation von Vergangenheit*, 67–76. Stuttgart: J. B. Metzler.

Lyne, R. O. A. M. 1987, *Further Voices in Vergil's* Aeneid. Oxford: Clarendon Press.

Maclean, I. 1986, 'Reading and Interpretation'. In Jefferson and Robey 1986: 122–44.
MacNeice, L. 1979, *Collected Poems*. London: Faber and Faber.
Malaise, M. 1974, 'La Traduction de Sinouhé B 160', *GM* 10, 29–34.
Malek, J. 1992, 'A Meeting of the Old and New: Saqqâra during the New Kingdom'. In A. B. Lloyd (ed.), *Studies in Pharaonic Religion and Society in Honour of Gwyn Griffiths*, 57–76. Occasional Publications 8. London: Egypt Exploration Society.
Malek, J., and Quirke, S. 1992, 'Memphis, 1991: Epigraphy', *JEA* 78, 13–18.
Mangan, M. 1996, *A Preface to Shakespeare's Comedies 1594–1603*. London and New York: Longman.
Manuelian, P. der 1992, 'Interpreting "The Shipwrecked Sailor"'. In I. Gamer-Wallert and W. Helck (eds), *Gegengabe: Festschrift für Emma Brunner-Traut*, 223–33. Tübingen: Attempto.
——, (ed.) 1996, *Studies in Honor of William Kelly Simpson*. Boston: Museum of Fine Arts.
Martin, G. T. 1985, *The Tomb-Chapels of Paser and Ra'ia at Saqqara*. Egypt Exploration Society Excavation Memoir 32. London: Egypt Exploration Society.
Martin, K. 1986, 'Vogelfang, -jagd, -netz, -steller', *LÄ* VI, 1051–4.
Martin-Pardey, E. 1982, 'Ptahhotep', *LÄ* IV, 1181.
Martindale, C. (ed.) 1997a, *The Cambridge Companion to Virgil*. Cambridge: Cambridge University Press.
——, 1997b, 'Introduction: "The Classic of All Europe"'. In Martindale 1997a: 1–18.
——, 1997c, 'Green Politics: The *Eclogues*'. In Martindale 1997a: 107–24.
Maspero, G. 1911 [1882], *Les Contes populaires de l'Égypte ancienne*. Paris: Guilmoto.
Mathieu, B. 1989, 'Études de métrique égyptienne I: Le Distique heptamétrique dans les chants d'amour', *RdE* 39, 63–82.
——, 1990, 'Études de métrique égyptienne II: Constraints métriques et production textuelle dans l'*Hymne à la crue du Nil*', *RdE* 41, 127–41.
——, 1991, 'Se souvenir de l'Occident (sḫ3 Jmnt.t): Une expression de la piété religieuse au Moyen Empire', *RdE* 42, 262–3.
——, 1993, 'Sur quelques ostraca hiératiques littéraires', *BIFAO* 93, 335–47.
——, 1994, 'Études de métrique égyptienne III: Une innovation métrique dans une "litanie" thébaine du Nouvel Empire', *RdE* 45, 139–54.

Mathieu, B. 1996a, *La Poésie amoureuse de l'Égypte Ancienne: Recherches sur un genre littéraire au Nouvel Empire*. BdE 115.
——, 1996b, 'La Complainte de Khâkhéperrê-séneb', *Égypte, Afrique et Orient* 2, 13–18.
——, 1999, 'Les Contes du Papyrus Westcar: Une interprétation', *Égypte, Afrique et Orient* 15, 29–40.
McDowell, A. 1992, 'Awareness of the Past in Deir el-Medîna'. In Demarée and Egberts 1992: 95–109.
——, 1996, 'Student Exercises from Deir el-Medina: The Dates'. In Manuelian 1996: 601–8.
——, 1999, *Village Life in Ancient Egypt: Laundry Lists and Love Songs*. Oxford: Clarendon Press.
McGann, J. L. 1995, 'Literature, Meaning, and the Discontinuity of Fact'. In Brown 1995: 45–9.
Meeks, D., and Favard-Meeks, C. 1996 [1993], *Daily Life of the Egyptian Gods* (G. M. Goshgarian, trans.). Ithaca and London: Cornell University Press.
Meltzer, E. S. 1994, 'The Art of the Storyteller in Papyrus Westcar: An Egyptian Mark Twain?'. In B. Bryan and D. Lorton (eds), *Essays in Egyptology in Honor of Hans Goedicke*, 169–75. San Antonio: Van Siclen Books.
Menu, B. 2000, 'Le *Dialogue d'un homme avec son âme*: Un débat d'idées dans l'Égypt ancienne', *Égypte, Afrique et Orient* 19, 17–36.
Meskell, L. 1997, 'The Irresistible Body and the Seduction of Archaeology'. In D. Montserrat (ed.), *Changing Bodies, Changing Meanings: Studies on the Human Body in Antiquity*, 139–61. London and New York: Routledge.
——, 1999, *Archaeologies of Social Life: Age, Sex, Class* et cetera *in Ancient Egypt*. Oxford: Blackwell.
Michaels, W. B. 1995, 'The Victims of the New Historicism'. In Brown 1995: 187–96.
Michalowski, P. 1989, *The Lamentation over the Destruction of Sumer and Ur*. Winona Lake IN: Eisenbrauns.
——, 1996, 'Sailing to Babylon, Reading the Dark Side of the Moon'. In Cooper and Schwartz 1996: 177–93.
Midant-Reynes, B. 1981, 'Les Noms du silex en Egyptien', *RdE* 33, 39–45.
Middleton, A. 1992, 'Medieval Studies'. In Greenblatt and Gunn 1992: 12–40.
Miller, P. 1982, *Sin and Judgement in the Prophets*. Chicago: Scholars Press.
Miosi, F. T. 1982, 'God, Fate and Free Will in Egyptian Wisdom Literature'. In G. E. Kadish and G. E. Freeman (eds), *Studies in Philology*

in Honour of Ronald James Williams: A Festschrift, 69–111. Toronto: SSEA.

Mitchell, D. 1993, 'Fit for a Queen? The Reception of *Gloriana*'. In libretto booklet to Argo recording of B. Britten's *Gloriana* (440 213–2). London: Decca.

Mitchell, W. J. T. (ed.) 1985a, *Against Theory: Literary Studies and the New Pragmatism*. Chicago: University of Chicago Press.

——, 1985b, 'Introduction: Pragmatic Theory'. In Mitchell 1985a: 1–10.

Mizener, A. 1959 [1939], 'Character and Action in The Case of Criseyde'. In E. Wagenknecht (ed.), *Chaucer: Modern Essays in Criticism*, 348–65. New York: Oxford University Press.

Moers, G. 1995, 'Der Brief des Wermai: Der Moskauer literarische Brief'. In E. Blumenthal *et al.*, *Mythen und Epen* III, 922–9, TUAT III:5.

——, 1996, *Der Aufbruch ins Fiktionale: Reisemotiv und Grenzüberschreitung in ägyptischen Erzählungen des Mittleren und Neuen Reiches*. Doctoral dissertation. Göttingen. (Published as Moers 2001.)

——, (ed.) 1999a, *Definitely: Egyptian Literature. Proceedings of the Symposion "Ancient Egyptian Literature: History and Forms", Los Angeles, March 24–26, 1995*. Lingua Aegyptiaca Studia Monographica 2. Göttingen: Seminar für Ägyptologie und Koptologie.

——, 1999b, 'Travel as Narrative in Egyptian Literature'. In Moers 1999a: 43–61.

——, 1999c, 'Fiktionalität und Intertextualität als Parameter ägyptologischer Literaturwissenschaft: Perspektiven und Grenzen der Anwendung zeitgenössischer Literaturtheorie'. In J. Assmann and Blumenthal 1999: 37–52.

——, 2000, '*Bei mir wird es Dir gut ergehen, denn Du wirst die Sprache Ägyptens hören!* Verschieden und doch gleich: Sprache als identitätsrelevanter Faktor im pharaonischen Ägypten'. In U. Sander and F. Paul (eds), *Muster und Funktionen kultureller Selbst- und Fremdwahrnehmung: Beiträge zur internationalen Geschichte der sprachlichen und literarischen Emanzipation*, 45–99. Göttingen Sonderforschungsbereich 529 "Internationalität nationaler Literaturen" B: Europäische Literaturen und internationale Prozesse 5. Göttingen: Wallstein.

——, 2001, *Fingierte Welten in der ägyptischen Literatur des 2. Jahrtausends vor Christus: Grenzüberschreitung, Reisemotiv und Fiktionalität*. PÄ 19.

——, in press, 'Self(-)Fashioning Identity: The Interplay of Reenactment and Memory in the *Complaints of Khakheperreseneb*', *LingAeg* 10.

Möller, G. 1909, *Hieratische Paläographie: Die ägyptische Buchschrift in ihrer Entwicklung von der fünften Dynastie bis zur römischen Kaiserzeit* I: *Bis zum Beginn der achtzehnten Dynastie*. Leipzig: J. C. Hinrichs.

Montrose, L. 1986, 'Renaissance Literary Studies and the Subject of History', *English Literary Renaissance* 16 (Winter), 5–12.

Montrose, L. 1988, '"Shaping Fantasies": Figurations of Gender and Power in Elizabethan Culture'. In S. Greenblatt (ed.), *Representing the English Renaissance*, 31–64. Berkeley and London: University of California Press.

——, 1989, 'Professing the Renaissance: The Poetics and Politics of Culture'. In H. A. Veeser (ed.), *The New Historicism*, 15–36. London: Routledge.

——, 1992, 'New Historicisms'. In Greenblatt and Gunn 1992: 392–418.

Morenz, L. 1994, 'Gottesunmittelbarkeit und ein skandalöses Suffixpronomen: Zum 13. Kapitel des Schiffbrüchigen', *GM* 141, 77–80.

——, 1996, *Beiträge zur ägyptischen Schriftlichkeitskultur des Mittleren Reiches und der Zweiten Zwischenzeit*. ÄAT 29.

——, 1997a, 'Eine Maxime aus der Sammlung weisheitlicher Sprüche des Papyrus Ramesseum II', *Discussions in Egyptology* 39, 65–70.

——, 1997b, 'Ein hathorisches Kultlied und ein königlicher Archetyp des Alten Reiches – Sinuhe B 270f. und eine Stele der späten XI. Dynastie (Louvre C 15)', *WdO* 28, 7–17.

——, 1997c, 'Ein Wortspiel mit dem Namen Chetys, des Assertors der *Lehre für Meri-ka-re* (Meri-ka-re, E 143 f.)', *GM* 159, 75–81.

——, 1997d, 'Kanaanäisches Lokalkolorit in der Sinuhe-Erzählung und die Vereinfachung des *Urtextes*', *Zeitschrift des Deutschen Palästina-Vereins* 113, 1–18.

——, 1998, 'Sa-mut / *kyky* und Menna, zwei reale Leser/Hörer des *Oasenmannes* aus dem Neuen Reich?', *GM* 165, 73–81.

——, 1999a, 'Geschichte als Literatur: Reflexe der Ersten Zwischenzeit in den *Mahnworten*'. In J. Assmann and Blumenthal 1999: 111–38.

——, 1999b, 'Humor', *SAK* 27, 261–9.

——, 2000, 'Zum Oasenmann – "Entspanntes Feld", Erzählung und Geschichte'. In Gnirs 2000a: 53–82.

Morenz, S. 1975 [1966], 'Die Bedeutungsentwicklung von [*jjt*] "Das, was kommt" zu "Unheil" und "Unrecht"'. In E. Blumenthal, S. Herrmann et al. (eds), *Religion und Geschichte des alten Ägypten: Gesammelte Aufsätze*, 343–59. Weimar: H. Böhlaus Nachfolger.

Morschauser, S. 1994, 'The Opening Lines of *K3-gm.n.í* (P. Prisse I, 1–3a)'. In B. Bryan and D. Lorton (eds), *Essays in Egyptology in Honor of Hans Goedicke*, 177–85. San Antonio: Van Siclen Books.

Müller, D. 1961, 'Der gute Hirte: Ein Beitrag zur Geschichte ägyptischer Bildrede', *ZÄS* 86, 126–44.

Müller, M. 1998, 'Egyptian Aesthetics in the Middle Kingdom'. In Eyre 1998: 785–92.

Murnane, W. J. 1977, *Ancient Egyptian Coregencies*. SAOC 40.

——, 1981, 'In Defense of the Middle Kingdom Double Dates', *BES* 3, 73–82.

Naville, H. E., and Hall, H. R. 1907, *The XIth Dynasty Temple at Deir el-Bahari* I. Memoir of the Egypt Exploration Fund 28. London: Egypt Exploration Fund.
Nemoianu, V. 1995, 'Literary History: Some Roads Not (Yet) Taken'. In Brown 1995: 13–22.
Newberry, P. E. 1899, *The Amherst Papyri*. London: Quaritch.
Newton, K. M. 1990, *Interpreting the Text: A Critical Introduction to the Theory and Practice of Literary Interpretation*. London: Harvester Wheatsheaf.
Nordh, K. 1996, *Aspects of Ancient Egyptian Curses and Blessings: Conceptual Background and Transmission*. Acta Universitatis Upsaliensis, Boreas 26. Uppsala: Uppsala University.
Nuttall, A. D. 1990, 'Power Dressing: On Greenblatt, *Shakespearean Negotiations*', Comparative Criticism 12, 265–72.

Obsomer, C. 1993, 'La Date de Nésou-Montou (Louvre C1)', *RdE* 44, 103–40.
——, 1995, *Sésostris Ier: Étude chronologique et historique du règne*. Connaissance de l'Égypte Ancienne 5. Brussels.
——, 1999, 'Sinouhé l'Égyptien et les raisons de son exil', *Le Muséon* 112, 207–71.
Ockinga, B. 1983, 'The Burden of Kha'kheperre'sonbu', *JEA* 69, 88–95.
——, 1984, *Die Gottebenbildlichkeit im alten Ägypten und im alten Testament*. ÄAT 7.
O'Connor, D. 1985, 'The "Cenotaphs" of the Middle Kingdom at Abydos'. In P. Posener-Kriéger (ed.), *Mélanges Gamal Eddin Mokhtar* II, 161–77. BdE 97.
Ogdon, J. R. 1982, 'CT VII, 36i r – Spell 836', *GM* 58, 59–64.
——, 1987, 'A Hitherto Unrecognised Metaphor of Death in Papyrus Berlin 3024', *GM* 100, 73–80.
O'Hara, J. J. 1997, 'Virgil's Style'. In Martindale 1997a: 241–58.
O'Keeffe, K. O'B. 1993, 'Texts and Works: Some Historical Questions on the Editing of Old English Verse'. In Cox and Reynolds 1993: 54–68.
Olsen, S. T. 1987, *The End of Literary Theory*. Cambridge: Cambridge University Press.
Omlin, J. A. 1971, *Der Papyrus 55001 und seine satirisch-erotischen Zeichnungen- und Inschriften*. Catalogo del Museo Egizio di Torino I: Monumenti e testi III. Turin: Pozzo.
Ong, W. J. 1982, *Orality and Literacy: The Technologizing of the Word*. New Accents. London: Methuen.
Oppenheim, A. L. 1977 [1964], *Ancient Mesopotamia: Portrait of a Dead Civilization*. Chicago and London: University of Chicago Press.

Orgel, S. 1987, *Shakespeare: The Tempest*. Oxford: Oxford University Press.
Osing, J. 1977a, 'Gespräch des Lebensmüden', *LÄ* II, 571–3.
——, 1977b, 'Gleichnis', *LÄ* II, 618–24.
——, 1977c, 'Glosse', *LÄ* II, 628–30.
——, 1992a, 'Zu zwei literarischen Werken des Mittleren Reiches'. In J. Osing and E. Rand Nielsen, *The Heritage of Ancient Egypt: Studies in Honour of Erik Iversen*, 101–19. Carsten Niebuhr Institute Publications 13. Copenhagen: Museum Tusculanum Press.
——, 1992b, *Das Grab des Nefersecheru in Zawyet Sultan*. AV 88.
——, 1992c, *Aspects de la culture pharaonique: Quatre leçons au Collège de France (Février-mars 1989)*. Mémoires de l'Académie des Inscriptions et Belles-lettres (n.s.) 12. Paris: Boccard.
Osing, J., and Dreyer, G. (ed.) 1987, *Form und Mass: Beiträge zur Literatur, Sprache und Kunst des alten Ägypten. Festschrift für Gerhard Fecht*. ÄAT 12.
Osing, J., and Rosati, G. 1998, *Papyri geroglifici e ieratici da Tebtynis*. Florence: Istituto Papirologico G. Vitelli.
Otto, E. 1951, *Der Vorwurf an Gott: Zur Entstehung der ägyptischen Auseinandersetzungsliteratur*. Vorträge der orientalistischen Tagung in Marburg: Ägyptologie. Hildesheim: Gerstenberg.
——, 1962, 'Zwei Paralleltexte zu TB 175', *CdE* 37/73, 249–56.
——, 1966, 'Die Geschichten des Sinuhe und des Schiffbrüchigen als "Lehrhafte Stücke"', *ZÄS* 93, 100–11.
——, 1969, 'Das "Goldene Zeitalter" in einem ägyptischen Text'. In P. Derchain (ed.), *Religions en Egypte hellénistique et romaine: Colloque de Strasbourg 16–18 Mai 1967*, 93–108. Travaux du Centre d'Etudes Supérieures Spécialisé d'Histoire des Religions de Strasbourg. Paris: Presses Universitaires de France.
——, 1975, 'Chacheperreseneb', *LÄ* I, 896–7.
——, 1977, 'Zur Komposition von Coffin Text Spell 1130'. In J. Assmann *et al.* 1977: 1–18.

Pamminger, P. 1993, 'Gottesworte und Zahlensymbolik in den "Klagen des Bauern"', *SAK* 20, 207–21.
Parant, R. 1982, *L'Affaire Sinouhé: Tentative d'approche de la justice répressive égyptienne au début du IIe millénaire av. J.C.* Aurillac: published by author.
Parkinson, R. B. 1988, 'The Tale of The Eloquent Peasant: A Commentary'. Doctoral dissertation, University of Oxford.
——, 1991a, *Voices from Ancient Egypt: An Anthology of Middle Kingdom Writings*. London: British Museum Press.
——, 1991b, 'Teachings, Discourses and Tales from the Middle Kingdom'. In Quirke 1991a: 91–122.

——, 1991c, *The Tale of the Eloquent Peasant*. Oxford: Griffith Institute.

——, 1991d, 'Images of Death: Interpreting the "Dialogue between a Man and His *Ba*"'. In *Sixth International Congress of Egyptology: Abstracts of Papers*, 318–19. Turin: Organizing Secretariat.

——, 1991e, 'The Date of the "Tale of the Eloquent Peasant"', *RdE* 42, 169–81.

——, 1992, 'Literary Form and the *Tale of the Eloquent Peasant*', *JEA* 78, 163–78.

——, 1995, '"Homosexual" Desire and Middle Kingdom Literature', *JEA* 81, 57–76.

——, 1996a, 'Individual and Society in Middle Kingdom Literature'. In Loprieno 1996a: 137–55.

——, 1996b, 'Types of Literature in the Middle Kingdom'. In Loprieno 1996a: 297–312.

——, 1996c, 'On a Proposed Survival of the "Lebensmüder" into the Christian Era', *CdE* 71/142, 389–92.

——, 1996d, '*Khakheperreseneb* and Traditional Belles Lettres'. In Manuelian 1996: 646–54.

——, 1997a, *The Tale of Sinuhe and Other Ancient Egyptian Poems 1940–1640 BC*. Oxford: Clarendon Press.

——, 1997b, 'The Text of *Khakheperreseneb*: New Readings of EA 5645, and an Unpublished Ostracon', *JEA* 83, 55–68.

——, 1999a, *Cracking Codes: The Rosetta Stone and Decipherment*. London: British Museum Press.

——, 1999b, 'Reading Ancient Egypt', *British Museum Magazine* 34, 12–15.

——, 1999c, 'The Dream and the Knot: Contextualizing Middle Kingdom Literature'. In Moers 1999a: 63–82.

——, 1999d, 'Two New "Literary" Texts on a Second Intermediate Period Papyrus? A Preliminary Account of P. BM EA 10475'. In J. Assmann and Blumenthal 1999: 177–96.

——, 1999e, 'Two or Three Literary Artefacts: EA 41650/47896, and 22878–9'. In W. V. Davies (ed.), *Studies in Egyptian Antiquities: A Tribute to T. G. H. James*, 49–57. British Museum Occasional Paper 123. London: British Museum Press.

——, 1999f, *The Tale of Sinuhe and Other Ancient Egyptian Poems 1940–1640 BC*. Oxford World's Classics. Oxford: Oxford University Press.

——, 2000a, '*Sinuhe* Speaks Again', *Egyptian Archaeology* 16, 44.

——, 2000b, 'Imposing Words: The Entrapment of Language in The Tale of the Eloquent Peasant'. In Gnirs 2000a: 27–51.

——, 2000c, '*The Teaching of King Amenemhat I* at el-Amarna: EA 57458 and 57479'. In A. Leahy and J. Tait, *Studies on Ancient Egypt in Honour*

of H. S. Smith, 221–6. Occasional Publications 13. London: Egypt Exploration Society.
Parkinson, R. B., and Quirke, S. 1995, *Papyrus*. Egyptian Bookshelf. London: British Museum Press.
Patanè, M. 1989, 'Quelques remarques sur Sinouhé', *BSEG* 13, 131–3.
——, 1991, 'Existe-t-il dans l'Égypte ancienne une littérature licencieuse?', *BSEG* 15, 91–3.
Patterson, A. 1984, *Censorship and Interpretation*. Madison: University of Wisconsin Press.
——, 1993, *Reading between the Lines*. London: Routledge.
Patterson, L. 1990, 'Literary History'. In F. Lentricchia and T. McLaughlin (eds), *Critical Terms for Literary Study*, 250–62. Chicago: University of Chicago Press.
Payne, R. O. 1973 [1963], *The Key of Remembrance: A Study of Chaucer's Poetics*. Westport CT: Greenwood Press.
Peet, T. E. 1931, *A Comparative Study of the Literature of Egypt, Palestine and Mesopotamia: Egypt's Contribution to the Literature of the Ancient World*. Schweich Lectures, 1929. London: Oxford University Press for British Academy.
Perdue, L. G. 1981, 'Liminality as a Social Setting for Wisdom Literature', *ZAW* 93, 114–26.
Perkins, D. 1995, 'Some Prospects for Literary History'. In Brown 1995: 63–9.
Perloff, M. 1995, 'Empiricism Once More'. In Brown 1995: 51–61.
Pestman, P. W. 1982, 'Who Were the Owners, in the "Community of Workmen", of the Chester Beatty Papyri?' In R. J. Demarée and J. J. Janssen (eds), *Gleanings from Deir el-Medîna*, 155–72. Leiden: Nederlands Instituut voor het Nabije Oosten.
Piccato, A. 1997, 'The Berlin Leather Roll and the Egyptian Sense of History', *LingAeg* 5, 137–59.
Pieper, M. 1927, *Die ägyptische Literatur*. Wildpark-Potsdam: Athenaion.
Pinch, G. 1993, *Votive Offerings to Hathor*. Oxford: Griffith Institute.
Piper, M. 1973, *Death in Venice*. Libretto to Benjamin Britten opera, Op. 88. London: Boosey and Hawkes.
Poignault, R. 1995, *L'Antiquité dans l'œuvre de Marguerite Yourcenar: Littérature, mythe et histoire*. Collection Latomus 228. Brussels.
Poláček, A. 1974, 'Lehre der Antike: Randglossen zu Ptaḥḥoteps Anstandsregeln'. In *Akten des XIII. internationalen Papyrologenkongresses*, 339–48. MBP 66.
Polz, F. 1995, 'Die Bildnisse Sesostris' III. und Amenemhets III.: Bemerkungen zur königlichen Rundplastik der späten 12. Dynastie', *MDAIK* 51, 227–54.

Porter C. 1988, 'Are We Being Historical Yet?', *South Atlantic Quarterly* 87, 743–86.
Posener, G. 1938, *Catalogue des ostraca hiératiques littéraires de Deir el Médineh* I: *(N°s 1001 à 1108)*. DFIFAO 1.
——, 1946, 'Admonitions 3^{14}', *RdE* 5, 254–5.
——, 1948, 'Annexe I: Deux ostraca littéraires d'un type particulier et le livre KMJ.T'. In van der Walle 1948: 41–50.
——, 1950a, 'Section finale d'une sagesse inconnue (Recherches littéraires, II)', *RdE* 7, 71–84.
——, 1950b, 'Trois passages de l'Enseignement à Mérikarê', *RdE* 7, 176–80.
——, 1951a, 'Les Richesses inconnues de la littérature égyptienne (Recherches littéraires, I)', *RdE* 6, 27–48.
——, 1951b, 'Sur l'emploi de l'encre rouge dans les manuscrits égyptiens', *JEA* 37, 75–80.
——, 1951c, *Catalogue des ostraca hiératiques littéraires de Deir el Médineh* II:1. DFIFAO 18.
——, 1951d, 'Ostraca inédits du Musée de Turin (Recherches littéraires III)', *RdE* 8, 171–89.
——, 1952a, 'Compléments aux "Richesses inconnues"', *RdE* 9, 117–20.
——, 1952b, 'Le Début de l'Enseignement de Hardjedef (Recherches littéraires, IV)', *RdE* 9, 109–17.
——, 1955, 'L'Exorde de l'instruction éducative d'Amennakhte (Recherches littéraires, V)', *RdE* 10, 61–72.
——, 1956, *Littérature et politique dans l'Égypte de la XIIe dynastie*. BEHE 307.
——, 1957, 'Le Conte de Néferkarè et du Général Siséné (Recherches littéraires, VI)', *RdE* 11, 119–37.
——, 1960, 'Une nouvelle histoire de revenant (Recherches littéraires, VII)', *RdE* 12, 75–82.
——, 1962, 'Histoire et Égypte ancienne', *Annales, Économies, Sociétés, Civilisations* 17, 631–46.
——, 1962–6, 'L'Enseignement pour le roi Mérikarê'. Summary of lecture course. *Annuaire du Collège de France* 62 (1962), 290–5; 63 (1963), 303–5; 64 (1964), 305–7; 65 (1965), 343–6; 66 (1966), 342–5.
——, 1963, 'L'Apport des textes littéraires à la connaissance de l'histoire égyptienne'. In S. Donadoni (ed.), *Le fonti indirette della storia egiziana*, 11–30. Studi Semitici 7. Rome: Centro di Studi Semitici, Università di Roma.
——, 1966, 'Quatre tablettes scolaires de Basse Epoque (Aménémopé et Hardjédef)', *RdE* 18, 45–65.
——, 1969, 'Fragment littéraire de Moscou', *MDAIK* 25, 101–6.

Posener, G. 1971, 'Literature'. In J. R. Harris (ed.), *The Legacy of Egypt*, 220–56. Oxford: Clarendon Press.

——, 1975, 'Les Ostraca numérotés et le Conte du Revenant', *Drevnii Vostok: sbornik* 1 (Fs. Korostovstev), 105–12. Moscow: izdatel'stvo 'Nauka'.

——, 1976, *L'Enseignement loyaliste: sagesse égyptienne du Moyen Empire*. Centre de Recherches d'Histoire et de Philologie II: Hautes études orientales 5. Geneva: Droz.

——, 1978 (ed.), J. Černý, *Papyrus hiératiques de Deir el-Médineh* I. DFIFAO 8.

——, 1977–80, *Catalogue des ostraca hiératiques littéraires de Deir el Médineh*. III: *N°ˢ 1267–1675*. DFIFAO 20.

——, 1979, 'L'Enseignement d'un Homme à son Fils'. In Hornung and Keel 1979: 308–16.

——, 1980a, 'L'Auteur de la Satire des Métiers'. In J. Vercoutter (ed.), *Livre du Centenaire: 1880–1980*, 55–9. MIFAO 104.

——, 1980b, 'Lehre des Djedefhor', *LÄ* III, 978–80.

——, 1980c, 'Lehre, Loyaliste', *LÄ* III, 982–3.

——, 1980d, 'Lehre eines Mannes an seinen Sohn', *LÄ* III, 984–6.

——, 1980e, 'Lehre für Merikare', *LÄ* III, 986–9.

——, 1985a, 'Pour la reconstruction de L'Enseignement d'un Homme à son Fils', *RdE* 36, 115–19.

——, 1987a, *Cinq Figurines d'envoûtement*. BdE 101.

——, 1987b, 'L'Enseignement d'un homme à son fils'. In Osing and Dreyer 1987: 361–7.

——, 1988, 'Découverte de l'ancienne Égypte', *BSFE* 112, 11–22.

Posener-Kriéger, P. 1972, 'Les Papyrus de l'Ancien Empire'. In S. Sauneron (ed.), *Textes et langages de l'Égypte pharaonique: Cent cinquante années de recherches 1822–1972, hommage à Jean-François Champollion*, 25–35. BdE 64/2.

Purdy, S. 1977, 'Sinuhe and the Question of Literary Types', *ZÄS* 104, 112–27.

Quack, J. F. 1990, 'Zwei Ostraka-Identifizierungen', *GM* 115, 83–4.

——, 1992, *Studien zur Lehre für Merikare*. GOF IV.23.

——, 1993, 'Beiträge zur Textkritik der Prophezeiung des Neferti', *GM* 135, 77–9.

——, 1994, *Die Lehren des Ani: Ein neuägyptischer Weisheitstext in seinem kulturellen Umfeld*. OBO 141.

——, 1997, 'Die Klage über die Zerstörung Ägyptens: Versuch einer Neudeutung der "Admonitions" im Vergleich zu den altorientalischen Städteklagen'. In B. Pongratz-Leisten, H. Kühne, and P. Xella (eds), *Ana šadî Labnāni lū allik: Beiträge zu altorientalischen und mittelmeerischen*

Kulturen, Festschrift für Wolfgang Röllig, 345–54. Kevelaer: Butzon and Bercker; Neukirchen-Vluyn: Neukirchener Verlag.

Quirke, S. 1990a, review of Loprieno 1988, *Discussions in Egyptology* 16, 89–95.

——, 1990b, *The Administration of Egypt in the Late Middle Kingdom: The Hieratic Documents*. New Malden: SIA.

——, 1991a (ed.), *Middle Kingdom Studies*. New Malden: SIA.

——, 1991b, 'Royal Power in the 13th Dynasty'. In Quirke 1991a: 123–39.

——, 1991c, '"Townsmen" in the Middle Kingdom: On the Term *s n niwt tn* in the Lahun Temple Accounts', *ZÄS* 118, 141–9.

——, 1996a, 'Narrative Literature'. In Loprieno 1996a: 263–76.

——, 1996b, 'Archive'. In Loprieno 1996a: 379–401.

——, 1999 (ed.), *Lahun Studies*. Reigate: SIA.

Ranke, H. 1954, 'Zu Bauer I, 64ff.', *ZÄS* 79, 72–3.

Rathke-Konrad, K. 1997, 'Wortverzeichnis und lexikostatistische Untersuchung der Lehre für König Merikare', *GM* 160, 85–109.

Redford, D. B. 1986, *Pharaonic King-lists, Annals and Daybooks: A Contribution to the Study of the Egyptian Sense of History*. SSEA Publication 4. Mississauga, Ont.: Benben.

——, 1987, 'The Tod Inscription of Senwosret I and Early 12th Dynasty Involvement in Nubia and the South', *JSSEA* 17, 36–55.

Renaud, O. 1988, 'Ipouer le mal-aimé', *BSEG* 12, 71–5.

——, 1991, *Le Dialogue du Désespéré avec son Âme: Une interprétation littéraire*. Cahiers de la Société d'Egyptologie 1. Geneva.

Rendsburg, G. A. 2000, 'Literary Devices in the Story of the Shipwrecked Sailor', *JAOS* 120, 13–23.

Reynolds, L. D., and Wilson, N. G. 1991 [1968], *Scribes and Scholars: A Guide to the Transmission of Greek and Latin Literature*. Oxford: Clarendon Press.

Richards, J. E. 1992, *Mortuary Variability and Social Differentiation in Middle Kingdom Egypt*. Doctoral dissertation, University of Pennsylvania. Ann Arbor: UMI.

——, 1997, 'Ancient Egyptian Mortuary Practice and the Study of Socioeconomic Differentiation'. In Lustig 1997: 33–42.

Richter-Aeroe, E. 1984, 'Sisenet und Phiops II.', *LÄ* V, 957.

Ritner, R. K. 1992, 'Egyptian Magic: Questions of Legitimacy, Religious Orthodoxy and Social Deviance'. In A. B. Lloyd (ed.), *Studies in Pharaonic Religion and Society in Honour of J. Gwyn Griffiths*, 189–200. Occasional Publications 8. London: Egypt Exploration Society.

——, 1993, *The Mechanics of Ancient Egyptian Magical Practice*. SAOC 54.

Ritter, V. 1999, 'Hordjédef ou le glorieux destin d'un prince oublié'. *Égypte, Afrique et Orient* 15, 41–50.
Robey, D. 1986a, 'Modern Linguistics and the Language of Literature'. In Jefferson and Robey 1986: 46–72.
——, 1986b, 'Anglo-American New Criticism'. In Jefferson and Robey 1986: 73–91.
Robins, G. 1996, 'Dress, Undress, and the Representation of Fertility and Potency in New Kingdom Egyptian Art'. In N. B. Kampen (ed.), *Sexuality in Ancient Art*, 27–40. Cambridge: Cambridge University Press.
Roccati, A. 1982a, *La Littérature historique sous l'Ancien Empire égyptien*. Paris: Editions du Cerf.
——, 1982b, 'Su un passo di Hardjédef', *JEA* 68, 16–19.
——, 1993, 'Plaidoyer pour le Paysan Plaideur'. In J.-M. Kruchten and C. Cannuyer (eds), *Individu, société et spiritualité dans l'Égypte pharaonique et copte: Mélanges offerts au Professeur Aristide Théodoridès*, 253–6. Ath, Bruxelles, Mons: Illustra.
——, 1994a, '[šmw šḥnw]'. In C. Berger et al. (eds), *Hommages à Jean Leclant* 1, 493–7. BdE 106.
——, 1994b, *Sapienza egizia: La letteratura educativa in Egitto durante il II millennio a. C.* Brescia: Paideia Editrice.
——, 2000, 'Réflexions sur la Satire des Métiers', *BSFE* 148, 5–17.
Römer, M. 1987, 'Der Kairener Hymnus an Amun-Re zur Gliederung von pBoulaq 17'. In Osing and Dreyer 1987: 405–28.
Ronen, R. 1994, *Possible Worlds in Literary Theory*. Literature, Culture, Theory 7. Cambridge: Cambridge University Press.
Rose, M. A. 1993, *Parody: Ancient, Modern, and Post-modern*. Literature, Culture, Theory 5. Cambridge: Cambridge University Press.
Rössler-Köhler, U. 1979, *Kapitel 17 des ägyptischen Totenbuchs: Untersuchungen zur Textgeschichte und Funktion eines Textes der altägyptischen Totenliteratur*. GOF IV.10.
Rowinska, E., and J. K. Winnicki 1992, 'Staatausdehnung (P 67–68) und Massnahmen zur Verstärkung der Nordostgrenze (P 106–109) in der "Lehre für den König Merikare"', *ZÄS* 119, 130–43.
Ryan, K. (ed.) 1996, *New Historicism and Cultural Materialism: A Reader*. London: Arnold.
Ryholt, K. S. B. 1997, *The Political Situation in Egypt during the Second Intermediate Period c. 1800–1550 B.C.* Carsten Niebuhr Institute Publications 20. Copenhagen: Museum Tusculanum Press.

Said, E. W. 1978, *Orientalism*. London: Routledge and Kegan Paul.
——, 1984, *The World, the Text and the Critic*. London: Faber and Faber.

Sallier, F. 1828, *Sur une découverte de Champollion dans des papyrus égyptiens.* Aix.

Sander-Hansen C. E. 1957, 'Bemerkungen zu der Sinuhe-Erzählung', *AcOr* 22, 142–9.

Säve-Söderbergh, T. 1949, *Studies in the Coptic Manichaean Psalm Book: Prosody and Mandaean Parallels.* Uppsala: Almqvist and Wiksell.

Schaefer, A 1986, 'Zur Entstehung der Mitregentschaft als Legitimationsprinzip von Herrschaft', *ZÄS* 113, 44–55.

Schama, S. 1995, *Landscape and Memory.* London: HarperCollins.

Schenkel, W. 1964, 'Eine neue Weisheitslehre?', *JEA* 50, 6–12.

——, 1965, *Memphis, Herakleopolis, Theben: Die epigraphischen Zeugnisse der 7.–11. Dynastie Ägyptens.* ÄA 12.

——, 1972, 'Zur Relevanz der altägyptischen Metrik', *MDAIK* 28, 103–7.

——, 1973, 'Ist der Wortschatz des "Lebensmüden" grösser als der des "Sinuhe"?', *GM* 5, 21–4.

——, 1975a, 'Repères chronologiques de l'histoire rédactionelle des *Coffin Texts*'. In G. Posener (ed.), *Actes du XXIXe congrès international des orientalistes: Égyptologie* 2, 98–103. Paris: L'Asiathèque.

——, 1975b, 'Die Bauinschrift Sesostris' I. im Satet-Tempel von Elephantine', *MDAIK* 31, 109–25.

——, 1984, 'Sonst-Jetzt: Variationen eines literarischen Formelements', *WdO* 15, 51–61.

——, 1986, 'Texttradierung, -kritik', *LÄ* VI, 459–62.

——, 1996, 'Ägyptische Literatur und ägyptologische Forschung: Eine wissenschaftsgeschichtliche Einleitung'. In Loprieno 1996a: 21–38.

——, 1999, '"Littérature et politique": Fragestellung oder Antwort? Zwei Diskussionbeiträge'. In J. Assmann and Blumenthal 1999: 63–74.

Schipper, B. U. 1998, 'Von der "Lehre des Sehetep-jb-Re" zur "Loyalistischen Lehre"', *ZÄS* 125, 161–79.

Schlichting, R. 1977, 'Hören', *LÄ* II, 1232–5.

Schlott, A. 1996, 'Einige Beobachtungen zu Mimik und Gestik von Singenden', *GM* 152, 55–70.

Schmid, H. H. 1966, *Wesen und Geschichte der Weisheit: Eine Untersuchung zur altorientalischen und israelitischen Weisheitsliteratur.* ZAW 101.

Schorr, E. 1974, 'Admonitions 9,3', *GM* 13 (1974), 29–30.

Schott, S. 1990, *Bücher und Bibliotheken im Alten Ägypten: Verzeichnis der Buch- und Spruchtitel und der Termini technici.* Wiesbaden: Harrassowitz.

Schulman, A. R. 1986, 'The So-called Poem on the King's Chariot Revisited', *JSSEA* 16, 19–35, 39–49.

Seibert, P. 1967, *Die Charakteristik: Untersuchungen zu einer altägyptischen Sprechsitte und ihren Ausprägungen in Folklore und Literatur I: Philologische Bearbeitung der Bezeugungen.* ÄA 17.

Seidlmayer, S. J. 1990, *Gräberfelder aus dem Übergang vom Alten zum Mittleren Reich: Studien zur Archäologie der Ersten Zwischenzeit*. SAGA 1.

——, 2000, 'Zu Fundort und Aufstellungskontext der groß Semna-Stele Sesostris' III.', *SAK* 28, 233–42.

Sethe, K. 1928a [1924], *Ägyptische Lesestücke zum Gebrauch im akademischen Unterricht: Texte des Mittleren Reiches*. Leipzig: J. C. Hinrichs.

——, 1928b, *Dramatische Texte zu altägyptischen Mysterienspielen*. UGAÄ 10.

Seyfried, K. J. 1984, 'Zur Inschrift des Hor (Wadi el-Hudi Nr. 1 (143))', *GM* 81, 55–64.

Shirun-Grumach, I. 1977, 'Parallelismus membrorum und Vers'. In J. Assmann *et al.* 1977: 463–92.

——, 1984, 'Sinuhe R 24: Wer rief?' In Junge 1984c: 621–9.

——, 1993, *Offenbarung, Orakel und Königsnovelle*. ÄAT 24.

Shupak, N. 1988, 'Instruction and Teaching Appellation in Egyptian Wisdom Literature (and Their Biblical Counterparts)', *SAK* Beiheft 4, 193–200.

——, 1992, 'A New Source for the Study of the Judiciary and Law of Ancient Egypt: "The Tale of the Eloquent Peasant"', *JNES* 51, 1–18.

——, 1993, *Where Can Wisdom Be Found? The Sage's Language in the Bible and in Ancient Egyptian Literature*. OBO 130.

Silverman, D. P. 1980, *Interrogative Constructions with jn and jn-jw in Old and Middle Egyptian*. Bibliotheca Aegyptia I. Malibu: Undena.

——, 1988, *The Tomb Chamber of ḥsw the Elder: The Inscribed Material at Kom el-Ḥisn* I. Winona Lake, IN: Eisenbrauns.

——, 1990, 'A Spell from an Abbreviated Version of the Book of the Two Ways in a Tomb of the Western Delta'. In Israelit-Groll 1990: 853–76.

——, 1996, 'Coffin Texts from Bersheh, Kom el Hisn, and Mendes'. In Willems 1996a: 129–41.

——, 1994, *Cultural Politics – Queer Reading*. London: Routledge.

Simpson, W. K. 1958a, 'Allusions to the Shipwrecked Sailor and the Eloquent Peasant in a Late Ramesside Text', *JAOS* 78, 50–5.

——, 1958b, 'A Hatnub Text of the Early Twelfth Dynasty', *MDAIK* 16, 298–309.

——, 1960, 'Papyrus Lythgoe: A Fragment of a Literary Text of the Middle Kingdom from el-Lisht', *JEA* 46, 65–70.

——, 1961, 'An Additional Fragment of a "Hatnub" stela', *JNES* 20, 25–30.

——, 1963a, *Papyrus Reisner I: The Records of a Building Project in the Reign of Sesostris I, Transcription and Commentary*. Boston: Museum of Fine Arts.

——, 1963b, 'The Vizier Weḥaʿu in P. Lythgoe and Ostr. Moscow 4478', *JEA* 49, 172.

——, 1972, 'Papyri of the Middle Kingdom'. In S. Sauneron (ed.), *Textes et langages de l'Egypte pharaonique* II, 63–72, BdE 64/2.

——, 1974, *The Terrace of the Great God at Abydos: The Offering Chapels of Dynasties 12 and 13*. Publications of the Pennsylvania-Yale Expedition to Egypt 5. New Haven: Peabody Museum; Philadelphia: University of Pennsylvania Museum.

——, 1980, 'Lischt', *LÄ* III, 1057–61.

——, 1981, 'The Memphite Epistolary Formula on a Jar Stand of the First Intermediate Period from Naga ed-Deir'. In W. K. Simpson and W. M. Davis (eds), *Studies in Ancient Egypt, the Aegean, and the Sudan: Essays in Honor of Dows Durham on the Occasion of His 90th Birthday, June 1, 1980*, 173–9. Boston: Museum of Fine Arts.

——, 1982, 'Pap. Westcar', *LÄ* IV, 744–6.

——, 1984a, 'Schiffbrüchiger', *LÄ* V, 619–22.

——, 1984b, 'Sinuhe', *LÄ* V, 960–65.

——, 1990, 'The Political Background of the Eloquent Peasant', *GM* 120, 95–9.

——, 1991, 'Mentuhotep, Vizier of Sesostris I, Patron of Art and Architecture', *MDAIK* 47, 331–40.

——, 1995. *Inscribed Material from the Pennsylvania–Yale Excavations at Abydos*. Publications of the Pennsylvania-Yale Expedition to Egypt 6. New Haven: Peabody Museum; Philadelphia: University of Pennsylvania Museum.

——, 1996, '*Belles Lettres* and Propaganda'. In Loprieno 1996a: 435–43.

Sinfield, A. 1992, *Faultlines: Cultural Materialism and the Politics of Dissident Reading*. Oxford: Clarendon Press.

Sitzler, D. 1995, *Vorwurf gegen Gott: Ein religiöses Motiv im Alten Orient (Ägypten und Mesopotamien)*. Studies in Oriental Religions 32. Wiesbaden: Harrassowitz.

Smith, B. R. 1991, *Homosexual Desire in Shakespeare's England: A Cultural Poetics*. Chicago and London: University of Chicago Press.

Smith, M. 1987, *The Mortuary Texts of Papyrus BM 10507*. Catalogue of Demotic Papyri in the British Museum 3. London: British Museum Press.

Smither, P. 1939, 'A New Reading of *Lebensmüde*, 131–2', *JEA* 25, 220.

von Soden, W. 1965, 'Das Fragen nach der Gerechtigkeit Gottes im Alten Orient', *MDOG* 96, 41–59.

Sontag, S. 1994 [1966], *Against Interpretation and Other Essays*. London: Vintage.

Sourvinou-Inwood, C. 1991, *'Reading' Greek Culture: Text and Images, Rituals and Myths*. Oxford: Clarendon Press.

Spalinger, A. J. 1984, 'An Alarming Parallel to the End of the Shipwrecked Sailor', *GM* 73, 91–5.

Spalinger, A. J. 1998, 'Orientations on *Sinuhe*', *SAK* 25, 311–39.
Spiegel, J. 1975, 'Admonitions', *LÄ* I, 65–6.
Spycher, L. 1982, 'Propaganda', *LÄ* IV, 1120–2.
Staehelin, E. 1970, 'Bindung und Entbindung: Erwägungen zu Papyrus Westcar 10, 2', *ZÄS* 96, 125–39.
Stallybrass, O. 1979, *E. M. Forster: A Passage to India*. Penguin Modern Classics. Harmondsworth, Penguin.
Stewart, H. M. 1979, *Egyptian Stelae, Reliefs and Paintings from the Petrie Collection*. II: *Archaic Period to Second Intermediate Period*. Warminster: Aris and Phillips.
Szpakowska, K. 2000, *The Perception of Dreams and Nightmares in Ancient Egypt: Old Kingdom to Third Intermediate Period*. Doctoral dissertation, University of California, Los Angeles.

Tacke, N. 2001, *Verspunkte als Gliederungsmittel in ramesidischen, Schülerhandschriften*. SAGA 22.
Tait, J. 1977, *Papyri from Tebtunis in Egyptian and Greek*. Texts from Excavations 3. London: Egypt Exploration Society.
Tarrant, R. J. 1997a, 'Aspects of Virgil's Reception in Antiquity'. In Martindale 1997a: 56–72.
——, 1997b, 'Poetry and Power: Virgil's Poetry in Contemporary Context'. In Martindale 1997a: 169–87.
Taylor, G. 1990, *Reinventing Shakespeare: A Cultural History from the Restoration to the Present*. London: Hogarth Press.
Tefnin, R. 1992, 'Les Yeux et les oreilles du Roi'. In M. Broze and Ph. Talon (eds), *L'Atelier de l'orfèvre: Mélanges offerts à Ph. Derchain*, 147–56. Leuven: Peeters.
Textor de Ravisi, Baron 1878, 'Recherches et conjectures sur la poésie pharaonique'. In *Congrès provincial des orientalistes français. Compte rendu.* Session 1, tome 2, 473–554. Saint Etienne: Théolier.
Théodoridès, A. 1958–60, 'La "Satire des Métiers" et les marchands', *Annuaire de l'Institut de Philologie et d'Histoire Orientales et Slaves* 15, 39–69.
——, 1984, 'L'Amnistie et la raison d'état dans les 'Aventures de Sinouhé' (début du IIe millénaire av. J.-C.)', *RIDA* 31, 75–144.
——, 1990, 'Sur une théorie du droit à la vie par la propriété privée', *Bulletin, Association Montoise d'Egyptologie* 1:2, 11–19.
Thériault, C. A. 1993, '*The Instruction of Amenemhat* as Propaganda', *JARCE* 30, 151–60.
Thissen, H. J. 1992, *Der verkommene Harfenspieler: Eine altägyptische Invektive (P. Wien KM 3877)*. Demotischen Studien 11. Sommerhausen: Gisela Zauzich.
Thomas, K. 1986, 'The Meaning of Literacy in Early Modern England'.

In G. Baumann (ed.), *The Written Word: Literacy in Transition*, 97–131. Oxford: Clarendon Press.

Till, W. 1961, *Koptische Grammatik (Saïdischer Dialekt)*. Lehrbücher für das Studium der Orientalischen Sprachen 1. Leipzig: Enzyklopädie.

Tobin, V. A. 1991, 'A Re-assessment of the *Lebensmüde*', *BiOr* 48, 341–63.

——, 1995, 'The Secret of Sinuhe', *JARCE* 32, 161–78.

Todorov, T. 1973, 'The Notion of Literature', *New Literary History* 5, 5–16.

——, 1976, 'The Origin of Genres', *New Literary History* 8, 159–70.

——, 1981, *Introduction to Poetics* (R. Howard, trans.). Brighton: Harvester Press.

Trigger, B. 1998, 'Archaeology and Epistemology: Dialoguing across the Darwinian Chasm', *American Journal of Archaeology* 102, 1–34.

Trilling, L. 1942, *E. M. Forster: A Study*. London: The Hogarth Press.

Troy, L. 1984, 'Good and Bad Women: Maxim 18/284–288 of the Instructions of Ptahhotep', *GM* 80, 77–81.

Turner, E. G., and Cockle, W. E. H. 1982, 'Complaint against a Policeman', *JEA* 68, 272–6.

van den Boorn, G. P. F. 1988, *The Duties of the Vizier: Civil Administration in the Early Middle Kingdom*. Studies in Egyptology. London and New York: Kegan Paul International.

van der Plas, D. 1984, 'On Criteria for the Dating of Egyptian Texts', *GM* 73, 49–56.

——, 1986, *L'Hymne à la crue du Nil*. 2 vols. Leiden: Nederlands Instituut voor het Nabije Oosten.

van der Walle, B. 1948, *La Transmission des textes littéraires égyptiens*. Brussels: Fondation égyptologique Reine Élisabeth.

——, 1985, 'Formules et poèmes numériques dans la littérature égyptienne', *CdE* 60/119–20, 371–8.

Vandersleyen, C. 1990, 'En relisant le Naufragé'. In Israelit-Groll 1990: 1019–24.

——, 1993, 'Tjarou', *GM* 136, 85–7.

——, 1995, *L'Égypte et la Vallée du Nil*. II: *De la fin de l'Ancien Empire à la fin du Nouvel Empire*. Nouvelle Clio: l'Histoire et ses problèmes. Paris: Presses Universitaires de France.

van Dijk, J. 1994, 'The Nocturnal Wanderings of King Neferkare'. In C. Berger *et al.* (eds), *Hommages à Jean Leclant* 4, 387–93. BdE 106/4.

Van Siclen, C. C. 1982, *The Chapel of Sesostris at Uronarti*. San Antonio: Van Siclen Books.

Vanstiphout, H. 1995, 'Memory and Literacy in Ancient Western Asia'. In J. Sasson *et al.* (eds), *Civilizations of the Ancient Near East*. New York, Charles Scribner's.

Verhoeven, U. 1996, 'Ein historischer "Sitz im Leben" für die Erzählung von Horus und Seth des Papyrus Chester Beatty I'. In M. Schade-Busch (ed.), *Wege öffnen: Festschrift für Rolf Gundlach zum 65. Geburtstag*, 347–65. ÄAT 35.

——, 1999, 'Von hieratischen Literaturwerken in der Spätzeit'. In J. Assmann and Blumenthal 1999: 255–66.

Vernus, P. 1970, 'Quelques exemples du type du "parvenu" dans l'Égypte ancienne', *BSFE* 59, 31–47.

——, 1978, 'Littérature et autobiographie: Les Inscriptions de *s3-mwt* surnommé *kyky*', *RdE* 30, 115–46.

——, 1982, 'Name', *LÄ* IV, 320–6.

——, 1984, 'Schreibtafel', *LÄ* V, 703–9.

——, 1986, 'Traum', *LÄ* VI, 745–9.

——, 1990a, 'La Date du *Paysan Eloquent*'. In Israelit-Groll 1990: 1033–47.

——, 1990b, *Future at Issue. Tense, Mood and Aspect in Middle Egyptian: Studies in Syntax and Semantics*. Yale Egyptological Studies 4. New Haven: Yale Egyptological Seminar.

——, 1991, 'Les "Décrets" royaux (*wḏ-nsw*): L'Énoncé d'auctoritas comme genre'. In *SAK* Beiheft 4, 239–46.

——, 1995a, *Essai sur la conscience de l'histoire dans l'Égypte pharaonique*. Bibliothèque de l'École des hautes études, Sciences historiques et philologiques 332. Paris: Honoré Champion.

——, 1995b, 'L'Intertextualité dans la culture pharaonique: L'Enseignement de Ptahhotep et le graffito d'jmny (Ouâdi Hammâmât n° 3042)', *GM* 147, 103–9.

——, 1996a, 'Langue littéraire et diglossie'. In Loprieno 1996a: 555–64.

——, 1996b, 'Le Début de l'Enseignement de Ptahhotep: Un nouveau manuscrit', *CRIPEL* 18, 119–40.

——, 1997, 'Le Vizir et le balancier: À propos de l'*Enseignement de Ptahhotep*'. In C. Berger and B. Mathieu, *Études sur l'Ancien Empire et la nécropole de Saqqâra dédiés à Jean-Philippe Lauer*, 437–43. Orientalia Monspeliensia 9. Montpellier: Université Paul Valéry.

——, 1999, 'Le Discours politique de l'*Enseignement de Ptahhotep*'. In J. Assmann and Blumenthal 1999: 139–52.

Veyne, P. 1988, *Roman Erotic Elegy: Love, Poetry, and the West* (D. Pellauer, trans.). Chicago and London: University of Chicago Press.

Volten, A. 1945, *Zwei altägyptische politische Schriften: Die Lehre für König Merikarê (Pap. Carlsberg VI) und die Lehre des Königs Amenemhet*. Analecta Aegyptiaca 4. Copenhagen: Einar Munksgaard.

von der Way, T. 1984, *Die Textüberlieferung Ramses' II. zur Qadeš-Schlacht: Analyse und Struktur*. HÄB 22.

Ward, W. 1982, *Index of Egyptian Administrative and Religious Titles of the Middle Kingdom*. Beirut: American University. (Cited by entry number.)

Wegner, J. W. 1996, 'The Nature and Chronology of the Senwosret III – Amenemhat III Regnal Succession: Some Considerations Based on New Evidence from the Mortuary Temple of Senwosret III at Abydos', *JNES* 55, 249–79.

Wellek, R., and Warren, A. 1962 [1949], *Theory of Literature*. Harmondsworth: Penguin.

Wells, S., Taylor, G., *et al.* 1987, *William Shakespeare: A Textual Companion*. Oxford: Clarendon Press.

Welsh, E. D. 1978, *The 'Lebensmüde' and Its Relationship to the Hedonistic Harpers' Songs of the Middle–New Kingdoms*. Doctoral dissertation, Brandeis University. Ann Arbor: UMI.

Wenig, S. 1969, 'Bertolt Brecht und das alte Ägypten', *ZÄS* 96, 63–6.

Wente, E. F. 1982, 'Mysticism in Pharaonic Egypt?', *JNES* 41, 161–79.

——, 1990, *Letters from Ancient Egypt*. Society of Biblical Literature: Writings from the Ancient World 1. Atlanta: Scholars Press.

Wessetzky, V. 1963, 'Sinuhes Flucht', *ZÄS* 90, 124–7.

Westendorf, W. 1973, 'Eine Formel des Totenbuches als Schreibfehler in der "Lehre des (Dua-)Cheti"', *GM* 5, 43–5.

——, 1977a, 'Noch einmal: Die "Wiedergeburt" des heimgekehrten Sinuhe', *SAK* 5, 293–304.

——, 1977b, 'Das strandende Schiff: Zur Lesung und Übersetzung von Bauer B1, 58 = R 101'. In J. Assmann *et al.* 1977: 503–9.

——, 1981, 'Die Menschen als Ebenbilder Pharaos: Bemerkungen zur "Lehre des Amenemhet" (Abschnitt V)', *GM* 46, 33–42.

——, 1986a, 'Theodizee', *LÄ* VI, 473–4.

——, 1986b, 'Einst – Jetzt – Einst oder: Die Rückkehr zum Ursprung', *WdO* 17, 5–8.

——, 1990, 'Die Insel des Schiffbrüchigen: Keine Halbinsel!' In Israelit-Groll 1990: 1056–64.

Wildung, D. 1969, *Die Rolle ägyptischer Könige im Bewusstsein ihrer Nachwelt I: Posthume Quellen über die Könige der ersten vier Dynastien*. MÄS 17.

——, 1977, *Imhotep und Amenhotep: Gottwerdung im alten Ägypten*. MÄS 36.

——, 1984, *Sesostris und Amenemhat: Ägypten im Mittleren Reich*. Munich: Hirmer.

——, (ed.) 1997, *Sudan: Ancient Kingdoms of the Nile* (P. der Manuelian, trans.). Exhibition catalogue. Paris and New York: Flammarion.

——, *et al.* 2000, *Ägypten 2000 v. Chr.: Die Geburt des Individuums*. Munich: Hirmer Verlag.

Willems, H. 1988, *Chests of Life: A Study of the Typology and Conceptual*

Development of Middle Kingdom Standard Class Coffins. Mededelingen en Verhandelingen van het Vooraziatisch-Egyptisch Genootschap (Gezelschap) 'Ex Orient Lux' (Leiden) 25.

Wildung, D. (ed.) 1996a, *The World of the Coffin Texts: Proceedings of the Symposium Held on the Occasion of the 100th Birthday of Adriaan de Buck, Leiden, December 17–19, 1992*. Leiden: Nederlands Instituut voor het Nabije Oosten.

Williams, R. 1977, *Marxism and Literature*. Oxford: Oxford University Press.

——, 1980, *Problems in Materialism and Culture: Selected Essays*. London: Verso and New Left Books.

——, 1981, 'Marxism, Structuralism and Literary Analysis', *New Left Review* 129, 51–66.

Williams, R. D. 1990 [1967], 'The Purpose of the *Aeneid*'. In Harrison 1990a: 21–36.

Williams, R. J. 1962, 'Reflections on the *Lebensmüde*', *JEA* 48, 49–56.

——, 1964, 'Literature as a Medium of Political Propaganda in Ancient Egypt'. In W. S. McCullough (ed.), *The Seed of Wisdom: Essays in Honour of T. J. Meek*, 14–30. Toronto: University of Toronto Press.

——, 1983 [1956], 'Theodicy in the Ancient Near East'. In J. Crenshaw (ed.), *Theodicy in the Old Testament*, 42–56. London: SPCK.

Wilson, J. A. 1951, *The Burden of Egypt*. Chicago: University of Chicago Press.

Wilson Knight, G. 1930, '*King Lear* and the Comedy of the Grotesque'. In G. Wilson Knight, *The Wheel of Fire: Essays in the Interpretation of Shakespeare's Sombre Tragedies*. London: Oxford University Press.

Wimsatt, W. K. 1964, *The Verbal Icon: Studies in the Meaning of Poetry*. New York: Noonday Press.

Wimsatt, W. K., and Beardsley, M. 1964, 'The Intentionalist Fallacy'. In Wimsatt 1964: 3–18.

Winlock, H. E. 1924, 'A Statue of Horemhab before His Accession', *JEA* 10, 1–5.

Woolf, V. (K. Flint, ed.) 1992, *The Waves*. Penguin Twentieth Century Classics. London: Penguin.

Wright, E. 1986, 'Modern Psychoanalytic Criticism'. In Jefferson and Robey 1986: 145–65.

Yourcenar, M. 1982, *Œuvres romanesques*. Bibliothèque de la Pléiade 303. Paris: Gallimard.

——, 1984 [1956], *Les Charités d'Alcippe*. Paris: Gallimard.

Yoyotte, J. 1952, 'À propos d'un monument copié par G. Daressy: Contribution à l'histoire littéraire', *BSFE* 11, 67–72.

——, 1961, review of Barns 1956, *RdE* 13, 114–20.

——, 1964, 'À propos du panthéon de Sinouhé (B 205–212)', *Kêmi* 17, 69–73.

Žába, Z. 1956, *Les Maximes de Ptaḥḥotep*. Prague: Académie tchécoslovaque des sciences, Section de la linguistique et de la littérature.

——, 1974, *The Rock Inscriptions of Lower Nubia (Czechoslovak Concession)*. Czechoslovak Institute of Egyptology in Prague and in Cairo Publications 1. Prague: Charles University of Prague.

Zandee, J. 1960, *Death as an Enemy: According to Ancient Egyptian Conceptions*. Studies in the History of Religions 5. Leiden: E. J. Brill.

——, 1992, *Der Amunhymnus des Papyrus Leiden I 344, verso*. Collections of the National Museum of Antiquities at Leiden 7. Leiden: Rijksmuseum van Oudheden.

Zettler, R. L. 1996, 'Written Documents as Excavated Artifacts and the Holistic Interpretation of the Mesopotamian Archaeological Record'. In Cooper and Schwartz 1996: 81–101.

Zetzel, J. E. G. 1997, 'Rome and Its Traditions'. In Martindale 1997a: 188–203.

Zumthor, P. 1986 [1980], *Speaking of the Middle Ages* (S. White, trans.). Lincoln, NE: University of Nebraska Press.

Index

All mentions of literary texts are listed. The main discussions are marked in **bold.**

Abydos   66, 68, 73, 76, 84, 97, 251–2, 318
Abydos Discourse   307–8
'Abydos formula'   121
administrative texts   55, 60–1, 71, 73, 105, 114, 116–17, 177, 294, 300, 302
aesthetic aspects   4, 19, 63, 84, 102, 104, 126–8, 180, 217, 272, 284, 287
allusions   48, 68–9, 73, 200, 319
   see also esoteric allusions
Althusser, Louis   7, 28–9, 272
ambiguity   18, 39, 83, 102, 104, 126, 153–4, 159, 180, 187–9, 202, 204, 221, 264, 272, 280
Amenemhat I, King   5, 8–9, 15, 45, 48–9, 91, 141, 152, 197, 280, 298–9, 304, 318, 322
Amenemhat I, Teaching of   8–11, 31, 46–7, 49, 53, 68, 72 n.10, 73, 76, 90–1, 117, 121, 152, 155, 161, 199 n.7, 205, 212 n.26, 236 n.1, 237–41, **241–8**, 252–3, 256, 259, 274, **316–17**
Amenemhat II, King   5, 49–50, 62, 298 n.5, 311–12
Amenemhat III, King   6, 49, 72–3, 313, 318
Amenemhat IV, King   6
Amenemhat, high priest   74 n.14, 145
Amenemope, Onomasticon of   76 n.16
Amenemope, Teaching of   68 n.2, 113–14, 116, 137, 154
Amennakht, scribe   30, 59, 76, 238–9

Amherst, P.   218, 309
Ani, Teaching of   69, 137
annals   55, 62
Annals of Amenemhat II,   62, 139, 227, 231, 298 n.5, 312
archaism   49, 313
archives, *see* libraries
Ashayet, princess   79
Assmann, Jan   17–19, 35, 49, 57–8, 62, 66, 69, 100, 130, 143, 195 n.2, 224, 235, 253, 272, 294
Asyut   68, 134, 207 n.16
Athens, P.   32, 45 n.1, 296, 308, 309, 314 n.21, 317, 320
audience   25, 78–81, 102–7, 237–8, 257 n.19, 265, 274–5, 278
audience response   25, 35, 81–5, 102–7, 166, 173, 179–81, 189–91, 194, 199–200, 215–16, 226, 237–41, 243, 247–8, 281–91
author, implied   24–5, 77–8
authorial intention   24–5, 37–8
authors and authorship   13, 24–5, 30–1, 52, 75–8, 237–9, 316–17, 320–1
autonomy, literary   19–20, 24, 28–9, 112, 122, 279

ba ('soul')   65, 94, 162, 250, 254
   see also A Man and His Ba
Baines, John   16, 18, 29, 55, 66–7, 99, 126, 288 n.8
Bakhtin, Mikhail   39, 64, 144, 184
Barthes, Roland   39, 41
Baxandall, Michael   84, 282
'Berlin library'   11, 52–3, 72, 115, 181, 297, 300, 309
el-Bersha   75, 131 n.1, 165

biographies, funerary   55, 58, 79, 87–8, 93–5, 118–19, 121–2, 131, 145, 149–50, 153–4, 157, 159, 165–7, 183, 197 n.4, 240, 242–3, 257–8, 260–2, 267, 276, 279–81, 298, 325
Blumenthal, Elke   18, 112, 196, 241
Book of the Dead
  other spells   244
  spell 175   135–6, 139, 217
Book of the Heavenly Cow   124, 130–1
boundaries   95, 157, 162, 166–7
Buau, official   72, 300 n.9
Building Inscription of Senwosret I   53, 63, 74, 140
building inscriptions   63
  see also Elephantine *and* Tod inscriptions of Senwosret I

Cairo Mythological Tale   142–3, **294–5**
carnival   144, 184, 187
  see also holiday
censorship   105
Champollion, Jean-François   3, 11
characterization   125–6, 152–3, 183–6
Cheops, King   97–8, 139–40, 182–7
Cheops' Court, Tale of   32, 47–8, 50, 56, 69, 82–5, 89, 96–8, 103, 114, 120–2, 125–6, **138–44**, 149, 161, 166 n.30, **182–92**, 195, 227, 231, 279, 289, **295–6**, 297, 304
Chester Beatty IV, P.   30, 94, 120 n.9, 137, 199, 255 n.44, 316, 322
  see also 'Eulogy of Dead Writers'
Chester Beatty papyri   117, 120 n.9 124, 208 n.17
circulation of poems   67–9, 76, 78
Coffin Texts   51, 53, 56 n.9, 61, 66, 72, 83, 94, 114, 117–18, 127 n.14, 131, 134–6, 142, 154 n.14, 157 n.18, 196, 205, 209 n.20, 210, 219 n.35–6, 221, 300, 316
Coffin Text spell 1130   131–5, 137–40, 185, 214, 221, 226, 244 n.7, 254–5
colophons   51–2, 67, 70–1, 75, 106, 125
commemorative inscriptions (*including* graffiti)   55, 62, 68, 73–4, 87–8, 93, 183, 194, 196, 198, 227, 236, 245, 267, 270–1, 279, 314, 318
compound genres   35–6, 226–32, 274, 311–12
containment   99–107, 181, 232–4, 286
Contending of the Belly and the Head   218, 309
co-regency   5, 8–10, 248
cosmos, sundered, *see* sundered cosmos
court, royal   61, 66–9, 72, 78, 80–1, 83–4, 167, 199, 227–8, 230, 232, 247–8, 257–8
criticism, ancient literary   4, 29–32, 279
Cultural Materialism   27–9, 40–1, 102
cultural poetics, *see* New Historicism
'cultural texts'   17–18, 107, 235, 285 n.6

'Daressy Fragment'   31, 205, 233, 304, 308, 317, 320–1
date of compositions   13, 45–50, 141–3, 193, 294–319
death as a theme   58–60, 96–7, 127–8, 134–6, 166, 212–13, 216–26, 260
decorum   9–10, 29, 63, 66, 86, 91–8, 105, 111, 129, 138, 144, 265, 275, 278–82
'defamiliarization'   26
Deir el-Bahri   72–3, 183, 236 n.1, 310
Deir el-Ballas   236 n.1, 298
Deir el-Medina   30–1, 53–4, 59, 68–70, 72, 76, 78 n.19, 84, n.29, 124, 238–9, 277 n.33, 296, 298, 313, 315, 322–3
Derchain, Philippe   19, 157, 183–4, 287, 288 n.8
Dévaud, Eugène   47, 294, 313 n.19, 314
dialogue, genre of   111, 138, 204–26, 308–10
differentiation, social, *see* social differentiation
differentiation, literary   15–16, 19–21, 23, 28–9, 30, 63, 74, 91–8, 122–8, 191–2, 237–41, 256–7, 272, 278–83
discourse
  genre of   18, 75–6, 82, 89–90, 108–12, 124, 138, 168–81, 193–234, 274, 303–8, 310–12

monumental, *see* monumental discourse
official, *see* official discourse
discrepancies, historical 48, 89, 182, 197, 248
Dra Abu el-Naga 70–2, 313
dream interpretation manuals 69, 124, 161, 281
dreams 96, 155, 161, 163, 188, 242, 244, 248, 280–2
'Duties of The Vizier' treatise 174 n.38, 176, 257
Dynasty, 11th 5, 31, 48–9, 63, 72, 79, 131, 182–3, 256, 300, 314, 316
Dynasty, 12th *passim*
Dynasty, 13th 3, 6–7, 68, 71, 97, 141, 232, 296, 304 *see also* Neferhotep
Dynasty, 17th 3, 7, 31

Eagleton, Terry 19, 27, 86, 105, 285
ecphrasis 166, 245
education 17–18, 53–5, 61, 69, 73, 84 n.29, 111, 115–17, 146, 233, 235–41, 247–8, 257–9, 272–7, 286–8, 322–5
Elephantine 3, 68, 323
  see also Heqaib
Elephantine inscription of Senwosret I 50, 63, 194, 242
elites 15, 58, 65–7, 69, 77–8, 81, 84, 107, 121, 215–6, 255, 257, 272, 274, 286
Eloquent Peasant, Tale of the 11, 33, 46–8, 50, 52–4, 56, 59, 62, 72, 77, 79–80, 82–4, 90, 93, 103, 109, 111–13, 115, 119–20, 122–8, 133, 135, 139, 141, 143, 145, 149, 154 n.14, **168–82**, 192, 194, 200–1, 206, 209, 210 n.23, 215, 218 n.34, 219, 221 n.38, 231, 238, 243, 248 n.11, 249, 259, 268–9, 272, 284, 288, **297**, 305, 307
empathy 128, 153, 167, 173, 179, 187, 215–16, 289–91
enemies 95, 130–1, 211–12, 251–6
entertainment 18, 27, 70, 83–5, 87, 91, 101–7, 143–6, 174–5, 189, 194–5, 198–200, 228–31, 233, 239–40, 275–7, 282, 288

'entrapment' 40, 102–7, 177–8, 216, 232
Erman, Adolf 12, 113, 309
esoteric allusions and aspects 74, 77, 80, 97–8, 105, 121, 139–40, 142, 182–9
eulogy 61, 63, 82, 84, 94, 103, 111–12, 156–7, 169–70, 173, 195, 198, 212 n.27, 227–8, 232, 240, 256, 267, 270–2, 276, 298, 312
'Eulogy of Dead Writers' 30–2, 45, 50, 69, 74, 89–92, 166, 265, 284, 304, 313, 314 n.21, 317, 320–1
Execration Texts and figures 62, 101, 103, 158
expectations, literary subversion of 94, 97–8, 140, 150–1, 191, 275, 280

faultlines 40, 106, 127, 164–5, 258, 270
Fecht, Gerhard 49, 113–17, 205, 211, 321
fictionality 8–10, 18, 31, 63, 76–7, 87–91, 140, 189, 197, 216, 237–9, 248, 266, 273, 278–82
First Intermediate Period 5, 14–15, 46–7, 49, 52 n.7, 64–5, 88, 91, 119, 134, 193
Fischer-Elfert, Hans-Werner 18, 270, 274, 295 n.1, 323
Fishing and Fowling, Account of 50, 84, 112, 146, **226–32**, 311, **312**
folktales and folk-compositions 11, 56, 111–12, 142
formulae 51, 56, 131, 141–2, 157, 167, 275, 323–5
Foucault, Michel 25–6, 28, 75, 77
Fowler, Alastair 21, 27, 33–6, 108–9, 111
Fowler, Discourse of the 49, 77, 110, 206 n.14, 230–1, **306–7**, 308
frames, literary 76–7, 78, 89, 167, 194–5, 227–8, 249, 273
free-play, *see* indeterminacy
frivolity 98, 145, 183–41, 187, 194, 231, 263, 279, 282, 288
  see also holiday
fugitives 95
functional context, *see* occasion
'fusion of horizons' 38, 41, 283, 289

gaps   25, 28, 83, 87, 92, 106, 126–7, 216, 272
Gardiner, A. H.   12, 33, 143, 205
Geertz, Clifford   17, 18 n.12, 41, 86, 136, 285, 289
gender   66–7, 75, 78, 95–6, 144, 244–5, 283
genre   18, 32–6, 55–6, 75, 108–12, 118, 129, 138, 150–1, 183, 202, 232–4, 277, 293
gestures in recitation   79
Ghost, Tale of a King and a   **301–2**
glosses   83, 198
governors, provincial (nomarchs)   5–6, 64–5, 200
graffiti, *see* commemorative inscriptions
Greenblatt, Stephen   20, 28, 39–40, 64–5, 99–102, 106, 179 n.47, 240, 275, 286, 288–90

Hapdjefai, nomarch   95
Haraga   67, 70, 297
'Harpist's Song of Intef'   31, 97 n.6, 217, 314, 320
harpist's songs   31, 56, 61, 79, 96–7, 134, 176 n.43, 205 n.12, 233, 280, 320
Hay, Tale of   50, 71, 142, **300–1**
heart   93–5, 132–3, 137, 159–61, 166–7, 174, 194, 201–4, 237, 239, 243–4, 252, 254, 258, 261–2, 264, 267, 277, 304–5
Heliopolis   139, 189, 196–7, 200
Heracleopolitan Period   56, 171–2, 248–57, 297, 315–6
  see also First Intermediate Period
Herdsman, Tale of the   46, 49, 61 n.13, 72, 79 n.20, 142, 230, **300**
Heqaib, chapel of   3, 63, 66, 132, 194, 208, 278
Heqanakht, official   27, 144, 275
hieratic script   47, 60–1, 73–4, 114–17, 323
high tradition   129–46, 149, 182–92, 228, 231–2, 276
Hirsch, E. D.   21, 37–41
history and historiography   9–10, 26, 37–8, 41, 62–3, 87–8, 184, 197–9, 200–1, 241–57, 287
  see also settings
holiday   59–60, 65–6, 73, 81, 141–4, 184, 189, 229
Hordedef, Prince   30–2, 45, 52, 76, 89–90, 120, 185–6, 320
Hordedef, Teaching of   49–50, 76, 115, **313–14**
Horus and Seth, Tale of   50, 71, 97, 143–4, 205, **294**
House of Life   69
House of Life, Tale of the   116, **302**, 312
humour   97–8, 103, 124, 142–6, 157, 163, 166, 182–8, 195, 215, 273–7, 284
hymns   30, 53, 59–61, 71, 82, 146, 228, 279, 308
  see also eulogy
Hymns to Senwosret III   61, 113, 119–20, 247, 301

ideology   14–16, 26, 28–9, 40–1, 86–7, 91–8, 112, 131, 216, 237–41, 248–9, 256, 259, 272. 279, 281–2, 285–6
illustrations   73–4, 80
imagery   122–4, 154, 188, 190, 209–10, 217–26, 244, 251. 255–6, 267–70, 272, 275, 278–83
Imhotep   30–2, 45, 320
indeterminacy   38–9, 284
individuality   65–6, 167
'Installation of the Vizier' treatise   100 n.8
Intef, Kings   31, 49, 84, 240, 314,
Intef, official   83, 95, 98, 113, 118–19, 259–60
intentionalist fallacy   24–5
interpretation   3, 10, 12, 20–1, 25, 36–42, 82–3, 101–2, 145, 203, 216, 277, 281, 283–91
interregnum   57, 59, 154, 164, 194, 280
intertextuality   18, 20, 29, 33, 36, 48, 60–3, 98, 118, 182, 229–30, 239, 272, 274–5
Ipuur, Dialogue of   32, 50, 56, 58–9, 78–9, 95, 97, 101, 111, 121, 124–5, 133–4,

140 n.10, 155 n.15, 156, 196, 199 n.7, **204–16**, 217, 221, 232, 243, 246, 253, 269, 274, **308–9**, 321
irony 83, 102, 124, 126–8, 157, 166, 174–81, 191, 252, 264, 280, 284
Iser, Wolfgang 21, 25, 27–8, 79, 83, 89, 92, 106, 126, 167, 282–3
Itj-tawi 5–7, 8 n.2, 72
see also Residence, royal

Jakobson, Roman 26, 122

Kagemni, Teaching for 46–7, 49–51, 70, 79, 82, 89, 133, 143, 181, 235, 260, 265, 271, 276–7, 282, **313**, 320
Kaires, official 30, 45, 313, 320–1
Kemit 48–9, 53, 73, 117, 236, 274, **322–5**
Khakheperreseneb, Words of 30, 32, 50, 90, 94, 104, 110–1, 121–2, 124–6, 134, 137, 172, **200–4**, 206, 212 n.28, 217, 229, 236, 249, **304–5**, 321
Khety, scribe 9, 30–2, 45, 76, 90–1, 284, 316–17
Khety, Teaching of 30, 45, 48–9, 50, 53, 65, 67, 69, 74 n.13, 77, 90–1, 112, 114, 129, 146, 229, 236 n.1, **273–7**, **317–18**, 319, 322–4
King and a Ghost, Tale of a **301–2**
'King as Sunpriest' treatise 62, 130, 247
kingship 5–6, 64–5, 130, 132, 159, 182–3, 187, 206, 215, 238, 240–1, 247, 253–6, 265–71, 275
'knot', *see* verse

el-Lahun 46, 61–2, 67–8, 70–1, 73, 113, 116–17, 142–3, 293 n.1, 294, 297, 300–3, 311, 322, 325
el-Lahun 'Wisdom Text' **311**
laments 46, 58–9, 79, 96–7, 110, 159, 193, 195–200, 201–4, 206–15, 217, 220–4, 242–4, 256, 267, 272, 274–5, 305
language 26–7, 31, 49, 66–7, 119–20, 138, 141, 143, 175–6, 228, 233, 289
Late Egyptian literature, general 145–6, 232–4

see also Late Egyptian tales; Miscellanies
Late Egyptian tales 70, 81, 117, 134, 142, 145–6
Late Period 55, 68, 296, 301
lector priest 71–2, 77–8, 118, 303–4
letters 27, 55, 61, 69, 79, 114, 117, 151 n.4, 159, 236, 264 n.24, 322–5
  to the dead 176 n.43, 242, 299 n.6, 325
Letter-teaching, genre of 324
libraries 30, 67–73
  institutional 67–9, 70 n.6, 71, 73
  private 69–73
  see also 'Berlin library'; 'Ramesseum library'
linear hieroglyphs 73, 117, 323
el-Lisht 5, 70, 299
  see also Residence, royal
Litany of Re 139
literacy 15, 64, 66–7, 70, 76–7, 80–1, 239, 274, 277, 325
literary theory, role of 7–8, 10, 12–42, 284–8
'literature' as term 4–5, 11, 22–9, 289
literature, origins of 55–60, 282–3
'little men' (*ndsw*) 65, 100, 185, 220–1, 282, 286,
local aspects of literary production 67–8, 78, 143–5, 238–9
Loprieno, Antonio 17–8, 39, 60, 65–6, 100, 122, 272
love-songs 54, 56, 70, 74 n.13, 79, 114, 145, 227 n.46, 231, 236, 304 n.11
low tradition 129–30, 138–46, 149, 175, 182–92, 232–4, 273–7
lowly wise men 56, 77, 142, 250
'Loyalist' Teaching 50, 52–3, 59, 69, 73–4, 76, 90, 94 n.3, 95, 123–4, 127, 175, 209, 229, 237–9, 246, **266–72**, 273–5, 281–2, **318–19**, 321
lyrics 26, 61, 145–6, 163–4, 221–5
Lythgoe, Tale of P. 70, 142, **299–300**

Maat ('Truth') 122–4, 128–38, 169–71, 179–80, 198, 202–3, 206, 210, 222, 237, 248–54, 260, 263, 266–8, 274

magic   31–2, 71, 100–1, 104, 120–1, 141–2, 165 n.28, 168–9, 185, 208 n.17, 255, 281, 294–5, 300
Man and His Ba, Dialogue of a   16, 50, 56–7, 72, 94, 110–1, 126, 127 n.14, 158 n.19, 165, 176 n.43, 189, 200, 202, 205, 211, 214, **216–26**, 231, **309–10**
Man for His Son, Teaching of a   47–8, 50, 76–7, 90, 93, 100 n.8, 123, 144, 199 n.7, 219 n.37, 221 n.39, 237, 266 n.6, **270–2**, 274, **319**
manuscripts   4, 11, 29, 36, 46–8, 50–5, 66–75, 105, 108, 112–17, 143, 181, 194, 235–6, 293, 299, 308–9, 320, 323
marsh landscape   140–1, 221–2, 230–1
Marxist theory   7, 25, 28–9, 92, 99
medical texts, *see* technical texts
Memphis   32, 296, 301, 303, 315–16, 317
 see also Saqqara
Menna, Letter of   54, 76, 238–9, 323
Merikare, Teaching for   7, 15, 47–50, 79 n.20, 90, 97, 100, 104, 119, 131–2, 134, 141, 161, 201, 208–9, 212–13, 236, 238–41, 243 n.5, 247 n.9, **248–57**, 268–9, 291, 311, **315–16**, 321
metre   35, 49, 112–17, 293
'middle class'   64–5
Miscellanies, Late Egyptian   63, 69, 115, 146, 228, 230, 233, 324
Moers, Gerald   18–19, 88–9, 11, 200–1, 282
monostichic arrangement, *see* stichic arrangement
Montuhotep, Kings   5, 53, 72, 182–3
Montuhotep, nomarch   100, 259
Montuwoser, steward   51, 80, 87, 120
monumental discourse   58, 62, 73, 86, 92, 242
 see also official discourse
musicians   56, 78–9, 84, 177, 187, 323
 see also harpist's songs
Mythological Tale   294 n.2, 311

Naga el-Deir   70
names and naming   119, 154, 163–5, 187, 194, 197–8, 200, 202, 256

Nefer[. . .], Tale of   168 n.33, **302**
Neferkare and Sasenet, Tale of   47, 50, 54, 79, 103, 142, 144, 177, 276 n.31, **296–7**, 301
Neferhotep I   6, 68, 296
 inscription of   68–9, 97–8, 123, 140, 201 n.8, 237
Nefersekheru, biography of   84, 122, 201
Neferti, Words of   15, 30–2, 45–7, 49, 59 n.12, 77–9, 89–90, 103–4, 110–1, 118, 121 n.11, 124, 140–1, 143–4, 165, 168 n.33, 172, 174, 183, 192, **193–200**, 201, 204, 207–8, 212, 241–2, 247, 256, 258 n.21, 265, 274, 284, **303–4**, 308
Nefru, Queen   150, 152, 298
Nefrusobek, Queen   6
negative anthropology   130, 137, 174, 212, 244
negative cosmology   130, 137, 166, 212, 244
Nemay, Tale of   **302–3**
New Critics   16, 23–4, 36–8
New Historicism   21–2, 28–9, 39–40, 102, 232, 286
New Kingdom   7. 9, 18, 31, 52, 58, 70, 74, 83, 96–7, 109, 114–17, 130, 141, 145–6, 205 n.12, 230, 232–4, 236, 274, 296–8, 300, 303–4, 310–2, 314–7, 318–9, 322
 see also Ramessid Period
New Year   60, 211
Nileflood, hymns to   53, 59, 59–60, 69, 144, 207–8

occasion ('*Sitz im Leben*')   17, 33, 35, 58–61, 81, 274–5
official discourse   9 n.6, 18, 58, 84–8, 90–8, 118–22, 131, 145, 152, 155–6, 167, 182–3, 192, 196, 198–9, 207, 219, 221, 227, 232–4, 242–3, 250, 255–7, 262, 269, 271, 276, 279–82
Old Kingdom   5, 35, 45–7, 49, 52 n.7, 55, 57, 60, 91. 96, 114, 131, 184, 257, 263, 295–6, 301, 313–5, 320

Ong, Walter J.   27, 57, 60
onomastica   62, 71, 73, 76 n.16, 110 n.2, 112, 230, 257, 277
oral compositions and transmission   50–1, 55–7, 74, 77, 111–12, 118, 142, 274–5
ostraca   53–5, 73, 115–17, 236, 274, 304, 320, 323
Otherworld   134–7, 170, 223–6, 246, 249 n.12, 250–1
Oxford Wisdom Text   236, 270, **310**

palaeography   47, 313
parables   212–13, 220–1
'paraphrase, heresy of'   16
parody   36, 102, 124, 139, 142, 183, 186, 227, 275–7
patronage   78, 105
'perfect speech'   82, 118, 140, 174–6, 179–81, 226, 259, 281, 303
'perfect to the heart'   82, 140, 181, 216
performance   51, 55–7, 63, 78–81, 125, 159, 167, 216, 247–8
  see also reading, act of
personal piety   65, 159, 233
petitioning   83, 168–77, 224, 228
philology   4, 12, 18–19, 26, 287
play, *see* entertainment
pleasure, *see* entertainment
Posener, Georges   13–15, 18, 21–3, 26, 33, 116–17
power, literature's relationship with   40–1, 98–107, 112, 119, 232–4, 240–1, 272, 277, 279
priest, lector, *see* lector priest
Prisse, P.   46–7, 49, 52, 70–1, 235, 298–9, 313–14
propaganda   3, 8–10 13–16, 40, 47, 98–101, 157, 198, 201, 232, 247–8, 279, 286, 317
prose   114
prototypes, literary   55–63
pseudonymy, *see* pseudepigraphy
pseudepigraphy   13, 90–1, 258, 317
Ptahemdjehuty, scribe   30, 321
Ptahhotep, Teaching of   30, 32, 45–52, 57, 70, 90, 93–6, 100, 104, 110, 112, 119022, 134, 136, 141. 144–5, 172 n.35, 176–7, 185, 190 n.59, 201, 235–7, 239, 241, 249, **257–66**, 267, 269, 271, 174–5, 280–1, 289, 311, **314–15**, 320
Pyramid Texts   55, 114

'Qadesh poem'   69–70
Qenherkhepshef, scribe   69, 277 n.33
quietness   93 172–3, 181
quotations   48–9, 68–9

'Ramesseum library'   52–3, 61–2, 70–2, 100, 111–12, 115–17, 181, 305, 310–11
Ramesseum II, Maxims of P.   53. 93, 111–12, 113, 116, 129–30, 146, 202, 237–8, **310**
Ramesseum Wisdom Fragment   116, **310–1**
Ramessid Period   30–2, 45. 49, 53–5, 60, 63, 68–9, 76, 84, 91, 111, 115, 134, 138, 145–6, 228, 230, 235–6, 273–4, 277, 308, 313, 315, 317, 320–1
reading, act of   3–4, 35, 79–80, 278–91
rebellion of humanity   130–2, 197, 209, 255–6
reception, modern   7–21, 33, 37–42, 118, 150–3, 162–3, 200, 205, 216–17, 223, 230, 235–7, 272, 278–91
reception, New Kingdom   29–32, 53–5, 89, 199, 232–4, 258, 319
'recite' (*šdj*)   79
recompense for literary activity   77, 82, 181, 1990
redactional activity   16, 45, 47–8, 51–5
redactional criticism   16, 77, 205, 308, 318
referentiality   7–10, 13, 25–7, 87–91, 202–4
refrains   111, 113, 120, 196, 206–9, 211, 214, 221–5, 227, 229, 274
registers of language and decorum   49, 120–1, 129–46, 159, 188, 191–2, 198, 225, 228, 231, 270, 274–7
relativization of values   133–4, 170–7
'relief' (*qb*)   83, 85, 140, 282

Renseneb, Discourse of 95, 110, **306**, 308
Residence, royal 70, 75, 142, 157–8, 168, 247, 251, 273, 276, 300, 317–18, 321–2
    see also Itj-tawi
response, literary 3, 77, 81–5, 99
    see also audience response
Retjenu 95, 103, 155, 157–8, 164 n.27, 306
rhetoric, *see* perfect speech
ritual texts 55, 61–2, 69, 71, 73–4, 79, 116–17, 230, 311
royal birth cycle 139, 187
Royal Eulogy of P. BM EA 10475 112, **312**
Royal Tale 63, 97–8, 140, 183, 186, 195, 205, 227, 240, 258, 312
rubrics 114–17, 150

Saqqara 31, 308, 311, 315 n.22, 320, *see also* Memphis
Sarenput I, nomarch 63, 94, 132, 165, 194, 208
Sasobek, Discourse of 49, 76, 93, 103–4, 110, 120, 132, 154–5, 168, 172, 200, 217, 228, 281, **305**, 308, 310
Satiric Letter of P. Anastasi I 32, 37, 51–3, 59–60, 62, 69, 82–3, 89, 115, 124–5, 163, 277, 280–1, 314 n.21, 324
satiric papyri 60, 195
Sehotepibre, official 73, 76–7, 84, 268, 270, 318
schools 18, 53–5, 69, 273
Semna stela 63, 74, 82 n.25, 86, 103, 243, 246, 252
Senwosret I 3, 5, 8–9, 49, 63, 75, 85, 131, 151, 156, 160–4, 193, 241–2, 246–8, 280, 296, 298, 316, 318–19, 322
Senwosret II 5, 49, 141, 200, 297, 304
Senwosret III 5–6, 86, 183
settings 45–7, 89, 171–2, 194, 198, 219, 237–8, 241, 248–9, 256–8, 263, 266, 273, 293
sexuality 95–6, 103, 141 143, 263, 283, 286, 290

Shipwrecked Sailor, Tale of the 14, 39, 46–7, 49, 52, 56, 61, 70–1, 80, 85, 89–90, 106, 114, 122, 124, 126 n.13, 129, 136, 138–42, 149, 157, 162, 166 n.30, **182–92**, 199 n.7, 201, 229–30, 235–6, **298–9**, 313
'significance' 37–8, 287, 289
Sile 77, 91, 317
Sinfield, Alan 28–9, 40–1, 64, 102–5, 119, 241, 286
'sing' (*ḥsj*) 79, 236
Sinuhe, Tale of 11–12, 18, 33, 47, 49, 52–4, 56, 63, 67, 70, 72–3, 80, 82 n.25, 85, 93, 95, 100, 103, 113, 115, 12, 126, 139, **149–68**, 183–4, 188, 205 n.12, 212, 217, 218 n.33, 219 n.33, 223, 230, 236, 247, 253, 267, 269 n.27, 279–81, 285, **297–8**, 311
Smith, Bruce 39, 92
Sneferu, King 84–5, 90, 126, 140, 182–5, 194–5, 198, 231, 303, 313
Sobekhotep, Kings 6, 296
social differentiation 5–7, 46, 64–7, 77–8, 80–1, 141, 143–4, 177, 195, 215–6, 240–1, 259, 261, 269–70, 274–5, 282
'sonst-jetz', *see* 'then-now' formulation
Sporting King, Account of the 12 n.9, 50, 84, 112, 122, 146, **226–32**, 276, **311–12**, 314
'stanza' (*ḥwt*) 114–15
stichic arrangement 112–17
structuralist theory 25–6
style 32, 35, 46, 112, 118–28
subversion 40–1, 94, 98–107, 232–4, 249, 279, 285–6
sundered cosmos 130–8, 155, 171, 197–8, 210, 254–5
suspension 104, 199, 226. 272, 279

tale, genre of 18, 109, 129, 138–46, 149–92, 232–4, 241, 267, 294–303
teaching, genre of 18, 57, 75–7, 82, 84 n.29, 90, 95, 99–100, 109–12, 232–77, 310–1, 313–21
technical texts 55, 62, 71, 73–4, 114, 257–8, 301

textual criticism, *see* redactional criticism
textual transmission   47–8, 50–5, 57, 69, 74, 274, 314
   open   53, 146
   see also circulation of poems
textuality   50–5, 57, 66, 74
Thebes   31–2, 46, 61, 63, 67, 70–2, 75, 81, 116, 235, 240, 271, 294, 296, 297, 299–301, 303–5, 306, 309–15, 317–9
   see also Deir el-Medina
'then-now' formulation   58–60, 110, 159, 220, 223
   see also laments
theodicy   97, 129–38, 156, 158, 168–74, 177–8, 188, 196, 204–16, 233, 254–7, 260, 270, 276–7, 297
titles   74–5, 109–12, 322
Tod inscription of Senwosret I   63, 131, 154, 166, 183, 194, 196, 209 n.20, 212, 213 n.30, 245, 249
Todorov, Tzvetan   26–7, 33, 55, 291
tombs, as provenances   11, 70–2, 297–9, 322 n.2
traditions, *see* high tradition; low tradition.
transmission, textual, *see* textual transmission
'transposition'   17–18, 57
travesties   77, 282

Underworld books   62
unity, textual and thematic   16, 32, 36–7, 77, 102, 125–6, 200, 205, 257, 260, 270, 281, 284
Useramen, Vizier   74 n.14–5, 258

variants, textual   47–8, 51–4, 236, 314
veracity   87–90, 155, 279–81
Vergil   16, 38, 41, 48, 60, 91, 99, 105, 111, 122, 126–7, 194, 197 n.5, 204, 239, 286
'verse' (*ts*)   113–14
verse, *see* metre
verse-points   115–17, 281

Wadi el-Hol   73
Wadi el-Hudi   267, 319
Wadi Hammamat   182–3, 263 n.23, 314
Westcar, P.   47, 295–6, 302, 312
Williams, Raymond   23, 27–9, 33–4, 88
women, role of 95
   see also gender
wordplay   124–5, 127–8, 143, 187, 197, 256, 264
writing   66, 141, 181, 282
   see also literacy
writing boards   236, 296, 304, 310

Yourcenar, Marguerite   13, 36, 55, 66, 78, 89, 149, 153, 223 n.41, 290

www.ingramcontent.com/pod-product-compliance
Ingram Content Group UK Ltd.
Pitfield, Milton Keynes, MK11 3LW, UK
UKHW022153170326
469109UK00006B/3515